ECONOMICS OF

POVERTY

INEQUALITY

AND

DISCRIMINATION

EDWARD NATHAN WOLFF

Professor of Economics

New York University

SOUTH-WESTERN College Publishing

An International Thomson Publishing Company

Acquisitions Editor: Jack C. Calhoun
Developmental Editor: Lois Boggs-Leavens
Production Editor: Karen L. Truman
Production House: Litten Editing and Production with Shepard Poorman
   Communications
Cover Design: Paul Neff Design
Cover Illustration: Diana Ong/Superstock
Marketing Manager: Scott D. Person

Copyright © 1997
by South-Western College Publishing
Cincinnati, Ohio

Library of Congress Cataloging-in-Publication Data:

Wolff, Edward N.
    Economics of poverty, inequality & discrimination / Edward N. Wolff.
        p.   cm.
    Includes bibliographical references and indexes.
    ISBN 0-538-84580-5 (alk. paper)
        1. Poor—United States.   2. Income distribution—United States.
    3. Poverty—United States.   4. Discrimination in employment—United
    States.   5. United States—Economic conditions—1981–   I. Title.
    HC110.P6W648   1996
    305.5'69'0973—dc20   96-9701
                                                               CIP

1 2 3 4 5 6 7 8 9 MT 4 3 2 1 0 9 8 7 6
Printed in the United States of America

International Thomson Publishing
South-Western College Publishing is an ITP Company.
The ITP trademark is used under license.

CONTENTS

*Sections denoted with an asterisk (*) contain more advanced material or special topics that may be omitted without losing continuity in the book.

Contents   v

PREFACE

This book developed as an outgrowth of my own course, "Poverty and Income Distribution," which I have taught at New York University on and off since 1977. The textbook incubated over many years. Because of a scarcity of textbooks in the field in the 1970s, I developed my own set of lecture notes, which I later distributed to students. Over time, with feedback from students (the course typically had 40 students per semester), the lecture notes evolved into this textbook. In this way, the textbook was constantly subjected to student reaction. Sections where exposition was unclear were refined and rewritten. Topics that did not seem of interest to students were dropped and new ones added. The data used in the book were periodically updated.

The book also changed focus over the years. In the late 1970s, there were only inklings of the dramatic changes that were to befall the American economy. The original focus of the course was on the measurement of inequality and poverty and explanations of inequality. Since the only well-developed models of inequality at that time were for labor markets, the course also had a heavy dose of labor economics. Moreover, at that time, the most widely used and most fully articulated model was human capital theory, so that considerable space was also devoted to this topic.

However, by the late 1980s, when the writing of this book began in earnest, the three-fold malady of falling real wages, stagnating living standards, and widening income disparities had become apparent. In addition, poverty rates, which had leveled off in the 1970s, began rising again in the 1980s. The numbers themselves tell a dramatic story. As a result, the book began to emphasize the actual statistics themselves as a way of telling the story of these disturbing changes in the American economy.

Some economists who teach in this field may feel that the book has, perhaps, an overdose of statistical evidence. Moreover, it is admittedly much harder to examine students on statistics than on economic theory. However, my own feeling is that numeracy is crucial in its own right. It is important to give students a feel for the actual magnitudes involved—that overall poverty rates are of the order of 10 to 15 percent; that poverty rates for black families are of the order of 30 percent; that the share of wealth held by the richest one percent of households is of the order of 40 percent; that the income of black families is about 60 percent the income of white families; etc. If nothing else, an awareness of these figures will help students become more knowledgeable citizens and help them better understand the statistics that are periodically reported in our major newspapers and magazines.

The book maintains a strong emphasis on the role of labor markets. There are two reasons for this. First, about three-quarters of personal income arises from labor activities. Second, many public policy programs, most notably social security, are linked either directly or indirectly to labor market activities. This may create some overlap between this text and traditional labor economics, but the stress here is different—much more on the relation between labor activity and inequality. In my treatment of the human capital model, for example, the stress is on the determination of earnings differences between individuals. The book also provides a wider coverage of models of the labor market than is found in more traditional labor economics courses. Institutional models are given particular attention here—such as internal and dual labor market theory, interindustry wage differentials and efficiency wage theory, and structural models—because of the recent stress on the demand side of the labor market as a source of earnings inequality.

A section of the book is devoted to the inequality of household wealth, which is my own research speciality. As it turns out, changes in inequality are much more dramatic in terms of household wealth than in terms of income. Indeed, it appears that changes in income inequality become magnified in terms of wealth disparities. There is again a heavy emphasis on the statistical evidence, though a chapter in this section treats the determinants of wealth differences between families. The major focus is on life-cycle theory, since it is still the primary model on this subject. However, there is also a lengthy discussion on the role of inheritances, since they also play an important role in explaining disparities in wealth holdings among households and also raise some crucial ethical issues.

Discrimination is also another persistent problem that seems unlikely to disappear over the next several decades, and a whole section of the book concentrates on this issue. The news is particularly distressful for black families, who after making some progress in closing the income gap relative to white families between the early 1960s and the mid-1970s now find their relative incomes at the same level as in the early 1960s. Poverty rates also remain much higher for blacks than for whites. The role of public policy, particularly affirmative action, in explaining the changing fortunes of minorities is given considerable emphasis in the book. This subject is especially topical today in light of recent decisions by the Supreme Court and recent attempts by members of Congress to dismantle the system.

The last part of the book treats the role of public policy on both poverty and income inequality. This tends to be the part of the course that elicits the most student interest and participation. Because of the political discourse on this subject and the emotions it raises, I have found it particularly useful to "lay out the facts." The first chapter of this part examines the social security system and the welfare system in some detail. Most students are surprised by the fact that the resources devoted to the former are many times those spent on welfare. The second chapter describes the workings of the U.S. tax system. Here, too, there is considerable surprise that the overall tax burden has changed relatively little over time and that the tax system as a whole appears to favor neither the rich nor the poor and is distributionally neutral.

International comparisons also play an important role in this book. It becomes clear throughout the text that among the industrialized countries of the world, the U.S. is really a special case both in terms of the level of inequality and the degree of increase of inequality during the 1980s. It also becomes apparent that U.S. poverty rates are exceptionally high when compared to countries at similar levels of development.

INCOME INEQUALITY AND POVERTY: ——MEASUREMENT AND TRENDS——

PART I

1

INTRODUCTION: ISSUES AND SCOPE OF BOOK

1.1 RECENT TRENDS IN LIVING STANDARDS, INEQUALITY, POVERTY, AND DISCRIMINATION

The last two decades have witnessed some disturbing changes in the standard of living and inequality in the United Sates. Perhaps the grimmest news is that the **real wage** (average wages and salaries adjusted for inflation) has been falling since 1973. Between 1973 and 1993, the real wage fell by 11 percent. This contrasts with the preceding years, 1950 to 1973, when real wages grew by 58 percent (see Chapter 2 for more details).

Changes in living standards have followed a somewhat different course. Living standards are normally measured by **income,** defined as the sum of the following: wages and salaries; interest, dividends, and rental receipts; and transfers such as social security benefits, unemployment insurance, and welfare payments. **Median family income** (the income of the average family, found in the middle of the distribution when families are ranked from lowest to highest in terms of income) remained virtually constant in real terms between 1973 and 1989 but then declined by 7 percent between 1989 and 1993. Despite falling real wages, living standards were maintained for a while by the growing labor force participation of wives. The percentage of wives with a job increased from 41 percent in 1970 to 57 percent in 1988. Among mothers with children in age group 6 to 17, the percentage at work grew from 55 percent in 1975 to 73 percent in 1988, and for mothers with children under the age of 6, the proportion at work increased from 39 to 56 percent over the same period. However, since 1989, this growth has slowed down, and with it, real living standards have fallen (see Chapters 2, 5, and 14).

Another troubling change is the turnaround in inequality witnessed in the United States over the last two decades. Inequality in the distribution of family income, which had remained virtually unchanged since the end of World War II until 1973, has increased sharply since then. The share of income of the top fifth of households climbed from 43.6 percent of all income in 1973 to 49.1 percent in 1994, with the share of the richest five percent rising from 16.6 to 21.2 percent, while the share of the poorest 20 percent fell from 4.2 to 3.6 percent (see Chapter 3).

What makes the rise in inequality particularly worrisome is that not only has the *relative* share of income fallen among the bottom half of the income distribution but their *absolute* income has fallen as well. The average income of the poorest fifth fell by 2.7 percent between 1973 and 1994 and that of the second poorest fifth by 3.8 percent, while that of the top fifth rose by 27.2 percent and that of the top 5 percent by a dramatic 44.2 percent. Once adjustments are made for changes in family size, the living standards of the bottom quintile declined by 18 percent from 1973 to 1994, while that of the top quintile rose by 32 percent (see Chapter 3). The poverty rate, which had declined from a postwar peak of 22 percent in 1960 to 12 percent by 1979, has since risen to 15.1 percent in 1993, about the same level as in 1966 (see Chapter 4).

Even more dramatic changes are evident for household **wealth** (the assets a family owns, such as a home, savings accounts, stocks, and bonds, less any outstanding debt). Inequality of household wealth has also been rising since the late 1970s in the United States. The share of total wealth owned by the top one percent almost doubled between 1976 and 1992. Between 1983 and 1989, in particular, its share increased from 33.7 to 38.9 percent. While **mean wealth** (total wealth divided by the number of families) grew by 23 percent in real terms over this period, median wealth increased by only 8 percent. Moreover, while the average net worth of the top three quintiles increased in real terms, the wealth of the bottom two quintiles suffered an absolute decline. All in all, the top 20 percent of wealth holders received 99 percent of the total gain in wealth over the period from 1983 to 1989, while the bottom 80 percent accounted for only 1 percent. The top one percent alone enjoyed 62 percent of wealth growth (see Chapter 10).

The main source of the rising inequality of family income and wealth appears to stem from changes in the structure of the labor market. Among male workers alone, wage disparities widened between the high-paid workers and the low-paid ones. Average real earnings of the bottom one-fifth of male workers fell by 9 percent between 1969 and 1979 and by another 17 percent between 1979 and 1989. In contrast, the earnings of the top fifth of male earners increased by 10 percent over the two decades.

Another indication of the dramatic changes taking place in the labor market is the sharp rise in the returns to education, particularly a college degree, that occurred during the 1980s. The differential in earnings between college graduates and high school graduates more than doubled among white males (with one to five years of work experience), from a ratio of 1.4 in 1980 to 1.9 in 1988. Among black men, the college premium increased from 1.7 to 2.0 (see Chapter 7).

Another disturbing finding is that the United States has now become the most unequal country among the advanced, industrialized countries of the world in terms of both income and wealth. One telling statistic is the ratio of the family income of the ninetieth percentile (the income of the family that ranks in the top ten percent of the income distribution) to that of the tenth percentile (the income of the family that ranks in the bottom ten percent of the income distribution). In 1986, this ratio was 5.9 in the United States. The second highest country was Canada, with a ratio of 4.0. The most equal country was Sweden, with a ratio of 2.7 (see Chapter 3). The United States also has the highest poverty rate among advanced countries. During the 1980s, it was about twice that of the United Kingdom's, $2^{1}/_{2}$ times that of West Germany, and over three times that of Norway and Sweden. Differences between the United States and other countries were particularly acute for one-person families.

In terms of wealth, the share of the top percentile in the United States in 1989 was 39 percent. This was much higher than in other countries with comparable data, including Canada, France, Sweden, and the United Kingdom. Moreover, this result contrasts rather sharply with the early part of the twentieth century (the 1920s, in particular) when wealth inequality was greater in Sweden and the United Kingdom than in the United States (see Chapter 10).

Marked differences also exist between different demographic groups in American society. For one, racial disparities in income have not only continued to persist over the last two decades but have actually been widening. In 1947, the ratio of median income between black and white families was 51 percent. This ratio increased between 1947 and 1975, reaching a peak of 62 percent. However, since that time, the relative income of black families has declined, and by 1993, it had fallen to 54 percent, the same ratio as in 1962. Indeed, in absolute terms (constant dollars), the median income of black families was the same in 1993 as it was in 1969.

However, black families have continued to make progress relative to white families in terms of wealth. The ratio of mean wealth between black and white families increased from 0.12 in 1962 to 0.33 in 1992, while the ratio of median wealth climbed from 0.04 to 0.20. Nevertheless, the wealth gap continues to remain considerably greater than the income gap (see Chapter 13).

One of the most important changes in the labor market has been the increasing participation rate of women. The percent of women in the labor force increased from 34 percent in 1950 to 58 percent in 1992. The participation rates have increased not only for single women but also for married women and, in particular, married women with young children. Another piece of good news is that despite the large increase in female employment, the gender gap in wages has been narrowing since 1970, and especially since 1980. Among full-time, full-year workers, the ratio of earnings between women and men increased from 0.60 in 1980 to 0.71 in 1992. One reason for these gains is that women have been entering professional occupations that were, until recently, almost completely dominated by men (see Chapter 14).

Not all women have done well over the last two decades. One group that has seen its fortunes deteriorate is female-headed households. Their number has increased dramatically since 1970. In 1988, 44 percent of black families with children were headed by a woman (no husband present), up from 31 percent in 1970. The comparable figures for white families were 13.0 percent in 1988 and 9.5 percent in 1970. This group also has the highest poverty rate of any demographic group, 32 percent in 1989. Moreover, in that year female-headed families accounted for over half of all poor families in the country (see Chapters 4 and 13).

Another group that has fared poorly over the last few decades is children (under the age of 18). The poverty rate among children has climbed from 14 percent in 1973 to 20 percent in 1989, whereas the overall poverty rate (for individuals) increased from 11.1 to 12.8 percent. One reason for this change is the growing number of children living in female-headed households. The percentage of black children living with only their mother increased from 22 percent in 1960 to 54 percent in 1988, and for white children, from 7 to 19 percent.

In contrast, the elderly (persons 65 years of age or older) represent what is, perhaps, the greatest success story of the last quarter century. The poverty rate of elderly families fell from 18 percent in 1969, almost double the national average, to 6.6 percent in 1989, well below the overall average. Much of their improvement was due to substantial increases in social security coverage and benefit levels (see Chapters 4 and 15).

1.2 CAUSES OF RISING INEQUALITY

The turnaround in inequality during the 1980s is particularly puzzling in light of the strong economic growth during the Reagan years. Normally, income inequality lessens during periods of prosperity and worsens during economic downturns. Except for the 1981–1982 recession, the decade of the 1980s was one of general prosperity, with stable economic growth. Moreover, the U.S. economy also experienced a reversal in productivity growth over the last decade. The period from 1973–1979 witnessed the slowest growth in labor productivity during the postwar period. Indeed, overall labor productivity growth fell from approximately 3 percent during the 1947–1967 years to under 1 percent from 1973 to 1979. However, productivity growth has been averaging about 2 percent per year over the last decade and a half, which is quite close to its twentieth century average.

Another anomalous phenomenon is the pattern of real wage growth. Historically, the average real wage has moved in line with average labor productivity. Real wages have remained virtually unchanged during the

1973–1987 years. This is understandable during the 1973–1979 period, when productivity was almost at a standstill, but not during the ensuing years, when productivity growth picked up.

The recent rise of inequality in light of sustained economic growth in the United States has spawned a considerable amount of literature. Why is inequality rising in this country? Is it also rising in other countries and, if so, to the same degree? Much of the rest of this book will return to this issue when we look at the various factors that affect income inequality. It is, perhaps, useful at this point to mention the major factors that will be considered in these studies.

Skill-Biased Technology Change

Perhaps the leading argument is that the last twenty years have seen a major technological revolution in this country, led by widespread computerization and the consequent penetration of information technology. This change has skewed the income distribution by placing a high premium on college-educated and skilled labor while reducing the demand for semiskilled and unskilled workers. One important piece of evidence is that the rate of return to a college education (the wage premium paid to a college graduate relative to a high school graduate) approximately doubled over the decade of the 1980s (see Chapter 7).

The Shift to Services

One of the notable changes in the composition of the labor force during the postwar period is the shift of jobs from goods-producing industries to services. The share of employment in services grew from 43 percent in 1950 to 72 percent in 1993. All of the employment growth during the 1980s occurred in the service sector. Some have argued that the dispersion of earnings is greater in services than in goods-producing industries because of the greater mix of professional and managerial jobs with relatively low-skilled clerical and manual work (see Chapters 5 and 9).

Declining Unionization

The proportion of employees represented by unions peaked in 1954, at 25.4 percent of the total labor force, and at 34.7 percent of the nonfarm labor force. After 1954, the trend was downward, and in 1993, only 15.8 percent were union members. Part of the reason for the decline in union representation is the de-industrialization that has occurred over the last couple of decades, because manufacturing industries in particular have had high unionization rates. Unions have historically negotiated collective bargaining agreements with narrow wage differentials between different types of jobs. This is one reason why the dispersion of earnings in manufacturing has tended to be lower than that of service industries. Their decline has led to widening differentials in the overall wage structure (see Chapter 8).

Growing International Trade

The increasing trade liberalization of the 1970s, 1980s, and 1990s has been cited as another factor of income inequality. Imports into the U.S. economy have grown from 5.5 percent of GDP in 1970 to 11.4 percent in 1993. According to standard trade theory, as trade increases, there is a growing tendency of factor prices—particularly, wages—to equalize across countries. This can take the form of rising wages among our trading partners as well as declining wages in our own labor force. As imports of manufactured products produced in low-income countries such as Indonesia, China, Thailand, Mexico, and Brazil increase, downward pressure is placed on the wages of unskilled and semiskilled workers in American manufacturing industries. This process explains both the falling average real wage of American workers (see Chapter 2) as well as the increasing gap between blue-collar workers and professionals who work in industries such as law, medicine, education, and business services that are well shielded from imports (see Chapter 9).

Downsizing and Outsourcing

Another suspect is the corporate restructuring that has taken place during the 1980s and 1990s. This process has taken two forms. First, permanent employees have gradually been replaced by part-time, temporary, and "leased" employees. Second, a number of important corporate functions such as maintenance, cafeteria services, legal services, and data processing that were traditionally performed by in-house employees have been outsourced (substituted for) by purchasing these operations from other companies. Both processes have reduced the relative number of permanent employees in large corporations. Corporate employees have traditionally enjoyed high wages, high benefits, job security, career-ladder type jobs, and good working conditions. This set of job characteristics is referred to as an internal or primary labor market. In contrast, wages tend to be low in secondary jobs found in part-time employment and small businesses. The shift of employment out of the primary labor force to the secondary labor market may have been another factor accounting for rising income inequality (see Chapter 8).

Public Policy Changes

The social safety net that has provided some degree of income maintenance to the low-income population has gradually frayed during the 1980s and 1990s. Welfare benefits have been falling in real terms (the average benefit in 1993 is down by 45 percent from 1970), and the percent of unemployed workers who receive unemployment compensation has also declined. Moreover, the minimum wage has fallen by 36 percent in real terms between its peak in 1968 and 1993. This has helped put downward pressure on the wages of unskilled workers and may account, in part, for the growing wage disparities between the unskilled and skilled workers and the decline in the average real wage since 1973 (see Chapters 9 and 15).

In contrast, changes in the tax code over the last two decades appear to have generally favored the rich over the middle class and the poor. The Tax Act of 1981 and the Tax Reform Act of 1986 lowered the tax rate paid by the rich (the top marginal tax rate) from 70 percent in 1980 to 28 percent in 1986, though it has since risen to 39.6 percent in 1994. The biggest increase in taxes has been from the social security tax, which primarily affects middle-class tax payers. However, some changes in the tax code have hurt the rich, including an increase in capital gains taxation, and some changes have bene-fited the poor, particularly the introduction of the Earned Income Tax Credit. Overall, however, it appears that the redistributional effects of the tax system—that is, the degree to which the rich are taxed more heavily than the poor—have lessened since the beginning of the 1980s. We shall analyze these changes in Chapter 16.

1.3 PLAN OF THIS TEXTBOOK

Is the standard of living still rising in the United States? Is inequality increasing or declining? Has poverty in this country attenuated or is it growing? What groups have fared well and what groups have done poorly? Is race and gender discrimination still a problem today? How unequal a country are we in comparison to other industrialized countries? Should we be concerned about inequality and poverty in our country? What factors are responsible for inequality? What role has public policy played? These and related questions will provide the general focus of this textbook.

This textbook will focus on historical trends in economic inequality, particularly since the early 1970s, and analyze the role of government policy and other factors on inequality movements. The book will also provide a public policy focus. It will examine the roles of transfer programs, the personal income tax system, the social security system, and anti-discrimination programs and policies, among others.

Comparisons of the United States with other countries will also be made where appropriate. This serves a two-fold purpose. The first is that it allows us to make an assessment about whether inequality is high or low compared to other nations with similar economic structures and development. Second, it allows us to draw inferences about the causes of growing inequality in the United States—whether these are structural in nature, thus affecting other industrialized countries, or whether they are a consequence of particular government policies followed in the United States and other countries. A more global concern of the book is whether there is growing disparity of income and economic well-being between the developed nations of the world and the less-developed ones.

The textbook serves as a self-contained course on income distribution and poverty, with additional emphasis on issues of discrimination. This book also contains sections on microeconomics (the derivation of the supply and demand curve for labor) and basic statistics.

The textbook is organized into five parts. The first part of the book treats the definition and measurement of income inequality and poverty and presents a statistical picture of the two. Part 2 investigates the role of labor markets in explaining differences in earnings among individuals. Part 3 considers differences in wealth holdings both as a factor accounting for differences in well-being among households and as another dimension of inequality in its own right. Part 4 explores the role of race and gender discrimination in accounting for differences in income and poverty rates. Part 5 considers the effect of public policy in both reducing inequality and alleviating poverty. Here, it should be noted that discussion of public policy is not confined to Part 5 but occurs throughout the textbook, particularly in Chapters 13 and 14 on discrimination.

Part 1 deals primarily with the measurement of inequality and poverty and their historical trends. Chapter 2 discusses how income and, more generally, the standard of living are measured. Basic concepts of national income accounting are discussed, as well as the measurement of personal income and alternative measures of personal well-being. Historical trends for the United States and comparisons with other countries are presented.

Chapter 3 develops basic measures of income inequality and presents a statistical overview. Standard indices of inequality are developed, including the Lorenz curve and the Gini coefficient. Particular attention is accorded to the rise in U.S. income inequality in more recent years. International comparisons are also included.

Chapter 4 presents a broad overview of issues in poverty. Three basic concepts of poverty are developed—absolute, relative, and subjective poverty lines. More recent issues in the measurement of poverty are canvassed, such as including noncash government benefits in the definition of family income. Trends in poverty rates are discussed, as well as comparisons of poverty incidence between black and white families and other demographic groupings. Particular attention is also paid to the changing composition of the poor in America, the "feminization of poverty," its rising incidence among children, and the development of an "underclass." International comparisons are also presented.

Part 2 looks at the role of the labor market as a source of income differences among individuals. Chapter 5 introduces the concept of the labor force, employment, and unemployment. It discusses trends in labor force participation patterns (who works and who does not), the composition of employment (the decline of manufacturing and the shift to services), and unemployment patterns (particularly by demographic characteristic). There is also some discussion of the sources of unemployment.

Chapter 6 introduces the standard neoclassical wage model, including the supply curve of labor, the demand schedule for labor, and the formation of an equilibrium. The human capital model is also developed, with the emphasis on the role of both schooling and on-the-job training in the determination of relative earnings.

Chapter 7 summarizes empirical work in the human capital tradition, which shows that schooling and experience play a major role in the determination of relative earnings. The value of a college education is highlighted. The recent rise in the returns to education is also given emphasis, as well as explanations for this occurrence. The contribution of human capital variables to overall earnings inequality is analyzed. Other interpretations of the schooling-earnings relation are also considered (such as job screening), as well as the connection between schooling and worker productivity. The last part treats the role of ability as a factor in determining wages and salaries.

Chapters 8 and 9 investigate the role of institutional factors in accounting for differentials in labor earnings. In Chapter 8, the role of labor unions is discussed. After a brief history of the trade union movement in the United States and trends in union membership, the chapter considers the economic role of unions. The first part of the chapter concludes with an analysis of whether unions have been effective in raising their members' earnings. The second part looks at the role of both internal labor markets and segmented labor markets in explaining earnings differences. Are there rigidities in wage structures within organizations (internal labor markets)? Do there exist noncompeting segments in the labor market with different wage structures? Do these barriers help explain the persistence of earnings differences between certain groups?

Chapter 9 looks at structural explanations for inequality in earnings. The first part considers the role of industrial mix in (regional) earnings inequality. The second part analyzes industry differences in wages and salaries. Do some industries pay more than others and, if so, why (efficiency wage theory)? The third part looks at occupational wage differences—particularly, their increasing spread in recent years. The last part assesses the role of structural factors in accounting for the recent increase in earnings inequality in the labor market.

Another major factor in accounting for differences in family well-being is household wealth. Part 3 treats the distribution of household wealth. Chapter 10 introduces the concept of household wealth. Important methodological issues are discussed in the second part, including the definition of wealth, the role of retirement income, and the availability of data sources. The next part presents evidence on long-term time trends in household wealth concentration in the United States and several European countries. More recent trends in U.S. wealth inequality are emphasized. The composition of household wealth is considered next, including trends in homeownership rates. Several economists have proposed composite measures of income and wealth as better indicators of well-being than income alone, and several alternative measures are presented.

The accumulation of household wealth depends not only on income but also on savings behavior, capital appreciation, and gifts and inheritances. Moreover, wealth is the direct source of property income, which is an important factor in accounting for disparities in family income. Chapter 11 considers some of the factors accounting for differences in wealth among families. Major emphasis is given to the life cycle model as an explanation of household savings. Since individuals work only part of their life, they have a strong incentive to accumulate wealth for their retirement years, which is one explanation for why older families are richer than younger ones. Bequests are another factor in explaining wealth differences, and their importance will also be assessed. The government itself plays a role in distributing wealth across generations through the social security system, and its role will be examined in the third part of the chapter.

Another major factor that explains differences in earnings and income between groups in our society is discrimination. This topic is covered in Part 4. In Chapter 12, we consider what discrimination means and how it is measured. Alternative models of discrimination are assessed, including taste for discrimination, statistical discrimination, and the overcrowding model of occupational segregation.

Chapter 13 presents evidence on trends in racial discrimination. Have blacks gained on whites in terms of wages, employment patterns, education, family income and wealth, and poverty incidence over the postwar period? Have Hispanic Americans made progress? This chapter then considers the principal factors in explaining changes in the economic status of black families, including migration from the South, gains in education, and changes in black family structure. The role and effectiveness of anti-discrimination government programs are also assessed.

Chapter 14 considers gender discrimination. Has the female-male wage gap declined since the end of World War II, and have women made gains in penetrating traditionally male occupations? This chapter discusses the major factors in explaining changes in the gender wage gap, including trends in female labor force participation rates, human capital differences, and occupational segregation. This chapter also investigates the effectiveness of anti-discrimination programs, with particular attention paid to issues of comparable worth.

Have government programs made a difference on inequality and poverty in the United States? The last part of the book considers the role of public policy on income and wealth inequality and poverty. Chapter 15 focuses on the role of public policy in alleviating poverty. The chapter begins with a brief history of the development of the income maintenance system in the United States. It then looks in detail at several of the major income support systems in the United States today: unemployment insurance, the social security system, Aid to Families with Dependent Children, manpower programs, and the minimum wage. The chapter ends with an overall assessment of these programs, particularly with regard to their effectiveness in reducing poverty.

Chapter 16 begins by raising the issue of why equality may be an important social goal. The next part provides a description of the system of taxation currently in place in the United States. It then considers the redistributional effects of government tax policy. Is the tax system progressive, regressive, or neutral? Does the system reduce or increase overall income inequality? The third part looks at the other side of the ledger, the effects of government disbursements. It considers the questions of which groups benefit from government expenditures and what are their distributional consequences.

2

Income, Earnings, and the Standard of Living

Is average income still rising in the United States? Does the United States still have the highest standard of living in the world? This chapter addresses these two issues and focuses, more generally, on how income and the standard of living are measured. We begin with a discussion of national income accounting and the measurement of personal income. We also present historical trends for the United States and comparisons of income levels with other countries. These topics are important for two reasons. First, in order to measure income inequality, it is first necessary to determine what income is. Likewise with poverty, which necessitates establishing an adequate concept of income in order to provide an operational definition of poverty. Second, trends in average income are just as important (perhaps more important) for well-being as changes in the inequality of income.

The major source of personal income is work. People earn a wage or salary for the time that they work. Wages and salaries—or, more broadly speaking, labor earnings—account for most of the personal income received in the United States and other developed countries today.

There are several other sources of personal income. One of the most common is interest income, which comes from savings accounts, government bonds, corporate securities, and the like. Another form of personal income is the dividends that are received from corporate stock ownership. Owners of small, unincorporated businesses receive business income. Real estate often yields rental income. Retirees who have participated in a pension plan receive pension income. There are also various "transfer payments" from the government. The most common source is social security income (more technically called "Old Age and Survivors Insurance," or OASI), which is also received by retired workers. Other forms are unemployment insurance benefits, which are paid to workers who are temporarily out of work, and welfare payments, which are given to destitute families.

Since the determination of income is the central focus of this book, it is important that we begin with a clear understanding of the concept of income. We shall do this by presenting a brief introduction to the National Income and Product Accounts (Section 2.1). The national accounts, as they are called for short, provide an overall conceptual framework for relating national income to the total product the nation produces—that is, Gross Domestic Product, or GDP. The national accounts use a double-entry book-keeping system in order to verify that total income always equals total product. In Section 2.2, personal income is defined and its relation to national income is discussed. Several tables are presented on the composition of personal income.

Section 2.3 introduces the concept of the standard of living. Alternative measures of the average well-being of a society are discussed. Such indices are found to be sensitive to the choice of welfare unit—the individual versus the family, for example—and the choice of income concept—before-tax versus after-tax income, for example. Several tables are presented which show the change in average welfare levels in the United States over time and compare the United States to other countries in the world.

In Section 2.4, we shift gears to a somewhat different concern—namely, factor shares or the functional distribution of income. Here, we are concerned with the form in which income is received—whether as wages and salaries or as income from property. Historical data are presented on trends in the wage and profit share from 1850 to the present.

Section 2.5 treats another dimension of well-being—household production. This concept refers to unpaid activities that occur within the household and provide direct utility to the family—cooking, cleaning, child care, home repair, and the like. These activities often substitute for market production. Section 2.6 raises a few technical issues on the measurement of income. A summary is provided in Section 2.7.

2.1 AN INTRODUCTION TO THE NATIONAL INCOME AND PRODUCT ACCOUNTS

The National Income and Product Accounts (NIPA, or "national accounts," for short) is an overall accounting statement of the performance of the economy over a given time period (usually a calendar year). Perhaps the most common measure from the national accounts is GDP, which shows the total output produced by a nation's economy in the course of a year. Other important measures are Net National Product (NNP), national income, personal income, and personal disposable income. All these measures appear quarterly (every three months) and are usually reported in major newspapers. The development of national accounts began during the 1930s. Their principal architect in the United States was the Russian-born economist Simon Kuznets, who was awarded the Nobel Prize for this achievement. Today, almost all the nations of the world publish official national accounts. In the United States, they are compiled by the Bureau of Economic Analysis, which is part of the Department of Commerce.

Perhaps the easiest way to understand the national accounts is through another accounting device—input-output analysis—that was also developed during the 1930s and by another Russian-born economist, Wassily Leontief. (He also received a Nobel Prize for this achievement.) An input-output system records the sales of goods not only to final users but also to intermediate users. These intermediate users are the producing industries of an economy, such as agriculture, mining, construction, manufacturing, transportation, and services. The transactions are recorded in a matrix form, so that each column of the interindustry portion of matrix shows the inputs required to produce a given level of output. The columns thus represent the technology of production. The rows of the matrix indicate how much each industry sells to other industries and final consumers. The rows thus show the distribution of the sales of each industry. In addition, beneath the interindustry portion of the matrix are rows showing the wages paid out and the gross profits received in each sector.

Diagram 2.1 presents a simplified input-output view of the economy. (The figures in the table are only illustrative.) There are only three producing sectors (or industries). The first sector produces raw materials, like iron ore, wood, and other basic materials. These are intermediate goods because they are used exclusively by other industries to produce their output. The second sector produces metal products. Some metal products like bolts and screws are intermediate goods, since they are inputs into other industries, while others such as stainless steel flatware are final goods, since they are purchased by households for their private consumption. The third sector produces food and clothing, which are consumption or final goods.

Let us first look at the columns of the three sectors. The total or gross output of the raw materials sector is $21 million. To produce this, the sector purchased $3 million of raw materials (trees, for example, are required to produce lumber) and $2 million worth of metal products. In addition, 1,000 workers were employed, who were paid a total of $9 million, and $65 million worth of capital was used. Capital consists of plant and equipment, which are distinguished from intermediate inputs in that they last much longer than the production period. (For example, when trees are transformed into lumber, the original trees no longer exist, whereas the circular saws used to cut the lumber continue to function.)

The total direct cost was $14 million (3 + 2 + 9). In addition, $1 million was paid out in indirect business taxes, such as sales and excise taxes. The remaining entry in the column is gross profits, which amounted to $6

Diagram 2.1 An Illustrative Input-Output Table of the Economy[a]

	Intermediate Users			Final Demand			
	Raw Materials	Metal Products	Food & Clothing	Consumption	Investment	Government	Totals
Raw materials	3	11	7	0	0	0	21
Metal products	2	4	1	13	5	7	32
Food and clothing	0	0	0	15	0	4	19
Wages and salaries	9	7	6				22
Gross profits	6	8	4				18
Indirect taxes (business)	1	2	1				4
Totals	21	32	19	28	5	11	

GDP = 28 + 5 + 11 = 22 + 18 + 4 = 44

<u>(Below the Line)</u>

Employment	1000	500	600		2100
Capital	65	80	35		180

[a]All figures are in millions of dollars, except for employment, which is in number of workers.

million. This item is often regarded as a return on capital. For this sector, the return on capital was 9.2 percent (6 divided by 65). It should now be apparent that the total value of output equals the sum of all the inputs used plus gross profits plus indirect business taxes.

The total output of the metal products industry is $32 million. To produce this, the industry used $11 million worth of raw materials and $4 million worth of metal products. It hired 500 workers, who were paid $7 million, paid out $2 million in indirect business taxes, and made $8 million in gross profits. Since its capital was worth $80 million, its rate of return was 10 percent (8/80). The major input into the food and clothing sector was raw materials, which amounted to $7 million out of a total output of $19 million. One million dollars' worth of metal products was also purchased, and $6 million in wages and $1 million in indirect business taxes were paid out. The gross profits in this sector totaled $4 million, or 11.4 percent on the capital stock.[1]

The rows of the matrix show where the output produced in each sector is sold. Thus, of the $21 million worth of raw materials produced, $3 million was sold to other raw material producers, $11 million to the metal products industry, $7 million to the food and clothing industry, and none to final demand. It should be noted that the row total for each sector must, by construction, equal the column total.[2] The metal products industry sells its output to both intermediate and final users. Of the $32 million produced, $7 million was sold to other industries and $25 million to final demand. In this table, final demand is divided into three components: household consumption, investment, and government expenditure.[3] Metal products are purchased by all three sources of final demand. Consumers purchased $13 million worth of housewares, appliances, and other metal products; $5 million worth of equipment and machinery was purchased for investment; and $7 million worth of defense hardware, filing cabinets, and the like was bought by the government. Finally, food and clothing were sold exclusively to final users. Fifteen million dollars' worth was bought by households and $4 million by the government (for police and armed force uniforms, food for troops, etc.).

Let us now see how the input-output table can be used to generate the national accounts. It is first important to distinguish between gross output and final output. The gross output (or, more technically, the gross domestic output) of a sector is the total value of the goods produced in the sector. This is recorded in both the first three column totals and the first three row totals. However, it should be apparent that the value of the gross output of a sector includes the value of goods produced by other industries during the period. Thus, the sum of gross output (in this case, 21 + 32 + 19 = 72) does not really represent anything, since the output of raw materials and metal products is double-counted. What is meaningful is the sum of the final output of the economy, since there is no double-counting involved. In this case, total household consumption was $28 million, total investment $5 million, and total government expenditure $11 million. The grand total was $44

---

[1] The columns of the input-output matrix have another interpretation. Suppose we divide the inter-industry entries in the matrix by their column total and designate this new matrix by the letter a:

$$a = \begin{pmatrix} 0.14 & 0.34 & 0.37 \\ 0.10 & 0.13 & 0.05 \\ 0.0 & 0.0 & 0.0 \end{pmatrix}$$

The a matrix, which is called the direct coefficient matrix, shows the technology of production used in each industry. For example, in the first industry, 14 cents' worth of raw materials is required for each dollar of output, while in the third industry, 37 cents is required. These coefficients are useful in projecting changes in industrial output that would result from changes in the pattern of demand.

[2] One may wonder about unsold goods produced by an industry. These are technically referred to as "inventories" and are recorded as a form of investment.

[3] The two components missing from final demand are exports and imports, where the latter is recorded as a negative flow (see Section 2.5).

million. The sum of final output is very familiar; it is called Gross Domestic Output, or GDP.

There are three components on the income side of the ledger: (1) wages and salaries, which summed to $22 million; (2) gross profits, which amounted to $18 million; and (3) indirect business taxes, which equaled $4 million. These three components taken together are also referred to as value added, since they represent the net addition to the value of the inter-industry inputs added by the factors of production. These three components are also income flows, since they are received by households, firms, and the government, respectively. The sum of value added equals $44 million, which is identical to GDP. (This should not be too surprising, since the intermediate flows are subtracted from both the column totals and row totals to arrive at their respective totals.) This is, in fact, the ingenious feature of the NIPA, that total product and total income must always be equal. This means that one can look at either income statements or product accounts to get a measure of the total output produced by the economy.

It is also possible to derive Net National Product, NNP, from these accounts. As indicated above, the full value of the capital stock is *not* included in the value of the final product or value added, since it is not fully consumed during the production period. In fact, in any given period, some portion of the capital stock wears out (machines and buildings do not last forever). This portion of the capital stock that is consumed during a period is called depreciation. The actual measure of "true economic depreciation" is a subject of much controversy. However, for national income accounting purposes, the measure is usually based on computations done by corporations for business income tax purposes. The Internal Revenue Service provides guidelines for depreciation, and these entries, called capital consumption allowances, are used as the basis of the measure of depreciation.

In Diagram 2.1, depreciation is included in the gross profits entry. The difference between gross profits and depreciation is often referred to as net profits. On the product side, the corresponding concept to depreciation is replacement investment. That is to say, the investment done by an economy during a given period consists of two parts: the first to replace worn out plant and equipment and the second to expand the capital stock. This second portion is referred to as net investment. NNP is thus equal to the sum of household consumption plus government expenditures plus net investment (plus exports less imports), which in turn equals the sum of labor earnings plus indirect business taxes plus **net profits.**

NNP is conceptually superior to GDP as a measure of the total final product of an economy, since it excludes that portion of new investment that is required simply to maintain the capital stock at its existing level.[4] However, because of the difficulty of measuring true economic deprecia-

_____

[4]GDP actually has the somewhat ironic property that the faster that capital goods are worn out, the higher the value of GDP is! An interesting class assignment would be to try to construct an example to show why this is so.

tion, GDP is the concept most often used to measure the overall performance of an economy.

2.2 THE SOURCES OF PERSONAL INCOME

In this book, we are interested primarily in personal income—that is, income received by families and individuals. Let us return to Diagram 2.1. As we noted above, the sum of national income must, of necessity, equal the sum of national product. However, it does not necessarily follow that the individual components of income equal the "corresponding" components of final demand. For example, total wages and salaries in Diagram 2.1 are $22 million, but total household consumption is higher, at $28 million. Gross profits are $18 million but total investment is only $5 million, while indirect business taxes total $4 million but government spending is $11 million. The reason for these differences is that the value-added categories of income do not really indicate the final recipient of the income. For example, income taxes are paid on wages and are remitted to the government. This is also true of a portion of the gross profits received by business. Moreover, part of the gross profits of firms are disbursed to individuals in the form of dividends and interest payments. Finally, part of the taxes received by the government are transferred to individuals in the form of social security benefits and the like.

In Diagram 2.2, we show how the value-added income categories can be schematically related to the final recipients of income. There are three different classes of recipients: (1) households, (2) businesses, and (3) governments. In our example, workers received $22 million in wages and salaries. Of this, we will assume that they paid $4 million in personal income taxes to the government. Gross profits received by businesses were $18 million. Of this, businesses paid $9 million in corporate income taxes and other business taxes to the government, leaving $9 million for the firms. Of this $9 million, businesses distributed $5 million to households in the form of dividends and retained $4 million, which represents the sum of undistributed firm profits and depreciation claimed by the businesses.

Finally, the government received $4 million in the form of indirect business taxes. It also collected $4 million of personal income taxes and $9 million in corporate taxes. The total receipts of government were thus $17 million. From this, the government transferred $7 million to households in the form of social security and the like. This transaction is recorded as a *negative* $7 million for the government and a (positive) $7 million for households. Notice that the row totals are identical to those of the corresponding value-added rows in Diagram 2.1. Moreover, since transfer payments always appear as a negative for one sector and a positive for another, on net, the sum of transfer payments must equal zero. The sum of value added still remains $44 million.

Let us now look at the column totals. The first column records the various sources of personal income. The first is wages and salaries. The second

Diagram 2.2   The Relation of Value Added to the Income of Households, Businesses, and the Government: An Illustrative Example

Value-Added Components (and Transfers)	Households	Final Recipients Businesses	Government	Total
1. Wage and salaries	18	0	4 (personal income taxes)	22
2. Gross profits	5 (dividends)	4	9 (corporate income taxes)	18
3. Indirect business taxes	0	0	4	4
4. Transfers	7	0	−7	0
Total income	30	4	10	44
Total spending[a]	28	5	11	44
Net savings (deficit)	2	−1	−1	0

[a]From the final demand columns of Diagram 2.1.

consists of dividends distributed from businesses. The third source in this example is transfer payments received from the government. The sum of household income was $30 million. This is referred to as personal disposable income, because the income taxes paid by families have already been subtracted, and this is the amount of money over which households have discretionary control. If we add back in the income taxes, we obtain what is called personal income, which totaled $34 million.[5]

In the second column of Diagram 2.2, the retained earnings of businesses (including depreciation allowances) totaled $4 million. In the third

_____

[5] To simplify the discussion, it was assumed that personal income taxes were paid only on wages and salaries. In actuality, income taxes are paid on total personal income, including dividends and some kinds of transfer payments.

column, the net receipts of the government after transfer payments amounted to $10 million. The sum of personal disposable income plus business retained earnings plus government net receipts was $44 million, identical to total value added.

Let us now compare the income of these three segments of the economy with the final demand columns of Diagram 2.1. The personal disposable income of households amounted to $30 million, whereas total household consumption was $28 million. The difference of $2 million is referred to as personal savings. Businesses, moreover, invested $5 million in new plant and equipment, but their retained earnings were only $4 million. The government spent $11 million on goods and services, yet its net receipts were only $10 million. The government, in other words, ran a deficit of $1 million.

We may wonder how the business sector was able to invest $5 million when its retained earnings were only $4 million and how the government managed to spend $11 million when its receipts were only $10 million. The answers lie in the fact that households saved $2 million. Thus, either directly through the purchase of corporate stocks and bonds and government securities or indirectly through deposits in banks, which in turn bought corporate and government securities, personal savings were used to finance the business and government deficits.

The Composition of Personal Income in the United States

Let us now turn to the actual U.S. economy. Table 2.1 shows the percentage composition of personal income for selected years since 1929. The first component is total labor earnings. This is the sum of not only wages and salaries received by employees but also of employer-paid fringe benefits, such as health insurance, life insurance, and pension contributions. Since these benefits are paid directly by the employer, they are not included in the employee's paycheck but still form part of total employee compensation.[6]

The second component is called proprietors' earnings. This component did not appear in Diagram 2.1 because we assumed that all business income was received by corporations. However, there are many businesses that are operated by single individuals (or partnerships) and are unincorporated. Income received by such self-employed individuals is considered personal income. These proprietors own farms, stores, and other small businesses.

The third component is the rental income received by individuals. This income comes from real estate and rental property owned by individuals (as

---

[6]An adjustment has also been made to exclude both the employee's and the employer's contribution for social insurance (mainly the social security contribution). The reason for the exclusion is that these contributions are transferred to other households in the form of social security benefits and the like. If we included both the social security contributions and benefits as part of personal income, we would essentially be counting the same flow twice.

Table 2.1 The Percentage Composition of Total Personal Income by Income Source, 1929–93[a]

Year	Total Labor Earnings[b]	Total Proprietors' Earnings[c]	Rental Income[d]	Dividends	Personal Interest Income	Transfer Payments	Total Income
1929	60.4	17.1	5.8	6.9	8.2	1.8	100.0
1940	64.2	16.2	3.5	5.2	6.8	4.0	100.0
1950	64.9	17.0	3.4	3.9	4.2	6.7	100.0
1960	67.1	12.7	3.7	3.2	6.1	7.2	100.0
1970	66.9	9.6	2.2	2.7	8.3	10.3	100.0
1980	63.0	8.0	0.3	2.3	12.0	14.4	100.0
1989	60.0	7.9	−0.3	2.9	15.3	14.3	100.0
1993	58.8	8.2	0.2	2.9	12.9	16.9	100.0

Addendum: Supplements to Wages and Salaries as a Percent of Total Wages and Salaries[e]

	All Supplements[f]	All Supplements Less Employer Contributions for Social Insurance
1929	1.4	1.2
1940	4.6	3.2
1950	5.6	3.6
1960	8.7	5.3
1970	12.1	7.1
1980	19.4	13.0
1989	19.9	11.7
1993	21.8	13.2

[a] Source: Council of Economic Advisers, *Economic Report of the President, 1994*, U.S. Government Printing Office, Washington, 1994.
[b] This is defined as the sum of wage and salary disbursements plus other labor income less personal contributions for social insurance, employer contributions to social insurance, and the excess of accruals over wage disbursements.
[c] With inventory valuation and capital consumption adjustments.
[d] With capital consumption adjustments.
[e] Source: Council of Economic Advisers, *Economic Report of the President, 1990, op. cit.*
[f] This is defined as the sum of employer contributions for social insurance and to private pension, health and welfare funds, workmen's compensation, and a few miscellaneous items.

opposed to corporations).[7] The next is dividends paid to owners of corporate stock. The fifth component is interest income that individuals receive

---

[7] There is a second part to this income category, which is "rent" imputed to owner-occupied homes. Since families that own their own homes do not (by definition) pay rent, the services received from owner-occupied housing would not be reflected in the national accounts. In order to
(continued)

on time and savings accounts, government bonds and other securities, corporate bonds, and other financial instruments. The last component is government transfer payments to families and individuals. Among the most common are social security payments, unemployment benefits, veterans' benefits, Aid to Families with Dependent Children, and food stamps. (We shall discuss these transfer programs more fully in Chapter 15.)

The data on personal income in Table 2.1 show some interesting trends. The proportion of personal income derived from labor earnings increased from 60 percent in 1929 to 67 percent in 1960 and then declined to 59 percent in 1993. Proprietors' income and other forms of self-employment earnings accounted for 17 percent of total personal income in 1929 but declined rather sharply to 8 percent in 1980, at which point it has stabilized. The downward trend reflects primarily the decline in the ownership of small, unincorporated farms as agriculture became more mechanized and large farms became more efficient to run.

Also showing declines are rental income and dividends. The former declined from 5.8 percent of total personal income in 1929 to 0.2 percent in 1993, while the latter fell from 6.9 percent in 1929 to 2.2 percent in 1970, though it has increased slightly since then. Interest income as a proportion of total personal income declined from 8 percent in 1929 to 4 percent in 1950 but has generally risen ever since, reaching 15 percent in 1989, though it has fallen back to 13 percent in 1993. Transfer payments show the most dramatic change. A little under 2 percent of total income in 1929, they rose to 4 percent in 1940, 7 percent in 1950, 10 percent in 1970, and 17 percent in 1993. (This component will be treated in greater detail in Chapter 15.)

The category labor earnings includes not only wages and salaries but also fringe benefits such as employer contributions for employees' health insurance, life insurance, and pension funds. One of the most important developments in the U.S. economy since 1929 is the increasing proportion of total labor compensation that has taken the form of fringe benefits and other supplements to wages and salaries. The first column of the Addendum to Table 2.1 shows all fringe benefits including employer contributions to social insurance (social security), as a percent of wages and salaries.[8] This ratio has increased almost continuously over time from 1.4 percent in 1929 to almost 22 percent in 1993. The second column shows the ratio of all fringe benefits, excluding employer contributions for social insurance, to wages and salaries. This ratio has also increased dramatically, from 1 percent in 1929 to 13 percent in 1993.

---

make owner-occupied housing consistent with rental housing, the NIPA estimates the market rental for owner-occupied housing and includes this "imputed rent" in national income. This imputation results in a better measure of national income. To make the income and product accounts balance, the NIPA then includes imputed rent on the product side as a measure of the output of the "rental and real estate" sector.

[8] Both the employee and the employer make equal contributions to the social security system. The employee's share is usually referred to as the employee's social security tax and is treated, like income taxes, as a tax on wages and salaries. It is therefore considered a part of wages and salaries, not a supplement. See Chapter 16 for more details.

2.3 THE STANDARD OF LIVING

Up until now, we have been discussing total flows, like GDP, NNP, and total personal income. Yet, what is really important for welfare is not the total output of a nation's economy but its average level of output, since this better indicates how well off the average citizen is. For example, if two economies have the same GDP and the first has half the population of the second, then it is apparent that the average citizen in the first country is better off.

The best way to measure the average standard of living is not easy to determine. Since any measure of an average level is a ratio, there are two considerations: what is the best measure of the numerator and what is the best measure of the denominator. There are four common measures for the numerator: GDP, NNP, total personal income, and personal disposable income. Let us consider the relative merits of each. The gross domestic product shows the total (final) product a nation produces in the course of a year. This measure includes not only the personal consumption of households but investment and government expenditure (and the excess of exports over imports). Personal consumption provides immediate benefits to individuals and families. Investment expenditure, on the other hand, is not consumed by individuals or families and therefore does not directly improve their current well-being. However, by expanding the capital stock, investments can increase future production and therefore future consumption possibilities. Because of this, investment expenditure can be considered an indirect contributor to future personal welfare.

Government expenditure can be considered as partly consumption and partly investment. For example, the police, fire, sanitation, power generation, educational, recreational, and public transit services provided by governments directly benefit individuals and families. Moreover, the road and highway construction, research and development, sewerage construction, and other forms of "social overhead expenditure" provided by the government sector expand the national capital stock and increase the potential for future consumption. Therefore, government expenditure can also be considered a contribution to either current personal well-being or future well-being. Thus, GDP is usually considered the most comprehensive measure of the contribution of a nation's economy to either the current or future well-being of its members.

As compared to GDP, NNP is usually considered a superior measure of a nation's annual output, since it subtracts from gross output the value of that part of the capital stock that wears out each year. The GDP measure, as mentioned above, has the somewhat unfortunate property that the faster the capital stock wears out, the greater the value of GDP. The difference between GDP and NNP is depreciation—or, more technically, the capital consumption allowance. Since there is no widely agreed-upon definition or measure of depreciation, the GDP measure is used more frequently than NNP, and we will also follow this convention.[9]

Total personal income measures that portion of national income that accrues directly to families. This measure is also referred to as before-tax family (or personal) income, because it includes the income and the personal taxes paid by individuals and families. Personal income is a better measure of *current* personal well-being than GDP or NNP, since it essentially excludes the investment portion of the national product. However, since this measure does include a portion of taxes, and therefore implicitly a portion of government spending, it is not a very pure measure of private welfare. Therefore, another measure has been devised, called **personal disposable income,** which equals total personal income less personal income tax and other tax payments. Personal disposable income is a better measure of current well-being from (private) consumption than personal income.

As far as the denominator is considered, there are two common candidates. The first is the number of people living in a country. This is normally called a **per capita** measure. The second is the number of families. The choice of concept depends on one's judgment as to which is the appropriate welfare unit. For many purposes, the individual is considered the relevant unit, and output per capita the relevant measure of the average standard of living, since it is individuals who think and feel and who experience utility. However, it is also true that consumption is an activity that is usually performed jointly by the members of a family. For example, a house is shared by family members. Therefore, there are certain "economies of consumption" realized in a family unit from the individual members sharing common resources. As a result, as a unit of consumption, the family is usually considered the appropriate concept, and the family unit is usually used in conjunction with personal income.

One problem with the use of the family unit as a measure of welfare is that family income provides different levels of welfare to families of different sizes. A family income of $30,000 provides a higher standard of living to a family of two than of four. As a result, some researchers have used a measure of family income adjusted for family size, called "equivalent income."

---

[9]There are a host of other issues connected with the measurement of average well-being. One that has been a subject of much recent discussion is that GDP may not accurately reflect the total final product an economy produces. There are essentially two separate issues involved. The first is that certain goods and services classified as final products are really intermediate products. Some items suggested for this category are defense spending, since it serves primarily to protect the resources and production facilities of a country, and work-related personal consumption expenditures such as commuting expenses. The second is that some activities that are not included in GDP should be added to measure welfare. One example is household work such as cooking, cleaning, and do-it-yourself activities. These activities increase personal welfare and act as substitutes for services provided by restaurants, repair shops, and the like that are paid for and therefore included in GDP. See the next section and Tobin and Nordhaus (1971) for further discussion.

This concept lies in between per capita income and family income and is probably the best indicator of well-being.[10]

Before looking at actual trends in the standard of living, it is first necessary to make another distinction—in this case, between "real" and "nominal" income. **Nominal income,** also called income in *current dollars,* records income in the actual value of that year. **Real income,** also called income in *constant dollars* or *constant prices,* adjusts the nominal income value for changes in prices over time. For example, if the price of bread rises between two years, the output value of bread in current dollars will increase even though there may be no corresponding increase in the number of loaves that are produced. Thus, it is important to distinguish between the current dollar value of output and real output, particularly if we are interested in how the economy has grown over time.

To measure real output, we convert the prices of each year into the prices of a arbitrarily chosen base period. This conversion is done by dividing output in current dollars for Year X by the price index for Year X. For example, actual data for the U.S. economy are shown below:

Year	GDP in Current Dollars (billions)	Price Index [1987 = 100]	GDP in 1987 Dollars (billions)
1980	$2,708	71.7	$3,776
1987	4,540	100.0	4,540
1993	6,374	124.2	5,133

To convert 1980 GDP in nominal dollars to GDP in 1987 dollars, we would divide $2,708 billion by 0.717, which yields $3,776 billion; and to convert 1993 GDP into 1987 prices, we divide $6,374 billion by 1.242, which yields $5,133 billion. This procedure is the best way of comparing the real output of different years.[11]

Table 2.2 shows four alternative measures of the average standard of living for the period 1929–1993 (see also Figures 2.1 and 2.2). The first column shows the growth of GDP per capita in constant (1993) dollars. Between 1929 and 1933, the period of the Great Depression, real GDP per capita declined by 32 percent, and it was not until 1940 that it regained its 1929 high. From 1939 to 1950, it grew at 3.4 percent per year, mainly due to

---

[10] We shall discuss this concept in more detail in Chapter 4.

[11] As with many other statistical questions, there are alternative ways to construct price indices. The problem would be very simple to solve if the economy produced only *one* product (and the "quality" of this product did not change over time). However, once there is more than one product, then the selection of the appropriate combination of output weights (as they are called) to use to construct the price index can make some difference in the measure of inflation.

Table 2.2 GDP and Personal Disposable Income Per Capita, Median Family Income, Mean Hourly Earnings, and Median Equivalent Family Income, 1929–1993[a]

Year	GDP Per Capital (1993$)	Personal Disposable Income Per Capita (1993$)	Median Family Income (1993$)	Mean Hourly Earnings[b] (1993$)	Median Equivalent Family Income[c]
1929	8,441	6,238			
1933	5,750	4,498			
1939	7,929	5,812			
1950	11,505	7,959	21,152	7.74	
1960	13,356	9,203	27,979	9.84	
1967	16,568	11,455	34,321	11.14	2.67
1973	18,771	13,786	39,220	12.22	3.15
1989	24,219	17,810	39,869	11.20	3.43
1993	24,574	18,222	37,078	10.83	3.29 [1992]

Average Annual Growth Rates (in percent)

1929–39	−0.6	−0.7			
1939–50	3.4	2.9			
1950–73	2.1	2.4	2.7	2.0	2.8 [1967–73]
1973–93	1.3	1.4	−0.3	−0.6	0.2 [1973–92]

[a] Sources: Council of Economic Advisers, *Economic Report of the President, 1994,* U.S. Government Printing Office, Washington, D.C., 1994. For median family income from 1947–66; U.S. Bureau of the Census: *Historical Statistics of the United States: Colonial Times to 1970,* Bicentennial Edition Part I, Washington, D.C., 1975.
[b] Hourly earnings are for total private nonagricultural production and nonsupervisory workers. The figures are adjusted for overtime in manufacturing and interindustry employment shifts.
[c] Expressed as a ratio to the poverty line. Source: U.S. Bureau of the Census, *Money Income of Households, Families, and Persons in the U.S., 1992,* Series P60–184, September, 1993.

the stimulating effects World War II had on the U.S. economy. Between 1950 and 1973, GDP per capita continued to increase at a substantial rate, 2.1 percent per year. However, between 1973 and 1993, the growth in GDP per capita slowed down to only 1.3 percent per year. Still, in 1993, GDP per capita was three times higher than in 1929 and over twice as high as in 1950.

The next column shows the growth in personal disposable income per capita. Here, too, we see a fairly precipitous drop in disposable income per capita between 1929 and 1933 and a gradual rise back to its 1929 level by 1940. The growth in disposable income per capita was slightly lower than

Figure 2.1 Real GDP & Personal Disposable Income Per Capita in 1993$, 1929–93

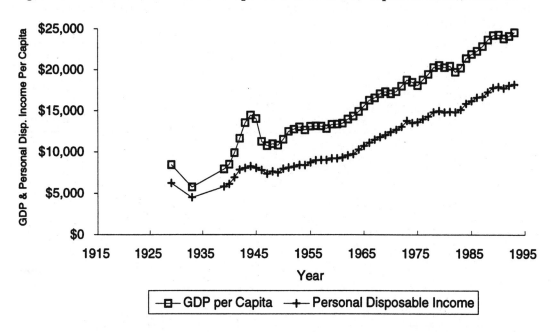

that of GDP per capita between 1939 and 1950 but slightly higher between 1950 and 1993.

The third column uses family income as the welfare measure. In addition, the *median* income level rather than the average or *mean* level is used. To compute the **mean** family **income level,** as we shall see in Chapter 3, we divide total income by the number of family units. To compute the **median income level,** we rank families by income and pick the income level of the family at the midpoint of the ordering. The median income level gives a better indication of what the average family receives than mean income. Its growth pattern differs from that of GDP or personal disposable income per capita. Between 1950 and 1973, median family income grew by 2.7 percent per year, greater than the other two measures. Over this period, family size was increasing substantially from the "baby boom," causing population to increase quite a bit faster than the number of families. However, between 1973 and 1993, median family income actually *declined in real terms.* In fact, between 1989 and 1993, median family income fell by 7 percent.

What has caused the growing rift between personal disposable income per capita and median family income since the early 1970s? There are two reasons. First, the number of families has been increasing much more rapidly than the number of individuals in the United States. This is partly a consequence of a falling birth rate, but it is also due to a large number of divorces and marital separations that have split families in two. The second reason is that the *median* has behaved quite differently than the *mean* over the last 20 years. Whereas the *average family* is hardly better off today than it

Part I Income Inequality and Poverty: Measurement and Trends

Figure 2.2 Hourly Wages, Median Family and Equivalent Income, Index (1977 = 100), 1947–93

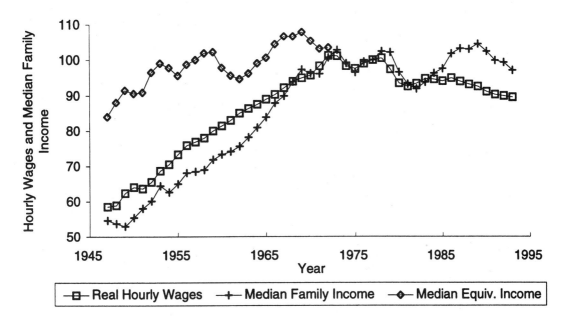

was two decades ago, mean income has been rising. This seems like a contradiction, but it isn't. The difference is due to the growing *inequality* in family incomes in the United States since the early 1970s. We shall have much more to say about this in the next chapter.

The fourth measure presented in Table 2.2 is average hourly labor earnings. Labor earnings, as we saw above, forms only a part of personal income and is therefore not really a measure of well-being. However, it is the major component of personal income. As a result, trends in wages and salaries are an important determinant of changes in personal income. Between 1950 and 1973, average hourly earnings increased by 2.0 percent per year, somewhat slower than median family income but still at a significant pace. However, since 1973, real hourly wages have been *declining*. They fell by 3.6 percent (altogether, not annually) from 1973 to 1979, and by another 8.0 percent from 1979 to 1993.

Why have real wages been declining since their peak in 1973? Economists have several explanations, which we shall discuss in later chapters (see Chapters 7, 8, and 9). However, we can explain why real wage trends differ from those of median family income. First, median family income has not fallen as much since 1973, because the number of two-earner families has been rising. In particular, the proportion of wives who have joined the labor force has risen dramatically over the last two decades (see Section 5.2). This is the principal explanation why family incomes have not fallen, despite the decline in real labor earnings. It is literally true, as some have said, that today it requires two people to work in order to provide the same income that one person could earn 20 years ago. The second reason is that, as we saw from Table 2.1, other forms of income have been increasing faster than labor earnings. In particular, property income and transfer income have both been rising relative to labor income. This factor helps explain why personal income per capita has actually been rising since the early 1970s, while real wages have been falling.

The last measure in Table 2.2 is median equivalent family income, expressed as a ratio to the poverty line (also see Figure 2.2). As noted above, this measures adjusts family income for size of family. This series begins only in 1967. Between 1967 and 1973, this index grew by 2.8 percent per year—at about the same rate as median (unadjusted) family income. From 1973 to 1989, it rose at 0.5 percent per year. In comparison, median family income remained virtually unchanged. The difference reflects the fact that average family size fell over this period. Between 1989 and 1992, median equivalent family income fell by 4 percent (in total), slightly less than unadjusted median family income.

International Comparisons of Per Capita Income

Does the United States still have the highest standard of living in the world? Have other countries been gaining on the United States? These and related issues have been a focus of recent policy debates in the United States and other countries around the world. Fortunately, there are some recent data available to provide an answer to this set of questions.

For the period 1960–1990, the Penn World Tables have provided excellent data on per capita GDP for 150 countries (see Summers and Heston, 1988, mentioned in the international data sources at the end of this chapter, for a description of the data). The figures for different countries are made comparable by an adjustment in terms of relative purchasing power parity (PPP), which reflects differences in the actual cost of living among countries, rather than currency exchange rates. The figures are expressed in units that Summers and Heston call "1985 international dollars," and the statistics are referred to as real Gross Domestic Product (GDP) per capita, or RGDP. These figures permit a comparison of the performance of the less-developed countries, the middle-income countries, and other groupings with that of the leading industrial countries.[12]

---

[12] There are two major problems in making cross-national comparisons of average living standards, especially between developed nations and underdeveloped ones. The first is that in underdeveloped countries, many items that contribute to the standard of living are not exchanged (such as food grown by the household) and therefore are not counted in the official national accounts statistics. The second is that people in different countries often consume very different commodities. For these two reasons, the official foreign exchange rate between two countries' currency rarely reflects the relative cost of maintaining comparable living standards. Instead, PPP indices have been developed to capture differences in actual costs of living for international comparisons of well-being.

Comparative data for selected countries are shown in Table 2.3 for both 1960 and 1990. The countries are ranked by their 1990 GDP per capita. Let us first look at the 1990 figures. According to the Summers and Heston data, the United States was first in terms of GDP per capita (also abbreviated RGDP), followed very closely by Canada and Switzerland. Norway, Japan, Sweden, West Germany, Hong Kong, Australia, and Finland were about 80 percent of the U.S. level, while the United Kingdom's RGDP was at 71 percent. The standard of living in Spain, Israel, and Taiwan was about half that of the United States, while Czechoslovakia and Greece were at one-third.

Among the "third-world countries," Venezuela was the richest, at 31 percent of the U.S. level, while Mexico was at 29 percent, Chile at 22 percent, and Brazil at 21 percent. Average income in the People's Republic of China was 13 percent of the U.S. level. Among the poorest countries in the world were Pakistan and Bangladesh at 7 percent and Nigeria at 4 percent of the American RGDP.

A comparison of the 1960 and 1990 figures does show that many countries of the world were "catching up" to the United States in average income. This can be seen in Column 5, where a ratio greater than unity indicates that a country's RGDP was increasing relative to the United States' between 1960 and 1990. All of the top 23 countries in 1990, with the exception of Switzerland, Australia, and New Zealand, gained on the United States over this period. Norway's RGDP relative to RGDP in the United States increased by 40 percent; the Federal Republic of Germany gained by 16 percent; France by 24 percent; Singapore by *252 percent*; Japan by *165 percent*; and Hong Kong by *245 percent*. Belgium, Finland, Austria, Italy, Spain, and Israel also made sizable gains on the United States. Average income in Czechoslovakia gained by *33 percent* on the United States level. Thailand's RGDP increased by 103 percent relative to the United States.

However, many countries fell even further behind the United States over this period. These include Venezuela, Argentina, and Chile, which suffered sizable losses, as did Peru. Some very poor countries, including the Philippines, Bangladesh, and Nigeria, also lost relative to the United States between 1960 and 1990.[13]

2.4 FACTOR SHARES

Factor shares, or the class distribution of income, refers to whether income is received in the form of wages or profits, irrespective of who gets it. A family may receive both salary income and some form of income from profits, such as dividends, interest, or rent. We are interested here in the *source* of the income, not its final disposition.

It is interesting to note that historically the term **income distribution** referred to the division of income between classes or factors. David Ricardo,

---

[13] See Baumol, Blackman, and Wolff (1989), Chapter 5, for more discussion of the "catch-up" or "convergence" phenomenon.

Table 2.3 Real GDP Per Capita (RGDP) for Selected Countries, 1960 and 1990[a]

Country	1960 RGDP Dollar Value (1)	1960 RGDP Percent of U.S. (2)	1990 RGDP Dollar Value (3)	1990 RGDP Percent of U.S. (4)	1960–90 Catch-up Rate [Col. (4) / Col. (2)] (5)
United States	9,774	100	18,399	100	1.00
Canada	7,288	75	17,419	95	1.27
Switzerland	9,637	99	17,007	92	0.94
Norway	5,656	58	14,909	81	1.40
Japan	2,976	30	14,827	81	2.65
Sweden	7,505	77	14,490	79	1.03
Germany, West	6,660	68	14,487	79	1.16
Hong Kong	2,222	23	14,412	78	3.45
Australia	7,880	81	14,311	78	0.96
Finland	5,384	55	14,216	77	1.40
France	5,981	61	13,931	76	1.24
Denmark	6,748	69	13,802	75	1.09
Belgium	5,554	57	13,588	74	1.30
United Kingdom	6,509	67	13,066	71	1.07
Netherlands	6,104	62	12,858	70	1.12
Austria	5,152	53	12,849	70	1.32
Italy	4,660	48	12,555	68	1.43
New Zealand	7,935	81	11,534	63	0.77
Singapore	1,653	17	10,956	60	3.52
Spain	3,165	32	9,662	53	1.62
Israel	3,348	34	8,639	47	1.37
Taiwan	1,359	14	8,513	46	3.33
Greece	2,066	21	6,678	36	1.72
Czechoslovakia	2,454	25	6,143	33	1.33
Venezuela	6,167	63	5,764	31	0.50
Mexico	2,798	29	5,376	29	1.02
Malaysia	1,381	14	4,896	27	1.88
Chile	2,898	30	3,988	22	0.73
Brazil	1,745	18	3,912	21	1.19
Turkey	1,594	16	3,711	20	1.24
Thailand	923	9	3,526	19	2.03
Argentina	3,294	34	3,505	19	0.57
South Africa	2,107	22	3,193	17	0.81
Colombia	1,657	17	3,188	17	1.02
China			2,326	13	
Peru	1,936	20	2,041	11	0.56
Indonesia	621	6	1,941	11	1.66
Egypt	769	8	1,838	10	1.27
Philippines	1,112	11	1,750	10	0.84
Pakistan	622	6	1,360	7	1.16
Bangladesh	803	8	1,206	7	0.80
Nigeria	557	6	775	4	0.74

[a]Source: Penn World Tables, Version 5.5, diskettes. Figures are in 1985 "International Dollars." Countries are ranked by 1990 RGDP.

writing in the early part of the nineteenth century, went so far as to argue that the primary aim of political economy (the original name for the field of economics) should be precisely to understand the factors that determined the distribution of income between classes.[14] Karl Marx, writing in the middle part of the nineteenth century, also focused a large part of his work on the determinants of the division of income between workers and capitalists.

With the development of neoclassical theory, which began in the latter part of the nineteenth century, income distribution continued to be viewed as the apportionment of the national income between classes, though the mechanisms they analyzed were quite different from the earlier classical writers. It was only in the twentieth century that attention shifted to the allocation of income among individuals or families—the so-called "*size* distribution of income." Today, the unqualified term *income distribution* typically refers to the size distribution of income. Class shares, on the other hand, are referred to as the "functional" distribution of income, since income is divided according to the factors in the production function.

It is also interesting to note that for the classical economists, the analysis of income distribution focused on "classes"—typically, the capitalists, workers, and, in some cases, the landowners. Income distribution was viewed as a consequence of historical forces and struggles between these social classes. With the neoclassical revolution in economic theory, income was seen as a return to a *factor* of production. Hence, income distribution became synonymous with "factor shares"—the share of the total product received by each factor. By its very structure, income distribution theory became, as a result, embedded in production theory.

Diagram 2.3 shows how the wage and profit shares are estimated. We begin with the broadest concept of national output, which is GDP (Gross Domestic Product). Subtracting from this the capital consumption allowance (depreciation), we obtain net national product (NNP). If indirect business taxes (and nontax liability) is then subtracted and several other minor adjustments made, national income (NI) is obtained. NI shows the total income generated in the economy and valued at factor cost. (See Section 2.6 for more details on measuring national income.)

There are three sources of national income: (1) person (including unincorporated businesses and not-for-profit institutions), (2) corporations, and (3) net interest in the economy.[15] Households receive three kinds of income

---

[14] In his case, there were three classes of interest: (1) workers, (2) capitalists, and (3) landowners.

[15] Households receive interest income on savings accounts, corporate bonds, government securities, and so on, and they pay interest on mortgages and consumer debt. The difference between what they receive and pay out is the net interest income of households. Likewise, corporations and the government sector both receive interest income and pay out interest on their debt. Each of these sectors has a net interest income. The sum of the net interest of households, corporations, and government is the net interest in the economy. If there is no interest received from or paid abroad, then the three sectors should cancel out, and economywide net interest should be zero. Because of imputations of interest to the financial sector, the net interest in the economy has historically been positive, though, until recently, relatively small.

Diagram 2.3 Accounting Framework for Measuring Factor Shares

Sources		
1. Persons	2. Corporations	3. Other
Wage and supplements Proprietors' income: Wage portion		
Proprietors' income: Profit portion Rental income	Corporate Profits	Net Interest
Indirect business tax and nontax liabilities Business transfers Current surpluses less subsidies of government enterprises		
Capital consumption allowance		

Wage share

Profit share

National income

NNP

GDP

from factors employed: (1) wages, salaries, and supplements on their labor; (2) proprietors' income on the equity invested in unincorporated businesses; and (3) rental income on land and other real estate. Corporations receive one form of income, profits, on their invested capital. The last component of NI is net interest in the economy. The wage share consists mainly of wages and fringe benefits. The property income or profit share consists mainly of rental income, corporate profits, and net interest. Proprietors' income is a hybrid category, since part of the income is from the proprietors' labor and the remainder is a pure profit on the invested capital. The labor portion is included in the wage share, and the profit portion in the property income share.

One of the earliest attempts to estimate the functional distribution of income was made by W. I. King in 1919. His estimates cover the period from 1850 to 1910 (see Table 2.4). In the 1850–1860 period, 37 percent of the national income was received by employees in the form of labor compensation (almost entirely wages) and 42 percent was received by proprietors (mainly self-employed farmers). In King's methodology, proprietor income was classified as labor income, and the sum of employee compensation and proprietors' income constituted the labor share. During 1850–1860, the wage share was 78 percent of the national income, while the property share was only 22 percent. According to King's estimates, employee compensation as a share of national income rose quite sharply between 1850 and 1910, and the share of proprietors' income correspondingly fell, reflecting the shift of workers from the farm to the factory. However, together the labor share remained almost unchanged between 1850 and 1910.

Estimates were later made by D. Gale Johnson (1954) for the period from 1900 to 1949. It is first instructive to compare his estimates for the 1900–1909 period with those of King for 1900–1910. Using different data sources and a slightly different measure of national income, Johnson's figure on the share of employee compensation in national income was higher than King's, and the share of proprietor income was correspondingly lower. Moreover, Johnson broke proprietor income into two components—estimated compensation to the labor input of the proprietor and a profit on the capital invested in the business. Taken together, Johnson's estimated wage share in this period was 69 percent, compared with King's 76 percent.

Johnson's calculations show a moderate rise in the wage share from 69 percent to 75 percent between 1900 and 1950. The share of employee compensation in total income rose over the period from 55 to 64 percent, while the share of proprietor income fell. Between 1900 and 1949, the property income share fell from 31 percent to 25 percent. This was largely due to the proportion of interest and rent in national income, which declined from 15 to 6 percent. The share of corporate profits in national income, on the other hand, rose from 7 to 13 percent.

An alternative estimate of the wage share for the early part of the twentieth century was made by Arthur Grant (1963). He restricted his estimate of national income to the product of the business sector only (excluding the government sector and imputed rent to owner-occupied housing). Moreover, he included all of proprietor income as property income. His computations, shown in Table 2.4, indicate an almost constant ratio of employee compensation in national income in the period from 1899 to 1929.

The author's estimates are also shown for the period from 1950 to 1993. Employee compensation as a percentage of total national income rose significantly from 68.5 percent in the 1950–1959 period to 75.4 percent in the years 1980–1983, though it since declined to 73.7 percent in 1993. If we append this series to Johnson's data, the estimates show an

Table 2.4 Estimates of the Functional Distribution of Income in the U.S., 1850–1993 (in percent)

Period and Source	Employee Compensation	Proprietor Income		Other Property Income	Total Labor	Total Property
		Labor	Profit			
A. King's Data[a]						
1850–60	36.5	41.6			78.1	21.9
1860–70	42.9	35.8			78.7	21.3
1870–80	50.1	26.4			76.5	23.5
1880–90	52.5	23.0			75.5	24.5
1890–1900	50.4	27.3			77.7	22.3
1900–10	47.2	28.8			76.0	24.0
B. Johnson's Data[b]						
1900–09	55.0	14.4	9.2	21.4	69.4	30.6
1910–19	53.2	14.9	9.3	22.6	68.1	31.9
1920–29	60.5	11.2	6.4	22.0	71.7	28.4
1930–39	66.8	9.7	5.3	18.1	76.5	23.4
1940–49	64.3	10.9	6.0	18.7	75.2	24.7
C. Grant's Data[c]						
1899–1909	49.1					
1909–19	46.4					
1919–29	49.5					
D. Economic Report of the President, 1995[d]						
1950–59	68.5	8.9	4.8	17.8	77.4	22.6
1960–69	70.8	6.5	3.5	19.2	77.3	22.7
1970–79	74.7	4.8	2.6	17.9	79.5	20.5
1980–83	75.4	3.2	1.7	19.7	78.6	21.4
1984–86	73.1	5.2	2.8	18.9	78.3	21.7
1987–89	73.0	5.3	2.9	18.8	78.3	21.7
1989–92	73.9	5.4	2.9	17.8	79.3	20.7
1993	73.7	5.6	3.0	17.7	79.3	20.7

[a] The original source is King (1919). The figures are as reported in Johnson (1954), p. 179.
[b] The source is Johnson (1954), p. 178.
[c] The source is Grant (1963), p. 279. The figures are the share of employee compensation in business production only.
[d] The source is own computations from the *Economic Report of the President, 1995*. Proprietors' income was split into a labor and property component by using Johnson's average proportion for the 1900–1949 period.

almost continuous rise in the share of employee compensation in national income since 1900, followed by a slight decline in the late 1980s and early 1990s. On the other hand, proprietor income as a proportion of national income fell precipitously from 14 percent in the 1950–1959 period to 5 percent in the 1980–1983 period, though it then increased to almost 9 percent by 1993. The author assumes that the apportionment of the income of the self-employed into a labor component and a profit component remained constant over the 1950–1988 period and was equal to the same ratio as in the 1940–1949 period. On the basis of this assumption, the total labor share remained almost unchanged over the post-1950 period at around 78 percent. The share of property income in national income averaged around 22 percent over the last four and a half decades.

Two other studies also give some interesting evidence on the wage and profit share. The first, by John Hotson (1963), investigated the labor share in the Canadian economy over the period 1926 to 1960. Hotson's measure of the wage and profit share was based on the average markup over wage costs in the business economy. The markup is the difference between the wages a business pays and the price it charges for its output. If material inputs are ignored, the markup is essentially equivalent to property income—corporate profits, rents, and interest. Hotson found that the average markup on wages in the business economy remained very stable between 1926 and 1960.

The second, by Jacques Lecaillon and Dimitrios Germidis (1975), is a cross-national study intended to link the level of development of a country to the wage share in national income. The nations considered in the study included underdeveloped, developing, and industrialized ones. The major finding is that a greater fraction of the active labor force was employed as wage labor rather than self-employed in more developed economies (as measured by per capita income), than in less developed ones. As a result, the share of employee compensation in national income generally increases with development, and the share of proprietors' income falls. This result is consistent with the statistical results for the United States over the last 30 years. A secondary finding is that the relation between the share of employee compensation in national income and the ratio of wage and salary workers to the active labor force is nonlinear (actually parabolic). As the latter ratio approaches unity, the employee compensation share asymptomatically approaches a constant less than one (0.70 in their study).

2.5 HOUSEHOLD PRODUCTION AND WELL-BEING

The contribution of household production to GNP is a well-established problem from the earliest days of national accounting (for example, Wesley Mitchell, 1921, considered this issue). Household work such as cooking, child care, home repairs, and cleaning increases the flow of goods and services and thus increases the national product and economic welfare. The value of such production is not included in the standard National Income and Product Accounts (NIPA). However, the value of such work is quite sizable, and its inclusion in the NIPA could have far-reaching implications for the level and distribution of national income and the growth of economic welfare over time. For example, the increasing participation of wives in the labor force means that they will have less time for household work. As a result, the use of traditional family income measures might lead to an *overstatement* of the growth of living standards over time, since part of the gains in labor earnings will be offset by a loss of home production.

There have been many attempts to estimate the value of household work. Estimates range from about 20 percent of GNP to over 50 percent. The estimates depend on the methodology used to measure the value of household work. There are two approaches that are commonly used. The first is based on the market price of services that the household provides. The second is based on the opportunity cost of the person performing the housework—the actual or potential earnings foregone by the individual performing the housework.

Defining Household Work

In both approaches, it is first necessary to define what is meant by home production. The definition of economic activity that underlies the NIPA is based on market transactions. Since household work is not paid for through a market transaction, it is excluded from the NIPA definition of economic activity. There are two more general definitions of economic activity that have been employed by economists working on this issue. The most comprehensive concept defines economic activity to include virtually all household activities, including leisure, that yield a utility to household members. A second, more restrictive concept defines economic activity to include only household production for which there is a clear market alternative—that is, which results in a good or service that could be purchased from the market. Cooking, for example, would fall in this category, since one could purchase a meal at a restaurant.

The latter definition is normally used in these studies, since the former would lead to serious problems in measuring household activity (how do you assign a value to TV watching?). Activities typically included in household work are meal preparation and cleanup, house cleaning, gardening, laundry, home repairs, child care and child teaching, medical care, bill paying, and shopping.

Once the list of household activities to include in household production is determined, it is still necessary to decide on how to measure their *quantity*. In principle, the amount of household work can be evaluated as a flow of inputs or a flow of outputs. However, there are virtually no data on output flows (for example, the number of meals served in a year by the average family). As a result, most researchers in this field have measured quantity in terms of the amount of *time* spent on the activity. Such data are usually based on "time-use studies," where a family is asked to fill in a diary indicating how they allocate their time during a typical week. The latter approach also has problems. First, almost all household activities require nonlabor inputs. For example, cooking requires a stove and utensils, and mowing the lawn requires a lawn mower. In principle, the value of nonlabor inputs should also be included in the valuation, but these are difficult to measure and are usually excluded. Second, two or more household activities may occur simultaneously. For example, babysitting is often combined with cooking, cleaning, or dishwashing. It is difficult to divide the time up between such concurrent activities. In practice, individuals are asked their primary activity during each time interval.

Market Cost Approach

When a household hires someone to perform household work, there is a cost involved—namely, the prevailing wage of the service performed. Thus, if a babysitter is engaged to look after the children, the family must pay the babysitter a given hourly wage. If a gardener is hired to care for the garden, the family must pay the gardener a given fee. In this approach, household work performed by family members is valued according to the going market wage for the given activity. As a result, the valuation of household production will vary, depending on the activity performed. It will likely be higher for repairing a car than vacuuming the house. There are, of course, difficult problems in making this type of valuation. First, such estimates are very sensitive to the type of occupation the researcher chooses as the appropriate market replacement. Second, even if one selects the proper market replacement, it is still necessary to determine the equivalent wage rate. For example, if a person paints his or her own house, should the work be valued at the wage rate of an experienced union painter, a nonunion painter, or a general laborer?

Opportunity Cost Approach

In this approach, it is assumed that an individual allocates time until the net return to an additional hour is equal in alternative employments. Since one use of time is to work for pay, in equilibrium, the marginal value of an hour of housework should equal the marginal return to an additional hour of paid work. According to this argument, housework should be valued at the going market wage for the individual performing the work. As a result, different activities performed by a household member will be assigned the same hourly value, irrespective of the type of activity. For example, babysitting and house painting are given the same valuation. On the other hand, the same work performed by two different household members will generally receive different valuations, depending on the respective wages that the individual can command in the market.

There are a number of problems with this approach also. First, since it is an equilibrium concept, it may not apply to persons who desire fewer or more hours of paid work or who are involuntarily unemployed. For example, it can be argued that the opportunity cost of an unemployed painter is lower than that of a painter actively working. Second, the opportunity cost of individuals *not* in the labor force can not be directly determined. For example, retirees do not normally have an opportunity wage available from paid work. In most applications it is assumed that every individual has an opportunity wage.

Estimates

Because the valuation of household production is normally based on special time-use surveys, which appear intermittently, there are no annual time series data available on the total magnitude of household services. However, there have been estimates done for several years by Martin Murphy (1978) for the United States. On the basis of the market cost approach, he calculated that the total value of household production amounted to 37 percent of the official GNP figure for 1960 and 34 percent for 1970. According to the opportunity cost calculations, household output increased GNP by 38 percent in 1960 and 37 percent in 1970. Thus, according to both indices, there was a slight decline in the relative value of household work during the 1980s, a trend that reflected the increased labor force participation of married women. Hans Adler and Oli Hawrylyshyn (1978) made similar calculations for Canada in 1961 and 1971. On the basis of the market cost method, the value of household work amounted to 40 percent of GNP in 1961 and 41 percent in 1971; according to opportunity cost calculations, the proportion fell from 44 percent in 1961 to 40 percent in 1971.

Several more recent studies [Chadeau (1985), Fitzgerald and Wicks (1990), Bonke (1992), Goldschmidt-Clermont (1993)] all confirm the earlier results. Based on newer data for the United States, as well as several other industrialized countries, such as Denmark, France, Germany, Switzerland, and Great Britain in the 1980s, these researchers have consistently found that the value of household work amounts to between 40 and 50 percent of GDP.

Another interesting dimension is afforded by looking at who contributes household labor. On the basis of the market cost approach, Murphy (1978) found that housewives provided 55 percent of the total value of household services in 1970, married men provided 16 percent, single women 23 percent, and single men 6 percent. Similar percentages were obtained from the opportunity cost approach. Thus, altogether, women were responsible for 78 percent of total household production and men only 22 percent. It will be interesting to see how these proportions have changed and will change in the future!

Diagram 2.4   An Illustrative Input-Output Table with Imports and Exports

| | Domestic Industries | | Final Demand | | | Total |
	Industry A	Industry B	Domestic[a]	Exports	Imports	Output
Industry A	4	7	1	3	0	15
Industry B	2	3	10	5	0	20
Imports	1	4	3	0	−8	0
Value added	8	6				14
Total output	15	20	14	8	−8	

GDP = 14 + 8 − 8 = 8 + 6 = 14

[a]Domestic final demand is defined as the sum of domestic consumption, investment, and government expenditure.

2.6 MISCELLANEOUS ISSUES IN NATIONAL ACCOUNTING*

Treatment of International Trade

In defining GDP in Section 2.1, we skipped over two separate issues. The first is the treatment of imports and exports. Imports consist of goods and services that are produced outside a given country (in our case, the United States) but purchased by industries or residents of the United States. Exports are goods or services produced in the United States but purchased by industries or residents of other countries. Let us return to a simplified input-output framework to show how these are handled (Diagram 2.4). There are two **domestic** (that is, U.S.) industries, A and B. Each purchases inputs from one another and also inputs imported from abroad to produce its respective output. The value of the imported inputs is recorded in a separate row, labeled "imports."[16] The cost of producing a domestic prod-

---

[16] In actual input-output accounting, imports are divided into two groups. The first are "competitive imports," which are imports that are directly substitutable for some domestic product, such as Saudi Arabian oil for American oil or Japanese steel for American steel. Competitive imports are added into the same row as their domestic substitutes and then subtracted in the import column of final demand. The second are "noncompetitive imports," which are those for which there are no comparable American products, such as Colombian coffee. These are recorded in a separate import row, as illustrated here.

uct includes not only the cost of domestic inputs and value added but also the cost of imported inputs. This is apparent in the computation of the column sums for total output in Industries A and B. Moreover, imports are also purchased directly by final consumers for personal consumption, investment, and government expenditure. Examples of these are Japanese cars and German machinery. This is shown by an entry in the import row in final demand. Finally, part of the output produced in the United States, such as American computers and American wheat, is exported to other countries. These transactions are recorded in a separate column of final demand.

GDP is a production concept and is defined as the total final output produced in a given *nation*. Therefore, goods and services produced abroad but consumed in a given nation are excluded from the value of GDP. This is done by subtracting the total value of imports, shown in the import column of final demand. In the example here, the total amount of imports is 8 and, as a result, there is a −8 in the import column. On the other side of the ledger, exports are included in GDP, since they are part of final output *produced* by a country. The fact that these goods and services are purchased abroad indicates only the **disposition** of the final product. Thus, GDP is defined to equal the sum of consumption, investment, government expenditure, and exports less imports. In the example here, GDP equals 14, which is the same as total value added, as it should be.

The second issue is somewhat more subtle and ultimately stems from the fact that in NIPA, total income must equal the total product. The problem arises because there are residents (and corporations) in a country that own income-producing property abroad. For example, an American may own stock in British Petroleum or Telefonos de Mexico. As a result, part of the income received each year by Americans comes from foreign production. The converse is also true—namely, that foreigners own stock in American companies and therefore part of the value added generated in the United States is remitted abroad (that is, sent out of the country). The actual physical production that takes place in a given country is not the same as the income its citizens receive, so that two different concepts of "national product" have developed.

The first, which we call Gross Domestic Product (GDP), measures the total final output produced in a nation defined as a particular geographical area. The second is called **Gross National Product (GNP)** and refers to the total income received by residents or corporations of a given country. To compute GNP, it is necessary to subtract from domestically generated value added (GDP) any dividends or other payments remitted abroad and to add any remittances from foreign countries received by American residents or corporations.[17] In order to adjust the product side of the accounts, a fictitious final product is created, called "the rest of the world sector." It is equal

---

[17] The major flow consists of profits made by foreign subsidiaries of U.S. companies that are remitted to the parent company.

to the net remittances from abroad and added to the domestically produced final product to balance the accounts.[18]

National Income at Factor Costs

All production is performed by **factors of production**—labor, capital, land, and other natural resources. (Intermediate inputs, which are also inputs in the production process, are themselves produced by factors of production and therefore reducible to them.) From this point of view, all income must originally accrue to these basic factors, in the form of wages, interest, profits, and rent. National income at factor costs, or "national income" for short, in this regard, is the total sum of payments to these factors.

The relation between GDP and national income is as follows: First, since national income is the sum of compensation to factors, depreciation is excluded, since it is a cost of production, not part of the return to capital. Second, indirect business taxes, such as sales taxes, and other payments to the government not levied on factor income are also excluded. The reason is that such indirect taxes are simply added to the price of a product and are not paid out of profits or wages. On the other hand, income and social security taxes would be included in national income, since they are assessed directly on factor income like wages and profits. Thus, national income at factor costs equals GDP less depreciation less indirect business taxes and similar payments to the government.

The Treatment of Capital Gains

Another concept of personal income is used by the Internal Revenue Service (IRS) for the computation of income taxes. The major difference between the IRS definition and the NIPA definition of personal income is that the IRS includes **capital gains** on the sale of property. A capital gain is the difference between the sale price of property, such as a house, land, or stock shares, and its original purchase price.[19] From the standpoint of the IRS, a capital gain on a sale represents money income to the seller and should therefore be subject to taxes like any other form of income. However, from the standpoint of the NIPA, the inclusion of capital gains in income would violate the identity between total income and total product, because there is no production corresponding to the capital gain.

Take the simple case of housing prices increasing from general inflation. A person will receive a capital gain on the sale of the house, and yet the house itself may have remained completely unchanged from the time of

---

[18] For the United States, GNP and GDP have historically been very close, and this distinction is not usually stressed. However, for many smaller economies, the two measures can differ substantially, and GDP is the preferred concept of national output, since it measures the actual production taking place in a country.

[19] Technically, capital gains refers to the difference between sale price and purchase price of property held for a predefined minimum period of time. Otherwise, the Internal Revenue Service calls this an "ordinary gain."

purchase. From the standpoint of the overall economy, no new product has been created, and therefore no additional income has been generated. Yet from the individual's standpoint, he or she could have bought a corporate bond with the same money that was used to pay for the house. In a world of perfect capital markets, the interest the person receives on the bond would be equal to the capital gain made on the house. From the standpoint of the IRS, it would make no sense to tax interest on corporate bonds if capital gains were not taxed, since an individual could switch wealth out of corporate bonds and into housing.[20]

A major political issue of recent years in the United States is the tax treatment of capital gains. Historically, capital gains have been subject to a lower tax rate than other components of personal income in the federal tax system. However, many Republicans argue that the tax rate should be made still lower (if not actually eliminated), because capital gains taxation discourages savings and therefore investment. Moreover, they argue that a large portion of capital gains is illusory insofar as it merely reflects overall price inflation. If a house doubles in value over ten years and all other prices double as well, then the house is no more valuable today than it was ten years ago, since its value would purchase the same goods. Several Republican leaders have also advocated that capital gains be "indexed" for changes in the overall price level.

However, as we shall see in Chapter 11, wealth is very unequally distributed in the United States, and capital gain income is highly concentrated among the wealthy. As a result, many Democrats argue that the main beneficiaries of a reduction of capital gains taxation would be the rich, who have already enjoyed major tax reductions on their income during the 1980s. They argue against a reduction in capital gains taxes on the basis of equity in the tax system. (See Chapter 16 for more discussion of the federal tax system.)

2.7 SUMMARY

The national accounts use a double-entry bookkeeping system in order to maintain an identity between total income and total product. This system is the basis of our measures of GDP and national income. Personal income is a component of national income. It consists of wage and salary earnings, proprietors' earnings, rental income, dividends, interest income, and government transfer payments.

The main component of personal income is labor earnings, historically between 60 and 67 percent. Proprietors' income accounted for 17 percent of total personal income in 1929 but today is only 8 percent. Rental income and dividends have also declined in importance, from 13 percent in 1929 to

---

[20]There is a secondary issue involved with capital gains. The IRS taxes only *realized* capital gains—that is, gains on the actual sale of property. But the market value of unsold property may also increase. Such increases, called *unrealized* capital gains, are not taxed by the IRS.

only 3 percent today. Interest income has amounted to as low as 4 percent of personal income but today is 13 percent. Transfer payments show the most dramatic change, rising from 2 percent of income in 1929 to 17 percent today.

There are different ways of measuring the standard of living. Three were presented in this chapter: (1) GDP per capita, (2) personal disposable income per capita, and (3) median family income. The first is based on total national output, including investment and government expenditures, while the second uses only after-tax personal income as the base. The third is based on pre-tax personal income but uses the family as the unit of welfare instead of the individual and reflects the income of the average family rather than mean income. A related index is average labor earnings, since this is the main component of personal income.

Two rather disturbing findings were reported in this chapter. The first is that mean hourly labor earnings, after increasing by 2.0 percent per year from 1950 to 1973, have been declining ever since. Real wages fell by 11 percent (altogether, not annually) between 1973 and 1993.

The second finding is that a somewhat similar pattern is evident for median family income (in real terms). Between 1950 and 1973, it grew by 2.7 percent per year, faster than real wages. However, over the years 1973 to 1989, median family income remained virtually unchanged and between 1989 and 1993 fell by 7 percent. The reasons that median family income remained constant over the 1973–1989 period, while real wages fell, are (1) the number of "two-earner" families rose and (2) nonlabor income— property and transfer income—increased faster than labor income. However, since 1989, the growth in two-earner families and nonlabor income have both slowed down.

In contrast, real GDP per capita increased at 2.1 percent per year between 1950 and 1973 and continued to grow between 1973 and 1993, though at a somewhat slower rate of 1.3 percent per year. Likewise, real personal disposable income per capita rose at 2.4 percent per year from 1950 to 1973 and at 1.4 percent per year from 1973 to 1993. There are two reasons why both GDP and personal disposable income per capita continued to grow after 1973 while median family income declined. The first is that the number of families has been increasing more rapidly than the number of individuals. The second is that income inequality has been rising since the early 1970s, so that mean income has grown faster than median income.

Median equivalent family income showed positive, albeit very modest, growth between 1973 and 1992, compared to an absolute decline in median unadjusted family income. The difference is due to the fact that average family size fell over this period.

The chapter also investigated differences in per capita income among countries of the world on the basis of purchasing power parity (PPP) rates. The figures indicate that in 1990 the United States had the highest living standard in the world. Canada and Switzerland were close to the United

States, while Germany's per capita income was 79 percent of the U.S. level and Japan's was 81 percent. Per capita income in the United Kingdom was 71 percent of the U.S. level, while Mexico's was only 29 percent. However, the statistics also indicate that many of the major countries of the world have been closing the income gap between themselves and the United States since 1960.

Attention was also given to the economywide division of national income between labor and property. It was found that the labor share increased between 1900 and 1950 and has since remained relatively constant at about 78 percent. The constancy of the wage share over the last 45 years is somewhat surprising in light of the fact that the real wage has been declining over the last 20 years.

REFERENCES

Adler, Hans J., and Oli Hawrylyshyn, "Estimates of the Value of Household Work Canada, 1961 and 1971," *Review of Income and Wealth*, Vol. 24, December 1978, pp. 333–355.

Baumol, William, Sue Anne Batey Blackman, and Edward N. Wolff, *Productivity and American Leadership: The Long View*, M.I.T. Press, Cambridge, Mass., 1989.

Bonke, Jens, "Distribution of Economic Resources—Implications of Including the Household Production," *Review of Income and Wealth*, Series 38, No. 3, September 1992, pp. 281–294.

Chadeau, Anne, "Measuring Household Activities: Some International Comparisons," *Review of Income and Wealth*, Series 31, No. 1, March 1985.

Fitzgerald, John, and John Wicks, "Measuring the Value of Household Output: A Comparison of Direct and Indirect Approaches," *Review of Income and Wealth*, Vol. 36, June 1990, pp. 129–141.

Goldschmidt-Clermont, Luisella, "Monetary Valuation of Non-Market Productive Time: Methodological Considerations," *Review of Income and Wealth*, Series 39, No. 4, December 1993, pp. 419–434.

Grant, Arthur, "Issues in Distribution Theory: The Measurement of Labor's Relative Share, 1899–1929," *Review of Economics and Statistics*, Vol. 45, No. 3, August 1963, pp. 273–279.

Hotson, John H., "The Constancy of the Wage Share: The Canadian Experience," *Review of Economics and Statistics*, Vol. 45, No. 1, February 1963, pp. 84–91.

Johnson, D. Gale, "The Functional Distribution of Income in the United States, 1850–1952," *Review of Economics and Statistics*, Vol. 36, No. 2, May 1954, pp. 175–182.

King, W. I., *The Wealth and Income of the People of the United States*, New York, 1919.

Lecaillon, Jacques, and Dimitrios Germidis, "Economic Development and the Wage Share in National Income," *International Labor Review,* Vol. 3, No. 5, May 1975, pp. 393–409.

Murphy, Martin, "The Value of Nonmarket Household Production: Opportunity Cost versus Market Cost Estimates," *Review of Income and Wealth,* Vol. 24, September 1978, pp. 243–255.

———, "Comparative Estimates of the Value of Household Work in the United States for 1976," *Review of Income and Wealth,* Vol. 28, March 1982, pp. 29–43.

Tobin, James, and William Nordhaus, *Economic Growth,* National Bureau of Economic Research Colloquium V, National Bureau of Economic Research, New York, 1971.

SUGGESTIONS FOR FURTHER READING

Clark, J. B., "Distribution as Determined by the Law of Rent," *Quarterly Journal of Economics,* Vol. 5, April 1891, pp. 289–318.

Eisner, Robert, *The Total Incomes System of Accounts,* University of Chicago Press, Chicago, 1989.

Juster, F. Thomas, and Frank Stafford, *Time, Goods, and Well-Being,* Institute for Social Research, University of Michigan, Ann Arbor, 1985.

Kalecki, Michael, "Class Struggle and the Distribution of National Income," *Kyklos,* Vol. 24, No. 1, 1971, pp. 1–9.

Mitchell, Wesley, *Income in the United States: Its Amount and Distribution, 1909–1919,* National Bureau of Economic Research, New York, 1921.

National Bureau of Economic Research, *The Behavior of Income Shares: Selected Theoretical and Empirical Issues,* National Bureau of Economic Research, New York, 1964.

Parker, R. H., and G. C. Harcourt, *Readings in the Concept and Measurement of Income,* Cambridge University Press, Cambridge, 1969.

Ruggles, Nancy, and Richard Ruggles, *The Design of Economic Accounts,* National Bureau of Economic Research, New York, 1970.

DATA SOURCES

Data Sources for the U.S. Economy

Council of Economic Advisers, *Economic Report of the President,* U.S. Government Printing Office, Washington, D.C. These volumes are available annually.

Survey of Current Business. Every year, the July issue of this publication contains detailed information on the National Income and Product Accounts.

U.S. Bureau of the Census, *Long-Term Economic Growth 1860–1970,* Washington, June 1973.

U.S. Bureau of the Census, *Historical Statistics of the United States, Colonial Times to 1970,* Part 2, U.S. Government Printing Office, Washington, D.C., 1975.

U.S. Bureau of the Census, *Statistical Abstract of the United States.* Available annually.

U.S. Bureau of the Census, Census of Population, *Subject Reports.* Various publications are available for each of the decennial censuses.

U.S. Bureau of the Census, *Current Population Reports.* Available annually.

U.S. Bureau of Labor Statistics, *Employment and Earnings,* U.S. Government Printing Office, Washington D.C. Available annually.

International Data Sources

Kravis, Irving, Alan Heston, and Robert Summers, *International Comparisons of Real Product and Purchasing Power,* World Bank, Baltimore, 1978.

Maddison, Angus, *Phases of Capitalist Development,* Oxford University Press, Oxford, 1982.

———, *Dynamic Forces in Capitalist Development,* Oxford University Press, Oxford, 1991.

Summers, Robert, and Alan Heston, "Improved International Comparisons of Real Product and Its Composition, 1950–1980," *Review of Income and Wealth,* Vol. 30, June 1984, pp. 207–262.

———, "A New Set of International Comparisons of Real Product and Prices: Estimates for 130 Countries, 1950–1985," *Review of Income and Wealth,* Series 34, March 1988, pp. 1–26.

———, "The Penn World Table (Mark V): An Expanded Set of International Comparisons," *Quarterly Journal of Economics,* Vol. 106, 1991, pp. 327–336.

World Bank, *World Development Report,* Oxford University Press, New York. Available annually.

World Bank, *World Tables,* Johns Hopkins University Press, Baltimore. Available annually.

DISCUSSION QUESTIONS

1. Explain the difference between gross output and gross domestic product (or GDP).
2. Why were time trends different for GDP per capita and median family income between 1973 and 1993?

3. What are the components of personal income? What has been the biggest change in the composition of personal income in the United States since 1929?
4. Explain the two methods used to value household work in relation to national accounts.
5. Suppose GDP and the price index for the United States are as follows:

Year	GDP in Current Dollars	Price Index [1980 = 100]
1975	$1,800	90
1980	2,000	100
1985	2,400	120

Calculate GDP in 1980 dollars for each of the three years. Calculate GDP in 1975 dollars for each of the three years.
6.* Explain why the definition of income used in the national income and product accounts excludes capital gains.

---

*The more advanced sections or questions are designated by an asterisk.

3

INCOME INEQUALITY: ITS MEASUREMENT, HISTORICAL TRENDS, AND INTERNATIONAL COMPARISONS

In Chapter 2, we developed the concept of mean earnings and median income. These measures are useful in tracking changes in the well-being of the average worker and the average family. This chapter focuses on the distribution or inequality of income. What does income inequality mean? Quite simply, it means that different people or families receive different amounts of income. In this chapter, our focus is on how great these differences are—that is, what the **dispersion** of income looks like. The term *income distribution* refers to a way of recording the differences in what people receive and of measuring the overall dispersion of income.

This chapter is primarily concerned with the measurement of income inequality. However, it will also investigate whether our country has become more equal or unequal in terms of income over time and how we compare to other countries of the world in terms of income inequality. Section 3.1 presents a brief review of basic statistics, and Section 3.2 develops the measurement of income inequality in some detail. Historical data on U.S. income inequality are shown in Section 3.3, while Section 3.4 presents comparisons between the United States and other countries. A summary is given in Section 3.5.

3.1 A REVIEW OF BASIC STATISTICS

In most studies, it is too costly to survey a full population (like the United States). Therefore, only a small percentage of the population is actually surveyed, and this we call a **sample.** In most cases, the sample is *randomly* drawn from the full population. It is hoped that this sample will be representative of the population, and that its statistics will be close to the actual population values.[1]

Mean, Variance, and Standard Deviation

The two most common statistics used to describe a sample are the mean and variance. The mean is a measure of the central tendency of a sample. In studying income distribution, a primary concern is the average level of income, since it reflects the average level of well-being of the population, as we discussed in Chapter 2. Suppose the sample size consists of n observations. Let X_1 refer to the first observation, X_2 to the second, and so on to X_n for the nth observation. The sample mean, $\overline{X}$, is defined as

$$\overline{X} = (X_1 + X_2 + \ldots + X_n)/n \tag{3.1}$$

where the three dots (. . .) mean "and so on to." An alternative expression is given by:

$$\overline{X} = \sum_{i=1}^{n} X_i / n \tag{3.2}$$

where the symbol Σ, which is the Greek letter "sigma," means "summation of X_i from i = 1 to i = n." The equations (3.1) and (3.2) are identical.

Another important concern about a sample is the *dispersion* of its values. The dispersion of income also has important implication for the well-being of a population.[2] The most common measure of dispersion is the variance of a sample. The sample variance, s^2, is given by:

$$s^2 = \sum_{i=1}^{n} (X_i - \overline{X})^2 / (n-1) \tag{3.3}$$

The term $(X_i - \overline{X})$ is called the deviation from the sample mean of each observation X_i and measures the discrepancy (difference) between the observation and the center of the sample. The more dispersed a sample is, the

---

[1]Another type of sampling technique is called a *stratified sample,* in which some subgroups of a population are sampled more heavily than others. This is a common technique used for analyses of wealth distribution, since a very small part of the population usually holds a very high percentage of the total wealth. In stratified samples, the overall population *weights* (that is, shares) must be known in advance from other sources in order to construct overall population statistics. See Chapter 12 for more discussion of stratified samples.

[2]This is also true of other variables. Take temperature, for example. New York City and San Francisco have about the same annual mean temperature, but the dispersion in temperature over the year is much greater in New York City. Even though the mean values are close, the fact that the dispersion is greater in New York City means that it has many more unpleasant (that is, hot or cold) days than San Francisco.

greater these deviations are and the higher the variance statistic. The reason that the deviations are squared is that the sum of the algebraic value of the deviations will always equal zero.[3] The sum of squared deviations is then divided by n − 1 to yield an estimate of the average squared deviation from the mean of the sample.[4] Without dividing by n − 1, the variance statistic would tend to increase merely as the sample size increased. The variance is also referred to as the mean squared deviation from the mean and is probably the most common indicator of sample dispersion.

An alternative measure, which is directly derived from the sample variance, is the sample standard deviation, denoted by *s* and defined as the square root of the variance. Its advantage over the variance measure is that it is of the same exponential order as the mean, since the variance is the average *squared* deviation and the standard deviation is the square root of this. As a result, it is meaningful to make a direct comparison between the standard deviation and mean of a distribution. One inequality measure, the coefficient of variation, is the ratio of the two, as we shall see below.

Distributions

So far the author has been using the term *distribution* rather loosely, but there is a technical meaning to the term. A distribution, or more formally a **frequency distribution,** refers to the frequency with which observations on a given variable fall within predefined categories of values for that variable. In the case of income, these categories are ranges of income, or **income classes.** In a sense, a frequency distribution is simply a convenient way of presenting statistical results for a variable with a wide range of values and for a sample with many observations.

Panel A of Table 3.1 presents data on the actual frequency distribution of family income in the United States in 1989. In that year, there were over 93 million family units in the country. Note first of all that the income classes are all defined to be mutually exclusive. Also note that the ranges of income that define each income class can differ in width. There are nine income classes in this distribution. The first eight are referred to as **close-ended classes,** since specific limits are denoted for these, while the last is called an **open-ended class,** since there is no defined upper limit. The first column of Table 3.1 shows the frequency with which the income observations fall into the designated classes. This distribution is also referred to as the **size distribution of income,** since it shows the frequency of income by size of income (as opposed to the "functional distribution" of income, which shows the shares of income received by labor and capital).

---

[3] The proof is as follows:

$$\sum_{i=1}^{n} (X_i - \overline{X}) = \sum_{i=1}^{n} X_i - \Sigma\, \overline{X} = n\overline{X} - n\overline{X} = 0$$

[4] For statistical reasons, it can be shown that division by n − 1 rather than by *n* yields an unbiased estimate of the population variance.

Table 3.1   Size Distribution of Total Family Income in the United States By Income Class and Percentile Rank, 1989[a]

A. Size Distribution of Income

Income Class	Frequency (in 1,000s)	Percentage Frequency	Cumulative Percentage Frequency	Percentage of Total Income By Income Class	Cumulative Percentage of Income
Under $5,000	4,947	5.3	5.3	0.4	0.4
$5,000–$9,999	9,615	10.3	15.6	2.1	2.5
$10,000–$14,999	9,055	9.7	25.3	3.3	5.8
$15,000–$24,999	16,709	17.9	43.2	9.8	15.6
$25,000–$34,999	14,842	15.9	59.1	13.1	28.7
$35,000–$49,999	16,149	17.3	76.4	20.1	48.8
$50,000–$74,999	13,535	14.5	90.9	24.8	73.6
$75,000–$99,999	4,761	5.1	96.0	12.2	85.8
$100,000 & over	3,641	3.9	100.0	14.2	100.0
All families	93,254	100.0		100.0	

B. Cumulative Percentage of Income by Percentiles

Percentiles	Cumulative Number of Families (in 1,000s)	Percentile Income Level	Cumulative Percentage of Income
10	9,335	$ 7,282	1.3
20	18,669	$ 12,268	4.0
30	28,004	$ 17,626	8.4
40	37,339	$ 23,212	13.8
50	46,674	$ 28,906	21.2
60	56,008	$ 35,780	29.7
70	65,343	$ 44,451	41.3
80	74,678	$ 56,207	55.0
90	84,012	$ 73,448	72.1
95	88,680	$ 95,098	83.4
99	92,414	$114,706	93.0
100	93,254		100.0

(continued)

Table 3.1 *(concluded)*

C. Income Shares by Quintiles

B. Quintile	Percentage Share of Total Income
Bottom	4.0
Second	9.9
Third	15.9
Fourth	25.2
Top	45.0
All	100.0

D. Other Statistics

1.	Median income	$28,906
2.	Mean income	$36,520
3.	Variance of income	$857,854,125
4.	Standard deviation of income	$29,289
5.	Kuznets (K) coefficient	0.305
6.	Coefficient of variation	0.802
7.	Gini coefficient	0.415
8.	Log variance of income	0.850
9.	Theil's "entropy" index	0.290
10.	Atkinson index (0.5)	0.145
	Atkinson index (0.8)	0.235
	Atkinson index (1.5)	0.442

[a]Source: U.S. Bureau of the Census, *Current Population Reports*, Series P-60, No. 169, *Money Income and Poverty Status in the United States: 1989*, U.S. Government Printing Office, Washington, D.C., 1990.

The second column shows the percentage frequency distribution. This is computed by dividing the actual frequency by the total number of observations. Thus, for example, 10.3 percent of all incomes fell in the $5,000–$9,999 income class, and 17.9 percent fell in $15,000–$24,999 income class. This income class is referred to as the **modal class,** since it has the largest frequency of observations. (The **mode** of a distribution is the income level with the largest frequency of cases.) The next column shows the cumulative percentage frequency. This is computed by summing the percentage frequency of the particular income class with those of lower income classes. The cumulative percentage frequency thus shows the proportion of the sample receiving income at or below a given income class. For example, 15.6 percent of the population received income below $10,000, and 59.1 percent received income below $35,000.

Figure 3.1 1989 Family Income Distribution (Based on midpoint of each income class)

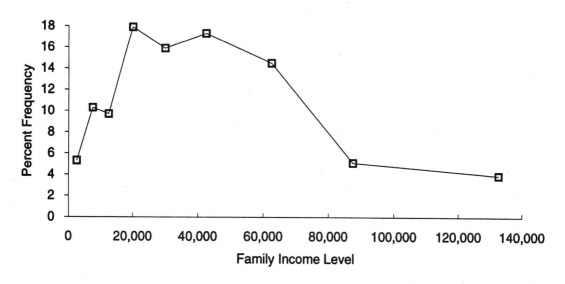

It is also possible to present the relative frequency distribution in graphical form, as shown in Figure 3.1. The vertical axis of the graph shows the percentage of the population in each income class, and the horizontal axis represents the income level. Here the midpoint of each income interval is used to represent the income class. The shape of this graph is very typical for an income distribution. Most of the observations are crowded on the left side of the graph, and the distribution peaks on the left side. The part of the distribution between zero income and the peak is referred to as the **lower tail** of the distribution. The right side, or **upper tail,** of the distribution is thinner and much longer than the lower tail. The basic shape of the distribution is often referred to as *asymmetrical* or *skewed to the right.* A **symmetrical distribution** is one in which a vertical line drawn through the center of the distribution yields a mirror image of the two sides. An **asymmetrical distribution** is one in which this is not true, where one side is longer or thinner or otherwise differently shaped than the other. An asymmetrical distribution in which one tail is longer than the other is also called a skewed distribution, and the direction of skewness is the side where the tail is longer. The point where the curve changes from being concave to the origin to convex to the origin is called the **inflection point.** After the inflection point, the curve asymptotically approaches the income axis.

Percentile Ranking

An alternative way of presenting the same data as in Panel A of Table 3.1 is in terms of percentile ordering, shown in Panel B. Percentiles are computed by first ordering the sample in terms of income from lowest to highest. The nth percentile is the income level such that n percent of the sample has income less than or equal to this level. In this case, 10 percent of U.S. families had incomes less than or equal to $7,282 in 1989; 20 percent of families (or 18.7 million) had incomes less than or equal to $12,268; and 50 percent of the sample had income less than or equal to $28,906. There is a special name for the 50th percentile, which is the **median,** since it is the middle income level of the distribution. Half of the sample is at or below this level, and the other half has income greater than this level. The median income, as we noted in Chapter 1, represents the level of well-being of the *average individual* or family.

The **mean** income level of families in 1989 was $36,520 (see Panel D), which is considerably higher than the median. The fact that the mean is higher than the median is typical of income distributions. This results from the fact that the income distribution is asymmetrical and, in particular, skewed to the right. If the distribution were symmetrical, then the median would be identical to the mean. Because the distribution has a long upper tail, there are some families in the population with incomes considerably further from the median than families on the lower tail. As a result, the computation of the mean income level is heavily weighted by these very rich people, even though they are few in number. The average income level of families in the population is almost always greater than the income level of the average family.

The second column of Panel B shows the percentage of the total income of all families whose income is at or below the given percentile level. For example, the bottom 10 percent of families in 1989 received (only) 1.3 percent of total family income; the bottom 50 percent received 21.2 percent of the total income, and so on. These computations will prove useful later in computing inequality measures.

Panel C of Table 3.1 shows a typical way in which income distributions are analyzed. A quintile is defined as 20 percentiles. The bottom quintile of a distribution refers to the bottom 20 percent of the sample; the second quintile to those ranked between the 20th and 40th percentile, and so on to the top (or fifth) quintile. The share of total income is computed for each quintile. The bottom quintile of U.S. families received 4.0 percent of total income; the second quintile, 9.9 percent; and the top quintile, 45.0 percent. The fact that the quintile shares are so different is one indication of considerable income inequality in the United States.

3.2 Inequality Measures

Economists have developed many measures of income inequality (see, for example, Amartya Sen, 1973, for a good review). In this section, we discuss the most common measures currently in use.

Concentration Measures

The simplest summary statistic on income inequality is the concentration ratio. This measures the percentage of total income received by the richest individuals—typically, the top 20 percent (quintile) of the income distribution, the top 10 percent (decile), the top 5 percent, or the top 1 percent. If there were perfect equality, each person by assumption would receive the same income and each percentile of the distribution would have one percent of total income. If there is inequality, then upper percentiles will receive more of total income than lower ones.

Panel C of Table 3.1 illustrates this point. The upper quintile of U.S. families in 1989 received 45.0 percent of total income, while the bottom quintile received only 4.0 percent. The second quintile received more than the lowest, the third more than the second, and the fourth more than the third. If there were perfect equality, each quintile would have received 20 percent of the total income. Since the difference in "quintile shares" is great, overall inequality is large.

Looking at overall quintile (or decile) shares is probably the best way to analyze the overall income distribution. However, sometimes it is convenient to use a single summary statistic. The usual way of doing this is to compute the percentage of the total income that accrues to the top income classes. There are four common measures. The first is the share of total income going to the top quintile, which in 1989 was 45.0 percent. The second is the share of income received by the top decile (10 percent), which was 27.9 percent. (This is computed from Panel B of Table 3.1 by subtracting the share of income going to the bottom 90 percent—0.721—from one.) The third is the share of the top 5 percent, which in 1989 was 16.6 percent, and the fourth is the share received by the top 1 percent, which was 7.0 percent.

Though these summary measures are very convenient and easy to compute, they reflect only the upper part of the distribution. Changes in the bottom part of the distribution—say, a redistribution of income from the middle classes to the lower class—would not be captured by these measures. Therefore, most researchers prefer to use summary inequality measures that reflect the full income distribution. One common measure is the **Kuznets coefficient.**

Kuznets Coefficient

This measure, developed by Simon Kuznets, who was also one of the founders of the modern system of national accounting, can be computed from the data shown in Table 3.1. The sample is first divided into n income classes (in this case, nine). The percentage frequency of the total families in each income class i, which we designate by f_i, as well as the share of total income received by income class i, which we designate by y_i, are then computed.

These are shown in the second and fourth columns of Table 3.1. If there were perfect equality in incomes, y_i would equal f_i for each income class i. (In fact, there would be only *one* income class.) If inequality is low, then the income shares and population shares would not differ by much. However, intuitively, we can see that the more inequality there is, the greater the differences would be between the population and income shares. In the case of the concentration measures, this was also true. If in one economy the top 5 percent receive 20 percent of the total income while in another economy the top 5 percent receive 12 percent of the income, the second economy would be considered more equal than the first.

The Kuznets coefficient K is computed by summing the absolute values of the difference between the population and income shares for each income class i:

$$K = \sum_{i=1}^{t} |f_i - y_i| / 2 \qquad (3.4)$$

where there are t income classes and the vertical bars "|" indicate absolute value. The reason that the absolute value rather than the actual algebraic difference is used is that the sum of the algebraic differences would always equal zero.[5] The summation is then divided by two in order to "normalize" its range between zero and one. To see this, note that in the case of perfect equality, $f_i = y_i$ for each income class i, and therefore K equals zero. On the other extreme, suppose one person has all the income in an economy and all the rest have zero income. In this case there would be two income classes. For the lower income class, $f_i \approx$ (approximately equals) 1.0 and $y_i = 0$; for the upper income class, $f_i \approx 0$ and $y_i = 1.0$. In this case, K would (almost) equal 1.0.

The range of the Kuznets coefficient is therefore from zero to one. The closer the measure is to one, the more inequality there is, and the closer to zero, the more equal the income distribution is. For the United States in 1989, K is equal to 0.305. Notice that the Kuznets coefficient reflects the entire income distribution, not just the upper tail as do the concentration measures. Changes in the bottom and middle parts of the distribution are therefore captured by the Kuznets coefficient. On the other hand, one major criticism of this measure is that it is very sensitive to the number of income classes used. The more income classes the original data are divided into, the higher the value of K. This feature makes it very difficult to compare income distributions drawn from different sources, which have different numbers or breakdowns of income classes.

---

[5]This can be proved by first noting that $\Sigma f_i = 1$ and $\Sigma y_i = 1$. Then:

$$\sum_{i=1}^{t} (f_i - y_i) = \sum_{i=1}^{t} f_i - \sum_{i=1}^{t} y_i = 1 - 1 = 0$$

A second criticism is that the Kuznets index does not conform to the **principle of transfers**—one of the principles economists cite to characterize a desirable inequality measure. According to this principle, a transfer of income from a richer to a poorer individual should always cause a decline in measured inequality.[6] If the inequality index shows no change, then the index is said to violate the principle of transfers. The Kuznets coefficient does violate this principle if transfers occur between individuals on the "same side" of the distribution—in particular, between individuals in income classes whose percentage frequencies are greater than their income shares (those with incomes under $35,000 in 1989) or between those in income classes whose percentage frequencies are less than their income shares ($35,000 or above in 1989). Transfers occurring between individuals below (or above) this point will cause no change in the Kuznets coefficient. The Kuznets coefficient will decrease only if the transfer is from someone above this point to someone below it.

Coefficient of Variation

The coefficient of variation, CV, is defined as the ratio of the standard deviation of income, SD(Y), to mean income, $\overline{Y}$:

$$CV = SD(Y) / \overline{Y} \tag{3.5}$$

As discussed in Section 3.2, the standard deviation of income is a measure of its dispersion. Why then divide the standard deviation of income by mean income? The reason is that a summary inequality measure should be a relative measure and, in particular, one that allows comparison between income distributions at different times and in different countries. It can be shown statistically that the standard deviation of a distribution moves proportionally with the mean of the distribution.[7] As a result, price inflation by itself

---

[6]Technically, this should hold as long as the amount of income transferred is low relative to the initial income levels. If it is too high (in particular, if it is greater than half the original difference between the two incomes), then the transfer will simply cause the original recipients to "switch places," with no effect on measured inequality.

[7]This can be proved formally as follows. Suppose there are two distributions of income, Y and Z, where $Z_i = aY_i$ for every observation i and a is a constant (scalar). Then, from equation (3.1),

$$\begin{aligned}\overline{Z} &= \Sigma\ Z_i\ /\ n = (Z_1 + Z_2 + \ldots + Z_n)\ /\ n \\ &= (aY_1 + aY_2 + \ldots + aY_n)\ /\ n \\ &= a\ \Sigma\ Y_i\ /\ n \\ &= a\overline{Y}\end{aligned}$$

From equation (3.3),

$$\begin{aligned}Var\ (Z) &= \Sigma\ (Z_i - \overline{Z})^2\ /\ n - 1 \\ &= \Sigma\ (aY_i - a\overline{Y})^2\ /\ n - 1 \\ &= a^2\ \Sigma\ (Y_i - \overline{Y})^2\ /\ n - 1 \\ &= a^2\ Var\ (Y)\end{aligned}$$

(continued)

would cause the standard deviation of income to rise over time. Dividing SD(Y) by $\overline{Y}$ standardizes the measure of income inequality and makes it invariant to changes in the overall price level. In technical terms, the CV is a **scale-free index,** another characteristic used by economists to characterize a desirable inequality measure.

The coefficient of variation of income for the United States in 1989 is equal to $29,289/$36,520 = 0.802. The coefficient of variation of income is typically close to one. If there is perfect equality in income, then the standard deviation is equal to zero and the CV also equals zero. At the other extreme, when all the income goes to one person, the CV approaches infinity (that is, increases without limit). One criticism of this measure is that it is unbounded.

Another criticism of this index is that the mean and standard deviation capture only two aspects ("moments") of an income distribution. If income were distributed normally, this information would be sufficient to fully describe such a distribution. Instead, income distributions are generally skewed to the right. This third moment of the distribution—its skewness—is not captured by the CV. Since income is concentrated in the upper tail of the distribution, changes in its thickness and its overall shape affect the inequality of income.

A third criticism is that the CV is more sensitive to changes in the upper tail of the income distribution than in the middle or lower tails. This can be seen by noting that the standard deviation is calculated by taking the sum of squared deviations from the mean. Consider the case where the sample mean is $20,000. Suppose the income of a person with $100,000 increases by $1,000. Then, the squared deviation increases by $161,000,000. On the other hand, if the income of a person with $8,000 increases by $1,000, the squared deviation rises by only $25,000,000. The same transfer of $1,000 has a much larger effect on the CV when it occurs in the upper tail of the distribution than at the bottom or middle.

The Lorenz Curve

The **Lorenz curve** is a graphical technique used to represent the relative size distribution of income (see Figure 3.2). We first draw a square. The horizontal dimension (axis) of the box represents the cumulative percentage of families (ordered from lowest to highest income), and the vertical dimension represents the cumulative percentage of income received by these families. A line connecting the opposite corners of the box between the points

---

Therefore,

$$SD(Z) = [Var(Z)]^{.5} = a\ SD(Y)$$

and

$$CV(Z) = SD(Z)\ /\ \overline{Z}$$
$$= a\ SD(Y)\ /\ aY$$
$$= CV(Y)$$

Figure 3.2   Lorenz Curve for 1989 Family Income Based on Percentile Data from Table 3.1

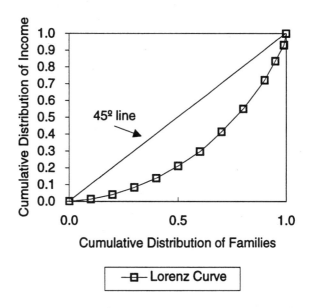

(0,0) and (1.0,1.0) is referred to as the 45° (degree) line, since in trigonometric terms it is 45° from the horizontal and vertical axes. It represents the Lorenz curve of perfect income equality, since if everyone receives the same income, the cumulative percent of income will exactly equal the cumulative percent of recipients. If there is less than perfect equality in income, the Lorenz curve will fall below the 45° line, because the lowest P percent of the income recipients will necessarily receive less than P percent of the total income.

The Lorenz curve for the U.S. income distribution in 1989 is shown in Figure 3.2. All Lorenz curves start at the (0,0) point (zero percent of the population receives zero percent of total income) and end at the (1.0,1.0) point (100 percent of the population receives 100 percent of income). In between, the 1989 curve passes through the point (0.10,0.013), since, from Table 3.1, the poorest 10 percent of U.S. families received 1.3 percent of total income. The curve also passes through the point (0.50,0.212), since the bottom half earned 21.2 percent of total income, and the point (0.90,0.721), since the bottom 90 percent obtained 72.1 percent of total income (or, alternatively, the top 10 percent earned 27.9 percent).

Lorenz curves can themselves be used to compare income distributions and assess the relative degree of income inequality. Two hypothetical non-intersecting curves are illustrated in Figure 3.3A, referring to countries A and B. In this case, we can say unambiguously that country A has less income inequality than country B. To see why, select any percentile rank in the cumulative distribution of families, say point P, then draw a vertical line

Figure 3.3A Illustrative Lorenz Curves (Nonintersecting)

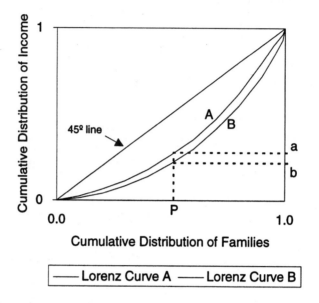

and note where it intersects curves A and B—in this case, at points *a* and *b*, respectively. As shown, *a* is greater than *b*. This means that the poorest P percent of families have a *greater* share of income in country A than in country B. Since the two curves do not intersect, this is true of every point P. This implies that at *every* percentile level, income is less concentrated in country A than in country B, and, hence, country B has greater income inequality than country A.

In Figure 3.3B the two Lorenz curves cross. The comparative degree of income inequality between the two countries, C and D, is ambiguous in this case. Consider two points on the horizontal axis, P_1 and P_2, and their corresponding points on the Lorenz curves for countries C and D. At point P_1, d_1 is greater than c_1, which means that the poorest P_1 percent of families has a greater share of income in country D than in country C. However, at point P_2, c_2 is greater than d_2, which implies that the poorest P_2 percent has a greater share of income in country C than in country D. In country C the upper income class has a smaller share of total income than in country D, but the lower income class also has a smaller share. In this case, there is no direct way of assessing the relative degree of inequality between the two countries based on a comparison of Lorenz curves alone.[8]

---

[8] This example illustrates why one should be cautious in using concentration measures such as the share of the upper 1, 5, or 10 percent of the income distribution as summary measures of income inequality.

Figure 3.3B Illustrative Lorenz Curves (Intersecting)

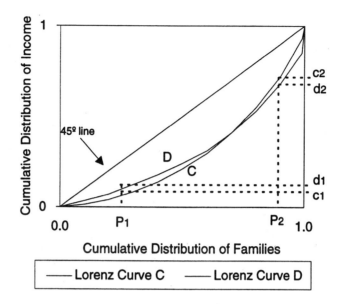

In the case of nonintersecting Lorenz curves, a graphical representation can give a convenient and unambiguous way of ranking income inequality between two countries or two points in time. However, graphs by themselves do not allow us to say, quantitatively, how much or little difference there is in equality between the two distributions. A summary measure of income inequality is desirable in order to make comparisons among countries or over time.

Gini Coefficient

One very common measure that is derived from the Lorenz curve is the Gini coefficient, which was devised by Corrado Gini in 1912 (the English translation of his original work, which was written in Italian, was published in 1936). The Gini coefficient is proportional to the area between the 45° line and the Lorenz curve. In the case of Figure 3.3A, country B would have a larger Gini coefficient than country A, reflecting its higher degree of inequality. A Lorenz curve further from the 45° line will always have a larger Gini coefficient, as it should. In the case of intersecting Lorenz curves, as in Figure 3.3B, the Gini coefficient will in general provide a measure that will rank one of the two countries as having greater inequality. However, though the Gini coefficient will provide an unambiguous ranking, there is some

Figure 3.4 Computation of the Gini Coefficient Based on 1989 U.S. Family Income Distribution

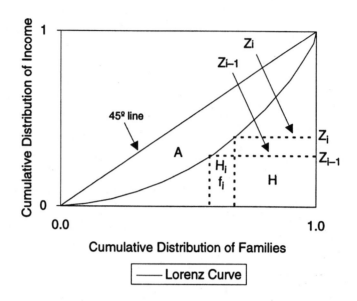

disagreement among economists about whether it is a meaningful measure in such a situation.[9]

The computation of the Gini coefficient from the 1989 U.S. family income distribution data is illustrated in Figure 3.4. The area A between the 45° line and the Lorenz curve is equal to 0.5 (the area of the lower right triangle, which equals half the area of the square) less the area H underneath the Lorenz curve:

$$A = 0.5 - H$$

The area H can be approximated by dividing it into trapezoids. One such trapezoid, H_i, is illustrated in Figure 3.4. The base of trapezoid H_i is equal to the difference between P_i (the cumulative percentage of income recipients up through income class i) and P_{i-1}, and thus to the percent of recipients in income class i, or f_i (the "f" stands for percent frequency). The shorter length of the trapezoid is equal to z_{i-1} (the cumulative percentage of income up through income class i − 1) and the longer length is equal to z_i. From elementary geometry, the area of a trapezoid is equal to its base multiplied by half the sum of its lengths:

---

[9] In particular, if one's value judgment is such that one is more concerned about the poor having too little than the rich having too much, one would consider country C to be more unequal than country D, since the poor have a smaller share of total income in C than in D. If, on the other hand, one objects more to the rich having too high a share of total income, then one would consider country D to have greater inequality. See the section on Atkinson's Measure for more discussion.

$$H_i = f_i(z_{i-1} + z_i) / 2$$

The area under the Lorenz curve is then given by:

$$H = \sum_{i=1}^{t} H_i = \sum_{i=1}^{t} f_i(z_{i-1} + z_i) / 2$$

for t income classes, where z_0 is defined as equal to zero. The area A is then given by:

$$A = \left[(1 - \sum_{i=1}^{t} f_i(z_{i-1} + z_i) \right] / 2$$

The Gini coefficient G is then derived by selecting a constant by which to multiply A so that G ranges from zero to one. To select the constant, note that complete equality is given by the 45° line, and in this case A would equal zero (since H would equal 0.5). The other extreme—total inequality of income—would occur if one person received all the total income of a country. Then the Lorenz "curve" would be described by the lower horizontal axis and the right vertical axis of the square. In this case, H would equal zero and A would equal 0.5. To standardize G, we thus choose a factor of 2:

$$G = 2 \cdot A$$

and, therefore,

$$G = 1 - \sum_{i=1}^{t} f_i(z_{i-1} + z_i) \tag{3.6}$$

Perfect equality would thus yield a value of zero for G, and complete inequality would yield a value of one. In the case of the 1989 U.S. family income distribution shown in Table 3.1, the Gini coefficient is equal to 0.415.[10]

One important characteristic of the Gini coefficient is that it is more sensitive to changes in the middle of the distribution than at either extreme. This is apparent by noting that from equation (3.6) the cumulative share of

---

[10]An alternative formulation of the Gini coefficient based on individual data is given by:

$$G = \sum_{i=1}^{n} \sum_{j=1}^{n} | Y_i - Y_j | / (2\bar{Y}n^2)$$

where Y_i is the income of individual i, n is the number of individuals, and $\bar{Y}$ is mean income.

income is, in effect, weighted by the percent of people in each income class. Since most people are in the middle income classes, changes in the middle portion of a given dollar amount have a greater impact in the computation of G than at the two extremes.[11]

Log Variance of Income*

The so-called "log variance of income" is actually the variance of the logarithm of income. We noted above that while the variance of income is a good measure of dispersion, it is not a good measure of relative income inequality, since it, as well as the standard deviation of income, tends to increase with mean income. The coefficient of variation measure corrects for this by dividing the standard deviation of income by the mean. There is an alternative way of correcting for this property, which is to use the logarithm of income instead of actual income. The variance of the logarithm of income can be shown to be scale-free (that is, independent of proportional changes in income), as follows. Let

$$Z_i = aY_i \text{ for each person } i,$$

where a is a constant and Y_i is income. Then:

$$\ln(Z_i) = \ln(a) + \ln(Y_i)$$
$$= a' + \ln(Y_i)$$

where "ln" stands for the natural logarithm and a' is a constant. Therefore:

$$\text{Var } [\ln(Z)] = \text{Var } [\ln(Y) + a'] = \text{Var } [\ln(Y)] \tag{3.7}$$

since the variance of the sum of a random variable and a constant is equal to the variance of the random variable. Thus, like the coefficient of variation, the log variance is an index of relative income dispersion. The log variance of income for the United States in 1989 is 0.850.

There is another justification for using the log variance measure. The common shape of an income distribution conforms somewhat closely to the log-normal distribution. A random variable has a log-normal distribution when the logarithm of the variable is normally distributed. A log-normal

---

[11] One interesting variant of the Gini coefficient was proposed by Morton Paglin in a 1975 article. He noted first that income tends to increase as families get older (see Chapter 7 for a discussion). He argued that because almost all families experience the same life cycle pattern, this source of income inequality is not of normative interest. As a result, an inequality measure should be adjusted to capture only differences of income among families at the same stage of their life cycle. He developed such a modified Gini coefficient, which is usually referred to as the "Paglin-Gini coefficient." However, Danziger, Haveman, and Smolensky (1977), as well as other researchers in this field, criticized Paglin's proposed measure because of analytical problems.

distribution can be fully characterized by its mean and its variance. If income has a log-normal distribution, its relative dispersion is fully captured by the log-variance measure.

There are four criticisms made of this index. First, if income does not conform closely to a log-normal distribution, then its skewness and the concentration of income in the upper tail is not adequately reflected in this measure. Second, its range of values, like that of the coefficient of variation, is unbounded.

Third, this measure violates the principle of transfers. In particular, if the same dollar amount is transferred from a very rich person to a rich person (both of whom have incomes significantly above mean income), the log variance will generally increase instead of decline. The reason is that changes in the logarithm of income depend on percentage changes in income, rather than changes in absolute dollar amounts.[12] A $1,000 change in income represents a larger percentage change for a rich person than for a very rich person. As a result, the decrease in the log variance from the loss of income to the richer of the two persons is actually less in absolute value than the increase in the log variance from the gain of income to the less rich individual. A fourth and related criticism is that the log-variance measure is more sensitive to changes of income in the lower part of the income distribution than in the upper part. The reason is similar. A decrease of $1,000 in income of a low-income person will produce a larger increase in the log variance than a $1,000 increase in the income of a high-income person.

The Theil Entropy Index*

The Theil entropy index of inequality is given by the following formula:

$$T = (1/n) \sum_{i=1}^{n} (Y_i/\overline{Y}) \ln(Y_i/\overline{Y})$$ (3.8)

where n is the size of the population, Y_i is the income of individual i, and $\overline{Y}$ is the mean income of the population. The rationale for this index stems from information theory. The underlying idea is that the more-surprising events have more information value. If an event is completely predictable, it has no information value; when it is less predictable, it has information content. When income is equally distributed or nearly so, income for any individual is predictable. When income is unequally distributed, however, it is less easy to predict the income of a randomly chosen individual, and a message which indicates what that individual's income is has information content.

---

[12] In terms of calculus,

$$d (\ln Y) = dY / Y$$

where dY / Y is the percentage change in income.

The formal derivation is as follows. Suppose that there are n mutually exclusive events which may occur with probability π_i, $i = 1, \ldots, n$, with $0 < \pi_i < 1$ and $\Sigma_i \pi_i = 1$. According to information theory, if a particular event is very rare, then the information value of a message saying it has occurred is valuable, while the information value of very common events is rated low. If $h(\pi_i)$ is a function that assigns an information value to the event, it will be decreasing in π_i. Another provision of this theory is that the information content of knowing that two statistically independent events i and j have taken place should be the sum of the values of the separate messages. Since the probability of i and j both occurring is $\pi_i \cdot \pi_j$, then it follows that the function h must have the property that

$$h(\pi_i \cdot \pi_j) = h(\pi_i) + h(\pi_j)$$

A function which has this property and which is decreasing in π is

$$h(\pi_i) = -\ln(\pi_i)$$

The expected information content ("entropy" or "disorder") of the whole system is given by the sum of $h(\pi)$ weighted by the respective probabilities:

$$S = \sum_{i=1}^{n} \pi_i \, h(\pi_i) = -\sum_{i=1}^{n} \pi_i \ln(\pi_i)$$

The maximum possible value of this function S is $\Sigma_i(1/n)h(1/n)$, which occurs when all events are equally likely.[13] The greater the "disorder"—that is, differing probabilities—that occurs, the more the value of S falls below the maximum. A function that expresses this relation is the entropy index E given by:

$$E = \sum_{i=1}^{n} (1/n) \, h(1/n) - \Sigma \, \pi_i \, h(\pi_i) = \sum_{i=1}^{n} \pi_i \, [\ln(\pi_i) - \ln(1/n)]$$

The function E will be higher the more disorder exists in the system.

The analogy between "disorder" and income inequality provides the rationale for using index E as the basis of an inequality index. In fact, the Theil function T is exactly equivalent to E if income shares $s_i = Y_i/(n\bar{Y})$, $i = 1, \ldots, n$, are substituted for the probabilities.[14]

---

[13] This can be proved by setting the first derivative of function S to zero and solving for $\pi_1 = \pi_2 = \ldots = \pi_n$ subject to the condition that $\lambda(\Sigma \pi_i - 1) = 0$ where λ is the Lagrange multiplier.

[14] The proof is that

$$E = \sum_{i=1}^{n} Y_i/(n\bar{Y}) \cdot [\ln(Y_i/n\bar{Y}) - \ln(1/n)] = (1/n) \sum_{i=1}^{n} (Y_i/\bar{Y}) \cdot \ln(Y_i/\bar{Y}) + \ln(n) - \ln(n)$$

The Theil index is the only index that satisfies the following three desirable characteristics of an inequality measure: (1) scale-free, (2) the principle of transfers, and (3) decomposability into between-group inequality and within-group inequality. The latter can be shown as follows:

$$T = \sum_g (n_g \bar{Y}_g / n\bar{Y}) \cdot T_g + (1/n) \sum_g (n_g \bar{Y}_g / \bar{Y}) \ln(\bar{Y}_g / \bar{Y}) \qquad (3.9)$$

where g is the number of groups, n_g is the number of individuals in group g, and $\bar{Y}_g$ is the mean income for group g. The first term of (3.9) is a weighted sum of the Theil indices of each group (that is, a weighted sum of **within-group inequality**), where the weight for each group g is group g's share of total income. The second term represents the **between-group inequality**, which is calculated by the Theil formula, as if each group were treated as an individual.[15]

There are two criticisms of the Theil index. First, in contrast to the Kuznets coefficient, the Gini coefficient, and the coefficient of variation, the Theil formula has no intuitive interpretation with regard to inequality. Second, like the Gini coefficient, the Theil index is more sensitive to changes in the middle of the income distribution than in the lower or upper tails. The reason is that, like the Gini index, the center of the distribution has a much larger weight in the calculation of the Theil index because of its large concentration of income recipients.

Atkinson's Measure*

Anthony Atkinson (1970) developed a family of inequality indices in order to explicitly introduce value judgments into the measurement of inequality. His index is given as follows:

$$A = 1 - [(1/n) \sum_{i=1}^{n} (Y_i/\bar{Y})^{1-\epsilon}]^{1/(1-\epsilon)} \qquad (3.10)$$

Atkinson notes that inequality measures implicitly involve value judgments and argues that these value judgments should be made explicit in choosing an inequality measure. Such a judgment should take the form of introducing a specific social welfare function and, in particular, specifying society's degree of inequality aversion. In his formulation, this amounts to the price that society is willing to pay in order to decrease income inequality.

Atkinson argues that if we are considering taking one dollar from a rich person and giving a certain proportion x to a poor person (the remainder being lost in the process), society ought to ask: "At what level of x do we

---

[15] According to this decomposition, inequality can be thought of as affected by three factors: (1) the proportion of the population in different groups, (2) inequality within groups, and (3) the variation of the group means around the overall mean.

cease to regard the redistribution as desirable?" If all the income transferred from the rich person actually gets to the poor individual (that is, $x = 1$), then any society which is in the least concerned about inequality will consider this redistribution as socially desirable. If only a small fraction of the dollar is actually received by the poor individual, then only a society which is particularly concerned about inequality will consider the transfer as socially desirable. The value of x is chosen so that society is indifferent between the actual degree of its inequality and a distribution in which everyone receives the same level of income but average income is only x percent of the actual average income.

Atkinson's measure of inequality requires a specification of ϵ, the degree of inequality aversion, where $x = 1/2^\epsilon$. The choice of a high value of ϵ (a low value of x) implies a high degree of inequality aversion and, in particular, a concern for the share of the bottom portion of the income distribution. In contrast, the choice of a relatively low value of ϵ implies that society has a low degree of inequality aversion and is particularly concerned with changes in the upper portion of the income distribution. The value of the Atkinson index for the United States in 1989 is 0.145 for an ϵ-value of 0.5, 0.235 for an ϵ-value of 0.8, and 0.442 for an ϵ-value of 1.5.

The major advantage of this measure is that it overcomes the ambiguity in relative inequality when Lorenz curves cross. The reason is that our choice of ϵ determines whether we are more concerned with inequality at the top of the distribution or inequality at the bottom. Thus, the Atkinson index gives an unambiguous ranking in inequality between countries or at different points in time, even when Lorenz curves cross (refer back to the section entitled "The Lorenz Curve").

This measure has been criticized on two grounds. First, it is very difficult to determine society's value of ϵ (its degree of inequality aversion). Thus, typically, a researcher will use different values of ϵ in computing the Atkinson index (as we did for the United States in 1989). The value of the Atkinson index is very sensitive to the value of ϵ, as we have just seen. Moreover, different values of ϵ will often produce different trends in the Atkinson index, as well as different rank orders among countries.

Second, there is a certain internal inconsistency in the Atkinson index. The formula for the index implies that total social utility is the sum of individual utility levels (that is, the index is additively separable) and that individual utility depends only on individual incomes. But if individual utility depends only on individual income, why would society be concerned with the relative distribution of income and why would it have any aversion to income inequality in general?

3.3 TIME TRENDS IN INCOME INEQUALITY IN THE UNITED STATES

One important social issue that has occupied both policy makers and the public at large is whether inequality in the United States has been declining

Table 3.2   The Percentage Share of Total Income Received by the Top Percentiles of Tax Units, 1913–1948[a]

Year	Top 1 Percent	Top 5 Percent	Top 10 Percent
1913	15.0	—	—
1920	12.3	22.1	30.6
1929	14.5	26.1	—
1933	12.1	24.7	—
1940	11.9	22.7	32.1
1945	8.8	17.4	23.7
1948	8.4	17.6	24.8

[a]Source: Simon Kuznets (1953). The statistics are based on Internal Revenue Service tax data.

or rising over time. There are good reasons for believing that greater economic equality is a social good (see Section 3.1 above for a discussion). Therefore, any movement towards increasing income equality might be viewed as a beneficial development for American society.

The earliest inequality statistics based on official government data that we have date back to 1913, the first year federal income taxes were paid in the United States. Table 3.2 shows the share of total income received by the top 1, 5, and 10 percent of tax units (filers) in the United States for selected years between 1913 and 1948. These results are based on Internal Revenue Service tax return data. The unit of observation is the tax return unit. In these years, most families and unrelated individuals filed a single tax return, so that the tax return unit tends to correspond to the family unit. (This is the most common unit used in income distribution analysis.)

Between 1913 and 1948, there was a clear trend towards greater equality in the distribution of income. Except for 1920, all three concentration measures fell almost continuously over time for the indicated years. The share of income received by the top 1 percent fell almost in half, from 15 percent of all income in 1913 to 8 percent in 1948. The share of total income received by the top 5 percent declined from 26 percent in 1929 to 18 percent in 1948, and the share of the top 10 percent from 32 percent in 1940 to 25 percent in 1948. The share of income received by the top income groups fell considerably between 1913 and 1948. Even so, the income distribution was still far from perfect equality in 1948, with the top 1 percent having one-twelfth of all income; the top 5 percent with one-sixth; and the top 10 percent with one-quarter.

Table 3.3 presents a more complete picture of the change in the size distribution of income between 1935 and 1950. In this case, the income distribution is broken down by quintile shares. The share of total income received by the top quintile declined from 52 percent to 46 percent of total

Table 3.3 Quintile Shares of Family Personal Income, 1935–1950[a]

| Year | Quintile | | | | | Total |
	Bottom	Second	Third	Fourth	Top	
1935	4.1	9.2	14.1	20.9	51.7	100.0
1941	4.1	9.5	15.3	22.3	48.8	100.0
1944	4.9	10.9	16.2	22.2	45.8	100.0
1946	5.0	11.1	16.0	21.8	46.1	100.0
1947	5.0	11.0	16.0	22.0	46.0	100.0
1950	4.8	11.0	16.2	22.3	45.7	100.0

[a]Source: Goldsmith, Jaszi, Kurtz, and Liebenberg (1954).

income between 1935 and 1950. This is consistent with the results of the previous table, which showed a decline in the concentration of income in the top group. Analyzing the other quintile shares will enable us to see which groups gained at the expense of the top quintile. The fourth quintile's share of total income increased from 20.9 to 22.3 percent, for a net gain of 1.4 percentage points, while the third quintile gained 2.1 percentage points and the second quintile 1.8 percentage points. The bottom quintile's share of total income rose by only 0.7 percentage points, from 4.1 to 4.8 percent of total income.

Between 1935 and 1950, there was a movement toward greater equality in income distribution. However, the redistribution occurred mainly between the top group and the middle income classes (quintiles two through four). The relative position of the lower income classes changed very little during this period. This has very important implications concerning the elimination of poverty, as we shall see in the next chapter.

Table 3.4 shows a somewhat more detailed picture of the decline in inequality during the interwar period in the United States. In this table, the income received by the top one percent of tax return units is decomposed by type of income, and this is compared to the total income from that source. Table 3.2 showed that the share of total income received by the top percentile declined from 15 to 8 percent between 1913 and 1948. Here, we can see that this decline characterized all income types, except self-employment (entrepreneurial and small business) income. Employee compensation, dividends, interest, rent, and total property income received by the top percentile all declined as a share of the total income of that type.

Another interesting aspect of this table is the *relative* sizes of the income shares by type of income. Note, first of all, that the top one percent received only a relatively small share of total wages and salaries (that is, employee compensation). This was not the major source of their income. Second, the top one percent received over half of total dividends over this period, and in

Table 3.4 The Percentage Share of Total Income by Income Type Received by the Top Percentile, 1917–1948[a]

Year		*Income Type*				
	Employee Compensation	*Self-Employment Income*	*Dividends*	*Interest*	*Rent*	*Total Property Income[b]*
1917	6.6	9.2	72.4	44.6	14.9	49.9
1920	5.8	13.8	72.4	32.6	14.9	42.2
1925	6.2	15.6	67.9	28.7	17.2	41.0
1929	6.2	16.2	66.0	31.1	17.2	44.5
1933	7.3	11.9	55.9	20.6	16.0	31.5
1940	6.4	14.8	63.2	23.7	13.0	37.7
1943	3.8	23.4	52.3	22.7	9.8	29.7
1945	3.4	23.0	—	—	9.1	28.0
1948	3.8	15.2	53.6	15.8	12.8	31.1

[a] Source: Kuznets (1953). The statistics are based on Internal Revenue Service tax data.
[b] Total property income is defined as the sum of dividends, interest, and rent.

1917 and 1920 almost three-quarters of all dividends. Third, the top percentile received about 15 percent of all self-employment and rental income over this period, though the share tended to fluctuate considerably from year to year. Fourth, their share of interest income showed the most substantial decline over this period, falling from 45 percent of total interest to 16 percent. Fifth, in 1917 this group received half of all property income (i.e., dividends from stock shares, interest from savings accounts and securities, and rent from rental property). By 1948, this ratio had fallen to about a third, which, though lower than its 1917 level, was still quite substantial. Thus, the falling share of the top groups in total income between the two world wars was due largely to the widening ownership of income-producing property (see Chapter 11 for more discussion of wealth trends).

Table 3.5 carries the story from the beginning of the postwar period through 1993. The Gini coefficient is used here as the measure of income inequality, and the unit of observation consists of families and unrelated individuals. In the period between 1947 and 1966, there is a modest downward trend in income inequality (also see Figure 3.5), with the Gini coefficient falling from 0.436 to 0.405. The share of total income received by the top 5 percent also declines from 17.5 to 15.2 percent. However, the trend is not uniform over these years, and, indeed, the Gini coefficient fluctuates back and forth between about 0.41 and 0.43. From 1966 (when the Gini coefficient reaches its lowest value of 0.405) to 1993, there is a clear upward trend in inequality. The Gini coefficient rises almost continuously over

Table 3.5 Measures of Household Income Inequality for Selected Years, 1947–1993[a]

Year	Gini Coefficient	Percent of Total Income Received by Top 5 Percent of Income Recipients
1947	0.436	17.5
1950	0.439	17.3
1955	0.423	16.4
1960	0.423	15.9
1965	0.416	15.5
1966	0.405	15.2
1970	0.414	15.6
1975	0.419	15.5
1980	0.428	15.3
1985	0.455	16.7
1986	0.458	17.0
1987	0.457	16.9
1988	0.458	17.0
1989	0.462	17.6
1990	0.459	17.3
1991	0.459	16.8
1992	0.464	17.3
1993	0.479	18.6

[a]Sources: 1947–87: Hayes, Slottje, Nieswladomy, and Wolff (1990); 1988–92: U.S. Bureau of the Census, *Money Income of Households, Families, and Persons in the U.S., 1992*, Series P60–184, September, 1993; and 1993: U.S. Bureau of the Census, *Income, Poverty, and Valuation of Noncash Benefits, 1993*, Series P60–188, February, 1995. The estimates are constructed from Current Population Report data for various years. The unit of observation is families and unrelated individuals.

these years, and by 1993 reaches 0.479—a value considerably greater than its value at the end of World War II. Most of the increase occurs after 1975, when its value was 0.419. The share of the top 5 percent also increases, from 15.2 to 18.6 percent, though its rise is not as dramatic as that of the Gini coefficient.

3.4 INEQUALITY COMPARISONS WITH OTHER COUNTRIES

We now consider U.S. income inequality in the light of the experiences of other countries in the world. Such an analysis provides some perspective on whether inequality in the United States is high or low, since inequality measures *per se* provide very little guidance. We shall consider various indices of

Figure 3.5   Gini Coefficients for Household Income, 1947–1993

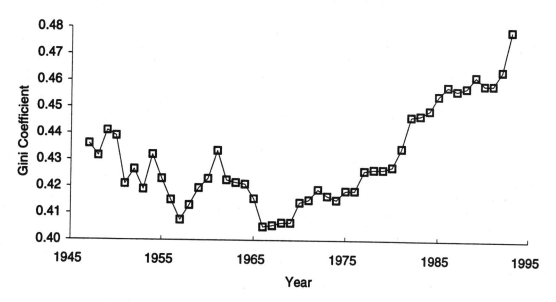

U.S. income inequality in comparison with those of other countries at similar levels of development and also with those at lower levels of development.

Table 3.6 provides some comparative data on 12 highly developed economies. These results are taken from one of the earliest comparative income studies (Malcolm Sawyer, 1976). Because this study did not attempt to make the income concepts in the various countries consistent, these results have to be interpreted with some caution.

Raw data on income distribution in the 12 nations were first converted into decile shares, and Gini coefficients were computed from the decile shares. Two different computations were performed. The first was on income before income taxes were paid, and the second was on income after income taxes were paid. Let us look at the pre-tax levels of inequality first. The three countries with the greatest amount of pre-tax inequality were France, the United States, and West Germany, in that order. All had Gini coefficients considerably above the average level for these twelve countries. Also high were the Netherlands and Canada. Considerably below this group was Norway, followed by Sweden, the United Kingdom, Japan, and Australia, which had the lowest level of pre-tax inequality.

The post-tax levels of income inequality were all lower than the respective pre-tax levels. This is as should be expected, since most income tax systems are *progressive*, which means that people with higher income pay a higher *proportion* of their income in the form of taxes. This means that the share of after-tax income received by the top income group is smaller than its share of before-tax income, and conversely for the lower income groups.

Table 3.6 Income Inequality in Selected Industrialized Countries, 1966–74[a]

Country	Year	Gini Coefficient[b] Pre-Tax Income	Post-Tax Income
1. Australia	1966–67	0.313	0.312
2. Canada	1969	0.382	0.354
3. France	1970	0.416	0.414
4. West Germany	1973	0.396	0.383
5. Italy	1969	—	0.398
6. Japan	1969	0.335	0.316
7. Netherlands	1967	0.385	0.354
8. Norway	1970	0.354	0.307
9. Spain	1973–74	—	0.355
10. Sweden	1972	0.346	0.302
11. United Kingdom	1973	0.344	0.318
12. United States	1972	0.404	0.381
Average	—	0.366	0.350

[a] Source: Sawyer (1976), Tables 5 and 6.
[b] The Gini coefficient computations are based on decile shares in the overall income distribution.

As a result, the after-tax Gini coefficient is lower than the before-tax Gini coefficient for each of the countries.[16]

However, as is evident from Table 3.6, the degree of progressivity of the tax system varies considerably across countries. France had the highest post-tax level of income inequality, and, in fact, the tax system had very little effect on income inequality in France. Italy had the second highest level of after-tax inequality, followed by West Germany and the United States. In the case of West Germany and the United States, the tax system had a moderate impact on reducing overall income inequality. Spain, the Netherlands, and Canada all ranked in the middle. In the case of both the Netherlands and Canada, the tax system made a fairly substantial contribution to reducing income inequality. The United Kingdom, Japan, Australia, Norway, and Sweden had the lowest levels of after-tax income inequality. For the two most equal countries, Norway and Sweden, the tax system had the biggest effect on reducing the level of income inequality among the twelve countries.

Table 3.7 shows the results of two studies which rely on the Luxembourg Income Study (LIS) database. This consists of surveys that were conducted

---

[16] The structure of the U.S. tax system and its impact on inequality will be discussed more fully in Chapter 16. For the moment, the student might try to prove that a proportional tax on income leaves the Gini coefficient unaffected.

Table 3.7 The Distribution of Income Among Advanced Countries Based on the Luxembourg Income Study (LIS) Data

I. Distribution of Family Income by Quintiles[a]

	Percentage Share of Income by Quintile					Gini Coefficient
	Lowest	Second	Third	Fourth	Top	
A. Distribution of Family Gross Income Among Quintiles of Families						
Canada	4.6	11.0	17.7	25.3	41.4	0.374
U.S.A.	3.8	9.8	16.6	25.3	44.5	0.412
U.K.	4.9	10.9	18.2	25.3	40.8	0.365
Germany[b]	4.4	10.2	15.9	22.6	46.9	0.429 (0.414)
Sweden	6.6	12.3	17.2	25.0	38.9	0.329
Norway	4.9	11.4	18.4	25.5	39.8	0.356
Israel	4.5	10.5	16.5	24.9	43.6	0.395
B. Distribution of Family Net Income Among Quintiles of Families						
Canada	5.3	11.8	18.1	24.6	39.7	0.348
U.S.A.	4.5	11.2	17.7	25.6	41.0	0.370
U.K.	5.8	11.5	18.2	25.0	39.5	0.343
Germany[b]	5.0	11.5	15.9	21.8	45.8	0.409 (0.389)
Sweden	8.0	13.2	17.4	24.5	36.9	0.292
Norway	6.3	12.8	18.9	25.3	36.7	0.311
Israel	6.0	12.1	17.9	24.5	39.5	0.338
C. Distribution of Family Equivalent Gross Income Among Quintiles of Persons						
Canada	6.7	12.6	17.5	24.0	39.2	0.327
U.S.A.	5.1	11.4	17.1	24.2	42.1	0.371
U.K.	7.9	13.0	17.9	23.7	37.5	0.297
Germany[b]	7.2	12.1	16.0	21.3	43.4	0.363 (0.352)
Sweden	9.4	14.6	18.5	23.3	34.3	0.249
Norway	8.1	13.6	17.9	23.4	37.0	0.289
Israel	6.1	10.3	15.9	23.7	44.0	0.382
D. Distribution of Family Equivalent Net Income Among Quintiles of Persons						
Canada	7.6	13.3	17.9	23.8	37.4	0.299
U.S.A.	6.1	12.8	18.1	24.4	38.6	0.326
U.K.	9.0	13.5	18.0	23.4	36.1	0.273
Germany[b]	7.5	12.7	16.1	20.7	43.0	0.355 (0.340)
Sweden	10.6	16.1	19.1	23.1	31.1	0.205
Norway	9.9	14.8	18.4	22.9	34.1	0.243
Israel	7.5	11.7	16.8	23.7	40.3	0.333

(continued)

Table 3.7 *(concluded)*

II. Inequality Measures for Disposable Income, Weighted by Persons, and the Rank Order (shown in parentheses) for Each Measure[c]

Country	Gini Coefficient	Coefficient of Variation	Theil Index	Atkinson's Index ($\epsilon = .8$)	($\epsilon = .5$)
U.S.A.	.330 (1)	.600 (2)	.182 (1)	.186 (1)	.099 (1)
Australia	.314 (2)	.584 (4)	.165 (2)	.151 (2)	.087 (2)
Netherlands	.302 (5)	.596 (3)	.159 (3)	.151 (2)	.083 (3)
Canada	.306 (3)	.569 (6)	.157 (4)	.144 (4)	.083 (3)
Switzerland	.292 (6)	.603 (1)	.154 (5)	.143 (5)	.079 (5)
U.K.	.303 (4)	.574 (5)	.153 (6)	.128 (6)	.078 (6)
Israel	.292 (6)	.564 (7)	.142 (7)	.114 (7)	.071 (7)
Germany	.280 (8)	.556 (8)	.134 (8)	.106 (8)	.066 (8)
Norway	.255 (10)	.484 (9)	.114 (9)	.105 (9)	.060 (9)
Sweden	.264 (9)	.474 (10)	.114 (9)	.104 (10)	.060 (9)

[a] Source: O'Higgins, Schmaus, and Stephenson (1989), Table 2. Panels A and B of Part I weight each family unit equally, while Panels C and D weight each individual equally. Income units are ranked by family gross income in Panel A, by family net income in Panel B, by gross equivalent income in Panel C, and by net equivalent income in Panel D.

[b] The German data are affected by a relatively large number of zero and negative incomes in the sample. A revised Gini coefficient which excludes income units with such incomes was calculated and is shown in parentheses.

[c] Source: Buhmann, Rainwater, Schmaus, and Smeeding (1988), Table 5. Countries are ranked from highest (U.S.) to lowest (Sweden) in terms of median disposable income.

in the late 1970s and early 1980s in 10 industrialized countries. In the case of the LIS data, considerable effort has been made to make the income concepts and the unit of observation consistent among the various country samples.

The results, interestingly, are fairly consistent with the earlier Sawyer study. Panel I shows the quintile shares for seven countries based on a 1989 study by Michael O'Higgins, Guenther Schmaus, and Geoffrey Stephenson. They are computed for both gross (before-tax) income and net (after payroll and income tax) income. In Panels A and B of Part I, each family unit is weighted equally, while Panels C and D weight each family by the number of individuals living in the family unit. Income units are ranked by family gross income in Panel A, by family net income in Panel B, by gross equivalent income in Panel C, and by net equivalent income in Panel D, where equivalent income adjusts family income for differences in family size.[17]

---

[17] See Chapter 4 for a discussion of equivalence classes and equivalent income.

By all four income concepts, the United States and Germany rank highest in terms of income inequality. Canada, the United Kingdom, Norway, and Israel form the middle group. Sweden is distinctly lower than any of the other countries in terms of family or individual income inequality.

Panel II shows five overall inequality measures for 10 advanced countries on the basis of a 1988 study by Brigitte Buhmann, Lee Rainwater, Guenther Schmaus, and Timothy Smeeding. By four of the five indices, the United States ranks highest in terms of income inequality and second according to the fifth index. Indeed, according to the first four of these indices, there is a considerable gap in inequality between the United States and the second-ranked country. Australia, the Netherlands, Canada, Switzerland, the United Kingdom, Israel, and Germany comprise a middle group, with a fairly narrow range of inequality among them. Norway and Sweden are distinctly more equal than the other eight countries.

Results compiled by Anthony Atkinson, Lee Rainwater, and Timothy Smeeding (forthcoming) on the basis of more recent LIS data are shown for 11 advanced countries in Table 3.8. These new computations also have the advantage of showing changes over the 1980s in the degree of inequality in the various countries. The calculations use a different indicator of inequality than the ones we have developed so far. The authors first compute the ratio of the income of the tenth percentile to the median income of that country (P10) and then the ratio of the income of the ninetieth percentile to the median income (P90). A small value for P10 indicates that the poor in the country have a relatively low level of income in comparison to the average family in that country. In 1986, among the eleven countries, the United States had the lowest value for P10, 34.7, meaning that the family ranked in the tenth percentile of the U.S. income distribution earned only 34.7 percent of the U.S. median income. In contrast, in the Netherlands in 1984, the tenth percentile received an income that was 61.5 percent of the median income in the Netherlands.

Conversely, a high value for P90 indicates that the rich in the country are particularly relatively well off in comparison to the average family. In 1986, the United States had the highest value of P90, 206.1, meaning that the ninetieth percentile received an income 2.061 times the median income of the United States. The lowest value of P90 was found for Sweden in 1987, a value of 151.5.

A high value of P90 and a low value of P10 both reflect a high degree of income inequality. A useful summary measure of overall inequality is the ratio of P90 to P10. In the late 1980s, the United States had by far the highest degree of inequality among the eleven countries—a ratio of 5.94—followed by Canada at 4.02 and Australia at 4.01. The lowest inequality was recorded in Sweden at 2.72, followed by Finland at 2.74 and Belgium at 2.79.

It is also interesting to compare changes in the ratio over time within a country. Here, too, the United States had by far the largest increase of inequality, from a ratio of 4.9 in 1979 to 5.9 in 1986. Changes were much

Table 3.8 The Ratio of the Ninetieth to the Tenth Percentile of Income Based on the Luxembourg Income Study (LIS) Data, 1979–1987[a]

Country	Year	Ratio of Percentile to Median Income (%) P10	P90	Ratio of P90 to P10
Australia	1981	46.0	186.3	4.05
	1985	46.5	186.5	4.01
Belgium	1985	59.3	162.5	2.74
	1988	58.5	163.2	2.79
Canada	1981	44.9	182.7	4.07
	1987	45.8	184.2	4.02
Finland	1987	58.9	152.7	2.59
	1990	57.0	156.2	2.74
France	1979	53.6	186.5	3.48
	1984	55.4	192.8	3.48
The Netherlands	1979	64.8	176.1	2.72
	1984	61.5	175.0	2.85
New Zealand	1983–84	53.2	189.6	3.56
	1987–88	53.6	186.6	3.48
Norway	1979	57.0	158.1	2.77
	1986	55.3	162.2	2.93
Sweden	1981	61.5	150.9	2.45
	1987	55.6	151.5	2.72
United Kingdom	1979	50.9	179.7	3.53
	1986	51.1	194.1	3.79
United States	1979	38.1	187.6	4.93
	1986	34.7	206.1	5.94

[a] Source: Atkinson, Rainwater, and Smeeding (forthcoming), Table 5. P10 shows the ratio of the income of the tenth percentile to the median income of that country, and P90 shows the ratio of the income of the ninetieth percentile to the median income of that country.

smaller for other countries. Moreover, of the eleven countries in the sample, seven showed an increase in inequality, three showed a decline, and one showed no change.

Table 3.9 presents relative income distribution figures for a selection of countries at various levels of development. These data have been collected by the World Bank. The countries are organized into four groups by the World Bank, depending on the country's per capita income level. No attempt has been made to make the underlying income concepts consistent. Moreover, in some cases, the income shares correspond to per capita

Table 3.9   Income Distribution Comparisons for Countries at Various Levels of Development, 1978–87[a]

Country	1985 GDP per capita[b] [U.S. = 100]	Year	Lowest	2nd	3rd	4th	Highest	Top 10%
			Percentage Share of Household Income[c] — Quintiles					

Country	1985 GDP per capita[b] [U.S. = 100]	Year	Lowest	2nd	3rd	4th	Highest	Top 10%
A. Low-Income Countries								
Bangladesh[d]	5.0	1981–82	9.3	13.1	16.8	21.8	39.0	24.9
India	4.5	1983	8.1	12.3	16.3	22.0	41.4	26.7
Pakistan[e]	8.1	1984–85	7.8	11.2	15.0	20.6	45.6	31.3
Ghana[d]	—	1987	6.5	10.9	15.7	22.3	44.6	29.1
Sri Lanka[f]	11.2	1985–86	4.8	8.5	12.1	18.4	56.1	43.0
Indonesia	—	1987	8.8	12.4	16.0	21.5	41.3	26.5
Average	6.0		7.6	11.4	15.3	21.1	44.7	30.3
B. Lower-Middle Income Countries								
Philippines[e]	10.8	1985	5.5	9.7	14.8	22.0	48.0	32.1
Cote d'Ivoire[d]	10.2	1986	5.0	8.0	13.1	21.3	52.7	36.3
Morocco[e]	13.1	1984–85	9.8	13.0	16.4	21.4	39.4	25.4
Guatemala	—	1979–81	5.5	8.6	12.2	18.7	55.0	40.8
Botswana	16.1	1985–86	2.5	6.5	11.8	20.2	59.0	42.8
Jamaica[d]	—	1988	5.4	9.9	14.4	21.2	49.2	33.4
Colombia[f]	—	1988	4.0	8.7	13.5	20.8	53.0	37.1
Peru[d]	—	1985	4.4	8.5	13.7	21.5	51.9	35.8
Costa Rica[f]	—	1986	3.3	8.3	13.2	20.7	54.5	38.8
Poland[f]	24.5	1987	9.7	14.2	18.0	22.9	35.2	21.0
Malaysia[f]	—	1987	4.6	9.3	13.9	21.2	51.2	34.8
Brazil	—	1983	2.4	5.7	10.7	18.6	62.6	46.2
Average	14.9		5.2	9.2	13.8	20.9	51.0	35.4
C. Upper-Middle Income Countries								
Hungary[f]	31.2	1983	10.9	15.3	18.7	22.8	32.4	18.7
Yugoslavia[f]	29.2	1987	6.1	11.0	16.5	23.7	42.8	26.6
Venezuela[f]	—	1987	4.7	9.2	14.0	21.5	50.6	34.2
Average	30.2		7.2	11.8	16.4	22.7	41.9	26.5
D. High-Income Economies								
Spain	46.0	1980–81	6.9	12.5	17.3	23.2	40.0	24.5
Israel	—	1979	6.0	12.1	17.8	24.5	39.6	23.5
Singapore	—	1982–83	5.1	9.9	14.6	21.4	48.9	33.5
Hong Kong	61.7	1980	5.4	10.8	15.2	21.6	47.0	31.3
New Zealand	60.9	1981–82	5.1	10.8	16.2	23.2	44.7	28.7

(continued)

Table 3.9 *(concluded)*

Country	1985 GDP per capita[b] [U.S. = 100]	Year	Lowest	2nd	3rd	4th	Highest	Top 10%
			Percentage Share of Household Income[c]					
			Quintiles					
D. High-Income Economies (continued)								
Australia	71.1	1985	4.4	11.1	17.5	24.8	42.2	25.8
United Kingdom	66.1	1979	5.8	11.5	18.2	25.0	39.5	23.3
Italy	65.6	1986	6.8	12.0	16.7	23.5	41.0	25.3
Belgium	64.7	1978–79	7.9	13.7	18.6	23.8	36.0	21.5
Netherlands	68.2	1983	6.9	13.2	17.9	23.7	38.3	23.0
France	69.3	1979	6.3	12.1	17.2	23.5	40.8	25.5
Canada	92.5	1987	5.7	11.8	17.7	24.6	40.2	24.1
Denmark	74.2	1981	5.4	12.0	18.4	25.6	38.6	22.3
Germany, Fed. Rep.	73.8	1984	6.8	12.7	17.8	24.1	38.7	23.4
Finland	69.5	1981	6.3	12.1	18.4	25.5	37.6	21.7
Sweden	76.9	1981	8.0	13.2	17.4	24.5	36.9	20.8
United States	100.0	1985	4.7	11.0	17.4	25.0	41.9	25.0
Norway	84.4	1979	6.2	12.8	18.9	25.3	36.7	21.2
Japan	71.5	1979	8.7	13.2	17.5	23.1	37.5	22.4
Switzerland	—	1982	5.2	11.7	16.4	22.1	44.6	29.8
Average	63.0		6.2	12.0	17.4	23.9	40.5	24.8

[a]Source: World Bank, *World Development Report 1990*, Oxford University Press, New York, 1990, Table 30.
[b]Conversion to U.S. dollars is based on the United Nations' International Comparison (ICP) purchasing power parity deflators. The data are preliminary Phase V results.
[c]These estimates should be treated with caution. See the technical notes for details of different distribution measures in the following footnotes.
[d]Per capita expenditure.
[e]Household expenditure.
[f]Per capita income.

income, in other cases to family income, and for some countries, to consumption expenditure rather than income.

Despite these drawbacks, the results are highly suggestive. The most equal countries in the world in terms of having the lowest concentration share of income among the top percentiles are the high-income ones, including the United States and other industrialized countries. The average share of the top quintile of this group was 41 percent and that of the top 10 percent was 25 percent. The low-income economies, including India, Pakistan, and Indonesia, are the second most equal group in this dimension. However, in terms of having the largest share of income going to the poorest groups, the low-income countries rank above the high-income ones (7.6

percent of total income earned by the bottom quintile versus 6.2 percent). Their average per capita income was only 6 percent of the U.S. level. The average share of the top quintile of these countries was 45 percent, and that of the top decile was 30 percent.

The most unequal countries are the lower-middle income group, which includes the Philippines, Colombia, Peru, Poland, and Brazil. Their average per capita income was about 15 percent of the U.S. level in 1985. The average share of income of the top quintile of countries in this group was 51 percent, compared to an average share of 41 percent for the advanced economies. Their average share of the top decile was 35 percent, compared to 25 percent for the high-income countries. For Brazil, which appears to be the most unequal country in the world, the share of the top quintile was 63 percent and that of the top decile was 46 percent.

The pattern of inequality shown in this table follows a well-known pattern referred to as the Kuznets curve. Simon Kuznets (1955) argued that inequality would tend to be low in a country at its early stages of development, rise as the country developed from a low-income to a middle-income status, and then decline as the country became a high-income, industrialized economy. He predicted an inverted "U-shaped" relation between income inequality and per capita income, a result which is consistent with the data in Table 3.9.

3.5 SUMMARY

Different inequality measures have their distinctive advantages and disadvantages. The concentration shares are indicative of the level of inequality at the top of the income distribution. The Kuznets coefficient is equally sensitive to changes across the entire income distribution but violates the principle of transfers. The coefficient of variation is more sensitive to changes at the top of the income distribution than at the middle or bottom. Both the Gini and Theil coefficients are more responsive to changes in the middle ranges of the distribution than at either tail. The log variance measure is more sensitive to movements in the lower portion of the distribution. The Atkinson index allows one to specify parametrically the portion of the distribution with which one is most concerned, but the measure is sensitive to the value of the parameter.

This chapter has presented data on time trends in income inequality in the United States. Inequality fell rather dramatically in the United States from the early part of this century through World War II. This was followed by a moderate decline from the late 1940s through the mid-1960s. However, this trend was reversed after this point. Inequality increased gradually from the mid-1960s through the mid-1970s and then rose sharply from the mid-1970s through the mid-1990s. The rise of income inequality in the United States since the 1970s is one of the most important social changes in its postwar development. This is particularly so in light of the major reduction in inequality that occurred during the first half of this century. This conclusion may seem surprising in light of the major efforts put forward by the federal government to redistribute income in favor of the lower income classes. This will be discussed more in Chapters 15 and 16.

This reversal in inequality trends has been coupled with a stagnation in real income growth since the mid-1970s, as we saw in Chapter 1. As a result, income stagnation and rising inequality have become a major concern of public policy today.

From an international perspective, the United States is today characterized by the highest level of income inequality among industrialized countries. This holds for both before-tax income and after-tax income as well. The fact that the United States still has the highest per capita income in the world (with the possible exception of Luxembourg) implies that the Kuznets curve is not always followed as countries develop. The only countries that appear to be distinctly more unequal than the United States are the lower-middle income group, including Colombia, Peru, and, particularly, Brazil.

REFERENCES AND BIBLIOGRAPHY

A. The Measurement of Inequality

Aitcheson, J. and J. A. C. Brown, *The Lognormal Distribution,* Cambridge University Press, Cambridge, 1957.

Arrow, K. J., *Social Choice and Individual Values,* Wiley, New York, 1963.

Atkinson, A. B., "On the Measurement of Inequality," *Journal of Economic Theory,* Vol. 2, 1970, pp. 244–263.

Atkinson, A. B. (ed.), *Wealth and Income Inequality,* Penguin Books, Harmondsworth, Middlesex, England, 1973.

———, *The Economics of Inequality,* Oxford University Press, Oxford, 1983.

———, and F. Bourguignon, "Income Distribution and Differences in Needs," in G. R. Feiwel (ed.), *Arrow and the Foundations of the Theory of Economic Policy,* Ch. 12., Macmillan, London, 1987.

———, and S. Jenkins, "The Steady-State Assumption and the Estimation of Distributional and Related Models," *Journal of Human Resources,* Vol. 19, No. 3, Summer 1984, pp. 358–376.

Berrebi, Z. M., and J. Silber, "Income Inequality Indices and Deprivation, a Generalization," *Quarterly Journal of Economics,* Vol. 100, 1985, pp. 807–810.

———, "Dispersion, Asymmetry and the Gini Index of Inequality," *International Economic Review,* Vol. 28, 1987, pp. 331–338.

Blackorby, C., and D. Donaldson, "Measures of Relative Equality and Their Meaning in Terms of Social Welfare," *Journal of Economic Theory,* Vol. 19, 1978, pp. 59–80.

Blinder, A. S., *Towards and Economic Theory of Income Distribution*, MIT Press, Cambridge, Mass., 1974.

Bourguignon, F., "Decomposable Inequality Measures," *Econometrica*, Vol. 47, 1979, pp. 901–920.

Chakravarty, S. R., "Extended Gini Indices of Inequality," *International Economic Review*, Vol. 29, 1988, pp. 147–156.

Champernowne, D. G., "A Model of Income Distribution," *Economic Journal*, Vol. 63, 1953, pp. 318–351. Reprinted in Champernowne, 1973, Appendix 6.

———, *The Distribution of Income Between Persons*, Cambridge University Press, Cambridge, 1973.

———, and F. A. Cowell, *Inequality and Income Distribution*, Cambridge University Press, Cambridge, 1990.

Cowell, F. A., *Measuring Inequality*, Phillip Allan, Oxford, 1977.

Creedy, J., *The Dynamics of Income Distribution*, Blackwell, Oxford, 1985.

Danziger, Sheldon, Robert Haveman, and Eugene Smolensky, "The Measurement and Trend of Inequality: Comment," *American Economic Review*, Vol. 67, June 1977, pp. 505–512.

Gini, Corrado, "On the Measure of Concentration with Special Reference to Income and Wealth," Abstracts of papers presented at the Cowles Commission Research Conference on Economics and Statistics, Colorado College Press, Colorado Springs, 1936.

Grubb, W. Norton, and Robert H. Wilson, "The Distribution of Wages and Salaries, 1960–80: The Contributions of Gender, Race, Sectoral Shifts and Regional Shifts," LBJ School of Public Affairs Working Paper No. 39, 1987.

Harrison, A. J., "Earnings by Size, a Tale of Two Distributions," *Review of Economic Studies*, Vol. 48, 1981, pp. 621–631.

Jenkins, Stephen, "The Measurement of Income Inequality," in Lars Osberg (ed.), *Readings on Economic Inequality*, M. E. Sharpe Inc., Armonk, N.Y., forthcoming.

Kakwani, N. C., *Income, Inequality and Poverty, Methods of Estimation and Policy Applications*, Oxford University Press, Oxford, 1980.

Lydall, H. F., *The Structure of Earnings*, Clarendon Press, Oxford, 1968.

———, "Theories of the Distribution of Earnings," in A. B. Atkinson (ed.), *The Personal Distribution of Incomes*, Ch. 1, Allen and Unwin for the Royal Economic Society, London, 1976.

Osberg, Lars, *Economic Inequality in the United States*, M. E. Sharpe Inc., Armonk, N.Y., 1984.

Paglin, Morton, "The Measurement and Trend of Inequality: A Basic Revision," *American Economic Review*, Vol. 65, September 1975, pp. 598–609.

Pareto, Vilfredo, *Cours d'Economie Politique*, Rouge, Lausanne, 1897.

Pen, Jan, *Income Distribution: Facts, Theories, Policies*, Praeger Publishers, New York, 1971.

Sahota, G. S., "Theories of Personal Income Distribution: A Survey," *Journal of Economic Literature*, Vol. 16, 1978, pp. 1–55.

Sen, Amartya, *On Economic Inequality,* Norton, New York, 1973.

Schultz, R. R., "On the Measurement of Income Inequality," *American Economic Review,* March 1951, pp. 107–122.

Shorrocks, A. F., "The Class of Additively Decomposable Inequality Measures," *Econometrica,* Vol. 48, 1980, pp. 613–625.

Taubman, P., *Income Distribution and Redistribution,* Addison-Wesley, Reading, Mass., 1978.

Yntema, D., "Measures of the Inequality in the Personal Distribution of Wealth or Income," *Journal of the American Statistical Association,* Vol. 28, 1933, pp. 423–433.

B. Income Distribution Statistics for the United States

Benus, J., and J. N. Morgan, "Time Period, Unit of Analysis and Income Concept in the Analysis of Income Distribution," in J. D. Smith (ed.), *The Personal Distribution of Income and Wealth,* NBER Studies in Income and Wealth, Vol. 39, Columbia University Press, New York, 1975, pp. 209–224.

Budd, Edward C., "Postwar Changes in the Size Distribution of Income in the U.S.," *American Economic Review,* Vol. 60, No. 2, May 1970, pp. 247–260.

Cowell, F. A., "The Structure of American Income Inequality," *Review of Income and Wealth,* Series 30, 1984, pp. 351–375.

Danziger, S. and M. K. Taussig, "The Income Unit and the Anatomy of Income Distribution," *Review of Income and Wealth,* Series 25, 1979, pp. 365–375.

Goldsmith, Selma, George Jaszi, Hyman Kurtz, and Maurice Liebenberg, "Size Distribution of Income Since the Mid-Thirties," *Review of Economics and Statistics,* Vol. 36, No. 1, February 1954.

Hayes, K. J., D. J. Slottje, Michael Nieswiadomy, and Edward N. Wolff, "The Relationship Between Productivity Changes and Economic Inequality in the U.S.," mimeo, 1990.

Internal Revenue Service, *Statistics of Income: Individual Income Tax Returns,* from 1948 to the present, U.S. Government Printing Office.

Kuznets, Simon, *Shares of Upper Income Groups in Income and Savings,* National Bureau of Economic Research, New York, 1953.

Menderhausen, H., "Changes in Income Distribution During the Great Depression," *Studies in Income and Wealth,* National Bureau of Economic Research, New York, 1946.

Miller, Herman P., *Income Distribution in the U.S., 1960,* U.S. Census Bureau Monograph, U.S. Government Printing Office, Washington, D.C., 1966.

———, *Rich Man, Poor Man,* Thomas V. Crowell, New York, 1971.

Radner, Daniel B. and John C. Hinrichs, "Size Distribution of Income in 1964, 1970, and 1971," *Survey of Current Business,* Vol. 50, 1974, pp. 19–31.

Schultz, T. Paul, "Secular Trends and Cyclical Behavior of Income Distribution in the U.S., 1944–1965," *Six Papers on the Size Distribution of Income and Wealth,* National Bureau of Economic Research, New York, 1969.

Soltow, Lee, "The Share of Lower Income Groups in Income," *Review of Economics and Statistics,* Vol. 47, November 1965, pp. 429–433.

Taussig, Michael K., "Trends in Inequality of Well-Offness in the United States Since World War II," *Conference on the Trend in Income Inequality in the U.S.,* Institute for Research on Poverty, Madison, Wisconsin, 1977.

U.S. Bureau of the Census, *Current Population Reports,* Series P-60 (Consumer Income), U.S. Government Printing Office, Washington, D.C., various issues and dates.

U.S. Bureau of the Census, *Trends in the Income of Families and Persons in the U.S., 1947–1964,* Technical Paper No. 17, U.S. Government Printing Office, Washington, D.C., 1967.

U.S. Bureau of the Census, *Money Income of Households, Families, and Persons in the U.S., 1992,* Series P60–184, U.S. Government Printing Office, Washington, D.C., September 1993.

U.S. Bureau of the Census, *Income, Poverty, and Valuation of Noncash Benefits, 1993,* Series P60–188, U.S. Government Printing Office, Washington, D.C., February 1995.

C. International Comparisons of Income Inequality

Atkinson, Anthony B., Lee Rainwater, and Timothy M. Smeeding, "Income Distribution in Advanced Economices: The Evidence from the Luxembourg Income Study (LIS)," *Review of Income and Wealth,* forthcoming.

Bergson, Abram, "Income Inequality under Soviet Socialism," *Journal of Economic Literature,* Vol. 22, September 1984, pp. 1052–1099.

Berry, Albert, "On Trends in the Gap Between Rich and Poor in Less Developed Countries: Why We Know so Little," *Review of Income and Wealth,* Series 31, No. 4, December 1985, pp. 337–354.

———, "Evidence on Relationships Among Alternative Measures of Concentration: A Tool for Analysis of LDC Inequality," *Review of Income and Wealth,* Series 33, No. 4, December 1987, pp. 417–429.

Buhmann, Brigitte, Lee Rainwater, Guenther Schmaus, and Timothy M. Smeeding, "Equivalence Scales, Well-Being, Inequality, and Poverty: Sensitivity Estimates Across Ten Countries Using the Luxembourg Income Study (LIS) Database," *Review of Income and Wealth,* Series 34, Number 2, June 1988.

Kuznets, Simon, "Economic Growth and Income Inequality," *American Economic Review,* Vol. 45, No. 1, March 1955, pp. 1–28.

Lecaillon, J., F. Paukert, C. Morrison, and D. Germidis, *Income Distribution and Economic Development, an Analytical Survey,* International Labor Organization, Geneva, 1984.

Luxembourg Income Study (LIS): datasets from various countries.

O'Higgins, Michael, Guenther Schmaus, and Geoffrey Stephenson, "Income Distribution and Redistribution: A Microdata Analysis for Seven Countries," *Review of Income and Wealth,* Series 35, Number 2, June 1989.

Radner, Daniel B., "Family, Income, Age, and Size of Unit: Selected International Comparisons," *Review of Income and Wealth,* Series 31, No. 2, June 1985, pp. 103–126.

Sawyer, Malcolm, "Income Distribution in OECD Countries," *OECD Economic Outlook: Occasional Studies,* July 1976.

Weisskoff, Richard, "Income Distribution and Economic Growth in Puerto Rico, Argentina, and Mexico," *Review of Income and Wealth,* Series 16, No. 4, December 1970, pp. 303–332.

World Bank, *World Development Report 1990,* Oxford University Press, New York, 1990.

Yotopoulos, Pan A., "Distributions of Real Income Within Countries and by World Income Classes," *Review of Income and Wealth,* Series 35, No. 4, December 1989, pp. 357–376.

DISCUSSION QUESTIONS

1. Some economists use the ratio of mean to median income as an index of inequality. Explain why this would be an appropriate measure.

2. Explain why the concentration ratio is not a comprehensive measure of income inequality.

3. If the Lorenz curves for country A and country B cross, how do you interpret their relative inequality levels?

4. Suppose a country has the following income distribution:

Income Class	Number of Families	Average Income
1.	50,000	$5,000
2.	100,000	10,000
3.	50,000	15,000

   a. Define and compute the coefficient of variation.
   b. Draw the Lorenz curve.
   c. Define and calculate the Gini coefficient.

5. Suppose country A and country B have the following income distribution:

| | Country A | | Country B | |
Income Class	Percent of Families	Percent of Total Income	Percent of Families	Percent of Total Income
1.	15	5	15	3
2.	20	10	20	8
3.	20	15	20	12
4.	20	20	20	20
5.	15	25	15	25
6.	10	25	10	32

    a. Draw the Lorenz curve for each country.

    b. Which country is more unequal and why?

6. Suppose country A has the following cumulative distribution of income:

Cumulative Percent of Families	Cumulative Percent of Total Income
20	5
40	15
50	27
60	30
80	50
90	70
95	90

Compute the quintile shares. What is the share of total income of the top 10 percent of families and of the top 5 percent of families?

7. Suppose that there are 50 people in a village and one person receives all the income and the other 49 have nothing. Show that the CV ≈ $7^1/_7$. Then, show that CV can be made even greater by increasing the sample size while maintaining the assumption that one person continues to receive all the income.

Chapter

4

POVERTY

Chapter 3 developed indices of overall income inequality, which measure disparities of income among all segments of society. However, there is particular concern among policy makers and the public at large about the status of the low-income population. Have the number of poor increased or declined over time? Are the poor materially better off today than they were 20 or 50 years ago? These questions have led to the development of metrics that attempt to capture both the extent and intensity of poverty in a country. Ever since the New Deal was launched in the 1930s, much of public policy in the United States has been directed at alleviating poverty. The success or failure of these programs, particularly the welfare system, has been a primary focus of recent intense political debate.

Chapter 4 discusses the measurement of poverty, presents statistics on trends in poverty and the make-up of the poverty population, and analyzes some of the causes of poverty. Section 4.1 treats the definition of poverty, the poverty line, and the overall poverty rate. Poverty trends for the United States are presented in Section 4.2. Section 4.3 presents empirical findings on the composition of the poor, the permanence of poverty, the extent of the underclass, and international differences in poverty incidence. In Section 4.4, other issues in measuring poverty are considered, such as the treatment of taxes and noncash government benefits. A summary is presented in Section 4.5. In Chapter 15, we shall consider in some detail the public policy measures that have been developed in the United States to alleviate poverty and evaluate their successes and failures.

4.1 THE MEASUREMENT OF POVERTY

The problem of defining and measuring poverty has been a subject of considerable research and debate over the last two decades. Two issues must be decided. The first is the identification of the poor, and the second is the aggregation of the individuals who fall into the poverty population into an overall index of poverty.

The Official U.S. Poverty Standard

It is helpful to discuss first how the poverty line is defined in the official U.S. government statistics. The official measure of the poverty line was developed by Mollie Orshansky in 1965 for the Social Security Administration. The index provided a range of income cutoffs adjusted for such factors as family size, farm versus nonfarm residence, age of the family head, and the number of children under 18. The threshold levels were designed to specify in dollar terms what a minimally "decent" level of consumption or "needs" would be for families of different types. The estimates were based primarily on food requirements. The Department of Agriculture estimated what constituted a minimally nutritionally sound diet (what it called the "economy food plan"). In 1955 the Department of Agriculture conducted a Survey of Food Consumption and determined that poor families of three or more individuals spent approximately one-third of their income on food. The poverty level of these families was then set at three times the cost of the minimally decent diet. For families of two individuals and persons living alone, the cost of this diet was multiplied by a slightly higher factor than three in order to adjust for the relatively larger fixed expenses (particularly housing) of these smaller households.

Until 1969, annual revisions of these poverty thresholds were based on price changes of the items included in the economy food plan. After 1969, the poverty lines were adjusted each year according to changes in the overall Consumer Price Index (CPI), instead of the cost of food alone. The poverty line of farm households was originally set at 70 percent of the corresponding nonfarm level because of the cheaper cost of food for farm families. In 1969 farm thresholds were raised to 85 percent of the corresponding nonfarm levels, and in 1981 a separate farm threshold was eliminated altogether.[1]

Table 4.1 shows the official **poverty lines** in current dollars for selected years and for selected family types. In 1993, a family of four was classified as poor if its income fell below $14,763, while a two-person family was considered poor if its income did not exceed $9,414. It is interesting to note that the poverty line does not rise proportionally with family size but less than

---

[1] Another distinction contained in the original poverty lines was for male-headed versus female-headed families. The thresholds for the former were set at a slightly higher level than that for the latter, because men were assumed to have higher dietary requirements. These two categories were eliminated in the official 1981 poverty lines.

Table 4.1 Official Poverty Thresholds for Nonfarm Families by Family Characteristic, in Current Dollars, 1959–1993[a]

Family Type	Year								
	1959	1963	1967	1972	1977	1982	1985	1989	1993
Singles	1,467	1,539	1,675	2,109	3,075	4,901	5,469	6,314	7,363
2 persons	1,894	1,988	2,168	2,724	3,951	6,281	6,998	8,075	9,414
3 persons	2,324	2,442	2,661	3,339	4,833	7,693	8,573	9,890	11,522
4 persons	2,973	3,128	3,410	4,275	6,191	9,862	10,989	12,675	14,763
5 persons	3,506	3,685	4,019	5,044	7,320	11,684	13,007	14,994	17,449
6 persons	3,944	4,135	4,516	5,673	8,261	13,207	14,696	16,927	19,718
7+ persons	4,849	5,092	5,092	6,983	10,216	15,036	16,656	—	
7 persons						15,036	16,656	19,127	22,383
8 persons						16,719	18,512	21,256	24,836
9 or more persons						19,698	22,083	25,296	29,529
Singles									
Under 65	1,505	1,581	1,722	2,168	3,152	5,019	5,593	6,452	7,518
65 and over	1,397	1,470	1,600	2,005	2,906	4,626	5,156	5,947	6,930

[a]Sources: *Social Security Bulletin,* Annual Statistical Supplement, various years.

proportionally. The reason is that many consumption items, such as housing and furniture, can be shared among family members. Thus, a house or an apartment required for a family of four does not have to be twice as large as one for a couple (there is no reason to have two kitchens, for example). As a result, there are **economies of consumption** built into the poverty thresholds. On the other hand, food and clothing needs tend to rise proportionally to family size, so that the poverty threshold does increase with the size of family. Moreover, the poverty line is lower for individuals aged 65 and over than for those under 65. This is based on the judgment that the dietary needs of older people are less than those of younger people.

There are several points of interest to note about the official poverty definition. First, the definition of the poverty line is based on the *family* as the basic consumer unit. Second, the underlying assumption is that the well-being of families (and also single individuals living alone) is related to their ability to purchase consumption goods and services. A family is considered poor if its consumption level falls below some pre-established minimal standard. This is referred to as a **needs-based** definition of poverty.

Third, the income a family receives is used to measure their ability to consume. As a result, family income levels are used to define the poverty standard. Fourth, the poverty thresholds for different family sizes ($9,414 for a two-person family and $14,763 for a family of four) are referred to as

equivalence classes or **equivalent income.** The assumption is that $9,414 is required to satisfy the same level of needs for a two-person family as $14,763 for a family of four. In this sense, the two incomes are equivalent in terms of the standard of living that can be attained.

Absolute versus Relative Poverty Thresholds

The official U.S. poverty lines are adjusted each year to reflect the change in the cost of living. Since they are fixed in real terms, the official thresholds are said to be *absolute* poverty thresholds. There are two major criticisms of the absolute poverty line. First, in so far as it is an absolute poverty standard, the determination of what the necessities of life are and what a minimum family diet should be is itself *relative*. Indeed, it is relative to a particular society at a particular time. As far as food requirements are concerned, nutritional needs depend in great measure on how active a person is, what kind of climate he or she lives in, the type of housing, and whether the standard is defined to simply ensure prolongation of life or to maintain a given standard of health. The estimated caloric intake for an adult man or woman can vary considerably depending on these factors.

Moreover, even given a minimal level of calories, it is possible to fulfill this requirement very cheaply if one could live on potatoes and raw vegetables alone. However, given the general dietary practices of the U.S. population, most of us would judge such a standard unreasonably low and would include poultry, some kinds of meat, and even some forms of dessert in a minimal diet. When it comes to other consumption items, the determination of what is a necessity is very much conditioned by the standards of a particular society. Today, indoor plumbing, a telephone, and electricity are considered basic necessities of life, while at the turn of the century this was certainly not the case. Even an absolute poverty standard depends on what is considered socially acceptable at a given point in time.

Second, such absolute poverty standards would, as a result, provide some very misleading statistics on poverty over a long stretch over time. For example, according to our current poverty standards, almost the entire U.S. population in 1880 would have been recorded as living below the poverty line. On the other hand, by current standards almost no one living in the year 2090 will show up below the poverty line.

As a result of these criticisms, many economists have recommended that the official poverty line be set equal to a certain percentage of median family income—say, 45 percent or 50 percent, as Victor Fuchs (1967) proposed. Any family falling below this income level would be classified as poor. The poverty line would be adjusted each year to reflect increases in the cost of living and changes in the **real** standard of living. Such a poverty line is referred to as a **relative** poverty standard, since it is tied to and changes with the average real standard of living. A relative poverty measure has the advantage that it adjusts for changes in what people perceive to be necessities and the requirements of a decent living standard.

According to Sheldon Danziger, Robert Haveman, and Robert Plotnick (1986), the official poverty threshold for a family of four stood at 46 percent of the median income in 1965, compared to 37 percent in 1983. If a relative poverty line was adopted at 46 percent of median income, they calculated that the poverty rate would have risen by 1.3 percentage points between 1965 and 1983. In comparison, the official poverty rate declined by 2.1 percentage points. In 1993, the poverty line for a four-person family was 40 percent of median family income, so that the discrepancy in poverty rates calculated from the official and relative measures would be somewhat less pronounced.

Calculations by Patricia Ruggles (1990, Table 4.3) show that between 1967 and 1972 the relative poverty threshold would have increased 12 percent faster than the official (absolute) poverty threshold, when real median family income was growing rapidly (see Table 1.2 above). However, between 1972 and 1987, the relative poverty line increased by only 2 percent relative to the official one, because real income growth was stagnant over these years. In periods when real incomes are growing very slowly, the difference between a relative poverty line and an absolute poverty standard is very small.

The relative poverty line, too, is subject to criticism—in particular, that by a relative poverty standard, the percentage of poor in the population would most likely remain fairly constant over time. As long as the overall income distribution retains the same basic shape over time (for example, the decile shares remain unchanged), then the percentage of families below 45 or 50 percent of the median would also remain constant. Such a result would mean that as the bottom of the income distribution became better off in real terms from economic growth, their poverty categorization would remain unchanged.[2]

Subjective Poverty Lines

Public opinion surveys have been conducted annually in the United States asking individuals what they consider to be an adequate amount of income to meet their needs. The income levels given in response have increased over time but not as fast as median income. This suggests that the average person thinks of poverty in terms of a mixture of an absolute and a relative poverty line.

This type of approach, based on individuals' own evaluation of income adequacy, has been formalized in what are referred to as subjective poverty lines. This technique was originally developed by Dutch economists in Leyden and is also referred to as the Leyden Poverty Line (see Aldi Hagenaars

---

[2]From another point of view, however, this may not necessarily be a criticism. If indeed poverty is a relative phenomenon and a family *perceives* itself as poor in relation to the average standard of living (see the next section), then it may make sense to say that the percentage of poor remains constant over time as long as the relative income distribution remains unchanged. From this point of view, reducing poverty becomes tantamount to reducing overall income inequality!

and Bernard van Praag, 1985, or Aldi Hagenaars, 1986, for a summary). The underlying idea is that to discover the minimum amount of income or consumption that individuals require to maintain what they consider to be an adequate standard of living, one should ask them directly. For the Leyden Poverty Line, the poverty line measure is based on survey responses to the following type of question (the so-called "Income Evaluation Question"):

"Please try to indicate what you consider to be an appropriate amount of money for each of the following cases. Under my (our) conditions, I would call an after-tax income of

$_____ very bad
$_____ bad
$_____ insufficient
$_____ sufficient
$_____ good
$_____ very good."

As might be anticipated, the response to such a question tends to vary with the level of an individual's income. The higher the person's income, the greater is the amount of income considered necessary for a minimal standard of living. The Dutch group found that the elasticity of the poverty line estimate with respect to income is about 0.6 (that is, individuals raise their estimate of a "just sufficient" amount of income by 60 cents for each additional dollar of income that they have). This variation appears due to the fact that estimates of needs depend directly on the usual consumption habits of families with a given level of income. Moreover, as with the standard poverty line, the estimate of needs varies directly with the size of the family unit (larger families require greater income to meet a "just-sufficient" level of consumption).

This approach has a certain amount of intuitive appeal, since poverty is in actuality a socially determined state and poverty thresholds represent the opinion of some group of policy makers of what constitutes a minimally decent standard of living. Since the responses to the question of what is a sufficient income increases with income, but not to the same degree, subjective measures may constitute an adequate compromise between absolute and relative poverty lines.

Formal Derivation of the Leyden Poverty Line* In this procedure, it is assumed that the six responses indicated above (very bad, bad, insufficient, sufficient, good, and very good) each represent equal divisions (quantiles) of individual welfare or utility. Since the interval is divided into six categories, the "just-sufficient" income level corresponds to the 50th percentile of the distribution. On the basis of the individual's response to this question, an individual welfare function can be derived, relating actual income levels to utility or welfare levels (this is also referred to as a "cardinal utility" function).

Formally, it is assumed that individuals evaluate income levels y according to a (cardinal) utility function $U(y)$. If a certain welfare level δ is chosen, then the income level $y_{\delta, i}$ can be determined for each individual i which satisfies:

$$U(y_{\delta, i}) = \delta.$$

The function U will be monotonically increasing in y (the higher the individual's income level, the greater the amount of income the individual will deem necessary to reach a certain utility level δ). In other words,

$$y_{\delta, i} = f(y_i, fs_i, \delta)$$

where the function f is increasing in y_i. The income level $y_{\delta, i}$ is also an increasing function of family size fs_i.

The welfare level δ^* is then chosen which corresponds to the "just-sufficient" income level (midway between the answers "insufficient" and "sufficient" of the Income Evaluation Question). The "national poverty line" y^* is then defined as the solution to the following equation

$$y^* = f(y^*, fs, \delta^*)$$

The basic idea is that for low-income individuals, the just-sufficient income level will be above their actual income level. Conversely, for middle- and high-income individuals, their just-sufficient income will be below their actual income level. At some income level, y^*, between the low- and middle-income levels, the just-sufficient income level recorded by the respondent will be exactly equal to y^*. The poverty level is then defined as that level of income which someone with *that level of income* will deem just sufficient for an adequate living standard. The poverty threshold will also vary according to family size.

One more technical assumption is needed to solve for the national poverty level—namely, that the individual welfare function is lognormal. It can then be shown that:

$$\ln y_{\delta, i} = \mu_i + \mu_\delta \sigma_i \tag{4.1}$$

where μ_i is the mean of the lognormal welfare distribution for individual i, σ_i is the standard deviation of the distribution, and μ_δ is the percentile of the standard normal distribution corresponding to welfare level δ. Moreover, empirically it has been found that

$$\mu_i = \beta_0 + \beta_1 \ln fs_i + \beta_2 \ln y_i \tag{4.2}$$

Figure 4.1   Solution for the National Poverty Line Using the Subjective Poverty Line Approach

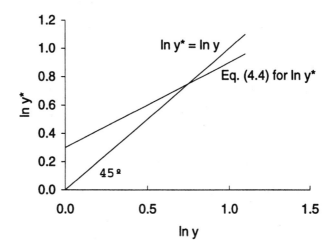

This equation can be estimated econometrically with the addition of a stochastic error term. As indicated above, the coefficient of ln y, the income elasticity of the poverty threshold, is normally found to be less than unity.

Substituting (4.1) into (4.2), one obtains:

$$\ln y_{\delta, i} = \beta_0 + \beta_1 \ln fs_i + \beta_2 \ln y_i + u_\delta \sigma_i \tag{4.3}$$

The parameter σ_i is then fixed at the national average, $\bar{\sigma}$. The national poverty line y* is then found by setting the welfare level equal to δ* and solving

$$\ln y^* = \beta_0 + \beta_1 \ln fs + \beta_2 \ln y^* + \mu_{\delta} \cdot \bar{\sigma} \tag{4.4}$$

The solution, y*, is illustrated in Figure 4.1 for a given family size fs. People whose income is less than y* are counted as poor, while people whose income is greater than or equal to y* are considered not poor.

Measurement of the Aggregate Poverty Rate

Once the actual poverty thresholds are decided upon, there still remains the question of how the overall poverty rate is to be defined. The most common measure is called the **head count.** On the basis of the poverty lines, we first classify family units as poor or not poor. We then count the number of *individuals* in families below the poverty line. The ratio of this count to the total population is defined as the **poverty rate.**

The head count measure of poverty has been criticized because it does not adjust for the relative severity of poverty among the poor—that is, for how much the income of the poor falls short of the poverty line. As a result, another index is the **poverty gap ratio,** defined as the ratio between the total amount of income by which the poor fall short of the poverty line and their total income if all the poor had incomes equal to the poverty line. For families of the same family size, this index would equal the ratio of the average shortfall of income below the poverty line to the poverty line itself. This measure thus reflects the *degree* of privation of the poor. If all or most poor families had incomes close to the poverty threshold, the poverty gap ratio would be low; if all or most had incomes considerably below the poverty line, this index would be high. The poverty gap ratio thus indicates the average amount of income that would be required to bring all poor families up to the poverty threshold.

Other indices have been devised which reflect both the number of poor and the poverty gap. Each by itself is somewhat inadequate. The head count measure does not indicate the severity of poverty. The poverty gap ratio does not indicate the number of individuals who are poor. One such alternative measure was proposed by Amartya Sen (1976), which combines these two dimensions of poverty as well as the degree of income inequality *among the poor.* The Sen index S of poverty incidence is given by:

$$S = H[R + (1 - R)G] \tag{4.5}$$

where H is the head count measure of the poverty rate, R is the poverty gap ratio, and G is the Gini coefficient of inequality among poor people only. The poverty gap measure captures the absolute deprivation of the poor population, while the Gini index captures their relative deprivation. According to this measure, the poverty incidence is greater the greater the proportion of individuals in poverty, the greater the shortfall in income below the poverty line,[3] and the greater the degree of inequality among the poor.

4.2 POVERTY TRENDS IN THE UNITED STATES

Table 4.2 and Figure 4.2 show poverty rate statistics from 1959 to 1993 for the whole population and by race and Hispanic origin. These are head count rates based on the official U.S. poverty lines for those years. For the full population, the reduction in the poverty rate has been quite dramatic. In 1959, 22 percent of individuals in the population were recorded as living below the poverty line. In 1973, the poverty rate had fallen to 11 percent, its lowest point since these statistics were first recorded. The major reduction in the poverty rate occurred between 1964 and 1969. This dramatic change

---

[3]Note that $\delta S/\delta R = H(1 - G)$, and G is always less than unity.

Table 4.2 Percentage of Persons in Poverty (Head Count Measure) by Race and Hispanic Origin, Selected Years, 1959–1993[a]

Year	All Races	Whites	Blacks	Hispanics[b]
1959	22.4	18.1	55.1	
1960	22.2	17.8		
1963	19.5	15.3		
1965	17.3	13.3		
1967	14.2	11.0	39.3	
1970	12.6	9.9	33.5	
1973	11.1	8.4	31.4	21.9
1975	12.3	9.7	31.3	26.9
1977	11.6	8.9	31.3	22.4
1980	13.0	10.2	32.5	25.7
1981	14.0	11.1	34.2	26.5
1982	15.0	12.0	35.6	29.9
1983	15.2	12.1	35.7	28.0
1984	14.4	11.5	33.8	28.4
1985	14.0	11.4	31.3	29.0
1986	13.6	11.0	31.1	27.3
1987	13.4	10.4	32.4	28.0
1988	13.0	10.1	31.3	26.7
1989	12.8	10.0	30.7	26.2
1990	13.5	10.7	31.9	28.1
1991	14.2	11.3	32.7	28.7
1992	14.8	11.9	33.4	29.6
1993	15.1	12.2	33.1	30.6

[a]Source: U.S. Bureau of the Census, Current Population Reports, Series P-60–188, *Income, Poverty, and Valuation of Noncash Benefits: 1993*, February 1995.
[b]Persons with Spanish surname may be of any race.

occurred during the same period that President Lyndon Johnson waged his "War on Poverty," but more on this in Chapter 15. After 1969, the overall poverty rate changed very little in the United States, until 1980, when it rose to 13 percent. The rate climbed during the early 1980s, peaking at 15 percent in 1983. After 1983, the poverty rate fell again, reaching 13 percent in 1989. However, since 1989, the poverty rate has again risen, and in 1993 stood at 15.1 percent, almost the same level as in 1966.

The poverty rate for white individuals was somewhat lower than for the full population. In 1959, 18.1 percent of white persons were classified as poor, compared to 22.4 percent for the full population; in 1973 the poverty rate for whites was 8.4 percent, compared to 11.1 percent overall; and in 1993, it was 12.2 percent, compared to 15.1 percent for the full population.

Figure 4.2   Percentage of Persons in Poverty by Race and Hispanic Origin, 1959–1993

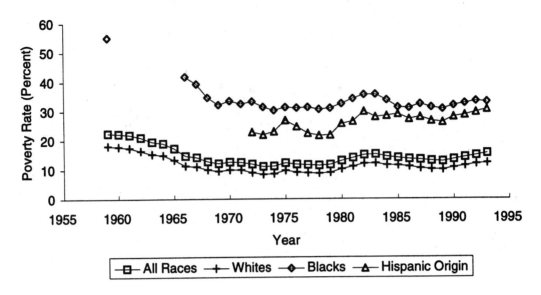

The poverty trends for whites mirrored the overall rate, with a gradual reduction between 1959 and 1964, a sharp drop between 1964 and 1968, almost no change until 1979, a steep rise between 1979 and 1983 followed by a moderate decline until 1989, and then a gradual increase during the early 1990s.

The poverty rate among the black population was about *three* times that of whites, and this ratio was maintained fairly consistently over the last three decades. In 1959, *over half* the black persons in the United States fell into the poverty category. By 1966, the poverty rate had fallen to 42 percent, by 1969 to 32 percent, and by 1978 to 31 percent, its low point. The rate increased during the early 1980s, declined again to 31 percent in 1989, but in 1993 was back to 33 percent.

In 1973, a new category was added to the official poverty statistics, which was for Hispanic families—that is, families with Spanish surnames. Their poverty rate has tended to be about twice the overall rate. It increased from 22 percent in 1973 to 27 percent in 1975, declined to 22 percent in 1979, increased to 29 percent in 1985, then fell to 26 percent in 1989, but by 1993 was close to 31 percent—almost the same level as in the black population.

However, it should be noted that even though the *incidence* of poverty is much greater among black persons than white persons, about *two-thirds* of the poor people in America since the early 1960s have been white. The reason, as might be evident, is that whites constitute the vast majority (close to 90 percent) of the U.S. population.

4.3 OTHER DIMENSIONS OF POVERTY

Composition of the Poor

Besides race, poverty incidence also differs substantially by age class and family type, as shown in Figure 4.3. The poverty rate among adults in age group 18 to 64 has been consistently lower than that for the general population. In 1959, their poverty rate was 17.0 percent, compared to 22.4 percent overall. In 1993, it was 12.4 percent, compared to 15.1 percent for the whole population. On the other hand, the poverty rate among children (under age 18) has been consistently higher than the poverty rate for adults. Moreover, the incidence of poverty has been increasing much more rapidly among children than among adults over the last two decades or so. Between 1973 and 1993, the poverty rate for children increased from 14.4 to 22.7 percent, whereas the overall poverty rate increased from 11.1 to only 15.1 percent. Indeed, since 1981, one-fifth or more of children in the United States have been found to be poor.

The poverty rate among elderly persons (ages 65 and over) has declined dramatically, from 35.2 percent in 1959 to 12.2 percent in 1993. In 1959, the

Figure 4.3 Poverty Rates of Persons by Family Type and Age Group, 1959–1993

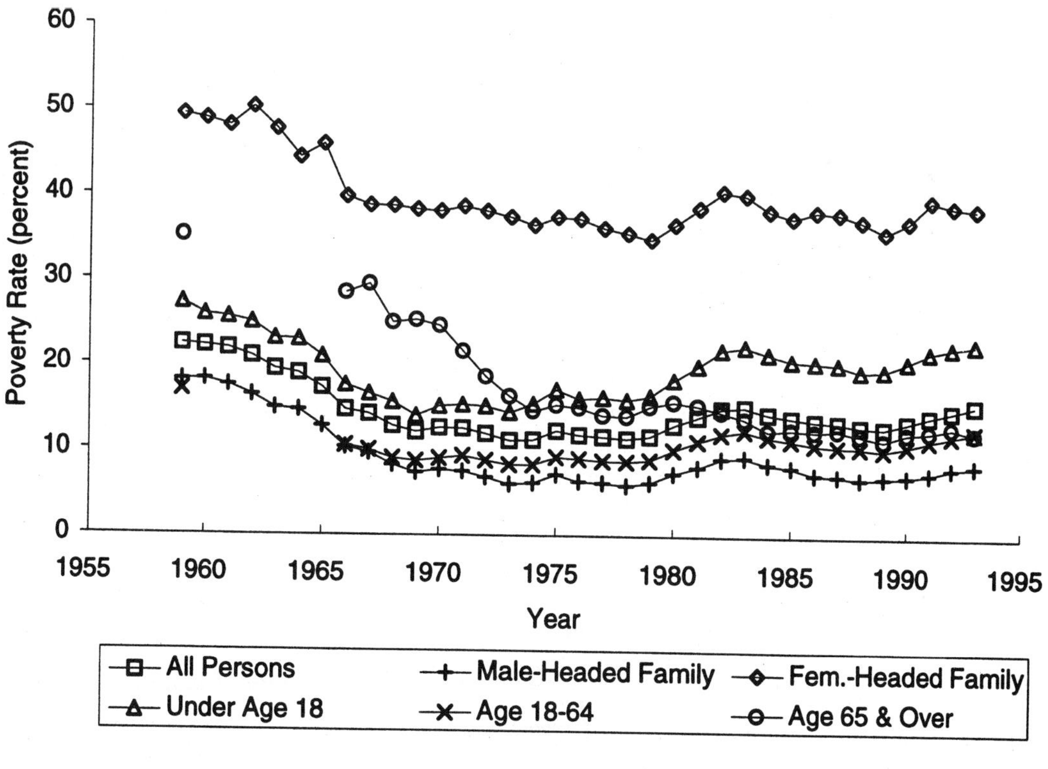

incidence of poverty among the elderly was greater than that among children and more than twice that among adults under age 65. By 1993, poverty incidence among the aged was about half the poverty rate of children and slightly lower than among persons ages 18 to 64.

Families are divided into two types, "male-headed families," consisting of married couples and single men, and female-headed households, comprised of unmarried women with children and single women.[4] Poverty incidence has been considerably higher among female-headed families than male-headed ones. In 1973, their poverty rate was over *six* times greater than for male-headed families, and in 1993, about *five* times as great. However, the poverty rate among female-headed families has not changed very much since 1973 (37.5 percent then compared to 38.7 percent in 1993).

Table 4.3 shows both the poverty incidence and the composition of the poverty population by demographic and labor force characteristics. This table includes data for families only (two or more related individuals living together).[5] There have been some notable changes since 1959. Between 1959 and 1989, the poverty rate increased among young families (under 25 years of age), while it declined for every other age group. However, despite this, the majority of poor families in 1989 were in the 25–44 age bracket, compared to 40 percent in 1959—a reflection of the large number of baby-boom families in this age group.

As was noted above, the poverty *rate* for female-headed families has not changed much since the late 1960s. However, by 1989, female-headed families constituted over *half* of all poor families, compared to less than a fourth in 1959. The reason for this is the rapid growth in the number of female-headed households in the population since the late 1950s.[6] This phenomenon has been called the **feminization of poverty,** which refers to the growth in the proportion of poor people who are found in female-headed families (as opposed to the increase in the incidence of poverty within this group).

Poverty rates also vary with the size of the family, even though the poverty line is adjusted for family size. In 1989, in particular, poverty incidence increased almost directly with family size. Very large families (seven or more persons) have had particularly high poverty rates (32.3 percent in 1989), because there are "many more mouths to feed." The major change since 1959 is that the poverty rate for two-person families has declined dramatically. This is mainly a reflection of declining poverty among elderly couples, who make up a large proportion of two-person families.

As we might expect, poverty incidence varies with employment status and work experience. The incidence of poverty is much higher among fami-

---

[4]The Census Bureau defines the head of a household to be the husband in the case of a married couple. Thus, by definition, female-headed families are those consisting of a mother with children.

[5]Note that Table 4.2 shows poverty rates for *persons,* so that the overall rates differ between the two tables.

[6]See Chapters 11 and 12 for more discussion of this trend.

Table 4.3 Poverty Rates for Families and the Composition of Poverty Among Families by Selected Household Characteristic and Year, 1959–1989[a]

Family Characteristics	Poverty Rate for Group (in percent)				The Number of Poor as a Percent of Total Poor[b]			
	1959	1969	1978	1989	1959	1969	1978	1989
1. All Families	18.5	9.7	9.1	10.3	100.0	100.0	100.0	100.0
2. Age of Household Head								
a. 14–24	26.9	14.8	18.5	30.4	7.5	10.6	13.4	12.8
b. 25–44	16.5	8.4	10.2	12.0	39.8	36.5	48.6	55.8
25–34				14.9				32.7
35–44				9.4				23.1
c. 45–54	15.0	6.5	6.7	6.3	17.3	14.0	13.8	10.9
d. 55–64	15.9	8.0	6.0	7.4	13.1	13.3	10.7	10.2
e. 65 & Over	30.0	17.7	8.4	6.6	22.4	25.5	13.5	10.4
3. Sex of Household Head								
a. Male	15.8	6.9	5.3	5.9	77.0	63.5	49.7	48.3
b. Female	42.6	32.6	31.4	32.2	23.0	36.5	50.3	51.7
4. Size of Family								
a. 2 persons	19.6	10.9	8.0	8.2	34.3	38.7	34.2	33.4
b. 3 persons	12.8	7.5	8.6	9.8	15.1	16.1	21.1	22.2
c. 4 persons	12.7	6.8	8.1	10.1	14.0	13.5	18.4	20.9
d. 5 persons	18.3	8.0	10.7	13.5	13.1	10.3	12.3	11.8
e. 6 persons	24.2	11.3	13.9	12.1	8.5	7.9	6.7	6.2
f. 7 or more persons	45.6	21.6	22.8	32.3	15.1	13.5	7.3	5.6
5. Employment Status of Household Head								
a. Not in labor force	40.8	26.7	20.9	21.1	38.8	52.7	52.4	51.5
b. Unemployed	33.7	18.0	24.9	31.7	6.7	4.2	8.0	9.7
c. Employed	12.8	5.3	4.9	5.6	54.5	43.1	39.7	38.5
6. Work Experience of Household Head								
a. Did not work	45.2	31.0	24.0	23.4	30.5	44.7	50.3	50.8
b. Part of the year	26.9	16.5	16.4	19.0	31.0	28.3	30.2	28.0
c. Whole year (not necessarily full-time)	10.6	3.7	2.7	3.5	36.6	25.9	18.8	20.9
d. Full-time, whole year	9.4	3.2	2.4	2.9	31.5	21.3	16.1	16.2

(continued)

Table 4.3 *(concluded)*

Family Characteristics	Poverty Rate for Group (in percent)				The Number of Poor as a Percent of Total Poor[b]			
	1959	1969	1978	1989	1959	1969	1978	1989
7. Educational Attainment of Head[c]								
a. No years of Schooling			33.4	45.6			2.3	1.8
b. Elementary: less than 8			20.3	25.5			18.2	14.1
c. Elementary: 8 years			12.2	15.9			10.8	7.0
d. High School: 1–3 years			14.4	19.2			20.7	20.2
e. High School: 4 years			6.6	8.9			23.0	30.5
f. College: 1 or more years			3.4	3.6			11.6	13.6
8. Residence								
a. Farm	42.8	17.5	10.9	9.6	17.8	8.5	4.2	2.0
b. Nonfarm	15.7	9.3	9.1	10.3	82.2	91.5	95.8	98.0
a. Central cities	13.7	9.8	12.7	14.9	25.2	32.1	37.6	41.8
b. Suburbs	9.6	5.3	5.3	6.4	16.7	20.0	23.1	29.7
c. Rural	28.2	14.8	10.8	12.5	58.1	47.9	39.3	28.5
Addendum								
Mean income deficit for all families (1978 $)	2,637	2,274	2,370	2,613				
Average poverty gap ratio for all families	0.431	0.375	0.415	0.462				

[a]Sources. 1959–78: U.S. Bureau of the Census, Current Population Reports, Series P-60, No. 124, *Characteristics of the Population Below the Poverty Level: 1978,* July 1980; Source: U.S. Bureau of the Census, Current Population Reports, Series P-60, No. 166, *Money Income and Poverty Status in the United States: 1989,* September 1990. Please note that this series was discontinued by the U.S. Bureau of the Census in 1989.
[b]Note that the distribution shares do not sum to unity for some groupings, because of the exclusion of certain subgroups.
[c]Includes only families with household heads 25 and over.

lies whose prime earner is unemployed or not in the labor force than among those in which he or she is employed. Interestingly, while the poverty rate has fallen since 1969 for families whose prime earner is not in the labor force, poverty incidence has increased among those whose prime earner is unemployed. Part of the reason, as we shall discuss in Chapter 15, is that government benefits for unemployed workers have deteriorated over the last twenty years or so. Despite this increase, families with an unemployed household head constituted only a very small proportion of poor families in 1989. About half the poor were families whose household head was not in the labor force, and about 40 percent those whose household head was employed.

The poverty rate for families in which the household head worked the whole year, and particularly full-time (35 hours per week or more) over the whole year, has been very low since 1969 (3.5 percent in 1989). The poverty rate for families whose prime earner worked only part of the year has been much higher (19 percent in 1989). In 1989, while half the poor families consisted of those whose prime earner did not work, 28 percent were composed of those in which the household head worked only part of the year, and the remaining 21 percent were composed of those whose household head worked the full year. Moreover, as to be expected, poverty rates varied inversely with the level of education of the household head. Despite this, about half the poor in 1989 consisted of families in which the household head had attended high school (but not beyond) and 31 percent of those whose household head had graduated from high school (but did not attend college).

The poverty rate among farm families has declined enormously, from 42.8 in 1959 to 9.6 percent in 1989. In 1989, they constituted only 2 percent of the poverty population, compared to 18 percent in 1959. Poverty incidence was also higher for urban and rural dwellers than suburbanites. However, one of the most dramatic changes since 1959 is that the proportion of poor families living in rural areas declined from 58 to 29 percent in 1989, while the proportion living in urban areas (central cities) increased from 25 to 42 percent. This is one of the reasons for the current concerns about urban poverty.

The last two lines in Table 4.3 show the mean income deficit and the poverty gap ratio. The income deficit is defined as the difference between the income of a family in poverty and its corresponding poverty line. The mean income deficit is the average of this for all families below the poverty line. In constant dollar terms, this statistic fell between 1959 and 1969, but by 1989, it had increased almost to its 1959 level. The poverty gap ratio (Section 4.1 "Measurement of the Aggregate Poverty Rate") also declined between 1959 and 1969, from 0.43 to 0.38, and then rose between 1969 and 1989. By 1989, it had reached 0.46, considerably higher than its 1959 level. So, even though the poverty rate (head count) was lower in 1989 than in 1959, the severity of poverty for those below the poverty line, as measured by the poverty gap, was greater.

Poverty Spells and the Permanence of Poverty

The official poverty definition is based on annual income flows. The *duration* of poverty is another important dimension to the problem of poverty. It is likely that a family that is poor for only a few months or a year experiences much less hardship than one that has been poor for many years. Several researchers have examined the extent of **permanent** or **chronic poverty** relative to **temporary poverty.**

Greg Duncan (1984) estimated on the basis of the Panel Survey of Income Dynamics (PSID) that only 20 to 25 percent of individuals classified as poor on the basis of the annual poverty definition were poor in eight out of the ten years between 1969 and 1978. Richard Coe (1978) defined persistent poverty to occur if the family's income was below the poverty line in every year between 1967 and 1975 and estimated that only about 12 percent of the annual poverty population would fall into this group. Martha Hill (1981), using the same definition for the ten years from 1969 to 1978, estimated that only about 6 percent of the official poverty group would be classified as persistently poor.

Joan Rodgers and John Rodgers (1993) found that between the late 1970s and the mid-1980s, not only did the overall poverty rate increase but poverty became more chronic and less transitory in nature. Using the PSID, they calculated that chronic poverty characterized 42.8 percent of the average annual poverty population during the 1975–1979 period and 47.1 percent during the 1982–1986 period. The rise in the proportion of the poor population who found themselves in permanent poverty rose among most demographic subgroups as well.

Another way of addressing this issue is to measure the duration of poverty spells. Mary Jo Bane and David Ellwood (1986) used the PSID to examine movements into and out of poverty. They found that among nonelderly people who are classified in poverty status in a given year, about 45 percent will leave poverty within one year; 70 percent will exit poverty within three years; and 87 percent within eight years. Yet, somewhat paradoxically, about half of the nonelderly poor at any given time are in the midst of a long spell of poverty. The reason for this apparent inconsistency is that the chronic poor remain in the poverty population year after year, while the temporary poor are only classified as part of the poverty population for a short period of time and are then replaced by other short-term poor.

They also found that the most common reason for a nonelderly family falling into poverty was a change in family composition, from the birth of a child, separation or divorce, or the establishment of a separate household unit (43 percent of poor families). The second most important cause was a decline in the earnings of the head of the family (38 percent). Exits from poverty are typically caused by the same events in the reverse direction, such as marriage or an increase in earnings of the family head.

The composition of the permanently poor is also of interest. Martha Hill (1981) calculated that 61 percent of the permanently poor between 1969 and 1978 were black; 49 percent were unmarried with children; 59 percent were nonelderly female, 22 percent were elderly female, and 4 percent elderly men; and 32 percent were disabled.

A recent study by Ann Stevens (1994) updated some of the earlier Bane and Ellwood results. She found that mobility out of poverty fell between 1970 and 1987, particularly among female-headed households. This means that poverty has become a more permanent condition among the poor, particularly among unwed mothers. Moreover, she found that half of all individuals who exited poverty fell back into poverty within five years. The tendency to experience repeated spells of poverty increased between 1970 and 1987 among families headed by white (though not black) females.

The Underclass

A related issue is the existence of an "underclass" in the United States. Michael Harrington's classic 1962 book, *The Other America,* first brought widespread attention to the "culture of poverty." He described this in terms of the sense of hopelessness, depression, loss of self-esteem, and pessimism for the future among the poor. William Julius Wilson's 1987 book, *The Truly Disadvantaged,* focused attention on what he called "dys-functional" social behavior among disadvantaged people living in inner-city "ghetto" areas. This is associated with a whole set of social problems, such as welfare dependency, dropping out of school, crime, drug culture, teenage pregnancy, almost permanent joblessness, and the presence of families headed largely by females. Wilson argued that, paradoxically, this may have occurred due to the success of anti-discrimination efforts, which have enabled successful blacks to move from the inner city areas, leaving a virtually homogeneous poor population behind. Whatever the reasons, the notion of an underclass is that there is a subset of the poor who have very different values, aspirations, and attitudes from the middle-class, and these characteristics produce behavior that prevents them from escaping poverty.

The underclass has been defined in various ways, and estimates of their size depend critically on the definition used. Most definitions use as one criterion residence in a low-income area (usually measured as an area where the poverty rate is 40 percent or greater). U.S. Census data identify which areas fall into this category. On the basis of this criterion, only about 7 percent of the poverty population would be considered as belonging to the underclass, and only about 15 percent of poor blacks (and about 5 percent of the black population as a whole). On the other hand, by whatever gauge is used, the size of the underclass appears to have grown. During the 1970s, the number of poor people living in low-income areas increased by 36 percent, while the overall number of poor grew by only 8 percent (see Isabel Sawhill, 1988, pp. 1108–1109 for more discussion). Erol Ricketts and Ronald Mincy (1990), using a similar definition, estimated that the number of people in the underclass in 1980 was roughly four times the number in 1970.

International Comparisons of Poverty Rates

There are a limited number of comparisons of poverty rates among countries. The main difficulty is that poverty line definitions vary considerably across nations, so that it would make little sense to make comparisons on the basis of official definitions in different places. One way of getting around this problem is to use a relative poverty line, defined as some percentage of the median income in a country. This has the virtue of providing the same standard across countries. Another difficulty in such comparisons is that different countries use different equivalence class adjustments, particularly for different family sizes, for their official poverty rates. An appropriate international comparison of poverty rates must also employ the same equivalence class adjustments in different countries.

A study by Timothy Smeeding, Lee Rainwater, Martin Rein, Richard Hauser and Gaston Schaber (1985) made both sets of adjustments. Their relative poverty line was set at one-half the median income for the country. They standardized the equivalence classes by family size on the basis of the official U.S. poverty lines. The calculations were based on the Luxembourg Income Study (LIS), which included data from the late 1970s and early 1980s.

Results are shown in Table 4.4 on both poverty rates and poverty gap ratios for seven countries for which the requisite data were available. The results are very interesting in placing U.S. poverty in an international perspective. The United States had the highest poverty rates of any of the seven countries. It was about twice that of the United Kingdom's, two and a half times that of West Germany, and over three times that of Norway and Sweden. Differences between the United States and other countries were particularly acute for one-person families. The poverty gap was also very high for the United States, though several other countries, including Sweden and Norway, also showed similar levels.

4.4 OTHER ISSUES IN THE MEASUREMENT OF POVERTY

There has been continuing controversy over the last two decades on the proper way to measure poverty. In Section 4.1, we discussed alternative ways of setting the poverty threshold. Three such proposals were put forward: an absolute poverty line, a relative poverty line, and a subjective poverty line.

The measurement problems treated in this section address the absolute poverty standard used in the official U.S. measure. The first two issues that are addressed concern the adjustment of the poverty line for differences in family size and the indexation of the poverty threshold over time for changes in the price level.

Once the poverty lines are decided, several questions arise as to the proper measure of resource availability that should be used to determine whether the poverty standard is met. The official U.S. statistics are based on annual family money income before taxes. The third issue considered here is the treatment of taxes, and the fourth is whether noncash government benefits, such as food stamps, housing subsidies, Medicare, and Medicaid, should be included in family income.

Families may also have other resources available besides (current) income to provide for their current consumption needs. In particular, many families own assets, such as houses, savings accounts, bonds, and other fi-

Table 4.4 International Comparisons of Poverty Rates and the Poverty Gap Ratio for Selected Countries[a]

Country	Total	Elderly Families	1-Parent Families	2-Parent Families	Other Families
A. *Percentage of Persons Who Are Poor*					
Canada	12.1	11.5	37.5	11.0	8.5
Israel[b]	14.5	23.8	11.8	14.9	5.5
Norway	4.8	4.6	12.6	3.4	5.7
Sweden	5.0	0.1	9.2	5.0	7.0
United Kingdom	8.8	18.1	29.1	6.5	4.1
United States	16.9	20.5	51.7	12.9	9.8
West Germany	6.0	9.3	18.1	3.9	5.4
B. *Percentage Poverty Gap Among Persons Living in Poverty*					
Canada	33.9	18.8	37.0	30.5	41.8
Israel[b]	16.3	13.4	13.7	20.4	13.3
Norway	40.8	48.3	27.7	29.2	47.6
Sweden	40.0	45.2	33.4	28.2	43.2
United Kingdom	16.0	10.9	17.7	10.8	24.3
United States	39.9	29.1	43.0	33.3	50.6
West Germany	30.6	28.5	31.4	23.2	48.4

[a]Source: Timothy M. Smeeding, Lee Rainwater, Martin Rein, Richard Hauser and Gaston Schaber (1985).

Income is based on income after transfers (post-transfer income). Poverty is defined as families or persons in families with equivalent income below one-half of median family equivalent income.

Families are defined as two or more persons living together who are related by blood, marriage or adoption, or single (unrelated) individuals. More than one family may occupy one household. Elderly families are those headed by a person age 65 or older. Single-parent families are nonelderly families with only one natural parent present and children under age 18. Two-parent families are nonelderly families with two natural parents and children under age 18. Other families are mainly nonelderly childless couples and nonelderly single individuals.

Totals may not equal sums across rows owing to rounding errors.
[b]Israeli figures are for urban populations only.

nancial assets. The fifth issue discussed below is the incorporation of household wealth in a measure of family resources used to measure poverty.

Because of taxes, noncash government benefits, and the availability of savings and service flows from housing and consumer durables, annual income may not be a good measure of the actual consumption level enjoyed by a household over the course of a year. A sixth issue concerns the use of actual family consumption instead of income in order to measure poverty status.

The official poverty calculations are based on annual income. A seventh issue concerns the choice of the accounting period. Some researchers have suggested that a shorter accounting period be used, such as a month, while others have suggested two- or three-year periods. As will be seen below, the measured poverty rate is quite sensitive to the period of analysis chosen. Several other measurement issues are considered in the last part of this section.[7]

Equivalence Scales

In constructing poverty thresholds for different family sizes and types, one must implicitly determine what levels of income are "equivalent" for them in terms of the needs that are satisfied. For example, according to the official U.S. poverty thresholds for 1993, a family of three requires $11,522 to obtain a minimally adequate standard of living, while a family of four requires $14,763 (see Table 4.1). These two incomes are considered equivalent for their respective family size. The full set of adjustment factors for different family sizes and types is referred to as an **equivalence scale**.

It is assumed that a larger family requires a greater income to achieve the same standard of living as a smaller one but that there are also economies of consumption as household size increases. The official U.S. poverty lines were set on the basis of food requirements. It was then assumed that other consumption needs varied more or less in the same proportion.

However, the resulting poverty thresholds have a rather irregular pattern with respect to family size. The poverty line for a family of three is set 22 percent greater than for a two-person family, while the threshold for a four-person family is 28 percent greater than for three persons. The threshold is set 13 percent greater for a six-person family than for five persons and also 13 percent greater for a family of seven than one of six. If there are economies of scale in consumption, then the differential between a two-person and three-person family should be greater than that between a four-person and three-person one. Moreover, it is not clear why the differential between a seven- and six-person family is the same as that between a six- and five-person family.

Another anomalous feature is that the poverty threshold for elderly couples is set lower than for nonelderly ones (the difference is 8 percent for the 1993 thresholds). Whereas it is true that food needs are less for elderly persons than nonelderly ones (this was found in the original 1955 Survey of Food Consumption), it is unlikely that their other needs are correspondingly less. This is particularly true for medical expenses, which are much higher for elderly people. Patricia Ruggles (1990) calculated that the poverty rate for elderly persons in 1984 would have been 12.7 percent, instead of the official rate of 10.3 percent, if the same poverty threshold were used for elderly people as for the nonelderly. Moreover, it is likely that consump-

---

[7]See also Isabel Sawhill's 1988 survey article and Patricia Ruggles' 1990 book, *Drawing the Line*, for more discussion of these issues.

tion needs vary among *all* age groups, not just between the elderly and nonelderly, so that equivalence class adjustments could be performed for young and middle-aged households as well as elderly ones.[8]

Choice of Price Index

The official U.S. poverty thresholds have been adjusted each year (after 1969) by the national Consumer Price Index (CPI). The use of the CPI has been questioned by researchers for three reasons. First, the CPI is based on the consumption expenditure patterns of the average household (actually, the average *urban* household). Since the consumption patterns of low-income families may differ from those of the average family (in particular, they consume a higher proportion of food, housing, and other necessities), it is not clear that the CPI is the most appropriate deflator for indexing the poverty thresholds. If the prices of food, housing, and other necessities rise at different rates than other consumption items, then the use of the CPI may be an inaccurate index of the actual change of purchasing power of the poor.

Second, for technical reasons, the CPI has been shown to have a bias with regard to the treatment of housing expenses. In particular, before 1983, the housing price index was based on the actual change in the price of *new houses* that were purchased on the market. However, only a small proportion of households buy a new house in a given year. For the vast majority of homeowners, the cost of housing depends on (usually fixed) mortgage rates, real estate taxes, utilities, and maintenance costs, while for renters, it depends on rent and utilities. This problem was particularly acute during the late 1970s and early 1980s, when the price of new housing was rising much faster than the costs of these other items.

In 1983, the Bureau of Labor Statistics changed its treatment of housing costs in the construction of the Consumer Price Index. Instead of using new housing prices, the Bureau of Labor Statistics substituted the change in the *rental* prices of housing. This series was felt to be more representative of the actual change in housing costs faced by most consumers.

This new treatment of housing costs was also used to adjust the CPI before 1983. This new series is referred to as the CPI-X_1 series. In most years before 1983, but particularly between 1977 and 1981, the annual change in CPI-X_1 was smaller than that of the official CPI. This change had the effect of reducing the measured percentage of persons in poverty, because the poverty thresholds are correspondingly lower. For example, the overall poverty rate in 1974 calculated on the basis of the CPI-X_1 is 10.4 percent, compared to the official rate of 11.2 percent. For 1978 the adjusted rate is 10.4 percent, compared to the official rate of 11.4 percent; for 1983, it is 13.7 percent, compared to 15.2 percent; and for 1993, 13.7 percent, compared to 15.1 percent. The adjusted poverty rates are about 1 to 1.5 percentage

---

[8] See Deaton and Muellbauer (1980) for a comprehensive treatment of equivalence scales.

points lower than the official ones. However, the time trends are very similar. For both series, the poverty rate shows a sharp increase from 1978 to 1983, and almost identical levels in 1993 as in 1983.

A third problem with the use of the national CPI in adjusting poverty thresholds over time is that the cost of living may vary rather considerably around the country. It requires less money income to attain the same standard of living in rural Mississippi in comparison to New York City. As a result, the official statistics likely overstate poverty in Mississippi and understate it in New York. Many researchers have proposed the use of state or local CPI indices to determine poverty rates in different localities.

The Treatment of Taxes

The official poverty measure is based on before-tax income. Economists believe that a better measure of resource availability is the actual amount of money families have to spend to meet their needs. This argument suggests that the resource measure should be based on **disposable** or **after-tax income.** This is particularly important for two reasons. First, the tax burden of low-income households has risen over time in the United States since the early 1960s, when the poverty population paid almost no income taxes because of the system of personal exemptions and the standard deduction. The trend over time was mainly due to so-called "bracket creep." Personal income tax schedule brackets tended to be fixed in nominal terms over time, so that inflation forced low-income households into higher marginal tax brackets even though there was no change in their real income (see Chapter 16 for a discussion of the U.S. tax system). As a result, by the early 1980s, tax liability started at incomes that were considerably below the poverty line. Also, the increase in the payroll tax has added to the burden of the low-income population. In 1984, a family of four earning poverty-level income was paying about 10 percent of its income in the form of payroll and income taxes (see Sawhill, 1988, p. 1079). However, the Tax Reform act of 1986 has since substantially lowered the personal income tax burdens of low-income families, and today income tax brackets are indexed for inflation.

Second, if the actual taxes paid differ among demographic groups, then comparisons of poverty rates across groups may also be misleading. This is particularly germane to comparisons of families of different sizes, since the number of income tax exemptions rises with the size of the family. This issue also affects poverty rate comparisons between elderly and nonelderly families, because the former receive an extra tax exemption and a major source of their income, social security income, is exempted from most income tax.

Patricia Ruggles (1990, Table 4.1) calculated the effects of excluding federal income taxes and payroll taxes from family income on the poverty rate. She found that the poverty rate for all individuals would have increased from its actual level of 13.6 percent in 1986 to 14.6 percent, or by one percentage point. Moreover, the poverty gap ratio would have increased by

4 percent. The changes are relatively small, because even though the tax burdens of low-income households have increased over time, they are still small relative to total family income.

The Treatment of Noncash Benefits

When the poverty line was first established in the early 1960s, noncash government benefits were virtually nonexistent. However, since that time, the Food Stamp Program, Medicare, and Medicaid were established, and these programs considerably augmented the amount of resources available to low-income households. If, in addition, housing subsidies and school lunches are included, total noncash benefits to poor households more than doubled between 1970 and 1986 and accounted for almost two-thirds of total assistance to the poor (see Sawhill, 1988, p. 1078).

Most researchers now agree that noncash benefits should be included in the measure of family income used to determine poverty status. A number of studies have constructed new measures of the poverty rate based on the inclusion of noncash benefits, and the U.S. Census Bureau publishes an alternative series of poverty rates on the basis of adjustments originally estimated by Timothy Smeeding (1982).

Despite this general agreement, there still remains the difficult question of how such in-kind benefits should be valued. One approach is to value them at their **market value**—that is, the price the consumer must pay to obtain the same item in the private market. However, such noncash benefits are not directly **fungible**—that is, they cannot be used like cash to purchase any commodity that the individual wishes. Consequently, their value to the individual may be less than their market value, since the person does not have discretion over how to spend the benefits. In fact, the recipient may be forced to consume too much medical care, for example, and not enough clothing.

Food stamps have been shown to be fairly fungible (indeed, many businesses will accept them in lieu of cash even for nonfood purchases). As a result, their value to the recipient may be close to their face value. The main problem in valuation is the treatment of medical expenses. If actual medical benefits received were added to cash income, this would have the paradoxical result of implying that sicker persons are better off than healthier ones. An alternative approach is to value medical benefits at their **insurance value**—that is, how much medical insurance a person would have to pay to achieve the same level of medical care. However, for elderly people, the insurance costs would be very high to replace Medicare and Medicaid. Indeed, studies have shown that adding the insurance value of these two programs to the incomes of the elderly would, by itself, be sufficient to lift almost all the elderly poor out of poverty! Moreover, medical benefits have very limited fungibility, so that their value to the recipient is likely to be considerably less than their insurance equivalent.

Despite these reservations, if we totally disregard the growth of medical benefits (as well as other noncash benefits) for low-income families over time, we will understate the improvement of their well-being. As a result, one compromise proposal put forward by Henry Aaron (1985) is a two-tiered poverty measure. For the first tier, the value of "cash-like" government benefits, such as food stamps, would be added to the family income measure. For the second tier, the availability of adequate medical coverage would be considered. If the person passed the poverty threshold based on the first measure but failed to have adequate medical coverage, the person would be classified as poor. A person would have to surpass both criteria to be considered not poor.

Some alternative calculations of the poverty rate made by the U.S. Census Bureau calculations are shown in Table 4.5. Two valuations are provided. In the first set, noncash benefits are valued at their private market value equivalent. For food stamps, this was set equal to the face value of the food coupons. For medical expenses, this was calculated as the actual medical expenditures paid out by the government divided by the number of individuals covered by the various programs. For housing subsidies, this was defined as the difference between the market rent for the housing unit and the actual rent paid by the recipient of the housing subsidy.

The second valuation is based on **recipient value,** which theoretically reflects the recipient's own valuation of the noncash benefit received. This was estimated in a fairly complex manner by comparing the expenditure patterns of the benefit recipient with a comparable family which did not receive the benefit. By comparing the expenditure patterns of the latter on similar items (food, medical care, and housing), the Census Bureau was able to impute a value of these benefits to the recipient.

The results clearly indicate that including the value of noncash government benefits in family income significantly lowers the measured poverty rate. The official poverty rate for the total population is 13.4 percent for 1987. When food and housing benefits are included at market value, the

Table 4.5 Alternative Measures of the Poverty Rate From Adding Noncash Government Benefits to Income, 1979–1987[a] (in percent)

Year	All Races	Whites	Blacks	Hispanics
Official Poverty Index				
1979	11.7	9.0	31.0	21.8
1980	13.0	10.2	32.5	25.7
1981	14.0	11.1	34.2	26.5
1982	15.0	12.0	35.6	29.9
1983	15.2	12.1	35.7	28.0
1984	14.4	11.5	33.8	28.4
1987	13.4	10.4	32.4	28.0

Table 4.5 *(concluded)*

Year	All Races	Whites	Blacks	Hispanics
Valuing Food and Housing Benefits Only at Market Value				
1979	9.7	7.8	23.5	17.4
1980	11.1	9.0	25.6	21.5
1981	12.3	9.9	28.9	22.8
1982	13.4	10.9	30.7	26.5
1983	13.9	11.3	30.6	25.6
1984	12.9	10.5	28.8	25.5
1987	12.0			
Valuing Food and Housing Benefits Only at Recipient Value				
1979	10.0	7.9	24.7	17.9
1980	11.4	9.2	26.5	22.2
1981	12.6	10.1	30.0	23.6
1982	13.7	11.1	31.7	27.2
1983	14.1	11.4	31.7	25.9
1984	13.2	10.7	30.1	26.0
1987	12.4			
Valuing Food, Housing Benefits, and All Medical Benefits at Market Value				
1979	6.8	5.6	14.9	12.0
1980	7.9	6.6	16.2	15.2
1981	9.0	7.4	19.7	16.8
1982	10.0	8.3	21.5	20.5
1983	10.3	8.7	21.2	19.9
1984	9.7	8.0	20.5	19.9
1987	8.5			
Valuing Food, Housing Benefits, and All Medical Benefits at Recipient Value				
1979	9.0	7.1	22.2	16.6
1980	10.4	8.4	24.2	20.5
1981	11.7	9.3	27.9	22.2
1982	12.7	10.3	29.3	26.1
1983	13.1	10.6	29.2	24.6
1984	12.2	9.8	28.3	24.7
1987	11.0			

[a]Sources. 1979–84: U.S. Bureau of the Census, Technical Paper 55, *Estimates of Poverty Including the Value of Noncash Benefits: 1984,* U.S. Government Printing Office, Washington, D.C., August 1985. 1987: U.S. Bureau of the Census, Technical Paper 58, *Estimates of Poverty Including the Value of Noncash Benefits: 1987,* U.S. Government Printing Office, Washington, D.C., 1988.

measured poverty rate falls to 12.0 percent; add to these the market value of all medical benefits, and the rate declines to 8.5 percent. A similar pattern is observed for other years and for valuation at recipient value. It is also of interest that valuation at recipient value produces a smaller decline in the poverty rate than market value. This is particularly true for medical benefits, whose recipient value is much smaller than its market value.

However, interestingly, the inclusion of noncash benefits in family income does not appear to alter the *trends* in the poverty rate. By all measures, the poverty rate increased between 1979 and 1983 and then declined thereafter to 1987. This was true for all families, and for whites, blacks, and Hispanic households separately.

A more elaborate calculation is shown in Table 4.6 for 1989. This table shows the effects of both including government transfers and netting out taxes on the measurement of the poverty rate. It has several steps. For all persons, the official poverty rate for 1989 is 12.8 percent. If all government transfer payments are excluded from income, the poverty rate jumps to 20.0

Table 4.6   The Effect of Taxes and Government Transfers on the Poverty Rate, 1989[a]

	All Races	Whites	Blacks	Hispanics
1. Official poverty rate	12.8	10.0	30.7	26.2
2. (1) less government transfers	20.0	17.2	38.2	31.3
3. (2) plus capital gains	19.9	17.2	38.1	31.0
4. (3) plus health insurance supplements to labor earnings	19.4	16.7	37.3	29.9
5. (4) less social security payroll taxes	20.3	17.6	38.3	32.5
6. (5) less federal income tax	20.1	17.3	37.8	31.7
7. (6) less state income tax	20.3	17.5	38.3	31.8
8. (7) plus non-means-tested government cash transfers	13.9	11.0	32.8	28.3
9. (8) plus Medicare[b]	13.4	10.5	31.8	27.7
10. (9) plus school lunches	13.4	10.5	31.7	27.7
11. (10) plus means-tested government cash transfers	12.5	9.9	29.3	26.0
12. (11) plus Medicaid[b]	11.7	9.3	27.7	24.3
13. (12) plus other noncash government transfers	10.4	8.3	23.9	21.5
14. (13) plus net imputed rent to owner-occupied housing	8.9	6.9	21.2	19.4

[a]Source: U.S. Bureau of the Census, Current Population Reports, Series P-60. No. 169-RD, *Measuring the Effect of Benefits and Taxes on Income and Poverty: 1989*, U.S. Government Printing Office, Washington, D.C., September 1990, Table 2.
[b]Based on market value valuation (see text for details).

percent. The adjustment for income taxes and payroll taxes paid, as was discussed above, has very little effect on the measured poverty rate. When non-means-tested government cash transfers, such as social security benefits, are added back to income, the measured poverty rate falls by 6.4 percentage points to 13.9 percent. The inclusion of Medicare benefits, valued at market value, reduces the poverty rate by another 0.5 percentage points; the inclusion of means-tested government transfers, particularly Aid to Families with Dependent Children (AFDC), reduces it by a further 0.9 percentage points; and the addition of the value of Medicaid, also at market value, by still another 0.8 percentage points. Finally, the inclusion of other noncash government transfers, particularly food stamps and housing subsidies, results in a further drop of 1.3 percentage points.[9]

In a sense, the results provide an answer to the often-asked question of why the poverty rate seems to remain so high after the huge increase in government spending on antipoverty programs. Part of the answer is that much of the improvement in the well-being of low-income families is not captured in our standard poverty measure. However, once we include the value of noncash government benefits, the poverty rates are, in fact, much lower than they were 20 years ago.

The Role of Household Wealth

Families may have access to consumption over and above their income if they have accumulated wealth. This may take two forms. First, if they have accumulated financial savings, they can draw on this during periods when their income is low. Second, families also receive consumption "services" from housing that they may own or from consumer durables, such as automobiles. If poverty is thought of as a deprivation of resources to acquire an adequate amount of consumption services, then it might make sense to include a wealth dimension in the measure of family resources used to construct the poverty rate.[10]

Several studies have attempted to do this. Usually, wealth is converted into an income flow by assuming a fixed rate of return (5 or 7 percent, for

---

[9]There are several other technical adjustments that are made. First, realized capital gains on assets that are sold, which is not normally counted as part of "Census income," is added to family income (see Chapter 2). In addition, health insurance premiums paid by employers for their wage and salary workers are also estimated and added to family income. Both of these adjustments have a negligible effect on the measured poverty rate. A still further adjustment is the inclusion of net imputed rent of owner-occupied housing. This is an estimation of the value of services provided to homeowners by the houses that they own. (Technically, it is defined as the equity in the house multiplied by the average rate on high-grade municipal bonds less imputed property taxes. See the next section for further discussion of "wealth adjustments" to the poverty definition). Another interesting point is that the subtraction of federal income taxes actually reduces the measured poverty rate for families. This is due to the fact that some low-income families receive the Earned Income Tax Credit (EITC), which increases their after-tax income. Also, see Chapter 15 for more discussion of government transfer programs to the poor.

[10]A related issue is that some families may be "poor" because they record a large accounting loss from their business. The author (1990) has estimated that only 4 to 5 percent of the poverty population in 1983 would fall into this group.

example), or it is converted into a lifetime annuity (that is, a constant income flow over the remaining lifetime of the individual so that the person's wealth is completely exhausted at the end of life). In addition, an implicit rent on owner-occupied housing is also computed. This is typically estimated as a set rate of return on the gross or net value of the home. In the author's work (Wolff, 1990), when a 5 percent rate of return was used, it was found that including an annuity along with household income reduced the estimated poverty rate by 8 percent and the further addition of imputed rent on homes reduced it by another 8 percent. Burton Weisbrod and Lee Hansen (1968) and Marilyn Moon (1977) obtained similar results. The drop in the poverty rate was substantially greater for elderly families, because they had higher wealth (and also a higher ratio of wealth to current income) than younger families. Similar calculations for 1962 showed an even higher percentage drop in the measured poverty rate (26 percent decline in 1962 compared to 16 percent in 1983) because of the declining wealth holdings of low-income families.

Consumption-Based Measures of Poverty

We have already discussed four reasons why before-tax money income may not be an adequate measure of the resources available to the low-income population. First, tax payments reduce the amount of income that can be used for consumption. Second, government noncash benefits may add to family resources. Third, families can draw from accumulated savings. Fourth, housing and consumer durables provide service flows that can directly benefit households. As a result, income may be a poor proxy for consumption, particularly among families with low income.

A related argument comes from the permanent income hypothesis developed by Milton Friedman (1957). He argues that income consists of two parts: permanent income, which represents the normal flow of resources to the family, and transitory income, which is subject to random fluctuations over time. Households base their consumption patterns on permanent income, rather than their actual income. The lower tail of the income distribution is likely to have a disproportionate number of households who have experienced a temporary reduction in income. As a result, low-income households generally have high ratios of consumption to income in order to maintain their normal standard of living.

Because of the problems with an income-based measure of poverty, Daniel Slesnick (1993) developed new indices of poverty using actual expenditure data drawn from the Consumer Expenditure Survey. His main conclusion is that consumption-based measures of poverty are substantially lower than the official income-based poverty rates. His estimate of the poverty rate for 1989 is 8.4 percent, compared to the official figure of 12.8 percent. The time trends were also different. Whereas the official numbers show poverty declining between 1960 and 1973 and then generally rising, his consumption-based index showed a general downward trend from 1960 to 1989. Moreover, the divergence between the official rate and the consumption-based poverty rate widened over time. He concluded that poverty in the United States had declined much more over the postwar period than the official figures had indicated.

A similar conclusion was reached by Susan Mayer and Christopher Jencks (1993) on the basis of a somewhat different approach. They argued that poverty measures should reflect whether families have adequate food, shelter, clothing, medical care, and education. They evaluated the welfare level of the low-income population using actual measures of material well-being such as food and clothing expenditures, housing conditions (the presence of indoor plumbing, for example), access to automobiles, telephones, and televisions, health status, and access to medical and dental care. Unlike the official poverty figures, they found no evidence of the deterioration in the living conditions of the poor during the 1980s and concluded that anti-poverty programs have been effective in providing for the basic needs of the low-income population.

The Accounting Period

The official poverty rate calculation is based on annual family income. If a family's total income for the year falls short of the poverty threshold (also based on annual income), the family is classified as poor. However, income flows tend to be very uneven over time. As a result, it is much more likely for a family to experience an income shortfall for a short period of time than an extended one. Such setbacks may be associated with sudden or temporary changes in a family's condition, such as divorce or separation, a period of unemployment, death or disability of a worker in the family, or the birth of a child. Thus, the choice of accounting period can make a crucial difference in both our measure of the poverty rate and our understanding of the causes and remedies for poverty.

Let us first consider the use of accounting periods longer than one year. To examine such an issue, one must rely on a panel survey, which covers the same set of families on a continuing basis. One such database is the Panel Survey of Income Dynamics (PSID), which has followed a sample of 5,000 families since 1968. A study by Greg Duncan (1984), based on the PSID, found that only a very small proportion (2.6 percent) of the sample population would be classified as poor in eight out of the ten years between 1969 and 1978. On the other hand, 24 percent of the population fell into poverty for at least one year over this period. Thus, as we saw in Section 4.3 above, the number of long-term poor is much smaller than the poverty population identified in a calendar year. If we use an accounting period longer than a year to define poverty, our estimate of the poverty rate will be correspondingly lowered.

Let us now look at the other side of the question, the use of accounting periods shorter than one year. It is first of interest to note that eligibility for many government welfare programs, such as Aid to Families with

Dependent Children (AFDC), is based on monthly income statements rather than annual income. These program designers were aware of the importance of short-term poverty, since even a temporary shortfall of income for many families may require immediate relief.

Research on this issue has been done by Patricia Ruggles (1990), on the basis of the Survey of Income and Program Participation, which provides monthly income data. Four indices were computed on the basis of 1984 data: (1) the percent poor on the basis of the official annual income definition; (2) the percent whose monthly income fell below the official poverty threshold in monthly terms (the annual threshold divided by 12) for all 12 months; (3) the percent whose monthly income fell below the official poverty threshold for at least one month; and (4) the average of the monthly poverty rates. She found sharp differences in the measures. The official poverty index yielded a 11.0 percent poverty rate in this sample. In contrast, only 5.9 percent of individuals were poor in all 12 months (the second index), while 26.2 percent were poor in at least one month (the third index). The average monthly poverty rate (the fourth index), in turn, was 13.7 percent. It is interesting that the proportion of poor based on the average of monthly rates was higher than the annual poverty index, because of the high proportion of individuals who fall into poverty in at least one month.

Measures of poverty are thus quite sensitive to the period that we consider appropriate in determining what constitutes deprivation of a "minimally adequate standard of living." The majority of poor people are in poverty for relatively short periods rather than over long stretches of time.

Other Issues

Another issue of measurement is the unit of analysis or the choice of the recipient unit. The official poverty line is based on the family unit. This choice is mainly due to the fact that a large amount of resource sharing occurs within the family unit. Thus, even though children do not typically earn any income themselves, they still have access to their parents' income. The same argument holds for nonworking wives. As a result, an individual's poverty status has traditionally depended on the total income of the family unit.

However, the nuclear family may have access to resources outside its immediate members. This is particularly so in the case of divorce if former wives receive alimony or their children receive child support from their father. In such a case, children may have access to resources from a father who no longer lives with them. Moreover, there still exists among certain segments of our population the "extended family system." In this regard, a nuclear family may receive assistance from the mother's or father's parents or other relatives. This may be especially true in times when a family is experiencing economic hardship. Though these issues are of direct interest, it has proven very difficult to obtain precise estimates of how they might affect the measured poverty rate.

Another issue concerns the value of leisure or nonmarket time (see Section 2.5). Low-income families, whose father and mother are both working full-time, may have relatively little time left over for home production or child care. In some sense, such a family is materially worse off than another family unit with the same money income but whose mother does not work and can devote more time to nonmarket activity. It would also be of interest to adjust poverty measures for the welfare loss stemming from the unavailability of time for home production.

A related issue concerns the existence of some family or household units with low incomes, such as college students, who may be classified as poor according to the official poverty index but who expect low incomes to be temporary until they begin their lifetime career. Because of this problem, Irwin Garfinkel and Robert Haveman (1977) took another approach to measure poverty, on the basis of what they call "earnings capacity." This measure is defined on the basis of 2,000 hours worked per year and on the wage that would be expected, given the person's schooling and occupation. Such a measure eliminates from the ranks of the poor the many young individuals with a high level of education and temporarily low incomes. However, low-skilled workers, who sometimes work more than 2,000 hours per year ("moonlighting" with two jobs or working excessive overtime) in order to compensate for low wages, do enter the ranks of poor, even if their annual earnings are above the poverty threshold.

4.5 SUMMARY

There are three common ways of setting the poverty line that are in common use: (1) an absolute standard, (2) a relative standard, and (3) a subjective standard. The official U.S. poverty threshold is based on an absolute poverty standard, which remains fixed over time in real terms. The relative poverty line is set as a fixed percentage of the median income, which may change over time if median income changes in real terms. The subjective poverty line is based on respondents' answers to questions regarding what they consider an adequate standard of living.

The official poverty index for the United States is based on annual before-tax cash income received by the family unit. Alternative ways have also been proposed to modify the existing poverty standard, and studies have shown that measures of poverty are sensitive to the criteria for both the poverty threshold and the definition of income used. Among the modifications that have been used are as follows: First, different equivalence class adjustments have been employed to differentiate the poverty thresholds among families of different sizes and types. Second, after-tax income has been proposed as a better measure of family resources than before-tax income, which is used in the official definition. Measured poverty incidence is slightly greater with after-tax income. Third, noncash government benefits—particularly, food stamps, Medicaid and Medicare benefits, and housing allowances—have also been added to family income. Such adjustments result in a considerably lower measure of poverty incidence, though the trend, at least since 1979, does not seem to be affected. Fourth, including a return on household wealth in the definition of income lowers the measured poverty rate by 10 to 20 percent. Fifth, using monthly income instead of annual income produces a higher poverty rate, whereas using income for several years as the base produces a lower rate.

Actual poverty trends for the United States show a gradual reduction between 1959 and 1964, a pronounced drop between 1964 and 1968, almost no change until 1979, a steep rise between 1979 and 1983, a moderate decline to 1989, and a subsequent increase. The poverty rate in 1993 was 15.1 percent, about the same level as in 1966. Poverty rates have been about three times as high for black persons as whites and $2^1/_2$ times as high for Hispanic individuals as whites. Poverty rates in the United States are considerably higher than other industrialized (OECD) countries.

Poverty rates for children have been considerably greater than those for adults. Between 1973 and 1993, the poverty rate among children increased faster than the adult rate. During the 1980s and early 1990s, one-fifth or more of children were poor. The big success story over the last three and a half decades has been the elderly, whose poverty rate fell from 35 percent in 1959, considerably above the overall rate, to 12 percent in 1989, below the overall rate.

Poverty incidence is 5 to 6 times greater for female-headed families than for male-headed ones. Though the poverty rate for female-headed households has not changed very much since the 1960s, more than half of all poor families were headed by a female in 1993, compared to less than one-fourth in 1959. The reason is the rapid growth in the total number of female-headed households in the United States since the late 1950s.

Though poverty incidence is much higher in families where the household head did not work, 40 percent of the poor in 1989 were in families in which the head did work, and 21 percent in households where the head worked the whole year.

Another dimension of poverty is its duration or "permanence." Only about 10 to 20 percent of poor families would be called permanently poor. About half of all poor families exit poverty within a year. The underclass, defined by residence in a low-income area, comprises only about 5 to 7 percent of all the poor. However, this proportion may have been increasing since the 1970s, since today over 40 percent of poor families live in urban areas, compared to 25 percent in 1959.

The analysis of the determinants of poverty is really part of the analysis of income determination, a subject which will occupy us for most of the remainder of the text. There are many complex issues involved in what causes poverty, and these are best left for later treatment. However, it is possible at this point to make some general observations on the incidence and implications of poverty. Age seems to have an important bearing on poverty status. One might expect that poverty among young people is due to the difficulty of finding a good job and therefore temporary, since better jobs are usually reserved for more experienced workers. On the other hand, the aged poor are often trapped in their poverty status, since well-paying jobs are usually unavailable to them due to laws, custom, or their lack of work capacity. Therefore, poverty occurring in old-age is usually more serious than when it happens when one is young.

Families headed by females have a very high incidence of poverty. The major reason is that the demands of child care often make the mother unavailable for work. Unwed mothers often become dependent on public assistance, though recently there has been some effort to make day care facilities and training programs available to single parents to allow them to work.

Children have recently had a very high incidence of poverty. Many of them live in single-parent households. There is also a high incidence of poverty in families with a large number of children. The mere fact that a family has many children means that the same income must be spread over more people.

Poverty status is very closely related to employment status. For those not in the labor force or unemployed, the incidence of poverty is very high. There are a number of reasons why an adult might not be in the labor force. One, just discussed, is that the person might be a single parent, whose time is tied up in child care. Other causes include sickness, disability, and old age. Unemployment may be due to a recession or to the fact that an individual may be unskilled or uneducated or lack the necessary skills to meet job requirements. Racial and gender discrimination may prevent a person from obtaining a job.

Many families in poverty are the working poor. This may be a consequence of part-time or part-year work or a result of working in a low wage job. In 1995, someone working full-time and full-year at the minimum wage would not earn enough income to keep a family of four above the poverty line. The incidence of low wage employment is particularly high among persons with limited schooling and skills, unattached individuals, females, minorities, and employees in seasonal or service industries. This issue leads directly to the question of the determination of earnings with which Part II of the book is concerned.

REFERENCES

Aaron, Henry, "The Foundations of the 'War on Poverty' Reexamined," *American Economic Review*, Vol. 57, No. 4, December 1967, pp. 1229–1240.

———, *Politics and the Professors: The Great Society in Perspective,* Brookings Institution, Washington, D.C., 1978.

———, "Comments on 'Evaluation of Census Bureau Procedures for the Measurement of Noncash Benefits,' " in *Conference on the Measurement of Noncash Benefits,* Vol. 1, U.S. Bureau of the Census, Washington, D.C., 1985, pp. 57–62.

Anderson, Martin, *The Political Economy of Welfare Reform in the United States*, Hoover Institute Press, Palo Alto, California, 1978.

Anderson, William Henry Locke, "Trickling Down: The Relationship Between Economic Growth and the Extent of Poverty Among American Families," *Quarterly Journal of Economics*, Vol. 78, No. 4, November 1964, pp. 511–524.

Atkinson, A. B., "Income Maintenance and Social Insurance: A Survey," in Alan Auerbach and Martin Feldstein (eds.), *Handbook of Public Economics*, Vol. 2, North Holland, Amsterdam and New York, 1987, Ch. 13, pp. 779–889.

———, "On the Measurement of Poverty," *Econometrica*, Vol. 55, 1987, pp. 749–764.

Bane, Mary Jo, and David Ellwood, "Slipping into and out of Poverty: The Dynamics of Spells," *Journal of Human Resources*, Vol. 21, No. 1, Winter, 1986, pp. 1–23.

Bassi, Laurie, and Orley Ashenfelter, "The Effect of Direct Job Creation and Training Programs on Low-Skilled Workers," in Sheldon H. Danziger and Daniel H. Weinberg (eds.), *Fighting Poverty*, 1986, pp. 133–151.

Beach, Charles, "Cyclical Sensitivity of Aggregate Income Inequality," *Review of Economics and Statistics*, Vol. 59, No. 1, February 1977, pp. 56–66.

Blackburn, McKinley L., "International Comparisons of Poverty," *American Economic Review Papers and Proceedings*, Vol. 84, No. 2, May 1994, pp. 371–374.

Blinder, Alan, "The Level and Distribution of Economic Well-Being," in Martin Feldstein (ed.), *The American Economy in Transition*, University of Chicago Press, Chicago, 1980, pp. 415–479.

———, and Howard Esaki, "Macroeconomic Activity and Income Distribution in the Postwar United States," *Review of Economics and Statistics*, Vol. 60, No. 4, November 1978, pp. 604–609.

Browning, Edgar K., and William R. Johnson, "The Trade-Off Between Equality and Efficiency," *Journal of Political Economy*, Vol. 92, No. 2, 1984, pp. 175–203.

Burtless, Gary, "Public Spending for the Poor: Trends, Prospects and Economic Limits," in Sheldon H. Danziger and Daniel H. Weinberg, (eds.) *Fighting Poverty*, 1986, pp. 18–49.

———, "In-Kind Transfers and the Trend in Poverty," in Douglas J. Besharov and Les Lenkowsky (eds.), *Understanding Poverty and Dependence*, Free Press, New York, forthcoming.

Chen, Shaochua, Gaurav Datt, and Martin Ravallion, "Is Poverty Increasing in the Developing World?" *Review of Income and Wealth*, Series 40, No. 4, December 1994, pp. 359–376.

Clark, S., R. Hemming, and D. Ulph, "On Indices for the Measurement of Poverty," *Economic Journal*, Vol. 91, 1981, pp. 515–526.

Coe, Richard, "Dependency and Poverty in the Short and Long Run," in Greg J. Duncan and James N. Morgan (eds.), *Five Thousand American Fam-*

ilies: Patterns of Economic Progress, Vol. VI, Institute for Social Research, Ann Arbor, Michigan, 1978, pp. 273–296.

Corcoran, Mary, *et al.,* "Myth and Reality: The Causes and Persistence of Poverty," *Journal of Policy Anal. Manage.,* Vol. 4, No. 4, Summer 1985, pp. 516–536.

Cowell, F. A., "Poverty Measures, Inequality and Decomposability," in D. Bos, M. Rose, and C. Seidl (eds.), *Welfare and Efficiency in Public Economics,* Springer Verlag, Heidelberg, 1988.

Danziger, Sheldon, "Recent Trends in Poverty and the Antipoverty Effectiveness of Income Transfers," in Sheldon Danziger and Kent Portney (eds.), *The Distributional Impacts of Public Policy,* Macmillan Press, London, 1987, pp. 33–45.

———, and Peter Gottschalk, "Do Rising Tides Lift All Boats? The Impact of Secular and Cyclical Changes in Poverty," *American Economic Review,* Vol. 76, No. 2, May 1986, pp. 405–410.

——— and ———, "Earnings Inequality, the Spatial Concentration of Poverty, and the Underclass," *American Economic Review,* Vol. 77, No. 2, May 1987, pp. 211–215.

Danziger, Sheldon, Robert Haveman, and Robert Plotnick, "How Income Transfer Programs Affect Work, Savings, and the Income Distribution: A Critical Review," *Journal of Economic Literature,* Vol. 19, No. 3, September 1981, pp. 975–1028.

———, ———, and ———, "Antipoverty Policy: Effects on the Poor and the Nonpoor," in Sheldon H. Danziger and Daniel H. Weinberg (eds.), *Fighting Poverty,* 1986, pp. 50–77.

Danziger, Sheldon, and Robert Plotnick, "The War on Income Poverty: Achievements and Failures," in Paul Sommers (ed.), *Welfare Reform in America,* Kluwer-Nijhoff, Boston and The Hague, 1982, pp. 31–52.

Danziger, Sheldon H., and Daniel H. Weinberg, *Fighting Poverty,* Harvard University Press, Cambridge, Mass., 1986.

Deaton, Angus S., and John Muellbauer, *Economics and Consumer Behavior,* Cambridge University Press, Cambridge, 1980.

Dooley, Martin, and Peter Gottschalk, "Earnings Inequality Among Males in the United States: Trends and the Effect of Labor Force Growth," *Journal of Political Economy,* Vol. 92, No. 1, February 1984, pp. 59–89.

———, "The Increasing Proportion of Men with Low Earnings in the United States," *Demography,* Vol. 22, No. 1, February 1985, pp. 25–34.

Duncan, Greg, *Years of Poverty, Years of Plenty,* University of Michigan Press, Ann Arbor, 1984.

———, and Saul D. Hoffman, "The Use and Effects of Welfare: A Survey of Recent Evidence," *Social Service Review,* forthcoming.

Duncan, Otis, David Featherman, and Beverly Duncan, *Socioeconomic Background and Achievement,* Seminar Press, 1972.

Ellwood, David, and Lawrence Summers, "Poverty in America: Is Welfare the Answer or the Problem?" in Sheldon H. Danziger and Daniel H. Weinberg (eds.), *Fighting Poverty,* 1986, pp. 78–105.

Fisher, F. M., "Household Equivalence Scales and Interpersonal Comparisons," *Review of Economic Studies,* Vol. 54, 1987, pp. 519–524.

Foster, J., and A. F. Shorrocks, "Poverty Orderings," *Econometrica,* Vol. 56, 1988, pp. 173–177.

Freeman, Richard, and Brian Hall, "Permanent Homelessness in America?" *Population Research Policy Review,* Vol. 6, 1987, pp. 3–27.

———, and David A. Wise (eds.), "The Youth Labor Market Problem: Its Nature, Causes and Consequences," NBER Conference Report, University of Chicago Press, Chicago, 1982.

Friedman, Milton, *A Theory of the Consumption Function,* Princeton University Press for the National Bureau of Economic Research, Princeton, N.J., 1957.

Fuchs, Victor, "Redefining Poverty and Redistributing Income," *The Public Interest,* Vol. 8, Summer 1967, pp. 88–95.

van der Gaag, Jacques, and Eugene Smolensky, "True Household Equivalence Scales and Characteristics of the Poor in the United States," *Review of Income and Wealth,* Vol. 28, No. 1, March 1982, pp. 17–28.

Garfinkel, Irwin, and Robert Haveman, *Earnings Capacity, Poverty, and Inequality,* Academic Press, New York, 1977.

Glazer, Nathan, "Education and Training Programs and Poverty," in H. Sheldon Danziger and Daniel H. Weinberg (eds.), *Fighting Poverty,* 1986, pp. 152–173.

Gottschalk, Peter, and Sheldon Danziger, "Macroeconomic Conditions, Income Transfers, and the Trend in Poverty," in D. Lee Bawden (ed.), *The Social Contract Revisited,* Urban Institute Press, Washington, D.C., 1984, pp. 185–215.

———, "A Framework for Evaluating the Effects of Economic Growth and Transfers on Poverty," *American Economic Review,* Vol. 75, No. 1, March 1985, pp. 153–161.

Gramlich, Edward M., "The Distributional Effects of Higher Unemployment," *Brookings Papers on Economic Activity,* Vol. 2, 1974, pp. 293–336.

Hagenaars, Aldi J. M., *The Perception of Poverty,* North-Holland Publishing Co., Amsterdam, 1986.

———, and Bernard M. S. van Praag, "A Synthesis of Poverty Line Definitions," *Review of Income and Wealth,* Series 31, No. 2, June 1985, pp. 139–154.

———, and Klaas de Vos, "The Definition and Measurement of Poverty," *Journal of Human Resources,* Vol. 23, No. 2, 1988, pp. 211–221.

Harrington, Michael, *The Other America,* Macmillan, New York, 1962.

Harrison, Bennett, and Barry Bluestone, *The Great U-Turn: Corporate Restructuring and the Polarization of America,* Basic Books, New York, forthcoming.

Harrison, Bennett, Chris Tilly, and Barry Bluestone, "Wage Inequality Takes a Great U-Turn," *Challenge,* March-April 1986, pp. 26–32.

Haveman, Robert (ed.), *A Decade of Federal Anti-Poverty Programs: Achievements, Failures, and Lessons,* Academic Press, New York, 1977.

Haveman, Robert, *Poverty Policy and Poverty Research: The Great Society and the Social Sciences,* University of Wisconsin Press, Madison, Wis., 1987.

Henle, Peter, and Paul Ryscavage, "The Distribution of Earned Income Among Men and Women, 1958–77," *Monthly Labor Review,* Vol. 103, No. 4, April 1980, pp. 3–10.

Hill, Martha S., "Some Dynamic Aspects of Poverty," in Martha S. Hill, Daniel H. Hill, and James N. Morgan (eds.), *Five Thousand American Families: Patterns of Economic Progress,* Vol. IX, Institute for Social Research, Ann Arbor, Michigan, 1981, pp. 93–120.

Hirsch, Barry, "Poverty and Economic Growth: Has Trickle Down Petered Out?" *Economic Inquiry,* Vol. 18, No. 1, January 1980, pp. 151–158.

Hoagland, William, "The Effectiveness of Current Transfer Programs in Reducing Poverty," in Paul Summers (ed.), *Welfare Reform in America,* Kluwer-Nijhoff, Boston and The Hague, 1982, pp. 53–75.

Jencks, Christopher (ed.), *Inequality,* Basic Books, New York, 1972.

Lampman, Robert, *Ends and Means of Reducing Income Poverty,* Academic Press, New York, 1971.

———, *Social Welfare Spending: Accounting for Changes from 1950 to 1978,* Academic Press, New York, 1984.

———, and Timothy Smeeding, "Inter-family Transfers as Alternatives to Government Transfers to Persons," *Review of Income Wealth,* Vol. 29, No. 1, March 1983, pp. 45–66.

Lazear, Edward, and Robert Michael, "Family Size and the Distribution of Real Per Capita Income," *American Economic Review,* Vol. 70, No. 1, March 1980, pp. 91–107.

Mayer, Susan E., "Living Conditions Among the Poor in Four Rich Countries," *Journal of Population Economics,* Vol. 6, 1993, pp. 261–286.

———, and Christopher Jencks, "Recent Trends in Economic Inequality in the United States: Income versus Expenditures versus Material Wellbeing," in Dimitri B. Papadimitriou and Edward N. Wolff (eds.), *Poverty and Prosperity in the USA in the Late Twentieth Century,* Macmillan Publishers, London, 1993.

McMahon, Patrick J., and John H. Tschetter, "The Declining Middle Class: A Further Analysis," *Monthly Labor Review,* Vol. 109, No. 9, September 1986, pp. 22–27.

Metcalf, Charles, "The Size Distribution of Personal Income During the Business Cycle," *American Economic Review,* Vol. 59, No. 4, September 1969, pp. 657–668.

Minarik, Joseph, "The Size Distribution of Income During Inflation," *Review of Income and Wealth,* Vol. 25, No. 4, December 1979, pp. 377–392.

Mirer, Thad, "The Effects of Macroeconomic Fluctuations on the Distribution of Income," *Review of Income and Wealth,* Vol. 19, No. 4, December 1973, pp. 385–406.

Moon, Marilyn (ed.), *The Measurement of Economic Welfare: Applications to the Aged,* Academic Press, New York, 1977.

Murray, Charles, *Losing Ground: American Social Policy, 1950–1980,* Basic Books, New York, 1984.

Orshansky, Mollie, "Counting the Poor: Another Look at the Poverty Profile," *Social Security Bulletin,* January 1965, Vol. 28, No. 1, pp. 3–29.

Patterson, James, *America's Struggle Against Poverty, 1900–1980,* Harvard University Press, Cambridge, Mass., 1981.

Pechman, Joseph, *Who Paid the Taxes, 1966–1985?* Brookings Institution, Washington, D.C., 1985.

Plant, Mark, "An Empirical Analysis of Welfare Dependence," *American Economic Review,* Vol. 74, No. 4, September 1984, pp. 673–684.

Plotnick, Robert, "Social Welfare Expenditures: How Much Help for the Poor?" *Policy Analysis,* Vol. 5, No. 3, Summer 1979, pp. 271–289.

———, "The Redistributive Impact of Cash Transfers," *Public Finance Quarterly,* Vol. 12, No. 1, January 1984, pp. 27–50.

———, and Felicity Skidmore, *Progress Against Poverty: A Review of the 1964–1974 Decade,* Academic Press, New York, 1975.

Pollak, Robert A., and J. Wales Terrence, "Welfare Comparisons and Equivalence Scales," *American Economic Review,* Vol. 69, No. 2, May 1979, pp. 216–221.

Ravallion, Martin, Gaurav Datt, and Dominique van de Walle, "Quantifying Absolute Poverty in the Developing World," *Review of Income and Wealth,* Series 37, No. 4, December 1991, pp. 345–361.

Reynolds, Morgan, and Eugene Smolensky, *Public Expenditures, Taxes and the Distribution of Income: The United States, 1950, 1961, 1970,* Academic Press, New York, 1977.

Ricketts, Erol R., and Ronald B. Mincy, "Growth of the Underclass, 1970–80," *Journal of Human Resources,* Vol. 25, No. 1, Winter 1990, pp. 137–145.

Rodgers, Joan R., and John L. Rodgers, "Chronic Poverty in the United States," *Journal of Human Resources,* Vol. 28, No. 1, Winter 1993, pp. 25–54.

Ruggles, Patricia, *Drawing the Line,* Urban Institute Press, Washington, D.C., 1990.

Sawhill, Isabel V., "Poverty in the United States: Why Is It So Persistent?" *Journal of Economic Literature,* Vol. 26, No. 3, September 1988, pp. 1073–1119.

Seidl, C., "Poverty Measurement: A Survey," in D. Bos, M. Rose, and C. Seidl (eds.), *Welfare and Efficiency in Public Economics,* Springer-Verlag, Heidelberg, 1988.

Sen, Amartya, "Poverty: An Ordinal Approach to Measurement," *Econometrica,* Vol. 44, No. 2, March 1976, pp. 219–232.

Sen, A., "Issues in the Measurement of Poverty," *Scandinavian Journal of Economics,* 1979, pp. 285–307.

Slesnick, Daniel T., "Gaining Ground: Poverty in the Postwar United States," *Journal of Political Economy,* Vol. 101, No. 1, 1993, pp. 1–38.

Smeeding, Timothy, "Alternative Methods for Valuing Selected In-Kind Benefits and Measuring Their Effect on Poverty," U.S. Bureau of the Census Technical Paper 50, U.S. Government Printing Office, Washington, D.C., 1982.

———, "The Antipoverty Effectiveness of In-Kind Transfers," *Journal of Human Resources,* Vol. 127, No. 3, Summer 1977, pp. 360–378.

———, and Marilyn Moon, "Valuing Government Expenditures: The Case of Medical Care Transfers and Poverty," *Review of Income and Wealth,* Series 26, No. 3, September 1980, pp. 305–324.

———, Lee Rainwater, Martin Rein, Richard Hauser and Gaston Schaber, "Income Poverty in Seven Countries: Initial Estimates from the LIS Database," in T. M. Smeeding, M. O'Higgins, and L. Rainwater (eds.), *Poverty, Inequality and Income Distribution in Comparative Perspective,* 1985.

Stevens, Ann Huff, "The Dynamics of Poverty Spells: Updating Bane and Ellwood," *American Economic Review Papers and Proceedings,* Vol. 84, No. 2, May 1994, pp. 34–37.

Taubman, Paul, *Income Distribution and Redistribution,* Addison-Wesley, Reading, Mass., 1978.

Thornton, James, Richard Agnello, and Charles Link, "Poverty and Economic Growth: Trickle Down Peters Out," *Economic Inquiry,* Vol. 16, No. 3, July 1978, pp. 385–394.

Thurow, Lester, *Generating Inequality: Mechanism of Distribution in the U.S. Economy,* Basic Books, New York, 1975.

Watts, Harold, "Have Our Measures of Poverty Become Poorer?" *Focus Institute for Research on Poverty,* Vol. 9, No. 2, Summer 1986, pp. 18–23.

Weinberg, Daniel, "Filling the 'Poverty Gap': Multiple Transfer Program Participation," *Journal of Human Resources,* Vol. 20, No. 1, Winter 1985, pp. 64–89.

———, "Filling the 'Poverty Gap,' 1979–1984: Multiple Transfer Program Participation," *Journal of Human Resources,* Vol. 22, No. 4, 1987, pp. 563–573.

Weisbrod, Burton A., and Lee W. Hansen, "An Income-Net Worth Approach to Measuring Economic Welfare," *American Economic Review,* Vol. 58, No. 5, December 1968, pp. 1315–1329.

Wilson, William Julius, *The Truly Disadvantaged: The Inner City, the Underclass, and Public Policy,* University of Chicago Press, Chicago, Ill., 1987.

———, and Kathryn Neckerman, "Poverty and Family Structure: The Widening Gap Between Evidence and Public Policy Issues," in Sheldon H. Danziger and Daniel H. Weinberg (eds.), *Fighting Poverty,* 1986, pp. 232–259.

Wolff, Edward N., "Wealth Holdings and Poverty Status in the U.S.," *Review of Income and Wealth,* Series 36, No. 2, June 1990, pp. 143–165.

Poverty Statistics

U.S. Bureau of the Census, *Characteristics of the Population Below the Poverty Level: 1980,* Current Population Reports, Series P-60, No. 133, U.S. Government Printing Office, Washington, D.C., 1982.

U.S. Bureau of the Census, *Estimates of Poverty Including the Value of Noncash Benefits: 1986*, Technical Paper 57, U.S. Government Printing Office, Washington, D.C., 1987.

U.S. Bureau of the Census, *Money Income and Poverty Status of Families and Persons in the United States, 1986*, Current Population Reports, Series P-60, No. 157, U.S. Government Printing Office, Washington, D.C., 1987.

U.S. Bureau of the Census, Current Population Reports, Series P-60, No. 166, *Money Income and Poverty Status in the United States*, U.S. Government Printing Office, Washington, D.C., various years.

U.S. Bureau of the Census, Current Population Reports, Series P-60, No. 169-RD, *Measuring the Effect of Benefits and Taxes on Income and Poverty: 1989*, U.S. Government Printing Office, Washington, D.C., various years.

U.S. Bureau of the Census, Current Population Reports, Series P-60–188, *Income, Poverty, and Valuation of Noncash Benefits: 1993*, U.S. Government Printing Office, Washington, D.C., February 1995.

DISCUSSION QUESTIONS

1. Discuss in what sense a subjective poverty line represents a "compromise" between an absolute and relative poverty standard.
2. Define the poverty gap ratio and the head count measure of poverty. What are the advantages and disadvantages of each?
3. Explain the apparent paradox that only a small percentage of individuals entering poverty will remain poor for a long period of time, yet about half of the poor at a given point in time are in the midst of a long spell of poverty.
4. Explain why a monthly poverty index would yield a higher average poverty rate over the course of a year than the official measure based on annual income.
5. What is the difference between market value and recipient value in evaluating noncash government benefits as part of family income?
6. Why does a consumption-based measure of poverty give a lower estimate of the overall poverty rate than one based on income?

THE ROLE OF
LABOR MARKETS

PART II

5

THE LABOR FORCE, EMPLOYMENT, AND UNEMPLOYMENT

One of the principal objectives of this book is to develop explanations as to why incomes differ among families and individuals. As we saw in Chapter 2, labor earnings have accounted for between 60 and 70 percent of personal income in the United States since the end of World War II. Much variation in family income derives from differences in pay. We are thus left with the question of why workers earn different amounts.

Part II of the book focuses on the role of the labor market in the determination of relative earnings. We approach this issue in stages. Before analyzing the determinants of wages and salaries, it is first necessary to consider the issue of who works and who does not. We begin, in Chapter 5, with the definitions of the labor force, employment, and unemployment. We also discuss trends in labor force participation patterns, the composition of employment, and the incidence of unemployment. Alternative explanations of unemployment are also considered in this chapter.

Chapter 6 develops the standard neoclassical model of wages, which establishes that in competitive equilibrium, workers are paid their marginal value product. The human capital model is also introduced in this chapter. This model treats schooling and training as investment decisions and leads to the conclusion that both factors will have a positive effect on wages. One implication is that differences in schooling and training will lead to differences in earnings and play an important role in accounting for inequality of income among families.

Chapter 7 surveys empirical work on the relation between schooling, experience, and earnings. Since training is hard to measure directly, years of worker experience are usually used as a "proxy" for training under the assumption that more experienced workers will, in general, have more training than less experienced ones. Empirical studies confirm that both schooling and experience are highly significant determinants of earnings. Returns to a college education, in particular, are highlighted and are found to be quite high. However, there are other reasons why schooling in general and a college education in particular might increase wages, and these other interpretations of the schooling-earnings relation, such as job screening, are also considered in this chapter.

Institutional factors also affect earnings, and these are treated in the next two chapters. Chapter 8 considers the effect of unions on labor earnings. Evidence is presented which indicates that union workers are paid more than comparable nonunion labor but that this differential has changed over time. Union membership rates have declined dramatically since the early 1950s, and this process may have contributed to falling real wages and rising inequality. This chapter also investigates the role of labor market segmentation on differences in earnings. The labor market is far from uniform and is often divided into noncompeting segments. Moreover, separate labor markets may exist within a large organization (internal labor markets). As a result, there may be little pressure for equalization of wages across such institutional boundaries, and wage differences for workers of equal skill may persist over time.

In Chapter 9, we look at the role of industrial structure in the inequality of earnings. Labor economists have noted for many years the peculiarity that workers of otherwise identical skill are often paid very different wages in different industries. These differentials tend to persist over time. We will consider several reasons that have been advanced for this finding, including: (1) degree of competition within an industry, (2) differences of industry profitability, and (3) differences in the ability to monitor or control workers (efficiency wage theory). One implication is that the industrial composition (that is, the distribution of employment among industries) of a region or country may bear directly on its average wages and its inequality of earnings.

This chapter lays out the basic groundwork for understanding changes in the composition of the labor force. Though the chapter is mainly factual in basis, it has clear connections with the major themes of the book—income inequality, poverty, and discrimination. Wherever possible, we will indicate the relation between labor force changes and the determinants of family income and poverty.

Section 5.1 introduces the concepts of the labor force, employment, and unemployment. Section 5.2 shows historical trends in labor force participation rates and rather dramatic changes in the demographic makeup of the labor force. Section 5.3 documents equally dramatic shifts in both the industrial and occupational composition of employment.

Section 5.4 presents historical trends on the unemployment rate and average duration of unemployment. Distinctions are made according to the reasons for unemployment, and some consideration is given to the "discouraged worker effect," as well as the relation between the unemployment rate and the vacancy rate. Section 5.5 documents considerable variation in the incidence of unemployment among age, gender, and racial groups, as well as by geographic region and occupation and industry of employment.

In Section 5.6, we discuss causes of unemployment. Four principal factors have been cited in the literature. The first, frictional unemployment, is ascribed to the lack of perfect information on job openings and the consequent search time required to find a new position. The second, seasonal unemployment, characterizes certain industries, like agriculture and tourism, where employment occurs on an irregular basis. The third, structural unemployment, refers to an imbalance between job vacancies by skill type and the qualifications of individuals looking for work. The fourth, demand-deficient unemployment, arises when the aggregate demand for output is not sufficient to absorb the full labor force in production.

The last section presents a summary of the chapter.

5.1 BASIC CONCEPTS OF THE LABOR FORCE, EMPLOYMENT, AND UNEMPLOYMENT

The population can be divided into two groups—those in the **labor force** and those not in the labor force. The former, in turn, can be subdivided into those at work or **employed** and the rest who are without a job or **unemployed**:

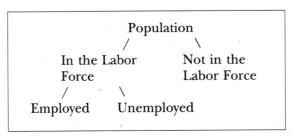

In the United States, the Bureau of Labor Statistics (BLS) of the Department of Labor is legally empowered to estimate and publish both the size of the labor force and the unemployment rate each month. It is instructive to consider the definitions it uses for these concepts.

Employment

The BLS definition of employment includes not only individuals with a paid job who are working for someone else but also self-employed individuals working in their own business, profession, or farm, and unpaid family members working in a family business 15 hours or more per week. Homemakers and those engaged in volunteer work for a religious or charitable organization are not counted as employed.

In computing **total employment,** BLS counts each employed person only once. Those individuals who hold more than one job are counted only in the job in which they work the most hours. It should be noted that total employment will, in general, differ from the total number of jobs in an economy. The former is a count of persons, while the latter is a count of the number of positions in the economy.

Unemployment

A person is considered unemployed if he or she did not work during a given week but was both available for and actively looking for work. An individual who made a specific effort to find work within the preceding four-week period, such as by registering at a public or private employment agency, writing application letters, and canvassing for work, is considered to be looking for work. BLS also defines a person as unemployed who has been temporarily laid off from a job and is waiting to be recalled or who is scheduled to start a new job soon.

BLS divides the unemployed into four categories depending on the reason for being unemployed.

1. A person is a **job loser** if employment ended involuntarily because of firing or layoff and the search for a new job begins immediately.
2. A person is a **job leaver** if the person quits or otherwise voluntarily terminates employment and begins to look for a new job immediately.
3. A person is a **re-entrant** if the person previously worked at a full-time job and was out of the labor force prior to looking for a new job.
4. A person is a **new entrant** if the person never worked at a full-time job.

The Labor Force

The "civilian" labor force is defined as the total of all civilians classified as either employed or unemployed. The "total" labor force includes, in addition, all members of the Armed Forces stationed either in the United States or abroad. The **unemployment rate** is defined as the ratio of the number of unemployed individuals to the number of individuals in the civilian labor force.

BLS divides all individuals 16 years of age or older who are not in the labor force into five categories: (1) engaged in housework, (2) in school, (3) unable to work because of long-term physical or mental illness, (4) retired, and (5) other. The last group includes so-called "discouraged workers," individuals who have essentially given up looking for work, because they believe that no jobs are available to them due to a lack of training or education or due to prevailing job market conditions. Some economists have argued that the unemployment count should include discouraged workers, since they would work if suitable jobs were available. As a result, the "true" unemployment rate may be considerably higher than the official unemployment rate.

Economists have raised several other concerns as well. First, both part-time and full-time workers are counted as employed workers. Yet, some part-time workers might be willing to work full-time if the opportunity arose and are therefore, in a sense, unemployed, or at least underemployed. A second issue is the asymmetric treatment of housemakers and domestic servants. The former are classified as "not in the labor force," while the latter are classified as employed workers. Yet, both perform the same type of "work"—the only difference is that the latter are paid for it (by someone else) while the former are not.[1] A third issue is the treatment of students, who, it is true, do not perform paid labor, yet are engaged in an activity that may presumably increase their future productivity. By this interpretation, students can be considered as engaged in an investment activity, and their time should be considered as work.[2]

Estimating Employment Statistics

The BLS is charged with the task of publishing monthly statistics on employment and unemployment. The data are based on the Current Population Survey (CPS), which is conducted for the BLS by the Bureau of the Census. The monthly survey is based on a scientifically selected sample of households, which is representative of the civilian noninstitutional population of the United States.

A brief history of the development of these statistics might prove illuminating. Before the 1930s, no official measurements were provided of unemployment. During the Great Depression, unemployment became a major and visible national problem, and this spurred the development of statistics to measure unemployment. During the early 1930s, estimates of the unemployment rate began to appear on the basis of a wide assortment of indirect techniques, but these estimates showed wide discrepancies. As a result, many research groups as well as the government started experimenting with direct survey techniques to measure the labor force, employment, and unemployment. In these surveys, individuals were asked a series of questions in order to classify them by labor force or employment status. In most of these attempts, unemployment was defined as the number of individuals who were not working but were "willing and able to work." However, this concept of

---

[1]Also, as a result, the income of domestic servants is counted in GDP, while the work performed by housewives is not. This leads to the further anomaly that if every pair of housewives could arrange to pay each other a "salary" while continuing to perform the same work, the level of GDP would increase while the amount of work actually performed would remain unchanged. See Section 2.5 for estimates of household production.

[2]See Section 6.2 for further discussion in the context of human capital theory.

unemployment was unsatisfactory and vague, since it appeared to depend heavily on the attitudes and interpretation of the individuals who were interviewed.

By the late 1930s, a more exact set of concepts of the labor force, employment, and unemployment was developed to make the measurement more objective. By these new criteria, an individual's classification was to depend on the actual activity in which he or she was engaged during the survey period—that is, on whether the person was working, actively looking for work, or involved in some other activity. The conventions were adopted by the Works Progress Administration (WPA) in 1940 for the first national sample survey of households. The original survey was called the Monthly Report on Unemployment and was administered by the WPA until 1943, when it was turned over to the Bureau of the Census. In 1943, the name of the survey changed to the Monthly Report on the Labor Force, and in 1948 it changed to its present name, the Current Population Survey (CPS). In 1959, the responsibility for analyzing and publishing the CPS employment statistics was transferred to the BLS, although the Census Bureau continues to administer the survey.

The CPS provides statistics on the civilian noninstitutional population who are 16 years of age or older. In addition to labor force statistics, the CPS also provides information on demographic, social, and economic characteristics of the population. The CPS is based on a monthly probability sample, which originally consisted of 47,000 households and in 1975 was expanded to 58,000 households. The time period covered in each monthly survey is a calendar week. The sample is designed to cover all states, which allows labor force statistics to be developed by state. In addition, the sample is designed to allow sufficient coverage of the largest 146 metropolitan areas (SMSAs), and labor force statistics are also published individually for each of these SMSAs. Besides total employment, unemployment, and the labor force, the CPS also provides a wealth of monthly statistics on hours worked, earnings, the composition of the labor force, and the composition of the population.

5.2 Labor Force Participation Rates

The labor force participation rate, or **LFPR,** is defined as the proportion of a particular population group that is in the labor force. In the aggregate, this concept is of limited interest, since the full population includes many groups who are not expected to work, such as children, the disabled, and the elderly. The usual participation rate statistics are those which show the labor force as a percent of the civilian noninstitutional population 16 years of age or older,[3] since it is from this population that the labor force is drawn. Generally speaking, the LFPR indicates the proportion of the population in the labor force that could be at work. Moreover, labor force participation is

---

[3]Until 1947, the relevant age group was those 14 years of age or older, but because of the change in child labor laws, the age bracket was raised to those 16 or older at that time.

often disaggregated into smaller population groups, such as gender, race, age, or education.

LFPR by Gender, Race, and Age

Table 5.1 and Figure 5.1 show historical trends of both the size of the labor force and the labor force participation rate since 1900. Between 1900 and 1993, the civilian labor force grew from 28.5 million to 128.0 million workers, or by a factor of 5.5. The labor force doubled in size between 1900 and 1941 and then doubled again between 1941 and 1985.

Over the same period, the overall LFPR also increased, from 56 to 66 percent. It remained virtually unchanged from 1900 to 1941, the start of American involvement in World War II. During the war years, the LFPR increased to 63 percent and then fell to 57 percent in 1946. After 1946, there was a gradual upward trend in the LFPR.

Beginning in 1948, it is possible to identify separately the trends in LFPR by gender. In 1948, the LFPR for males was 87 percent, and for females 33 percent. Between 1948 and 1993, there was an almost steady drop in the LFPR of males, from 87 to 75 percent. For females, the trend was exactly the opposite, increasing almost steadily from 33 to 58 percent. The

Table 5.1   The Civilian Labor Force and Labor Force Participation Rates, 1900–1993[a]

Year	Labor Force (in millions)[b]	Participation Rates (in percent)[c]		
		All	Male	Female
1900	28.5	55.5		
1910	36.9	57.4		
1920	41.7	55.6		
1930	48.8	55.0		
1940	56.2	56.0		
1950	62.2	59.2	86.4	33.9
1960	69.6	59.4	83.3	37.7
1970	82.8	60.4	79.7	43.3
1980	106.9	63.8	77.4	51.5
1993	128.0	66.2	75.2	57.9

[a]Sources: U.S. Department of Commerce, Bureau of the Census, *Historical Statistics of the United States: Colonial Times to 1970*, Bicentennial Edition, Part 1, Washington, D.C., 1975; Council of Economic Advisers, *Economic Report of the President, 1994.*
[b]Before 1948, the data refer to all members of the labor force 14 years of age or older; and for 1948 and after, to all labor force members 16 years or older.
[c]Before 1948, the participation rate is defined as the ratio of the civilian labor force to the civilian noninstitutional population 14 years of age or older; and for 1948 and after, it refers to the same ratio for those 16 years of age or older.

Figure 5.1 Labor Force Participation Rates (Overall and by Gender), 1900–1994

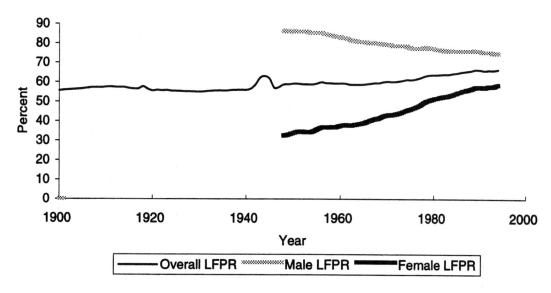

increase in the aggregate LFPR in the postwar period was thus due to the increasing labor force participation of females, dominating the declining rate for males. In 1948, females accounted for 27 percent of the labor force, in 1977 for 41 percent, and in 1993 for 46 percent.

The top of Table 5.2 presents some detail on the age distribution of the labor force. In 1950, 19 percent of the labor force was under the age of 25. By 1977, the figure had risen to 24 percent, but in 1994, the figure was under 17 percent. The percentage of the labor force in the prime working ages of 25 to 54 fell from 64 in 1950 to 61 in 1977 but then increased to 72 percent in 1994. These two trends largely reflect the progression of the "baby boomers," first as new entrants into the labor force during the 1970s and then as middle-aged workers in the 1980s. During the 1980s, the number of new entrants, members of the "baby dearth generation," fell sharply.

Older workers declined rather steadily as a share of the labor force. The proportion in age group 55–64 fell from 12 percent in 1950 to 9 percent in 1994, and the proportion 65 years of age or older fell from 4.9 to 2.9 percent. This trend was largely a consequence, as we shall see in Chapter 15, of improved social security and other retirement benefits.

There were also important changes in the racial and gender makeup of the labor force. White males, who constituted 63 percent of the labor force in 1954, fell to about half in 1985 and to 48 percent in 1994. Black males comprised a fairly constant 6 to 7 percent of the labor force. White females, in contrast, increased their representation in the labor force, from 27 per-

Table 5.2 Percentage Composition of the Labor Force by Age, Gender, and Race, 1950–1994[a]

	Year			
	1950	1970	1988	1994
Age Class				
Under 25	18.5	21.6	18.5	16.5
25–54	64.3	61.0	69.1	71.6
55–64	12.3	13.6	9.7	8.9
65+	4.9	3.9	2.7	2.9
Total	100.0	100.0	100.0	100.0
Race and Gender Group				
White Males	62.5[b]	55.6	47.9	48.3
Black Males	6.6[b]	6.3	6.5	5.6
White Females	26.8[b]	33.3	39.2	40.1
Black Females	4.1[b]	4.9	6.4	5.9
Total	100.0	100.0	100.0	100.0

[a] Sources: Bureau of Labor Statistics, *Handbook of Labor Statistics, 1989,* 1990, Bulletin 2340; and Bureau of Labor Statistics, *Employment and Earnings,* January 1995.
[b] 1954.

cent in 1954 to 40 percent in 1994, and black females also increased as a share of the labor force from 4.1 percent in 1954 to 5.9 percent in 1994.

Table 5.3, along with Figures 5.2 and 5.3, provides additional highlights of some of the important changes in the demographic makeup of the labor force. In this table, labor force participation rates (LFPR) are recorded separately by age group, gender, and race in 1954 and 1994. There are striking differences in the LFPR among white males in different age groups. In 1954, about half of 16–17 year-old white males were in the labor force, about 70 percent in the 18–19 age bracket, over 95 percent in the 25–54 age bracket, close to 90 percent in the 55–64 age group, and 40 percent of the elderly.

Between 1954 and 1994, the LFPR of white male teenagers showed little change, while the LFPR of prime-age (25 to 54) white males showed a slight decline. The biggest change occurred for older men. Among white males aged 55 to 64, the participation rate began to decline in the early 1960s and dropped almost steadily from 88 percent in 1961 to 66 percent in 1994. This decline is attributable to the increase in social security and pension benefits available for early retirement. There was also an almost continuous drop in the LFPR of white males 65 and over, from 48 percent in 1947 to 17 percent in 1994. This is likewise a consequence of the continual improvement in retirement benefits over this period.

Table 5.3   Civilian Labor Force Participation Rates by Age, Gender, and Race Groups, 1954 and 1994[a]

| | White Males | | Nonwhite Males | | | White Females | | Nonwhite Females | | |
| | | | Both | Black | Hisp. | | | Both | Black | Hisp. |
Age Group	1954	1994	1954	1994	1994	1954	1994	1954	1994	1994
16–17	47.1	47.8	46.7	30.1	34.5	29.3	46.1	24.5	29.9	28.5
18–19	70.5	68.1	78.4	53.2	66.1	52.1	64.3	37.7	43.2	48.1
20–24	86.3	85.5	91.1	73.9	88.0	44.4	73.4	49.6	64.5	57.9
25–34	97.5	93.9	96.3	86.2	92.5	32.5	74.9	49.7	71.9	60.5
35–44	98.2	93.9	96.6	85.9	91.5	39.3	77.5	57.5	76.4	66.4
45–54	96.8	90.3	93.2	79.1	85.7	39.8	75.2	53.4	71.3	61.4
55–64	89.1	66.4	83.0	54.5	63.6	29.1	49.4	41.2	45.3	38.1
65 & older	40.4	17.2	41.2	12.7	14.4	9.1	9.2	12.2	9.2	7.9
Total	85.6	75.9	85.2	69.1	79.2	33.3	58.9	46.1	58.7	52.9

[a]Sources: Bureau of Labor Statistics, *Handbook of Labor Statistics 1989,* 1990, Bulletin 2340; Bureau of Labor Statistics, *Employment and Earnings,* January 1995; and worksheets provided by the Bureau of Labor Statistics.

The LFPR show the same pattern across age groups for nonwhite males, rising with age, peaking in the 25–54 age bracket, and then declining with age. However, historical trends differ between 1954 and 1977. Overall, the LFPR of nonwhite males dropped from 85 percent in 1954 to 71 percent in 1977 and then declined slightly more to 69 percent among black males in 1994. The decline in the LFPR of nonwhite teenagers was particularly marked, reflecting in part the increasing time spent in school. The drop in participation rates among prime-aged nonwhite males was also sharp. This change may, in part, be attributable to the discouraged worker effect—that is, the withdrawal from the labor force of individuals whose skills or schooling are insufficient to allow suitable employment.

Two other factors have been cited to explain the lower LFPR of nonwhite males relative to white males over the last two decades. The first is a higher incidence of disability among nonwhite males. The second is that a higher percentage of nonwhite males are single than white males, and participation rates tend to be lower among single men than among married men. It is also interesting to note that Hispanic males had about the same participation rates as white (non-Hispanic) males in 1994. We shall discuss differences in LFPR by race in more detail in Chapter 13.

The pattern of labor force participation by age group is considerably different for females than for males, and among white females there have been notable changes in the postwar period. Among white females, the labor force pattern of the 1950s was characterized by a peak participation rate

Figure 5.2 Male Labor Force Participation Rates by Age Group, 1947–1994

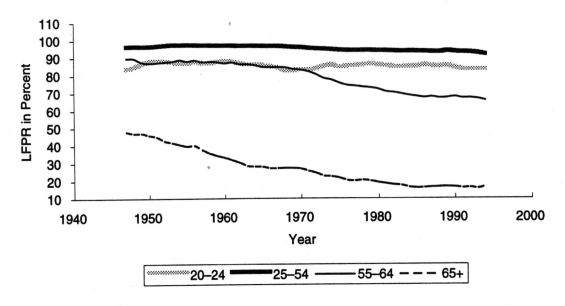

Figure 5.3 Female Labor Force Participation Rates by Age Group, 1947–1994

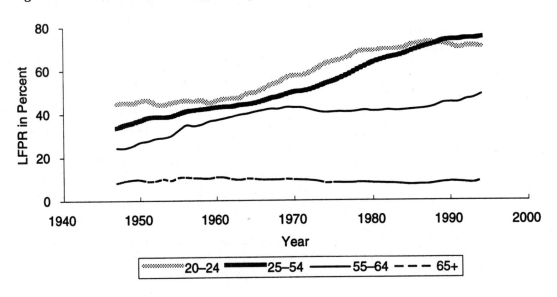

in the 18–19 year age bracket. The participation rate declined during the child-bearing years (ages 20–34), then increased during the child-rearing years (35–54), and then declined again after age 54. This pattern generally characterized white female labor force behavior until the early 1960s. After this point, there was a rapid acceleration in labor force participation among all age groups, though particularly among those in the child-bearing and child-rearing age groups. Overall, the LFPR of white females increased from 33 percent in 1954 to 59 percent in 1994. By 1994, participation rates for white females had a very similar structure to those of men, rising with age, peaking in the 35–44 age group, and then declining with age.

The major reasons for this change in labor force behavior are that a larger share of newly married women continued to work after marriage and that an increasing number of married women returned to work while their children were young. A number of explanations have been offered. The first is that the housewife's productivity in the home has been greatly amplified by the greater availability of home appliances, processed foods, and various outside services like child care, restaurants, and cleaning. As a result, much of the woman's time has been freed from housework, allowing more time for outside employment. A second reason is that there has been a secular decline in the average work week, and a shorter work week has allowed an increasing number of married women to hold a full-time or part-time job while working in the home.

A third factor is the trend toward smaller families, which began in the 1950s, and the resultant reduction in child-care responsibilities. A fourth reason is that traditional roles in American society, particularly those for females, have undergone a major transformation in the last 20 years, and as a result, it is more socially acceptable for married women to work. A fifth factor is that during the postwar period there has been a large increase in the demand for traditional female jobs, such as secretarial, teaching, nursing, and health care workers, coupled with rising real wages for these positions.

The labor force patterns of nonwhite females were considerably different from those of white females in 1954, and historical changes have been less pronounced. In 1954, the LFPR of nonwhite females by age group was similar to that of males, increasing with age, peaking in the 35–44 age bracket, and then declining with age. The overall LFPR for nonwhite females was 46 percent in 1954, compared to 33 percent for white females. Between 1954 and 1994, the LFPR rose from 46 percent for nonwhite females to 59 percent for black females (and 53 percent for Hispanic women). Upward trends characterized every age group, except 65 and over, but they were less pronounced for nonwhite females. By 1994, both the overall LFPR and the pattern of LFPR by age group were very similar among nonwhite and white females.

One seeming paradox is that despite the rising LFPR of women and the growing share of women in the labor force, women's wages have been catching up to those of men, particularly since 1970. Yet, this may not be as surprising as it appears, since one reason why more women are working is that their earnings have been rising. Another is that male wages have been declining in real terms since the early 1970s. We shall return to the topic of gender differences in earnings and LFPR in more detail in Chapter 14.

Two-Earner Households

As noted above, one of the most striking changes in labor force behavior in the postwar period has been the large increase in participation rates among married women. This trend is highlighted in Table 5.4, which shows the number of families with two or more wage earners. Between 1954 and 1993, the number of such families almost tripled, whereas the total number of families grew by 70 percent. As a result, the proportion of families with two or more earners increased from 44 to 64 percent.

Results are also shown for the number of families in which both the husband and wife worked. Between 1967 and 1987, their number grew by 55 percent, and the proportion of married couple families in which both husband and wife worked increased from 44 to 57 percent. By the 1980s, the "typical" married family was one in which both spouses were at work.

The growth in two-earner families helps to explain the apparent anomaly that while real wages have been declining since 1973, median family income has remained relatively constant, at least until 1989 (see Chapter 2

Table 5.4   Number of Families with Two or More Wage Earners, 1954–1993[a]

Year	All Two-Earner Families		Husband-Wife Earners	
	Number (1,000s)	Percent of Total Families	Number (1,000s)	Percent of Married Couple Families
1954	16,872	43.6		
1958	19,742	47.9		
1962	22,143	49.6		
1967	26,380	52.9	18,888	43.6
1972	28,706	53.0	21,279	45.7
1976	30,171	52.5	23,104	48.0
1979	32,949	55.0	25,595	52.1
1983	33,473	53.5	26,119	52.1
1987	37,085	56.5	29,369	56.6
1993	43,593	63.6		

[a] Sources: U.S. Bureau of the Census, Current Population Reports, Series P-60, Nos. 20, 24, 27, 30, 33, 35, 37, 39, 41, 43, 47, 51, 53, 59, 66, 75, 80, 85, 90, 97, 101, 105, 114, 118, 123.; U.S. Department of Labor, Bureau of Labor Statistics, *Handbook of Labor Statistics 1989*, 1990, Bulletin 2340; U.S. Bureau of the Census, *Income, Poverty, and Valuation of Noncash Benefits: 1993*, Series P60–168, February 1995.

for more details). The increased labor force participation of wives has helped compensate for the falling income of their husbands. Moreover, the increasing presence of working wives in the labor force is one factor explaining the widening disparities of family income since the 1970s, particularly between married couples and single men and women. According to data from the U.S. Census Bureau (provided on Internet), the median income of households with two earners was almost twice as great as those with only one earner in 1993 ($49,430 versus $25,560).

Educational Attainment of the Labor Force

Another striking trend is the increasing educational attainment of the labor force, as documented in Table 5.5. The median years of schooling of the entire labor force increased from 10.9 years in 1952, to 12.7 in 1982, and to 13.3 in 1994. In 1952, 38 percent of the labor force had not attended any high school, but by 1994, the proportion was only 4 percent. While 43 percent of workers had graduated high school in 1952, close to 90 percent of the labor force were high school graduates in 1992. In 1952, 16 percent of the labor force had attended some college, whereas over half did in 1994. By 1994, almost one-quarter of the labor force consisted of college graduates.

The gains in educational attainment were even more pronounced among nonwhite males than in the labor force as a whole. In 1952, their median level of schooling was 7.2 years. In 1962, it had risen to 9.0 years. By 1977, it was 12.1 years, and in 1984, the median was 12.4 years for black males and 12.0 for Hispanic males.[4] In 1952, only 32 percent of the nonwhite male labor force had more than an elementary school education, whereas in 1994, the figure had risen to 96 percent for black males. Only 15 percent of the nonwhite male labor force had graduated from high school in 1952, compared to 83 percent for black males in 1994. While only 5 percent had attended some college in 1952, 40 percent of black male workers completed at least one year of college in 1994, and 14 percent had graduated from college.

By 1994, the gap in educational attainment between black and white males had narrowed considerably. There are two reasons that explain this important development. The first is the greatly expanded educational opportunities provided to nonwhites that began with the 1954 Supreme Court decision to desegregate public schools. These opportunities continued with federal legislation during the 1960s, particularly the Civil Rights Act of 1964, which provided increasing access to educational institutions for nonwhites. The second is the "dropout" of many older, poorly educated black males from the labor force. The gains made by black men in educational performance is one principal reason why the gap in earnings between them and white men has narrowed over the postwar period. See Chapter 13 for more discussion of racial differences in earnings and educational attainment.

---

[4]More recent data for this series are not available.

Table 5.5 The Educational Attainment of the Labor Force, 1952–1994[a]
(in percent)

	Elem. School	H.S. 1–3	H.S. 4 Yrs.	Coll. 1–3	Coll. 4+	Total[b]	Median Years of Schooling
1. All Workers							
1952	37.5	18.5	26.6	8.3	7.9	100.0	10.9
1972	15.2	16.6	40.0	14.0	14.1	100.0	12.5
1994	4.0	8.8	34.7	29.3	23.3	100.0	13.3
2. White Males							
1952	38.2	18.9	24.6	8.4	8.5	100.0	10.8
1972	16.0	16.1	36.8	14.9	16.3	100.0	12.5
1994	4.9	9.2	33.4	26.4	26.1	100.0	—
3. Nonwhite Males							
1952	68.1	15.0	9.5	3.4	1.9	100.0	7.2
1972	29.0	24.0	30.0	8.8	8.1	100.0	11.6
1994: Blacks	4.0	12.8	43.4	25.9	13.9	100.0	—
4. White Females							
1952	26.3	18.4	36.9	9.6	8.3	100.0	12.1
1972	10.7	15.1	47.7	14.2	12.3	100.0	12.5
1994	2.9	7.7	35.1	31.0	23.4	100.0	—
5. Nonwhite Females							
1952	61.6	17.1	12.6	4.0	3.6	100.0	8.1
1972	19.8	24.2	37.2	10.5	8.3	100.0	12.2
1994: Blacks	2.1	10.8	38.6	32.5	16.0	100.0	—

[a] Sources: Bureau of Labor Statistics, *Handbook of Labor Statistics 1978,* 1979, Bulletin 2000; Bureau of Labor Statistics, *Handbook of Labor Statistics 1985,* 1986, Bulletin 2217; Bureau of Labor Statistics, *Handbook of Labor Statistics 1989,* 1990, Bulletin 2340; and worksheets provided by the Bureau of Labor Statistics.
[b] Includes workers with no schooling (not shown separately).

Historical trends for white females also differ from those for white males. The median level of schooling of white females in the labor force was already 12.1 in 1952, considerably higher than that for white males. However, schooling levels grew more slowly for white females in the labor force, and by 1984, median years of schooling were identical for the two groups, 12.8 years.

Here, one must be careful how to interpret these trends. The increase in educational attainment of the white male labor force reflects the growth in schooling levels of the white male population as a whole during this period. In contrast, trends in educational attainment of the white female labor force reflect both increases in the educational attainment of white women as a whole as well as changes in their labor force participation behavior. In 1952, the typical pattern among white females was to work for a number of years after graduating high school until marriage and then drop out of the labor force. Older women with less schooling had already left the labor force.

Between 1952 and 1994, the labor force participation rate among females of all age groups had increased considerably, and the educational composition of the white female labor force was more representative of the white female population as a whole. In particular, older women with less schooling either remained in the labor force or entered (reentered) the labor force during the 1970s and 1980s. The relatively slow increase in the schooling level of the white female labor force occurred because increases in educational attainment among white females as a whole were offset by a growing proportion of less educated white female laborers.

Trends in schooling among the nonwhite female labor force were similar to those of nonwhite males. The median years of schooling rose from 8.1 years in 1952 to 10.5 in 1962 and to 12.6 in 1984 for black females and 12.3 years for Hispanic females. By 1994, the gap in schooling levels between nonwhite and white females in the labor force had narrowed substantially. Gains in schooling among nonwhite females in the labor force are attributable to, first, greatly expanded educational opportunities for nonwhites, and, second, to the exit from the labor force of a large number of poorly educated nonwhite females.

5.3 THE INDUSTRIAL AND OCCUPATIONAL COMPOSITION OF EMPLOYMENT

The structure of employment in the United States has changed substantially since the end of World War II, and this is indicative of the changing nature of work and industrial activity in the U.S. economy. Table 5.6 shows the distribution of employment among industries over the period 1950 to 1993. One of the most dramatic changes has been in agriculture, which accounted for 14 percent of employment in 1950 and only 3 percent in 1993. This relative decline has been going on for at least the last 100 years. In 1929, for example, the fraction of total employment accounted for by agriculture was 22 percent. The proportion fell to 14 percent in 1947, 8 percent in 1960, and 4 percent in 1978. The major decline in employment in the agricultural sector was from the exodus of owners of small farms and their families.[5]

The share of employment in mining also declined between 1950 and 1993, from 1.7 to 0.5 percent, while the proportion of workers in construction remained roughly constant over the period, about 4 percent. Another

---

[5] Another implication of their exodus was that the proportion of self-employed workers (and also unpaid family members) in the labor force has fallen considerably since the turn of the century.

Table 5.6 Percentage Distribution of Employment by Major Industry, 1950, 1970, and 1993[a]

	1950	1970	1993
Agriculture	13.7	4.7	2.7
Mining	1.7	0.8	0.5
Construction	4.5	4.8	4.0
Manufacturing	29.1	26.1	15.7
Transportation and public utilities	7.7	6.1	5.0
Wholesale and retail trade	17.9	20.2	22.8
Finance, insurance, and real estate	3.6	4.9	5.8
Services	10.2	15.5	26.7
Government	11.5	16.9	16.6
Total	100.0	100.0	100.0

[a] Source: Council of Economic Advisers, *Economic Report of the President, 1994.*

major change occurred in manufacturing, whose share of total employment fell by almost half, from 29 percent in 1950 to 16 percent in 1993. In absolute terms, employment in manufacturing peaked in 1980 at 20.3 million workers and has since fallen to 17.8 million in 1993. Much discussion has recently ensued over this development, which has been labeled by some as the "deindustrialization" of America. However, it should be noted that much of the decline in employment in manufacturing is due to the high (labor) productivity growth of this sector. In fact, manufacturing accounted for almost the same share of total output in the early 1990s as it did in the early 1950s.[6] The share of employment in transport and public utilities also fell over this period, from 7.7 to 5.0 percent.

If the share of employment fell in agriculture, mining, manufacturing, and transport and utilities, where did it increase? The answer is the service sectors, which absorbed most of the growth of employment in the postwar period. The proportion of total employment in wholesale and retail trade increased from 18 to 23 percent. The percent in finance, insurance, and real estate increased from 3.6 to 5.8. The percent on government payrolls increased from 12 to 17, and the share in other services (personal and business) from 10 to 27 percent. In summary, two major developments characterized the postwar period. The first was the shrinking share of workers employed in agriculture and manufacturing, and the second was the shift of the work force out of goods-producing sectors and into services.

---

[6] If a sector's output share remains constant and its labor productivity growth is greater than average, then its share of total employment must, of consequence, fall. This mechanism is often referred to as the "unbalanced growth" effect. See Baumol, Blackman, and Wolff (1989), Chapter 6, for more discussion.

Another way of dividing up the labor force is by occupation. Occupations are indicative of the type of work a person does (accountants, teachers, truck drivers, laborers, etc.), while the industry classification is indicative of the type of product the worker produces. There is, of course, some correspondence between the occupation and industry categories. For example, some occupational groups like "farm laborers" are found only in certain industries (in this case, agriculture). However, other occupational categories, such as clerical workers, are found in a large number of industries, so that occupational trends in employment may differ from industrial trends.

Table 5.7 shows the occupational distribution of employment from 1900 to 1993. Some of the changes have been quite dramatic. Professional and technical workers doubled as a share of employment from 4.3 percent in 1900 to 8.6 percent in 1950, and they almost doubled again to 17.5 percent in 1993. Managers and administrators also increased substantially as a proportion of the work force, from 6 percent in 1900 to 13 percent in 1993. Clerical workers likewise showed a sharp increase in their share, from 3 to 16 percent. A much higher proportion of the labor force was also engaged as sales workers by 1993, with most of the increase apparently occurring

Table 5.7 The Percentage Distribution of Employment by Occupational Group, 1900–1993[a]

Occupational Group	1900	1950	1970	1993
Professional, Technical, and Kindred	4.3	8.6	13.8	17.5
Administrators and Managers except Farm	5.8	8.7	10.2	12.9
Clerical	3.0	12.3	17.4	15.6
Sales	4.5	7.0	6.1	11.9
Craft & Kindred	10.5	14.2	12.8	11.2
Operatives	12.8	20.4	18.2	10.4
Laborers, Nonfarm	12.5	6.6	5.0	3.9
Private Household	5.4	2.6	2.0	0.8
Service except Private Household	3.6	7.8	10.5	13.1
Farmers & Farm Managers	20.0	7.4	2.1	] 2.8
Farm Laborers	17.8	4.4	1.8	
Total	100.0	100.0	100.0	100.0

[a] Sources: U.S. Department of Commerce, Bureau of the Census, *Historical Statistics of the U.S.: Colonial Times to 1970*, Bicentennial Edition, Part 2, Washington, D.C., 1978; Bureau of Labor Statistics, *Handbook of Labor Statistics 1978*, 1979, Bulletin 2000; and U.S. Bureau of the Census, *Statistical Abstract of the United States, 1994.*

during the 1980s.[7] The other major increase occurred for service workers (excluding private household workers), whose share rose from 4 percent in 1900 to 13 percent in 1993.

The proportion of the labor force employed as craftsmen and operatives (that is, machine and transportation operators) remained more or less constant over the years from 1900 to 1993. The other occupational categories all declined substantially as a share of employment. Nonfarm laborers (that is, unskilled workers except those employed on the farm) fell from 13 percent of employment to 4 percent. Domestic servants and other household workers declined as a proportion of the employed labor force from 5 percent in 1900 to only 1 percent in 1993. Finally, farmers, farm managers, and farm laborers fell from 38 percent of total employment in 1900 to only 3 percent in 1993. In sum, the twentieth century witnessed a huge reduction in the share of unskilled and farm labor as a share of total employment and a corresponding increase in the share of white-collar workers, including professional, managerial, clerical, and sales workers.

Changes in the occupational composition of the labor force are connected to shifts in the industrial pattern of employment. The relative decline of employment in goods-producing industries, which are particularly intensive in their use of blue-collar workers, is one reason for the relative decline in the number of craft workers, operatives, and laborers in the workforce since 1950. The shift to services helps to explain the postwar rise in the share of professionals, administrators, clerical workers, and sales workers in the labor force.

Employment shifts also help account for recent trends in real wages and the distribution of labor earnings. First, since wages tend to be higher in goods-producing industries—particularly, manufacturing—than in services, the shift to services is one factor responsible for the declining real wage in the United States since 1973. Second, the dispersion of earnings is generally higher in service industries than in goods-producing sectors, so that this change also accounts, in part, for the rising earnings inequality of the 1980s and 1990s. We shall return to these developments in Chapter 9, when we consider the relation between industrial patterns of employment and earnings differences.

5.4 MEASURES OF UNEMPLOYMENT AND HISTORICAL TRENDS

Figure 5.4 shows the unemployment rate for selected years between 1900 and 1993.[8] Between 1900 and 1947, peaks (high points) and troughs (low

---

[7]The data show an increase in the share of sales workers from 6 percent in 1977 to 12 percent in 1988. However, these numbers should be interpreted with some caution, because the Census Bureau changed its classification of sales jobs during the 1980s.

[8]The data sources are: U.S. Department of Labor, Employment and Training Administration, *1976 Employment and Training Report of the President,* Transmitted to Congress 1976, U.S. Government

(continued)

Figure 5.4   The Unemployment Rate, 1900–1993

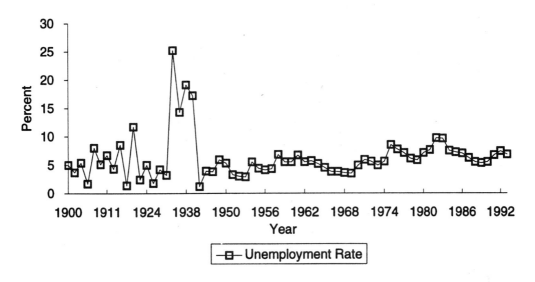

points) in the unemployment rate are shown. All years after 1947 are shown. The most striking result is the sharp cyclical changes in the unemployment rate. This is most evident during the Great Depression. In 1929, the number of unemployed was 1.6 million and the unemployment rate was 3.2 percent. By 1933, the number of unemployed reached its twentieth-century peak of 12.8 million and the unemployment rate hit 25.2 percent. The unemployment rate fell slowly during the 1930s, and it was not until 1942, after the United States had entered World War II, that the unemployment rate fell under 5 percent. In 1944, the unemployment rate reached its lowest point ever at 1.2 percent.

By 1946, after the war had ended, the unemployment rate climbed back to 3.9 percent, and in the postwar period it resumed its cyclical pattern. In 1982, the unemployment rate reached 9.7 percent, its highest level in the postwar period.[9] Moreover, for the first time since the Great Depression, the number of unemployed exceeded 10 million. By the late 1980s, the unemployment rate had again fallen to the 5–6 percent range. During the 1992

Printing Office; U.S. Department of Labor, Bureau of Labor Statistics, *Handbook of Labor Statistics 1978*, Bulletin No. 2000, June 1979; and *Economic Report of the President, 1994*.

The labor force, employment, and unemployment are defined for those 14 years of age or older for 1900–1960, and after that for those 16 years or older. In both cases, the statistics include only the civilian labor force. The definitions of employment and unemployment were modified somewhat in 1957. As a result, approximately 200,000 to 300,000 workers who were formerly classified as employed were reclassified as unemployed.

[9]This was the average unemployment rate for that year. The unemployment rate peaked in November and December of 1982 at 10.7 percent.

recession, the unemployment rate climbed to 7.4 percent, though it has since declined to under 6 percent.

As noted in Section 5.1, the BLS (beginning in 1967) has categorized the unemployed into four groups, depending on the reason for their joblessness. The four groups are the following: (1) *job losers,* who lose their job because they are fired (terminated due to poor work performance) or laid off (terminated because the job itself is eliminated); (2) *job leavers,* who voluntarily quit a job; (3) *re-entrants,* who were previously in the labor force and are now reentering it; and (4) *new entrants,* who are entering the labor market for the first time. One striking result, as shown in Table 5.8, is that typically one-third to two-fifths of the unemployed consists of those who are newly entering or reentering the labor market. These are individuals who have not lost jobs but are looking for work for the first time or after an extended period of being outside the labor force.[10]

Individuals who involuntarily lost their jobs typically accounted for about half of the unemployed over the years 1967 to 1993. Of these, many were on "temporary layoff"—that is, subject to immediate recall by their

Table 5.8   Percentage Distribution of Unemployment by Reason for Unemployment, Selected Years, 1967–1993[a]

| Year | Unemployment Rate [%] | Reason for Unemployment [percent] | | | | Unemployment Duration in Weeks | |
		Job Losers	Job Leavers	Re-entrants	New Entrants	Mean	Median
1950	5.3					12.1	
1960	5.5					12.8	
1967	3.8	41.3	14.7	31.8	13.3	8.7	2.3
1970	4.9	44.2	13.4	30.0	12.3	8.6	4.9
1973	4.9	38.8	15.6	30.7	14.9	10.0	5.2
1976	7.7	49.7	12.2	26.0	12.1	15.8	8.2
1979	5.8	42.9	14.3	29.4	13.3	10.8	5.4
1982	9.7	58.7	7.9	22.3	11.1	15.6	8.7
1985	7.4	49.8	10.6	27.1	12.5	15.6	6.8
1988	5.5	46.1	14.7	27.0	12.2	13.5	5.9
1990	5.5	48.3	14.8	27.4	9.5	12.1	5.4
1992	7.4	56.4	10.4	23.7	9.5	17.9	8.8
1993	6.8	54.6	10.8	24.6	10.0	18.1	8.4

[a] Source: Council of Economic Advisers, *Economic Report of the President, 1994.*

---

[10] In some countries, new entrants and reentrants are not officially counted among the unemployed.

employers. Workers who voluntarily quit their jobs typically accounted for about 10 percent of the unemployed.[11]

There is also a fairly strong relation between the reasons for unemployment and the overall jobless rate. In periods of low unemployment, like 1967, 1970, and 1973, the proportion of the unemployed who were job losers was relatively low. In periods of high unemployment, like 1982 and 1992, layoffs increase, and this becomes the primary cause of unemployment. Moreover, during economic downturns, the number of workers who voluntarily quit a job without having another job in line becomes much smaller, since the probability of finding a new job is much lower when the overall unemployment rate is high.

Another important dimension of joblessness is the *duration* of unemployment. This is the length of time during which an individual remains jobless. The economic impact of unemployment on family resources increases the longer someone is without a job. Short spells of unemployment cause relatively little economic hardship, while long periods of unemployment can be devastating to a family.

In 1948, 1953, and 1969, when the unemployment rate was under 4 percent, the mean duration of unemployment was less than 9 weeks. Moreover, over half the unemployed were out of work for less than 5 weeks. In high unemployment years, like 1975, 1982, 1983, and 1992, the average duration of unemployment was over 14 weeks. Indeed, in 1983, it reached 20 weeks. Moreover, in these four years about a third of the unemployed were out of work for 15 weeks or more. This indicates that periods of high unemployment cause particular hardships on families, because not only are a lot of people out of work but many remain out of work for long periods of time.

It is also interesting to compare the *median* duration of unemployment with its mean duration. The median duration refers to the length of time out of work for the average unemployed worker (while the mean duration is the arithmetic average of unemployment spells of all workers unemployed at a point in time). Median duration was typically half of the mean duration. This indicates that most workers who are unemployed find new work in a relatively short period of time, while the "hard-core" unemployed may remain jobless for a considerable length of time. Even in 1983, half of all unemployed workers found work in 10 weeks or less. The reason that the mean duration was so high that year is that a substantial proportion of the unemployed remained out of work for 6 months or more.

The official unemployment rate is often considered to understate the "true" level of unemployment, because some of the unemployed are "hidden." There are two reasons for this. First, there are some individuals who would like to work but believe that no (suitable) jobs are available and therefore do not actively look for work. These individuals are referred to as "discouraged workers." Discouraged workers are not officially counted in

---

[11] It should be noted that workers who voluntarily leave their job to take new ones or to leave the labor force entirely are not counted as unemployed.

either the ranks of the unemployed or in the labor force. Second, there are many part-time workers who would like to work full time but cannot because the requisite full-time jobs are not available. These individuals are officially counted as employed workers but should probably be considered "underemployed."

Table 5.9 provides estimates which adjust the unemployment rate for these two groups of individuals. The number of discouraged workers is added to both the labor force and the unemployment count in the adjusted unemployment rate. The part-time "unemployed" are already counted in the official labor force figure and are added to the ranks of the unemployed in the adjusted unemployment rate. The inclusion of discouraged workers and the part-time unemployed in the ranks of the unemployed makes a substantial difference in the unemployment rate calculation. In a special study conducted for years 1969 to 1975, these adjustments added between 3 and 5 percentage points to the official unemployment rate. The main effect comes from including the part-time unemployed, which typically outnumber discouraged workers by four to one. Recently, the Bureau of Labor Sta-

Table 5.9   The Unemployment Rate Adjusted for Discouraged and Part-Time Unemployed Workers, 1969–1975 and 1994[a]

Year	Official Unemployment Rate (%)	Official Number of Unemployed Workers (1,000s)	Number of Discouraged Workers (1,000s)	Number of Part-Time "Unemployed" (1,000s)	Adjusted Unemployment Rate[b] (%)
1969	3.5	2,831	574	2,056	6.7
1970	4.9	4,088	638	2,443	8.6
1971	5.9	4,993	774	2,675	9.9
1972	5.6	4,840	765	2,624	9.4
1973	4.9	4,304	679	2,519	8.4
1974	5.6	5,076	686	2,943	9.5
1975	8.5	7,830	1,082	3,748	13.5
1980	7.1				10.1
1985	7.2				10.6
1990	5.5				8.2
1994	5.4	7,112	400	4,400	9.0

[a] Sources: 1969–1975: Bureau of Labor Statistics, *Employment and Training Report of the President, 1976*; 1980–90: U.S. Department of Labor, *Report on the American Workforce*, 1994; and 1994: Bureau of Labor Statistics news release of unemployment statistics for December 1994.

[b] This is defined as the ratio of the sum of the official number of unemployed workers plus the number of discouraged workers plus the number of part-time "unemployed" to the sum of the official labor force plus the number of discouraged workers.

tistics has included its own estimates of hidden unemployment. In 1994, the inclusion of discouraged workers and workers who worked part-time because they could not find full-time jobs increased the unemployment rate from its official level of 5.4 percent to 9.0 percent.[12]

Another issue of some import is the relation between job vacancies and unemployment. It is quite possible for there to exist unemployed workers and job vacancies at the same time and in the same location. This is often due to mismatches between the skills required for the job openings and the (existing) skills of the unemployed workers. For example, while openings in technical fields may require very specific backgrounds, the qualifications may not be available among the ranks of the unemployed. Likewise, while vacancies may exist for unskilled jobs, unemployed workers who have received substantial training may not be willing to fill these positions.

The telling statistic is the ratio of the number of vacant positions available at a given point in time to the number of unemployed individuals. This variable is very crucial in disentangling the effects of structural and frictional causes of unemployment from those of inadequate demand (Keynesian) unemployment (see Section 5.6 below). A high vacancy/unemployment ratio would suggest that there are plenty of jobs available relative to the number of people looking for work. It would also suggest that the primary reason for unemployment is that the skills of the job seekers are not in balance with the skills required for the vacant positions (structural unemployment) or that workers are in transition from one job to another (frictional unemployment). A low ratio, on the other hand, would suggest that there simply are not enough jobs available for those looking and the problem is an inadequate number of jobs (Keynesian unemployment).

In an analysis of job vacancies and unemployment, Abraham (1983) found that during the mid-1960s there were approximately 2.5 unemployed individuals per vacant job. During the early 1970s, the ratio grew to 4.0 unemployed per vacancy, and in the late 1970s, 5.0 unemployed persons per vacant position. Abraham concluded that during the 1970s the main source of unemployment was an inadequate number of jobs being created relative to the number of people seeking work.[13]

There is a clear connection between unemployment and poverty. As we saw in Section 4.3, the poverty rate is five to six times greater in a family where the household head is unemployed than in one where he or she is employed (31.7 versus 5.6 percent in 1989). The incidence of poverty is also about four times as great in a family in which the household head is not in the labor force as one in which the person is employed (21.1 versus 5.6

---

[12]A related problem in counting the unemployed is "disguised" unemployment, which refers to lower skill jobs held by workers whose skills or training would qualify them for higher positions. Official statistics on unemployment do not reflect this form of underemployment. Overqualified workers may have been particularly prevalent during the Depression of the 1930s, when many college graduates, for example, held low-level clerical and sales jobs.

[13]Also, see Schwartz, Cohen, and Grimes (1986) for comments on the Abraham study and Abraham (1986) for a reply.

percent in 1989). As a result, discouraged workers who leave the work force entirely also encounter a very high frequency of poverty.

The duration of unemployment also makes a difference with regard to both poverty and family income. From Section 4.3, the poverty rate among families in which the household head did not work at all is about eight times as great as one in which the head worked the entire year (23.4 versus 3.2 percent in 1989). It is about six times as great among families where the household head worked only part of the year compared to one where the person worked the full year (19.0 versus 3.2 percent in 1989). According to data from the U.S. Census Bureau (provided on Internet), the median income of households where the household head worked full-year was $44,834 in 1993, compared to $24,450 where the head worked only part-year and $14,787 where the head did not work at all.

5.5 THE INCIDENCE OF UNEMPLOYMENT

Substantial variation exists in the degree of unemployment experienced by different groups of workers. Unemployment rates vary by age, race, gender, experience level, region of the country, occupation, and industry. During periods of high unemployment, some groups may suffer particularly hard while others not at all. During periods of low overall unemployment, some groups may still experience a high incidence of joblessness. In some recessions, unemployment may be very high in certain regions of the country (such as the Midwest during the 1982–1983 downturn and California during the 1992 recession) but low in other parts of the country (the "sunbelt" in 1982 and the Midwest in 1992). The structure of unemployment may also vary across the business cycle and from one business cycle to another.

Jobless Rates by Demographic Characteristic

Table 5.10 shows unemployment rates by age, gender, and race in 1957, 1977, and 1994. In 1957 and 1977, the unemployment rate was lower for white males than for white females. Indeed, the gap in unemployment rates between these two groups widened considerably over this 20-year stretch, from 0.7 to 1.8 percentage points. The increasing gap is largely due to the falling labor force participation rate of white males and the rising participation rate of white females over this period. In particular, older white males who lose jobs have dropped out of the labor force in greater numbers over time, thus reducing their unemployment rate. Meanwhile, the rising number of white females entering or reentering the labor force has increased their overall jobless rate, since entrants and reentrants have a higher incidence of unemployment than experienced workers. However, by 1994, the jobless rate for the two groups was almost identical.

The unemployment rate among black workers was about double that of whites in 1957, 1977, and 1994. This large difference is partly accounted for by differences in education and skills and partly by discrimination. As shown

Table 5.10   Unemployment Rates by Age, Gender, and Race, 1957, 1977 and 1994[a] (in percent)

Age	White Males	White Females	Black[b] Males	Black[b] Females
1957				
16–17 years	11.9	11.9	16.3	18.3
18–19	11.2	7.9	20.0	21.3
20–24	7.1	5.1	12.7	12.2
25–34	2.7	4.7	8.5	8.1
35–44	2.5	3.7	6.4	4.7
45–54	3.0	3.0	6.2	4.2
55–64	3.4	3.0	5.5	4.0
65 and over	8.2	3.5	5.0	4.3
All	3.6	4.3	8.3	7.3
1977				
16–17 years	17.6	18.2	38.7	44.7
18–19	13.0	14.2	36.1	37.4
20–24	9.3	9.3	21.7	23.6
25–34	5.0	6.7	10.6	12.9
35–44	3.1	5.3	6.1	8.5
45–54	3.0	5.0	5.2	5.6
55–64	3.3	4.4	6.4	4.9
65 and over	4.9	4.9	8.3	3.6
All	5.5	7.3	12.4	14.0
1994				
16–17 years	18.5	16.6	39.3	32.9
18–19	14.7	11.8	36.5	32.5
20–24	8.8	7.4	19.4	19.6
25–34	5.2	5.1	10.6	11.7
35–44	3.9	4.2	9.1	8.0
45–54	3.7	3.7	6.5	4.9
55–64	4.1	3.7	6.0	4.9
65 and over	3.7	3.9	8.2	4.4
All	5.4	5.2	12.0	11.0

[a] Sources: U.S. Department of Labor, Bureau of Labor Statistics, *Handbook of Labor Statistics, 1978,* 1979, Bulletin 2000; U.S. Department of Labor, Bureau of Labor Statistics, *Handbook of Labor Statistics 1989,* 1990, Bulletin 2340; and Bureau of Labor Statistics worksheets.
[b] Nonwhites in 1957.

in Table 5.5, nonwhite workers had considerably less schooling than the white labor force in the 1950s. Though by the mid-1990s blacks in the labor force had just about caught up to whites in terms of median years of schooling, they still fell short with regard to the proportion who had graduated from college.

An additional factor that has been cited to account for the difference in unemployment rates between whites and blacks is the high level of black migration, particularly out of the rural South. The argument is that new migrants to a region tend to experience greater unemployment than long-term residents, since the former are less aware of available jobs and have no job experience in the region. However, black migration from the South diminished considerably during the 1980s and 1990s, yet the large racial differential in unemployment rates continued to persist, suggesting that discrimination may account for a large part of the racial disparity. Moreover, the higher incidence of unemployment among black workers is an important factor accounting for the lower family income of black families relative to white ones (see Chapter 13 for more discussion).

Unemployment rates also show considerable variation among age groups. For all four race-gender groups, the highest unemployment rates were found among teenagers. The age group with the second highest unemployment rate was the 20 to 24 year-old group (with the exception of white males in 1957), followed by age group 25–34. Joblessness was lowest for those 35 and over.

The likelihood of unemployment tends to decline with age. The explanation is that teenagers, who are largely new entrants in the labor force, ordinarily experience a period of frictional unemployment while searching for a job (see the next section). In periods of layoff, teenagers are often the first to be let go, since they tend to have the least seniority. As workers age, they gain experience and are more likely to find a job that they find suitable. As a result, older workers are less vulnerable to layoffs because of their seniority and are less likely to quit because of dissatisfaction with their job. Moreover, if they do quit or lose their job, they are more likely to withdraw from the labor force than younger workers.[14]

Another striking result is the sharp increase in the unemployment rate among teenagers between 1957 and 1977, particularly among black youths. One explanation is that the number of teenagers entering the labor market between 1957 and 1977 increased considerably because of the postwar baby boom. The increase in the new teenager entrants was greater than the labor market could absorb. Indeed, during the 1982–83 recession, the black youth unemployment rate climbed to close to 50 percent. However, by 1994 jobless incidence among young people had subsided somewhat.

Peter Doeringer and Michael Piore (1975) argued that the increasing unemployment rate among youths, particularly black youths, during the

---

[14]Also, see Ehrenberg (1980) for an interesting analysis of sources of differences in unemployment rates between the various sex-race groups.

1960s and 1970s reflected the closing down of employment opportunities in the primary labor market. This is evidenced, in part, by the low unemployment rates of prime-age males (mainly white males), which seem to imply that the primary labor market was essentially full during the 1970s. Youths entering the labor force were apparently forced into the secondary labor market. The high youth unemployment rate was thus partially attributable to the temporary nature of most secondary jobs and their concomitant high turnover. In addition, for those young people who did manage to find and to hold onto jobs, the training they received was minimal and the advancement opportunities limited. Doeringer and Piore predicted that such early labor market experiences could eventually have unfortunate consequences as these young workers matured into prime-age workers.[15]

The higher unemployment rates among younger workers is also reflected in a higher incidence of poverty. According to data from the U.S. Census Bureau (provided on Internet), the poverty rate among persons aged 18 to 24 was 19.1 percent in 1993, compared to 12.2 percent for age group 25 to 44 and 9.4 percent for age group 45 to 64.

Another striking difference in unemployment rates is by marital status. As shown in Table 5.11, men who never married experienced unemployment rates more than double that among all males. This held true in both recessionary years and full-employment years. In contrast, married men faced unemployment rates that were only about two-thirds the rate for all men. Unemployment rates for men who were widowed, divorced, or separated were higher than the average male unemployment rate but lower than that for single men. One explanation of this difference in jobless rates is that married men, particularly those with children, have greater financial responsibilities. Thus they are likely to search harder for a job and accept a job position more quickly but are less likely to quit a job than unmarried men. Moreover, an employer may prefer married men over unmarried men because the former are less likely to quit their jobs.[16]

The same pattern held among women. Married women experienced lower jobless rates than widowed, divorced, or separated females, and the latter group had lower unemployment rates than single (and never married) women. The differentials in unemployment rates by marital status were not as pronounced among women as among men. The explanation is that unmarried women, particularly those with children to support (female

---

[15] Several studies have attempted to assess the effect of youth unemployment on the eventual wages and career paths achieved in adulthood. Four earlier papers (Stevenson (1978), Osterman (1978), Antos and Mellow (1978), and Becker and Hills (1980)) and several of the papers contained in Freeman and Wise (1982) and Freeman and Holzer (1986) tried to determine whether adult males who had experienced unemployment while teenagers had a higher probability of being unemployed and receiving lower wages than adult males who had not. The results indicate that such long-lasting adverse effects were in evidence among black males but not among white males.

[16] Also, married men are, on average, older than men who are single. As we saw from the previous table, jobless rates are lower among men 25 years and older than those under 25. However, econometric studies have generally found that, even after controlling for differences in age, married men have lower unemployment rates than singles.

Table 5.11 Unemployment Rates by Marital Status, Selected Years, 1956–1994[a] (in percent)

Marital Status	1956	1961	1969	1975	1988	1994
1. All	3.8	6.7	3.5	8.5	5.5	6.1
2. *Males*						
a. All males	3.5	6.5	2.8	7.9	5.5	6.2
b. Single	7.7	13.1	8.0	16.1	9.9	
c. Married, spouse present	2.3	4.6	1.5	5.1	3.3	4.4
d. Widowed, divorced or separated	6.2	10.3	4.0	11.0	7.0	
3. *Females*						
a. All females	4.3	7.2	4.7	9.3	5.6	6.0
b. Single	5.3	8.7	7.3	13.0	8.6	
c. Married, spouse present	3.6	6.4	3.9	7.9	3.9	4.6
d. Widowed, divorced or separated	5.0	7.4	4.0	8.9	6.3	
e. Female head of household	—	—	4.4	10.0	8.1	8.9

[a] Sources: Bureau of Labor Statistics, *Handbook of Labor Statistics 1979,* December 1980, Bulletin 2070; *Economic Report of the President, 1984*; Bureau of Labor Statistics, *Handbook of Labor Statistics 1990,* August 1989, Bulletin 2340; and *Monthly Labor Review,* statistical supplement.

heads of households, shown in line e), are likely to experience much greater financial pressure than married women. As a result, single women are more apt to be looking for a job than married ones. Moreover, married women who involuntarily lose their job often leave the labor force entirely, since there is usually another income in the family. Hence they do not show up in the unemployment statistics. In contrast, single women who lose their job will generally have to search for a new one and will thus be counted among the unemployed.

Here, again, poverty rates tend to mirror the unemployment experience of different demographic groups. According to data from the U.S. Census Bureau (provided on Internet), the poverty rate among husbands and wives living together was only 2.0 percent in 1993, compared to 8.7 percent among single men living alone, 9.5 percent among single women living alone, and 28.6 percent in female-headed households with children.

Unemployment by Industry, Occupation, and Region

The incidence of unemployment also shows large variation by industry of (last) employment. This is particularly true during recessionary times when certain industries are impacted more heavily than others. Comparative jobless rates are shown by major sector of the economy for four low unemployment years and two recession years (1958 and 1975) in Table 5.12. The construction sector has had the highest unemployment rate (in 1975 it reached 18.1 percent!), followed generally by agriculture. The jobless rate among mining workers varied over time—below average in 1948, 1969, 1975, and 1994, above average in 1988, and much higher than the overall rate in 1958. The jobless rate in manufacturing was about average during peak years but quite high during the two recession years 1958 and 1975.

The jobless rate in transportation and utilities tended to be below the national rate, and that in the trade sector tended to be slightly above the overall rate. Both the finance, insurance, and real estate sector and the government sector had unemployment rates considerably below the overall level (about half the national rate in most years). Unemployment in the service sector had a counter-cyclical pattern, at or above the national level during prosperity and below the national level during economic downturns.

Table 5.12   Unemployment Rates by Industry for Selected Years, 1948–1994[a] (in percent)

	Year					
	1948	*1958*	*1969*	*1975*	*1988*	*1994*
1. All workers	3.8	6.8	3.5	8.5	5.5	6.1
2. Agriculture	5.5	10.3	6.0	10.3	5.2	11.3
3. Mining	3.0	10.9	2.8	4.0	7.9	5.4
4. Construction	8.7	15.3	6.0	18.1	10.6	11.8
5. Manufacturing	4.2	9.3	3.3	10.9	5.3	5.6
6. Transportation and Utilities	3.5	6.1	2.1	5.6	3.9	4.8
7. Trade	4.7	6.8	4.1	8.7	6.2	7.4
8. Finance, Insurance & Real Estate	1.8	2.8	2.1	4.9	3.0	3.6
9. Services	4.8	5.7	3.5	7.1	4.9	6.1
10. Government	2.2	2.5	1.9	4.0	2.8	3.4

[a]Based on industry of last employment. Sources: Bureau of Labor Statistics, *Handbook of Labor Statistics 1979*, December 1980, Bulletin 2070; Bureau of Labor Statistics, *Handbook of Labor Statistics 1990*, Bulletin 2340; and *Monthly Labor Review*, March 1995, statistical supplement.

Unemployment rates also vary by occupation, as shown in Table 5.13.[17] The incidence of unemployment among white-collar workers was considerably lower than for blue-collar or service workers. Managers and administrators experienced the lowest rate of joblessness, about a third of the overall rate. Professional and technical workers also enjoyed a very low rate of unemployment. The incidence of joblessness among sales and clerical workers also fell below that for all workers.

The unemployment for blue-collar workers was greater than the overall rate. The differential was particularly wide during recession years, reflecting reduced demand for construction and manufactured products. There were considerable differences in the incidence of joblessness among the five blue-collar categories. Craft and skilled workers had the lowest unemployment rate in this group. The jobless rate for the skilled trades was about equal to the national average during economic downturns and fell below

Table 5.13 Unemployment Rates by Occupation for Selected Years, 1958–1979[a] (in percent)

	Year			
Occupation	1958	1969	1975	1979
1. *All workers*	6.8	3.5	8.5	5.8
2. *White-collar workers*				
a) All white-collar	3.1	2.1	4.7	3.3
b) Professional and technical	2.0	1.3	3.2	2.4
c) Managers and administrators	1.7	0.9	3.0	2.1
d) Sales	4.1	2.9	5.8	3.9
e) Clerical	4.4	3.0	6.6	4.6
3. *Blue-collar workers*				
a) All blue-collar	10.2	3.9	11.7	6.9
b) Craft and kindred	6.8	2.2	8.3	4.5
c) Operatives	11.0	4.4	13.2	7.7
d) Nonfarm laborers	15.1	6.7	15.6	10.8
4. *Service workers*				
a) All service workers	6.9	4.2	8.6	7.1
b) Private household workers	5.6	3.6	5.4	4.8
c) Other service workers	7.4	4.3	8.9	7.3
5. Farmers and farm laborers	3.2	1.9	3.5	3.8

[a]Based on occupation held in last job. Source: Bureau of Labor Statistics, *Handbook of Labor Statistics 1979*, December 1980, Bulletin 2070.

[17]Unfortunately, the Bureau of Labor Statistics discontinued this series in the 1980s.

the national average during periods of prosperity. The jobless rate for operatives was considerably above the level for all workers, while that for the unskilled nonfarm labor was almost double the national rate. The level of unemployment among service workers was about the same level as the overall rate during times of high unemployment and somewhat greater than average during low unemployment periods. Farmers and farm laborers experienced jobless rates about half that for all workers.

The general pattern that emerges from Table 5.13 is that unemployment rates are considerably lower in occupations that require either substantial training, such as the craft trades, or high levels of schooling, such as the professions. (The only exception is farm labor, a relatively low-skilled occupation.) An explanation of this comes from the internal labor market model (see Chapter 8). The argument is that firms invest more heavily in their primary labor force, who tend to be white-collar and skilled workers, than in their secondary labor force, who tend to be semiskilled and unskilled workers. As a result, during downturns, firms are likely to lay off their less skilled workers first. Another explanation of the difference in unemployment rates among skill groups is that unemployed skilled workers usually have an easier time finding a new job than jobless workers with little or no skills.

One reason for the higher unemployment rates of black workers is that they are disproportionately represented in the lower-skilled occupations, particularly as unskilled laborers and service workers. However, this is only part of the story, because even within occupation, black workers generally experience higher jobless rates than comparable white workers. This is also true between black workers and white workers with the same schooling, experience level, and on-the-job training. Differences in jobless rates is another aspect of labor market discrimination experienced by black workers (see Part 3 of the book for more discussion).

Differences in industrial and occupational mix among regions of the country cause major differences in the jobless rate experienced by various localities in the United States. As shown in Table 5.14, in 1975, which was a recession year with a national unemployment rate of 8.5 percent, the unemployment rate was 9.5 percent in the Northeast, 7.7 percent in the South, 7.9 percent in the North Central states, and 9.2 percent in the West. The variation in jobless rates by state was even greater. The highest state unemployment rate was 11.2 percent in Massachusetts that year, and the lowest was 3.6 percent in North Dakota. Even within regions of the country, there were large differences in jobless rates. In the South, unemployment rates ranged from a low of 5.6 percent in Texas to a high of 10.7 percent in Florida, and in the West the range was from 4.2 percent in Wyoming to 12.1 percent in Arizona.

In 1994, which was a relatively low unemployment year for the nation as a whole, there was again a large spread in jobless rates. The lowest rate of unemployment occurred in Nebraska, at 2.6 percent, and the highest in Louisiana, at 8.1 percent. In many cases, states that had high unemployment rates in one year experienced low unemployment in the other year. This was

Table 5.14   Unemployment Rates by Selected States, 1975 and 1994[a]
(in percent)

State	Year	
	1975	*1994*
United States	8.5	6.1
1. *Northeast*	9.5	
Massachusetts	11.2	5.5
New Hampshire	9.0	3.8
New York	9.5	6.3
Pennsylvania	8.3	5.9
2. *South*	7.7	
Delaware	9.7	4.5
Florida	10.7	6.8
Oklahoma	7.2	5.7
Texas	5.6	5.5
3. *North Central*	7.9	
Illinois	7.1	5.0
Michigan	12.5	4.6
Nebraska	4.2	2.6
North Dakota	3.6	3.1
4. *West*	9.2	
Alaska	6.9	7.4
Arizona	12.1	6.1
California	9.9	7.7
Wyoming	4.2	4.5

[a] Source: Bureau of Labor Statistics, *Handbook of Labor Statistics 1979,* December 1980, Bulletin 2070; and *Monthly Labor Review,* March 1995, statistical supplement. The states are classified into four regions by the Bureau of Labor Statistics.

the case for Massachusetts, whose jobless rate was the second highest in 1975 but below average in 1994, and Alaska, whose rate of joblessness was lower than average in 1975 but among the highest in 1994. Such switches in a state's relative unemployment ranking may reflect changes in demand composition, particularly between a recession year and a boom year. Over the long term, these shifts often reflect changes in industrial composition, as, for example, in New Hampshire and Massachusetts, where light industries such as electronics have been gradually replacing textiles and shoes.

Regional variations in unemployment are also reflected in regional differences in poverty incidence. In 1993, for example, poverty rates were well under the national average in the low-unemployment states of Massachusetts, New Hampshire, Delaware, North Dakota, and Wyoming, and above average in the high unemployment states of New York and California.

5.6 Causes of Unemployment

What causes unemployment? This subject has occupied economic writings for the last hundred years. Today, economists identify four different types of unemployment: (1) frictional, (2) seasonal, (3) structural, and (4) deficient aggregate demand. These distinctions are important because each type leads to a different form of policy remedy.

Frictional Unemployment

Frictional unemployment refers to joblessness caused by a temporary lack of smoothness in job transitions. This type of unemployment often characterizes workers who have quit their job and are actively searching for a new one and to new entrants and reentrants to the labor force who are searching for a position. It is also associated with search time for a new job, since longer search time increases the amount of frictional unemployment. Frictional unemployment is related to cyclical movements in the economy and structural change. In principle, better job vacancy information and better employment markets could reduce the level of frictional unemployment. Since frictional unemployment arises when workers change jobs or enter the job market, this type of unemployment is viewed as "voluntary" insofar as workers quit one position to search for another.

Frictional unemployment occurs because the labor market is dynamic and constantly changing and information on available jobs is imperfect. As a result, it takes time for a jobless worker to find an appropriate new job. This is true even if the size of the labor force is unchanging, since some workers will leave the labor force while new people enter it. In addition, shifts in demand composition will cause some industries to lay off workers and others to look for new employees. Because information is imperfect, matches between individuals looking for work and employers seeking to hire cannot be instantly made. Thus, even if the aggregate demand for labor equals the aggregate supply, unemployed workers and job vacancies may simultaneously exist.

Because of frictional unemployment, there will still be some unemployment even when then economy is operating at "full employment." However, the level of frictional unemployment is particularly sensitive to the kinds of job placement services and institutional arrangements that exist in the labor market. In the United Kingdom, the unemployment rate was under 3 percent during much of the 1960s, and, in West Germany, it fell under *1 percent* in both 1963 and 1973. The lower unemployment rates in these two countries reflect the fact that employers are required by law to register all job vacancies with the government. In the United States, the level of frictional unemployment could be reduced by similar requirements and through the use of a computerized network of job vacancy information.

Seasonal Unemployment

Another source of joblessness is seasonal fluctuations in business activity. This **seasonal unemployment** is usually associated with climatic changes or seasonal changes in behavior. The most obvious example is agriculture, where the level of employment varies according to the weather and the growing seasons of different crops. This is particularly true during harvesting, when the demand for farm labor is very high. As a result, many workers migrate from one place to another to meet the harvesting schedule of crops in different regions of the country.

Another industry affected by weather conditions is construction in the Northeast and the Midwest. During winter months, construction slows down considerably in these states, as does its employment. Food processing is also directly affected by weather, since many fruits and vegetables must be canned soon after picking. The tourist industry is likewise extremely seasonal in nature. Buying habits also change over the seasons. This is particularly true in retailing, where a large proportion of activity is directly related to the Christmas season. (In many stores, a third to nearly half the sales take place during the month of December.) The garment industry is also affected by the seasonal change in fashions. Likewise, employment in the automobile industry usually falls during the summer, as the factories are retooled for the new model year.

Seasonal declines in employment in one industry or location do not necessarily produce a corresponding rise in joblessness. Migratory farm workers may, for example, continue to find employment by traveling south during harvesting season. Moreover, workers laid off in one industry due to seasonal factors may find work in another industry in a seasonal upswing. Some seasonal workers may quit the labor force after being laid off (for example, students working in the tourist trade during the summer and returning to school in the fall or housewives employed in the retail trade during the Christmas season). However, seasonal shifts in employment may not be sufficient to offer employment to all workers laid off for seasonal reasons.

Seasonal employment may also arise due to shifts in the supply of labor. In particular, the labor force usually expands during the summer as students pour into the labor market looking for work, and it contracts during the fall as young people return to school.[18]

---

[18]Because of the importance of such seasonal fluctuations in output and employment, many official government statistics are seasonally adjusted to allow comparisons with other periods of the

(continued)

Structural Unemployment

Another source of unemployment is from discrepancies that arise between the job skills required by existing industries and the job skills possessed by the labor force. **Structural unemployment** is usually a local phenomenon and arises from three principal causes. The first is shifts in the structure of product demand either across industries or across regions of the country. This will cause workers to be laid off in one industry (or locality), and it will cause vacancies to occur in another industry (or locality). In many cases, the new positions require skills different than those the displaced workers possess. In such cases, the displaced workers would remain jobless even though vacancies exist in their local labor market. A classic example is Appalachia in the 1960s, where the shift of jobs away from low-skilled positions left many uneducated residents jobless. This type of unemployment differs from frictional unemployment, because unemployment is not eliminated by continued search or better information. Structural unemployment is ultimately a result of a mismatch between the skills of the labor force in a given locality and the skills in demand.

A second cause of structural unemployment is technological change, which may render some kinds of specialized skills obsolete. The development of the automobile industry in the early part of this century, for example, made blacksmithing and related trades virtually obsolete. The widespread use of computers over the last two decades has displaced many kinds of clerical skills (telephone operators and stenographers, for example). Displaced workers with specialized skills may be unable to use them in other industries and may remain jobless because they have no suitable substitute skills. It should be noted, however, that technological change does not necessarily lead to structural unemployment or, indeed, to joblessness. Though technological change is normally laborsaving (that is, it leads to the substitution of capital for labor), the reduced costs of production, if passed on to the consumer in lowered prices, will increase product demand. They may also cause employment in the firm or industry to expand (depending on the elasticity of the product demand curve).

A third source of structural unemployment emanates from the supply side. Demographic changes and changes in the labor force participation rates may change the composition of skills in the labor force. For example, during the 1970s, there was a large influx of young people (the baby boom generation) and first-time female workers into the labor force. As a result, there was a higher concentration of less experienced and lower skilled workers in the labor force which were out of balance with the skills in demand by industry.

The existence of both frictional and structural unemployment may cause joblessness to occur even if the aggregate demand for labor is in balance

---

year. The student should not confuse seasonal fluctuation with cyclical fluctuations, since the former occur on a regular basis each year whereas the latter occur on an irregular basis depending on aggregate demand conditions.

with the aggregate supply of labor. This level of joblessness is referred to as the "full-employment" unemployment rate or the **natural rate of unemployment**. There has been some debate among macroeconomists in recent years about exactly what the natural rate of employment is. However, most believe that the full-employment unemployment rate has risen since the late 1950s. Robert Gordon (1981), for example, has estimated that the natural rate of unemployment rate was 4.3 percent in 1957, 4.9 percent in 1968, and 5.6 percent in 1979. Analysis by Chinhui Juhn, Kevin Murphy, and Robert Topel (1991) led them to the conclusion that the natural rate may have settled at about 5 percent during the late 1980s, while Charles Adams and David Coe (1992) estimated a natural rate of 5.75 percent for the late 1980s.

There are two major reasons why the natural rate may have risen between the 1950s and the 1980s. The first is the growing proportion of females in the labor force, who, on average, have less experience and labor market skills than male workers. This has increased the difficulty of job placements, particularly among new entrants and reentrants to the labor force. Second, there were significant changes in technology and industrial structure in the 1970s and 1980s from the widespread introduction of computers and information technology. This has caused many skills to become obsolete, particularly in the clerical occupations, and increased the difficulty of matching skills among unemployed workers with those skills required by the new technology.

Demand-Deficient (Keynesian) Unemployment

A fourth major cause of unemployment is a decline in aggregate demand, known as **demand-deficient (Keynesian) unemployment.** Also referred to as cyclical unemployment, this type of joblessness occurs in business cycle downturns when the aggregate demand for products and, correspondingly, that for labor falls. One of Keynes' major contributions was to analyze this form of unemployment. The high unemployment rates of the Great Depression (reaching 25 percent) were attributable to deficient demand, as were the high unemployment rates associated with postwar recessions (primarily 1958 at 6.8 percent, 1961 at 6.7 percent, 1975 at 8.5 percent, 1982–1983 at 9.7 and 9.6 percent, and 1992 at 7.4 percent).

When aggregate demand falls, firms in industries with reduced demand respond in two ways. First, they may temporarily lay off workers. In many cases, such workers are subject to immediate recall by the company. Second, they may stop replacing employees who voluntarily quit the firm. For both reasons, the number of unemployed will increase, as will the unemployment rate. In principle, if wages were perfectly flexible, the real wage should fall in the face of such mounting unemployment, and the jobless rate should decline. Yet, in actuality, real wages are not downward flexible, and the macroeconomic response to falling aggregate demand is rising unemployment.

There are three major reasons why money wages at least may be quite rigid in the short run. First, collective bargaining agreements in unionized industries do not allow the employer to unilaterally reduce wages. This explanation, however, begs the question of why unions would prefer layoffs to a reduction in wages in the face of reduced demand. The rationale is that in most union agreements, the last hired are the first to be let go during layoffs. The most experienced workers are normally the last to be laid off. Therefore, most layoffs affect only a small percentage of union members, and these are likely to be the newest ones. A reduction of wages, on the other hand, will affect all union members, including the most experienced. Union leaders, who are themselves likely to be drawn from the ranks of the most experienced, will tend to support their interests over those of the new members. As a result, unions will likewise favor a policy of layoffs over across-the-board wage reductions (see Medoff [1979] for some evidence).

Second, in nonunion firms, the employer will often favor a policy of layoffs over across-the-board wage reductions. The rationale comes from internal labor market theory. The argument is that because firms invest heavily in firm-specific training, they are reluctant to lose their most experienced employees. A wage reduction, even if temporary, might induce these workers to look for work in another firm or, if they stay, to reduce their morale and work effort. In contrast, a policy of laying off the least experienced employees would not be particularly detrimental to the firm, since these are precisely the employees in which the firm has invested least. Thus, from the nonunionized firm's point of view, layoffs would be a preferable alternative to an across-the-board reduction in wages.

Third, employees in a nonunion firm may also prefer a layoff policy to a wage reduction one. The argument comes from implicit contract theory. Assume that, on average, employees are risk-averse—that is, they prefer a stream of steady income that is fairly certain to one that is on average higher (that is, its expected value is greater) but is more uncertain (that is, subject to greater variability over time). Such employees might engage in an implicit contract (not an explicit one, as in the case of unionized workers) with their employer so that most recent hires are laid off first in the case of economic downturns. However, their wages will not be reduced and the experienced labor force will be kept on except in circumstances that threaten the firm with bankruptcy. This is essentially a form of insurance in which the employee, except for an initial period after he (she) is first hired, is generally guaranteed stable earnings over time. In exchange for such lower risk, the employees should be willing to accept a lower average wage. Thus, the employer is also on average better off, since the firm's labor costs would be reduced by such an (implicit) arrangement.[19]

---

[19] This is true only in the case where the proportion of employees subject to layoffs is small. If it is large, the employer might be better off paying higher wages during good times and reducing wages during hard times.

The Debate over the Causes
of Unemployment

There is an extended debate among economists over the relative importance of these four causes of unemployment. Most economists do believe, however, that each of these four sources can exist at a given point in time and, indeed, they may all coexist simultaneously during certain periods. Frictional, seasonal, and structural unemployment can occur even when the aggregate demand for labor equals the aggregate supply. Frictional unemployment arises because members of the labor force may be out of work while searching for a (new) job. This type of unemployment is ultimately due to the facts that the job structure is constantly changing and that information about job vacancies is imperfect. Seasonal unemployment arises from the seasonal nature of many industries and occupations. Structural unemployment is due to the possibility that imbalances may occur within certain occupational or geographical labor markets between supply and demand for labor. In contrast, demand-deficient unemployment reflects an imbalance in the aggregate labor market. Such joblessness is due to a drop in the aggregate demand for goods and services and hence for labor.

The disagreement among economists is not about the possibility that each of these types of unemployment may arise but about the *quantitative* importance of each in explaining the unemployment rate at a given point in time. This is not simply an academic debate, since it will guide the choice of appropriate government policies to reduce the level of joblessness. If unemployment is largely frictional in nature, the appropriate policy response would be to improve information about job vacancies and employment placement services. If joblessness is largely structural in nature, the appropriate policy might be to encourage workers to move to locations where jobs are available or to retrain workers in skills that are in demand. If unemployment is due to deficient demand, the proper response is to pursue macroeconomic policies that increase aggregate demand. In a Keynesian world, these include increasing government spending and reducing taxes; in a monetarist world, these include increasing the rate at which the money supply grows and reducing the interest rate.

Most economists believe that the large cyclical swings in unemployment are due to changes in aggregate demand. The high unemployment rates during the early 1930s were due to deficient demand (see Figure 5.4). During the postwar period, the unemployment rate fluctuated in a range from 2.9 percent in 1953 to 9.7 percent in 1983. The jobless rate fell below 4 percent in 1947, 1948, 1951, 1952, 1953, and 1966 to 1969. These were periods of high aggregate demand, which produced tight labor markets. (Not surprisingly, most were during the Korean War and the Vietnam War.) The jobless rate climbed above 6 percent in 1958 and 1961, and above 8 percent in 1975 and 1982–1983. These were all recession years, caused by low aggregate demand.

During the low unemployment years, it is probably safe to say that all unemployment was due to frictional, seasonal, and structural unemployment. During the high unemployment years, these factors still played a role, though it is hard to determine exactly their relative importance.

"Structuralists" argue that two factors have led to greater occupational and geographical imbalances in the labor market. The first is the introduction of computers and automation and the spread of information technology that has caused the displacement of a large number of skilled and semiskilled workers. The second is the increasing shift to services in the American economy, which tends to make many goods-related skills obsolete. Charles Killingsworth (1965) referred to this phenomenon as the "labor market twist," whereby the new jobs created called for educated labor while the workers displaced by automation were largely unskilled.

Frictional sources of unemployment have been receiving increasing emphasis since the 1970s. Motivated partly by the perceived failure of government fiscal and monetary policy to reduce unemployment, the "frictionalists" emphasized the search process as a major source of unemployment. They advanced the argument that most unemployment tends to be of short duration. Based on data from 1969 to 1975, it was found that in four of these years, over half the unemployed remained jobless less than five weeks. Between 1948 and 1966, the average spell of unemployment was 5.5 weeks. Moreover, it was found that most unemployment was concentrated in relatively few individuals. For example, in 1973, when the annual unemployment rate stood at 4.9 percent, 13 percent of the experienced labor force had one or more periods of joblessness. Of these, a third had two or more spells, and a half of the latter group had three or more spells. The inference drawn was that unemployment was not an aggregate problem but was concentrated among a few workers who frequently experienced short spells of unemployment. These spells were interpreted as search periods.

By emphasizing the search process, the frictionalists made the workers and the institutions that fostered inflexibilities in reservation wages the primary culprits of unemployment. Joblessness was viewed as primarily "voluntary." Such institutional factors as union-induced wage rigidities, the minimum wage law, and the unemployment insurance system were also seen as responsible for unemployment, since they served to prolong the job search process. The idea of a "natural" rate of unemployment surfaced in this literature. Moreover, as we discussed above, the natural rate was seen to rise during the 1960s and the 1970s due to the changing demographic composition of the labor force.

The debate between voluntary or frictional unemployment versus involuntary or demand-deficient unemployment can be resolved, in part, by looking at vacancy data. If unemployment were entirely due to frictional causes, then the number of vacancies should equal or exceed the number of workers looking for jobs. Indeed, the vacancies should match the unemployed workers both in terms of skill requirements and location. (Otherwise, we would have structural unemployment.) If, on the other hand, the number of jobless workers exceeds the number of vacancies, this can be taken as an indicator of demand-deficient unemployment. One of the most careful studies of this issue was done by Abraham (1983), discussed in Section 5.4 above. She found that during the low-unemployment years, the ratio of unemployed individuals to job vacancies was about 2.5, and during the 1970s, the ratio ranged from 4.0 to 5.0. This suggests that demand-deficient unemployment has become more important than frictional causes over time.

Moreover, even if there are frictional and structural sources for unemployment, it is still possible for Keynesian type macroeconomic policies to reduce the jobless rate. In the case of frictional unemployment, stimulating aggregate demand will increase the number of job vacancies and thereby reduce the average search time of workers, *ceteris paribus* (all other things being held the same). In the case of structural unemployment, increasing aggregate demand will create additional job vacancies, some of which may match the skills and area of residence of the structurally unemployed. Macroeconomic policy, in conjunction with government retraining and relocation programs, could further facilitate labor market adjustments needed to remove imbalance between excess supplies of certain skills and excess demand for others.

5.7 SUMMARY

The overall labor force participation rate of a nation indicates the proportion of the population that could be at work that is in the labor force. It is one important determinant of the average income per capita of a country. We saw that for the United States, the civilian labor force grew from 28.5 million in 1900 to 128.0 million workers in 1993, or by a factor of 4.5. Over the same period, the overall LFPR increased from 56 to 66 percent, with most of it occurring after World War II. The trends were different for men and women. The male LFPR declined from 87 percent in 1948 to 75 percent in 1993, while the female LFPR rose from 33 to 58 percent. In 1948, females accounted for 27 percent of the labor force, while in 1993 for 46 percent.

During the 1960s and 1970s, the proportion of young workers in the labor force increased due to the large influx of baby boomers into the work force. In the 1980s and early 1990s, the number of new entrants, members of the "baby dearth generation," fell dramatically. Throughout the postwar period, the proportion of older workers in the labor force declined sharply.

The educational attainment of the labor force increased substantially during the postwar period. The median years of schooling for the whole labor force rose from 10.9 years in 1952 to 13.3 in 1994. The proportion of the labor force who had not attended high school fell from 38 percent in 1952 to 4 percent in 1994; the proportion who were high school graduates or better rose from 43 to 87 percent; and the proportion who had attended some college increased from 16 to 53 percent. For black men, the gains in educational attainment were particularly dramatic, with their median schooling level increasing from 7.2 years in 1952 to 12.4 years in 1984 and the proportion graduating from high school rising from 15 to 83 percent.

There were important changes in the industrial and occupational composition of the labor force over the twentieth century. The proportion employed in agriculture fell dramatically. There was also a substantial shift in the composition of the work force out of goods-producing sectors and into services. This was accompanied by a large reduction in the relative share of unskilled workers and farm workers in the labor force and a large increase in the relative share of white-collar workers, particularly professional, managerial, clerical, and sales workers.

The definition of the unemployment rate is the ratio of the number of unemployed to the total labor force. There have been sharp cyclical movements in the unemployment rate over this century. This is most evident during the Great Depression. In 1929, the unemployment rate was 3.2 percent, but by 1933, it had climbed to 25.2 percent. The unemployment rate fell slowly during the 1930s, and in 1944, it reached its lowest point ever at 1.2 percent. By 1946, after the war had ended, the unemployment rate climbed back to 3.9 percent and resumed its cyclical pattern. In 1982, the unemployment rate reached its highest level in the postwar period of 9.7 percent, but by the mid-1990s, the unemployment rate had again fallen under 6 percent.

Typically, a third to 40 percent of the unemployed consists of persons who are newly entering the labor market or reentering it. Individuals who involuntarily lost their jobs account for about half of the unemployed. The remaining 10 percent or so consist of workers who voluntarily quit their jobs.

There is considerable variation in jobless rates by demographic group. The unemployment rate for blacks has been about double that of whites. Among age groups, the unemployment rate was greatest for teenagers, second highest for the 20- to 24-year-old group, third highest for the 25–34 years range, and lowest for those 35 and over. The likelihood of unemployment tends to decline with experience.

Economists have identified four different causes of unemployment types: (1) frictional, (2) seasonal, (3) structural, and (4) deficient aggregate demand. Frictional unemployment arises because members of the labor force may be out of work while searching for a (new) job. This type of unemployment is ultimately due to the facts that the job structure is constantly changing and information about job vacancies is imperfect. Seasonal unemployment arises from the seasonal nature of many industries and occupations. Structural unemployment is due to the possibility that imbalances may occur within certain occupational or geographical labor markets between supply and demand for labor. Demand-deficient unemployment reflects an imbalance in the aggregate labor market and is due to a drop in the aggregate demand for goods and services and, as a result, for labor.

During low-unemployment periods, it is likely that all of unemployment is due to frictional, seasonal, and structural unemployment. During the high unemployment years, these factors still play a role, but demand deficiency is likely the major factor.

Though the next four chapters of the book will focus on earnings differences as a source of income inequality, it should be emphasized that both labor force participation and unemployment also play a crucial role in inequality and, especially, poverty. As we saw in Chapter 4, the incidence of poverty is much higher in families whose adult members do not work than in those in which they are employed. A low labor force participation rate is a particularly acute problem among female-headed households, elderly families, and individuals with disabilities, chronic illnesses, and criminal records. A high incidence of unemployment is pervasive among teenagers and young families and individuals with low levels of schooling and training. The large differences in unemployment rates between white and black workers may also be due, in part, to racial discrimination. Special government programs may be called for to enable these groups to participate more fully in the labor market (see Chapter 15 for more discussion).

REFERENCES AND BIBLIOGRAPHY

A. Employment and Labor Force Participation

Akerlof, George, and Brian Main, "Experience-Weighted Measure of Employment and Unemployment Durations," *American Economic Review*, Vol. 71, December 1981, pp. 1003–1011.

Antos, Joseph, and Wesley Mellow, "The Youth Labor Market: A Dynamic Overview," Bureau of Labor Statistics, February 1978, mimeo.

Bailey, Martin, "Wages and Employment Under Uncertain Demand," *Review of Economic Studies*, Vol. 41, January 1974, pp. 37–50.

Baumol, William J., Sue Anne Batey Blackman, and Edward N. Wolff, *Productivity and American Leadership: The Long View*, MIT Press, Cambridge, Mass., 1989.

Ben-Porath, Yoram, "Labor Force Participation Rates and the Supply of Labor," *Journal of Political Economy*, Vol. 81, May–June 1973, pp. 697–704.

Blau, Francine, and Lawrence Kahn, "Unionism, Seniority, and Turnover," *Industrial Relations*, Vol. 23, 1983.

Bowen, William, and T. Aldrich Finegan, *The Economics of Labor Force Participation*, Princeton University Press, Princeton, NJ, 1969.

Cain, Glen G., *Married Women in the Labor Force: An Economic Analysis*, University of Chicago Press, Chicago, Ill., 1966.

Clark, Kim B., and Lawrence H. Summers, "Demographic Differences in Cyclical Employment Variation," *Journal of Human Resources*, Vol. 16, No. 1, Winter 1981, pp. 61–79.

Fishman, Betty G., and Leo Fishman, *Employment, Unemployment and Economic Growth,* Crowell, New York, 1969.

Franklin, N. N., "Employment and Unemployment: Views and Policies, 1919–1969," *International Labor Review,* Vol. 99, March 1969.

Freeman, Richard B., and David A. Wise, *The Youth Labor Market Problem: Its Nature, Causes, and Consequences,* University of Chicago Press, Chicago, 1982.

Gordon, Robert, *Macroeconomics,* Little, Brown, Boston, various editions.

Gordon, Robert J., and Robert E. Hall, "Arthur M. Okun, 1928–1980," *Brookings Papers on Economic Activity,* 1980–1981, pp. 1–5.

Kreps, Juanita, *Sex in the Marketplace: American Women at Work,* Johns Hopkins Press, Baltimore, Md., 1971.

Mincer, Jacob, "Labor Force Participation of Married Women: A Study of Labor Supply," in *Aspects of Labor Economics,* National Bureau of Economic Research, New York, 1962.

————, "Labor Force Participation and Unemployment: A Review of Recent Evidence" in Robert and Margaret Gordon (eds.), *Prosperity and Unemployment,* John Wiley, New York, 1966.

Morly, Jean, "Some Remarks on the Concepts of Employment, Underemployment and Unemployment," *International Labor Review,* Vol. 105, February 1972.

National Commission on Employment and Unemployment Statistics, *Counting the Labor Force,* U.S. Government Printing Office, Washington, D.C., 1979.

Okun, Arthur, "Potential GNP: Its Measurement and Significance," reprinted in Arthur Okun (ed.), *The Political Economy of Prosperity,* The Brookings Institution, Washington, D.C., 1970.

Owen, John D., *The American Work Force Since 1920,* Heath-Lexington Books, Lexington, MA, 1986.

President's Committee to Appraise Employment and Unemployment Statistics, *Measuring Employment and Unemployment,* U.S. Government Printing Office, Washington, D.C., 1962.

Stein, Robert, "Reasons for Nonparticipation in the Labor Force," *Monthly Labor Review,* Vol. 90, July 1967.

Stevenson, Wayne, "The Relationship Between Early Work Experience and Future Employability," in Avril Adams and Garth Magnum (eds.), *The Lingering Crisis of Youth Unemployment,* W. E. Upjohn Institute, Kalamazoo, Mich., 1978.

Strand, Kenneth, and Thomas Dernburg, "Cyclical Variation in Civilian Labor Force Participation," *Review of Economics and Statistics,* Vol. 46, No. 4, November 1964, pp. 378–391.

Tella, Alfred J., "The Relation of Labor Force to Employment," *Industrial and Labor Relations Review,* Vol. 17, April 1964, pp. 454–469.

————, "Labor Force Sensitivity to Employment by Age, Sex," *Industrial Relations,* Vol. 4, February 1965, pp. 69–83.

U.S. Department of Labor, *Manpower Report of the President, 1973*, U.S. Government Printing Office, Washington, D.C., March 1973.

Waldman, Elizabeth, and Kathryn Gover, "Marital and Family Characteristics of the Labor Force," *Monthly Labor Review*, Vol. 95, April 1972.

Wolfbein, Seymour, *Employment and Unemployment in the United States*, Science Research Associates, Chicago, 1962.

B. Unemployment

Abraham, Katherine, "Structural/Frictional vs. Deficient Demand Unemployment: Some New Evidence," *American Economic Review*, Vol. 83, No. 4, September 1983, pp. 708–724.

————, "Structural/Frictional vs. Deficient Demand Unemployment: Reply," *American Economic Review*, Vol. 76, No. 1, March 1986, pp. 273–276.

Adams, Avril, and Garth Magnum, *The Lingering Crisis of Youth Unemployment*, W. E. Upjohn Institute, Kalamazoo, Mich., 1978.

Adams, Charles, and David Coe, "A Systems Approach to Estimating the Natural Rate of Unemployment and Potential Output for the United States," *IMF Staff Papers*, Vol. 37, No. 2, June 1990, pp. 232–293.

Akerlof, George, and Brian Main, "Unemployment Spells and Unemployment Experience," *American Economic Review*, Vol. 70, 1980, pp. 885–893.

Azariadis, Costas, "Implicit Contracts and Underemployment Equilibria," *Journal of Political Economy*, Vol. 83, December 1975, pp. 1183–1202.

Becker, Brian, and Stephen Hills, "Teenage Unemployment: Some Evidence on the Long-Run Effects on Wages," *Journal of Human Resources*, Vol. 15, Summer 1980, pp. 354–372.

Benjamin, Daniel, and Levis Kochin, "Searching for an Explanation of Unemployment in Interwar Britain," *Journal of Political Economy*, Vol. 87, June 1979, pp. 441–478.

Bergmann, Barbara, and David E. Kaun, *Structural Unemployment in the United States*, U.S. Department of Commerce, U.S. Government Printing Office, Washington, D.C., 1966.

Breggar, John E., "Unemployment Statistics and What They Mean," *Monthly Labor Review*, Vol. 94, November 1971.

Clark, Kim B., and Lawrence H. Summers, "The Dynamics of Youth Unemployment," in Richard Freeman and David Wise (eds.), *The Youth Labor Market Problem: Its Nature, Causes, and Consequences, op. cit.*, 1982.

Corcoran, Mary, and Martha S. Hill, "Reoccurrence of Unemployment Spells Among Adult Men," *Journal of Human Resources*, Vol. 20, Spring 1985, pp. 165–183.

Doeringer, Peter B., and Michael J. Piore, "Unemployment and the Dual Labor Market," *The Public Interest*, Vol. 38, Winter 1975, pp. 74–75.

Eckstein, Otto, "Aggregate Demand and the Current Unemployment Problem," in A. M. Ross (ed.), *Unemployment and the American Economy*, John Wiley and Sons, New York, 1963.

Ehrenberg, Ronald G., "The Demographic Structure of Unemployment Rates and Labor Market Transition Probabilities," *Research in Labor Economics,* Vol. 3, 1980, pp. 241–243.

Feinberg, Robert, "Risk Aversion, Risk, and the Duration of Unemployment," *Review of Economics and Statistics,* Vol. 59, 1977.

Feldstein, Martin, "The Economics of the New Unemployment," *Public Interest,* Vol. 33, Fall 1973, pp. 3–42.

———, "The Importance of Temporary Layoffs: An Empirical Analysis," *Brookings Papers on Economic Activity,* No. 3, 1975, pp. 725–744.

———, "Temporary Layoffs in the Theory of Unemployment," *Journal of Political Economy,* Vol. 84, October 1976, pp. 937–957.

Flaim, Paul O., "Discouraged Workers and Changes in Unemployment," *Monthly Labor Review,* Vol. 96, No. 3, March 1973.

Freeman, Richard B., and Harry J. Holzer, *The Black Youth Unemployment Crisis,* University of Chicago Press, Chicago, 1986.

Friedlander, Stanley, *Unemployment in the Urban Core,* Praeger, New York, 1972.

Gallaway, Lowell, "Labor Mobility, Resource Allocation and Structural Unemployment," *American Economic Review,* Vol. 53, September 1963.

Gilpatrick, Eleanor, *Structural Unemployment and Aggregate Demand: A Study of Employment and Unemployment in the United States, 1948–1964,* John Hopkins Press, Baltimore, Md., 1966.

Gilroy, Curtis, "Job Losers, Leavers, and Entrants: Traits and Trends," *Monthly Labor Review,* Vol. 96, August 1973.

Gordon, David, *Theories of Poverty and Underemployment: Orthodox, Radical, and Dual Labor Market Perspectives,* D.C. Heath, Lexington, Mass., 1972.

Gordon, Robert A., and Margaret S. Gordon (eds.), *Prosperity and Unemployment,* John Wiley and Sons, New York, 1966.

Gordon, Robert J., "Unemployment and Potential Output in the 1980s," *Brookings Papers on Economic Activity,* Vol. 2, 1984, pp. 537–563.

Hall, Robert E., "Why Is the Unemployment Rate So High at Full Employment?" *Brookings Papers on Economic Activity,* No. 3, 1970, pp. 369–402.

Hammermesh, Daniel S., *Jobless Pay and the Economy,* Johns Hopkins University Press, Baltimore, Md., 1977.

Harrison, Bennett, "Ghetto Economic Development: A Survey," *Journal of Economic Literature,* Vol. 12, March 1974, pp. 1–37.

Hurd, Michael, "A Compensation Measure of the Cost of Unemployment to the Unemployed," *Quarterly Journal of Economics,* Vol. 95, 1980, pp. 225–244.

Johnson, G. E., and P. R. G. Layard, "The Natural Rate of Unemployment: Explanation and Policy," in Orley C. Ashenfelter and Richard Layard (eds.), *Handbook of Labor Economics,* Vol. II, North-Holland, New York, 1986.

Juhn, Chinhui, Kevin M. Murphy, and Robert H. Topel, "Why Has the Natural Rate of Unemployment Increased over Time?" *Brookings Papers on Economic Activity,* No. 2, 1991, pp. 75–126.

Katz, Arnold, "Schooling, Age, and Length of Unemployment," *Industrial and Labor Relations Review,* Vol. 27, 1974.

Killingsworth, Charles C., "Automation, Jobs, and Manpower: The Case for Structural Unemployment," in Garth L. Magnum (ed.), *The Manpower Revolution: Its Policy Consequences,* Doubleday, Garden City, N.Y., 1965.

Marston, Steven T., "Employment Instability and High Unemployment Rates," *Brookings Paper on Economic Activity,* 1976, No. 1, pp. 169–203.

Mattila, J. Peter, "Job Quitting and Frictional Unemployment," *American Economic Review,* Vol. 64, March 1974, pp. 235–239.

Medoff, James, "Layoffs and Alternatives Under Trade Unions in United States Manufacturing," *American Economic Review,* Vol. 69, June 1979, pp. 380–395.

Mortensen, Dale T., "Job Search, the Duration of Unemployment, and the Phillips Curve," *American Economic Review,* Vol. 60, December 1970, pp. 847–862.

———, "Job Search and Labor Market Analysis," in Orley C. Ashenfelter and Richard Layard (eds.), *Handbook of Labor Economics,* Vol. II, North-Holland, New York, 1986.

Osberg, Lars, Richard Apostle, and Don Clairmont, "The Incidence and Duration of Individual Unemployment: Supply Side or Demand Side?" *Cambridge Journal of Economics,* Vol. 10, 1986, pp. 13–33.

Osterman, Paul, "Race Differences in Male Youth Unemployment," in U.S. Department of Labor, *Conference Report on Youth Unemployment: Its Measurement and Meaning,* U.S. Government Printing Office, Washington, D.C., 1978.

Rosen, Carol, "Hidden Unemployment and Related Issues," *Monthly Labor Review,* Vol. 96, No. 3, March 1973.

Rowthorn, Bob, and Andrew Glyn, "The Diversity of Unemployment Experience Since 1973," *Structural Change and Economic Dynamics,* Vol. 1, No. 1, June 1990, pp. 57–89.

Schwartz, Arthur R., Malcolm S. Cohen, and Donald R. Grimes, "Structural/Frictional vs. Deficient Demand Unemployment: Comment," *American Economic Review,* Vol. 76, No. 1, March 1986, pp. 268–272.

Sider, Hal, "Unemployment Duration and Incidence," *American Economic Review,* Vol. 75, No. 3, June 1985, pp. 461–472.

Simler, N. J., "Long-Term Unemployment, the Structural Hypothesis, and Public Policy," *American Economic Review,* Vol. 54, December 1964.

———, "Hidden Unemployment 1953–1962: A Quantitative Analysis by Age and Sex," *American Economic Review,* Vol. 56, March 1966.

———, and Alfred Tella, "Labor Reserves and the Phillips Curve," *Review of Economics and Statistics,* Vol. 50, No. 1, February 1968, pp. 32–49.

Sorkin, Alan L., *Education, Unemployment, and Economic Growth,* Lexington Books, Lexington, Mass., 1974.

Summers, Lawrence H., "Why Is the Unemployment Rate So Very High Near Full Employment?" *Brookings Papers on Economic Activity,* Vol. 2, 1986, pp. 339–383.

————, "Relative Wages, Efficiency Wages, and Keynesian Unemployment," *American Economic Review Papers and Proceedings*, Vol. 78, No. 2, May 1988, pp. 383–388.

U.S. Congress, Joint Economic Committee, *The Extent and Nature of Frictional Unemployment*, Bureau of Labor Statistics, Washington, D.C., 1959.

U.S. Congressional Budget Office, *Youth Unemployment: The Outlook and Some Policy Strategies*, U.S. Government Printing Office, Washington, D.C., April 1978.

Warden, Charles, "Unemployment Compensation: The Massachusetts Experience," in Otto Eckstein (ed.), *Studies in the Economics of Income Maintenance*, The Brookings Institution, Washington, D.C., 1967.

Welch, Finis, "What Have We Learned from Empirical Studies of Unemployment Insurance?" *Industrial and Labor Relations Review*, Vol. 30, July 1977, pp. 451–461.

DISCUSSION QUESTIONS

1. Give three reasons why the LFPR of men and women appear to be converging over time.
2. Describe the principal changes in the occupational and industrial makeup of the labor force since 1950.
3. Explain why the mean duration of unemployment is higher than its median duration. What does this imply about the composition of the unemployed population?
4. Discuss three sources of structural unemployment.
5. Explain why and how the official unemployment rate might need adjustment for discouraged workers and part-time employment.

6

LABOR SUPPLY, LABOR DEMAND, AND HUMAN CAPITAL THEORY

We begin our formal analysis of the labor market in this chapter. Section 6.1 develops the standard neoclassical model. The supply curve of labor and demand curve for labor are derived, as well as the formation of an equilibrium wage. The human capital model is discussed in Section 6.2. It is an extension of the neoclassical model, which treats schooling and training as an investment decision on the part of workers and leads to a theory of relative wages. A summary is provided in the concluding section.

6.1 THE NEOCLASSICAL THEORY OF WAGES

In the **neoclassical model,** the amount of labor an individual is willing to supply is a function of the wage rate, and the amount of labor firms are willing to purchase is also a function of the wage rate. Under conditions of **perfect competition,** an **equilibrium** or **market wage** will form at the point where the supply and demand curves cross. It is also possible to derive an equilibrium wage under other special conditions when perfect competition fails to hold.

It might be noted at the outset that there are alternative models that have been developed to explain differentials in earnings. (These will be developed in subsequent chapters.) The neoclassical model is based upon a set of assumptions that may not hold in a number of circumstances. The two most important assumptions of the model are (1) perfect competition among firms and workers and (2) perfect information. The assumption of perfect competition among firms implies that there are a large number of firms in an industry, capital is free to move between firms, and there is free entry into and exit from each industry. Perfect competition among workers means that there is free entry into the labor market and unrestricted mobility among alternative employment opportunities. Perfect information implies that workers are fully aware of alternative job opportunities and that firms are fully aware of the characteristics of the available labor pool. Each of these assumptions, as we shall see below, plays a crucial role in the determination of the equilibrium wage.

This section is divided into four parts. The first part develops the labor supply curve. The second part presents the theory of labor demand. The third part explains how the equilibrium wage is formed. The concept of equilibrium is first discussed, and then the formation of equilibrium is developed under alternative assumptions about the labor market. In the fourth part, some extensions of the neoclassical model are considered.

The Supply of Labor

The theory of the household serves as the basis for the analysis of labor supply, and the labor supply curve is derived from the household's trade-off between income and leisure. The basic unit of analysis is the household or family. Though the family is a complex social entity which decides how to allocate its time among a range of activities, including housework, child care, personal health, recreation, schooling, and market work, we shall be concerned here only with the decisions regarding paid labor. Moreover, such decisions regarding labor market participation are made more complex by the fact that decisions by a husband or wife depend on those made by the other spouse. For simplicity, it will be assumed that each family member makes the decisions regarding his or her labor supply independently of other family members.

Formally, we shall define **labor supply** as time sold by an individual in the market in exchange for wages or salary (wages, for short). Basically, the individual faces a trade-off in allocating his or her time between paid labor and nonmarket activities, which will be lumped together under the rubric leisure. Since wages can be used to purchase goods and services, the trade-off reduces to one between real income and leisure.

This trade-off can be represented by a utility function which gives the level of utility or well-being U as a function of real income Y (income, for short) and hours of leisure H:

$$U = U(Y, H) \qquad (6.1)$$

The utility function can be represented by indifference curves. An indifference curve shows those combinations of income and hours of leisure among which an individual is indifferent—that is, which lead to the same level of utility. Such an indifference mapping is shown in Diagram 6.1. The vertical

Diagram 6.1 Indifference Curves for Income and Leisure

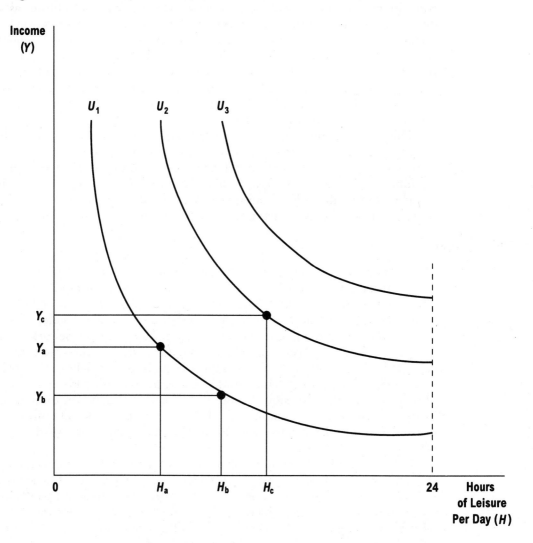

axis represents income, and the horizontal axis represents hours of leisure. For purposes of interpretation, it is necessary to think of both axes in terms of a particular time period, such as a day. Since there are only 24 hours in a day, the horizontal axis has a maximum value of 24 hours.

The curved lines (designated U_1, U_2, and U_3) are the indifference curves. Curves lying further from the origin represent higher levels of utility, since more of both leisure *and* income can be attained. In this case, since $Y_c > Y_a$, and $H_c > H_a$, then the indifference curve U_2 must represent a higher level of utility than U_1.[1] On the other hand, the combination Y_a and H_a yields the same level of utility, U_1, as the combination Y_b and H_b and, as a result, is on the same indifference curve.

Indifference curves have a **negative slope.** In other words, if some income is given up, more hours of leisure are necessary to reach the same utility level. In this case, $Y_b < Y_a$ but $H_b > H_a$. The absolute value of the slope of an indifference curve is referred to as the **marginal rate of substitution of income for leisure (MRS),** since it shows that amount of income that must be added to compensate for the loss of a given amount of leisure.[2] It is also assumed that indifference curves are **convex to the origin.** This means that the more income an individual has, the more income he is willing to give up for an extra hour of leisure to achieve the same utility level. Conversely, the less income she has, the greater the amount of leisure she is willing to give up for an extra dollar of income.[3]

The MRS represents the amount of income the individual is willing to give up for an extra hour of leisure. The actual **market wage rate** indicates how much additional income a worker *could* obtain for an additional hour of work. It is assumed that workers sell their labor in a competitive labor market at a fixed market-determined wage rate. This condition can be conveniently represented by a **budget line** or **budget constraint,** as shown in Diagram 6.2. We have used the same axes as in Diagram 6.1. The person's maximum income is Y_{max}, which indicates how much the person could earn if the person spent 24 hours working (had no hours of leisure). At the other extreme, if the person did not work at all, income would be zero. The slope of the line, $\Delta Y / \Delta H$, is the wage rate w, since it shows the change in earnings per hour worked. Note that the budget line is a straight line because the wage rate is assumed to be fixed and not to vary with the number of hours worked (for example, overtime pay is the same as regular pay). Note also that at a particular point, such as (Y_d, H_d), $L_d = 24 - H_d$ is the number of hours worked per day.

The choice of the hours of work for a particular individual depends on the prevailing wage rate and the individual's utility function. This is illustrated in Diagram 6.3 by the budget line at the prevailing wage rate and the person's indifference map. Points A and B, for example, lie on both the budget line and indifference curve U_1. Though the individual could choose either of these points, he could reach a higher level of utility, U_2, at point P, where he would work $\overline{L} = 24 - \overline{H}$ hours and receive an income of $\overline{Y}$. In fact, given the prevailing wage rate w, U_2 is the highest level of utility that could

---

[1] It should be noted that it is not necessary to assign actual (cardinal) values to these curves. It is sufficient for this analysis that U_2 simply represents a higher level of utility than U_1, and U_3 represents a higher level than U_2—that is, that utility curves have an ordinal ranking.

[2] In terms of calculus, the slope is dY/dH.

[3] In other words, the MRS between income and leisure declines with income. Another way of describing this relation is to say that leisure and income are "imperfect substitutes." If the two were perfect substitutes, the indifference curve would be a straight line, and the MRS would be the same at every point on the line. (The student should try to verify this.)

Diagram 6.2   The Budget Line for a Representative Worker

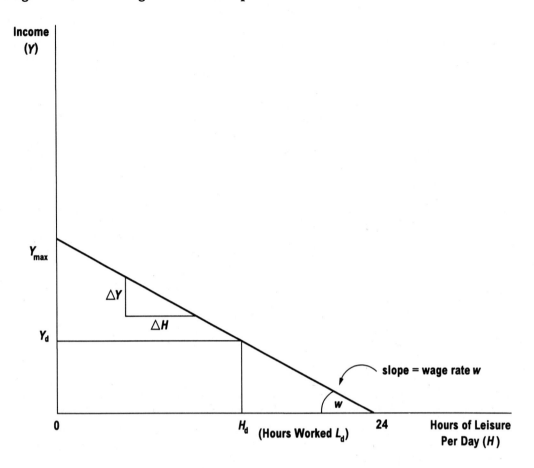

be attained. Point P maximizes the person's utility. Indeed, even though U_3 represents a higher level of utility, it cannot be reached at the prevailing wage rate. The point P is the point at which the indifference curve is *tangent* to the budget line, whose slope is the prevailing wage rate w. Since the slope of the indifference curve is also the MRS between income and leisure, the condition of maximizing utility is given by:

$$MRS = w \qquad (6.2)$$

At this point, the individual cannot increase his or her utility by working less hours or more hours.[4]

---

[4]For simplicity, we are ignoring the issue of whether the individual may decide not to work at all.

Part II   The Role of Labor Markets

Diagram 6.3 The Choice of Hours of Work at a Given Wage Rate

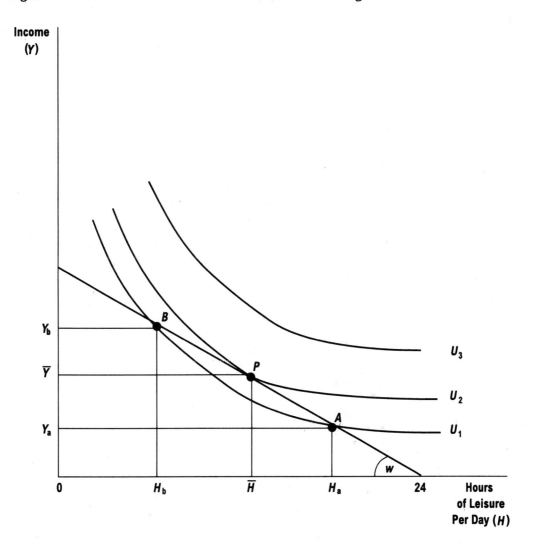

Supply Curve of Labor. We can now generate the **supply curve of labor,** which shows how many hours an individual will work at any given wage rate. Three budget lines are drawn in Diagram 6.4 at three different wage rates—w_1, w_2, and w_3, where $w_3 > w_2 > w_1$. At wage rate w_1, the individual will choose H_1 hours of leisure or $L_1 = 24 - H_1$ hours of work; at w_2, the individual would choose to work $L_2 = 24 - H_2$ hours of work; and at w_3, $L_3 = 24 - H_3$ hours of work. H_2 is less than H_1, but H_3 is greater than H_2. In fact, it is not possible to predict from theory alone whether an increase in the wage rate will lead

Diagram 6.4   The Choice of Hours of Work at Different Wage Rates

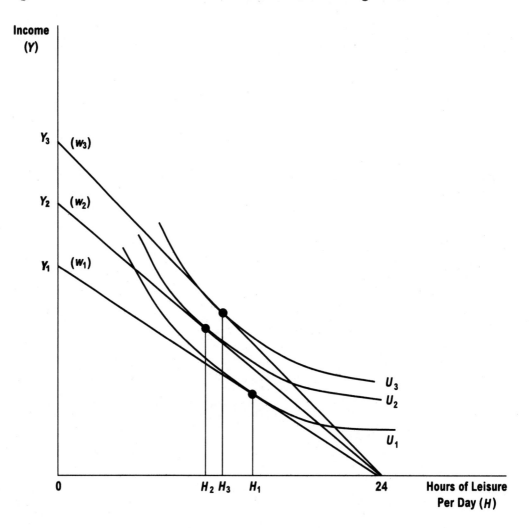

to more or less hours of work. In this illustration, hours of work decline when the wage rate rises from w_2 to w_3.

Further analysis reveals why one cannot predict what happens to hours worked when the wage rate changes. In Diagram 6.5, we have replicated the two budget lines for w_1 and w_2 shown in Diagram 6.4, as well as the indifference curves U_1 and U_2. For wage rate w_1, $24 - H_1$ hours would be supplied, and for w_2, $24 - H_2$ hours. Let us now draw a line parallel to the budget line for wage rate w_1 and tangent to the indifference curve U_2. This new line has slope w_1 and intersects the vertical axis at Y^*. If we draw a vertical line at 24

Diagram 6.5 The Substitution and Income Effects Resulting from a Change in the Wage Rate

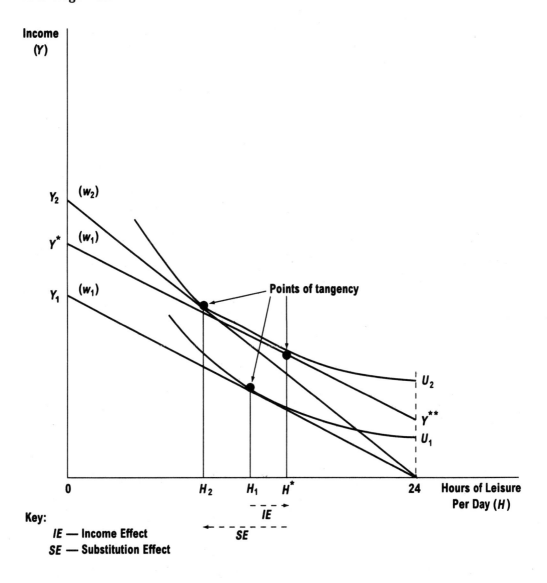

Key:

IE — Income Effect

SE — Substitution Effect

hours, this line would intersect it at Y^{**}. From elementary geometry, Y^{**} would equal $Y^* - Y_1$.

We can now decompose the change in hours worked resulting from a wage increase from w_1 to w_2 into two components. The first is equivalent to a movement of the budget line from its original position at Y_1 to Y^*Y^{**}. The line Y^*Y^{**} can be interpreted as the budget constraint that would prevail if the individual continued to face wage w_1 but was given a "lump-sum payment" (such as a bequest or annuity) of Y**. Y** is the amount of extra income required to allow the individual to attain the new level of utility at the old wage rate of w_1. This new budget line, by construction, yields a utility level of U_2. The hours of work *always* decline—in this case, from $24 - H_1$ to $24 - H_*$.[5] This change is called the **income effect,** since it shows how much additional income the person would require to reach the new utility level (or "real income" level) at the old wage rate.

The second component is equivalent to the movement of the budget line from Y*Y** to its final position at Y_2. This represents the increase of the wage rate to w_2. Notice that since the indifference curve is convex, the point of tangency must move to the left. Thus, the hours of work will *always* increase when the wage rises—in this case, from $24 - H_1$ to $24 - H_2$. This change is called the **substitution effect**—that is, the effect of substituting the new wage rate for the old wage rate while keeping the utility level constant. It essentially tracks the change in hours worked from a change in the wage rate, while the budget constraint also changes in such a way as to keep utility constant.

With an increase in the wage rate, the income effect always leads to a reduction in hours of work, while the substitution effect always leads to an increase in hours of work. The net effect, which is the sum of the two, may therefore either increase or decrease hours supplied. This is equivalent to saying that the net effect is theoretically indeterminant.

It is uncertain what the supply curve of labor looks like. However, there is empirical evidence that it looks something like Diagram 6.6.[6] This curve shows the amount of hours that would be supplied by an individual at different wage rates. It is usually thought that over low levels of wages the substitution effect dominates the income effect and the supply curve slopes upward to the right. However, in the upper range, the income effect is dominant, and the supply curve slopes upward to the left. This is referred to as the **backward-bending supply curve.** Thus, it is quite possible that at a high enough wage, as the wage rate increases, hours worked will decline.

To derive the aggregate or *market* supply curve for the whole labor force, we sum up the curves for the individual workers. This is accomplished by selecting a wage rate *w* and then adding together the hours that would be supplied by each individual at wage rate *w*. When this addition is done for all possible wage rates *w*, we have the market supply curve of labor.

It has been implicitly assumed in the derivation that the "quality" of labor is fixed. The full labor supply decision involves not only how many hours to work (if any) but also what quality of labor to supply. This latter decision often involves deciding on how much schooling or training to acquire. In this sense, the supply curve of labor we have just derived is the **short-run supply curve,** since the quality of labor is assumed fixed. The **long-**

---

[5]This is true as long as leisure is a "normal" good. In this case, normality means that as income rises, the demand for leisure increases.

[6]See the excellent survey of empirical work on this subject in Killingsworth (1983), Chapter 3.

Diagram 6.6   The Supply Curve of Hours Worked for an Individual Worker

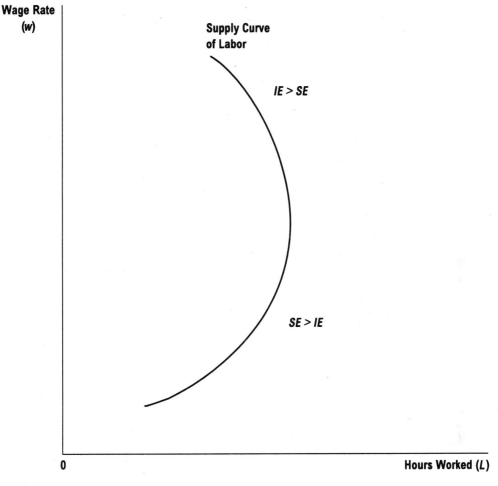

Key:
  IE — Income Effect
  SE — Substitution Effect

run supply curve of labor would reflect not only the amount of labor offered for sale but also the amount of schooling and training. We shall have
more to say about this in Section 6.2.[7]

---

[7]Another qualification is that we have assumed that an individual can choose the number of
hours to work. In reality, most individuals are required to work a certain number of hours per week
by their company.

The Demand for Labor

The basic unit of analysis is the firm, and the labor demand curve is derived from the firm's production function. A firm's demand for labor depends on the demand for its *output*. The relation between a firm's output and its labor input can be conveniently represented by the firm's **production function.** For convenience, it will be assumed that there are only two factors of production: labor, L, and capital, K. Then, the firm's production function F is given by:

$$Q = F(L,K)$$

As with the utility function, it is helpful to look at the combinations of the inputs that yield the same level of output. Such a set of points is called an **isoquant.** Isoquants for three different levels of output are illustrated in Diagram 6.7. Capital is recorded on the vertical axis, and labor on the horizontal axis. The curves in the diagram show the combinations of inputs that are needed to produce the indicated level of output. Unlike indifference curves, isoquants represent actual quantities of output. Thus, the combination K_a of capital and L_a of labor will produce Q_1 units of output, as will K_b of capital and L_b of labor. It should also be apparent that $Q_2 > Q_1$ and $Q_3 > Q_2$. Consider, for example, the combination K_c and L_c on isoquant Q_2. Since $K_c > K_a$ and $L_c > L_a$, then the level of output achievable with K_c and L_c must be greater than with K_a and L_a.[8]

There are two important properties of the isoquant, which are very similar to those for the indifference curve. First, the isoquant has a negative slope. When one factor of production is reduced, the other factor must be increased in order to maintain the same level of output. In Diagram 6.7, for example, points A and B are on the same isoquant. Since K_a is greater than K_b, then L_b must be less than L_a. The slope of the isoquant indicates how much labor must be added per unit reduction of capital in order to maintain production at a given level. This slope (actually, its absolute value) is referred to as the **marginal rate of technical substitution of capital for labor (MRTS).**

Second, the isoquant is *convex* to the origin. The slope of the isoquant becomes smaller as the amount of labor increases. The economic interpretation of this is that more labor must be added to compensate for a unit re-

---

[8]There are two additional points that should be mentioned. First, there may be production points that entail both more capital and more labor in order to produce Q_1 than some other point, say A, on the isoquant for Q_1. Though such points are *technically* feasible, they are not *economically* feasible, since they would involve a higher cost at all input prices than point A and would not be chosen by a firm. These points are not shown in Diagram 6.7. Second, both output and inputs are actually measured for a given time period, such as a year. Thus, the input of capital is better thought of as an input of capital *services* and labor as labor *services* for the given time period.

Diagram 6.7 Isoquants of Capital and Labor in a Firm's Production Function

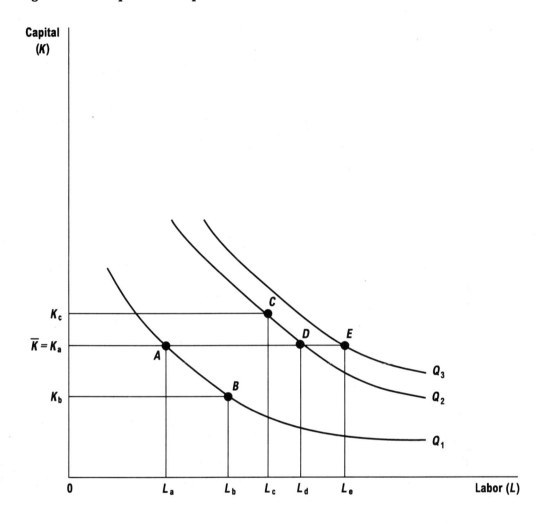

duction in capital as production becomes more labor-intensive.[9] In other words, the slope (the absolute value) of the isoquant, MRTS, declines as labor increases.

The production function shows the combination of inputs which can *technologically* produce various levels of output. The actual choice of input combination depends on *economic* variables, particularly the relative price of the inputs. In order to solve the problem, three assumptions must be made.

_____

[9] Or, conversely, more capital must be added to compensate for a unit loss of labor as production becomes more capital-intensive.

The first is that firms operate in a competitive market, and no firm is dominant enough to set the price of either the output of its industry or the inputs in the industry. Firms are *price-takers* in the market. The second is that firms are profit-maximizers. The third is that when the wage is fixed at the market level, the firm can hire as much labor as it wants at that wage (i.e., the supply curve of labor to the firm is perfectly elastic).

We first show the short-run analysis, when the firm's capital is fixed at say $\overline{K} = K_a$, as shown in Diagram 6.7. With K_a units of capital and an input of L_a units of labor, output will equal Q_1 (point A); with L_d labor, output will be Q_2 (point D); and with L_e labor, Q_3 (point E) will be produced. By drawing all possible isoquants in Diagram 6.7, we could determine what level of output would be produced with K_a units of capital and any amount of labor.

For analytical reasons it is more useful to derive the relation between the change in labor input and the change in output. This can be obtained in a very similar manner. Instead of noting the actual level of output corresponding to each level of labor input, one can instead note the *change in output* corresponding to *each unit change* in labor input. This variable is referred to as the **marginal physical product of labor,** MPP_L,

$$MPP_L = \Delta Q / \Delta L = \Delta F(L,\overline{K}) / \Delta L \qquad (6.3)$$

since it shows the (marginal) change in output per unit change in labor (with capital held fixed).[10]

The MPP_L curve is shown in Diagram 6.8. Initially, as more labor is added to a fixed amount of capital, the rate at which output increases may itself increase, because labor becomes more specialized and skilled. However, after a point, the change in output per unit increase in labor starts to decline, as the **law of diminishing returns** becomes operative. An alternative way of stating this is that, with the amount of capital fixed, as the capital-labor ratio declines, so does the MPP_L. The classic example is the increase of employment on a fixed amount of agricultural land ("capital"). As more and more labor is hired to farm a given amount of acreage, the incremental yield per new worker will decline (and continue to decline) after a point.

The curve for the **average physical product of labor,** APP_L, is also shown in Diagram 6.8. This is computed from the function $Q = F(L,\overline{K})$ by dividing output by the amount of labor:

$$APP_L = Q/L = F(L,\overline{K}) / L \qquad (6.4)$$

Note that the point P at which the MPP_L curve crosses the APP_L curve is the point at which the average product of labor is a maximum. The reason is that to the left of point P, $MPP_L > APP_L$, which means that the marginal increase in output per unit increase of labor is greater than the average

---

[10] In terms of calculus, $MPP_L = \partial F(L,K) / \partial L$, where "$\partial$" is the sign for the partial derivative.

Diagram 6.8 The Marginal and Average Physical Product of Labor (with Capital Fixed)

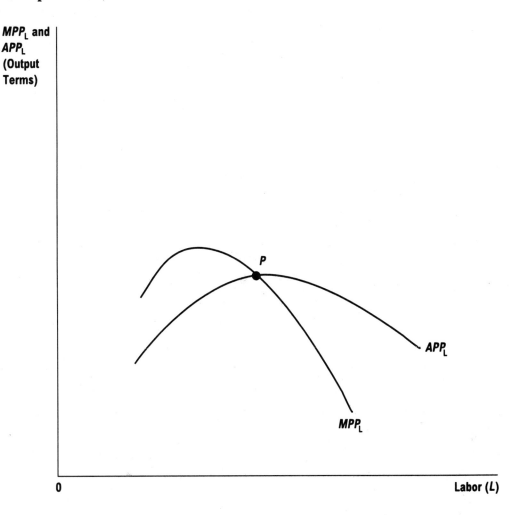

product of labor. If you add a number to a series which is greater than the original mean, then the mean must increase (the student should verify this with an arithmetic example). Thus, to the left of point P, the APP_L curve is rising. To the right of point P, the opposite is true. The $MPP_L < APP_L$, which causes the average product of labor curve to decline.

How much labor would a firm hire at a given wage w? To answer this, we must go one step further and convert the physical product curve of labor into *value terms*. A firm's total revenue TR is equal to the quantity it produces multiplied by the price of its output, p:

$$TR = p \cdot Q \tag{6.5}$$

Define the **marginal value product of labor,** MVP_L, as the additional *revenue* the firm receives from employing an additional worker, and the *average value product of labor,* AVP_L, as the average revenue the firm receives per worker. Under perfect competition, the MVP_L is thus equal to the MPP_L multiplied by the output price, and likewise, the AVP_L equals the APP_L multiplied by the price:[11]

$$MVP_L = MPP_L \cdot p \qquad (6.6)$$

$$AVP_L = APP_L \cdot p \qquad (6.7)$$

The MVP_L and AVP_L curves are shown in Diagram 6.9. The value product curves look almost identical to the corresponding physical product curves—the only difference is that the former are measured in dollars, whereas the latter are measured in physical quantities.

We can now derive the short-run demand curve for labor. A profit-maximizing firm will continue to hire labor as long as the extra or **marginal revenue** (MR) it can obtain is greater than the extra or **marginal cost** (MC) of the additional input. The condition of profit-maximizing is given by:

$$MR = MC \qquad (6.8)$$

Beyond this point, the extra cost incurred by the firm will be greater than the extra revenues it receives, and the firm's profit will decline.

In the case of its labor input, the marginal cost of hiring an additional worker in a competitive labor market is the wage w. The marginal revenue generated by the additional employee is MVP_L in a competitive output market. Therefore, the firm will continue to hire additional labor until:

$$MVP_L = w \qquad (6.9)$$

This is the condition of profit maximization for the firm. This is shown in Diagram 6.9 for wage w_a. At this wage, the firm will hire L_a workers.

The short-run demand curve for labor, D_L, which shows the amount of labor a firm will hire at each wage level, is the MVP_L curve of labor, with one qualification. The firm will hire L_a workers at wage w_a only if their average revenue is greater that their average cost, since only then will the firm make a profit. The average revenue of labor is given by the AVP_L curve in Diagram 6.9, while the average cost of labor is its wage rate. At wage rate w_a, the average revenue of labor (point B) is greater than its average cost, and

---

[11] In a competitive market, the price of a firm's output is set in the market and is independent of the quantity of output it produces.

Diagram 6.9   Short-Run Demand Curve for Labor

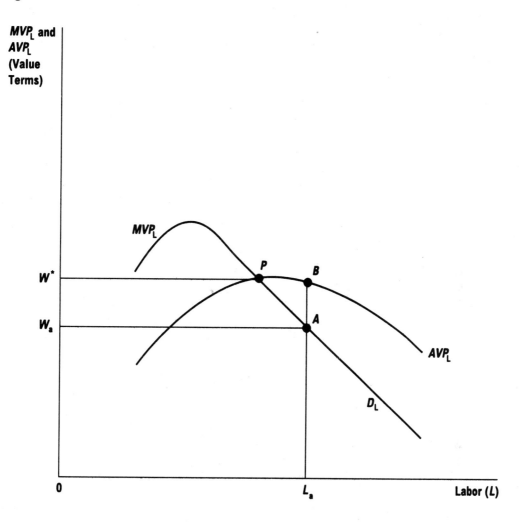

therefore, the firm will hire L_a workers.[12] This is the case up to wage rate w*, since here (point P) the wage is equal to the AVP_L. Above w*, the MVP_L = w > AVP_L, and the firm would lose money by hiring any workers at all. Therefore, the firm would hire no labor for w > w* and, instead, shut down the plant. The demand curve for labor is thus that portion of the MVP_L curve that lies below point P. Its most important characteristic is that it slopes downward to the right. This means that as the wage falls, the quantity

---

[12]Technically, we would have to add a second condition that the other variable costs of the firm are also covered.

Chapter 6   Labor Supply, Labor Demand, and Human Capital Theory   195

of labor demanded increases, and as the wage rises, quantity of labor demanded falls off.

The short-run market demand curve is constructed in analogous fashion to the market supply curve of labor. In this case, we sum up the demand curves for the individual firms. This is accomplished by selecting a wage rate w and then adding together the labor that each firm would hire at this wage.

Long-Run Demand Curve for Labor*

The long-run demand curve for labor is somewhat more complicated to derive, and the formal analysis will not be done here. However, the major properties of the demand curve can be discussed. In the long run, it is assumed that firms can adjust the amount of capital they own. For simplicity, it is also assumed that the price of capital as well as the price of the firm's output are fixed by the market. Let us suppose that the firm is in equilibrium and the wage rate falls. In the short run, with the firm's capital fixed, the firm will hire additional workers until the MVP_L equals the new wage rate. However, with capital flexible, the firm may decide to change not only the amount of labor it employs but also the amount of capital.

The immediate effect of the decreased wage is to make the cost of producing the original level of output cheaper. In fact, the firm could produce the original level of output even more cheaply by substituting labor for capital—that is, increasing its employment while reducing its capital. This is called the **substitution effect.** However, since the cost of production is now lowered, the firm could increase its profit by expanding its production (by assumption, the price of the firm's output is fixed). This is called the **scale effect** and is accomplished both by hiring even more workers and buying additional capital.

The relation between the short-run and long-run demand curves for labor is illustrated in Diagram 6.10. Suppose the wage rate is initially w_1, and the firm's capital stock is K_1. The firm will therefore hire L_1 workers, since point A is on its short-run demand curve MVP_L with a capital of K_1. At point A, the marginal value product of labor is equal to w_1. Now suppose the wage falls to w_2. In the short run, with capital fixed at K_1, the firm will hire L_2 workers, since at point B, the marginal value product of labor, with capital fixed at K_1, is equal to w_2. However, in the long run, the firm will also adjust its capital stock. In particular, with the wage rate lowered, the firm will adjust its capital stock to K_2. The marginal value product curve for labor shifts to the right to MVP_L (K_2).[13] $MVP_L(K_2)$ is now the new short-run demand

[13]Analytically, it is impossible to determine whether K_2 will be greater than K_1. The reason is that the substitution effect and scale effect cause capital to change in the opposite direction. The substitution effect, by itself, will cause the new level of capital to be smaller than the original level, but the scale effect causes the capital to increase from expanded production. It cannot be predicted which of the two effects is dominant. Despite this, it is possible to prove mathematically that the $MVP_L(K_2)$ curve will always lie to the right of the $MVP_L(K_1)$ curve.

Diagram 6.10   The Long-Run Demand Curve for Labor

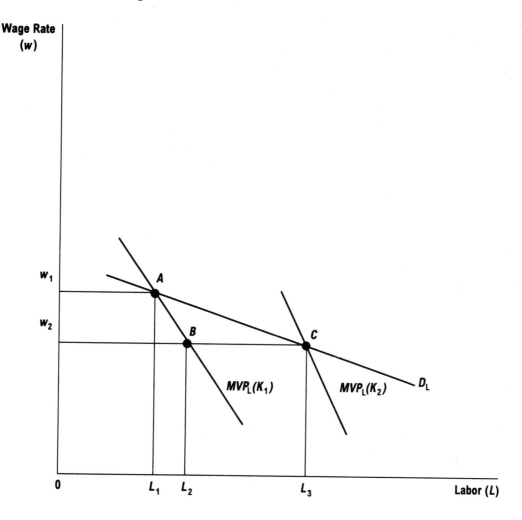

curve for labor, and the firm will hire L_3 workers, since at point C, the marginal value product of labor equals w_2.

The long-run demand curve for labor, indicated by D_L, is the line joining the equilibrium points of the short-run MVP_L curves. At wage w_1, the short-run equilibrium is L_1 labor; at w_2, the short-run equilibrium is L_2 labor. The long-run demand curve D_L thus runs through points A and C. There are two properties of the long-run demand curve. First, like the short-run demand curves, D_L slopes downward to the right, which means that as the wage falls, more labor is hired. Second, the long-run demand curve D_L is *flatter* (or *more elastic*) than the short-run demand curves. This means that a fall in the wage rate will cause more workers to be hired in the long-run than in the short-run, and conversely if the wage rises.

The Formation of an Equilibrium Wage in a Competitive Market

Under the assumptions of competitive markets, how do the supply and demand curves interact to determine the wage level? The solution is shown in Diagram 6.11. The market supply curve S_L shows how much labor will be offered for sale at each wage rate,[14] while the market demand curve D_L shows how much labor firms will hire at each wage rate. Both the supply curve and the demand curve are derived under the assumption of perfect competition. The *equilibrium* (or market-clearing) wage $\bar{w}$ is the wage level at which the supply and demand curves intersect, and the equilibrium employment level $\bar{L}$ is the corresponding employment.

Wage $\bar{w}$ is an equilibrium wage because the amount of labor workers wish to sell at $\bar{w}$ equals the amount of labor firms want to hire at this wage. In this case, the labor market has cleared. At a higher wage, say w_1, the quantity of labor supplied would be greater than the quantity of labor demanded. As a result, some workers who offer their services will be unable to work all the hours they wish, or they will be unemployed. Some of them may therefore offer to work at a lower wage, and this will cause the wage to fall to $\bar{w}$. Conversely, if the wage were at w_2, the quantity demanded would be greater than the quantity supplied. Firms would bid up the wage until the wage once again equaled $\bar{w}$. At equilibrium, then, both firms and the workforce are satisfied with the level of employment, and no household or firm has an incentive to change.[15]

There are two important properties of the equilibrium wage. First, since the supply curve indicates the set of points at which the marginal rate of substitution (MRS) between income and leisure equals the wage, the first property is:

$$\text{MRS} = \bar{w} \tag{6.10}$$

Second, since the demand curve indicates the set of points at which the marginal value product of labor equals the wage, the second property is:

$$\text{MVP}_L = \bar{w} \tag{6.11}$$

---

[14] To simplify the analysis, we will ignore the "backward-bending" part of the labor supply curve. Equivalently, we are assuming that the demand curve does not intersect the supply curve in its backward-bending portion.

[15] The point of intersection of the D_L and the S_L curves in Diagram 6.11 is not only an equilibrium point but a *stable* equilibrium. This means that if the wage deviates from $\bar{w}$, the dynamics of the labor market would bring the wage back to $\bar{w}$. In contrast, an unstable equilibrium would imply that if the wage deviated from $\bar{w}$, the dynamics would cause the wage to move further away from $\bar{w}$. The wage $\bar{w}$ is still an equilibrium wage, since there would be no reason to change if it were $\bar{w}$.

Diagram 6.11   The Formation of the Short-Run Equilibrium Wage in a Competitive Market

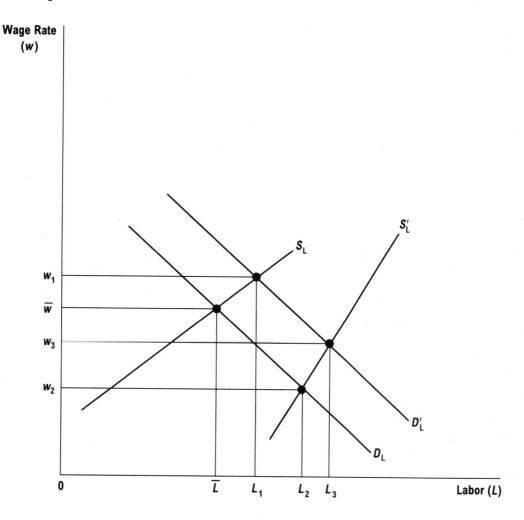

Thus, the point of equilibrium in the labor market is the wage at which the marginal rate of substitution between income and leisure for each worker equals the marginal value product of labor in each firm and both are equal to the wage.

It might be instructive to analyze what happens to the wage and employment if the demand and supply curves for labor shift. Suppose, as illustrated in Diagram 6.11, the demand curve shifts to the right to D'_L. This indicates that at a given wage, firms wish to hire more workers, perhaps because production has expanded or technology has changed. A shift in demand to D'_L will cause both the wage to rise to w_1 and employment to increase to L_1.

Suppose the supply curve shifted to the right to S'_L. This means that at a given wage, more labor is offered for sale, perhaps because the population has increased or people's trade-off between income and leisure has changed. Employment will increase from $\bar{L}$ to L_2, but the wage will drop from $\bar{w}$ to w_2. Finally, consider the case when both the supply curve and demand curve shift to the right (D'_L and S'_L). In this case, employment will always rise (in this case, to L_3), but the wage may either rise or fall (in this case, to w_3).

Equilibrium Wage in Noncompetitive Markets*

We have assumed throughout the chapter that both firms and workers operate in perfectly competitive markets. We shall consider two cases here when these assumptions do not hold. The first is the case when a firm is a monopolist in the product market. The second is the case when the firm is the sole buyer of labor.

The Case of the Monopolist   A **monopolist** is a firm that is the sole seller of a good or service in a particular product market. The firm is a *price-maker* rather than a price-taker. The monopolist can determine the price of its output by controlling the quantity it produces. The monopolist's demand curve is identical to the industry's demand curve and is downward sloping, as indicated by the curve DD′ in Diagram 6.12. Therefore, the more output that is offered for sale, the lower will be the market-clearing price.

As for a competitive firm, a profit-maximizing monopolist will produce at that level of output where its marginal revenue (MR) equals its marginal cost (MC). For a competitive firm, the marginal revenue obtained from selling an additional product is equal to the *fixed* product price. For a monopolist, the situation is more complicated. If the output price remained fixed, then the marginal revenue for an additional unit sold would equal the price. However, since the demand curve is downward-sloping, an increase in output also causes the price at which the additional unit of output and *all other units of output to fall.* Thus, the additional (marginal) revenue for an additional unit of output is less than the original output price. The marginal revenue curve (MR) thus lies below the demand curve DD′. For example, for a given output level, say Q_1, the marginal revenue MR_1 is less than the output price p_1.[16]

---

[16] Mathematically, this can be shown as follows. As for a competitive firm, total revenue (TR) is given by:

$$TR = p \cdot Q$$

The marginal revenue (MR) is the change in total revenue per unit change in output and is given by:

$$MR = \partial(TR)/\partial Q = p + Q\, \partial p/\partial Q$$

(continued)

Diagram 6.12   The Product Demand and Marginal Revenue Curve of a Monopolist

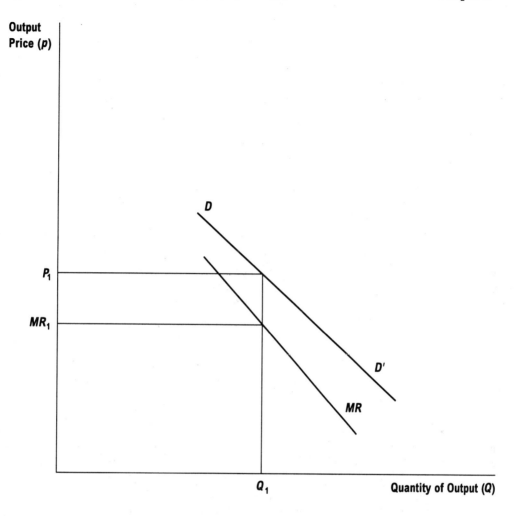

What is the monopolist's short-run demand curve for labor? As for a competitive firm, the additional output produced by another worker is MPP_L. In a competitive industry, the marginal value product of labor MVP_L is computed by multiplying MPP_L by the constant market output price p. For the monopolist, the marginal revenue product of labor, MRP_L^m, is computed by multiplying the MPP_L by the monopolist's marginal revenue from selling one more unit of output. On the cost side, the marginal cost, MC, of hiring

---

Since the demand curve is downward-sloping, the term $\partial p / \partial Q$, the change in price per unit change of output, is always negative. As a result, MR is always less than p. Indeed, it is possible for MR to be negative if the price falls enough for a unit increase in output. At this point, the demand curve is said to be "elastic."

an additional worker is, as for a competitive firm, the wage w. Therefore, the demand curve for labor by a monopolist is given by the equation:

$$MRP_L^m = MPP_L \cdot MR = w \text{ (monopolist)} \qquad (6.12)$$

This curve should be contrasted with the demand curve for labor in a firm in a competitive industry, given by:

$$MVP_L = MPP_L \cdot p = w \text{ (competitive firm)} \qquad (6.13)$$

Since MR is always less than the output price p, the monopolist's demand curve for labor, D_L^m, always lies below that of a corresponding competitive industry with the same demand for output, D_L^c, as illustrated in Diagram 6.13.[17] As a result, both the equilibrium wage rate (w_m) and employment level (L_m) for a monopolist would be smaller than the corresponding wage rate (w_c) and employment (L_c) in a competitive industry.

Somewhat paradoxically, monopolistic industries tend to pay higher wages in reality than do competitive ones. This suggests that there are other, more complicated, factors involved in wage formation than simple supply and demand analysis would suggest. These factors will be considered more fully in Chapter 9.

The Case of the Monopsonist A **monopsonist** is a firm which is the sole buyer in a market. Here, we consider the case of a market in which there is only one firm that hires labor. Though such situations are relatively rare in actuality,[18] they present an interesting case for analysis.

The characteristic feature of the monopsonistic labor market is that the supply curve of labor that the firm faces is the same as the supply curve of the industry (S_L in Diagram 6.14). For a competitive firm, the marginal cost of hiring an additional worker is a fixed wage. For a monopsonist, the marginal cost is higher, since it must offer a higher wage to induce more people to work. Its marginal cost of labor, MC_L^{mn}, is thus equal to the original wage plus the increase in the wage multiplied by total employment, since every worker receives the higher wage. The MC_L^{mn} curve therefore lies above the supply curve S_L.[19]

---

[17]This implicitly assumes that the monopolist has the same production function (that is, uses the same technology) as the competitive firm.

[18]Examples are "company towns," where there is essentially one major employer. These are sometimes found in rural areas with resource-intensive production, such as Appalachia coal country, and in small textile towns in the South, such as the Bibb mill in Bibb City, Georgia.

[19]In technical terms, the total cost of labor, TC_L, is given by:

$$TC_L = w \cdot L$$

Then, the marginal cost of labor is the change in total cost per unit change in employment and is given by:

(continued)

Diagram 6.13   The Demand Curve for Labor in a Monopoly and in a Competitive Industry

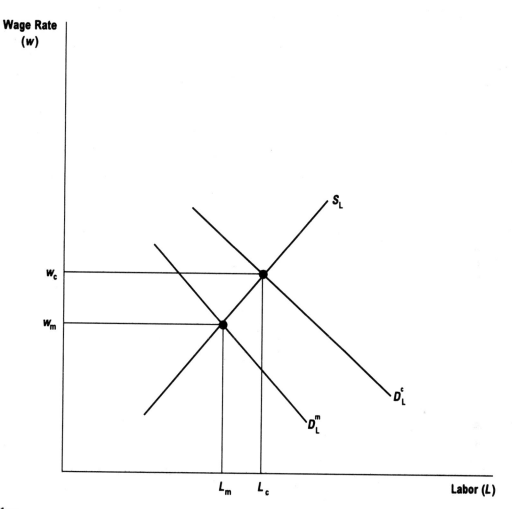

Key:
   m — monopoly
   c — competitive industry

$$MC_L = \partial(TC_L)/\partial L = w + L \, \partial w/\partial L$$

Since the supply curve of labor is upward-sloping, the term $\partial w/\partial L$, the change in the wage rate per unit change of employment, is always positive along this curve. As a result, MC_L is always greater than w.

Diagram 6.14   The Supply and Marginal Cost Curves of Labor in a Monopsony

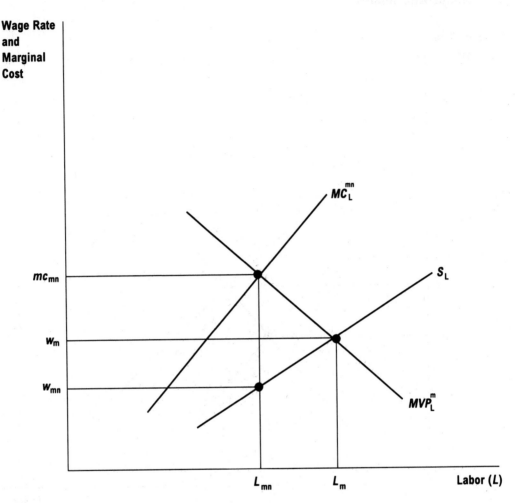

Key:
mn — monopsony
m — monopoly

Suppose the monopsonist also enjoys a monopoly position in the product market in which it sells. Its marginal value product of labor MVP_L^m curve is indicated in Diagram 6.14. The condition of profit maximization is given by equating marginal revenue to marginal cost:

$$MVP_L^m = MC_L^{mn}$$

In the case illustrated here, this occurs at an employment level L_{mn}, since at this point the MVP_L^m and MC_L^{mn} curves intersect. The wage offered at the point of profit-maximization is w_{mn}, which is below the marginal cost of labor and also below labor's marginal value product. In a monopsony, labor is paid less than its marginal value product. In contrast, for a monopolist who is not a monopsonist but operates in a competitive labor market, the equilibrium wage w_m and employment L_m are given by the point at which the S_L and MVP_L^m curves cross. As shown in Diagram 6.14, the nonmonopsonist would offer a higher wage and employ more workers than the monopsonist.[20]

Extensions of the Neoclassical Model

At this level of analysis, the neoclassical model cannot provide much guidance toward an understanding of the determination of relative wages or the distribution of earnings, since labor is treated as a single, homogeneous factor of production. Moreover, the assumptions of the model, particularly those of competition and perfect information, are very restrictive and do not allow much theoretical leverage in accounting for differences among people.

However, the model can be extended in several directions to explain inequality of earnings. In each of the extensions, one or more of the basic assumptions of the neoclassical model is relaxed. One way is to distinguish individuals according to their productive ability. The three most important characteristics are schooling, training, and ability. Differences in productive abilities serve as one explanation of why earnings vary among different workers. This approach will be treated more fully in Section 6.2 and in the next chapter.

Another way is to assume that firms have imperfect information on the productive abilities of potential employees. As a result, firms may use observable characteristics of job applicants as a guide to or "signal" of their true abilities. In some versions, schooling is considered to be an important screening device (see Section 7.4). In other versions, labor market discrimination against minorities and females is explained as a response to imperfect information (see Section 12.4).

A third way is to relax the assumption that labor markets are fully competitive. One example was provided above by the case of the monopsonist, though such cases are relatively rare. A more important consideration is the role of unions (Section 8.1) and labor market segmentation (see Section 8.2).

These three cases by no means represent an exhaustive list of the ways in which the neoclassical model has been extended to account for differences of earnings among workers. In subsequent chapters, we shall consider these

---

[20] Technically speaking, the monopsonist has no demand curve for labor. The reason is that the monopsonist determines simultaneously the equilibrium level of employment and the wage rate. Given the supply curve of labor and the firm's technology, there is only *one* wage rate and employment level at which the firm is willing to operate.

variants of the basic neoclassical model as well as several alternative theories that have been developed to explain the inequality of labor earnings.

6.2 THE HUMAN CAPITAL MODEL

Though elements of human capital theory can be traced back to Adam Smith's *Wealth of Nations* (written in 1776), its modern formulation is largely credited to Theodore Schultz, who coined the phrase in a 1961 article. It is also credited to Gary Becker, who produced the first systematic exposition of the model in a 1964 book, entitled *Human Capital*. The **human capital model** is actually an extension of the neoclassical model of wage determination to the *long-run supply curve of labor*. The emphasis here is on the determination of the marginal productivity of labor.

In the human capital model, each individual makes an investment decision about how much schooling and training to acquire. Both schooling and training are assumed to increase the productivity of the worker. The benefit of acquiring increased skills is to augment marginal productivity and (future) wages. However, there is a cost involved. An individual normally forgoes earnings while studying in school, as well as spending money on books, supplies, and tuition. A rational individual will therefore choose to invest in her human capital as long as the rate of return on her investment is greater than the prevailing discount rate. The notion that the acquisition of skills is an investment decision is the central concept of human capital theory. One direct implication is that differences in human capital help explain why earnings differ among workers.

The first part of this section introduces the basic human capital model and develops the concept of the rate of return to human capital. The second part extends the human capital model to the acquisition of on-the-job training. In the third part, some additional implications of the human capital model are explored.

The Rate of Return to Human Capital

Human capital theory is really a special application of capital theory. In the basic model, individuals are viewed as choosing between two possible courses of action: either working or investing in new skills. In the simplest form of the model, the choice is made between working and schooling. Schooling increases a person's skills, future productivity on the job, and future wage. There are two types of cost associated with schooling. The first are the direct expenses of schooling—tuition, books, and supplies. The second is **foregone earnings**—the income that could have been earned if the person had been working instead of in school. This is also called the *opportunity cost* or the *indirect costs* of schooling.

How does an individual decide whether to continue in school? In human capital theory, the choice is viewed as an investment decision. The added skills acquired from schooling increase the person's stock of human capital. Like other capital, human capital commands a certain return in the market place, computed as the difference between the added income and its cost. If the rate of return is sufficiently high, the investor will undertake the investment by remaining in school. If the return is too low, the person will quit school and enter the labor force.

Consider the case of a high school graduate at age 18 deciding between college and work. Suppose he can earn $30,000 a year if he goes to work but can earn $39,000 with a four-year college degree. We will assume for now that his earnings do not change over time and that he retires at age 65. For the moment, we will also assume that a college education is free—that is, there are no tuition fees or expenses for books or supplies. These "earnings profiles" are illustrated in Diagram 6.15. Note that if he goes to college, he earns nothing between ages 18 and 22.

Should the person go to college? At first glance, it would seem to make sense. Her lifetime earnings would be $1,677,000 [(65 − 22) × $39,000], compared to $1,410,000 [(65 − 18) × $30,000] if she went directly to work. But this is not really the correct way to make the comparison.

Suppose the (real) market interest rate is 5 percent.[21] A person with $30,000 in 1995 could invest the money at 5 percent, and in 1996, the investment would be worth $31,500 (1.05 × $30,000). In other words, to have $31,500 next year, a person needs to invest only $30,000 today. The amount $30,000 is referred to as the **present value** of $31,500 in 1996, since this would be the value in 1995 of having $31,500 in 1996.

With a market interest rate of 5 percent (and perfect capital markets[22]), a rational person would be indifferent between $30,000 today and $31,500 next year. The reason is that if you had $30,000 today, you could invest it and earn $31,500 next year, or if you borrowed $30,000 today, you would have to pay back $31,500 next year. In other words, if you had $30,000 today, you could *exchange* it for $31,500 next year, and vice versa.

Thus, the correct way of comparing two alternative income streams is to look at their present values. Let V_h be the present value of the total lifetime earnings of the high school graduate:[23]

$$V_h = \$30,000 + \frac{\$30,000}{1.05} + \frac{\$30,000}{(1.05)^2} + \ldots + \frac{\$30,000}{(1.05)^{46}}$$

The 5 percent interest rate is also referred to as the **discount rate,** since this is the rate at which a person would discount future earnings. Algebraically,

---

[21] The "nominal" interest rate is the interest rate actually recorded on a savings account or loan. The "real" interest rate is the difference between the nominal interest rate and the inflation rate. This is analogous to the difference between nominal growth rates of output and real growth rates of output, discussed in Chapter 2. Throughout this chapter, we will assume all interest rates are in real terms.

[22] The assumption of perfect capital markets means that anyone can lend or borrow money at the same interest rate.

[23] It is assumed that the salary is paid at the beginning of the year.

Diagram 6.15 Hypothetical Earnings Profiles of a High School Graduate and a College Graduate

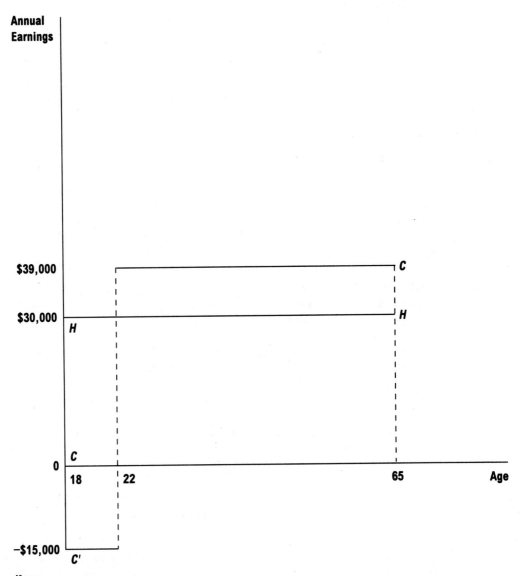

Key:

   HH — High School Graduate

   CC — College Graduate (no tuition or other college costs)

   C'C — College Graduate ($15,000 per year in college costs)

this summation is a geometric series with a ratio of 1/1.05. Using the formula for a sum of a finite geometric series[24], we obtain:

$$V_h = \frac{30,000 - 30,000/(1.05)^{47}}{1 - 1/1.05} = \$566,402$$

This means that an investment today of $566,402 at 5 percent per year will yield an income (annuity) stream of $30,000 per year over the next 47 years. At the end of this time period, the initial investment would be totally exhausted.

The present value of the lifetime earnings of the college graduate, V_c, is given by:

$$V_c = \frac{\$39,000}{(1.05)^4} + \frac{\$39,000}{(1.05)^5} + \ldots + \frac{\$39,000}{(1.05)^{46}}$$

Note that the first term in the series is divided by $(1.05)^4$, since the college graduate does not start working until age 22 (four years from now). As a result, the present value of the college graduate's first year's earnings is worth only $32,085 today. Using the same formula for the sum of a geometric series, we obtain:

$$V_c = \frac{\$32,085 - \$32,085/(1.05)^{43}}{1 - 1/1.05} = \$591,116$$

Under these assumptions, a college education would still be the better choice.

Let us now assume that tuition and supplies cost $15,000 per year for a college education. The net earnings profile for the college graduate is now C'C in Diagram 6.15. From age 18 to 22, the person's net earnings are actually negative, since college tuition must be paid. After age 22, the earnings profile is identical to CC. In this case, the present value of the direct costs of four years of college, D_c, is

$$D_c = \$15,000 + \frac{\$15,000}{1.05} + \frac{\$15,000}{(1.05)^2} + \frac{\$15,000}{(1.05)^3} = \$55,848$$

---

[24]A geometric series is one in which each term (except the first) is a fixed multiple of the preceding term. The formula for the sum S is given by:

$$S = \frac{a - aq^n}{1 - q}$$

where a is the first term of the series, q the ratio between one term and the next lower term, and n the number of terms.

and the present value V_c' of his net earnings stream is given by:

$$V_{c'} = V_c - D_c = \$591,116 - \$55,848 = \$535,268$$

V'_c is now less than V_h, so that in this case the rational choice would be to start work immediately after high school.

It should now be apparent that the present value calculation depends critically on the market interest rate. If the interest rate changes, so does the present value of the earnings profile. Suppose that the market interest rate falls to 3 percent. Then,

$$V_{h,.03} = \$30,000 + \frac{\$30,000}{(1.03)} + \frac{\$30,000}{(1.03)^2} + \ldots + \frac{\$30,000}{(1.03)^{46}} = \$773,264$$

The present value of the earnings stream increases when the interest rate falls from 5 to 3 percent. The reason is that future earnings are discounted less at a lower interest rate.

The same is true, of course, of the earnings stream for the college graduate. The interesting question is whether the present value of the earnings stream is still greater for the college graduate than for the high school graduate at the lower interest rate. Since the college graduate defers more of his earnings to the future than the high school graduate, the college graduate should be better off relative to the high school graduate from a drop in the interest rate because future earnings now count more. For earnings stream CC, then:

$$V_{c,.03} = \frac{\$39,000}{(1.05)^4} + \frac{\$39,000}{(1.05)^5} + \ldots + \frac{\$39,000}{(1.05)^{46}} = \$855,927$$

With a 3 percent market interest rate, college becomes even more attractive (assuming no tuition costs) than working at age 18, since the ratio of present values V_c/V_h is now 1.11 ($\$855,927$ / $\$773,264$), compared to 1.04 ($\$591,116$ / $\$566,402$) at a 5 percent interest rate. The gain from going to college is greater at the lower interest rate.

What if the student had to pay $\$15,000$ per year in college costs? At a 5 percent interest rate, it made sense to go straight to work after high school. At a 3 percent interest rate, $D_{c,.03} = \$57,431$ and $V_{c'} = \$798,496$. At a 3 percent interest rate, college would now be preferable to working even with college costs of $\$15,000$ per year.

Let us now see what would happen if the market interest rate rises to 7 percent. $V_{h,.07} = \$439,500$ and $V_{c,.07} = \$430,002$. At a 7 percent market interest rate, it would no longer make sense for the 18-year-old to go to college even if it were free. The reason is that at the higher interest rate, future earnings of the college graduate are discounted even more.

The Internal Rate of Return   A somewhat different way of viewing the decision to go to college is to ask at what interest rate an 18-year-old would be indifferent between college and working. This interest rate is called the internal rate of return to a college education. If the internal rate of return to college is greater than the market interest rate, then it would pay the 18-year-old to invest in college. This decision-making process is analogous to a firm's choosing among alternative investment opportunities.

The internal rate of return is defined as the rate which would equalize the lifetime earnings of the high school and college graduate. In the case of free college tuition, the internal rate of return, $\bar{r}$, is given by:

$$V_{c,\bar{r}} = V_{h,\bar{r}}$$

or, as in the example above,

$$\sum_{t=4}^{46} \frac{\$39,000}{(1+\bar{r})^t} - \sum_{t=0}^{46} \frac{\$30,000}{(1+\bar{r})^t} = 0$$

This equation has no simple analytical solution. However, we know that $\bar{r}$ must lie between 5 percent and 7 percent, because at 5 percent, lifetime earnings are greater for the college graduate, while at 7 percent, they are greater for the high school graduate. By trying different values of $\bar{r}$ in this range, we can obtain a solution, which is $\bar{r}$ = 6.4 percent.

On-the-Job Training

Another form of human capital investment is on-the-job training. For some jobs, formal training programs are provided by the company. Skilled trades, such as machinists, plumbers, and electricians, offer special apprenticeship programs, which allow a beginning worker to acquire the skills of the trade while working. The medical professions have required training programs for doctors—internships and residencies. Many companies also provide special training for junior executives and computer programmers. In other cases, workers are trained *informally* while on the job. This training is often done by the worker's supervisor or her fellow workers. A newly hired factory worker must be taught how to operate equipment in the plant. A secretary must learn the procedures and forms used in a company.

On-the-job training increases a worker's productivity in much the same way as formal schooling. Moreover, like formal schooling, on-the-job training entails both direct and indirect costs. Direct costs include payments for the instructor, equipment, and materials used in the training program. The indirect (opportunity) cost is the foregone production resulting from the fact that the worker's time is absorbed in training instead of engaged in direct production.

The major difference between on-the-job training costs and those of formal schooling is that all or part of the former may be borne by the *firm*. In the previous section, we showed that in competitive equilibrium, the wage is equal to the worker's marginal value product. We will now see that this condition may not hold if there are training costs involved.

Let us see what differences training costs would make. The standard neoclassical model implicitly assumes that production in each period is independent of other periods. However, if a firm trains a worker in one period and this affects the firm's output in subsequent periods, then this assumption no longer holds.

In particular, from the firm's point of view, the total revenue generated by a worker (its marginal value product, MVP) must be sufficient to recoup its total expenditure on the worker, including both wages (w) and the direct costs of training (TC). To simplify the discussion, suppose the firm operates in two periods and provides training in only the first period. Then, in equilibrium,

$$MVP_1 + MVP_2 = w_1 + w_2 + TC \qquad (6.14)$$

where the subscript refers to the time period.[25]

To see how this equation is interpreted, it is first necessary to distinguish between two kinds of on-the-job training—**specific training** and **general training.** Specific training is entirely firm-specific and nontransferable to other firms. There are several examples. One is training that familiarizes a new secretary in a company with the forms, coding procedures, filing procedures, and other organizational matters that are specific to that company. A second is training a new factory hire with the use of a very specific (perhaps, custom-made) piece of machinery. A third is military training in advanced weaponry or learning how to operate a tank. Specific training can be formally defined as that which increases the marginal productivity of the worker in the worker's own firm but which has no effect on the worker's potential productivity in other firms.

At the opposite extreme is general training, which is formally defined as training that increases the marginal productivity of the trainee both in the firm providing the training as well as in other firms that may hire the worker. There are several examples of general training. First, a plumber apprenticed to one firm will receive skills that can be transferred to other plumbing companies. Second, a programmer trained by one company can usually use the skills that are acquired in other companies. Third, surgeons who receive training in one hospital can use these skills in other hospitals or private practice. General training increases the worker's marginal product in the firm providing the training, as well as in competing firms.

---

[25] Also, for simplicity, it is assumed that the discount rate is zero.

Let us first consider the implications of firm-specific training. From the employer's point of view, specific training is very useful, since it increases the employee's future productivity on the job. The employer would thus be willing to absorb the full training costs insofar as the return is greater than or equal to the cost of the training. On the other hand, from the *employee's* point of view, the wage that can be commanded in a competing firm is *not* changed by specific training (by assumption, it increases the worker's wage in *only* the firm in which the worker is employed). As a result, the employee cannot rely on a higher outside wage offer to increase the wage being paid by his current employer. Therefore, the employee is essentially *indifferent* with regard to specific training. However, the employee is *not* willing to pay for specific training by accepting a lower wage, since there is no direct benefit for him. For these reasons, it is the employer who winds up paying the costs of specific training.

In terms of equation (6.14), the worker will accept a first period wage, w_1, that is no lower than her marginal value product in that period, MVP_1. As a result, $w_1 = MVP_1$, and therefore,

$$MVP_2 - w_2 = TC \quad \text{[the case of specific training]} \tag{6.15a}$$

In other words, the employer will recoup the costs of training by paying the worker a wage less than her marginal value product in period 2. This is the only condition under which a profit-maximizing firm would be willing to invest in an employee's specific training.

In contrast, general training, by assumption, increases the worker's marginal product not only in the worker's own firm but also in competing firms. After the worker acquires general training, other firms would be willing to pay a wage equal to his higher marginal product. The firm providing this type of training would also have to pay the higher wage, because otherwise the employee would change jobs. As a result, the firm has no incentive to pay for general training. However, the worker does have an incentive, since general training will increase his future productivity and therefore his future wage.

In terms of (6.14), this argument implies that in the case of general training, w_2 must equal MVP_2. Therefore,

$$w_1 = MVP_1 - TC \quad \text{[the case of general training]} \tag{6.15b}$$

In other words, the earnings of the worker would be reduced by the cost of the training while he was engaged in training. The *employee* would essentially wind up paying the cost of the training by receiving a lower wage during the training period, though he would make it up later in the form of higher wages.

In summary, in the case of specific training, the employer absorbs all the costs of training, while in the case of general training, the employee absorbs the cost. In both cases, the costs consist of direct costs paid for instruction, materials, and equipment, and indirect costs in the form of the foregone output of the worker while in training. In the case of specific training, the wage equals the worker's marginal value product during the training period but is less than the worker's marginal value product in subsequent periods. In the case of general training, the wage is less than the worker's marginal value product during the training period but equals the worker's marginal value product in subsequent periods.

In actuality, most forms of training lie between these two extremes and are neither completely firm-specific nor completely general. As a result, both the employee and the employer typically absorb portions of the training cost, though the relative proportions vary, depending on how general or specific the training is. This has important implications for the shape of the age-earnings profile, as we shall discuss below.

Moreover, in the case of specific training, there are two reasons why an employee might be very interested in it, even though it may not increase her current wage. The first is that the mere fact that an employer has invested in the worker's training makes the worker much more valued by the firm than a new hire. The firm will not want to jeopardize its investment by losing the employee. Therefore, specific training may significantly reduce the likelihood that an employer will discharge the worker. This has important implications regarding the structure of internal labor markets, as we shall see in Section 8.2.

Second, by raising the worker's marginal product in later periods, specific training may also increase her future wage. The reason is that the employee, by threatening to quit the firm and hence causing the firm to lose its investment, could induce the firm to pay more than the worker's opportunity cost in another firm. This is another implication of internal labor markets, as we shall see in Section 8.2.

Additional Implications of the Human Capital Model

Basic Assumptions of the Model   As in the neoclassical model, the derivation of the human capital model depends on four key assumptions: (1) perfect competition among firms and workers, (2) perfect information and foresight on the part of both firms and workers, (3) perfect rationality on the part of firms and employees, and (4) perfect capital markets. It might be instructive to consider cases where these assumptions fail to hold. With regard to perfect competition, most occupations have free entry; a few do not. The most prominent example is doctors, where entry is restricted by limits placed on medical school openings. In this case, we would expect the internal rate of return in the medical professions to be higher than in other fields, because restrictions on entry will prevent people from entering this lucrative profession. Another result will be an excess demand for places in medical schools.[26]

Another important assumption of the human capital model is that capital markets are perfect—that is, everyone can borrow money at the same interest rate to finance a college education. This assumption is particularly vital in the schooling model, since the cost of the investment in terms of both direct costs and foregone earnings can be quite high. Yet, capital markets for student loans are not perfect, since there are limitations on the amount that can be borrowed. Moreover, the cost of college financing differs among students—those from a rich family often have parents willing to pay for it, while others might have to take out loans. Such imperfections in the capital market would mean that different students faced different market interest rates, depending on their circumstances (and for those who could not obtain funds, the interest rate would be effectively *infinite*). As a result, students with the same potential rate of return on a college education may make different schooling decisions, depending on the actual interest rate they faced. Consequently, there may be no tendency toward equilibrium in the schooling "market" (see the last section of this part for more discussion of equilibrium in the human capital market).

The joint assumptions of perfect information and rationality may not always apply to high school seniors deciding on whether to attend college. How many of you have made the necessary calculations to decide to attend college or go to work? Moreover, if you had made these computations, how many of you would actually have been guided by the results of your calculations?

Though very few students actually make the complicated calculations of the return to a college degree, most are aware of earnings differences between college graduates and high school graduates. Studies have shown that when differentials are high, a larger percentage of high school graduates go on to college than when differentials are small (see, for example, Freeman, 1976). Moreover, decisions about professional school, such as law, medicine, business, or engineering, are even more sensitive to the relative earnings of these professions (also see Freeman, 1976).

What if a student pursues education simply for its own sake (the love of learning perhaps)? Would this be considered irrational behavior according to the human capital market? Not necessarily, because education has both an investment and a *consumption* component. Part of the reason that many students go to school is to acquire knowledge. An art history or music appreciation course may not have any direct relevance to a student's future

---

[26] The entry restrictions may also enable doctors to charge fees above what would be feasible in a competitive market. Medical schools could capture part of this "excess profit" by charging higher direct tuition fees. In fact, by raising direct costs of a medical education sufficiently high, medical schools could drive the internal rate of return to medical training back to a competitive level. However, because of competition for students among medical schools, medical schools are unable to do this, thus allowing doctors to capture the "rent" from restricted entry.

career but may greatly add to the student's enjoyment of life later on. Thus, even if the direct monetary reward were not great from attending college, other "psychic" benefits could well justify the expenditure.

A Theory of Relative Earnings   One immediate implication of the human capital schooling model is that *annual earnings will differ according to the educational attainment of the worker.* This follows directly from the human capital model, since schooling, by assumption, increases the marginal productivity of the worker. Moreover, an individual would not be willing to invest in additional schooling unless earnings were increased. Thus, we should find systematic differences in earnings between those with different amounts of schooling. In other words, schooling should help explain some of the variation in annual earnings among workers.

A second implication, which emerges from the on-the-job training model, is that labor earnings should be positively related to *work experience.* This result follows from the analysis of *general* training. During the training period, the worker's earnings are effectively reduced by the costs of the training. After the training period, the worker's marginal product and earnings both rise over time. Most workers obtain some form of on-the-job training, and it is normally a mixture of both specific and general skills. In addition, though formal training may last for only a short period of time, most workers continue to learn informally on the job. Therefore, for most workers, we would expect their productivity and earnings to rise with years of experience in the labor force.[27] As a result, years of experience is a second factor which should help account for the variation in labor earnings.

Policy Implications   Human capital theory has had a strong influence on public policy throughout the world. Many public programs have emphasized the acquisition of human capital as one mechanism for combating poverty. As we demonstrated in Section 4.3, there is a strong correlation between low levels of schooling and poverty rates. As a result, many government programs have been implemented to increase the schooling and training of the low-income population. In the United States, special programs for poor children, such as *Head Start,* have been devised to prepare preschool children from poor families for elementary school education. Efforts have been made to reduce the dropout rate among high school age students. Student loan programs have been designed to encourage college-age students from low-income families to attend college. For low-income adults, special manpower training programs have been developed to increase their marketable skills. In Section 15.5, we shall discuss these programs in greater detail.

---

[27] This is true up to a point. As we shall discuss in Section 7.1, after a certain age, human capital may actually start to depreciate, as skills become obsolete, and earnings may fall with experience after this point.

The Formation of an Equilibrium in the Human Capital Market* Let us return to the computation of the internal rate of return to schooling. Suppose it turns out that the internal rate of return to a college education is below the market interest rate. Why would anyone attend college?[28] Or, conversely, suppose the internal rate of return exceeded the market interest rate. Why would anyone go to work after high school? Both predictions are nonsensical, since they would imply that everyone should attend college or no one should attend college. Are there any mechanisms that ensure that an equilibrium is formed in the human capital market?

In fact, there are two such mechanisms at work. The first is market interest rate adjustments. We have implicitly assumed that it was fixed. Actually, it changes according to the supply of and demand for funds. Suppose the current market interest rate were lower than the rate of return to a college education. There would then be a great incentive to go to college. As a result, the quantity of college loans demanded would be high with many students seeking college loans, and the market interest rate would rise. In equilibrium, the interest rate would equal the internal rate of return. Conversely, if the internal rate of return to a college education were below the market interest rate, the quantity of college loans demanded would fall, and so would the interest rate.

The second mechanism involves changes in the earnings differential between high school and college graduates. We had implicitly assumed in the first section above that they were fixed. However, suppose the return to a college education is very high. The market response would be an increase in the number of college students. As a result, the supply of college graduates would increase relative to the number of high school graduates in the labor market. As we discussed in Section 6.1, the marginal product of a factor of production depends not only on its productivity but also on its supply. In general, the marginal product of a factor will decline as its use increases relative to other factors of production (the law of diminishing marginal returns). In this case, an increase in the number of college graduates relative to high school graduates would cause the earnings of the former to decline relative to the latter. A decline in the earnings differential would, in turn, cause the internal rate of return to a college education to fall, and in equilibrium it would be brought back in line with the market interest rate.

Equilibrium will then occur when the present value of the earnings streams of different educational levels are equal. This can come about from a change in the interest rate and/or a change in earnings differentials between educational groups. This also implies that in equilibrium the present value of *lifetime earnings* will be equal for all schooling groups (as long as the assumptions of the human capital model spelled out in the beginning of the third part of this section hold). This statement should not be confused with our previous assertion that annual earnings will differ systematically between

---

[28] We shall assume that there are no consumption benefits to a college education.

levels of schooling. Indeed, the human capital model predicts that *annual* earnings will differ. What should be equalized is the present value of discounted lifetime earnings among workers. In the human capital model, then, the true measure of economic inequality is that of lifetime earnings, not annual earnings, since the latter may differ among workers with the same lifetime incomes.

In a sense, the human capital equilibrium may now be too rigid. In equilibrium, the present value of lifetime earnings net of training costs at different levels of schooling will be equal (as long as all the assumptions hold). However, this implies that individuals will be *indifferent* between going to college or working immediately after high school. In this sense, the human capital model is *indeterminant*. There is no way to determine levels of schooling for individuals, the distribution of schooling, and therefore the distribution of labor earnings, since the latter depends on the distribution of human capital.

Gary Becker (1967) suggests a solution to this problem by relaxing two of the assumptions of the human capital model. This can be conveniently represented in terms of the supply of and demand for schooling, as shown in Diagram 6.16. Let us consider the supply curve first. Recall that one of the key assumptions of the human capital model is that there are perfect capital markets. This means that all students face the same interest rate when borrowing funds for their education. Suppose that this is not the case and that different individuals face different costs in borrowing funds. Such differences in *opportunities* for acquiring human capital can be interpreted as differences in the *supply curve* for human capital.

Consider three different individuals, facing supply curves SC_1, SC_2, and SC_3. It should first be noted that the supply curves slope upward. This means that early years of schooling can be financed at relatively low costs—probably from family financing—and later years at higher costs—probably from taking out a loan. Individual 1 faces the highest costs of acquiring funds, SC_1. This person comes from a poor family and cannot rely on family funds to finance much schooling. The interest rate becomes infinite at some point if he cannot get any loans. Individual 2, from a middle-income family, faces supply curve SC_2. Early years of schooling can be financed at relatively low costs from her family. Later years can be financed with the help of low-cost government loans, and still later years through relatively high-cost bank loans. Individual 3, from a rich family, faces a lower supply curve for funds. He can rely on family resources for most of his school financing and on low-cost government loans for the remainder. To finance a given level of schooling, individual 1 must pay the highest interest rate, individual 2 the second highest, and individual 3 the lowest.

The demand curve for schooling depends largely on a person's ability.[29] In the basic model, it is implicitly assumed that a given level of schooling will

---

[29] It may also depend on differences in preferences for the nonpecuniary aspects of work that require training.

Diagram 6.16 Supply and Demand Curves for Schooling of Three Individuals

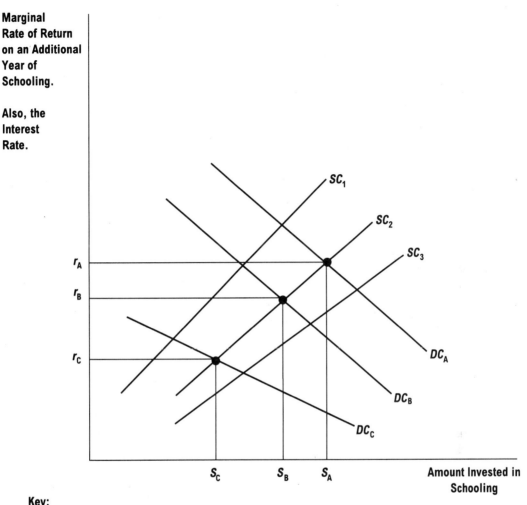

Marginal
Rate of Return
on an Additional
Year of
Schooling.

Also, the
Interest
Rate.

Key:
SC — Supply Curve for Schooling
DC — Demand Curve for Schooling

produce the same level of skill for everyone. Suppose that individuals differ in "native intelligence" and can convert a given level of schooling into different levels of skill.[30] This, in turn, implies that individuals with the same schooling attainment can earn different amounts. As a result, the **marginal rate of return** (additional earnings) from an additional year of schooling can differ among students.

---

[30] These differences could, for example, be reflected in school grades.

These differences can be represented by a demand curve for schooling, as illustrated in Diagram 6.16. It should first be noted that the demand curve slopes downward to the right. This means that there are diminishing returns to investment in schooling. Primary school generally provides the most essential and productive skills of work life (reading, writing, and arithmetic). High school and college supply more advanced literacy, reasoning, and mathematical skills, which while still important, tend to have a smaller *incremental* impact on later productivity. As a result, the marginal return to schooling tends to decline with years of schooling.

Individual A has the most ability, and the corresponding demand curve, DC_A, is the highest of the three, indicating the greatest return for a given level of schooling. Individual B is of average ability, and the corresponding demand curve, DC_B, is in the middle. Individual C has the lowest ability and receives the lowest return for a given schooling investment. Thus, for a given schooling investment, individual A obtains the highest return, followed by B and C.

We can now determine the equilibrium level of schooling investment each individual would make. First, suppose that all individuals A, B, and C face the same supply curve for funds, SC_2. Then, as shown in Diagram 6.16, individual A would acquire S_A years of schooling, since at this point the marginal cost of funds would equal the marginal return to an additional year of schooling, r_A. Individual B would choose S_B years of schooling. S_B is less than S_A, because individual B has lower ability. Individual C, who has the least ability, would acquire the lowest level of schooling, S_C.

Of course, if individuals have both different demand curves and face different supply curves for funds, then the situation becomes even more complicated. In the case of three individuals, there are nine possible combinations of supply and demand curves.[31] Each individual would invest in additional human capital until the marginal return from an additional year equaled his marginal cost of funds. The interplay of supply and demand curves faced by each individual would then determine the level of human capital acquisition, and this, in turn, would close the human capital model.[32]

6.3 SUMMARY

The first section of this chapter developed the neoclassical model of wages. The labor supply curve is derived from an individual's trade-off between income and leisure. This trade-off can be represented by a set of indifference curves between income and hours of leisure. The absolute value of the

---

[31] Actually, the supply and demand curves for human capital may not be entirely independent. For example, ability, as we argued, affects the demand curve for human capital. It may also affect the supply curve, if brighter students have a better chance of getting a scholarship and thereby lowering the cost of funding their schooling.

[32] An alternative way of "closing" the model is to introduce the fact that young people may differ in their personal discount rate. Some individuals have a very strong preference for immediate gratification, while others are more willing to defer consumption. A student will leave school when the return to an additional year of schooling falls below her personal discount rate.

slope of the indifference curve is the marginal rate of substitution between income and leisure, MRS. The marginal rate of substitution represents the amount of income the individual is willing to give up for an extra hour of leisure. The market wage rate indicates how much additional income a worker can obtain for an additional hour of work. This condition can be represented by a budget line. The choice of hours of work for a particular individual depends on the prevailing wage rate and the individual's utility function. At a given wage rate w, an individual will choose those hours of leisure at which the indifference curve is tangent to the budget line. This condition is given by: MRS = w.

The supply curve of labor shows the number of hours an individual will work at each wage rate. An increase in the wage rate can be decomposed into two effects: (1) an income effect, which reduces the number of hours worked, and (2) a substitution effect, which increases the hours worked. Since the two effects go in opposite directions, it is not possible to predict whether hours of work will increase or decrease from an increase in the wage rate. Most economists think (and there is some evidence to support them) that the supply curve of labor is backward-bending—first sloping upward to the right and then sloping upward to the left.

The demand curve for labor is derived from a firm's production function. A profit-maximizing firm will hire labor up to the point where its marginal revenue equals its marginal cost. In competitive markets, the marginal revenue from an additional unit of labor is given by the marginal value product of labor, MVP_L, and the marginal cost by the wage rate. In the short run, with capital fixed, the demand curve for labor is given by the firm's marginal value product of labor curve. The demand curve slopes downward to the right.

Market equilibrium is determined by the intersection of the supply and demand curves for labor. In equilibrium, MRS = MVP_L = w. If the demand curve for labor shifts to the right, both the wage rate and employment will rise. If the supply curve of labor shifts to the right, employment will increase but the wage rate will fall.

The human capital model is an extension of neoclassical theory which derives the long-run supply curve of labor. In the model, each individual is viewed as making an investment decision about how much schooling and training to acquire. Both schooling and training increase the productivity of the worker and therefore future wages. However, the investment involves two types of costs: (1) indirect costs in the form of foregone earnings and (2) direct costs in the form of tuition, fees, and related expenses. The idea that the acquisition of skills is an investment decision is the central concept of human capital theory.

In the case of a college education, a high school senior would decide whether to continue in school or go to work by comparing the alternative lifetime earnings streams. Each earnings stream is converted into a present value by discounting future earnings at the market interest rate. The student would rationally choose the course of action which yielded the highest present value. An alternative calculation is based on the internal rate of return, which is defined as the discount rate which would equalize the lifetime earnings of the high school and college graduate. If the internal rate of return were higher than the market interest rate, the optimal choice would be to attend college.

Another form of human capital investment is on-the-job training. This also increases a worker's future productivity and entails both direct costs—payments for the instructor, materials, etc.—and indirect costs—the production foregone while the worker is training. The main difference between this form of human capital and schooling is that part of the costs may be borne by the employer instead of the individual.

Two kinds of training were distinguished. The first is firm-specific training, which increases the worker's productivity only in the firm where he is working. In this case, the employer absorbs all the costs of training but recoups it by paying a wage less than the worker's marginal value product after the training period. The second is general training, which provides skills that are transferable outside the firm. In this case, the employee pays the training cost in the form of a reduced wage while training but makes up for it in the form of higher wages later on.

Differences in human capital help explain why earnings vary among workers. There are two reasons. First, workers who attain a higher level of education will have higher productivity and will therefore command higher wages in the labor market. They also require higher wages to compensate them for the costs of additional schooling. Second, insofar as workers acquire general training while on the job, earnings should be positively correlated with years of work experience.

REFERENCES AND OTHER SUGGESTED READINGS

A. Neoclassical Model

Ehrenberg, Ronald G., and Robert S. Smith, *Modern Labor Economics: Theory and Public Policy,* Scott, Foresman, and Company, Glenview, Illinois, latest edition of publication.

Fleisher, Belton M., and Thomas J. Kniesner, *Labor Economics: Theory, Evidence, and Policy,* Prentice-Hall Inc., Englewood Cliffs, New Jersey, latest edition.

Hammermesh, Daniel S., and Albert Rees, *The Economics of Work and Pay,* Harper and Row Publishers, New York, latest edition.

Killingsworth, Mark R., *Labor Supply,* Cambridge University Press, Cambridge, 1983.

B. Human Capital Theory

Becker, Gary S., *Human Capital: A Theoretical and Empirical Analysis,* Columbia University Press and National Bureau of Economic Research, New York, 1964; and 2nd edition, 1975.

————, *Human Capital and the Personal Distribution of Income,* University of Michigan Press, Ann Arbor, 1967.

————, "A Theory of Social Interactions," *Journal of Political Economy,* Vol. 82, No. 6, November-December 1974, pp. 1063–1094.

Ben-Porath, Yoram, "The Production of Human Capital and the Life-Cycle of Earnings," *Journal of Political Economy,* Vol. 57, August 1967.

————, "The Production of Human Capital Over Time," in Lee Hansen (ed.), *Education, Income, and Human Capital,* Columbia University Press and National Bureau of Economic Research, New York, 1970.

Blinder, Alan S., and Yoram Weiss, *Human Capital and Labor Supply: A Synthesis,* Princeton University Press, Princeton, 1974.

Freeman, Richard, *The Overeducated American,* Academic Press, New York, 1976.

Ghez, Gilbert R., and Gary S. Becker, *The Allocation of Time and Goods Over the Life Cycle,* Princeton University Press and the National Bureau of Economic Research, Princeton, 1975.

Haley, William J., "Human Capital: The Choice Between Investment and Income," *American Economic Review,* Vol. 63, No. 5, December 1973, pp. 929–944.

Heckman, James J., "A Life Cycle Model of Earnings, Learning and Consumption," *Journal of Political Economy,* 1976.

Mincer, Jacob, "The Distribution of Labor Incomes: A Survey with Special Reference to the Human Capital Approach," *Journal of Economic Literature,* Vol. 8, No. 1, March 1970, pp. 1–26.

Rosen, Sherwin, "Human Capital: A Survey of Empirical Research," in Ronald Ehrenberg (ed.), *Research in Labor Economics,* Vol. 1, JAI Press, Greenwich, CT, 1977, pp. 3–39.

Schultz, Theodore W., "Capital Formation by Education," *Journal of Political Economy,* Vol. 68, No. 6, December 1960, pp. 571–583.

————, "Investment in Human Capital," *American Economic Review,* Vol. 51, No. 1, March 1961, pp. 1–17.

————, *Investment in Human Capital: The Role of Education and of Research,* The Free Press, New York, 1971.

Smith, Adam, *The Wealth of Nations,* University Paperbacks, Nuthuen, London, 1961 (originally published in 1776).

DISCUSSION QUESTIONS

1. Discuss why the effect of an increase in the wage rate on hours worked is theoretically indeterminant.

2. Give an arithmetic example to show why the MPP_L curve crosses the APP_L curve at the latter's maximum value. Why would the firm hire no labor if the wage rate is greater than the point at which the AVP_L curve crosses the MVP_L curve?

3. Compute the present value of lifetime earnings at age 18 for a high school graduate who works immediately after graduating high school at age 18 and one who attends college for four years after graduating high school if the annual earnings of the former is $40,000 (assumed constant over time) and that of the college graduate is $50,000 (assumed constant over time) at:
    a. a three, five, and seven percent rate of interest, with no direct costs of college
    b. a three, five, and seven percent rate of interest, with college costing $10,000 per year. Explain in each of these cases whether it would make sense to attend college.
4. Explain why according to the human capital model general training will increase the worker's future earnings whereas specific training will not.
5. Why would fewer high school graduates go on to college if the (real) rate of interest increases?

7

Empirical Work on and Alternative Views of the Relation of Schooling, Experience, and Earnings

One of the strong points of human capital theory is that it has observable and testable implications. We mentioned one in the previous chapter: annual earnings should increase with both education and the experience level of the worker. Moreover, as we shall see in subsequent sections, the relation between earnings, schooling, and experience should assume a certain functional form. A vast amount of empirical research has gone into statistically estimating these earnings functions. A second implication of human capital theory that we shall consider here is that the present value of lifetime earnings for different educational groups should be equal. A third is that differences in earnings between workers should reflect differences in their productivity. A fourth implication is that the inequality of the overall earnings distribution should be related to the distribution of both schooling and experience levels among workers.

In this chapter, we shall begin by examining the statistical evidence on the relation between earnings, schooling, and experience. Section 7.1 presents basic statistical results on age-earnings profiles by schooling level for males and females and for different racial groups. We also present estimates of the rate of return to schooling (the first part). Our times-series for the United States extends from the mid-1950s to the early 1990s. Estimates from other countries are also shown. The second part presents figures on the present value of lifetime earnings for different educational and occupational groups.

In Section 7.2, we discuss how the schooling-earnings function is derived and present econometric estimates of the rate of return to schooling. We also show how the earnings function can be extended to include experience, and regression estimates of the extended earnings function are also shown. Section 7.3 considers the role of ability in the determination of earnings. Ability is viewed as an additional factor that, along with schooling and experience, determines labor earnings. In this section, we also review some of the studies that have attempted to assess the contribution of ability to earnings.

Section 7.4 assesses the relation between earnings and worker productivity. In the human capital model, schooling is believed to increase worker earnings, because it makes workers more productive. The same is true for experience on the job. We first review evidence concerning the relation between experience and direct indicators of worker productivity on the job. We then consider other interpretations for the observed positive association between schooling and earnings. These include the screening model of schooling, education as a transmitter of family background, and schooling as a socializing mechanism.

Section 7.5 considers the relation between the inequality of earnings and the distribution of human capital. We first derive the algebraic relationship between the two. We then consider whether the recent rise in income inequality can be attributed in whole or in part to changes in the distribution of schooling and experience levels in the workforce. Concluding remarks are made in Section 7.6.

7.1 Earnings, Schooling, and Experience

Figures 7.1 through 7.4 show mean earnings among year-round (50 to 52 weeks), full-time (35 hours per week or more) workers for white males, black males, white females, and black females in 1989. The data source is the 1990 Census of Population. Human capital theory predicts that earnings will rise with schooling and experience. While educational attainment is very easy to establish on a survey questionnaire, it is difficult to obtain a good estimate of a person's total years of work experience (excluding time out of the labor force or out of a job). Therefore, age is often used as a "proxy" for experience, since work experience normally increases with a person's age.[1]

In every case shown in the four figures, average earnings increased with schooling level. This conforms with the predictions of human capital theory. The relation between earnings and age is more complex. Gary Becker (1964) presents three arguments why the age-earnings profile should slope upwards—that is, why earnings should increase with age. They all stem from the theory of on-the-job training. First, because working lives are finite, people will invest in their training as early as possible in their working life so they will have a longer period in which to recoup their investment. This

---

[1]This relation is more reliable for men than for women, since historically many mothers have left the labor force when their children were young and re-entered it when their children were older. See Chapter 11 for further discussion of estimating female experience levels.

Figure 7.1   Age–Earnings Profiles, 1989, White Males, Full-Year, Full-Time Workers

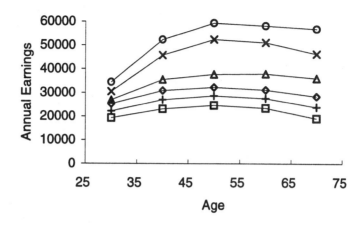

Figure 7.2   Age–Earnings Profiles, 1989, Black Males, Full-Year, Full-Time Workers

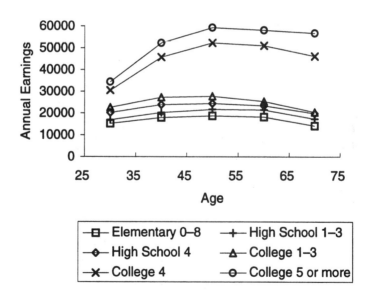

Figure 7.3   Age–Earnings Profiles, 1989, White Females, Full-Year, Full-Time Workers

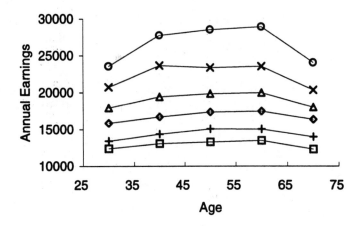

Figure 7.4   Age–Earnings Profiles, 1989, Black Females, Full-Year, Full-Time Workers

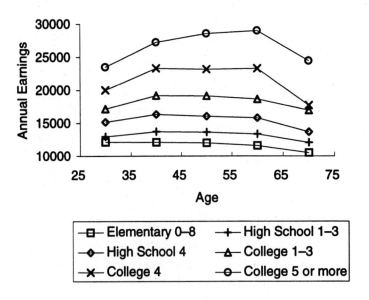

can be seen in Section 6.2, where the present value of lifetime income is computed as the sum of discounted future earnings. An investment in human capital late in one's working life will increase earnings for only a few remaining years and therefore will not add much to lifetime earnings.[2]

Second, because future earnings are discounted in computing the present value of lifetime earnings, the gains in labor earnings from an investment late in one's working life have a much smaller weight in lifetime earnings than from an earlier investment. This is due to the fact that the discount factor increases exponentially with age (see Section 6.2). Therefore, earnings later in one's working life count less in computing lifetime earnings.

Third, because earnings normally increase with age due to early investments in human capital, the opportunity cost of investing in human capital likewise increases with age. The source of this increase is the rising penalty in foregone earnings. Early in life, when wages are low, the opportunity cost of one hour of training is also low. However, late in life, when one's earnings are high, the opportunity cost of giving up an hour of pay for an hour of training is much greater.[3] For these three reasons, then, workers will invest early in their on-the-job training, and earnings should therefore rise with their experience on the job and, on average, with their age.[4]

There is another part to the age-earnings relation. Jacob Mincer (1974) argues that human capital, like other forms of capital, will depreciate over time. For example, many skills acquired 30 or 40 years ago are now obsolete. This is particularly true of fields with rapidly changing technology, like medicine and computer science. In most fields, there is a gradual obsolescence of skills over time. Also, with physical labor, there is a gradual attrition of strength and dexterity as people age beyond a certain point. For professional athletes, this point can occur in their late 20s or early 30s.

---

[2]Another implication of this argument is that capital investment should rise as working life increases. The reason is that an investment in human capital can be recaptured over a longer period of time. This implies that, *ceteris paribus*, the internal rate of return to a given investment, C, will be higher. The internal rate of return $\bar{r}$ is approximately given by:

$$\bar{r} = (k/C) \cdot [1 - (1 + \bar{r})^{-n}]$$

where k is the net increase in earnings resulting from the investment C and n is the number of years of working life. As n becomes larger, the term $(1 + \bar{r})^{-n}$ becomes smaller and therefore $\bar{r}$ becomes larger. In the limit, as n gets increasingly larger, $\bar{r}$ approaches k/C, the ratio of the net increment in earnings to the initial investment C. One reason for the average work life to increase is that the median life span is rising. This has particular relevance for developing countries where, according to the human capital model, decreasing mortality rates should cause increases in investment in education and training.

[3]Another reason might be that an individual's capacity for learning declines with age because of biological and psychological factors. This argument, however, is difficult to substantiate.

[4]By this argument, one might wonder why workers do not complete all their human capital investment as quickly as possible, say before age 22. One answer comes from Yoram Ben-Porath (1967), who argues that the marginal cost curve of producing human capital is upward-sloping within each period. For example, trying to cram all the training required to become a surgeon into, say, a one-year time span would be very expensive because the training costs would rise astronomically (even assuming that a person could absorb all the training in such a short time span). Since individuals will invest until the marginal gain (in this case, the net increase in earnings) equals the marginal cost, they will tend to spread out their human capital investment to keep the cost down.

Thus, there are two counteracting influences on the age-earnings profile. On the one hand, workers acquire new skills and upgrade old skills through on-the-job training. On the other hand, old skills depreciate over time through obsolescence. The human capital model thus predicts that the age-earnings profile will be concave from below—that is, it will slope upward during the early working years, peak, and then slope downward in later working life. The age-earnings profiles illustrated in Figures 7.1–7.4 by schooling level generally conform to this pattern.[5] For all four demographic groups, mean earnings by schooling group rise with age, peak around age 50 to 60, and then fall.

Another interesting aspect of age-earnings profiles is that they tend to be steeper for more educated workers. Among 25–34 year-olds, average earnings for the different schooling groups were relatively close. In the 35–44 age group, mean earnings were slightly more dispersed among schooling groups, and for the 45–54 and 55–64 age brackets, the dispersion increased even more. The reason for this increasing variation in earnings between schooling groups is the different rates of growth of earnings with age. The earnings profiles are decidedly flatter for the less educated than the more educated workers. This is true for all four race-gender groups.

An explanation for this is provided by Mincer (1970). He argues that the increasing steepness of the age-earnings profile with schooling level is due to a positive association between schooling and "post-schooling investment" (that is, on-the-job training). Higher-educated workers will take jobs where there is ample opportunity to acquire new skills on the job. Less educated workers, on the other hand, tend to work in positions with little opportunity for on-the-job training. College graduates, for example, will generally work in professional and managerial jobs, while high school graduates may take clerical or semiskilled jobs and those with less schooling even lower-skilled positions. As a result, more educated workers will, on average, acquire more post-schooling investment and their earnings will rise more steeply over time than those with less schooling.[6]

---

[5]One technical qualification should be mentioned. The data shown here came from a "cross-sectional" sample—that is, one in which people of different ages are observed at a single point of time (in this case, 1989). The age-earnings profile predicted by the human capital model, on the other hand, refers to the time path of earnings of a single individual over time. A sample that includes such data is called a "longitudinal sample." Since no longitudinal data source now exists which traces a person's entire working-life, most of the empirical tests are made on the basis of cross-sectional samples such as the 1990 Census of Population. However, it can be demonstrated that under general conditions if the longitudinal age-earnings profiles are concave downward, then the cross-sectional profiles will also be shaped concave downward.

[6]Another implication is that earnings will peak later in life for the more educated workers. This is also generally confirmed by the data, particularly for white males. Technically, it should also be noted that the argument implies that the actual *dollar increases* in earnings over time will be greater for the more educated than the less educated, because there is a positive correlation between the dollar value of the post-schooling investment and school investment. On the other hand, the *percentage increase* in earnings over time is much closer between schooling groups, because this depends on the amount of post-schooling investment *relative* to schooling investment.

Rates of Return to Schooling

Another way of comparing age-earnings profiles by schooling level is to compute rates of return to schooling. One of the earliest studies was conducted by Giora Hanoch (1967) for white and nonwhite males using 1960 Census of Population data. Some of his results are presented in Table 7.1. Each cell of the matrix shows the rate of return from completing the schooling level on the left margin of the table in comparison to completing the schooling level indicated at the top of the table. For example, among white males, the completion of one to three years of high school resulted in a 16 percent rate of return relative to eight years of elementary school. From the diagonal of the matrix, graduating from high school produced a 16 percent rate of return over one to three years of high school. Completing one to three years of college yielded a 7 percent rate of return over graduating high school, and graduating college a 12 percent rate of return over one to three years of college. The marginal rate of return to graduate school for white males was a relatively low 7 percent. In comparison to a high school degree, the rate of return to a four-year college degree was 10 percent, and 9 percent to graduate school.

Similar tabulations, provided by Richard Raymond and Michael Sesnowitz (1975), for all males in 1969, are shown in Table 7.2. These estimates are based on 1970 Census of Population data. They also include an "ability adjustment" to control for the fact that more educated individuals generally have greater natural ability than less educated ones (see Section 7.3). The Raymond and Sesnowitz figures are higher than those cited from Hanoch in the previous table. The newer estimates indicate that rate of return to attending college over graduating high school was 15–17 percent in 1969; and the return to graduating college over three years of college was 31 to 39 percent.

Table 7.1 Internal Rates of Return by Schooling Levels for White Males in the Non-South United States, 1959[a]

Higher Schooling Level in Each Comparison	Lower Schooling Level in Each Comparison				
	Elem. 8	H.S. 1–3	H.S. 4	Coll. 1–3	Coll. 4
High School 1–3	0.16				
High School 4	0.16	0.16			
College 1–3	0.11	0.10	0.07		
College 4	0.12	0.11	0.10	0.12	
College 5 or more	0.10	0.10	0.09	0.10	0.07

[a] Source: Giora Hanoch, "An Economic Analysis of Earnings and Schooling," *Journal of Human Resources*, Vol. 2, No. 3, Summer 1967, pp. 310–329.

Table 7.2   Internal Rates of Return to Schooling for Males, 1969[a]

Higher Educational Level	Lower Educational Level		
	High School 4	College 1–2	College 3
A. 25 Percent Ability Adjustment			
College 1–2	0.146		
College 3	0.115	0.082	
College 4	0.157	0.164	0.308
B. 15 Percent Ability Adjustment			
College 1–2	0.156		
College 3	0.121	0.087	
College 4	0.168	0.176	0.341
C. No Ability Adjustment			
College 1–2	0.168		
College 3	0.129	0.094	
College 4	0.179	0.193	0.388

[a] Source: Richard Raymond and Michael Sesnowitz, "The Returns to Investments in Higher Education: Some New Evidence," *Journal of Human Resources*, Volume 10, Number 2, Spring 1975, pp. 139–154.

Part of the reason for the difference in estimates is that the rate of return to schooling tends to fluctuate over time in response to changes in both demand and supply conditions. A time series on estimated returns to both high school and college from 1956 to 1979 is shown in Table 7.3, based on the work of J. Peter Mattila (1984). The data source are Current Population Reports for the respective years. The returns are presented in index number form, where 1956 is set to 100.0. The data show a steady increase in the returns to a high school degree over one to three years of high school. In 1979, the return to four years of high school was almost twice that of 1956. In contrast, the return to a college degree (relative to one to three years of college) increased from 1956 through 1972, declined rather sharply between 1972 and 1974, remained low during the mid-1970s, and then started to increase in the late 1970s. For college dropouts (relative to high school graduates), returns fell during the mid-1950s, increased during the 1960s, and then declined again during the 1970s.

There was considerable discussion generated by the collapse in returns to a college education in the 1970s. Richard Freeman, in a 1976 book entitled *The Over-Educated American*, documented both the rising returns to a college degree during the 1960s and its subsequent decline in the 1970s. He argued that during the 1960s, returns increased, despite a large increase in

Table 7.3 Rate of Return to Schooling Indices for Males, 1956–1979[a]
(1956 = 100)

Year	Finishing High School (RORH)	Starting College (RORC)	Continuing College (RORCC)
1956	100.0	100.0	100.0
1957	108.8	96.3	100.1
1958	117.2	94.3	101.0
1959	125.1	93.9	102.7
1960	132.2	94.8	105.0
1961	138.4	96.7	107.9
1962	143.9	99.6	111.2
1963	148.4	102.8	114.6
1964	152.3	105.8	117.4
1965	155.4	108.7	120.0
1966	157.9	112.2	123.9
1967	160.0	114.3	126.1
1968	161.6	115.7	128.0
1969	163.0	115.5	128.4
1970	164.3	114.3	128.5
1971	165.5	111.8	127.8
1972	166.6	107.7	126.2
1973	168.0	102.2	124.2
1974	183.2	96.3	105.7
1975	190.6	95.5	106.1
1976	195.6	94.3	106.7
1977	198.3	93.9	109.0
1978	198.5	94.1	112.7
1979	196.0	94.9	117.9

[a] Source: J. Peter Mattila, Determinants of Male School Enrollments: A Time-Series Analysis, *Review of Economics and Statistics*, Vol. 64, Number 2, May 1984, pp. 242–251.
Key:
RORH—return to completing the fourth year of high school versus having one to three years of high school.
RORC—return to starting college versus having completed the fourth year of high school.
RORCC—return to obtaining four or more years of college versus one to three years of college.

the number of college graduates, because of a rapidly growing demand for college graduates. This was due, in turn, to the growth in sectors and activities that were intensive in their use of college-educated workers. For example, in 1970, 31 percent of all employees in the financial sector had college degrees, compared to 6 percent in the automobile industry. If those industries that are intensive in their use of graduates, such as finance, grow rapidly, then the market demand for college graduates will increase. If these sectors grow slowly, then the market demand will likewise grow slowly.

During the 1960s, several sectors and activities which employed a high proportion of college graduates grew rapidly. These included finance, aerospace, research and development, and the education sector itself, which is very intensive in college manpower. Freeman calculated that between 1960 and 1969, college manpower-intensive sectors grew at 4.4 percent per year, while other sectors grew at only 2 percent per year. This large growth in demand caused the return to a college education to rise.

However, during the 1970s, these demand forces weakened, as the growth of the education, public administration, aircraft, and computer sectors fell off. College manpower-intensive sectors grew at only 2.8 percent per year from 1969 to 1974, while other sectors increased at 2.0 percent per year. Moreover, there was a large surge in the number of college graduates, as the baby-boom generation reached college age.

The result was an excess supply of college-educated workers relative to the demand, causing college-level earnings to drop relative to those of high school graduates. Among male year-round, full-time employees, college graduates earned 53 percent more than high-school graduates in 1969 but only 35 percent more in 1974. For recent graduates, the premium fell from 35 percent in 1969 to 16 percent in 1972. Moreover, for the class of 1972, only 45 percent of males with B.A. degrees were able to obtain professional jobs upon graduation, compared to 71 percent in 1968. The fraction of college graduates working as professionals or managers declined from 76 percent in 1969 to 68 percent in 1974.

During the 1980s, the picture changed once again. Comparisons between 1979 and 1988 are shown in Table 7.4, based on work by McKinley L. Blackburn, David E. Bloom, and Richard B. Freeman (1991). The figures show earnings differentials (rather than rates of return) between college graduates and high-school-educated workers in the two years. The data are based on annual earnings for full-time, year-round workers. The differentials are standardized for age, marital status, region, and occupation. The original data sources are the Current Population Surveys for 1980 and 1989. The results show that the earnings of college graduates relative to both high school dropouts and high school graduates increased from 1979 to 1988. This was true for all four demographic groups shown in the table—white males, black males, white females, and black females. Interestingly, the relative earnings of college graduates increased more for whites than for blacks over this period.

The results are consistent with several other studies that have documented rising returns to a college education during the 1980s. Kevin Murphy and Finis Welch (1993) calculated that the ratio of average hourly wages between white male college and high school graduates with one to five years of experience increased from 1.4 in 1978 to 1.8 in 1985, though it fell off

Table 7.4   Standardized Earnings Differentials Between Schooling Groups, 1979 and 1988[a]

	College 4 Relative To High School 1–3		College 4 Relative To High School 4	
	1979	*1988*	*1979*	*1988*
1. White Males	.51	.66	.28	.38
2. Black Males	.56	.58	.34	.41
3. White Females	.55	.72	.35	.46
4. Black Females	.67	.73	.45	.49

[a] Source: McKinley L. Blackburn, David E. Bloom, and Richard B. Freeman, "The Distribution of Labor Market Outcomes: Measuring and Explaining Trends and Patterns in the 1980s for Selected Demographic Groups in the United States," mimeo, February, 1991, Table 3. The data are based on annual earnings for full-time, year-round workers. The differentials are standardized for age, marital status, region, and occupation. The original data sources are the Current Population Surveys for 1980 and 1989.

slightly to 1.75 in 1990. Mary Coleman (1993) also generally found large increases in the college earnings premium between 1980 and 1988 for workers with one to five years of experience—from 1.4 to 1.9 for white men, 1.6 to 1.9 for white women, and 1.7 to 2.0 for black men—though no change for black women (1.9 in both years).

The large relative gains of college graduates during the 1980s reflect both supply and demand factors. Though college enrollment rates did not decline appreciably during the 1980s, the number of people of college-age years did, as the "baby boom" gave way to the "baby dearth." Thus, the number of new college graduates declined during the 1980s. Moreover, many of the industries that experienced the most rapid rate of employment growth during the 1980s—including health, government, finance and banking, and business and professional services—were all intensive in their use of college graduates. Thus, both supply and demand factors helped fuel the growing returns to a college education.

Table 7.5 presents comparisons of rates of returns to education for different regions of the world on the basis of work by George Psacharopoulos (1985). The figures are based on studies of a large number of countries conducted mainly for the 1960s and the 1970s. The figures in Table 7.5 are averages of the returns computed for individual countries within each group. Two different sets of returns are calculated. The first is the social rate of return, based on the total cost of education, from both public and private sources, at each schooling level. The second, the private rate of return, is based on the costs of education to individual students, after the public subsidy to education is deducted.

Table 7.5 Average Rates of Return to Education by Region of the World and Level of Education[a]

Region	Social Returns			Private Returns		
	Primary	Secondary	Higher	Primary	Secondary	Higher
Africa	.26	.17	.13	.45	.26	.32
Asia	.27	.15	.13	.31	.15	.18
Latin America	.26	.18	.16	.32	.23	.23
Middle-Income	.13	.10	.08	.17	.13	.13
High-Income	—	.11	.09	—	.12	.12

[a]Source: George Psacharopoulos, "Returns to Education: A further International Update and Implications," *Journal of Human Resources*, Vol. 20, No. 4, Fall 1985, pp. 583–604, Table 1.

The results indicate that for all regions of the world, social returns are greater to primary education than to secondary school, and greater to secondary than higher education. The main reason for the very high return to primary schooling is the substantial productivity differential between literate and illiterate workers. The data also show that returns to education are substantially higher for low-income regions of the world—Africa, Asia, and Latin America—than for middle-income and high-income countries. For example, the social return to a high school education was 70 percent higher in Africa than in the middle-income countries. The reason is the greater scarcity of human capital relative to physical capital in poor regions of the world. The figures also show that private returns are higher than social returns. The differences are particularly great for the poor regions of the world and for higher education in all regions. The differences reflect the greater public subsidy to education in poor countries than in richer ones, and the greater public subsidy for higher education than for lower levels of schooling.

Policy Implications Insofar as one accepts the assumptions of the human capital model, these rates of return could serve to give some guidance to social policy. For developing countries, particularly Africa and Latin America, the implications are clear that underinvestment exists at all levels of education. This argument is documented by the fact the social returns to schooling are considerably higher than normal rates of return to investment in physical capital (plant and equipment). Primary school appears to be the top priority, since its social return far exceeds that for secondary or college education. This also shows the importance of increasing literacy rates in less developed countries. The results also suggest that secondary schooling is given more priority than higher education in poorer countries. Interestingly, similar results of high rates of return to schooling were found for non-white males for the United States. This suggests that for the United States, heavy investment is warranted in the education of black Americans, particularly at the secondary school level.

Results for advanced economies like the United States indicate that education is still a good investment, if not an "extraordinary" investment. Returns of the order of 10 to 12 percent are comparable to those obtained in private investment in physical capital. Returns to college, in particular, have been increasing during the 1980s and are now as high as they were during the 1960s. This reinforces the importance of continued investment in education in the United States.

Lifetime Earnings

Another important implication of the human capital model is that the present value of the discounted stream of lifetime earnings ("lifetime earnings," for short) should be equal among schooling groups if the basic assumptions of the model are true (see Section 6.2). In actuality, many of the assumptions of the human capital do not hold. Capital markets are not perfect. Because of trade unions and the like, the labor market is not perfectly competitive, and "native ability" may be correlated with schooling achievements. Any one of these three conditions would cause some inequality in lifetime earnings between schooling groups. However, for the human capital model to be at all reliable, there should be relatively small differences in lifetime earnings among these groups.

Four sets of estimates are presented on lifetime earnings in Table 7.6. The first, from James Morgan and Martin David (1963), is based on the 1959 Survey Research Center National Sample. It shows lifetime earnings in 1959 dollars at different levels of educational attainment for white males. Differences in estimated lifetime earnings between schooling groups were quite small in this study. The percentage difference between lowest ($86,900) and highest ($101,700) was only 17 percent. Moreover, if we exclude the group with nonacademic training, lifetime earnings ranged from $91,000 to $102,000, a relatively narrow range.

The second, from Bruce Wilkinson (1966), is based on the 1961 Canadian Census and shows lifetime earnings in 1961 Canadian dollars at different educational levels for selected occupations for males. In this study, the variation in lifetime earnings between different schooling groups within occupation was quite small. For laborers, the range was $33,000–$36,000; for carpenters, $41,000–$44,000; for compositors and typesetters, $57,000–$61,000; for technicians, $57,000–$61,000; and for engineers, $72,000–$77,000. The maximum percentage difference in lifetime earnings was only 9 percent (for laborers). However, there were considerable differences in lifetime earnings between occupations, ranging from the mid $30,000s for laborers to the low $70,000s for engineers. Since the human capital model does predict that lifetime earnings will be equal not only for different

Table 7.6 Estimates of Lifetime Earnings by Schooling Group

Educational Level	Lifetime Earnings
A. Morgan and David (1963)[a]	
Grades 0–8	$ 96,000
Grades 9–11	96,950
Grade 12	90,300
Grade 12 and non-academic training	86,900
College, no degree	91,100
College, bachelor's degree	100,450
College, advanced degree	101,700
B. Wilkinson (1966)[b]	
(1) Laborers	
No high school	33,300
Some high school	36,200
Four years high school	36,400
(2) Carpenters	
No high school	41,100
Some high school	42,700
Four years high school	44,300
(3) Compositors and Typesetters	
No high school	57,600
Some high school	60,100
Four years high school	57,200
(4) Draftsmen	
No high school	59,300
Some high school	60,500
Four years high school	57,200
(5) Science and Engineering Technicians	
Four years high school	60,800
Some college	56,800
College degree	56,700
(6) Engineers	
Four years high school	72,500
Some college	71,800
College degree	76,500

(continued)

Table 7.6 *(concluded)*

C. *Lillard (1977)*[c]

Ability Level	Years of Schooling								
	12	13	14	15	16	17	18	19	20
1. Discount Rate = 0.03									
Low	252	251	252	254	255	256	257	258	259
Average	260	255	256	259	264	271	279	289	300
High	270	268	269	273	280	288	298	310	322
3. Discount Rate = 0.05									
Low	163	159	156	154	152	151	149	147	146
Average	166	160	157	156	157	158	161	165	169
High	171	165	163	163	165	168	172	177	182

D. *1989 Survey of Consumer Finances*[d]

Educational Level	White Males	Nonwhite Males	Females
Grades 0–11	895	653	454
High School 4	1,221	876	659
College 1–3	1,308	1,043	737
College 4	2,195	1,370	927
College 5 or more	2,770	2,341	1,248
Gini Coefficients			
Annual Earnings	0.50	0.41	0.40
Lifetime Earnings	0.31	0.23	0.22

[a] Source: James Morgan and Martin David, "Education and Income," *Quarterly Journal of Economics*, Vol. 77, No. 3, August 1963, pp. 423–437. Lifetime earnings is computed as the present value at age 15 of future earnings discounted at an interest rate of 4 percent, assuming 2,000 hours worked per year until age 65. Adjustments were made for differences in the social characteristics of workers, labor market condition, past mobility, and supervisory responsibility.

[b] Source: Bruce W. Wilkinson, "Present Values of Lifetime Earnings for Different Occupations," *Journal of Political Economy*, Vol. 74, No. 6, December 1966, pp. 556–572. Lifetime earnings is computed as the present value at age 14 of future earnings (after income taxes) discounted at an interest rate of 5 percent.

[c] Source: Lee A. Lillard, "Inequality: Earnings vs. Human Wealth," American Economic Review, March 1977, Vol. 67, No. 2, pp. 42–53, Table 1. The figures show lifetime earnings in thousands of 1970 dollars by years of schooling, assuming full retirement at age 66 and with average values for social variables.

[d] Source: Author's calculations from the 1989 Survey of Consumer Finances. The figures show lifetime earnings in thousands of 1989 dollars for individuals aged 35 in 1989 by years of schooling, assuming full retirement at age 65, a one percent growth rate in real earnings, and a two percent discount rate.

schooling levels but also for different types of job training, this result would not be consistent with the human capital model.

The third set, from Lee Lillard (1977), is derived from the NBER-Thorndike sample. This is a longitudinal or panel data set, which follows the same set of individuals over time. In this case, men who were born between 1917 and 1925 and who volunteered for the Air Force in 1943 were surveyed in 1943 and one to four times more after that until 1970. On the basis of these data, lifetime earnings were estimated for each individual in the sample. Estimates were standardized for social and demographic factors, including parent's education, religion, and number of siblings, as well as an ability index based on the Armed Forces Qualification Tests (AFQT).

The results show that there is variation in lifetime earnings between schooling groups even among individuals with the same ability level. However, here, again, the variation is not very great. One way of measuring the extent of variation is to compute the Gini coefficient for lifetime earnings. Lillard calculated a value of 0.19 for the Gini coefficient of lifetime earnings for the 4,699 individuals in the sample (the results were very similar for the different discount rates used in the analysis). In contrast, the Gini coefficient for annual earnings by age group averaged 0.28. Thus, inequality in lifetime earnings was about one-third less than that of annual earnings.[7]

The author's calculations based on the 1989 Survey of Consumer Finances show considerably more variation in lifetime earnings by schooling group than the previous sets. Among white males, there is an almost two-fold difference between the lifetime earnings of college graduates and those of high school graduates. For nonwhite males, the ratio is 1.6 and for females, 1.4. However, as in the other studies, the inequality of lifetime earnings is about a third to a half less than that of annual earnings.

In summary, these studies do show that there is variation in lifetime earnings among schooling groups. However, the variation in average lifetime earnings by schooling group is considerably smaller than that of average annual earnings, and inequality of lifetime earnings among all individuals is less than that of annual earnings.

These results have two important implications. First, they indicate that a substantial portion of the differences in annual earnings among individuals evens out over the lifetime. This is partly due to the fact that different educational groups have different lifetime earnings trajectories. It is also a result of the fact that annual income has both a permanent and transitory component. The transitory component tends to wash out over the lifetime, so that the variation in permanent income among individuals is less than that of annual income.

Second, from a policy perspective, should we be unduly concerned with increases in the inequality of annual incomes if lifetime (or permanent) income is more equally distributed? It probably makes more sense to con-

---

[7]Calculations by Friesen and Miller (1983) produced similar results. In 1962, the Gini coefficient for annual income was 0.36 and that for lifetime earnings was 0.21.

sider differences in lifetime income and resources as the more relevant measure of inequality for public policy, since this is what determines the long-term welfare of families. In this regard, it would be of interest to know whether inequality in lifetime income has also been rising in recent years.

7.2 THE SCHOOLING-EARNINGS FUNCTION*

Jacob Mincer (1970, 1974) contributed much of the basic work in deriving a specific functional relation between an individual's level of schooling and labor earnings. Following Mincer, let us assume that a worker with S years of schooling earns E_S per year and that earnings are constant over time. Assume also that the direct schooling costs are zero—that is, the only cost of schooling is foregone earnings—and that there is no further investment in human capital after the completion of schooling. If working life is n years and the market rate of interest is r, then the present discounted value of the stream of future earnings, V_S, is given by:

$$V_S = \sum_{t=s+1}^{s+n} \frac{E_S}{(1+r)^t} \tag{7.1}$$

It is now convenient to convert equation (7.1) into a continuous form. To do this requires some calculus. Instead of assuming that earnings are paid each year, we assume that they are received continuously over time. Therefore, the present value of lifetime earnings, V_S, becomes:

$$V_S = \int_s^{s+n} E_S\, e^{-rt}\, dt \tag{7.2}$$

where "$\int$" is the integral sign and e is the natural number.

Equation (7.2) can be solved to obtain

$$V_S = \frac{1}{r} E_S\, e^{-rS} (1 - e^{-rn}) \tag{7.3}$$

The present value of earnings, $V_{S'}$, for a worker with S' years of schooling is given by:

$$V_{S'} = \frac{1}{r} E_{S'}\, e^{-rS'} (1 - e^{-rn'}) \tag{7.4}$$

where $E_{S'}$ is annual earnings (assumed constant over life) corresponding to S' years of schooling and n' is the person's working life in years.

By the assumptions of the human capital model, V_S must equal $V_{S'}$ in equilibrium. Therefore, from equations (7.3) and (7.4),

Chapter 7 Empirical Work and Alternative Views

$$\frac{1}{r} E_S e^{-rS} (1 - e^{-rn}) = \frac{1}{r} E_{S'} e^{-rS'} (1-e^{-rn'})$$

Rearranging terms, we obtain an expression for the relative annual earnings between the two workers:

$$\frac{E_S}{E_{S'}} = \frac{-e^{rS'} (1 - e^{-rn'})}{-e^{rS} (1 - e^{-rn})} \tag{7.5}$$

This ratio can be simplified under either of two conditions. First, if despite the fact that the two individuals have different amounts of schooling, they work the same number of years, then $n' = n$ and the two expressions in parentheses are equal. Second, if as recent data suggest, differences in working life are small and n and n' are large, then the difference in the value of the two expressions in parentheses is very small and can be conveniently ignored.[8] Under either condition, equation (7.5) can be simplified to:

$$\frac{E_S}{E_{S'}} = e^{r(S - S')} \tag{7.6}$$

If we now let S' be the zero schooling level and take the natural logarithms (ln) of both sides of equation (7.6), we obtain:

$$\ln E_S = \ln E_0 + rS \tag{7.7}$$

Equation (7.7) is the basic earnings function of the human capital model.

Before considering the uses of the earnings equation (7.7), let us consider three implications of equation (7.6). First, the ratio $E_S/E_{S'}$ is greater than one if S is greater than S'. In other words, workers with more schooling should receive higher earnings. Second, the ratio $E_S/E_{S'}$ is a positive function of r. The higher the discount rate, the greater the increase in earnings must be to compensate for an additional year of schooling (and hence foregone earnings). This point was illustrated in the various numerical examples presented in Section 6.2. Third, the equation indicates that earnings differences are multiplicative between schooling levels. In other words, an additional year of schooling is associated with a certain *percentage* increase in earnings, rather than a certain absolute dollar amount. Or, by equation (7.7), there is a log-linear relation between earnings and schooling.

Equation (7.7) lends itself very readily to econometric analysis. If E_i refers to the earnings of individual i and S_i refers to the person's level of schooling, then the regression model becomes:

---

[8] As Mincer (1970) notes, the main reason why more educated workers receive higher annual earnings than less educated ones is the postponement of earnings early in life rather than a shorter payoff period.

$$\ln E_i = b_0 + b_1 S_i + u_i \tag{7.8}$$

where b_0 and b_1 are parameter coefficients to be estimated and u_i is a random error term. The coefficient estimator b_1 is of particular interest, since it is the estimated rate of return to schooling (that is, it corresponds to the variable r in equation 7.7). The random error term u_i is supposed to pick up individual differences in earnings capacity, from differences in abilities, quality of schooling, family background, and the like.

Mincer (1974) applied this model to a sample of white, nonfarm male workers drawn from the 1960 Census of Population. As he notes, the equation is really incomplete, since there is no variable for experience or other sources of post-schooling investment. Since the existence of on-the-job training or post-schooling investment will cause earnings to rise over time for each schooling group, the assumption of constant earnings E_S over time will be violated. However, Mincer found that after about eight years of work experience, the average earnings of most schooling groups were close to their average lifetime value.[9] Therefore, choosing a sample of workers with eight or so years of experience could provide a fairly valid test of the schooling model.

The results of these regressions are shown in Table 7.7, as well as those of an additional form with the logarithm of weeks worked (ln W) added.[10] The coefficient of schooling—that is, the estimated rate of return—was highly significant in each regression. The estimated rates of return ranged from 10 percent to 17 percent, which was similar to the range that Hanoch and Raymond and Sesnowitz found (see Tables 7.1 and 7.2). The coefficient of weeks worked was also highly significant. The coefficient of determination of the regression (R^2), which is the statistic that measures the amount of variation in the dependent variation (explained by the independent variables of the regression), was very high for this type of individual data. For the forms without ln W, the R^2 ranged from 0.26 to 0.33, and in the forms with ln W, the range was 0.51 to 0.60.

The Extended Earnings Function

As Jacob Mincer notes, the schooling model is an incomplete specification for the human capital model, because no variable is included to reflect on-the-job training or other forms of post-schooling investment. Therefore, to complete the model, some variable or variables must be included to capture such training. Unfortunately, it is very difficult to observe the amount of training an individual receives, and most data sources include no such esti-

---

[9] In more technical terms, the average earnings of a schooling group after about eight years of experience tended to equal that amount of annual earnings in a constant income stream whose present value equals the present value of the actual stream of lifetime earnings. Mincer called this number of years the "overtaking years of experience."

[10] Since the left-hand variable, logarithm of earnings, will vary with the number of weeks worked, this was considered a "natural" variable to add to the regression specification.

Table 7.7 Regressions of Annual Earnings on Schooling and Weeks Worked for White, Nonfarm Males with 6 to 10 Years of Experience[a]

Years of Experience	Number of Observations	Regression Results[b]	R^2
8	790	(1) $\ln E = 6.36 + 0.162\ S$ (16.4)	0.306
		(2) $\ln E = 2.14 + 0.115\ S + 1.27\ \ln W$ (15.1) (21.0)	0.575
6–10	3,689	(3) $\ln E = 6.75 + 0.133\ S$ (36.1)	0.261
		(4) $\ln E = 2.07 + 0.104\ S + 1.31\ \ln W$ (34.0) (43.4)	0.511
7–9	2,124	(5) $\ln E = 6.30 + 0.165\ S$ (26.5)	0.328
		(6) $\ln E = 1.89 + 0.121\ S + 1.29\ \ln W$ (24.6) (30.6)	0.596

[a] Source: Jacob Mincer, *Schooling, Experience, and Earnings*, National Bureau of Economic Research, New York 1974, p. 53. The results are based on the 1/1,000 sample of the 1960 U.S. Census of Population.
[b] Key: (1) ln E: natural logarithm of earnings; (2) S: schooling; (3) ln W: natural logarithm of weeks worked; and (4) R^2: coefficient of determination. Figures in parentheses are t-ratios.

mates. Actually, very few data sources have reliable estimates even of the amount of work experience someone has had. Therefore, some additional assumptions must be made on the amount of post-schooling investment workers receive in order to obtain a form that can be estimated.

As Gary Becker argued, investment in human capital should decline over the life cycle, at least beyond an early stage, primarily because the pay-off period is limited (see Section 7.1). The actual form of the investment function cannot be directly predicted by the human capital model. However, Mincer (1974) proposed four possibilities. The two most widely used are discussed below.

Define X as years of experience and k_X as the amount of time devoted to post-schooling investment at X years of experience. Then, the total amount of time devoted to post-schooling investment from the first year of work through X years of work, K_X, is given by:

$$K_X = \int_{t=0}^{X} k_t\ dt \tag{7.9}$$

For the same reason as with the schooling model, earnings will increase exponentially with the total amount of post-schooling investment. Therefore, the logarithm of earnings of someone with S years of schooling and X years of experience is given by:

$$\ln E_{S,X} = \ln E_0 + rS + r'K_X \qquad (7.10)$$

where r is the rate of return to schooling and r' is the rate of return to post-schooling investment.

Two possible relations between post-schooling investment and experience are as follows. First, suppose post-schooling investment declines as a linear function of time. Then:

$$k_X = k_0 - (k_0/T) X \qquad (7.11)$$

where T is the total period of post-schooling investment. In this case,

$$K_X = k_0 X - (k_0/2T) X^2$$

and

$$\ln E_{S,X} = \ln E_0 + rS + r'k_0 X - (r'k_0/2T) X^2 \qquad (7.12)$$

This relation is referred to as a *parabolic* earnings function, since there is both an experience (X) and an experience-squared (X^2) term in the function. This implies that earnings will rise with experience for a time, level off, and then decline towards the end of the working life.

Second, suppose post-schooling investment declines exponentially with experience:

$$k_X = k_0 e^{-gX} \qquad (7.13)$$

where g is a parameter indicating the rate of decline of investment. Then:

$$K_X = k_0/g - (k_0/g) e^{-gX}$$

and

$$\ln E_{S,X} = (\ln E_0 + r'k_0/g) + rS - (r'k_0/g) e^{-gX} \qquad (7.14)$$

Equation (7.14) is referred to as a **Gompertz curve**. In this form, earnings increase with experience, though the rate of increase declines continuously over time. This, like the parabolic function, causes the shape of the earnings profile to be concave downward. Moreover, for technical reasons, the term $-k_0^2 e^{-2gX}/2$ is usually added to equation (7.14).[11]

The actual estimating forms of the parabolic and Gompertz forms look much simpler. For the parabolic form, the regression equation is:

$$\ln E_i = b_0 + b_1 S_i + b_2 X_i + b_3 X^2_i + u_i \qquad (7.15)$$

where the subscript i refers to individual i, the parameters b_0, b_1, b_2, and b_3 are coefficients to be estimated, and u_i is a random error term. For the Gompertz form, the regression equation is:

$$\ln E_i = b_0 + b_1 S_i + b_2 e^{-gX_i} + b_3 e^{-2gX_i} + u_i \qquad (7.16)$$

Mincer estimated these two regression forms on a sample of 31,093 white, nonfarm, nonstudent males up to age 65 drawn from the 1960 Census of Population. The results of several of the forms are shown in Table 7.8. The first line shows the results of estimating the simple schooling equation on the full sample. Though the schooling variable is still very significant, the R^2 is much lower than when the sample is restricted to a given number of years of experience (see Table 7.7). The second line shows the results of estimating the parabolic earnings function. The goodness of fit for the equation is 0.29, considerably higher than for the simple schooling model. Moreover, the schooling and experience variables are both extremely significant. The last four lines show the results of various Gompertz forms. Since there is no way of directly estimating the parameter g, the rate at which postschooling investment declines with experience, Mincer tried a number of values ranging from 0.05 to 0.30. The two values of g with the best fit were 0.10 and 0.15. Results for both values are shown. In specifications (3) and (4), both the schooling and experience variables are highly significant, and the R^2 is over 30 percent. In equations (5) and (6), the variables e^{-2gX} and the logarithm of weeks are added, and the R^2 jumps to 55 percent.

These results of Mincer, shown in Tables 7.7 and 7.8, have often been cited as confirmation of the human capital model. However, there are a number of criticisms of these results. First, including weeks worked as an explanatory variable for annual earnings will overstate the explanatory power of the model, since the real issue is difference in compensation rates explained by schooling achievement and experience.[12] As a result, the fair

---

[11] It is also possible to introduce a depreciation term into the two earnings equations. Suppose human capital depreciates at a rate δ per year. Then the parabolic earnings equation becomes:

$$\ln E_{S,X} = \ln E_0 = (r - \delta)S + (r'k^*_0 - \delta) X - (r'k^*_0/2T^*) X^2$$

where T^* is the gross investment period. The Gompertz earnings function becomes:

$$\ln E_{S,X} = \ln E_0 + (r - \delta)S - \delta X + (r'k^*_0/g) (1 - e^{-gx})$$

[12] An alternative specification might have had the logarithm of weekly earnings ($\ln E/W$) as the dependent variable.

Table 7.8 Regressions of Annual Earnings on Schooling, Experience, and Weeks Worked for White Nonfarm, Nonstudent Males up to Age 65[a]

Regression Results[b]	R^2
(1) $\ln E = 7.58 + 0.070\ S$ $\quad\quad\quad\quad\quad (43.8)$	0.067
(2) $\ln E = 6.20 + 0.107\ S + 0.081\ X - 0.0012\ X^2$ $\quad\quad\quad\quad\quad (72.3)\quad\quad (75.5)\quad\quad\quad (55.8)$	0.285
(3) $\ln E = 7.43 + 0.110\ S - 1.651\ e^{-.15x}$ $\quad\quad\quad\quad\quad (77.6)\quad\quad (102.3)$	0.313
(4) $\ln E = 7.52 + 0.113\ S - 1.521\ e^{-.10x}$ $\quad\quad\quad\quad\quad (74.3)\quad\quad (101.4)$	0.307
(5) $\ln E = 7.43 + 0.108\ S - 1.172\ e^{-.15x} - 0.324 e^{-.30x} + 1.183\ \ln W$ $\quad\quad\quad\quad\quad (65.4)\quad\quad (16.8)\quad\quad\quad\quad (10.2)\quad\quad\quad\quad (105.4)$	0.546
(6) $\ln E = 7.50 + 0.111\ S - 1.291\ e^{-.10x} - 0.162\ e^{-.20x} + 1.174\ \ln W$ $\quad\quad\quad\quad\quad (65.0)\quad\quad (3.5)\quad\quad\quad\quad (16.0)\quad\quad\quad\quad (107.3)$	0.551

[a] Source: Jacob Mincer, *Schooling, Experience, and Earnings*, National Bureau of Economic Research, New York, 1974, p. 92. The results are based on the 1/1,000 sample of the 1960 U.S. Census of Population. The sample size is 31,093.
[b] Key: (1) ln E: natural logarithm of earnings; (2) S: schooling; (3) X: experience; (4) ln W: natural logarithm of weeks worked; and (5) R^2: coefficient of determination. Figures in parentheses are t-ratios.

measure of the explanatory power of the model is between 26 and 33 percent which, though still high, leaves at least two-thirds of the variation unexplained. Jencks, *et al.* (1972), for example, argued that the amount of unexplained variation was so large as to make schooling an ineffective weapon to reduce overall economic inequality. Second, the sample chosen was restricted to white males (employed in nonagricultural industries) in their prime working years. Most of the labor force—females, minorities, and agricultural workers—was therefore excluded in the test. Indeed, subsequent work has shown that the human capital earnings model does not work nearly as well for females and minorities as it does for white males.

7.3 ABILITY AND EARNINGS

The idea of a positive association between ability and earnings is an intuitive one. People who are more able should be more productive on the job and therefore command higher pay in the workplace. In the neoclassical model, workers with more ability have higher marginal products and therefore command higher wages. Many early models of income distribution were based almost exclusively on the distribution of ability in the population.[13]

---

[13] See, for example, Ammon (1895), Taussig (1915), Roy (1950), and Mandelbrot (1962).

The main difficulty with these models is in defining "ability." If ability and productivity are simply synonymous, then we are left with a truism or tautology without explanatory content. Unless we can explain what ability is or what determines it independently of what someone earns, we are left with a theory without economic content. Consider the old saw, "If you're so smart, why aren't you rich?" If "being rich" *means* "being smart," then there is no way of verifying that intelligence is positively related to labor earnings. We shall return to this point later.

In this section, we consider the relation between schooling, ability, and earnings. There are both theoretical and statistical issues involved. Suppose that ability affects productivity on the job and thereby pay and that ability also affects school performance. Then, how do we determine the independent effects of ability and schooling on a worker's productivity and earnings? More particularly, if we are in a human capital framework, how do we determine the rate of return to schooling independently of the return to ability? As will be seen, on the statistical level, this is equivalent to asking the question: How do we separate out the coefficients of schooling and ability on earnings? The failure to do this correctly will result in the commission of a potentially serious error in estimating the returns to education, called a specification bias.

In many models, ability is included along with schooling, experience, and other personal characteristics as independent determinants of a person's earnings. Unlike the traditional variables used in such models, there are two types of problems associated with the ability variable. First, as mentioned above, it is very difficult to define innate or natural ability and even more difficult to measure it. Most studies treat ability as synonymous with cognitive ability and measure it using standardized tests such as IQ or school achievement tests. But even with such tests, it is very difficult to separate out "innate intelligence" from that produced by home environment or by schooling itself.

The second difficulty in the use of the ability variable is that ability may not only influence a person's earnings directly—that is, through its impact on job performance—but indirectly through its effect on schooling achievement. The path diagram shown in Diagram 7.1 may help clarify the problem. Path (a) reflects the fact that ability may affect schooling attainment for two reasons. First, more able students will, in general, achieve a higher level of potential productivity from a given amount of schooling. Second, partly as a consequence of the first, the more able student will generally acquire more schooling than the less able student. Ability will, therefore, affect both a student's achievement from schooling and the level of schooling attained.

Ability will indirectly affect earnings via path (b) according to its effect on the amount of human capital acquired. Those with more human capital will, on average, command higher wages in the labor market. At the same time, by path (c), ability will directly affect earnings, independently of school-acquired skills. A worker with more ability may simply perform better on the job than someone who is less able.

Diagram 7.1 Path Diagram of Ability, Schooling, and Earnings

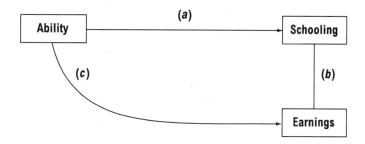

Econometrically, the most straightforward way of assessing the independent effects of ability and schooling on earnings is to estimate two equations of the following form:

(1) $$\ln E_i = a_0 + a_1 S_i \qquad (7.17a)$$

(2) $$\ln E_i = b_0 + b_1 S_i + b_2 A_i \qquad (7.17b)$$

where A_i is the ability level of individual i. The first equation is the standard human capital earnings function, where the coefficient a_1 is the estimated rate of return to schooling. The second equation includes an ability variable as an independent determinant of earnings.

If the model illustrated in Diagram 7.1 is correct, then we would expect that schooling and ability will be positively correlated (related), since those with more ability will, on average, acquire more schooling. As a result, equation (1) will lead to an overstatement of the "true" impact of schooling on earnings, since part of the estimated effect of schooling on earnings is due to the greater ability of the more educated worker. The estimated rate of return to schooling from equation (1) will be biased upward—that is, will be too high.[14] Equation (2) corrects for this bias by including the ability variable. The coefficient b_1 is therefore a better estimate of the rate of return to

---

[14]Technically, this is called a "specification bias" or an "omitted variable" bias, since equation (1) is incorrectly specified by the exclusion of an ability variable. There is another, more subtle, error in estimation associated with this problem, which is called a "self-selection bias," or a "selectivity bias." This problem arises not from an omitted variable in the basic schooling model but rather from the fact that the sample itself is unrepresentative of the full population. For example, if we observe earnings for a sample of college graduates in a given year but have no information on their ability, their earnings will reflect both their schooling achievement and their unobserved ability. Presumably, because this group of people went on to finish college, their ability or set of talents is, on average, different than a sample of high school graduates. Therefore, the earnings the group of high school graduates would have received had they completed college would not be the same as the actual earnings received by the college graduates. In general, the earnings would be lower. On the other hand, the earnings actually received by the high school graduates would, in general, be
(continued)

schooling. The coefficient b_1 will be lower than a_1, since part of the effect of schooling on earnings estimated in (1) will be properly attributed to ability. Gary Becker, in his 1964 book, *Human Capital,* thought that rates of return to schooling were probably overstated by about one-third because of the exclusion of an ability variable. However, there was no hard evidence available at that time on which to base this presumption. Since then, a number of studies have tried to estimate the size of the bias.

Several studies were based on the NBER-Thorndike sample. This sample consisted of men who had taken a battery of tests called the Armed Forces Qualification Test (AFQT), which were used to select candidates for the Army Air Force during World War II. These tests measured various abilities such as mathematical and reasoning skills, physical coordination, reaction to stress, and spatial perception. In 1955, Thorndike and Hagen conducted a survey of 17,000 of those who took the test in 1943 to see how useful these tests were in predicting future vocational success. In 1969, the National Bureau of Economic Research conducted a follow-up survey to determine their vocational achievement in that year. About 4,700 of the original 17,000 responded to the follow-up questionnaire. This sample is useful for estimating equation (2), since the database provides observations on both schooling and ability.

Paul Taubman and Terrence Wales (1974) conducted one of the first studies using the NBER-Thorndike sample. They found that the inclusion of all the ability measures in the model reduced the estimated rate of return to schooling by about 30 percent. This figure is quite close to Gary Becker's original guess. Looking more at the full range of ability measures provided by the AFQT, they also found that ability was a significant determinant of earnings for all schooling groups. Of the various measures of ability that they used, mathematical ability had the strongest effect on earnings.

As with the testing of many hypotheses in economics, results vary according to the sample of data and methodology used. John Hause (1972, 1975), using the same NBER-Thorndike sample, found a smaller bias in estimating the rate of return to schooling, though his work concentrated primarily on measures of cognitive ability. Zvi Griliches and William Mason (1972) also reported a relatively small effect of AFQT scores using a sample of World War II veterans. On the other hand, Lee Hansen, Burton Weisbrod, and William Scanlon (1970) estimated a larger effect, a bias of about 50 percent, when the NBER-Thorndike sample was extended to include individuals who had taken but failed the AFQT.

---

different than the earnings the sample of college graduates would have received had they gone to work immediately after graduating high school.

In the human capital model, such a computation of forgone earnings is necessary to estimate the rate of return to additional schooling (see Section 6.2). This argument indicates that such computations of the rate of return to schooling based on only the observed earnings of high school and college graduates is not really valid. This error is called a selectivity bias because the sample of high school and college graduates select themselves based on, for us, unobserved attributes. Heckman (1976) and Willis and Rosen (1979) both developed statistical techniques for correcting this problem.

Other data sources have also been used. Orley Ashenfelter and Joseph Mooney (1968) compiled data on a sample of 1,322 Woodrow Wilson Fellows appointed between 1958 and 1960, with salary data reported for 1966. Adding SAT scores as their ability variable, the coefficient on the schooling variable declined very little. David Wise (1975) used a sample consisting of college graduates working in a large corporation. He found that schooling level had a significant effect on a person's initial salary but not on its rate of growth over time in the firm. On the other hand, school quality and class rank (interpreted as measures of ability) were very significant in affecting salary growth over time but not in the determination of starting salary. Similar results were reported by Lewis Solmon (1975) and Paul Wachtel (1975), both using the NBER-Thorndike sample, and Ethel Jones and John Jackson (1990) in a study of graduates in business administration.

In sum, there is general agreement among economists about the importance of innate ability in the determination of earnings. Almost all agree that it affects earnings directly through its effect on job performance and indirectly through its effect on schooling achievement, though specific estimates do differ on its importance. On average, rates of return to schooling estimated without an ability variable included in the equation are probably overstated by about a third, as Becker had originally speculated.

The concern about the ability bias in estimating rates of return to education is not only of academic interest but can also have a direct bearing on public policy issues. As we discussed in Section 6.2, human capital theory has had and continues to have a direct bearing on social policy. This is particularly true for the emphasis on schooling as a mechanism to alleviate poverty and reduce inequality. Moreover, it has important implications for economic growth, since investments in human capital and physical capital appear to be the two major determinants of output growth. As a result, accurate estimates of the rate of return to schooling do have direct relevance for public decisions regarding educational expenditures and, particularly, educational programs such as student loans. This concern will be addressed below again, when we consider other interpretations of the relation between schooling and earnings.

The Nature vs. Nurture Controversy

In our discussion of ability models, we have sidestepped one major and very controversial issue: What determines individual ability? Debate on this question has a long history, though it has heated up considerably in the last two decades. The central issue is whether ability, particularly intelligence, is genetically inherited or whether it is due to environment, particularly a child's family background. Much of the difficulty with resolving this issue is that, statistically, it is very hard to separate the influence of genetic factors from environment. The exception is the study of twins, where it is possible to control for genetic makeup.

Cyril Burt undertook one of the first studies of identical twins, some of whom were bought up in the same home and some of whom were raised separately. He was also one of the earliest proponents of the "nature" view. The twin sample allows the most direct test of the heritability of ability, since identical twins have the same genetic makeup.[15] If identical twins raised in different environments achieve the same (or nearly the same) IQ score, then it is possible to attribute the determination of intelligence to heredity alone. If, on the other hand, pairs raised in different homes have different IQ's, then the environment would be seen to have a major impact.[16] Cyril Burt determined from his study that genetic influences were paramount in determining intelligence. However, it was subsequently learned that Burt, who had already believed in the extreme importance of genetic makeup, simply falsified his data to obtain the desired result. Therefore, Burt's work has been completely discredited (see Kamin [1974] or Hearnshaw [1979] for more on Cyril Burt).

In more recent years, Arthur Jensen (1969, 1970) and William Shockley (1970), and Richard Herrnstein and Charles Murray (1994) have resurrected the Burt position that genetic differences are the primary cause of differences in intelligence. Their work is particularly controversial, since it attributes a large part of the lower economic status achieved by blacks to genetic differences between blacks and whites. Much of their analysis is based on the rather strong assumption that gene pools have evolved independently in the black and white populations. However, their work has been generally criticized for its failure to control adequately for the effects of home environment versus genetic endowment in explaining both intelligence and economic performance.

Paul Taubman (1976) produced the first widely accepted study of the role of genetics versus home background on earnings. (In 1950, he surveyed 2,000 twins, including both identical and fraternal pairs, who were about 50 years old at the time.) Taubman's interest was to determine how much of the difference in earnings—not measured intelligence as Burt had done—could be attributed to family background and how much to intelligence. All of the twins in Taubman's samples were raised in the same home, so that family background could be controlled for. If genetics were very important in determining economic success, then identical twins should have earnings that were more similar than fraternal twins. For statistical reasons,[17] Taubman could compute only a range of possible effects, and he concluded that between 18 and 41 percent of the variation in earnings was due to heredity. His overall conclusion is that environment is more important than heredity in the determination of earnings. In a later study, the econometri-

---

[15] This is not 100 percent true, because there is the possibility of genetic mutation during the development of the embryo.

[16] Since some statistical variations in IQ scores were expected even among twins raised in the same home, this variation was used as a control for the statistical analysis of twins raised apart.

[17] In particular, his model was econometrically underidentified so that additional assumptions were required to estimate the model.

cian Goldberger (1979), using the same data but making different though equally reasonable assumptions, concluded that *no* part of the difference in earnings was due to genetic differences.[18]

Studies by Harold Lydall (1968) and Samuel Bowles and Valerie Nelson (1974) examined similar issues but relied on samples of the full population (rather than twins), which included measures of both home environment and intelligence. Lydall (1968) argued that family background and, in particular, the social class into which a child is born largely influence measured intelligence. Intelligence testing always takes place after a child has reached a certain age, so that home environment and other environmental influences like schooling cannot be directly separated out from heredity. Moreover, since most intelligence tests are couched in language, the literacy and the use of language in the home are very likely to make a difference in the child's measured intelligence. In this regard, socio-economic class makes an important difference.

Another indicator of intelligence is school achievement. Here, too, social class has a large impact. Greater emphasis on education is placed by higher socio-economic classes than by poor families, and their children achieve greater socialization into the work habits required in most school systems. Social class also has a direct bearing on the quality of schooling received by the child. In his survey of various data on this issue, Lydall concluded that between 20 and 30 percent of measured intelligence could be attributed to the socio-economic class of the parents.

Bowles and Nelson (1974) employed a recursive system to assess the role of socio-economic background and intelligence in the determination of earnings. They estimated a four-equation system, which is summarized in Diagram 7.2. They argued that ability, as measured in their case by IQ, affects earnings directly and indirectly through its relation to years of schooling. However, they also argued that family background affects these relations in three ways. First, they distinguished between "genotypic IQ" or innate ability and measured childhood IQ. They argued that family background affects actual measured IQ, because parental literacy and education have a direct bearing on early childhood development. Second, family background has a direct bearing on schooling attainment, because financial resources differ among families as well as their emphasis on education. Third, family background affects earnings directly, because family connections and the like can make an important difference in the jobs obtained.

Their principal findings are, first, that independent of socio-economic background, measured childhood IQ exercised a substantial direct effect on schooling attainment but had a much smaller impact on income and

---

[18] It has also been pointed out that twins are not a very representative sample of the population as a whole. The major reason is that a twin on average probably gets less attention from parents and spends more time with siblings than other children. Therefore, results from twin studies may not be generalizable to the full population.

Diagram 7.2 Path Diagram of Ability, Socio-Economic Background, Schooling, and Earnings

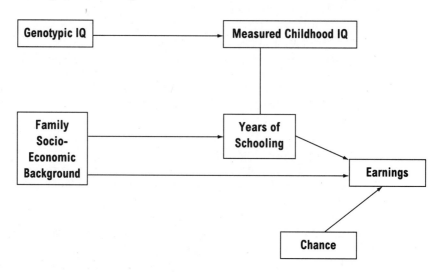

occupational status. Second, considering both direct and indirect effects, variations in childhood IQ were less important than variations in socio-economic background in determining schooling attainment, occupational status, and income. Third, the observed intergenerational transmission of educational and economic status was attributable primarily to the direct impact of education. Thus, even if IQ is largely hereditary, its role in explaining economic status is still relatively small.

In sum, the nature vs. nurture controversy still remains unresolved. The reason is that statistically it is very difficult to control for all the genetic and environmental variables necessary to perform a conclusive test. Most social scientists take the view that both sets of factors are important in determining ability, particularly intelligence, as well as economic success. Perhaps, the vehemence with which this issue has been contested is due to the rather extreme policy implications some analysts have drawn. Some of those who support the heredity position have suggested that the only way to increase the average intelligence level of society and to reduce inequality is through eugenics—that is, the selective breeding of the population. Some have even suggested that this selection should be done on the basis of race. However, Goldberger (1979) has wisely pointed out that even *if* it could be shown that genetics were the primary factor in determining ability or intelligence, it does not follow that such genetically based handicaps could not be overcome. A good example is that someone born with poor eyesight can have this problem corrected through the acquisition of eyeglasses.

7.4 PRODUCTIVITY AND EARNINGS

We have until now been rather reticent about an important linkage in the human capital model of earnings. Let us review Gary Becker's argument, presented in Section 6.2, about the effect of increased schooling on labor earnings. There are two sides to the argument. On the one hand, the reason why a student would spend an extra year in school and forgo a year's worth of earnings is that the resultant wage will be higher after the extra year of school. On the other hand, the reason why a firm will pay more to a better-schooled worker is that the individual's *productivity will be higher*. This reflects a basic proposition of neoclassical theory that all factors of production are paid their marginal product. Therefore, from the firm's point of view, the only justification for paying a worker with greater schooling more is that his or her productivity is higher. The same argument must also hold for paying a higher wage for a worker with greater post-schooling investment, and, in general, for paying higher wages to those with greater human capital. Schematically, the "productivity linkage" can be illustrated as follows:

The evidence that has been presented in this chapter establishes a relation between human capital and earnings. Figures 7.1 through 7.4 on age-earnings profiles by schooling level and Mincer's regression results (Tables 7.7 and 7.8) establish a direct, positive relation between an individual's earnings and schooling and experience. However, these results do *not* establish the reason for this positive relation. Indeed, there may be other mechanisms or explanations for these observed relations.

Experience, Productivity, and Earnings

We shall first consider evidence concerning the relation between a worker's training and productivity on the job. There have been several studies that have tried to develop more or less direct measures of worker productivity on the job. The first, by Stanley Horowitz and Allan Sherman (1980), examined the relations between the maintenance record of various ships in the U.S. Navy and the training and experience of maintenance personnel. Their measure of worker productivity was based on how well the ships were maintained. For this, the authors used the amount of "downtime" of the ship— that is, the amount of time it was laid up for repairs. The less downtime, the better maintained the ship was.

The authors examined the records of 91 Navy vessels in 1972, 1973, and 1974. They also examined the personnel records of sailors who worked in the following maintenance occupations: boiler technician, machinist's mate, fire-control technician, gunner's mate, sonar technician, and torpedoman's mate. The economists were particularly interested in three characteristics of these sailors: length of service in the Navy, sea experience, and the amount of advanced training. Through regression analysis, they were able to relate the personal characteristics of the crew members in these occupational categories to the ship's downtime. They found that all three characteristics were statistically significant. In other words, greater length of service in the Navy, greater sea experience, and a greater amount of advanced training each led to improved ship maintenance. Therefore, the authors concluded that both experience and training had a positive effect on worker productivity.

A second study, by James Medoff and Katherine Abraham (1981), reached the opposite conclusion. They obtained personnel records from a large U.S. manufacturing firm. They selected a sample of white male managerial and professional employees from company records. Besides information on education, length of company service, age, current salary, and salary history, the personnel files also contained a performance rating for each worker. The performance evaluation was done by the employee's immediate superior, who was asked to rate the worker "both to his contributions in terms of the standards of his job and against others performing similar work at similar levels." The authors used this performance rating as a measure of the worker's productivity on the job. Of course, performance evaluations are to some degree subjective, but the authors concluded that, on the whole, these performance ratings by one's superior were a fairly objective measure of how much each employee contributed in his work.

The authors then performed two types of regression analysis. First, they investigated the relation between experience in the company, earnings, and performance rating for their sample of employees in a given year. In their cross-sectional analysis, they found that among managers and professionals performing tasks of similar difficulty, greater experience in the company was associated with significantly higher relative earnings, but *not* with higher rated performance. Second, they investigated the relation between the same three variables over time for employees staying in a given job. They found in their longitudinal analysis that among those managers and professionals remaining in a job, relative earnings rose but relative performance either remained constant or declined with the passage of time. They concluded that though earnings did rise with experience for their sample, growth in earnings was *not* due to higher productivity on the job.

In a later study, Medoff and Abraham (1983) conducted a special survey to evaluate the effects of years of service in a firm and worker productivity on the probability of a worker being promoted in the firm. They surveyed personnel directors at 1,025 American companies who were listed in the 1981 edition of Standard and Poor's Register (firms with 50 or more employees). They asked them, somewhat indirectly, about the importance of length of service in promotion decisions. They also obtained personnel records from two companies, which contained information on job promotion and performance ratings of the individual workers. They found, from both sources of data, that seniority, independently of job performance or productivity, played a significant role in promotion decisions. This was true for both union and nonunion employees.

In a 1984 study, Cheryl Maranto and Robert Rodgers examined data on wage claims investigations of a state labor department to examine the effects of work experience on job performance. The main task of field investigators is to recover unpaid wages that employers allegedly owe to employees. Aggrieved employees are allowed to submit claims to this department in order to collect unpaid wages. The investigator's job is to convince employers to make legitimate payments to their workers. With practice and experimentation, investigators should be expected to increase the proportion of outstanding wage claims that are collected from employers. Using the proportion of wage claims that are collected as an index of the investigator's productivity, Maranto and Rodgers found that investigators become significantly more productive during the first six years of their job tenure.

A 1985 study by Bruce Dunson examined a similar issue for a group of civilian middle managers and professionals in the Department of Defense. His productivity measure was a performance rating scheme employed by the Defense Department. He found that more experienced workers were paid more than those with fewer years of experience but, once controlling for experience, performance ratings had no relation to worker pay.

A different approach was employed by James Brown in a 1989 study. The Michigan Panel Survey of Income Dynamics (PSID) asked respondents in 1976 and 1979 the following question: "On a job like yours, how long would it take the average new person to become fully trained and qualified?" On the basis of this question and corresponding information on length of experience in the current position, Brown could identify those workers who were currently in training, as well as the total time spent in training. His main finding was that wage growth within positions ceased with the completion of the training period. He concluded that on-the-job training explained a substantial proportion of the total wage growth experienced in a given job position.

In sum, the findings of various tests above on the relation between experience on the job and on-the-job productivity have been mixed. Some of the studies show that job productivity is positively related to a worker's experience, and they conclude that training is responsible for the positive association between earnings and job experience. The others also find that earnings grow with experience, but find no evidence that this growth in earnings is due to higher productivity among more experienced workers.

Other Interpretations of the Relation Between Schooling and Earnings

In the case of schooling, there have been several other theories proposed to explain the observed positive association between educational attainment and earnings. In this section, we consider three such interpretations of schooling: as a screening device, as a transmitter of family background, and as a socializing mechanism.

Education as a Screening Device   Since 1973, with the appearance of Kenneth Arrow's article "Higher Education as a Filter," several signaling or screening models have been developed in which schooling is viewed as an informational device. The underlying assumption of these models is that there is imperfect information in the labor market. In particular, while potential employees differ in their ability with regard to a particular job, employers have no direct way of (imperfect information in) assessing a prospective employee's productive abilities. Positions are therefore "allocated on the basis of imperfect indicators or surrogates for productive capability or potential," as Michael Spence (1981) notes in his survey of the literature on the subject. Educational attainment is one of the primary sources of information used by a firm to gauge an employee's likely success on the job.

It is also assumed that beyond a certain point,[19] schooling does not improve an individual's productive capacity. Rather, it functions as a signaling device to identify preexisting talents. A prospective employer who has no direct way of assessing an applicant's productive abilities uses educational attainment as an indicator of the employee's expected productivity. Thus, schooling functions as an identification device by indicating for prospective employers those (future) workers who are most likely to perform well in their jobs. In this sense, the educational system acts as a "screening" mechanism for prospective employees.

Employers will therefore pay more to applicants with more schooling (or hire them in favor of less educated applicants), not because (or solely because) education enhances their productivity but because it identifies the more productive workers. A necessary corollary of this argument, as Spence (1973) notes, is that for the job market to remain in equilibrium, the more educated workers will, in fact, have to demonstrate greater productivity on the job. Otherwise, it would not be rational for an employer to continue to use education as a screening device. Thus, the abilities that are necessary for superior school performance must be the same as those that are necessary for superior work performance.

This argument is directly contrary to human capital theory. In the human capital model, employers pay more to those employees with more schooling because education increases their productivity. Human capital theory thus views schooling as *productivity-augmenting*. In the screening model, schooling is viewed to provide information to a prospective employer about which students would likely perform better in a job, but

---

[19] It is usually noted that the basic skills learned in elementary and, perhaps, high school—particularly, reading, writing, and arithmetic—are necessary for most occupations. Subjects taught in more advanced schooling, particularly in college, are less relevant to the skills required in the workplace.

schooling does not itself increase the individual's productivity. The observed positive relation between schooling and earnings is then due to the identification or screening function of education, rather than to a productivity-augmenting process.

In both models, it still pays the individual student to seek greater schooling. In the human capital model, the reason for the greater earnings is higher productivity. In the screening model, the reason is to identify himself or herself as a potentially superior worker. In both models, then, a firm would be willing to pay a better-educated worker a higher salary, though for very different reasons. In both models, moreover, schooling has a certain implied **private rate of return** for the individual student, since it increases the individual's earnings. The implications concerning the **social rate of return** are very different in the two models, as we will discuss in Section 7.6.

The problem then arises of how to discriminate between the human capital and the screening model. What kind of test can be devised in order to show that one is true and the other false (or, perhaps, neither is true)? In other words, is it possible to derive distinct testable hypotheses from the two models? If we can, then we will be able to determine empirically which of the two models better explains the observed relation between schooling and earnings.

Several ingenious attempts have been made over the years to discriminate between the two models. Richard Layard and George Psacharopoulos (1974) argued that if the screening hypothesis is true, then educational differentials in earnings should not rise with age, since employers should have better information about older employees' abilities. Instead, they found that earnings differences between workers of different schooling levels did increase with age, with earnings rising faster for more educated workers.

David Wise (1975) made a similar argument. He argued that if college quality (selectivity) were used only as a screening device, then earnings should rise no faster over time for graduates of higher-quality colleges than lower-quality ones. Instead, using data on college graduates working in a large corporation, he found that after controlling for the undergraduate grade point average (GPA), earnings increased faster for those who had attended more selective colleges than less selective ones. Ethel Jones and John Jackson (1990) reached similar conclusions on the basis of a sample of business school graduates.

Another approach was taken by James Albrecht (1974), who compared the success of applicants for a given position between those inside an organization (the Internal Revenue Service office in San Francisco) with those outside the organization. He reasoned that the office would have better information on inside candidates than on outside ones. Therefore, if education were used as a screening device, schooling should have less bearing on the hiring decision of inside applicants than outside ones. He found no confirmation for this hypothesis.

Kenneth Wolpin (1977) took another tack. His reasoning was that students planning to go into their own business will acquire less schooling than those planning to work for an employer, since the former will stay in school long enough to satisfy the needs of their work, whereas the latter will acquire additional schooling to signal a prospective employer. Wolpin made two predictions based on the screening hypothesis. First, self-employed workers will have a lower mean schooling than salaried workers. Second, the increment in earnings from schooling will be lower for self-employed than salaried employees. Using the NBER-Thorndyke sample and estimating separate earnings equations for salaried and self-employed workers, he found no confirmation of these predictions.

Eugene Kroch and Kriss Sjoblom (1994) developed an ingenious test to discriminate between the two models. They argued that if the screening hypothesis were correct, then earnings should be related to *relative* schooling rank rather than to the absolute level of schooling as predicted by the human capital model. Using data from the Panel Survey of Income Dynamics and the 1972 Current Population Survey Exact Match File, they estimated earnings regressions, which included both schooling level and an individual's rank in the distribution of schooling for his or her age cohort as independent variables. Unfortunately, the tests were not conclusive, though the authors felt that evidence was slightly more in favor of the human capital model than the screening model.

Though most of the empirical work to date seems to favor the human capital model over the screening model, these results must be interpreted with some caution. The main reason is that both models predict that the better educated will receive higher earnings *and* that the better educated will also be more productive on the job (Spence's corollary). The point of dispute is whether the additional schooling *causes* the increase in worker productivity by transmitting work-related skills or is merely correlated with it. Comparisons of job performance and earnings over time between workers of different educational attainment (or between those inside and those outside an organization) cannot discriminate between causation and correlation. Wolpin's tests avoid the pitfalls of the previous studies by selecting two groups—self-employed workers and salaried employees—whose behavior would differ under the screening model. However, for his test to be conclusive, the student must know ahead of time whether he or she will be self-employed or working for someone else.

Thus, in general, it has proven very difficult to devise a decisive test of the screening versus human capital hypothesis. A direct empirical test of this mechanism has so far proven allusive. This is why Mark Blaug (1989), for example, speaks of "the observational equivalence of human capital theory and screening models."

Family Background Another interpretation of the functioning of the educational system is that it helps maintain the class structure between generations. Children of rich parents become rich by hooking into the "old boys' network" and thereby developing the necessary contacts for high-paying jobs. Conversely, the children of poor parents are excluded from such contacts and wind up in poor-paying jobs. This view was developed by Samuel Bowles in four articles (1970, 1971, 1972, 1974) and later expanded into a book-length treatise in a work with Herbert Gintis (1976). The argument is similar to that of the signaling model. Employers screen prospective job candidates on the basis of their educational attainment. Moreover, schooling does not in itself enhance the productive skills of future workers. However, here, education is used to screen family background, rather than unobserved natural ability.

Bowles' 1972 paper highlights the relation between earnings, socio-economic status, and schooling. He argues that one of the primary objectives of the wealthy is to preserve their dominant position. This means, in part, that a rich family will try to ensure that their children remain in the dominant class. Moreover, by preserving class background, the wealthy can better attempt to legitimate their position. If classes are stable between generations, a society will view one class as possessing power and authority and therefore entitled to it, while the subordinate class will become resigned to its position. The preservation of class origins is one means of ensuring the maintenance of power by the rich.

From this point of view, the educational system is considered one means of preserving class background. Children from higher social classes are channeled into one part of the educational system and segregated from lower social classes. A kind of "old boys' network" is set up whereby children of rich parents meet other children of rich parents and through these contacts are funneled on to the higher-paying jobs. Conversely, the children of poorer parents never make these contacts and are thereby shut off from the upper slots in the job hierarchy.

To implement this model, Bowles estimated a recursive system of the form:

(1) $$S_i = \alpha X_i$$

(2) $$E_i = \beta_0 S_i + \beta X$$

where S_i is years of schooling, E_i annual income, and X_i a vector of variables reflecting the respondent's socio-economic background. Among the variables used for socio-economic background were: (1) the occupational status of the father or family head of the respondent, (2) the educational attainment of the father or family head of the respondent, and (3) the parents' annual income.

Bowles found that the socio-economic status of a child's family was a very significant determinant of the child's educational attainment. Those from the upper social classes acquired significantly more schooling than those from poorer backgrounds. This suggests that schooling opportunity is strongly correlated with family background. Moreover, Bowles found that once family background was controlled for, schooling achievement explained relatively little about a person's earnings. A person's family background was a more important determinant of relative income than schooling achievement. Bowles concluded that "the educational system is a major vehicle for the transmission of economic status from one generation to the next" (p. s240).[20]

Schooling as a Socializing Mechanism   A third interpretation is that the schooling system, rather than developing the cognitive skills necessary for work, instead helps mold personality traits, such as discipline, subordination, the willingness to accept hierarchy and authority, punctuality, and motivation according to external rewards, which are needed in the factory and office. The social structure of the school mirrors that of the factory and office. According to this view, schools do transform future workers in productive ways, as the human capital model maintains. However, the mechanism is seen to be quite different.

Herbert Gintis, in a 1971 article and later in his 1976 book with Bowles, argued that one function of the educational organization is to "replicate the relationships of dominance and subordinancy in the economic sphere" (Bowles and Gintis, 1976, p. 125). There is therefore a fairly direct correspondence between the social relations embodied in the school and those in the workplace. The social experience of the schooling process, and not merely the actual content of the subjects, is central to this function. The school system is considered a socializing mechanism. In particular, the educational organization tries to produce personality traits that are compatible with and required for work in the factory or office. In this way, a workforce that can fit into and function within the social organization of work is created.

Gintis argued that the social organization of schooling "by requiring the student to function routinely and over long periods of time in role situations comprising specific situations on the part of the teacher, other students, and administrators tends to elicit uniformities of response codified in individual personality" (1971, p. 272). Moreover, "the system of grading, by rewarding certain classroom behavior patterns and penalizing others, tends to reinforce certain modes of individual response to social situations" (1971, p. 272). Gintis found that the following traits seemed to be positively rewarded in the educational process: perseverance, self-control, social leadership, suppression of aggression, sharing, deferred gratification, and responsibility. On the other hand, the following traits were negatively

---

[20] In quantitative terms, Bowles estimated that 52 percent of the variation in schooling achievement was explained by the family background variables. Moreover, family background accounted directly for 13 percent of the variation of earnings and indirectly for another 15 percent via its impact on schooling achievement. On the other hand, once family background was controlled for, schooling achievement explained only two percent of the variation of earnings. Similar findings were reported in the Bowles and Nelson (1974) paper, discussed in Section 7.2. A recent paper by Behrman and Taubman (1990) looked at a related issue, the correlation between children's adult earnings and their parent's income. On the basis of the Panel Survey of Income Dynamics, they calculated correlations of over 50 percent.

rewarded: independence and self-reliance, initiative, complexity of thought, originality, independence of judgment, and creativity.

Gintis summarized the personality traits that are positively reinforced in the schooling as four types: (1) subordinateness, (2) discipline, (3) supremacy of cognitive over affective modes of response, and (4) motivation according to external reward. First, subordinateness and the proper respect for authority are induced by the strict hierarchical structure of the school as embodied in the administrator-teacher-student relation. The teacher acts as an authority figure to the student, rewarding or penalizing him or her for actions, and the student comes to accept this loss of autonomy. Such behavior is required for a worker to function effectively in the bureaucratic organization of work. Second, the educational system rewards such traits as regularity, punctuality, and quiescence—in a word, discipline—in its students. Such traits are also of obvious value in the factory or office environment. Third, a rational matter-of-fact or cognitive way of reacting to a situation is rewarded in the school system as opposed to an emotional, personal, or irrational way of behaving. This trait is also desirable in the factory or office, where work is dehumanized and people are expected to act more like machines than emotional beings. Finally, students are trained to be motivated more by the external reward for an action (a "good grade," for example) than by the actual satisfaction from the action itself ("learning," for example). Such a mode of action is useful in the work world, where workers are motivated not by the intrinsic pleasure of the work process but rather by the promise of a raise or the threat of being fired.

7.5 EARNINGS INEQUALITY AND HUMAN CAPITAL*

The human capital model lends itself directly to a theory of the inequality of labor earnings. This follows directly from equation (7.7). Since the logarithm of earnings is proportional to the level of schooling, then the log variance of earnings is a linear function of the variance of schooling:

$$\ln (\text{Var } E) = r^2 \ln (\text{Var } S) \tag{7.18}$$

where ln is the natural logarithm, Var is the variance, and r is the rate of return to schooling.[21] As we discussed in Section 3.3, the log variance is often used directly as a measure of income inequality.

It is of interest to note that the schooling model provides one explanation for an asymmetric distribution of earnings. One of the almost universal characteristics of observed distributions of earnings is that they are skewed to the right (see Section 3.2). For many theories of income distribution, this has presented a paradox. For example, in a simple model of ability, earnings

---

[21] Technically, it is necessary to assume that the rate of return to schooling is fixed.

are assumed to be proportional to a worker's ability. But most measures of ability, such as IQ, are shown to be normally, and therefore symmetrically, distributed.

Suppose schooling levels are normally distributed among the working population. Then, by equation (7.18), earnings will be lognormally distributed, since the logarithm of earnings rises proportionally to the level of schooling. One characteristic of the lognormal distribution is that it is skewed to the right. More generally, if years of schooling has a symmetric distribution (though not necessarily normal), then earnings will be positively (rightward) skewed. Indeed, unless the distribution of schooling is highly skewed to the left, the distribution of earnings will have a positive skew (see Mincer 1970).

We can also extend this model to include experience. If we use equation (7.12) but ignore the X^2 term, then it follows that:

$$\ln (\text{Var } E) = r^2 \ln (\text{Var } S) + (r'k_0)^2 \ln (\text{Var } X) + 2c \cdot \text{Cov}(S, X) \qquad (7.19)$$

where r' is the rate of return to experience, k_0 and c are constants, and $\text{Cov}(S, X)$ is the covariance between schooling and experience.

Have changes in the distribution of human capital played a role in explaining the rising income inequality of the 1980s and 1990s? The surface evidence does not appear to support this hypothesis. Empirically, it has been shown that when the average level of schooling is low, the distribution of schooling tends to be skewed to the right and the variance of schooling high. When average schooling levels rise, the skewness in the distribution of schooling becomes smaller and its variance declines.

Older cohorts (groups) of workers in the United States have had a low average schooling level and therefore a distribution of schooling skewed to the right. However, the schooling level of entering cohorts of workers has risen over time, thereby raising the average level of schooling in the workforce and lowering its dispersion (see Chapter 5). During the 1980s, rising education should have lowered overall earnings inequality, rather than raising it.

Two studies—Jacob Mincer (1991) and Kevin Murphy and Finis Welch (1992)—found that the declining number of college graduates entering the labor market during the 1980s—the "baby bust" generation—played a role in explaining the rising premium to a college education. The reason is that a decline in the share of college graduates in the labor force will, *ceteris paribus*, cause the earnings differential between college graduates and high school graduates to increase (see Section 6.2). From the point of view of human capital theory, the key factor explaining rising earnings inequality is the steep rise in the rate of return to schooling, particularly a college degree. In terms of equation 7.18, the explanation is that r^2 has risen sharply, rather than that the Var (S) has increased. In this regard, both studies noted that the change in the demographic composition of the labor force by itself could not account for the full increase in the return to education observed over the decade. The studies concluded that changes in the demand for educated workers was the principal cause of the rising return to schooling.

7.6 Summary and Concluding Remarks

The evidence presented in this chapter provides strong support for the hypotheses that more educated workers received greater earnings and that experience leads to greater earnings. These relations are confirmed by the age-earnings profiles shown in Figures 7.1 through 7.4 and the regression results presented in Table 7.7 and 7.8. Moreover, the estimated rates of return to both schooling and experience are found to be quite high—in the neighborhood of 10 to 15 percent for the United States and even higher in less developed countries. The rate of return to a college education, in particular, increased sharply during the 1950s and 1960s, fell dramatically in the 1970s, and increased substantially again during the 1980s and early 1990s. This evidence has powerful implications for public policy, particularly the role of schooling in increasing income and reducing both poverty and income inequality.

However, there are several important qualifications to these results. The first concerns the role of ability. Insofar as students with more natural ability both do better in school and acquire more schooling, part of the estimated return to schooling can be due to ability rather than the skills acquired in the schooling process. Though the evidence varies, it appears that about one-third of the estimated return to schooling is due to ability differences among students.

Second, even after controlling for the effects of ability, it must still be established that not only is there a positive association between a worker's *productivity* on the job and educational attainment but also that it is the schooling process itself that has augmented the worker's productivity. The most damaging counterclaim comes from the screening model, where it is argued that schooling merely signals greater "innate" ability rather than produces additional skills. It is argued that employers cannot directly assess the productive ability of potential employees (that is, there is imperfect information in the labor market) and use schooling achievement to identify the potentially productive workers.

The screening model thus provides an explanation of the observed positive relation between schooling and earnings. If the screening argument is true, it raises some serious doubts about the social productivity of the education process. Empirically, it is very difficult to distinguish between the screening model and the human capital model, because in both, the more educated must not only be more productive but demonstrate their greater productivity on the job for the labor market to be in equilibrium. Thus, the empirical implications of the human capital and screening models are almost identical. However, from our own casual observation, we can think of examples where formal schooling seems to be specifically job-related, such as vocational schools, secretarial schools, business schools, law schools, and medical schools. However, there are also examples of schooling whose content seems very far removed from any conceivable job the student is eventually likely to take. Some examples are high school social studies or a liberal arts college course in philosophy or linguistics. On net, the truth probably lies in between the extreme forms of these two models. Some aspects of schooling do provide job-related skills, while others do not.

If the screening model is true in whole or even in part, then a discrepancy may arise between the "private" and "social" rate of return to schooling, where the former is the net benefit of schooling to the individual and the latter is its net benefit to society. The private return reflects the increased earnings from additional schooling to the individual. The social return, in contrast, reflects the increased stock of productive skills in the economy as a whole from its investment in schooling. If schooling serves merely as a signaling device, then society receives no benefit from the increased schooling that individuals acquire. As a result, the social return to schooling may be significantly lower than its private return. This distinction has important implications for economic policy. It may, for example, make little sense for society to spur its rate of "human capital" formation on the basis of a high private return to education if the social return is low. Such a policy may be particularly misguided for a developing country where a large divergence may occur between the private and social returns to education.

Another interpretation of the role of schooling is that it serves to maintain socio-economic status from one generation to another. The educational system provides a network of contacts, which enables children of rich families to obtain high-paying jobs and excludes children from poor families. According to this view, schooling is also used as a signaling device, through screening is done on the basis of class background rather than innate ability. Earnings are not related to productivity or "what you know" but to "who you know"!

The evidence does indicate a significant intergenerational correlation in terms of both educational attainment and income. Yet, in criticism, the correlations are not perfect, and there is still a substantial amount of intergenerational mobility in terms of educational achievement and socioeconomic status. Some children of poor families do become rich and make it into the top levels of the corporate ladder, and conversely, children of rich parents often wind up in a lower economic stratum. The issues are how much mobility there actually is between generations and how much would constitute a refutation of this thesis.

Moreover, the fact that family background affects a person's schooling achievement and earnings can be and actually is incorporated in the human capital model. Gary Becker, in *Human Capital,* talks of the family as one social mechanism by which human capital is produced. The type of influences, training, and instruction that a child receives in the home is viewed as a major source of human capital production, in addition to the schooling system. As a result, the human capital model would predict that children from rich family backgrounds acquire more capital in the home than those from poor families. The high correlation between family background and earnings is also consistent with the human capital model. In this case, too, it would be very difficult to distinguish empirically between the two explanations, and there is probably some truth in both views.

A third explanation is that the schooling process is a socializing mechanism, molding personality traits that allow a worker to perform effectively in the office or factory, rather than developing cognitive skills. In this regard, too, it is possible to think of cases where schooling provides very specific job-related skills, such as medical or law school, and cases where it does not, such as social studies courses in grade school.

There is also conflicting evidence on the role of experience in generating higher earnings. The statistical data show that workers with more experience and seniority earn higher wages. However, it is not clear whether this is due to the greater productivity of older workers.

Human capital theory leads directly to a model of earnings inequality, where the degree of inequality is proportional to both the variance of schooling and the variance of experience. Changes in the distribution of schooling of the workforce during the 1980s did not play a direct role in explaining the rising income inequality over the decade, since the variance of schooling declined. However, the declining number of college graduates entering the labor force over this period has been found to be one factor accounting for the rising return to a college education.

REFERENCES AND BIBLIOGRAPHY

A. Education, Experience, and Earnings

Becker, Gary S., *Human Capital: A Theoretical and Empirical Analysis,* Columbia University Press, New York, and National Bureau of Economic Research, 1964.

Becker, Gary S., and Barry R. Chiswick, "Education and the Distribution of Income," *American Economic Review,* Vol. 56, No. 2, May 1966, pp. 358–369.

Ben-Porath, Yoram, "The Production of Human Capital and the Life-Cycle of Earnings," *Journal of Political Economy,* Vol. 57, August 1967.

Blackburn, McKinley L., David E. Bloom, and Richard B. Freeman, "The Distribution of Labor Market Outcomes: Measuring and Explaining Trends and Patterns in the 1980s for Selected Demographic Groups in the United States," mimeo, February 1991.

Chiswick, Barry R., *Income Inequality,* Columbia University Press and National Bureau of Economic Research, New York, 1974.

Chiswick, Barry R., and Jacob Mincer, "Time Series Changes in Personal Income Inequality in the U.S. from 1939, with Projections to 1985," *Jour-*

nal of Political Economy, Vol. 80, No. 3, Part II, May/June 1972, pp. 534–537.

Coleman, Mary T., "Movements in the Earnings-Schooling Relationship, 1940–1988, Journal of Human Resources, Vol. 28, No. 2, Summer 1993, pp. 660–680.

Creedy, John, "Income Changes Over the Life-Cycle," Oxford Economic Papers, Vol. 26 (New Series), No. 3, November 1974, pp. 405–423.

Dean, Edwin (ed.), Education and Economic Productivity, Ballinger Publishing Company, Cambridge, Mass., 1984.

Freeman, Richard B., The Over-Educated American, Academic Press, New York, 1976.

Friesen, Peter H., and Danny Miller, "Annual Inequality and Lifetime Inequality," Quarterly Journal of Economics, Vol. 98, No. 1, 1983, pp. 139–155.

Griliches, Zvi, "Estimating Returns to Schooling: Some Econometric Problems," Presidential Address, Econometric Society, Toronto, 1975.

Grubb, W. Norton, "The Varied Economic Returns to Postsecondary Education: New Evidence from the Class of 1972," Journal of Human Resources, Vol. 28, No. 2, Spring 1993, pp. 367–382.

Hancock, Keith, and Sue Richardson, "Discount Rates and the Distribution of Lifetime Earnings," Journal of Human Resources, Vol. 20, No. 3, Summer 1985, pp. 346–360.

Hanoch, Giora, "An Economic Analysis of Earnings and Schooling," Journal of Human Resources, Vol. 2, No. 3, Summer 1967, pp. 310–329.

Hansen, W. Lee, "Total Private Rates of Return to Investment in Education," Journal of Political Economy, April 1963.

——, Burton A. Weisbrod, and William J. Scanlon, "Schooling and Earnings of Low Achievers," American Economic Review, Vol. 50, No. 3, September 1970, pp. 409–418.

Heckman, James J., "Estimates of a Human Capital Production Function Embedded in a Life Cycle Model of Labor Supply," in N. Terleckyj (ed.), Household Production and Consumption, Columbia University Press and National Bureau of Economic Research, New York, 1976.

——, a Life-Cycle Model of Earnings, Learning, and Consumption," Journal of Political Economy, Vol. 84, No. 4, Part 2, August 1976, pp. S11-S44.

——, and Solomon Polachek, "Empirical Evidence on the Functional Form of the Earnings Schooling Relationship," Journal of the American Statistical Association, Vol. 69, June 1974, pp. 350–354.

Houthakker, Hendrik, "Education and Income," Review of Economics and Statistics, 1959.

Hunt, S., "Income Determinants for College Graduates and the Return to Educational Investment," Yale Economic Essays, 1963.

Jencks, Christopher, et al., Inequality: A Reassessment of the Effect of Family and Schooling in America, Basic Books Inc., New York, 1972.

Johnson, George E., and Frank Stafford, "Social Returns to Quantity and Quality of Schooling," Journal of Human Resources, Vol. 8, No. 2, Spring 1973, pp. 139–155.

Johnson, Thomas, "Returns from Investment in Human Capital," *American Economic Review*, Vol. 50, No. 4, September 1970, pp. 546–560.

Kane, Thomas J., and Cecilia Elena Rouse, "Comment on W. Norton Grubb 'The Varied Economic Returns to Postsecondary Education: New Evidence from the Class of 1972,' " *Journal of Human Resources*, Vol. 30, No. 1, Winter 1995, pp. 205–221.

Levhavi, David, and Yoram Weiss, "The Effect of Risk on the Investment in Human Capital," *American Economic Review*, Vol. 64, No. 6, December 1974, pp. 950–963.

Lillard, Lee A., "Inequality: Earnings vs. Human Wealth," *American Economic Review*, Vol. 67, No. 2, March 1977, pp. 42–53.

————, "The Distribution of Earnings and Human Wealth in a Life-Cycle Context," in F. Thomas Juster (ed.), *The Distribution of Economic Well-Being*, Studies in Income and Wealth, Vol. 41, Ballinger Publishing Company, Cambridge, Mass., 1977.

Lindsay, C. M., "Measuring Human Capital Returns," *Journal of Political Economy*, 1971.

Mattila, J. Peter, "Determinants of Male School Enrollments: A Time-Series Analysis," *Review of Economics and Statistics*, Vol. 64, No. 2, May 1984, pp. 242–251.

Mincer, Jacob, "Investment in Human Capital and the Personal Income Distribution," *Journal of Political Economy*, August 1958.

————, "On the Job Training: Costs, Returns and Some Implications," *Journal of Political Economy*, October 1962, No. 5, Part 2, October 1962, pp. 50–79.

————, "The Distribution of Labor Incomes: A Survey with Special Reference to the Human Capital Approach," *Journal of Economic Literature*, Vol. 8, No. 1, March 1970, pp. 1–26.

————, "Comment: Overeducation or Undereducation," in Edwin Dean (ed.), *Education and Economic Productivity*, Ballinger Publishing Company, Cambridge, Mass., 1984.

————, and Solomon Polachek, "Family Investments in Human Capital: Earnings of Women," *Journal of Political Economy*, Vol. 82, No. 2, Part II, March/April 1974, pp. S76–S108.

————, *Schooling, Experience, and Earnings*, National Bureau of Economic Research, New York, 1974.

————, "Human Capital, Technology, and the Wage Structure: What Do Time Series Show?" NBER Working Paper No. 3581, January 1991.

Morgan, James, and Martin David, "Education and Income," *Quarterly Journal of Economics*, Vol. 77, No. 3, August 1963, pp. 423–437.

Murphy, Kevin M., and Finis Welch, "The Structure of Wages," *Quarterly Journal of Economics*, Vol. 107, No. 1, February 1992, pp. 285–326.

Murphy, Kevin M., and Finis Welch, "Inequality and Relative Wages," *American Economic Review Papers and Proceedings*, Vol. 83, No. 2, May 1993, pp. 104–109.

Psacharopoulos, George, "Returns to Education: A Further International Update and Implications," *Journal of Human Resources*, Vol. 20, No. 4, Fall 1985, pp. 583–604.

Raymond, Richard, and Michael Sesnowitz, "The Returns to Investments in Higher Education: Some New Evidence," *Journal of Human Resources*, Vol. 10, No. 2, Spring 1975, pp. 139–154.

Rosen, Sherwin, "Measuring the Obsolescence of Knowledge," in F. Thomas Juster (ed.), *Education, Income, and Human Behavior*, McGraw-Hill, New York, 1975.

———, "Learning and Experience in the Labor Market," *Journal of Human Resources*, 1972.

———, "A Theory of Life Earnings," *Journal of Political Economy*, Vol. 84, No. 4, Part 2, August 1976, pp. 545–568.

Shaw, Kathryn L., "A Formulation of the Earnings Function Using the Concept of Occupational Investment," *Journal of Human Resources*, Vol. 19, No. 3, Summer 1984, pp. 319–340.

Weisbrod, Burton A., and Peter Karpov, "Monetary Returns to College Education, Student Ability and College Quality," *Review of Economics and Statistics*, Vol. 50, No. 4, November 1968, pp. 491–510.

Welch, Finis, "Education in Production," *Journal of Political Economy*, Vol. 78, No. 1, January/February 1970, pp. 35–59.

———, "Black-White Differences in Returns to Schooling," *American Economic Review*, Vol. 63, No. 5, December 1973, pp. 893–907.

———, "Relationships Between Income and Schooling," *Review of Research and Education*, 1974.

Wilkinson, Bruce W., "Present Values of Lifetime Earnings for Different Occupations," *Journal of Political Economy*, Vol. 74, No. 6, December 1966, pp. 556–572.

Willis, Robert J., "Wage Determinants: A Survey and Reinterpretation of Human Capital Earnings Functions," in Orley Ashenfelter and Richard Layard (eds.), *Handbook of Labor Economics*, North-Holland Press, Amsterdam, 1986.

B. Ability and Earnings

Ammon, O., *Die Gesellschaftsordung und ihre naturlichen Grundlagen*, Jena, 1895.

Ashenfelter, Orley, and Alan Krueger, "Estimates of the Economic Returns to Schooling from a New Sample of Twins," *American Economic Review*, Vol. 84, No. 5, December 1994, pp. 1157–1173.

Ashenfelter, Orley, and Joseph D. Mooney, "Graduate Education, Ability, and Earnings," *Review of Economics and Statistics*, Vol. 50, No. 1, February 1968, pp. 76–86.

Boissiere, M., J. B. Knight, and R. H. Sabot, "Earnings, Schooling, Ability, and Cognitive Skills," *American Economic Review*, Vol. 75, No. 5, December 1985, pp. 1016–1030.

Bound, John, Zvi Griliches, and Bronwyn H. Hall, "Wages, Schooling and IQ of Brothers and Sisters: Do the Family Factors Differ?" *International Economic Review*, Vol. 27, No. 1, February 1986, pp. 77–105.

Bowles, Samuel, and Valerie Nelson, "The 'Inheritance of IQ' and the Intergenerational Reproduction of Economic Inequality," *Review of Economics and Statistics*, Vol. 56, No. 1, February 1974, pp. 39–51.

Filer, Randall K., "The Influence of Effective Human Capital on the Wage Equation," in Ronald G. Ehrenberg (ed.), *Research in Labor Economics*, Vol. 4, JAI Press, Greenwich, Conn., 1981, pp. 367–416.

Goldberger, A. S., "Hereditability," *Economica*, Vol. 46, 1979, pp. 327–347.

Griliches, Zvi, and William M. Mason, "Education, Income, and Ability," *Journal of Political Economy*, Vol. 80, No. 3, Part II, May/June 1972, pp. S74–S103.

Hansen, Lee, Burton Weisbrod, and William Scanlon, "Schooling and Earnings of Low Achievers," *American Economic Review*, Vol. 60, No. 3, June 1970, pp. 409–418.

Hause, John, "Earnings Profile: Ability and Schooling," *Journal of Political Economy*, Vol. 80, No. 3, Part II, May/June 1972, pp. S108–S138.

———, "Ability and Schooling as Determinants of Lifetime Earnings," in F. Thomas Juster (ed.), *Education, Income, and Human Behavior*, McGraw Hill, New York, 1975.

Hearnshaw, L. S., *Cyril Burt, Psychologist*, Cornell University Press, Ithaca, New York, 1979.

Heckman, James J., "The Common Structure of Statistical Models of Truncation, Sample Selection and Limited Dependent Variables and a Simple Estimator for Such Models," *Annals of Economic and Social Measurement*, Vol. 5, Fall 1976, pp. 475–492.

Herrnstein, Richard, and Charles Murray, *The Bell Curve*, Basic Books, New York, 1994.

Jensen, A. R., "How Much Can We Boost IQ and Scholastic Achievement," *Harvard Educational Review*, Vol. 39, No. 1, Winter 1969, pp. 1–123.

———, "Learning Ability, Intelligence, and Educability," in V. L. Allen (ed.), *Psychological Factors in Poverty*, Markham Publishing Co., Chicago, 1970.

Kamin, Leo H., *The Science and Politics of IQ*, John Wiley & Sons, New York, 1974.

Lydall, H. F., *The Structure of Earnings*, Clarendon Press, Oxford, 1968.

Mandelbrot, B., "Paretian Distributions and Income Maximization," *Quarterly Journal of Economics*, February 1962.

Roy, A. D., "The Distribution of Earnings and of Individual Output," *Economic Journal*, Vol. 60, September 1950.

Schockley, W., "A 'Try Simplest Case' Approach to the Heredity-Poverty-Crime Problem," in V. L. Allen (ed.), *Psychological Factors in Poverty*, Markham Publishing Co., Chicago, 1970.

Solmon, Lewis J., "The Definition of College Quality and Its Impact on Earnings," *Explorations in Economic Research*, Vol. 2, No. 4, Fall 1975, pp. 537–589.

Taubman, Paul, "The Determinants of Earnings: Genetics, Family and Other Environments: A Study of White Male Twins," *American Economic Review*, Vol. 66, No. 5, December 1976, pp. 858–870.

Taussig, F. W., *Principles of Economics*, Macmillan Co., New York, 1915.

Wachtel, Paul, "The Effect of School Quality on Achievement, Attainment Levels, and Lifetime Earnings," *Explorations in Economic Research*, Vol. 2, No. 4, Fall 1975, pp. 502–536.

Willis, Robert J., and Sherwin Rosen, "Education and Self-Selection," *Journal of Political Economy*, Vol. 87, No. 5, Part 2, 1979, pp. S7–S36.

Wise, David, "Academic Achievement and Job Performance," *American Economic Review*, Vol. 65, No. 3, June 1975, pp. 350–366.

C. Age, Earnings, and Productivity

Abraham, Katherine G., "Job Duration, Seniority, and Earnings," *American Economic Review*, Vol. 77, No. 3, June 1987, pp. 278–297.

Altonji, Joseph, and Robert Shakotko, "Do Wages Rise with Job Seniority," NBER Working Paper No. 1616, May 1985.

Brown, James N., "Why Do Wages increase with Tenure? On-the-Job Training and Life-Cycle Wage Growth Observed Within Firms," *American Economic Review*, Vol. 79, No. 5, December 1989, pp. 971–991.

Dunson, Bruce H., "Pay, Experience, and Productivity: The Government Sector Case," *Journal of Human Resources*, Vol. 20, No. 1, Winter 1985, pp. 153–160.

Horowitz, Stanley A., and Allan Sherman, "A Direct Measure of the Relationship Between Human Capital and Productivity," *Journal of Human Resources*, Vol. 15, No. 1, Winter 1980, pp. 67–76.

Hutchens, Robert M., "Seniority, Wages and Productivity: A Turbulent Decade," *Journal of Economic Perspectives*, Vol. 3, No. 4, Fall 1989, pp. 49–64.

Kotlikoff, Laurence J., "Estimating a Firm's Age-Productivity Profile Using the Present Value of Workers' Earnings," *Quarterly Journal of Economics*, Vol. 107, No. 4, November 1992, pp 1215–1242.

Maranto, Cheryl L., and Robert C. Rodgers, "Does Work Experience Increase Productivity? A Test of the On-the-Job Training Hypothesis, *Journal of Human Resources*, Vol. 19, No. 3, Summer 1984, pp. 341–357.

Medoff, James L., and Katherine G. Abraham, "Experience, Performance, and Earnings," *Quarterly Journal of Economics*, Vol. 95, December 1980, pp. 703–736.

———, "Are Those Paid More Really More Productive? The Case of Experience," *Journal of Human Resources*, Vol. 16, No. 2, Spring 1981, pp. 186–216.

———, "Years of Service and Probability of Promotion," NBER Working Paper No. 1191, August 1983.

———, "Length of Service, Terminations and the Nature of the Employment Relationship," NBER Working Paper No. 1086, March 1983.

D. Other Interpretations of the Relation between Schooling and Earnings

Albrecht, James, "The Use of Educational Information by Employers," Econometric Society Meeting, Winter 1974.

————, "Interpreting the Returns to Education," Columbia University Department of Economics Discussion Paper No. 77–7811, January 1978.

————, "A Procedure for Testing the Signalling Hypothesis," Columbia University Department of Economics Discussion Paper No. 77–7811, February 1978.

Arrow, Kenneth, "Higher Education as a Filter," *Journal of Public Economics*, Vol. 2, No. 3, July 1973, pp. 193–216.

Behrman, Jere E., and Paul Taubman, "The Intergenerational Correlation between Children's Adult Earnings and Their Parents' Income: Results from the Michigan Panel Survey of Income Dynamics," *Review of Income and Wealth*, Series 36, No. 2, June 1990, pp. 115–128.

Blaug, Mark, "Review of Economics of Education," *Journal of Human Resources*, Vol. 24, No. 2, Spring 1989, pp. 331–335.

Bowles, Samuel, "Towards an Educational Production Function," in W. Lee Hansen (ed.), *Education, Income, and Human Capital*, National Bureau of Economic Research, New York, 1970.

————, "Unequal Education and the Reproduction of the Social Division of Labor," *Review of Radical Political Economy*, Vol. 3, No. 4, Fall-Winter 1971, pp. 1–30.

————, "Schooling and Inequality from Generation to Generation," *Journal of Political Economy*, Vol. 80, No. 3, Part II, May/June 1972, pp. S219–S251.

————, "The Integration of Higher Education into the Wage Labor System," *Review of Radical Political Economy*, Vol. 6, No. 1, Spring 1974, pp. 100–133.

————, and Herbert Gintis, *Schooling in Capitalist America*, Basic Books, New York, 1976.

————, and Herbert Gintis, "The Problem with Human Capital Theory," *American Economic Review*, Vol. 65, No. 2, May 1975, pp. 74–82.

Eckhaus, Richard, "Estimation of the Return to Education with Hourly Standardized Incomes," *Quarterly Journal of Economics*, Vol. 87, No. 1, February 1973, pp. 121–131.

————, *Estimating the Returns to Education: A Disaggregated Approach*, Technical Report, Carnegie Commission on Higher Education, 1973.

Gintis, Herbert, "Education, Technology, and the Characteristics of Worker Productivity," *American Economic Review*, Vol. 61, No. 2, May 1971, pp. 266–279.

Jones, Ethel B., and John D. Jackson, "College Grades and Labor Market Rewards," *Journal of Human Resources*, Vol. 25, No. 2, Spring 1990, pp. 253–266.

Kroch, Eugene A., and Kriss Sjoblom, "Schooling as Human Capital or a Signal," *Journal of Human Resources*, Vol. 39, No. 1, Winter 1994, pp. 156–180.

Lang, Kevin, "Does the Human-Capital/Educational-Sorting Debate Matter for Development Policy?" *American Economic Review*, Vol. 84, No. 1, March 1994, pp. 353–358.

Layard, Richard, and George Psacharopoulos, "The Screening Hypothesis and the Return to Education," *Journal of Political Economy*, Vol. 82, No. 5, September-October 1974, pp. 985–998.

Lazear, Edward, "Academic Achievement and Job Performance: Note," *American Economic Review*, Vol. 67, No. 2, March 1977, pp. 252–254.

Riley, John, "Competitive Signalling," *Journal of Economic Theory*, Vol. 10, 1975, pp. 175–186.

———, "Information, Screening, and Human Capital," *American Economic Review*, Vol. 66, No. 2, May 1976, pp. 254–260.

———, "Testing the Educational Screening Hypothesis," *Journal of Political Economy*, Vol. 87 (Supplement), 1979, pp. S227–S251.

Ross, Stephen, Paul Taubman, and Michael Wachter, "Learning by Observing the Distribution of Wages," in Sherwin Rosen (ed.), *Studies in Labor Markets*, Chicago University Press, Chicago, 1981, pp. 359–386.

Saloner, Garth, "Old Boy Networks as Screening Mechanisms," *Journal of Labor Economics*, Vol. 3, No. 3, July 1985, pp. 255–267.

Spence, Michael, "Job Market Signalling," *Quarterly Journal of Economics*, Vol. 87, No. 3, August 1973, pp. 355–374.

———, "Signalling, Screening, and Information," in Sherwin Rosen (ed.), *Studies in Labor Markets*, Chicago University Press, Chicago, 1981.

Stiglitz, Joseph, "The Theory of 'Screening,' Education, and the Distribution of Income," *American Economic Review*, Vol. 65, No. 3, June 1975, pp. 283–300.

Taubman, Paul, and Terrence Wales, "Higher Education, Mental Ability and Screening," *Journal of Political Economy*, Vol. 81, No. 1, January-February 1973, pp. 28–55.

———, and ———, *Higher Education and Earnings*, McGraw Hill, New York, 1974.

Weiss, Andrew, "Testing the Sorting Model of Education," NBER Working Paper No. 1420, August 1984.

———, "High School Graduation, Performance, and Earnings," NBER Working Paper No. 1595, April 1985.

Wolff, Edward N., "Schooling and Occupational Earnings," *Review of Income and Wealth*, Series 23, No. 3, September 1977, pp. 259–278.

Wolpin, Kenneth, "Education and Screening," *American Economic Review*, Vol. 67, No. 5, December 1977, pp. 949–958.

DISCUSSION QUESTIONS

1. Discuss three reasons why, according to human capital theory, individuals will invest in schooling early in their life rather than later.

2. What is the characteristic shape of the age-earnings profile? From the standpoint of the human capital model, explain why it has the characteristic shape and why the peak is later for more highly educated workers.

3. Explain why the failure to control for differences in individual ability may lead to an overstatement of the returns to schooling.

4. Compare and contrast the implications of the human capital and screening models with regard to the relation between an individual's schooling level and the person's earnings. What are the implications for the social rate of return to schooling in each model?

5. Discuss three ways in which family background may affect educational attainment and earnings.

8

OTHER SOURCES OF INEQUALITY IN LABOR EARNINGS: UNIONS AND LABOR MARKET SEGMENTATION

Chapters 6 and 7 examined the role of individual characteristics in explaining differences in earnings among the working population. In this chapter and the next, we will focus on institutional factors that might account for why workers earn different incomes.

We begin this chapter with a treatment of labor unions. These are associations of workers that try to improve the wages, fringe benefits, and working conditions of their members through collective bargaining and other means. By 1993, less than 16 percent of all employees were represented by some form of union in the United States. This figure is considerably below that of many Western European countries, where the proportion of workers in unions reaches 90 percent. However, trade unions are still believed to have a significant effect on wages and employment in the United States.

Section 8.1 examines the economic role of trade unions and surveys the pertinent evidence on their role in the economy. The first part presents a brief history of trade unions in the United States, including the growth in union membership and their occupational and industrial distribution. The second part discusses the current economic role of unions. The next two parts develop the neoclassical model of trade unions regarding wages and employment. The last part reviews evidence about the relative wages of union versus nonunion workers and the relation of unions to the overall distribution of earnings.

Another important institutional feature is labor market segmentation. Section 8.2 develops the dual labor market model characterized by two distinct groups of workers. The **primary labor market** is found in large organizations where jobs require substantial training, provide security and steady advancement, and pay high wages and benefits. In the **secondary labor market,** jobs require little education and training and pay low wages, and worker turnover is high. Many people employed in the secondary market are trapped in a vicious cycle of low training, low wages, and chronic poverty.

Both the decline in unionism and the rise in secondary employment are believed to have contributed to the rise of inequality in the United States since the early 1970s. Section 8.3 presents some evidence on this issue, as well as providing a summary of the chapter.

8.1 THE ECONOMIC ROLE OF LABOR UNIONS: ARE UNIONS EFFECTIVE IN RAISING WAGES?

A Brief History of Trade Unionism in the United States

Local craft unions first appeared in the United States in the 1790s. These associations were called "societies" or "bodies" in the beginning, and their membership consisted largely of skilled artisans in the towns and cities. These early unions were local and organized by trade, such as carpenters, printers, or shoemakers. The motivation for forming such unions was to promote better wages and fewer hours of work. Strikes were used by these workers as a means of inducing employers to meet their demands. However, this weapon was not always effective, since courts during that period often ruled that strikes were illegal.

The year 1827 marks the first attempt at the formation of **federations** of labor unions, which in this case was an organization of local unions across craft and industry lines in the city of Philadelphia. Such citywide labor federations became more involved in political issues than in collective bargaining disputes. A National Trades Union, representing an association of city federations, was formed in 1834, and one of its major objectives was to achieve a ten-hour day for federal government employees.

Both the number of trade unions and trade membership grew during the 1830s until the panic of 1837, when many local trade unions, as well as the National Trades Union, disappeared. The ebb and flow of union membership in response to macroeconomic conditions is a recurring theme in American trade union history until 1930. When the economy was prosperous, labor was scarce and profits were high, and, as a result, employers were more willing to meet union demands for higher wages and better working conditions. Union membership therefore grew during boom periods. During depressions, jobs were scarce and profits low and, as a result, employers were less willing to meet union demands and workers were more willing to work for lower wages. Unions therefore lost their effectiveness during downturns and union membership declined.

The 1850s saw the formation of the first *national* trade union, the National Typographical Union. This was followed in suit by the formation of national trade unions among machinists, locomotive engineers, stonecutters, cigar makers, and blacksmiths. These national unions were formed along craft (or trade) lines and were originally loose associations of local trade unions, with bargaining still done on the local level. Soon, however, the national level of the union became predominant, with most of union policy set at this level.

The rationale for the formation of national unions was that product makers were becoming national in scope. This was a result of the tremendous improvements in communication and transportation, particularly through the building of canals and railroads. This development sufficiently lowered transportation costs so that goods produced in one part of the country could compete successfully with locally produced goods. As a result, goods made in low-wage areas could undersell those produced in high-wage ones. Local unions could not successfully control wages, since these could be undermined by wage standards set in other parts of the country. National trade unions, on the other hand, could standardize wage rates across localities.

The Formation of the American Federation of Labor (AFL) Begun in 1881, the AFL soon became the dominant labor organization on the American scene, a position it has held to this day. It started as a loose federation of several national craft unions. Much of its success was due to its stress on economic activity, particularly wages, hours, and working conditions, rather than on political activity. The AFL granted a charter to each of its national unions, which gave the union the exclusive right to organize workers within a particular occupation or trade.

The AFL was led by Samuel Gompers of the cigar-makers union, who served as its president from 1886 until 1925. The period 1897 to 1904 witnessed a dramatic increase in union membership from 447,000 to 2,073,000 members (see Rees, 1977). Much of this occurred in the railroads, mining, and building industry. This increase was partly due to the prosperity of the period and partly due to the successful use of collective bargaining between employers and unions.

After 1904, union membership continued to grow, but at a slower rate. One major reason was that in 1908, the Supreme Court in a case involving the Danbury (Connecticut) Hatters Union ruled that it was illegal for the union to engage in a consumer boycott against nonunion producers of hats. This decision was based on the Sherman Antitrust Act, passed in 1890, which prohibited "restraint of trade" in interstate commerce.[1]

The tight labor markets caused by World War I brought another spurt in union membership, and by 1920, membership had passed the 5 million

---

[1] This rather strained interpretation of the antitrust act was not reversed by the Supreme Court until 1940.

mark. This increase was partly aided by the passage of the Clayton Act in 1914, which included clauses that exempted labor unions from the antitrust acts. A major achievement during this period was the passage of the Adamson Act in 1916, which set an eight-hour day for railroad employees. The eight-hour day quickly spread as a standard in other industries.

A recession in 1921 brought a sharp reduction in union membership, and despite prosperity from 1923 to 1929, membership stagnated. In 1929, membership stood at 3.5 million, compared to 5.0 million in 1920. One major reason was that companies were improving working conditions, wages, and benefits for nonunionized workers, partly as a means to forestall unionization.

The Great Depression and Its Aftermath   The depression that began in 1929 was a tremendous shock to the U.S. economy. By 1933 output had fallen by half, and the unemployment rate stood at 25 percent. Unions were also adversely affected by this turn of events, with membership falling from 3.5 million in 1929 to 2.7 million in 1933.

The New Deal inaugurated with the election of Franklin Roosevelt was to have a major and lasting impact on industrial relations. In 1933, the National Industrial Recovery Act was enacted, which for the first time explicitly gave labor the legal right to organize into unions and to engage in collective bargaining with management. Though in 1935 the Supreme Court found the National Industrial Recovery Act unconstitutional, later that year a new law was passed, called the National Labor Relations Act or Wagner Act, which again made it legal for workers to organize and bargain collectively. The law also prohibited employers from blacklisting or otherwise discriminating against union members and provided an institutional mechanism, the National Labor Relation Board, for adjudicating complaints against management. In 1937, the Supreme Court declared the Wagner Act constitutional, which further strengthened the union movement. Between 1933 and 1941, union membership increased from 2.7 million to 10.2 million.

Concomitant with the renewed vigor of the union movement were growing divisions within the AFL. The problem arose from the presence of two different principles used to organize workers—the trade (or craft) and the industry (irrespective of occupation). Almost all the early unions were organized around trades. The mining and clothing workers were organized according to the industry principle. As unionization penetrated new industries, such as automobiles and rubber, jurisdictional fights arose. A schism thus formed in the AFL, with the industrial unions breaking off and forming the Congress of Industrial Organizations (CIO), under the leadership of John Lewis. It was not until 1955 that the two groups came back together to form a single organization, the AFL-CIO.

During World War II, union membership leaped once again, from 10.2 million in 1941 to 14.3 million in 1945. After the war, unions demanded large wage increases, and a resulting wave of strikes swept across the country. Partially as a result of this, public sentiment seemed to shift against labor, and this lead to the passage of the Taft-Hartley Labor-Management Relations Act of 1947. This Act shifted the balance of bargaining power back toward management by, for example, making unions as well as employers prosecutable for unfair labor practices and allowing the decertification of unions. The Taft-Hartley Act probably helped slow the growth of union membership, for by 1956 membership had grown to only 17.5 million workers.

Trends in Union Membership

Figure 8.1 summarizes the trends in union membership since 1930. Though the *number* of union members increased in almost every year since 1933, this was not true of the more telling statistic, union membership as a percent of the labor force. In 1933, 5.2 percent of the total labor force and 11.3 percent of the nonagricultural labor force was represented by unions of one form or another.[2] This proportion increased in almost every year until 1954, when union membership as a fraction of the total labor force peaked at 25.4 percent and as a fraction of the nonfarm labor force at 34.7 percent. After 1954, the trend was basically downward. By 1960, the proportion stood at 23.6 percent of the total labor force and 31.4 percent of the nonfarm labor force; by 1978 the proportion stood at 19.7 percent of the total labor force

Figure 8.1   Union Membership as a Proportion of the Labor Force, 1930–1993

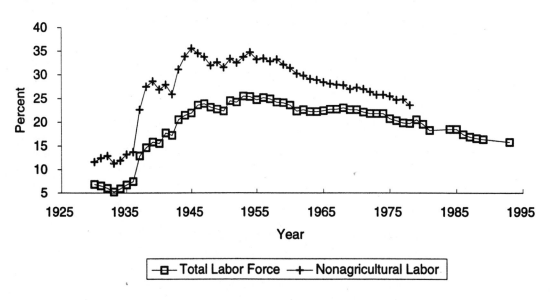

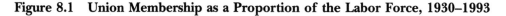

---

[2]Union membership as a percent of the nonfarm work force has always been higher, because the agricultural sector has had very low union representation.

Part II   The Role of Labor Markets

and 23.6 percent of the non-farm work force; and at 16.6 percent of the total labor force in 1988 and 15.8 percent in 1993.

Table 8.1 provides details on trends in unionization by occupational group. The most heavily unionized occupations during the 1950s and 1960s were the blue-collar trades. Foremost among them were operatives such as machine operators and truck drivers (over 80 percent in 1950 and over 70 percent in 1960). Second in line were unskilled labor such as assembly line workers (56 percent in 1950 and 29 percent in 1960). About a third of craftsmen and skilled workers were in unions in 1950, and this proportion increased to slightly over 40 percent in 1960. About a fifth of all service workers were represented by unions in 1950, and this proportion fell to 16 percent in 1960.

The white-collar occupations generally had lower union representation than blue-collar workers. Clerical workers were the most unionized white-collar group, at 18 percent in 1950 and 13 percent in 1960. Professional, technical, and kindred workers, including nurses, health technicians and teachers, were the second most unionized group, at a little over 10 percent in 1950 and 1960. The other two white collar occupational groups, managers and salesworkers, had almost no union representation in the two years. Finally, it should be noted that farmers, agricultural workers, and private household workers also had almost no union members in 1950 and 1960.

Though the occupational classification scheme for the 1980s and 1990s differs from the earlier one, it is still possible to make some comparisons. Perhaps, the most dramatic change was the fall in union representation for the blue-collar trades. The unionization rate fell to about 25 percent among craft, operative, and unskilled workers by 1993. Union representation for service workers also declined, to 14 percent.

In contrast, among the white-collar occupations, unionization either held its own or showed gains. In 1989, 22 percent of professional specialities and 12 percent of technical trades were organized. Unionization among sales workers increased from 3 percent in 1960 to 5 percent in 1989. Unions also penetrated the agricultural sector, reaching 5.1 percent in 1993.

By and large, unions have maintained their strength in areas where they were strong by the close of World War II but have failed to penetrate new sectors of the economy with one major exception. This exception is the government and the nonprofit sector, including universities and hospitals, in which union membership increased dramatically in the 1960s and 1970s. This is particularly true for state and local government employees, where the passage of new laws giving them the right to organize and bargain collectively greatly aided the process. In 1956, as shown in Table 8.2, 5 percent of all union members worked for the government. By 1993, this proportion had grown to 42 percent. Moreover, the percent of public employees organized in unions grew from 11 percent in 1960 to 38 percent in 1993 (also, see Freeman, 1986, for more discussion).

There were other notable changes in the distribution of union membership. In 1956, half of union workers were found in manufacturing (and the

Table 8.1   Union Membership as a Percentage of the Labor Force by Occupation, Selected Years, 1950–1993[a]

Category	1950	1960
1. Professional, technical, and kindred workers	11.9	10.6
2. Managers and administrators	0.3	0.5
3. Salesworkers	1.7	2.9
4. Clerical and kindred workers	17.6	12.5
5. Craftsmen and kindred workers	32.9	40.8
6. Operatives	82.4	73.6
7. Laborers, except farm	56.2	28.8
8. Farm laborers and foremen	1.2	2.2
9. Farmers and farm managers	—	—
10. Service workers	20.5	16.4
11. Private household workers	—	—
Overall	22.3	23.6

Category	1984	1989	1993
1. Executive, administrative, and managerial	6.3	6.2	] 14.9
2. Professional specialty	23.4	22.4	
3. Technicians and related support	12.2	12.0	
4. Sales occupations	6.3	5.1	] 10.4
5. Administrative support, incl. clerical	14.0	13.0	
6. Protective service	38.7	38.3	] 13.8
7. Service, except protective service	11.7	9.6	
8. Precision production, craft, and repair	30.1	26.3	25.6
9. Machine operators, assemblers, and inspectors	35.4	28.8	
10. Transportation and material moving	34.7	28.9	] 24.7
11. Handlers, equipment cleaners, helpers, and laborers	27.4	23.9	
12. Farming, forestry, and fishing	5.5	3.8	5.1
Overall	18.5	16.4	15.8

[a] Sources: Troy (1965); U.S. Bureau of the Census, *U.S. Census of the Population: 1950, Occupation by Industry*, 1954; U.S. Bureau of the Census, *U.S. Census of the Population: 1960*, "Occupation by Industry," Report PC(2)-72, 1963; U.S. Bureau of Labor Statistics, *Employment and Earnings*, January 1985; U.S. Bureau of Labor Statistics, *Employment and Earnings*, January 1990; U.S. Department of Commerce, *Statistical Abstract of the United States, 1994.*

Table 8.2 Union Membership by Industry as a Percent of Total Union Membership, Selected Years, 1956–1993[a]

Industry	1956	1960	1970	1978	1983	1993
A. *Nonmanufacturing Industries*	51.3	52.3	55.8	63.0	70.1	78.4
1. Mining & quarrying	2.9	3.3	1.8	2.0	1.0	0.6
2. Construction	11.7	12.6	12.5	13.6	6.4	5.6
3. Transportation	15.1	14.2	11.9	8.2 ⎤		
4. Telephone & telegraph	2.4	2.3	2.4	2.6 ⎥ 12.3 ⎤ 11.6		
5. Electric & gas utilities	1.8	1.5	1.5	1.6 ⎦		
6. Wholesale and retail trade	4.9	4.7	7.6	8.1	8.9	8.2
7. Finance & insurance[b]	0.3	0.4	0.3	0.2	0.9	0.8
8. Services	6.7	7.1	6.3	9.4	8.0	9.2
9. Agriculture & fishing	0.4	0.3	0.1	0.2	0.3	0.1
10. Government	5.1	5.9	11.3	17.1	32.3	42.3
B. *Manufacturing Industries*	48.8	47.6	44.2	37.0	29.9	21.6
11. Food, beverage, tobacco		5.8	4.7	3.0		
12. Clothing, textiles, leather		6.8	5.8	4.4		
13. Furniture, lumber, wood products, paper		4.6	4.2	3.9		
14. Printing & publishing		1.9	1.8	1.3		
15. Petrol, chemicals, rubber		3.0	3.4	2.7		
16. Stone, clay, glass		1.4	1.4	1.3		
17. Metals, machinery, equipment (except transportation equipment)		16.0	16.3	13.4		
18. Transportation equipment		7.3	5.5	5.2		
19. Other manufacturing		0.8	1.1	1.8		
C. *Total*	100.0	100.0	100.0	100.0	100.0	100.0

Addendum: Union Membership as a Percent of Employment by Industry

					1983	1993
1. Mining & quarrying					20.7	16.0
2. Construction					27.5	20.0
3. Transportation and utilities					42.4	30.5
4. Wholesale and retail trade					8.7	6.3
5. Finance, insurance, and real estate					2.9	1.9
6. Services					7.7	5.8
7. Agriculture & fishing					3.4	1.6
8. Government					36.7	37.7
9. Manufacturing					27.8	19.2
Total					20.1	15.8

[a] Source: U.S. Bureau of Labor Statistics, *Handbook of Labor Statistics, 1978*; U.S. Department of Commerce, *Statistical Abstract of the United States, 1994.*
[b] This sector includes real estate beginning in 1968.

other half in nonmanufacturing). However, by 1993, over three-quarters of organized workers were in nonmanufacturing. Almost all the manufacturing sectors lost in terms of their relative share of union workers.

Among the nonmanufacturing sectors, the picture was mixed. Twelve percent of union members were employed in transportation and utilities in 1993, down from 19 percent in 1956. The proportion of union workers employed in construction declined from 12 percent in 1956 to 6 percent in 1993. In contrast, 5 percent of union members were employed in the trade sector in 1956; by 1993 the proportion had reached 8 percent. The fraction of organized workers employed in services increased from 7 percent in 1956 to 9 percent in 1993.

What is also striking is that the percent of employees organized in unions fell in every major sector between 1983 and 1993 except government (see the Addendum to Table 8.2). In mining, the proportion fell from 21 to 16 percent; in construction, from 28 to 20 percent; in transportation and utilities, from 42 to 31 percent; and in manufacturing, from 28 to 19 percent. The share of government workers represented by a union increased from 37 to 38 percent.

In sum, in 1993 less than 40 percent of all union membership was found in construction, transportation, utilities, and manufacturing, compared to almost 80 percent in 1956. On the other hand, three service sectors—trade, general services, and government—accounted for 17 percent of all union membership in 1956 and 60 percent in 1993. Within these services, public sector trade unions showed the most rapid gains.

The Decline in Trade Unionism   Why has unionization fallen so sharply in the United States since the mid-1950s? Several studies have attempted to answer this question. Several factors have been identified as contributing to the process. The first is that since the end of World War II, employment has grown much more rapidly in the white-collar occupations, which were and have remained relatively less unionized, than in the blue-collar trades, the traditional area of union strength. William Dickens and Jonathan Leonard (1985) found that about a third of the decline in the union membership rate was due to plant closures, layoffs, and slower growth in basic manufacturing industries. However, this explains only part of the trend, since the unionization rate of the core union sectors—mining, manufacturing, construction, and transportation—also fell, particularly in the 1970s (see below).

A second factor is that union organizing activity has fallen off since the 1950s, particularly during the 1970s. Dickens and Leonard (1985) found that the number of workers involved in new union certification elections declined during the 1970s, while the labor force grew. A third and related factor is the decline in the success rate of union organizing efforts. The success rate, defined as the number of eligible voters in union elections choosing unions as a percentage of all eligible workers, also dropped between the mid-1950s and the early 1980s.

Other factors include the deregulation of transportation industries; changes in public attitudes toward unions; increased government regulation of the labor market, substituting for union rules; change in labor relations of corporations to forestall unionization attempts, particularly increased anti-union activity; and changes in government industrial relations policies, particularly the Reagan administration's opposition to the air traffic controllers' strike in 1982. Richard Freeman (1988) felt that increased corporate opposition to unionization attempts, including maintaining high wages and good benefits for nonunion workers, was a major factor. Melvin Reder (1988) stressed the role of deregulation of key industries. George Neumann and Ellen Rissman (1984) argued that government provision of services traditionally supplied by unions (particularly social welfare expenditures) played a major role in reducing union membership.

The experience of other industrialized countries has been strikingly different in regard to unionization (see Freeman, 1988). In several countries, the unionization rate (the percent of nonagricultural workers in unions) has increased dramatically since 1970: in Denmark, from 66 to 98 percent in 1984–1985; in Sweden, from 79 to 95 percent; and in Finland, from 56 to 85 percent. Other countries have experienced a moderate increase in or stable level of union density over this period, including Germany (37 to 42 percent), France (22 to 28 percent), Italy (39 to 45 percent); Canada (32 to 37 percent), Switzerland (31 to 35 percent), and the United Kingdom (51 to 52 percent). Among the industrialized countries, the United States experienced the largest decline in unionism during the 1970s and 1980s and had the lowest percentage of unionization by the mid-1980s (see also Freeman, 1989, for more discussion). We shall return to this point in Section 8.3.

The Economic Role of Labor Unions

Despite their recent decline, unions are still a major institution on the American economic scene. On the surface, at least, their endurance would seem to indicate that unions provide important benefits for labor. The question then arises as to what unions actually do. What functions do they perform? What are their goals? We shall look at these issues in this section. In the next section, we shall present a more formal analysis of their economic function in the labor market. In the last section, we shall investigate the evidence as to their success.

Union Organization   Before discussing the functioning of unions, it is useful to provide a brief overview of their organization and structure. As noted in the previous section, there are, in general, two broad classes of unions. The first is the trade or craft union, which includes members of the same occupations or related occupations. Some craft unions may be localized in a single industry but most cut across industry lines. The second is the industrial union, which encompasses all workers in a particular industry, regardless of occupation or skill.

Unions are organized in several layers. The smallest unit is the **bargaining unit,** which consists of a group of employees who are exclusively represented by a union in collective bargaining over compensation, hours, and working conditions. The contract or collective agreement reached between the union and the employer governs the relationship between the employer and the employee with respect to these matters. In most cases, the bargaining unit is established as a result of an initial representation election, held by the National Labor Relations Board (NLRB). One type of bargaining unit in manufacturing consists of production and maintenance workers in a single plant. Perhaps more common in manufacturing is the single-employer unit, where the bargaining unit may include all the plants owned by a given firm, as in the automobile industry. In nonmanufacturing sectors, the more typical bargaining unit cuts across employer lines and consists of employees in a particular industry, such as trucking, who are located in a specific geographical area.

The vertical structure of unions is usually in three layers—the local union at the bottom, the national union in the middle, and the federation (AFL-CIO) at the top. The local union is usually a subordinate unit to a national union. In industrial unions, the local union usually covers a geographical region such as a city or metropolitan area. In cases where the product market is restricted to a local geographical area, as in construction, local transit, restaurants, and entertainment, the local unions are usually the primary bargaining unit. In cases where the product market is national in scope, as in automobiles, the principal bargaining unit is usually the national union, and the function of the local union is usually confined to administering the collective agreement at that level.

The next level is the national union, which is typically the strongest and most important of the three levels. There are three reasons for this. First, the AFL-CIO normally grants the charter to a national union, which gives it the exclusive right to organize a given industry or craft. Second, because most product markets are national in scope, it is the national union that for strategic reasons does the bargaining in the industry or trade. Third, union dues are usually paid directly to the national union.

The top layer is the federation, which today is the AFL-CIO. The federation's primary function is to act as the spokesman for labor, particularly on the political scene. In many ways, the AFL-CIO acts as a lobby for labor in national politics. The federation does not engage in collective bargaining; this function is performed by the national unions. Its primary organizational power is its ability to grant jurisdictional charters to new unions.

Collective Bargaining   The most important function performed by labor unions is to bargain collectively with employers to reach an agreement on the terms of employment of the members of the union. Agreements usually cover wages, hours, and working conditions, as well as other relevant matters, such as security clauses to prevent nonunion members from being hired; seniority (i.e., length of service) policy, particularly in regard to wage differentials, the order of layoffs and recalls, and transfer policies; complaints and grievance procedures; and fringe benefits, including vacations, sick time, pensions, and health benefits. On the other side of the table, management is also concerned with work rules—that is, control over the productive process. These involve the freedom to assign workers to different jobs, control over machine speed, the right to introduce new technology in a plant, and the freedom to subcontract certain services, such as maintenance.

Strikes and Other Union Weapons The strike is by far the most powerful weapon a union has to win its negotiating demands. A strike is a decision made by a union to withhold labor from one or more workplaces. The usual reason for a strike is that an old contract has expired and negotiations with an employer have failed to provide a new contract. During a strike, workers do not receive wages or other employer-provided benefits, and the employer is stuck with idle plant and equipment. There is therefore a considerable cost associated with strikes. Strikes may also cause resources to lay idle in supplying and using industries (a strike in the railroad industry could idle steelworkers if there are no other means of shipping steel).

Once a strike is in effect, unions try to keep the pressure on employers by preventing any work from taking place in the plant or company. Until about 1940, employers often tried to break a strike by hiring new employees to replace the strikers. Unions, on the other hand, engaged in picketing to stop the "scabs" from working, and this often led to violence. Since the start of World War II, employers have very rarely resorted to this tactic. In some basic service industries, like telephones, supervisory personnel may keep service going during a strike, but in most other industries operations are discontinued.

A strike ends when a settlement is reached between the union and employer, which normally takes the form of a new contract. The factors determining both the timing and terms of the settlement are complex. On the union side, the main determinant is the ability of the workers to hold out financially. Many large unions have strike funds for this purpose. On the other side, employers will lose money as their plant and equipment lie idle. If production is completely halted, they will continue to lose money during the strike.

There are other weapons in labor's arsenal besides the planned strike. There is the "wildcat strike," which often occurs spontaneously by a local union without authorization from above. Wildcat strikes are usually called in violation of an existing collective bargaining agreement. They are sometimes ignited by a local grievance against a particular employer (over safety conditions, for example), but sometimes they are motivated by dissatisfaction with the national union. The primary aim, in both cases, is to win added concessions for the workers. Another tactic is the "slowdown," whereby workers will purposely slow down the pace of work in order to reduce output. This tactic is also used to gain concessions from management.

Less direct tactics include the use of "union labels" and boycotts. A union label is often put on consumer goods made by a union in order to encourage consumers who are sympathetic with the goals of organized labor to buy only union goods. A "boycott" is the converse of this, for it attempts to discourage consumers from buying nonunion products. These are, in general, weak weapons, though the United Farm Workers in California were fairly successful in using the boycott to help organize farm workers in grape and lettuce production in the 1970s.

Analysis of Trade Union Objectives

Trade unions have two conflicting goals. The first is to raise the wages of its members as high as possible, and the second is to increase its membership as much as possible. These two aims conflict because the demand curve for labor slopes downward (see Chapter 6), and thus, increasing the wage will reduce employment.

This trade-off can be represented by a set of **indifference curves** (see Figure 8.2). I_1, I_2, I_3, and I_4 show the combination of wage rates and employment levels that are equally preferred by the union. The fact that the indifference curves slope downward indicates that a union is willing to accept a lower wage rate in return for a higher level of employment and hence a larger membership. The points on the indifference curve I_2 are each preferred to the points on I_1, since for each point on I_1, there is a point on I_2 representing both a higher wage rate and a higher employment level. The curve I_2 therefore represents a higher level of utility than I_1, and likewise I_3 is higher than I_2, and I_4 higher than I_3.

The industry labor demand curve is represented by the line D_L. Point P is the point of tangency between the demand curve for labor and indifference curve I_3. The curve I_3 thus represents the highest utility level attainable by the union, given the shape and position of the labor demand curve. The corresponding wage rate w_o and employment level L_o are the union's preferred level of each. Of course, the actual level will be the result of collective bargaining between the union and the employer. In almost all labor contracts, it is the wage rate that is fixed, not the level of employment. The latter remains at the firm's discretion. The union (if it knows the true demand curve D_L) will try to negotiate the wage w_o, with the anticipation that the employers will hire L_o workers at w_o (since that is what the demand curve for labor represents). The employer, on the other hand, may wish a lower wage, and the settlement will depend on the negotiations.

Labor Market Impact of Trade Unions   The effect of a union on a labor market can perhaps be most easily understood by a comparison with the perfectly competitive labor market. In Figure 8.3 we have indicated the industry supply curve for labor under pure competition by S_L (see Chapter 6). The equilibrium wage in this situation will be w^*, and the equilibrium quantity of labor L^*.

Figure 8.2 Indifference Curve Representation of a Union's Wage and Employment Preferences

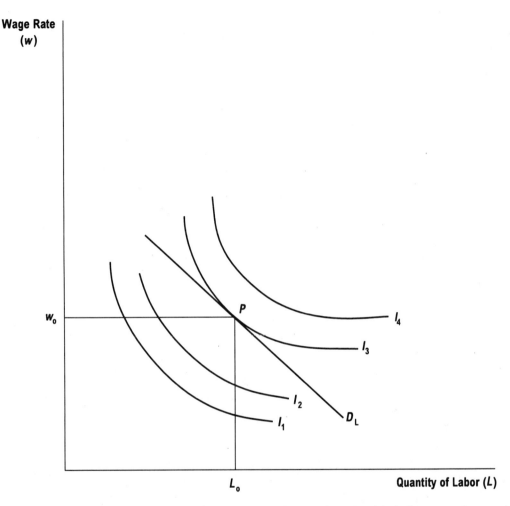

Suppose now a union organizes the workers in this industry and negotiates a wage rate w_1, which is greater (as it hopefully should be) than the prevailing equilibrium wage w^*. The firms in the industry will therefore reduce employment until the quantity of labor is equal to L_1. However, at the wage rate w_u, workers will be willing to supply L_2 of labor. L_2 will be greater than the competitive equilibrium level L^*, since the higher wage w_u will attract additional workers to the industry.

The initial effect of unionization is to create an excess supply of labor in the industry—that is, a larger number of workers willing to work at the prevailing wage than the number actually hired. In a perfectly competitive situation, this excess supply would cause the wage to be bid down until w^* is reached. However, with a union present, the wage cannot be changed, since

Figure 8.3   Demand and Supply Curves for Labor Under Perfect Competition and Under Unionization

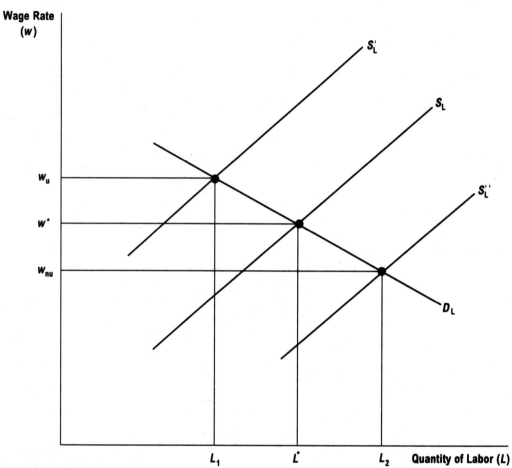

Key:
S_L — Supply curve for labor under perfect competition
$S_L^{'}$ — Supply curve for union labor
$S_L^{''}$ — Supply curve for nonunion labor
w^{*} — Wage under perfect competition
w_u — Wage for union labor
w_{nu} — Wage for nonunion labor

Part II   The Role of Labor Markets

the union is a monopsonist. What happens to the excess workers? They either remain unemployed or find work in another sector of the economy. The eventual effect of unionization in this industry is then to *shift the supply curve of labor to the left,* as indicated by S_L'. In other words, the primary effect of a union is to *restrict* the supply of labor flowing into an industry, which thereby allows the union to maintain a wage level higher than the competitive one. An important side effect is that the supply of labor in nonunionized sectors will thereby be increased (that is, the supply curve of labor in the nonunionized sector will move to the right, S_L''). This will lower the wage rate in the nonunionized sector, from w^* to w_{nu}. The wage rate advantage of unionized workers over nonunionized ones thus comes from the following *two* effects: the restriction of the supply of labor to the unionized sector and the expansion of the labor supply to the nonunionized sector.

Marshall's Rules   The effect of unions on wages was analyzed by the great English economist Alfred Marshall in his classic text, *Principles of Economics* (8th edition, Macmillan Co., New York, 1920.) Marshall analyzed four factors that influence the strength of unions (in his day, primarily craft unions), which today are called "Marshall's rules." The wage and employment effects of unionization depend on the **elasticity of demand** for union labor. The elasticity of demand is defined as the ratio of the percentage change in the quantity of labor demanded to the percentage change in the wage rate. The elasticity measure is one way of characterizing the *slope* of the demand curve.[3] A demand curve with a flat slope has a high elasticity and is said to be "elastic." This means that a small change in the wage rate will cause a large change in the quantity of labor demanded. In the extreme case, when the demand curve is horizontal, its elasticity is infinite. A demand curve with a very steep slope is said to be "inelastic," since a large change in the wage rate will cause only a small change in the quantity demanded. In the extreme case, when the demand curve is vertical, its elasticity is zero.[4]

Marshall's basic principle is that the more inelastic the demand curve for union labor, the smaller the impact on employment of a given percentage change in the wage rate and therefore the larger wage gains are likely to come from unionization. The rationale is that if the demand curve is elastic, then unions will be hesitant to push for a large increase in wages for fear of losing many jobs and hence members. If the labor demand curve is inelastic, on the other hand, unions will push for much higher wages since the expected loss in jobs will be small. Union strength will then be higher the more inelastic the demand curve for its members.

---

[3] Strictly speaking, the elasticity is a point measure, and its value normally varies along the demand curve. Loosely speaking, it can be used to characterize the overall shape of a demand curve. It should also be noted that the elasticity measure is negative in the case of a demand curve, since an increase in the wage rate will cause a decrease in employment, but one normally drops the negative sign when citing an elasticity.

[4] The dividing line between an elastic and inelastic demand curve is one of "unitary elasticity," which means an x percent change in the wage will cause an exactly x percent change in employment in the opposite direction.

The demand for labor is a "derived demand" (see Chapter 6) and, in particular, depends on labor's substitutability with other factors of production and on the demand curve for the product of the firm. Marshall used the theory of derived demand for labor to determine the factors that affect the elasticity of labor. His four conditions or rules are as follows:

Rule 1. The demand curve for labor is more inelastic the more "essential" union labor is in the production process—that is, the less substitutable other factors of production are for union labor. This condition would characterize many of the skilled construction trades, such as plumbers, electricians, and masons, for whom it is difficult to substitute other types of labor or equipment. Unions should thus be strong in the craft trades.

Rule 2. The more inelastic the product demand curve, the more inelastic the demand curve for the union workers. If the *product* demand curve is inelastic, then a large increase in its price will cause only a small decrease in the quantity of the product sold. A large wage increase, translated into a large output price increase, would not substantially reduce output and therefore the employment of union members.

This condition has two interpretations. First, if a union has organized all the firms in a particular industry, then the relevant product demand curve is that of the industry. Second, if an industry is only partially organized, then the relevant product demand curve is that of the firm. The demand curve for a firm's product is much more elastic than the industry demand curve, since the product of competing firms is easily substitutable (see models of monopolistic competition). This factor helps to explain why unions that succeed in organizing only part of an industry are often quite weak. It also helps to account for phenomena such as "union labels" (see above), which are a way of persuading consumers to discriminate between union and nonunion products (like apparel) and thus make the demand curve for the union product more inelastic.

Rule 2 helps explain why unions are particularly prevalent in oligopolistic and monopolistic industries, since their product demand curve is generally inelastic (see Chapter 6 again). This condition also helps account for the rapid growth of unions in the public sector, since the government enjoys perhaps the greatest degree of monopolization of any industrial sector. Growing international competition has also slowly eroded the strong oligopoly position of many domestic manufacturing firms over the last two decades. This is particularly notable in automobiles, steel, and electronics, where imports have made striking gains. This has made the product demand curve in these industries more elastic and further weakened unions.

Rule 3. The demand for union labor is more inelastic the lower the share of union wages in the total cost of production. If the share is low, a large increase in union wages will cause only a small increase in the cost (and hence price) of the product. This principle is particularly important when the product demand curve is elastic, since by rule 2, if the demand curve is inelastic, the reduction in employment will be low even for a large increase in the product price. The third principle tends to reinforce the view that craft unions will be stronger than industrial unions, since craft trades normally account for a smaller percentage of total costs than industrial unions.

Rule 4. The demand curve for union labor is more inelastic the more inelastic are the supply curves of substitutable factors of production. If wages go up, firms will generally try to substitute other factors of production, such as nonunion labor, machinery, and materials. If the supply curve of the other factors is inelastic, then the firm will have to pay higher prices for them and thus be more reluctant to substitute for union labor. This principle is particularly important when the first principle fails to hold—that is, when there are good technological substitutes for union labor. This condition may differ in the short run and long run. In the short run, capital equipment is sunk (that is, fixed), and its supply curve is inelastic. Over the long run, a company can buy new capital equipment, and the supply curve of capital is more elastic. Union strength may therefore be greater in the short run than the long run.

The Effect of Unions on Wages: The Evidence

Marshall's four conditions can be used to determine which occupations and industries unions might be most effective in raising wages. Table 8.3 shows the ratio of earnings between union and nonunion employees in 1993. It should be noted that these data do not adjust for any other factors that might influence earnings, such as schooling, experience, geographic region, and so on (see below). The biggest differential is found among service workers, among whom union members earned, on average, 80 percent more than nonunion workers. Other large differences characterized farming, forestry, and fishing workers (65 percent); operators, fabricators, and laborers (56 percent); and precision, craft, and repair workers (42 percent). Unionized technical, sales, and administrative support workers averaged 25 percent more in earnings than their nonunion counterparts. In managerial and professional jobs, there was almost no difference in earnings between union and nonunion workers.

Panel B presents similar industry statistics. The largest differential occurred in construction, where union members enjoyed a 63 percent advantage over nonunion workers. In wholesale and retail trade, the union workers earned 34 percent more. In manufacturing, transportation and public utilities, services, and government, the union edge varied between 13 and 24 percent, while in mining and in finance, insurance, and real estate, there were no significant differences in earnings. Within the entire labor force, union members earned 35 percent more than nonunion workers.

Table 8.3 Median Weekly Earnings by Union Status and Percent Union Members by Occupation and Industry, 1993[a]

	Median Weekly Earnings		Earnings Ratio	Percent Union Members
	Union Members	Nonunion		
A. Occupation				
Managerial and professional	$696	$670	1.04	14.9
Technical, sales, and administrative support	509	408	1.25	10.4
Service occupations	478	265	1.80	13.8
Precision, production, craft, and repair	642	453	1.42	25.6
Operators, fabricators, & laborers	501	321	1.56	24.7
Farming, forestry, and fishing	436	264	1.65	5.1
B. Industry				
Mining	631	657	0.96	16.0
Construction	692	425	1.63	20.0
Manufacturing	505	448	1.13	19.2
Transportation & public utilities	640	516	1.24	30.5
Wholesale & retail trade	465	347	1.34	6.3
Finance, insurance, & real estate	484	490	0.99	1.9
Services	482	416	1.16	5.8
Government workers	602	498	1.21	37.7
Overall	575	426	1.35	15.8

[a] Source: U.S. Department of Commerce, *Statistical Abstract of the United States, 1994.*

Econometric studies of union-nonunion earnings disparities attempt to standardize the union and nonunion samples for a variety of factors, such as schooling, experience, and skill differences, that might affect earnings independently of union membership. The most comprehensive and systematic review of this subject is H. Gregg Lewis's 1963 book, *Unionism and Relative Wages in the United States.*[5]

[5] For other surveys of the literature, see Parsley (1980) and Lewis (1986).

The statistical studies on union wage effects generally show a lower union wage advantage than the estimates derived from the unadjusted data. The reason is that union workers tend to be more skilled and experienced than nonunion ones. Adrian Throop (1968) adjusted earnings for differences in skill level between the unionized and nonunionized sectors. Using aggregate industry data, Throop found that with this adjustment, the union wage advantage fell to 22 percent in 1950 and 26 percent in 1960.

Leonard Weiss (1966), using 1960 Census of Population data, estimated a 20 percent union wage effect among male craftsmen and operatives. Frank Stafford (1968) estimated a union wage effect between 18 and 52 percent for all wage and salary workers in the same year. Richard Freeman and James Medoff (1984, p. 46) presented several estimates of the union wage effect for the decade of the 1970s on the basis of the Panel Survey of Income Dynamics, the Current Population Survey, and the National Longitudinal Survey. These ranged from 21 to 32 percent.

There has also been considerable variation in the union-nonunion wage spread over time. According to estimates provided by John Pencavel and Catherine Hartsog (1984), the differential was particularly high during the 1920s (23 percent in 1920–1924 and 35 percent in 1925–1929), the 1930s (50 percent in 1930–1934 and 22 percent in 1935–1939), and the period 1955–1969 (about 20 percent), but small during the 1940s (under 5 percent) and the 1970s (under 8 percent). They estimated that over the years from 1920 to 1980, the union wage advantage averaged about 17 percent.[6]

The "Threat Effect"   One criticism that has been raised about many of the studies of union wage differentials concerns the implicit assumption that unionization in one sector will leave unchanged or even lower the wages of the nonunionized sector. This assumption is based on the model developed in the fourth part (Analysis of Trade Union Objectives) (Figure 8.3), where an increase in the wage of unionized labor causes a reduction of employment in the unionized sector, a resulting increase in the supply of workers to the nonunionized sectors, and thereby a fall in nonunion wages. An alternative possibility is that unionization in one sector will induce employers in the nonunionized sector to *raise* wages because of the *fear or threat* of unionization. Companies may try to keep wages and benefits on a par with unionized companies in order to forestall the introduction of unions. Increases in wages in "key" organized industries may be imitated by the nonunionized sectors. If contagion to the nonunion industries is widespread, the observed union-nonunion wage differential may *understate* the true union wage effect, because nonunion wages may also rise from increased unionization (see Flanagan, 1976, for more discussion).

The threat effect has important implications because it suggests that unions may influence wages not only in the unionized sectors but in many

---

[6]See also Freeman and Medoff (1984) for comparative estimates. The Freeman-Medoff figures are similar to those of Pencavel and Hartsog, except for the 1970s. Freeman and Medoff found a union wage advantage of 19 percent for the early 1970s and 30 percent for the late 1970s.

nonunionized segments of the labor markets as well. Moreover, the decline of unionism in the United States may depress wages among nonunionized workers because the threat of unionization has also subsided. However, evidence on the threat effect has been inconclusive so far (see Mitchell, 1980, Freeman and Medoff, 1981, Freeman and Medoff, 1984, and Neumark and Wachter, 1992).[7]

Inequality of Earnings Somewhat surprisingly, though unions generally raise the wages of their members relative to nonunion workers, unionization may actually reduce overall earnings inequality. Lewis (1963) proposed four reasons for this. First, unions raise the earnings of production workers who are generally in unions relative to the higher wages of professional and managerial workers who are not generally found in unions. Second, unions tend to equalize wage rates for a given skill or occupational category both among firms and among different geographical locations. Third, unions tend to reduce the spread in wages among different classes of unionized workers within a company. Fourth, unions tend to even out wages within a skill or occupational class among individuals with different personal characteristics.

The evidence seems to indicate that unionization reduces the inequality of earnings among all workers, though the effect is probably very modest. Freeman (1980), using data from the 1973, 1974, and 1975 Current Population Surveys, found that wage inequality among union workers was substantially smaller than among nonunion workers. He also found that unions decreased the wage differential between unionized blue-collar workers and nonunionized white-collar workers. In two separate studies Thomas Hyclak (1979 and 1980) confirmed that unions tended to reduce overall inequality. In the first, he found a positive association between the extent of unionization and the level of earnings equality in metropolitan areas. In the second, he found a positive association between the degree of income equality and the degree of unionization across the states of the United States.

Robert Plotnick (1982), using a time-series of Current Population Survey data, found that wage inequality among male workers was higher when the unionization rate was lower. Michael Podursky (1983), using the 1971 Current Population Survey, found, as in previous studies, that collective bargaining agreements reduced the dispersion of income among union families. However, because union families tend to be found in the middle-income range, the union impact on overall family income inequality was negligible. Lawrence Kahn and Michael Curme (1987) argued that, because of the threat effect, nonunion firms most at risk from unionization will raise the wages of workers who would benefit most from a union. As a consequence, the dispersion of nonunion wages should be lower in sectors where the likelihood of unionization is greater. Using the 1979 Current Population

---

[7]Another issue is the effect of unionization on total labor compensation, including fringe benefits. The consensus seems to be that the union effect on fringe benefits is even greater than that on wages (see Freeman, 1981, or Freeman and Medoff, 1984, for example).

Survey, they found confirmation that the inequality of earnings among non-union employees was lower in more highly unionized industries.

Freeman and Medoff (1984) concluded on the basis of their own work and the work of other researchers that trade unionism in the United States reduced overall wage inequality by about 3 percent. This effect was primarily due to the demand of unions for standard rates of pay within and across establishments.

8.2 SEGMENTED LABOR MARKETS

Peter Doeringer and Michael Piore developed the dual labor market in their 1971 book, *Internal Labor Markets and Manpower Analysis.* They argued that there are two distinct labor markets effectively operating in the economy. In the primary labor market, training requirements are high. These jobs are primarily career-type positions in large, highly structured organizations. There are fairly well established entry positions and standard promotional ladders. These positions form an **internal labor market.** Wage policy for these positions is set by the organization, and internal consistency in wage levels is usually considered more important than consistency with the external labor market. As a result, relative salaries at different positions remain fairly stable over time. Schooling and experience are important in determining the wage level at which a prospective employee is hired, but they play a subordinate role in advancement once the individual has entered the internal labor market.

The secondary labor market consists of jobs which require little or no training. These jobs offer low wages, and worker turnover is generally very high. The secondary labor market consists largely of marginal workers whose attachments to the labor force is tangential. Blacks and other minorities, females, students, teenagers, the aged, the disabled, part-time workers, and the poorly educated are considerably overrepresented in this market. These workers receive little on-the-job training and may, as a result, have low wages throughout their work life.

The first part presents a discussion of internal labor markets. The second part develops the dual labor market model. The third part considers other models of labor market segmentation. In the last part, some criticisms of the dual labor market model are addressed.

Internal Labor Markets

The term "internal labor markets" was coined by Clark Kerr in a 1954 article entitled "The Balkanization of Labor Markets." He emphasized the importance of institutional rules in the operation of the labor market. Kerr argued that rules and procedures followed by large organizations set sharp boundaries between the internal and external labor market and, in particular, defined points of entry. Employees in an internal market do not compete directly against outside workers. Employers usually make the "admission decisions" determining who may enter the organization, though unions can exert some influence. Inside the internal market, labor mobility is largely dictated by organizational rules. Seniority plays a large role in advancement, particularly for production workers. Wage rates are set according to institutional rules and do not necessarily reflect supply and demand conditions in the external labor market.[8]

Doeringer and Piore (1971) revived the internal labor market model, though they emphasized the role of large organizations on wage setting and employment patterns. Doeringer and Piore define an internal labor market as "an administrative unit within which the pricing and allocation of labor is governed by a set of administrative rules and procedures." Ports of entry and exit mediate between the internal and external labor markets. Other jobs are filled by promotions and transfers and are thus shielded from the external labor market. In a sense, internal markets represent "industrial feudalism," where each "fiefdom" is relatively insulated from others. Doeringer and Piore estimated that about 80 percent of the employed labor force in the 1960s was located in internal labor markets.

The Structure of Internal Labor Markets Internal labor markets are characterized by four factors: (1) ports of entry, (2) exit ports, (3) promotional ladders, and (4) wage structure. With regard to the first factor, there is a well-defined and limited number of positions into which workers from the external labor market are hired. Internal labor markets also have specific exit rules. These rules are designed to control involuntary movements out of the internal labor market. With the exception of the military, workers are always free to quit a job or leave a position. These are voluntary terminations. However, there are also involuntary terminations, consisting of layoffs (both temporary and permanent), discharge for failure to perform one's work adequately, and compulsory retirement. Such work rules determine the various exit points in the job structure and the conditions under which the discharge can occur.

The third characteristic of internal markets is that they typically have well-defined promotional ladders. A promotional ladder indicates the normal progression of jobs through which advancement takes place. These ladders usually consist of related jobs requiring similar but increasingly more advanced skills. Promotion may depend on ability, but more often on seniority.

The fourth characteristic is a relatively rigid wage structure, which does not respond or change much in relation to changes in outside conditions like unemployment and shifting wage rates. Internal consistency in the wage structure is therefore considered more important than external consistency.

Rationale for Internal Labor Markets There are three factors primarily responsible for the development and structure of internal labor markets:

---

[8] Lloyd Reynolds (1951) and John Dunlop (1957) also developed early models of internal labor markets.

(1) skill specificity, (2) on-the-job training, and (3) customary law. The first of these, skill specificity, is related to the concept of specific training developed in human capital theory by Gary Becker (see Chapter 6). Specific training is defined as training that increases the productivity of a worker in a particular firm but which would not be useful in other firms. General training increases the marginal productivity of the worker by the same amount in the firm providing the training as in other firms. For Doeringer and Piore, on the other hand, the terms "specific" and "general" refer to skills and, in particular, to the frequency with which various skills can be used within different internal markets. A completely specific skill is one which is used within a single job classification in a single enterprise; a completely general skill is one which is required for every job in every company.

Skill specificity increases the proportion of training costs borne by the employer, as opposed to the worker. The reason for this is that as skills become more specific, it becomes increasingly difficult for the worker to use these skills in other employments. As a result, the worker has less incentive to invest in such training, and an increasingly higher proportion of the training cost will be borne by the employer, the more specific the skill (see Gary Becker's argument for specific training in Chapter 6). A second implication is that skill specificity increases the absolute costs of such training. The reason is that the less often a particular skill is used in the labor market, the less frequently workers are trained in that skill and, as a result, economies of scale in such training cannot be obtained. Both of these effects enhance the importance of a stable work force and give the employer an incentive to reduce worker turnover.

The second factor is the need for on-the-job-training. In the human capital literature, on-the-job training is viewed primarily as an extension of formal education with the major difference that the location of the investment in human capital is shifted to the workplace. In contrast, Doeringer and Piore emphasize the process of training, which they regard as very different from formal schooling. They find that the vast majority of blue-collar job skills are acquired on the job. Learning to operate a piece of equipment, for example, requires demonstration from fellow workers. A new employee in a repair or maintenance team will typically learn the job by serving as an assistant to a more experienced worker. Almost all on-the-job training in a plant is informal. The "instructor" is usually the foreman or an experienced workman. Participants in the training process thus spend part of their time in training and the rest in the production process.

The informal nature of on-the-job training is closely related to skill specificity. Such specificity leads to this type of training, since the number of trainees for a particular job is typically small. Also, since skill specificity often takes the form of unrecorded knowledge, the transmission of such skills must come from those already working on the job, who are in possession of the required knowledge. Training also has an effect on skill specificity. On-the-job training makes possible increasing specificity in skills and further specialization in tasks. Skills can also change over time as they are passed from one worker to the next. Such a process leads to innovations and greater productivity. In addition, machine operators and maintenance staff often modify equipment on their own without written record, and this knowledge can be passed on to new employees by informal training.

The third factor leading to the formation of internal labor markets is custom. Custom is an unwritten set of workplace rules based primarily on past practice or precedent. These rules can govern a variety of aspects of the work relationship. Such customary practices grow out of a stable work force in an internal labor market. Stable employment leads to the formation of social groups or communities in the work place, and this, in turn, leads to the development of unwritten behavioral rules governing the interaction of members of the group. These boost morale and impart a stabilizing influence to workplace rules and, in particular, to those affecting wage and employment policy. One result is that such internal allocation rules create a fairly rigid wage structure in the internal market, and this wage structure is unresponsive to pressures from the external labor market.

The development of internal labor markets provides economic benefits to both the employees and the employer. Workers benefit from increased job and wage security and the likelihood of promotion. Because employers must invest resources in workers for the acquisition of specific skills, employers are reluctant to discharge workers and lose their investment. In addition, customary rules and work practices guarantee workers a considerable degree of job security and certainty in wage setting and help to maintain a relatively stable wage structure over time. Internal labor markets also have well established paths for advancement. Movement up such promotional ladders is often based on seniority, which increases the prospects of advancement with age. A secondary benefit of internal labor markets is that they provide equity and due process for employees. These increase morale and minimize grievances.

The employer also benefits from the existence of internal labor markets. The major advantage is the reduction in worker turnover. Because of skill specificity, the training costs borne by the employer are substantial. Reducing turnover thus lowers overall training costs.

Employers reduce turnover by making job security and advancement depend on the worker's length of service. (For example, layoffs are usually done in reverse order of seniority.) Employers typically assign their most senior employees to those positions which have the most turnover cost. Also, this system provides an incentive for workers to train new employees, since there is no fear that the new workers will replace the established ones.

Internal labor markets, as a result, provide job security to workers and stability to employers. Insofar as such a system leads to reduced training and associated turnover costs, it lowers the cost of production and leads to efficiencies. However, this system can also lead to inefficiencies. This is particularly so when promotion chains come to be viewed as customary by employees and hence equitable. Promotion can then become based strictly on seniority, not ability, which tends to reduce efficiency. Another consequence is that employees may resist the introduction of new technology, since this tends to upset previously established work rules.

Internal labor markets also preserve a relatively rigid wage structure. This is so because any wage structure which exists for a period of time begins to take on a customary status. Such a wage structure is looked upon as normal and equitable by the workers. Any attempt to change the overall wage structure may therefore reduce worker morale or generate opposition in the form of strikes. Thus, short-run cost savings that employers can receive by hiring cheap "outside" labor may be far outweighed by the costs associated with a loss of worker morale.

Doeringer and Piore argue that the internal consistency of wages far outweighs their relation to the external labor market. Even at the entry ports, maintaining a regular relation between these wage rates and others in the internal structure receives a higher priority than responding to changing supply conditions of labor. Thus, even if a surplus of car mechanics develops in the external labor market, the entry wage for mechanics will not go down but will maintain its customary relation to other wages in the internal structure.

Internal markets thus help keep wage inequality low. The breakdown of internal labor markets that seems to have occurred since the late 1970s may be one factor explaining rising earnings inequality over this period. We will return to this point in Section 8.3.

The Dual Labor Market Model

Dual and segmented labor market theory may be said to date back to the work of John Stuart Mill (1848). He argued that there existed "noncompeting groups" within the labor market, which accounted for the persistence of wage differentials over long periods of time between industries, among occupations, and among firms within the same industry. These noncompeting groups were formed as the result of certain exogenous forces which erected barriers between various groups of workers in the labor force and prevented the long-run equalizing tendencies of the market place to occur over time. This caused mobility of labor between these segments of the labor force to be so limited that wage differences could remain over long stretches of time.

This theory was resurrected in the 1960s. One version, the dual labor market model, was developed by Doeringer and Piore (1971). They defined the primary market by four characteristics: First, wages and fringe benefits are high. Second, working conditions are safe and clean. Third, employment is stable, and there are considerable opportunities for promotion. Fourth, there is equity in pay scales, due process in work rules, and channels available for grievances. These conditions characterize the internal labor market described above.

The secondary market is characterized by opposite traits. First, wages are low and fringe benefits almost nonexistent. Second, secondary jobs generally have poor working conditions. Third, there is relatively little job security and hence high turnover in secondary employment. Fourth, advancement opportunities are limited. Fifth, work rules are generally arbitrary and supervision can be autocratic. One example of secondary labor markets is the hiring hall for temporary labor found in urban areas. The work is unskilled; hiring is done on a first-come, first-served basis; and no assurance of continued employment is made. Other examples are janitorial jobs in large companies, menial jobs in the health industry, stitching jobs in the clothing industry, laboring jobs in construction or steel, wood yard work in paper mills, temporary packaging jobs in manufacturing, dishwashing, domestic work, and seasonal agricultural jobs such as fruit picking.

Rationale for a Secondary Labor Market We have seen why an internal labor market might be advantageous to both employee and employer alike. Why would a secondary labor market be beneficial? Some employees prefer unstable employment. One example is the working mother whose primary concern is her family and whose earnings go to supplement those of her husband. Many mothers expect to work for only short periods of time, either until another child is born or some purchase, like a car, can be made. For them, jobs which tolerate absenteeism or lateness may be quite desirable. Students are a second example. Their principal activity is school and they usually seek part-time, temporary, or summer employment. A third example is individuals who take on second jobs (i.e., "moonlight") in order to supplement their primary income.

From the employer viewpoint, the main advantage of secondary jobs is that they require little training. As a result, there is no incentive for the employer to build up a stable work force for these jobs, and the employer is willing to trade off high turnover for low wages. Since little employer investment in training is required, the costs of turnover are relatively small. This is further reinforced by the fact that secondary jobs rarely carry termination benefits such as severance pay or unemployment insurance. Firms often view secondary jobs as an alternative to subcontracting. Instead of adjusting output to the temporary vicissitudes of demand by subcontracting out part of the work, the firm can adjust by expanding and contracting its secondary work force.

The Makeup and Consequences of the Secondary Labor Market Doeringer and Piore identified four segments of the secondary labor force. The first are adults with stable but low-wage work experience. A large percentage of black workers are in this group, particularly black females, as well as Hispanics and recent immigrants. The second are teenagers with relatively little work experience. Urban black teenagers are particularly overrepresented in this group. The third are adults who, for health or other reasons, have a long history of job loss and absenteeism. The fourth consists of groups who face well-defined barriers to long-term stable employment. Besides mothers with young children, students working part-time, and second job holders are the elderly, alcoholics and addicts, those who are poorly educated or illiterate, the disabled, and welfare recipients.

Though students and mothers with young children are in the secondary labor force temporarily and will eventually enter the primary work force, the other groups often remain trapped in the secondary work force. This entrapment may come about from race or gender discrimination, an unstable prior work history, the lack of appropriate educational credentials, a criminal record, and so on. Once in the secondary job market, secondary employment can become a self-perpetuating phenomenon. Secondary jobs tend to be short-lived, and the secondary work force experiences high turnover. Secondary employment tends to be unpleasant so that these workers develop a "bad" attitude about work. Due to the poor prospects for advancement, there is little incentive for developing a good work record and little opportunity for upgrading skills. Because of an unstable employment history, poor work habits, and the lack of skills, a secondary worker is unable to obtain employment in the primary labor market. This **feed-back cycle** then becomes a vicious circle, where employers have little incentive to train these workers and these workers see little to be gained by training since their job prospects are so poor. Once in secondary employment, it becomes very difficult to pull out. From the viewpoint of dual labor market theory, this vicious cycle is the principal problem of the working poor.

An Extension of the Dual Labor Market Model

One interesting invariant was developed by Michael Reich, David Gordon, and Richard Edwards (1973), who divide the primary segment into "subordinate" and "independent" jobs. The former are fairly routinized positions like factory and office jobs. The latter are positions which require creative or problem-solving talents and are typically professional jobs.

Reich, Gordon, and Edwards argued that labor market segmentation arose out of a historical process in which economic and social forces encouraged the segregation of the labor market into distinct components, each with its own labor market characteristics and behavioral roles. Segmentation developed during the transition from competitive to monopoly capitalism in the 1890s and the first decade of the twentieth century. The same two decades saw the development of the large oligopolistic corporations that still dominate the American economy today. These corporations felt threatened by the increasing militancy of the labor force. They argued that these large companies "actively and consciously fostered labor market segmentation in order to 'divide and conquer' the labor force." In addition, the competitive efforts of large companies to increase their market share led to a dichotomization of the industrial structure which reinforced the segmentation of the labor force.

The new form of organization taken by these large corporations consisted of bureaucratic control. Whole new structures of stratified jobs were introduced, with a clearly delineated hierarchy of positions. Power and control were exercised from the top of the hierarchy down through the ranks. Within the global corporation, internal labor markets were carved out in various pockets. Unions were often given authority to allocate jobs in selected internal labor markets in order to soften union resistance to this new form of organization. Ethnic and racial lines were often employed to separate groups of workers into different internal labor markets. More recently, education credentials were introduced to separate workers into different sectors of the job structure—particularly between blue-collar and white-collar jobs. These strategies were all conscious attempts on the part of the management of the large corporations to divide and segment the labor force.

Concomitant with these developments within the large corporation was the growing bifurcation in industrial structure. Giant corporations grew to occupy the monopolistic core of the American economy. These large corporations were highly capital-intensive and functioned effectively only when there was stable demand. On the periphery developed a competitive fringe of firms. These firms were typically small and had low capital intensity. Their function was to absorb fluctuations in demand which the large corporations could not. When demand rose rapidly, the large companies would subcontract out part of the work to the smaller firms, and during periods of contraction, the small firms would absorb most of the reduced demand.

The stable work environment of the monopoly core thus developed into the primary labor market. The instability that characterized the competitive fringe helped create the secondary labor market (see also Gordon, 1972, for a fuller discussion).

Paul Osterman (1975) provided empirical support for the Reich, Gordon, and Edwards model. Osterman classified occupations into three segments: (1) primary sector consisting of upper-tier jobs in which the employee had a great degree of autonomy and personal participation in the work process, (2) primary sector consisting of lower-tier jobs in which the employee had relatively little autonomy or participation in the work process, and (3) secondary sector.

Osterman drew a sample of workers for each segment from the 1967 Survey of Economic Opportunity. His main interest was to ascertain whether the determinants of earnings were the same or different in each of the three segments. Human capital earnings functions were used: individual earnings were regressed on schooling, age, the square of age, race, weeks worked, hours worked per week, and industry dummy variables. Osterman found that human capital characteristics explained the variation of earnings very well for the upper tier of the primary segment ($R^2 = 0.48$), moderately well for the lower tier of the primary segment ($R^2 = 0.25$), but not at all for secondary workers. For the secondary segment, only the amount of time worked was found to be a statistically significant determinant of earnings. The implication is that there are very significant differences in the factors which determine earnings within these three segments, and this result, in turn, supports the existence of distinct labor market segments.

Later studies, using more recent data, continued to provide strong empirical confirmation for the existence of distinct labor market segments, including Russel Rumberger and Martin Carnoy (1980) and William Dickens and Kevin Lang (1985). Dickens and Lang also find that in the primary labor market, the wage profile is similar to that predicted by human capital theory, whereas in the secondary market, the wage profile is almost completely flat—that is, wages are almost completely independent of schooling and experience. They also find support for the hypothesis that there exist noneconomic barriers that prevent minorities from entering the primary labor segment.

An Evaluation of Labor Market Segmentation

One problem in evaluating segmented labor market theory is that different versions use different principles with which to define segments. Some economists focused on the characteristics of the job—employment stability (Piore) or control over working time (Gordon), for example. Others classified workers by occupations and look at occupational characteristics (Osterman). Others looked at divisions by industry—for example, large corporations versus small competitive firms (Reich, Gordon, and Edwards). Piore emphasized differences in technology as the basis of segmentation—large capital-intensive production processes which require long production runs versus small labor-intensive production processes which arc adaptable to short production runs. Others attempted to combine both industrial and occupational characteristics as the basis of segmentation (Rumberger and Carnoy, 1980). Still others look to the existence of workers with loose labor market attachment as the basis of classifying secondary workers (Bluestone, 1970, Wachtel and Betsey, 1972, and Wachter, 1972).[9]

Traditional economists often ask whether there are really distinct "segments" in the labor market or a continuum of job characteristics which differ among a spectrum of jobs. They also question whether the barriers which are posted between segments are, in fact, permanent or temporary. Along this line, Glen Cain (1975, 1976) argued that segmented labor market theory can be viewed as a discussion of imperfections and temporary disequilibria in a neoclassical framework. Cain raised a number of "challenges" to dual labor market theory. First, is there really very little mobility of workers between segments of the labor market? If not, then dual labor market theory should be seriously questioned. Second, is labor market discrimination really a conscious attempt by employers to "divide and conquer" the work force by creating artificial divisions? Cain felt that prelabor market discrimination, due to segregated housing and schools and cultural

---

[9]Another view is provided by Bulow and Summers (1986), who view segmentation as deriving from the employer's need to motivate workers. They argued that firms are willing to pay primary workers a wage premium in order to elicit effort. See the next chapter for more discussion in the context of efficiency wage theory.

differences, is a sounder explanation of occupational and wage differences between races and genders.

Third, Cain called into question the notion that unemployment and instability are intrinsic to certain (secondary) jobs. Rather, he argued that these phenomena can be more adequately explained by neoclassical theories of job search. Fourth, wage rigidities and protected labor markets can be easily interpreted within the neoclassical framework as market imperfections. In the long run, economic forces should erode such artificial barriers between labor market segments and make internal labor market wages more responsive to external labor market conditions.

Despite the interpretation that labor market segments represent market imperfections, the point remains that there exist *qualitative* differences in the characteristics of jobs in the American labor market. There are "good" jobs on the top and "bad" jobs on the bottom of the job ladder. The econometric evidence supports the existence of fundamental differences in factors which determine wages in the primary and secondary labor market segments. One can, of course, argue about the exact position of the line that separates the two segments, but this problem characterizes most classification systems in economics.

8.3 SUMMARY

Unions and labor market segmentation both play an important role in wage determination. With regard to unionization, four general conclusions can be drawn. First, there is some disparity about the relative wage effects of particular unions in different industries and trades. Union workers tend to earn to earn 15 to 25 percent more than nonunion employees, after controlling for other worker characteristics. Second, the union wage advantage has changed over time. It was high during the 1950s and 1960s but low during the 1970s.

Third, the relative wage effects of unions do tend to vary among individual industries and crafts according to Marshall's rules. The largest effect occurs in the construction trades, of the order of 30 to 40 percent, where, because of the specialized skills involved, the demand curve for union labor is inelastic. Among operatives and laborers, the union effect is in the order of 15 to 20 percent. The union effect in heavy manufacturing is smaller than in construction. In competitive industries such as clothing, unions have very little effect on relative wages. Fourth, unionization tends to reduce overall earnings inequality, though the effect is relatively small.

Has the decline of unionism in the United States been one factor responsible for declining real wages and rising earnings inequality over the last two decades? Time-series evidence for the United States does not appear to support this argument. Real wages have been falling since 1973, while union membership as a proportion of the labor force peaked in 1954 and has been going down ever since. Moreover, unionism's decline predated the rise in earnings inequality since the mid-1970s. Still, two studies, Richard

Freeman (1991) and David Card (1992), using time-series data for the United States, surmised that about one-fifth of the increase in wage inequality among male workers in the 1980s was attributable to declines in unionism, particularly among lower wage workers.

Several studies which examined international differences in earnings inequality among industrialized countries have concluded that the degree of unionization plays a major role. Freeman (1991) found that industrial wages in the 1980s were more dispersed in countries that were less heavily unionized and that between 1978 and 1987, the change in inequality was negatively correlated with the initial level of unionization. Maury Gittleman and Edward Wolff (1993) also reported that those countries with low levels of unionization were the ones that experienced the greatest increase in industry wage inequality. Francine Blau and Lawrence Kahn (1994) concluded that the lower level of overall wage inequality among male workers found in other OECD countries in comparison to the United States in the 1980s was due, in part, to their greater degree of unionization and to their use of centralized systems of collective bargaining which extend the terms of union contracts to nonunion workers.

Another important source of earnings differences among workers is found to lie in the existence of relatively distinct labor market segments. Workers employed in the primary labor market enjoy high wages, good fringe benefits, stable employment and advancement possibilities, good working conditions, and due process in work rules. The secondary market is characterized by low wages and almost nonexistent fringe benefits, little job security and high turnover, limited advancement opportunities, poor working conditions, and arbitrary work rules. In the primary labor market, the wage profile is similar to that predicted by human capital theory, with earnings higher for more educated workers and increasing over time with experience. In the secondary market, wages show little gain from increased schooling or experience. There is also evidence that there exist both economic and noneconomic barriers that prevent secondary workers from entering the primary labor segment.

Many secondary workers often remain trapped in the secondary work force throughout their work-lives. Secondary jobs tend to be short-lived, and therefore the secondary work force experiences high turnover. Because the prospects for advancement are limited, there is little incentive or opportunity for upgrading skills. Because of an unstable employment pattern and the lack of skills, a secondary worker is unable to obtain employment in the primary labor market. This cycle becomes a vicious circle, where employers have little incentive to train secondary workers and these workers have little motivation for training. As a result, many of these workers are unable to escape the secondary labor market.

The breakdown of internal labor markets and the rise in secondary employment that seem to have occurred since the late 1970s may be other factors explaining rising earnings inequality over this period. Internal markets, by standardizing wage differentials among different classes of labor, help keep wage differences low. Wage inequality may be positively related to the proportion of secondary workers in total employment, since these are generally the lowest paid members in the labor force.

Though there is no hard statistical evidence on this issue, anecdotal evidence seems to suggest that the industrial restructuring of the 1980s—particularly, the "downsizing" of the core manufacturing industries—may have reduced the scope of internal labor markets. Moreover, the number of so-called contingent workers—those who work part-time or part-year—has risen as a share of total employment, from 14 percent in 1979 to 18 percent in 1994.[10] Though contingent workers are not identical with secondary employees, there is likely to be considerable overlap between the two groups. Circumstantial evidence thus seems to suggest that the primary labor market is shrinking and the secondary labor market is correspondingly rising.

REFERENCES AND BIBLIOGRAPHY

A. Unionization

Ashenfelter, Orley, "Racial Discrimination and Trade Unions," *Journal of Political Economy*, Vol. 80, May/June 1972, pp. 435–464.

Barbash, Jack, *American Unions: Structure, Government and Politics*, Random House, New York, 1967.

Bernstein, Irving, "The Growth of American Unions," *American Economic Review*, Vol. 44, No. 3, June 1954, pp. 301–318.

Blau, Francine D., and Lawrence M. Kahn, "International Differences in Male Wage Inequality: Institutions versus Market Forces," NBER Working Paper No. 4678, March 1994.

Boskin, Michael J., "Unions and Relative Real Wages," *American Economic Review*, Vol. 62, No. 3, June 1972, pp. 466–472.

Card, David, "The Effect of Unions on the Distribution of Wages: Redistribution or Relabeling?" NBER Working Paper No. 4195, October 1992.

Chamberlain, Neil W., and James W. Kuhn, *Collective Bargaining*, 2nd. ed., McGraw-Hill, New York, 1965.

Curme, Michael A., Barry T. Hirsch, and David A. Macpherson, "Union Membership and Contract Coverage in the United States, 1983–1988," *Industrial and Labor Relations Review*, Vol. 44, No. 1, October 1990.

Dickens, William T., and Jonathan S. Leonard, "Accounting for the Decline in Union Membership, 1950–1980," *Industrial and Labor Relations Review*, Vol. 38, No. 3, April 1985, pp. 323–334.

Dunlop, John T., *Wage Determination Under Trade Unions*, Macmillan Co., New York, 1944.

---

[10] The source for these figures is the *Monthly Labor Review*, statistical appendices.

Farber, Henry S., "The Analysis of Union Behavior," NBER Working Paper No. 1502, November 1984.

Flanagan, Robert J., "Wage Interdependence in Unionized Labor Markets," *Brookings Papers on Economic Activity,* 3, 1976, pp. 635–673.

Freeman, Richard, "Unionism and the Dispersion of Wages," *Industrial and Labor Relations Review,* Vol. 35, October 1980, pp. 3–23.

———, "The Effect of Trade Unionism on Fringe Benefits," *Industrial and Labor Relations Review,* Vol. 34, July 1981.

———, "Unionism Comes to the Public Sector," *Journal of Economic Literature,* Vol. 24, March 1986, pp. 41–86.

———, "Contraction and Expansion: The Divergence of Private Sector and Public Sector Unionism in the United States," *Journal of Economic Perspectives,* Vol. 2, No. 2, Spring 1988, pp. 63–88.

———, "On the Divergence of Unionism Among Developed Countries," NBER Working Paper No. 2817, January 1989.

———, "How Much Has De-Unionization Contributed to the Rise in Male Earnings Inequality?" NBER Working Paper No. 3826, August 1991.

———, and James L. Medoff, "The Impact of the Percentage Organized on Union and Nonunion Wages," *Review of Economics and Statistics,* Vol. 63, No. 4, November 1981, pp. 561–572.

———, and James L. Medoff, *What Do Unions Do?,* Basic Books, New York, 1984.

Galenson, Walter, *The CIO Challenge to the AFL,* Harvard University Press, Cambridge, Mass., 1960.

Gittleman, Maury, and Edward N. Wolff, "International Comparisons of Interindustry Wage Differentials," *Review of Income and Wealth,* Series 39, No. 3, September 1993, pp. 295–312.

Hildebrand, George H., *American Unionism: An Historical and Analytical Survey,* Addison-Wesley, Reading, Mass., 1979.

Hirsch, Barr T., and John L. Neufeld, "Nominal and Real Wage Differentials and the Effects of Industry and SMSA Density: 1973–1983," *Journal of Human Resources,* Vol. 22, No. 1, Winter 1987, pp. 138–148.

Hyclak, Thomas, "The Effect of Unions on Earnings Inequality in Local Labor Markets," *Industrial and Labor Relations Review,* Vol. 33, No. 1, October 1979, pp. 77–84.

———, "Unions and Income Inequality: Some Cross-State Evidence," *Industrial Relations,* Vol. 19, No. 2, Spring 1980, pp. 212–215.

Johnson, George E., "Economic Analysis of Trade Unionism," *American Economic Review,* Vol. 65, No. 2, May 1975, pp. 23–28.

Johnson, Harry G., and Peter Miezkowski, "The Effects of Unionizations on the Distribution of Income: A General Equilibrium Approach," *The Quarterly Journal of Economics,* Vol. 84, No. 4, November 1970, pp. 539–561.

Kahn, Lawrence M., and Michael Curme, *Review of Economics and Statistics,* Vol. 69, No. 4, November 1987, pp. 600–607.

Kerr, Clark, "Trade Unionism and Distributive Shares," *American Economic Review,* Vol. 44, No. 2, May 1954, pp. 279–292.

————, *Labor Markets and Wage Determination*, University of California Press, Berkeley, CA, 1977.

Kokkelenberg, Edward C., and Donna R. Sockell, "Union Membership in the United States, 1973–1981," *Industrial and Labor Relations Review*, Vol. 38, No. 4, July 1985.

Lewis, H. G., *Unionism and Relative Wages in the United States*, University of Chicago Press, Chicago, 1963.

————, *Union Relative Wage Effects: A Survey*, University of Chicago Press, Chicago, 1986.

Marshall, Alfred, *Principles of Economics*, 8th ed., Macmillan Co., New York, 1920.

Mellow, Wesley, "Unionism and Wages: A Longitudinal Analysis," *Review of Economics and Statistics*, Vol. 63, No. 1, February 1981, pp. 43–52.

Mitchell, Daniel J. B., *Union Wages and Inflation*, Brookings Institution, Washington, D.C., 1980.

————, "Shifting Norms in Wage Determination," *Brookings Papers on Economic Activity*, 2, 1985, pp. 575–608.

Neumann, George R., and Ellen R. Rissman, "Where Have All the Union Members Gone?" *Journal of Labor Economics*, Vol. 2, No. 2, April 1984, pp. 175–192.

Neumark, David, and Michael L. Wachter, "Union Threat Effects and Nonunion Industry Wage Differentials," mimeo, University of Pennsylvania, September 1992.

Oaxaca, Ronald, "Estimation of Union/Non-Union Differentials Within Occupational/Regional Subgroups," *Journal of Human Resources*, Vol. 10, Fall 1975, pp. 529–536.

Parsley, C. J., "Labor Union Effects on Wage Gains: A Survey of Recent Literature," *Journal of Economic Literature*, Vol. 18, March 1980, pp. 1–31.

Pencavel, John, and Catherine E. Hartsog, "A Reconsideration of the Effects of Unionism on Relative Wages and Employment in the United States, 1920–1980," NBER Working Paper No. 1316, March 1984.

Perlman, Selig, *History of Trade Unionism in the United States*, Augustus M. Kelley, New York, 1950.

Pettengill, John, *Labor Relations and the Inequality of Earned Income*, North Holland Elsevier, Amsterdam, 1979.

Plotnick, Robert, "Trends in Male Earnings Inequality," *Southern Economic Journal*, Vol. 48, No. 3, 1982, pp. 724–732.

Podursky, Michael, "Unions and Family Income Inequality," *Journal of Human Resources*, Vol. 18, No. 4, Fall 1983, pp. 574–591.

Reder, Melvin W., "The Rise and Fall of Unions: The Public Sector and the Private," *Journal of Economic Perspectives*, Vol. 2, No. 2, Spring 1988, pp. 89–110.

Rees, Albert, *The Economics of Trade Unions*, 2nd. ed., University of Chicago Press, Chicago, 1977.

Shapiro, David, "Relative Wage Effects of Unions in the Public and Private Sectors," *Industrial Labor Relations Review,* January 1978, Vol. 31, No. 2, pp. 193–204.

Slichter, Sumner H., James J. Healy, and E. Robert Livernash, *The Impact of Collective Bargaining on Management,* The Brookings Institution, Washington, D.C., 1960.

Stafford, Frank, "Concentration and Labor Earnings: Comment," *American Economic Review,* Vol. 58, March 1968, pp. 174–181.

Taft, Philip, *Organized Labor in American History,* Harper & Row, New York, 1960.

Throop, Adrian, "The Union-Nonunion Wage Differential and Cost-Push Inflation," *American Economic Review,* Vol. 58, No. 1, March 1968, pp. 79–99.

Troy, Leo, *Trade Union Membership, 1892–1962,* National Bureau of Economic Research, New York, 1965.

Ulman, Lloyd, *The Rise of National Trade Unions,* Harvard University Press, Cambridge, Mass., 1955.

U.S. Bureau of Labor Statistics, *Handbook of Labor Statistics, 1978,* Bulletin No. 2000, Government Printing Office, Washington, D.C., June 1979.

U.S. Bureau of Labor Statistics, *Employment and Earnings,* U.S. Government Printing Office, Washington, D.C., January 1985.

U.S. Bureau of Labor Statistics, *Employment and Earnings,* U.S. Government Printing Office, Washington, D.C., January 1990.

U.S. Bureau of the Census, *U.S. Census of the Population: 1950,* Vol. IV, Special Reports Part I, Chapter C, Occupation by Industry, U.S. Government Printing Office, Washington, D.C., 1954.

U.S. Bureau of the Census, *U.S. Census of the Population: 1960,* Subject Reports "Occupation by Industry," Final Report PC(2)-72, U.S. Government Printing Office, Washington, D.C., 1963.

U.S. Department of Commerce, *Statistical Abstract of the United States, 1994,* U.S. Government Printing Office, Washington, D.C., September 1994.

Weiss, Leonard, "Concentration and Labor Earnings," *American Economic Review,* Vol. 56, March 1966, pp. 96–117.

Wolman, Leo, *Ebb and Flow in Trade Unionism,* National Bureau of Economic Research, New York, 1936.

B. Segmented and Internal Labor Market Theory

Alexander, Arthur J., "Income, Experience, and the Structure of Internal Labor Markets," *Quarterly Journal of Economics,* Vol. 88, No. 350, February 1974, pp. 63–85.

Bluestone, Barry, "The Tripartite Economy: Labor Markets and the Working Poor," *Poverty and Human Resources,* July-August 1970, pp. 15–35.

Bulow, Jeremy I., and Lawrence H. Summers, "A Theory of Dual Labor Markets with Application to Industrial Policy, Discrimination, and Keynesian Unemployment," *Journal of Labor Economics,* Vol. 4, 1986, pp. 376–414.

Cain, Glen, "The Challenge of Dual and Radical Theories of the Labor Market to Orthodox Theory," *American Economic Review,* Vol. 65, No. 2, May 1975, pp. 16–22.

———, "The Challenge of Segmented Labor Market Theories to Orthodox Theory," *Journal of Economic Literature,* Vol. 14, No. 4, December 1976, pp. 1215–1257.

Dickens, William T., and Kevin Lang, "A Test of Dual Labor Market Theory," *American Economic Review,* Vol. 75, No. 4, September 1985, pp. 792–805.

——— and ———, "The Reemergence of Segmented Labor Market Theory," *American Economic Review Papers and Proceedings,* Vol. 78, No. 2, May 1988, pp. 129–134.

Doeringer, Peter B., "Determinants of the Structure of Industrial-Type Internal Labor Markets," *Industrial and Labor Relations Review,* 1967.

———, and Michael J. Piore, *Internal Labor Markets and Manpower Analysis,* D.C. Heath and Company, Lexington, Mass., 1971.

Dunlop, John T., "Wage Contours," in George W. Taylor and Frank C. Pierson (eds.), *New Concepts of Wages Determination,* McGraw-Hill, Inc., New York, 1957.

Elbaum, Bernard, "The Internalization of Labor Markets: Causes and Consequences," *American Economic Review,* Vol. 73, No. 2, May 1983, pp. 260–265.

Gordon, David, *Theories of Poverty and Underemployment,* D.C. Heath, Lexington, Mass., 1972.

Kerr, Clark, "The Balkinization of Labor Markets," in E. Wight Bakke (ed.), *Labor Mobility and Economic Opportunity,* MIT Press, Cambridge, MA, 1954.

Manwaring, Tom, "The Extended Internal Labour Market," *Cambridge Journal of Economics,* Vol. 8, No. 2, June 1984, pp. 161–187.

Mill, John Stuart, *Principles of Political Economy,* Vol. I, Revised Edition, The Colonial Press, New York, (1848) 1900.

Nickell, S. J., "Wage Structures and Quit Rates," *International Economic Review,* Vol. 17, No. 1, February 1976, pp. 191–203.

Osterman, Paul, "An Empirical Study of Labor Market Segmentation," *Industrial and Labor Relations Review,* Vol. 28, No. 4, July 1975, pp. 508–523.

——— (ed.), *Internal Labor Markets,* MIT Press, Cambridge, MA, 1984.

Piore, Michael J., "The Impact of the Labor Market Upon the Design and Selection of Productive Techniques Within the Manufacturing Plant," *Quarterly Journal of Economics,* Vol. 82, No. 4, November 1968, pp. 602–620.

———, "On-the-Job Training and Adjustments to Technological Change," *Journal of Human Resources,* Fall 1968.

———, "On-the-Job Training in a Dual Labor Market," in Arnold R. Weber *et al.* (eds.), *Public-Private Manpower Policies,* Industrial Relations Research Association, Madison, Wisc., 1969.

———, "Fragments of a 'Sociological' Theory of Wages," *American Economic Review,* Vol. 63, No. 2, May 1973, pp. 377–384.

———, "Notes for a Theory of Labor Market Stratification" in Richard C. Edwards, Michael Reich, and David Gordon (eds.), *Labor Market Segmentation,* D.C. Heath & Co., Lexington, Mass., 1975.

———, "Labor Market Segmentation: To What Paradigm Does It Belong?" *American Economic Review,* Vol. 73, No. 2, May 1983, pp. 249–253.

Reich, Michael, David M. Gordon, and Richard C. Edwards, "A Theory of Labor Market Segmentation," *American Economic Review,* Vol. 63, No. 2, May 1973, pp. 359–365.

———, "Segmented Labour: Time Series Hypothesis and Evidence," *Cambridge Journal of Economics,* Vol. 8, No. 1, March 1984, pp. 63–81.

Reynolds, Lloyd, *The Structure of Labor Markets: Wages and Labor Mobility in Theory and Practice,* Greenwood Press, Westport, Conn., 1951.

Rumberger, Russel W., and Martin Carnoy, "Segmentation in the U.S. Labour Market: Its Effects on the Mobility and Earnings of Whites and Blacks," *Cambridge Journal of Economics,* Vol. 4, 1980, pp. 117–132.

Vietorisz, Thomas, and Bennett Harrison, "Labor Market Segmentation: Positive Feedback and Divergent Development," *American Economic Review,* Vol. 63, No. 2, May 1973, pp. 366–376.

Wachtel, Howard M., and Charles Betsey, "Employment at Low Wages," *Review of Economics and Statistics,* Vol. 54, No. 2, May 1972, pp. 121–129.

Wachter, Michael L., "A Labor Supply Model for Secondary Workers," *Review of Economics and Statistics,* Vol. 54, No. 2, May 1972, pp. 141–151.

Williamson, Oliver E., "The Internal Labor Market: An Alternative Interpretation," *Markets and Hierarchies: Analysis and Antitrust Implications,* The Free Press, New York, 1971.

DISCUSSION QUESTIONS

1. Explain how the elasticity of demand for labor in a particular industry affects the potential strength of a union in that industry.
2. Discuss how unions affect the union-nonunion wage differential through their impact on the labor supply. How does the so-called "threat effect" affect the union-nonunion wage differential?
3. Briefly discuss Alfred Marshall's "Four Rules" with regard to the factors that influence the strength of unions. How are these rules related to actual union-nonunion wage differential observed in the American economy by industry?
4. Discuss three reasons why the unionization rate has declined in the United States since the early 1950s.
5. Explain why internal labor markets might help to maintain a low level of wage inequality.

9

STRUCTURAL MODELS OF EARNINGS INEQUALITY

Structural models emphasize the effects of industrial composition, occupational mix, technology, regional characteristics, market structure, plant size, per capita income, and other institutional characteristics on earnings. They assume that the overall distribution of earnings is determined primarily by the job structure of an economy. Changes in the inequality of earnings occur chiefly when the job structure changes.

It is helpful to contrast structural models with human capital theory. In the latter, the distribution of earnings is determined by the distribution of human capital—that is, of schooling, experience, and ability. These are all characteristics of the supply of labor. Changes in supply characteristics of labor are held to be responsible for changes in the overall distribution of earnings. In contrast, structural theories stress the demand for labor. Changes in structural characteristics, such as the industrial mix of a region, affect the demand for labor. For example, a shift in consumer demand toward medical care and away from housing will affect the overall job structure (more doctors and nurses and fewer carpenters, plumbers, and electricians) and therefore the distribution of labor earnings. A secondary theme is that human capital factors such as schooling and experience have less bearing on the overall distribution of income. Empirical research in this vein often considers the relative importance of structural characteristics and human capital factors in explaining the distribution of earnings.

The simplest type of structural model is the fixed coefficient manpower model. It is assumed that each industry has a characteristic technology, which determines the industry's job structure—that is, the number of workers of different types necessary to produce a unit of output. For example, manufacturing the Boeing 747 requires so many aeronautical engineers, welders, machinists, electricians, mechanics, and so on. Furthermore, it is assumed that the occupational mix in each industry is constant (fixed) over time and that the relative wage rates paid to each occupation are also fixed. The overall distribution of earnings then becomes completely determined by the mix of industries in the economy. As the pattern of demand shifts over time, so will the industrial composition of the economy and, consequently, so will the overall occupational skill mix. In this model, the distribution of labor earnings becomes an exclusive function of the composition of output. This example represents the extreme form of the structural model. Other models allow for effects of changing labor supply on earnings.[1]

Structural elements permeate the internal labor market model. In the internal labor market, jobs within large organizations have well-defined entry ports, promotional ladders, and exit points. These structures are largely due to the kinds of technology in use and customary rules. The need for specific skills in an organization and the resulting requirements for on-the-job training lead to the formation of rigid job ladders and wage scales. This is reinforced by custom, since, once this structure is in place for a time, workers are apt to resist attempts to change it.

The formation of dual labor markets is also viewed as the outcome of structural forces. The 1890s saw the structure of many industries becoming characterized by a dichotomization of firms. In the core were large corporations with a clearly delineated hierarchy of jobs, high-capital intensity, and long production runs. On the periphery developed a competitive fringe of small firms, characterized by low-capital intensity, short production runs, and a relatively unstructured job hierarchy. The duality of the job market developed as a result of differences in technology between the large monopolistic firms and the small competitive ones.

Section 9.1 discusses the effects of industrial structure on earnings inequality. Several approaches are investigated, including the role of agricultural and service employment in the variation of income among states in the United States. There are significant and persistent industry differences in the wages paid even for the same kind of work. Section 9.2 explores some of the factors that play a role, including differences in industry productivity, market power, profitability, and firm size. A more recent approach, efficiency wage theory, offers the rationale that paying higher wages helps to raise a firm's profitability. Section 9.3 treats a related concern, the pattern of occupational wages over time. Studies have emphasized the influence of increasing education and technological change on changes in occupational skill differentials.

---

[1] Richard Freeman (1980) found that the fixed-coefficient model predicted employment by occupation relatively well, accounting for about 45 percent of the change in employment by occupation between 1960 and 1970 at a detailed 3-digit occupational level (about 300 occupations).

The last section of the chapter considers the implications of structural change for rising earnings inequality in the United States since the mid-1970s. Three factors are relevant. The first is the continuing shift of employment shares from goods-producing industries, particularly manufacturing, to services. The second factor is a substantial widening of industry wage differentials since the 1970s. The third is a similar trend in occupational earnings, whose dispersions have also risen over the last two decades.

9.1 INDUSTRIAL STRUCTURE AND WAGE INEQUALITY

State and Regional Differences in Inequality

Several studies have analyzed the effects of industrial composition on regional earnings. The models used in these studies generally assume that industries differ in average wages. If employment in a region is concentrated in a few industries, then wage dispersion will generally be low. If it is spread out over many industries, then inequality will typically be high. The greater the mix of industries with different wage levels, the greater will be the dispersion of income in a region. One special case occurs when there is a sector, such as agriculture, which pays low wages. Then, income inequality will be greater in regions in which the proportion of the labor force employed in agriculture is greater.[2] The same argument applies for a high-wage sector such as finance.

The early studies on this topic were particularly focused on agricultural employment, since its share of total employment fell rapidly, from 14 to 5 percent between 1950 and 1970. Ahmed Al-Samarrie and Herman Miller (1967) used five explanatory variables in their analysis: (1) the relative importance of agriculture in the state's economy measured by the proportion of the state's income originating in agriculture, (2) the percent of property income in the total personal income of the state, (3) the median years of schooling of the adult population, (4) the percent of nonwhites in the state's population, and (5) the extent of labor force participation in the state measured by the percent of the civilian population employed. A multiple regression was used. The data sources were the 1950 and 1960 Censuses of Population. For each year, over 80 percent of the state-to-state variation in income inequality was explained by these variables (that is, the R^2 exceeded 0.8).

The proportion of nonwhites in the population was the most important variable in the regression and had a positive relation to inequality.[3] The second most important variable was the percent of income originating in agri-

---

[2]That is to say, as long as agriculture accounts for less than half of the total employment. Technically speaking, the degree of income inequality is a quadratic function of the percent employed in agriculture, first rising and then falling.

[3]The degree of importance was measured by the beta coefficient, defined as the product of the regression coefficient and the standard deviation of the independent variable divided by the standard deviation of the dependent variable.

culture, which also had a positive effect on inequality. This variable was less important in the 1960 regression than in the 1950 one, reflecting agriculture's decline as a source of income and employment in the U.S. economy. Median years of schooling was also a significant variable, and states with higher levels of schooling tended to have lower levels of income inequality.[4] Another interesting finding was that states with a high per capita income and a high degree of industrialization had less income inequality, on average, than states with low per capita income.[5]

Joseph Newhouse (1971) reported considerable variation in income distribution by state. He developed a model to relate the income distribution within a state to its industrial mix. He assumed that an industry's wage structure was invariant across geographical regions—that is, that local labor market conditions did not affect industry wages. He indicated three reasons for this. The first reason is that the technology within an industry is probably very similar across regions. The facts that factory jobs are very specialized as to industry, that technological information is highly disseminated around the nation, and that factories typically train the local labor force it hires to meet its skill needs imply that the skill mix of an industry will be uniform throughout the country. This factor, however, is not sufficient to guarantee the same industry wage distribution across regions, which leads us to the second reason. The second reason is that there is no regional variation in pay for each job. If an industry's output is sold in a national product market, regional variations in wages will be eliminated. Firms in different regions will face the same demand curve for their product, and the marginal revenue product of workers and thus the wage will be the same in each region (see Chapter 6). The third reason is that there are many industrial unions organized by product market, and during negotiations, they try to eliminate regional differentials in wages.

The empirical application of the model relied on a combined factor analysis—multiple regression technique. The dependent variable was the proportion of income in each income class by state, and the explanatory (independent) variables were the proportions of total state employment located in each of 31 industries. Newhouse reported that 88 percent of the variation in income distribution by state was explained by differences in the industrial mix of employment.

In a 1976 paper, Donald Smith and E. James Jennings also examined the effect of the industrial composition of employment on state income inequality. Their work is particularly interesting because it covers a much longer

---

[4]It was also found that income concentration was higher in states with lower rates of labor force participation and with a higher proportion of property income in the state's income, though the latter variable was significant only in 1950.

[5]In related work, Aigner and Heins (1967) and Conlisk (1967), both using 1960 Census of Population data, also found that income inequality was lower in states with a higher mean income. This result is consistent with the Kuznets hypothesis, which maintains that in the course of normal economic development, countries are likely to experience widening economic inequality in the early stages and declining inequality in the latter stages. See Kuznets (1955) for details.

period than the other studies, 1920–1970. They computed the Gini coefficient for each state in 1920, 1950, 1960, and 1970. The model they used was somewhat different than the others we have considered. Rather than comparing the level of income inequality by state, they compared the change in the Gini coefficient over time. The change in income inequality within each state was then regressed on the (weighted) change in sectoral employment in each state. For both the 1920–1950 period and the 1950–1960 period, the change in the distribution of employment between agriculture and nonagriculture was found to be a significant determinant of the change in state income inequality. However, by 1960, agricultural employment had become quite small in the U.S. economy, but employment in the service sector was becoming increasingly important (see Chapter 5). As a consequence, they found that for the 1960–1970 period, the change in the employment mix between the service and nonservice sector was the most important determinant of changes in income inequality.

Michael Farbman (1973) investigated determinants of the degree of income concentration in the South. Using 1960 Census of Population data, he computed the Gini coefficient of income inequality for 1,156 counties in 12 southern states. His model was similar to Al-Samarrie and Miller's model, except his structural variable was the percent of the labor force employed in middle-level occupations, defined as craft, clerical, and operative (such as truck drivers) jobs. Farbman argued that the dispersion of earnings was very high both among professional and technical workers and among service and low-skilled workers. However, earnings in the middle-level occupations tended to have a relatively narrow dispersion. He found that this variable was statistically significant and the most important determinant of interregional inequality in the South.

Regional Differences in Income Levels

Significant differences exist not only in regional inequality but also in regional income levels. In the United States before 1980, average incomes were generally higher in the northern and western states than in the South.

In a 1965 study, Jeffrey Williamson developed the argument that regional income differentials tend to widen over time as a nation develops, reach a maximum, and then decline during advanced stages of development. He argued that uneven development of regions is one cause of interregional differences in average incomes. Some regions industrialize more quickly than others, and as a result, their per capita income rises faster than the income of stagnant regions. In the early stages of development, some regions will shoot rapidly ahead of others, causing large disparities in regional incomes. Eventually, through labor migration, capital migration, technological diffusion, and government policy, the backward regions will start to industrialize and their per capita income will begin to catch up with the leading regions. This is what happened during the 1970s and 1980s in the United States, when the "Sunbelt" caught up with (and, in some cases, surpassed) the "Snowbelt."

Williamson used the percentage of agricultural employees in a region as the indicator of its level of development. On the basis of regional data for seven countries (Great Britain, Austria, Sweden, Brazil, Italy, Canada, and Finland), he found that per capita income was lower in regions with higher percentages of their labor force employed in agriculture. As the backward areas industrialized, their per capita income converged on the advanced regions.

Alan Green (1969), expanding Williamson's analysis for the case of Canada, disaggregated the economy into three sectors: (1) agriculture, (2) mining and manufacturing, and (3) the service sector. In Canada the share of the labor employed in agriculture declined from 53 to 24 percent between 1890 and 1956, while the share in mining and manufacturing increased from 16 to 20 percent. However, by province there were considerable differences in both the share of employment in the three sectors and their trend over time.

He examined the provincial industry mix in Canada over the period from 1890 to 1956 to determine how much of interregional differences in per capita income could be explained by differences in industrial composition. Between 1890 and 1929, provincial differences in the sectoral mix of employment widened considerably, and this was accompanied by a widening regional income gap. Between 1929 and 1956, there was some convergence in the industrial mix among the provinces, and this was associated with a decrease in income differentials among the regions. The main conclusion was that regional differences in income levels in Canada were largely due to the increasing concentration of mining and manufacturing in a few provinces.

Another interesting study of regional income differences was conducted by Gerald Scully (1969). One of his major objectives was to explain why wage rates in the manufacturing sector were higher in the North than in the South. Using the 1958 Census of Manufactures, he found that state-to-state variation in manufacturing wages was attributable to four factors: (1) the capital-labor ratio in the industry, (2) the average schooling level of workers in the industry, (3) nonwhites as a percent of the industry's labor force, and (4) females as a percent of the industry's labor force.

He found that differences in the mean schooling level of workers and the proportion of nonwhite workers played a significant role in explaining the higher wages in the North than the South. However, the most significant factor was the difference in industry composition between the North and the South. In 1958, high-wage manufacturing industries, such as machinery, equipment, and chemicals, tended to be concentrated in the North, while low-wage manufacturing industries, such as textiles, apparel, and lumber tended to be concentrated in the South. This study also confirmed the importance of differences in industrial mix in accounting for wage differences between regions.

Eric Hanushek (1973) also investigated interregional differences in earnings. He was particularly concerned with the relative importance of structural versus human capital factors in the determination of regional earnings. He used a 1969 sample of males who had taken the Armed Forces Qualification Test (AFQT). He estimated a human capital earnings function, where the logarithm of earnings was regressed on years of schooling, years of experience, and ability (as measured by the AFQT). He computed separate earnings functions for 150 distinct regions. He found that the rate of return to human capital varied considerably by region.

He then considered to what degree differences in the mean earnings in each of these areas were due to differences in the average amount of human capital (as measured by years of schooling, years of experience, and ability) and to differences in the rate of return to human capital among regions. His main result was that 80 percent of the interregional variation in earnings was attributable to differences in returns to human capital but less than 6 percent could be attributed to differences in human capital.

What causes differences in the return to human capital? He speculated that these differentials were largely due to differences in the industrial structure of a region. The industrial makeup of an area will determine its available employment opportunities, and this, in conjunction with the supply of human capital in the region, will determine the measured returns to human capital.

In a follow-up article, Hanushek (1981) used 1970 Census of Population data to estimate earnings functions for 341 regions of the country. As in the earlier paper, he found significant differences in regional earnings functions—both in the level and the shape of the earnings profile. Hanushek then used regression analysis to relate regional differences in earnings functions to structural differences in local labor markets, particularly differences in industrial mix and labor productivity. He used the proportion of the local work force employed in manufacturing, construction, and government to measure industrial composition. His major finding was that regional variation in industrial makeup was significant in explaining differences in regional earnings functions.[6]

Industrial Composition and Rising Earnings Inequality of the 1980s

The sharp rise in earnings inequality during the 1980s and the continuing shift of employment out of goods-producing industries and into services rekindled interest in the effect of industrial composition on income distribution. As reported in Table 5.4 of Chapter 5, the proportion of workers employed in industry fell from 43 percent in 1970 to 28 percent in 1993, and correspondingly, the share in services rose from 57 to 72 percent.

---

[6] He also found that differences in the local cost of living and the local unemployment rate were statistically significant.

McKinley Blackburn, David Bloom, and Richard Freeman (1990) were among the first investigators to argue that interindustry employment shifts played a major role in explaining the rising return to education during the 1980s (which we noted in Chapter 7). Using a decomposition analysis, they analyzed the effect of changes in employment patterns for 43 (two-digit) industries over the period 1979 to 1987 on the demand for workers of different educational levels. They calculated that about one-quarter to one-third of the rise in the premium associated with a college education could be attributed to shifts in employment by industry. A similar finding was reported by John Bound and George Johnson (1992) on the basis of 17 industries for the period 1979 to 1988.

Lawrence Katz and Kevin Murphy (1992) concluded that interindustry employment shifts played a major role in rising inequality. Between 1967 and 1987, industries which depended most heavily on college-educated manpower, such as professional, medical, and business services, finance, insurance, and real estate, and education and welfare, had the largest relative increases of employment. Those industries that relied primarily on less educated workers, such as manufacturing, agriculture, and mining, showed declines in their employment shares. This change in industrial composition shifted demand in favor of college-educated workers and against less-educated workers. They concluded that structural change accounted for a large part of the increase in college graduates' earnings relative to other educational groups and to rising overall earnings inequality for the period.

Chinhui Juhn (1994) analyzed the effects of industrial change on earnings inequality for the period 1940 to 1990. Using decennial Census of Population data, Juhn found that the demand for highly educated and skilled male workers increased no faster from changes in industrial composition during the 1980s than in the previous four decades. However, the peculiar feature of the 1980s is that the demand for male workers in the middle-skill categories, such as found in manufacturing, contracted severely during the 1980s. Juhn concluded that it was the decline in medium-skill jobs, rather than a sharp increase in highly skilled ones, that was primarily responsible for the rising wage inequality over this period.

Work by Lawrence Mishel and Jared Bernstein showed that industrial shifts were important in explaining the widening pay gap between white-collar and blue-collar workers. They first reported that hourly compensation (wages plus benefits) in 1993 averaged $20.22 in goods-producing industries and only $15.51 in services (see Table 9.1). Moreover, while employment grew by 38 percent in service industries between 1979 and 1993, it contracted by 12 percent among goods producers.

They then analyzed what would have happened to the pay of white-collar and blue-collar workers if the occupation and industry composition of employment had remained unchanged between 1980 and 1989 and compared this to the actual changes in pay for the two groups over the period. The difference is a measure of the effect of employment composition shifts on average pay. They estimated that employment shifts by themselves

Table 9.1 Employment Growth by Industry, 1979–1993 [a]

Industry	Employment (1,000s)		Percent Growth in Employment	Average Hourly Compensation in 1993
	1979	1993		
Goods Producing	26,461	23,256	−12.1%	$20.22
Manufacturing	21,040	18,003	−14.4%	20.09
Construction	4,463	4,642	4.0%	19.71
Mining	958	611	−36.2%	—
Services	63,363	87,269	37.7%	15.51
Transportation, utilities, and communications	5,136	5,787	12.7%	24.07
Finance, insurance, and real estate	4,975	6,712	34.9%	20.37
General services	17,112	30,278	76.9%	16.34
Trade	20,193	25,675	27.1%	11.33
Government	15,947	18,816	18.0%	—
Total	89,823	110,525	23.0%	16.70

[a] Source: Author's calculations from data presented in Lawrence Mishel and Jared Bernstein, *The State of Working America 1994–1995*, 1994.

lowered the hourly compensation of blue-collar workers by 6.9 percent while it raised the hourly compensation of white-collar workers by 0.6 percent. They concluded that employment shifts were partly responsible for the widening compensation gap between blue-collar and white-collar workers. Interestingly, they also found that employment shifts caused the average compensation among all workers to decline by 3.4 percent.

9.2 INDUSTRY WAGE DIFFERENTIALS

In the last section, we have considered a number of structural models which have shown the effect of industry mix on income inequality. In most of these, it was implicitly assumed that the wage structure within industry remained stable over time. With a fixed industry wage structure, the change in industrial composition would be entirely responsible for changes in the overall distribution of earnings.

Three questions immediately arise. First, how stable are relative wages between industries over time? Second, what factors account for differences in earnings among industries? Third, if industry wage differentials do change over time, what factors are responsible for these changes?

Relative Industry Wages

Interest in these issues dates back to 1950. According to neoclassical price theory, in equilibrium, industries in the same location should pay the same wage to each type of labor. Wage differences between locations for a given skill should reflect only interregional differences in the cost of living. There should also be no difference in average industry wage levels except as these differences are correlated with the skill mix (see Reder, 1962).

However, the early studies showed that industries in the same locality paid different wages for essentially the same work. Sumner Slichter (1950) reported that the wages of common labor in Cleveland ranged from 50 cents to $1.09 per hour in February, 1947. John Dunlop (1957) found that the union scale for truck drivers in Boston in July, 1953, ranged from $1.27 to $2.49 per hour, depending on what was being transported. As Slichter (1950) noted, there appeared to be "regularities" in the interindustry wage structure that did not appear to conform to neoclassical wage theory.

Several papers investigated how stable industry wage differentials remained over time. In one study based on Census of Manufacturing data, Donald Cullen (1956) concluded that the industry wage structure had remained remarkably stable over the first half of the twentieth century.

Several tests were made. The first test was based on the change in industry rankings with respect to their average wage paid over the period 1899 to 1950. Industries were ranked from lowest to highest on the basis of average pay. The result was clear that the rank order of industries changed very slowly over time.[7]

In the second test, industries were divided into a high-wage group and a low-wage group. The fourteen industries that comprised the high-wage group in 1899 were still members of that group in 1950. Moreover, ten of the fifteen low-paying industries in 1899 were still in the low-paying group in 1950.

The third set of tests was based on two measures of the dispersion of the industry wage structure: (1) the interquartile range divided by the median, and (2) the high-low percent differential. The high-low percent differential is defined as the median of the 21 industries forming the top 25 percent of the earnings distribution divided by the median of the 21 industries forming the bottom 25 percent of the earnings structure. Both measures remained remarkably stable over time. The interquartile range fell by only 7.3 percent over the entire period from 1899 to 1950, while the high-low percent differential declined by only 3.3 percent.[8]

---

[7]Using rank order in 1899 as the base, Cullen found that the rank correlation coefficient declined from 0.94 in 1904 to 0.66 in 1950.

[8]Another important result that emerged from this study is that there is no evidence that unionization has made the wage structure more rigid. The rate of change in the relative positions of industries, as measured by the rank correlation, was no greater in 1930–1950, a period of expanding unionization, than in prior years, when unionization was not expanding.

Explanations of Interindustry Wage Differences

Several factors have been proposed to account for differences in industry wages. These include industry productivity levels and productivity growth rates, employment growth rates, the share of labor costs in total value added, the degree of monopolization of an industry, the concentration ratio, market power, unionization, and the average firm size in an industry.

One of the earliest articles in this line of research was published by John Dunlop in 1948. He investigated changes in mean manufacturing wages by industry and found them to be significantly correlated with changes in worker productivity. One reason, he argued, was the use of piece-rate incentive schemes in many industries, whereby the worker is paid according to his or her output. He also suggested that the skill mix of an industry would affect the average wage it paid.

Slichter (1950) analyzed 1937 hourly wage data for ten manufacturing industries. He observed that the hourly earnings of male unskilled workers were high in industries where the wages of semiskilled and skilled workers were also high. This result indicated that high-wage industries tended to pay above-average wages to all grades of labor. He found that the wage levels of unskilled male workers were high where the value added per worker was high, confirming the Dunlop result that wages were higher in industries with higher productivity. He also found that the wages of male unskilled workers were generally lower in industries where the labor costs were a higher share of sales revenue. His explanation was that management had to be much more careful in giving wage increases in industries where labor costs were a high percentage of total costs.

Joseph Garbarino, in a paper also published in 1950, examined the effect of industry concentration and the extent of unionization on industry wages. He viewed the former as a measure of market power in the product market and the latter an indicator of market power in the labor market. He argued that in concentrated industries, workers should be able to capture part of the increase in productivity growth in the form of wage gains, since the firms had considerable market power.[9] Moreover, in heavily unionized industries, workers should likewise be able to capture a portion of productivity growth in the form of increased wages because of the union's market power. In contrast, in industries with little market power in both the product and labor markets, wages would not rise from productivity gains. Using industry wage data for the period 1923–1945, Garbarino found that, as predicted, concentration and unionization were both significant and positive explanatory factors of industry wage movements. He also found that industries that were growing faster in terms of employment had higher than average wages increases.

---

[9]Recall from Section 6.1 that the neoclassical theory of wages predicts just the opposite—namely, that monopolies will pay lower wages than competitive industries.

Richard Perlman (1956) followed up the work of Garbarino in investigating the relation between productivity growth and wage movements. His method was to replace the separate measures of industrial concentration and "physical" productivity growth with a single measure of "value productivity," defined as total sales in dollars per person-hour of work. There were two advantages to this approach. First, a more general concept of market power than industry concentration was ascribed to this measure, including the effects of advertising and barriers to entry. Second, increases in the value productivity measure reflected both increases in physical productivity and the ability of an industry to absorb some of the increased physical productivity in the form of profits and/or wages.

In a perfectly competitive industry, increases in physical productivity would result in a proportional decline in the product price and hence no increase in the industry's profits or wages. Insofar as an industry has market power, it can appropriate part of the physical productivity gain in the form of increased profits and/or wages levels. The value productivity measure could thus be interpreted to reflect an industry's "ability to pay" higher wages. Using a sample of manufacturing industries at the two-digit SIC level, he found that wage increases were highly correlated with changes in the value productivity measure in both the 1937–1947 and 1947–1952 periods. This result provided strong confirmation of the positive effects of productivity growth and market power on industry wage growth.

Saul Fabricant, in a 1959 paper, also analyzed the relation between physical productivity and industry wages. He computed a (rank) correlation of 0.26 between the industry productivity level and the average industry labor compensation for a sample of 80 industries over the period from 1899 to 1947. This result, like Perlman's, indicated a positive relation between physical productivity and wages across industry, although Fabricant's coefficient was not quite significant at the 5 percent level. Fabricant also found a positive rank correlation coefficient of 0.21 between industry wages and the amount of labor employed in the industry for 33 industries for the period 1899 to 1953, though the coefficient was not statistically significant. This result thus weakly suggested that industries that were expanding more rapidly tended to pay higher wages.

In a major study published in 1960, William Bowen also looked at the relation between wages and employment growth. Using a sample of 20 two-digit manufacturing industries over six subperiods between 1947 and 1959, he computed correlation coefficients between the percentage change in earnings and the percentage growth in employment. The coefficients were generally positive when unemployment was low. However, in periods of high unemployment, the results were mixed. Bowen's results indicated that during periods of labor scarcity, wage increases were highest in the industries expanding most rapidly. This result is consistent with neoclassical wage theory, which would explain such a result by an upward-sloping, short-run supply curve for labor. However, during recessions, there was no evidence that wages increased less rapidly in those industries with the greatest reductions in employment. This result is not consistent with the neoclassical model.[10]

The Later Literature   The later literature on interindustry wages differs from the earlier material in two important ways. First, it reflected the influence of human capital theory. In addition to such factors as productivity growth, employment growth, market power, the concentration ratio, unionization, and firm size, the later studies included measures of schooling and other forms of human capital in the list of variables used to explain industry wages. Second, most of the modern literature used multiple regression analysis to separate out the influence of the various factors on industry wages.

In a 1966 study, Leonard Weiss investigated the relation between earnings and industrial concentration. He argued that industries with greater concentration (a higher degree of monopolization) would pay higher wages, because more concentrated industries tend to have higher profits than less concentrated ones. Industries with high profits, whether from monopolization or some other cause, tend to attract trade unions, since potential wage gains are high. High labor earnings would then result from unionization or from the attempt by companies to forestall the introduction of unions. Low-profit companies, in contrast, would pay lower wages, because the threat of labor unions would be smaller and because such companies have smaller profits out of which to offer increased wages. One implication of this line of reasoning was that more concentrated industries would pay higher wages for labor of the same occupation or skill level.

Using 1960 Census of Population data, Weiss regressed the mean wages in each industry on the industry's concentration ratio,[11] its degree of unionization, and a set of other variables that affected the wages paid in an industry.[12] The sample was then divided by occupation group. The results showed that a higher concentration ratio led to higher mean wages for almost every occupational grouping. This relation, moreover, was statistically significant in almost every case.[13]

Weiss carried the analysis one step further by raising the issue of whether concentrated industries paying high wages attract "superior" workers. To answer this question, he added variables to the regression model measuring the human capital of the workers in each industry. These human

---

[10] See also Reder (1962) for a good review of the pre-1960 literature on industry wage differentials.

[11] The concentration ratio was measured by the ratio of the sales accounted for by the top four firms in an industry to the total sales of the industry.

[12] Other variables included the growth rate of employment in the industry, the percentage of employees in establishments with 250 or more employees, and a dummy variable to indicate the variability of employment in an industry over the business cycle.

[13] The effect of unionization on the mean wage was generally positive. Moreover, it was generally stronger in less concentrated industries. This result was consistent with the original argument, which was that concentrated industries may pay high wages either because of the presence of unions or the *threat* of unionization. Thus, nonunionized companies that fear unionization will also pay high wages. See Section 8.1 for a discussion of the threat effect.

capital variables were generally significant. Moreover, when they were introduced into the regression model, the concentration variable became statistically insignificant. Weiss concluded that the higher labor earnings associated with concentration in an industry could be explained by the higher level of human capital of these workers.[14]

A related study was conducted by Thomas Pugel in 1980. He argued that more concentrated industries paid higher wages because of greater "ability to pay" to achieve the firm's objectives. These goals can include the achievement of low turnover rates of the labor force, increasing worker morale to promote higher work performance, and the creation of a pool of available labor for periods of intense demand. Since concentrated industries are generally more profitable than competitive industries, they have the ability to pay higher wages in order to achieve these aims.

Pugel argued that, in fact, this argument is based on the relative profitability of different industries. It is true that more concentrated industries tend to have higher profit rates than less concentrated ones, but there are other elements of market power, besides concentration, that affect profitability. As a result, Pugel argued, economic profitability may be a better summary measure for analyzing the effects of market power on labor compensation.

Using a variety of data sources for 1968–1970, Pugel estimated two regression equations. In the first, the logarithm of the industry's mean hourly wages was regressed on the concentration ratio of the industry, its degree of unionization, the percentage of the industry's labor force employed in large establishments, and various measures of employee human capital. In the second equation, the same set of variables was used except that industry profitability was substituted for the industry concentration ratio. The major finding was that industry profitability was a more significant determinant of industry wages than the concentration ratio. Pugel estimated that about 14 percent of the excess profits industries earn due to market imperfections are "returned" to workers in the form of higher wages. Another result is that the concentration ratio variable became statistically insignificant as a determinant of industry wages once the median years of schooling in the industry's labor force was included in the regression equation. This was similar to Weiss's finding. However, the profitability variable remained statistically significant even after the schooling variable was included in the equation.

The Effects of Plant and Firm Size   In both the Weiss and Pugel studies, a variable was included in the model to reflect the size of firms or plants in

---

[14]As with many other hypotheses in economics, there are contradictory findings in the empirical literature. Like Weiss (1966), Ashenfelter and Johnson (1972) found that the concentration ratio variable became statistically insignificant once variables reflecting human capital were included in the regression equation. On the other hand, Dalton and Ford (1977) found that the concentration ratio remained significant, while Haworth and Reuther (1978) found that it remained significant for a 1958 (recession year) sample but not for 1967.

industries. A study that focused on the effect of plant size on industry wages was conducted by Stanley Masters in 1969. Masters argued that firms normally set minimum standards when hiring employees. A worker must usually demonstrate that he or she can meet these standards in order to be retained by the firm. The higher these minimum standards, the higher the wages the firm must be willing to pay.

Masters then argued that large plants will have higher standards than small plants. One reason is that in a large plant, the production process is subdivided into more tasks than in a small plant. Therefore, coordination is more difficult in a large plant and, as a result, more formal work rules and greater regimentation of the work force is required. Higher wages must be paid to obtain workers who are willing to tolerate this greater regimentation. Second, larger plants will generally have more expensive capital equipment. To avoid damage, large plants will hire more dependable workers and thus set higher standards than small plants. Third, unionization is more likely at a large plant than at a small one, because the potential gains in membership are greater. Therefore, a large plant may be willing to pay higher wages in order to avoid unionization.[15]

Masters tested these hypotheses using 1963 Census of Manufactures data for 417 manufacturing industries. In his regression model, the dependent variable was average hourly earnings for production workers. The plant size variable was the percentage of the total labor force of the industry working in establishments of 1,000 or more employees. After controlling for the industry's concentration ratio, the degree of unionization in the industry, and other industry characteristics, he found a positive and highly significant relation between industry wages and the plant size variable.

In a later study, Wesley Mellow (1981) investigated the relation between wages and firm size. Firm size is different from plant size, since a firm may own more than one plant (or establishment). A large firm could conceivably operate many small plants or establishments, though in actuality, large firms tend to own large plants and small firms tend to own small plants. The reasons why large firms pay high wages are similar to those for why large plants and concentrated industries pay high wages: large firms usually have high profitability, are desirable targets for unionization, and tend to have high standards for hiring.

Using 1979 Current Population Survey data, Mellow regressed individual wages on various human capital variables as well as on variables indicating union status and the size of the firm in terms of employment. The database covered all workers, not just those in manufacturing. His principal finding was that employer size had a significant and independent effect on wages. This was true even after controlling for the worker's human capital

---

[15] A related argument is that large plants tend to have more layers in their job hierarchy than small plants. If wages increase the higher the rung of the job ladder and the bottom wage is the same in large plants and small ones, then, *ceteris paribus*, average wages will be higher in larger plants.

and other measures of labor quality, as well as for industry concentration, unionization, and occupation/industrial status. The wage premium to employer size was found to be quite substantial. After other factors were controlled for, wages were 16 percent higher when employer size exceeded 1,000 employees, and 8 percent higher when employer size was in the 500–999 range, compared to the smallest employer size of 25 employees or less. This wage premium of large firms characterized all sectors of the economy.[16]

Derek Leslie (1985) followed up some of the earlier literature on the effects of productivity growth on interindustry wage differentials. He examined the behavior of real wages in 20 (two-digit) U.S. manufacturing industries over the period from 1948 to 1976. Among these industries, he found no significant relationship between the growth of real wages and an industry's rate of productivity growth (as measured by total factor productivity). He concluded that gains from productivity growth are shared by all industries, a result that is consistent with the competitive neoclassical model.

Recent Trends and Efficiency Wage Theory

One of the more notable developments of the 1980s has been an end to the stability of industry wage differentials that prevailed since World War II. According to estimates provided by Alan Krueger and Lawrence Summers (1988) on the basis of 42 (two-digit) industries, the standard deviation of industry wage differentials increased by 30 percent between 1979 and 1984. On the other hand, the ranking of industries according to the wage premium that they paid changed very little over this period. Thus, the increasing dispersion of industry wage differences was a result of a *widening* of pre-existing differentials, rather than a reordering of high- and low-wage industries.

The figures shown in Table 9.2 confirm the same pattern. In 1985, the industry wage differential, defined as the percentage difference between the industry's average wage and the average wage in the whole economy, ranged from a low of −71 percent in agriculture to a high of 55 percent in electricity, gas, and water. In 1970, the differentials ranged from −68 percent in agriculture to 39 percent in construction. The dispersion of industry wage differentials (measured by the log variance) increased from 0.092 in 1970 to 0.118 in 1985, or by 29 percent. However, the ranking of industries in terms of wages was very close in the two years. The correlation coefficient of the industry wage differentials in the two years was 0.97, and the rank correlation coefficient was also 0.97.

Partly in order to explain this new phenomenon, a new model of wage determination, called "efficiency wage theory," was developed by a number of economists. Though there are some differences among versions of the theory, the common feature of efficiency wage theory is that paying higher

---

[16]Later studies have also confirmed the effects of both plant and employer size on industry wages. See, for example, Evans and Leighton (1989), Brown and Medoff (1989), and Dunne and Roberts (1990).

Table 9.2 Industry Wage Differentials for the United States, 1970 and 1985[a]

	1970	1985	Percentage Change
Electricity, gas, & water	0.374	0.553	47.7
Mining	0.287	0.525	82.7
Basic metal products	0.317	0.484	52.8
Chemicals	0.310	0.429	38.3
Machinery & equipment	0.282	0.385	36.4
Transport, storage, & communication	0.251	0.344	37.2
Nonmetallic mineral products	0.155	0.253	63.6
Finance & insurance	0.091	0.227	149.0
Paper, printing, & publishing	0.178	0.198	11.2
Food, beverages, & tobacco	0.063	0.153	143.8
Construction	0.385	0.149	−61.3
Producers of government services	0.014	0.034	150.4
Real estate	0.003	0.015	334.7
Other manufactured products	−0.035	−0.038	7.7
Wood & wood products	−0.066	−0.065	−1.0
Community, social, & personal services	−0.365	−0.293	−9.8
Textiles	−0.260	−0.310	19.3
Wholesale & retail trade	−0.166	−0.314	88.9
Restaurants & hotels	−0.489	−0.484	−1.0
Agriculture	−0.682	−0.707	3.7
Inequality of industry wages[b]	0.092	0.118	28.6
Correlation with 1970		0.97	
Rank correlation with 1970		0.97	

[a] Source: Gittleman and Wolff (1993), computed from the OECD International Sectoral Data Base. The industry wage differential for industry i, d_i, is defined as the percentage difference between the industry's average wage and the average wage for the whole economy. The industries are ranked by the industry wage differential in 1985.
[b] Inequality is measured by the unweighted variance of the logarithm of industry wage differentials d_i.

wages helps to increase a firm's profitability. There are four factors cited to explain the benefits received by a firm from paying higher wages: (1) the **shirking model**: eliciting increased effort (especially if the monitoring costs of workers are high); (2) the **turnover model**: reducing turnover costs; (3) the **selection model**: attracting a higher-quality workforce; and (4) the **sociological model**: improving worker morale. Since the benefits of each of these factors will differ across industries, the theory implies that different industries will, in general, pay different wages for the same work.

The factors that receive the most attention vary by model. According to the shirking model, high wages will be paid in industries where monitoring is difficult and where it is costly if workers do not perform up to standard. Walter Oi (1983), like Masters (1969), suggests that this would be the case in large establishments, where monitoring may be difficult. In addition, the cost of mistakes is likely to be large in industries with expensive equipment (which, in turn, may be related to the capital intensity of production or to situations where shirking by one worker affects the performance of other workers).

According to the turnover model, wages will be high in industries where the costs of training and therefore turnover are high. The selection model predicts high pay in industries where it is difficult to directly evaluate labor quality. The sociological model implies that wages will be high in industries where worker morale is important and where a firm's evident ability to pay would lead workers to perceive that they were being treated unfairly (see Dickens and Katz, 1987b, for more discussion).

These models, with the exception of the sociological model, predict that wage premium would differ across jobs within an industry depending on, for example, the ease of monitoring, the amount of firm- or industry-specific human capital needed, or differences in recruiting costs. In contrast, studies of industry wages typically find that industry wage differentials are almost the same among jobs within an industry. To reconcile the two, the theory often includes the additional consideration that the amount of effort supplied by workers may also depend on how fairly they feel they are being treated. Their treatment, in turn, depends on how other workers in the firm or industry are compensated and how firms are doing in terms of profitability (see for example, Akerlof, 1984). This last consideration may explain the "rent sharing" discussed above (high-profit industries pay high wages), since a firm may fear that if workers perceive that they are not being fairly compensated, they may withhold effort.

In an influential paper, Krueger and Summers (1988) provided strong econometric evidence that industry wage differentials were statistically significant and persistent over time, even after controlling for differences in worker characteristics among industries. On the basis of the 1974, 1979, and 1984 Current Population Surveys, cross-sectional wage equations were estimated with industry (dummy) variables, as well as schooling levels, experience levels, demographic characteristics, and working conditions among workers. The authors found that, after controlling for these latter effects, the industry variables remained statistically significant and explained a substantial amount of the variation of earnings among workers. They concluded that industry wage differences could not be explained away by differences in worker attributes but, instead, appeared to depend on specific industry characteristics.

Krueger and Summers (1987) then provided a comprehensive analysis of industry wage differences in the United States and concluded that the industry wage structure reflected the sharing of rents with workers. These rents may be the result of monopoly power, returns to intangible assets, or returns to capital already in place. Where rents per worker (that is, profitability) were greatest, wage rates tended to be highest.

In a historical study of the introduction of a five-dollar per day wage rate in the Ford Motor Company in 1914, Donald Raff and Lawrence Summers (1987) found supporting evidence for efficiency wage theory. The new rate doubled the pay for most of the workers in the factory. The authors found strong evidence that the new wages, by increasing morale, lowered worker turnover, increased worker productivity, and, as a result, increased the profitability of the firm. Krueger and Summers (1988) also found that high industry wages were correlated with low worker turnover.

Linda Bell and Richard Freeman, using industry wage data for the United States, reported a sharp increase in the dispersion of industry wages not only for the economy as a whole but also within manufacturing and services over the period 1970 and 1987. Using regression analysis, they calculated that about 60 percent of the rise in interindustry wage dispersion can be attributed to changes in human capital (education and age) and occupational mix within industry. However, even after controlling for these effects, they found a positive and significant relation between changes in industry wages and increases in industry productivity. They concluded that a strong link between wages and productivity reflected rent-sharing behavior of the type predicted by efficiency wage theory.

David Levine (1992) used company data provided by 250 large North American manufacturers (mostly Fortune 500 companies) to analyze the relation between assessments made by managers of the relative wages paid to their workers and changes in worker productivity. Controlling for worker quality, he found a positive relation between relative wages and productivity. As predicted by efficiency wage theory, the resultant increase in productivity was sufficient to pay for the higher wages of the workers.

9.3 Occupational Wage Differentials

In the last section, we focused on differences in earnings among industries in the United States. Throughout this literature, it was assumed, either explicitly or implicitly, that, *ceteris paribus,* average industry wages should vary directly with the skill level of the industry. Indeed, in long-run equilibrium in a perfectly competitive neoclassical world, mean wage difference should reflect *only* differences in average skill levels. Of course, in actuality, this is not the case, and other factors are important in accounting for occupational wage differences.

In this section, we are interested in differences in earnings between skill levels or *occupations,* which are also referred to as **skill margins.** There are three questions of particular interest. First, what factors account for differences in earnings between skill levels? Second, have skill margins remained roughly stable over time? Third, if not, what factors account for changes in wage differentials between skill levels?

The skill margin is defined as the ratio of the mean (or median) wage of skilled workers to that of unskilled workers. The skill margin is also referred to as the "skill differential" or as the "wage differential according to skill." The consensus seems to be that skill margins in the United States have narrowed from the turn of the century until 1950 or so. However, the decline in the skill differential over this period was not continuous, and during some shorter periods the skill margin has risen. From 1950 until 1980 or so, skill differentials tended to remain constant. However, during the 1980s, there is strong evidence that skill margins have been increasing.

Historical Studies

Before examining the U.S. experience, let us first consider long-term historical studies of skill margins in other countries. In a series of papers, Phelps Brown and Hopkins (1955, 1956, and 1959) investigated the skill differential in southern England over the period from 1300 to 1914 (see Phelps Brown [1977] for a summary of these studies). They found that the skill differential remained roughly constant at 1.5 over this entire period. This ratio was affected by special historical circumstances, such as the Black Death, which caused a doubling of the skill margin during the latter half of the fourteenth century, but the ratio returned to 1.5 by 1412.[17]

Phelps Brown also computed skill differentials for Germany, France, and the United States in the period 1860 to 1910. The differentials were computed between a skilled manual worker and his helper or a laborer. The results do not indicate a coherent trend in wage differentials over this period.

From about 1914 through the 1960s, the pattern of wage differentials did change. It appears that in some countries, the skill margin narrowed significantly if one compares the skill ratio at the beginning and the end of the period. This was true of the United States and the United Kingdom. However, Canada and France did not display such a trend in skill differentials. Moreover, in a 1968 book, Ozanne argued that even in the United States, there had not been a continual decline in skill margins but rather a series of troughs and peaks that other researchers have isolated as trends. Phelps Brown acknowledged the erratic behavior of skill margins noted by Ozanne but claimed that the skill margin still exhibited a secular downward trend.

Trends in the United States in the Twentieth Century

Harry Ober (1948) was one of the first to look systematically at skill differentials in the United States. The study examined the period from 1907 to

---

[17]Moreover, this 50 percent differential seemed to prevail over most of Europe during much of the period. There were a couple of notable exceptions, where the skill margin narrowed. This occurred in Valencia, Spain, in the late 1500s and in Augsburg, Germany, in the early 1700s. The reason for this decline in the skill differential was a large population increase.

1947. Three skills classes were considered: skilled, semiskilled, and unskilled jobs. Semiskilled workers were further subdivided into two groups, depending on their degree of responsibility in identifying problems in the normal work process and repairing malfunctions. Unskilled workers were also subdivided, depending on the physical arduousness of the work.

In 1947, wage rates for skilled occupations were, on average, 55 percent greater than unskilled wages; wages of the first tier of semiskilled workers were 35 percent greater, those of the second tier were 15 percent higher, and wages of unskilled jobs requiring heavy labor were 15 percent greater. He also found a pronounced narrowing of the skill differentials over the period. In 1907, skilled workers were earning twice that of unskilled workers, but by 1947, the ratio had fallen to 1.55. However, the trend was not uniform over these years. The greatest portion of this decline took place between 1907 and 1917. During the depression of the early 1930s, the trend reversed and skilled differentials widened, but by 1940 the skill differentials began to narrow again.

Melvin Reder (1955) argued that the cyclical movements observed for skill margins could be explained by changes in the supply and the demand for labor. During periods of expansion, such as wartime, gross shortages of labor arise, which cause wage rates for the most skilled to rise. The increase in pay for the most skilled jobs attracts new applicants, who were previously unable to overcome the strict barriers to these positions. Because of labor shortages, the existing standards are relaxed and previously unqualified workers are accepted for these jobs.

This process of substituting less for more skilled workers causes a shortage of supply at the next lower grade of labor. As this process continues down the occupational ladder, each occupation is filled by personnel of a lower skill level until the lowest occupation level is reached, where further substitution of less for more skilled workers can no longer take place. The lowest grade of labor, the unskilled, would then experience a proportionately greater increase in the demand for their services, bidding up their wages relative to the skilled and narrowing the skill differentials.[18]

When the expansion eases, a reverse process of "downward bumping" occurs, which results in a relative increase in the supply of labor available for the lowest grade of labor. This leads to a widening of wage differentials. Ober's results confirm this argument. Both world war periods were characterized by a dramatic narrowing of the skill differential, while the depression of the 1930s saw a significant increase in the wage differential.

Both Reder and Phelps Brown argued that the skill differential had narrowed over the long term. Reder's explanation is that the laboring class is becoming better educated over time because of the increasing availability of schooling. The rising educational level of the working class increases the ease of substituting less skilled labor for more skilled workers. The supply of

---

[18]This assumes that the unemployment rate is sufficiently low so that all the reserves of labor have been fully absorbed in production.

completely unskilled labor will fall, due to the increased substitutability, and hence the relative wage of the unskilled will increase, narrowing the wage differential.

Another reason for the long-run decline in the skill margin is the mechanization and specialization of skills. These tend to reduce the demand for the broadly skilled laborer who requires long periods of training to achieve that skill capability. The rise of the specialized worker, requiring shorter training periods, further increases skill substitutability. These two developments—the improvement in educational standards and increased mechanization—exert downward pressure on the wage of skilled workers and upward pressure on those of the unskilled.

Richard Perlman (1958) disputed this interpretation of the effects of technological change on skill margins. First, he argued, there is not as much substitution between skill groups as there is substitution within the highly skilled group. As a result, the decline in the demand for one highly skilled occupation is likely to be accompanied by an increase in demand for another highly skilled group. This will cause the former's wage to fall and the latter's to rise but, on net, not affect the average wage of skilled workers as a group. Second, the reason why the wage differentials between broad skill groups have remained relatively constant is that technological change results in an increased demand for "new skills" and a decreased demand for "old skills." This shift in the demand occurs across the full spectrum of the occupational ladder—at the highly skilled, semiskilled, and unskilled levels. As a consequence, there is no relative shift in demand among the three broad-skilled groups and no resulting change in relative wage levels among the three groups.

Like Reder, Phelps Brown considered education to be the primary reason for the decline in the skill margin, but he took issue with Reder on the effects of technological change. The effect of technological change and innovation, according to Phelps Brown, is not as unambiguous as Reder implied. On the other hand, many skilled occupations are becoming less skilled due to mechanization. For example, craft workers can be replaced by semiskilled operatives due to automation—a process that is referred to as "de-skilling." On the other hand, there is a decreasing number of jobs that can use completely unskilled labor. These two effects, he argued, would lead to a decline in the skill differential.

Ober had a different argument. He believed that there had been more mechanization of unskilled tasks in industry than of skilled tasks. This mechanization was primarily aimed at relieving labor of arduous lifting and loading tasks. These innovations, consisting of such devices as forklifts, hoists, and steam shovels, as well as improvements in the organization of production processes, made it possible to better compensate the unskilled. But more importantly, according to Ober, mechanization and organizational improvements made it possible for many unskilled operators to become specialized and move up to the semiskilled category. These effects helped reduce the skill differential.

In a 1960 paper, Paul Keat discussed the period 1903 to 1956, both peak years in the business cycle. Keats computed the coefficient of variation (see Chapter 3) among wage rates by occupation in each year. It showed a 42 percent decline for the full economy. He also calculated the coefficient of variation in occupational wages within each industry in 1903 and 1956. The measure declined in all but two industries, and the decline ranged from 27 to 78 percent.[19]

Relatively little work on skill margins has been done since the early 1960s. The major reason for this is the shift in the focus of labor economics to the human capital model and the consequent attention to differentials in earnings between schooling groups, as opposed to skill or occupational groups. However, a few studies have appeared since 1960, which focus primarily on the postwar period. A study by Donald Blackmore in 1968 compared the earnings of skilled and unskilled workers in manufacturing. He found that the ratio in wages between these two groups fell from 2.1 in 1907 to 1.4 in 1953, but between 1953 and 1967, the skill margin remained virtually unchanged. In a 1980 study, Virginia Ward compared the wage levels of janitors to more skilled occupations in manufacturing establishments. Ward found that the skill margin remained stable from 1962 to 1967 and then narrowed slightly from 1967 to 1976.

In a 1991 study, Maury Gittleman found that skill margins increased rather substantially between 1979 and 1987. On the basis of the 1973, 1979, and 1987 Current Population Surveys, he computed the standard deviation of earnings among full-time, full-year employees in 49 occupations in each year. He found that dispersion in occupational earnings first declined by 15 percent between 1973 and 1979 and then increased by 26 percent between 1979 and 1987.[20] On net, the dispersion in occupational earnings was higher in 1987 than in 1973. As with industry wage differentials, a sharp increase in occupational wage differentials occurred in the 1980s, after almost $3\frac{1}{2}$ decades of relative stability.

Recent work has focused on a related phenomenon, called the "winner-take-all" effect. Two papers by Sherwin Rosen, published in 1981 and 1986, provided the theoretical underpinnings for this line of research. His object was to explain a peculiar feature of certain labor markets, such as sports and entertainment, wherein a relatively small number of "superstars" earn enormous compensation and dominate the activities of their fields. This is true despite the fact that the superstars may be only slightly more talented than the next rung of workers in their field, so differences in pay between the top performers and the rest could exist even though there are only relatively small differences in productivity. Rosen argued that a small difference in talent could make a huge difference in outcomes. This would be the case in competitive sports, where the most talented team or player would win the championship and the others would lose. In law, also,

---

[19] For males alone, the coefficient showed a decline of 40 percent.

[20] For male workers alone, the corresponding figures are 14 percent and 30 percent.

Part II   The Role of Labor Markets

the difference between winning and losing a case could mean millions of dollars to the client.

Rosen also argued that such a market might be efficient because it would provide very large incentives to excel. Having a tournament with a very lucrative first prize will give all the participants something to shoot for and may, as a result, elicit exceptional effort from the players. In a large corporation, for example, providing huge compensation for the top executive spot (the chief executive officer, or CEO) will give workers a tremendous incentive to perform. This will be the case even if the top position goes to someone who is only marginally more talented than the other employees in a company (see also Adler, 1985, for a different justification).

As developed by Robert Frank and Philip Cook in a 1995 book, the key feature of this argument is that winner-take-all markets are becoming more pervasive in the American economy. Though these markets were historically features of entertainment, sports, and the arts, they are now found in law, journalism, medicine, consulting, investment banking, corporate management, publishing, design, and fashion. One pertinent statistic is that in 1993, CEOs of top corporations earned *120 times as much as the average worker,* compared to 35 times as much in the mid-1970s. Another statistic is that the number of workers earning more than $120,000 in 1990 dollars doubled between 1980 and 1990 (from half a million to one million). Indeed, 40 percent of the growth in earnings was captured by the top one percent of earners between 1973 and 1993, a period when the median wage fell by 15 percent in real terms. Frank and Cook argue that the increasing prevalence of winner-take-all markets primarily accounts for the increasing concentration of income at the very top of the income distribution.

9.4 SUMMARY

This chapter has covered a wide range of topics that can be loosely grouped under the rubric of structural theories of income distribution. The unifying thread that runs through these works is the importance of the demand side of the labor market. In particular, these works have emphasized aspects of the labor market that reflect technology, industrial composition, market structure, plant size, and regional characteristics. Structural change, such as the shift of employment among industries in the economy, affects the demand for labor and the distribution of wages.

The studies surveyed in Section 9.1 lend strong support to the argument that the industrial or occupational distribution of employment is a significant determinant of regional differences in both income inequality and average earnings. In the early studies, particular attention was given to the proportion of the labor force employed in agriculture. In the later ones, measures of the entire mix of industries in a region were discussed.

The evidence presented in Section 9.2 generally supports the view that industry wage differentials have remained fairly stable over long periods of time in the United States, except for the last two decades or so, when they have widened. The earlier studies emphasized the importance of structural and institutional characteristics as determinants of industry wage differences. These include industrial concentration, market power, firm size, and unionization. The earlier literature also investigated other economic factors such as profitability, employment growth, and productivity in accounting for wage differences between industries. These factors were all generally found to be positively and significantly related to the industry wage level (or rate of wage growth).

The later literature, while continuing to include these factors as determinants of industry wages, added human capital as another determinant of industry wage differences. It was almost universally found that industries with higher average levels of human capital (particularly as measured by the mean or median level of schooling of the workers in the industry) had higher-than-average wages. Moreover, in some studies, though not in all, it was found that the concentration ratio and other structural variables became statistically insignificant as determinants of industry wages once human capital was included as an explanatory variable. However, when a variable measuring ability to pay was used to measure industry market power, this variable remained significant even when schooling was added as an independent factor.

Recent work on this subject has generally emanated from efficiency wage theory. The common thread in these models is that paying higher wages helps to increase a firm's profitability. The reasons are that higher wages may elicit increased effort, reduce worker turnover, attract a better-quality workforce, and improve worker morale. These arguments help to explain the "rent sharing" observed across industries—namely, that high-profit industries typically pay high wages.

In Section 9.3, strong evidence was found that wage differentials according to skill level declined from the turn of the century to the 1950s. Estimates of the decline in the skill margin range from 24 to 31 percent. The period from 1950 to 1980 was characterized by relatively stable skill margins. Since 1980, skill margins have been widening.

Three explanations were advanced for the secular trend in the skill margin. One focuses on the supply side and attributes changes to the increasing level of education of the lower-skilled portion of the work force. On the one hand, this increases the ease of substituting less skilled for more skilled workers, and, on the other hand, decreases the supply of totally unskilled labor. Both forces would tend to narrow the spread in wages among the various skill levels. A second explanation stresses the demand side, and, in particular, the effects of technological change. Here, too, there are two effects. First, automation tends to reduce the demand for highly skilled workers who require many years of training. Second, the introduction of new technology is also accompanied by some upgrading of previously unskilled jobs, since even the lowest jobs on the hierarchy entail some training with advanced technology. These two forces would also tend to narrow skill differentials. A third explanation is institutional in nature and emphasizes the effects of the social minimum and the legislated minimum wage. A secular increase in wage floors would also serve to lower the skill margins.

How do the findings reported in this chapter with regard to industrial composition, industry wage differentials, and occupational wage margins relate to growing inequality in labor earnings since the mid-1970s? All three effects appear to play a role in explaining rising income inequality over this period. Several studies have concluded that the shift in industrial composition over these years favored highly skilled and college-educated workers relative to low and medium skilled and less educated ones. This would account both for rising inequality and the increasing returns to a college education.

The dispersion in industry wage differentials remained almost unchanged from 1940 through the mid-1970s and then increased sharply, particularly during the 1980s. Changes in industry wages appear to be strongly linked to industry productivity and profitability movements and reflect the rent-sharing behavior of the type predicted by efficiency wage theory. Skill margins also remained remarkably stable between 1950 and the 1970s, and then showed a pronounced widening starting in the late 1970s. This trend is probably attributable to recent changes in technology which favor more educated workers and is related to the rising premium to a college education. Recent work has also found evidence of the growing tendency of the labor market to pay exceptionally high wages to superstars, even though their productivity may be only marginally superior to the next rung of workers.

REFERENCES AND BIBLIOGRAPHY

A. Industry Wage Differentials, Occupational Wage Differentials, and Structural and Related Models

Adler, Moshe, "Stardom and Talent," *American Economic Review*, Vol. 75, No. 1, March 1985, pp. 208–212.

Aigner, D. J., and A. J. Heins, "On the Determinants of Income Inequality," *American Economic Review*, Vol. 57, No. 1, March 1967, pp. 175–181.

Al-Samarrie, Ahmed, and Herman P. Miller, "State Differentials in Income Concentration," *American Economic Review*, Vol. 57, No. 1, March 1967, pp. 59–72.

Allen, Steven G., "Relative Wage Variability in the United States, 1860–1983," *Review of Economics and Statistics*, Vol. 69, No. 4, November 1987, pp. 617–626.

Ashenfelter, Orley, and George E. Johnson, "Unionism, Relative Wages, and Labor Quality in U.S. Manufacturing Industries," *International Economic Review*, Vol. 13, October 1972, pp. 488–503.

Barsky, Carl, "Occupational Wage Levels Cluster in Petroleum Refineries," *Monthly Labor Review*, June 1977, pp. 54–56.

Bell, Philip, "Cyclical Variations and Trends in Occupational Wage Differentials in American Industry Since 1914," *Review of Economics and Statistics,* Vol. 33, No. 4, November 1951, pp. 329–337.

Blackburn, McKinley L., David E. Bloom, and Richard B. Freeman, "The Declining Economic Position of Less Skilled American Men," in Gary Burtless (ed.), *A Future of Lousy Jobs?* The Brookings Institution, Washington, D.C., 1990.

Blackmore, Donald, "Occupational Wage Relationships in Metropolitan Areas," *Monthly Labor Review,* December 1968, pp. 29–36.

Bound, John, and George Johnson, "Changes in the Structure of Wages in the 1960s: An Evaluation of Alternative Explanations," *American Economic Review,* Vol. 82, No. 3, June 1992, pp. 371–392.

Bowen, William G., *The Wage-price Issue: A Theoretical Analysis,* Princeton University Press, Princeton, NJ, 1960.

Bradfield, Michael, "Necessary and Sufficient Conditions to Explain Equilibrium Regional Wage Differentials," *Journal of Regional Science,* Vol. 16, No. 2, 1976.

Brown, Charles, "Education and Jobs: An Interpretation," *The Journal of Human Resources,* Vol. 13, No. 3, Summer 1978, pp. 416–421.

Brown, Charles, and James Medoff, "The Employer Size-wage Effect," *Journal of Political Economy,* Vol. 97, No. 5, October 1989, pp. 1027–1059.

Conlisk, John, "Some Cross-state Evidence on Income Inequality," *Review of Economics and Statistics,* Vol. 49, No. 1, February 1967, pp. 115–118.

Cullen, Donald, "The Interindustry Wage Structure, 1899–1950," *American Economic Review,* Vol. 46, June 1956, pp. 353–369.

Dalton, James A., and E. J. Ford Jr., "Concentration and Labor Earnings in Manufacturing and Utilities," *Industrial and Labor Relations Review,* Vol. 31, October 1977, pp. 45–60.

Douty, H. M., "Wage Differentials: Forces and Counterforces," *Monthly Labor Review,* March 1968, pp. 74–81.

Dunlop, John, "Productivity and the Wage Structure," in *Income, Employment, and Public Policy,* W. W. Norton, New York, 1948, pp. 341–362.

———, "Wage Contours," in George W. Taylor and Frank C. Pierson (eds.), *New Concepts of Wage Determination,* McGraw-Hill, New York, 1957.

Dunne, Timothy, and Mark J. Roberts, "Wages and the Risk of Plant Closures," U.S. Bureau of the Census Discussion Paper No. 90–96, July 1990.

Elliott, R. F., and Fallick, J. C., "Pay Differentials in Perspective: A Note on Manual and Nonmanual Pay Over the Period 1951–1975," *Economic Journal,* Vol. 89, June 1979, pp. 377–384.

Evans, David S., and Linda S. Leighton, "Why Do Small Firms Pay Less?" *Journal of Human Resources,* Vol. 24, No. 2, Spring 1989, pp. 299–318.

Evans, Robert, "Wage Differentials, Excess Demand for Labor, and Inflation: A Note," *Review of Economics and Statistics,* Vol. 45, February 1963, pp. 95–98.

Fabricant, Solomon, *Basic Facts on Productivity Change,* Occasional Paper 63, NBER, New York, 1959.

Farbman, Michael, "Income Concentration in the Southern United States," *Review of Economics and Statistics,* Vol. 55, No. 3, August 1973, pp. 333–340.

———, "The Size and Distribution of Family Income in U.S. SMSA's, 1959," *Review of Income and Wealth,* Series 21, No. 2, June 1975, pp. 217–238.

Frank, Robert H., and Philip J. Cook, *The Winner-Take-All Society,* The Free Press, New York, 1995.

Freeman, Richard B., *The Over-Educated American,* Academic Press, New York, 1976.

———, "An Empirical Analysis of the Fixed Coefficient: 'Manpower Requirements' Model, 1960–1970," *Journal of Human Resources,* Vol. 15, No. 2, Winter 1980, pp. 176–199.

Garbarino, Joseph W., "A Theory of Interindustry Wage Structure Variation," *Quarterly Journal of Economics,* Vol. 64, May 1950, pp. 282–305.

Gittleman, Maury, "Changes in the Rate of Return to Education in the U.S., 1973–1987: The Role of Occupational Factors," mimeo, New York University, November 1991.

Gittleman, Maury, and Edward N. Wolff, "International Comparisons of Inter-Industry Wage Differentials," *Review of Income and Wealth,* Series 39, No. 3, September 1993, pp. 295–312.

Green, Alan G., "Regional Inequality, Structural Change, and Economic Growth in Canada—1890–1956," *Economic Development and Cultural Change,* Vol. 89, No. 2, February 1969, pp. 136–155.

Groshen, Erica L., "Five Reasons Why Wages Vary Among Employers," *Industrial Relations,* Vol. 30, No. 3, Fall 1991, pp. 350–381.

Gunter, H., "Changes in Occupational Wage Differentials," *International Labor Review,* Vol. 89, No. 2, February 1964, pp. 136–155.

Hanushek, Eric A., "Regional Differences in the Structure of Earnings," *Review of Economics and Statistics,* Vol. 55, No. 2, May 1973, pp. 204–213.

———, "Alternative Models of Earnings Determination and Labor Market Structures," *Journal of Human Resources,* Vol. 16, No. 2, Spring 1981, pp. 238–259.

Haworth, Charles T., and David W. Rasmussen, "Human Capital and Interindustry Wages in Manufacturing," *Review of Economics and Statistics,* Vol. 53, November 1971, pp. 376–380.

Haworth, Charles T., and Carol Jean Reuther, "Industrial Concentration and Interindustry Wage Determination," *Review of Economics and Statistics,* February 1978, pp. 85–95.

Juhn, Chinhui, "Wage Inequality and Industrial Change: Evidence from Five Decades," NBER Working Paper No. 4684, March 1994.

Katz, Lawrence F., and Kevin M. Murphy, "Changes in Relative Wages, 1963–1987: Supply and Demand Factors," *Quarterly Journal of Economics,* Vol. 107, No. 1, February 1992, pp. 35–78.

Keat, Paul, "Long-Run Changes in Occupational Wage Structure, 1900–1956," *Journal of Political Economy,* Vol. 68, No. 6, December 1960, pp. 584–600.

Kuznets, Simon, "Economic Growth and Income Inequality," *American Economic Review,* Vol. 45, No. 1, March 1955, pp. 1–28.

Lawson, Tony, "On the Stability of the Interindustry Structure of Earnings in the U.K.: 1954–1978," *Cambridge Journal of Economics,* Vol. 6, No. 3, September 1982, pp. 249–266.

Leslie, Derek, "Real Wage Growth, Technical Change, and Competition in the Labor Market," *Review of Economics And Statistics,* Vol. 67, No. 4, November 1985, pp. 640–647.

Lester, Richard, "Pay Differentials by Size of Establishment," *Industrial Relations,* October 1967, pp. 57–67.

Levinson, Harry M., "Post-War Movement in Prices and Wages in Manufacturing Industry," Study Paper No. 4, Joint Economic Committee, U.S. Congress, 1960.

————, "Unionism, Concentration, and Wage Changes: Toward a Unified Theory," *Industrial and Labor Relations Review,* Vol. 20, January 1967.

Lewis, Earl L., "Occupational Wage Levels in 20 Labor Markets," Fall 1952–Spring 1953," *Monthly Labor Review,* November 1952, pp. 1281–1284.

Lydall, H. B., *The Structure of Earnings,* Clarendon Press, Oxford, 1968.

Maher, John E., "The Wage Pattern in the United States, 1946–1957," *Industrial and Labor Relations Review,* Vol. 15, No. 1, October 1961, pp. 489–494.

Masters, Stanley H., "An Interindustry Analysis of Wages and Plant Size," *Review of Economics and Statistics,* Vol. 51, No. 3, August 1969, pp. 341–345.

Mellow, Wesley, "Employer Size and Wages," Bureau of Labor Statistics Working Paper No. 116, April 1981.

Meyers, F., and R. L. Bowlby, "The Interindustry Wage Structure and Productivity," *Industrial and Labor Relations Review,* October 1953, pp. 26–39.

Mishel, Lawrence, and Jared Bernstein, *The State of Working America 1994–1995,* M. E. Sharpe, Armonk, NY, 1994.

Muntz, Earl E., "The Decline in Wage Differentials Based on Skill in the United States," *International Labor Review,* June 1955, pp. 576–592.

Newhouse, Joseph P., "A Simple Hypothesis of Income Distribution," *Journal of Human Resources,* Vol. 6, No. 1, Winter 1971, pp. 52–74.

Ober, Harry, "Occupational Wage Differentials, 1907–1947," *Monthly Labor Review,* August 1948, pp. 127–134.

Ozanne, R., *Wages in Practice and Theory: McCormick and International Harvester, 1860–1960,* Union of Wisconsin Press, Madison, Wis., 1968.

Perlman, Richard, "Value Productivity and Interindustry Wage Structure," *Industrial and Labor Relations Review,* Vol. 40, No. 2, May 1958, pp. 107–115.

Phelps Brown, E. H., and S. V. Hopkins, "Seven Centuries of Building Wages," *Economica,* Vol. 22, No. 87, August 1955, pp. 195–206.

Phelps Brown, Henry, *The Inequality of Pay,* Oxford University Press, Oxford, 1977.

————, "Seven Centuries of the Prices of Consumables, Compared with Builders' Wage Rates," *Economica,* Vol. 23, No. 92, November 1956, pp. 296–314.

———, "Builders' Wage Rates, Prices, and Population: Some Further Evidence," *Economica,* Vol. 26, No. 101, February 1959, pp. 18–38.

Porter, Felice, "Occupational Pay Relationships and Employment in Textile Mills," *Monthly Labor Review,* June 1977, pp. 51–53.

Pugel, Thomas A., "Profitability, Concentration, and the Interindustry Variation in Wages," *Review of Economics and Statistics,* Vol. 62, No. 2, May 1980, pp. 248–253.

Reder, Melvin W., "The Theory of Occupational Wage Differentials," *American Economic Review,* Vol. 45, No. 5, December 1955, pp. 833–852.

———, "Wage Differentials: Theory of Measurement," in *Aspects of Labor Economics,* Princeton University Press, Princeton, 1962.

Reilly, Kevin T., "Human Capital and Information: The Employer Size-wage Effect," *Journal of Human Resources,* Vol. 30, No. 1, Winter 1995, pp. 1–17.

Rosen, Sherwin, "The Economics of Superstars," *American Economic Review,* Vol. 71, No. 5, December 1986, pp. 845–858.

———, "Prizes and Incentives in Elimination Tournaments," *American Economic Review,* Vol. 76, No. 4, September 1981, pp. 701–715.

Ross, Arthur W., "The Influence of Unionism Upon Earnings," *Quarterly Journal of Economics,* Vol. 62, February 1948.

———, and William Goldner, "Forces Affecting the Interindustry Wage Structure," *Quarterly Journal of Economics,* Vol. 64, May 1950, pp. 245–281.

Sahota, Glen S., "Theories of Personal Income Distribution: A Survey," *Journal of Economic Literature,* Vol. 16, March 1978, pp. 1–55.

Scully, Gerald W., "Interstate Wage Differentials: A Cross Section Analysis," *American Economic Review,* Vol. 59, No. 5, December 1969, pp. 757–773.

Segal, Martin, "The Relation Between Union Wage Impact and Market Structure," *Quarterly Journal of Economics,* Vol. 78, February 1964.

Sieling, Mark S., "Interpreting Pay Structures Through Matrix Application," *Monthly Labor Review,* November 1979, pp. 41–45.

Slichter, Sumner, "Notes on the Structure of Wages," *Review of Economics and Statistics,* Vol. 22, February 1950, pp. 80–89.

Smith, Donald Mitchell, and E. James Jennings, "The Distribution of State Income: Differential Growth of Sectoral Employment," *American Economic Review,* Vol. 66, No. 4, September 1976, pp. 717–722.

Tachibanaki, Toshiaki, "Wage Determination in Japanese Manufacturing Industries—Structural Change and Wage Differentials," *International Economic Review,* Vol. 16, No. 3, October 1975, pp. 562–586.

Taira, Koji, "Wage Differentials in Developing Countries: A Survey of Findings," *International Labor Review,* May 1966, pp. 281–301.

Tarling, Roger, and Frank Wilkinson, "Changes in the Inter-Industry Structure of Earnings in the Post-War Period," *Cambridge Journal of Economics,* Vol. 6, No. 3, September 1982, pp. 231–248.

Thurow, Lester C., *Generating Inequality,* Basic Books, New York, 1975.

———, and Roger E. B. Lucas, *The American Distribution of Income: A Structural Problem,* Joint Economic Committee of Congress, March 1972.

Tinbergen, Jan, "A Positive and Normative Theory of Income Distribution," *Review of Income and Wealth,* Series 16, No. 3, September 1970.

———, *Income Distribution Analysis and Policies,* 1975.

Wachter, M., "Cyclical Variation in the Interindustry Wage Structure," *American Economic Review,* Vol. 60, 1970, pp. 75–84.

Ward, Virginia, L., "Measuring Wage Relationships Among Selected Occupations," *Monthly Labor Review,* May 1980, pp. 21–25.

Weiss, Leonard W., "Concentration and Labor Earnings," *American Economic Review,* Vol. 56, No. 1, March 1966, pp. 96–117.

Williamson, Jeffrey G., "Regional Inequality and the Process of National Development," *Economic Development and Cultural Change,* Vol. 13, No. 4, Part 2, July 1965, pp. 3–84.

———, "The Sources of American Inequality, 1896–1948," *Review of Economics and Statistics,* Vol. 58, No. 4, November 1976, pp. 387–397.

Wolff, Edward N., "On the Relation Between Jobs and School-Acquired Skills," *Contemporary Sociology,* Vol. 8, No. 1, January 1979, pp. 12–14.

B. Efficiency Wage Theory

Akerlof, G. A., "Gift Exchange and Efficiency Wages: Four Views," *American Economic Review,* Vol. 74, 1984, pp. 79–83.

Bell, Linda, and Richard B. Freeman, "Does a Flexible Industry Wage Structure Increase Employment: the U.S. Experience," NBER Working Paper No. 1601, April 1985.

———, "The Causes of Increasing Interindustry Wage Dispersion in the United States," *Industrial and Labor Relations Review,* Vol. 44, No. 2, January 1991, pp. 275–287.

Dickens, William T., and Lawrence F. Katz, "Interindustry Wage Differences and Industry Characteristics," in Kevin Lang and Jonathan Leonard (eds.), *Unemployment and the Structure of Labor Markets,* Basil Blackwell, Oxford, 1987(a).

———, "Interindustry Wage Differences and Theories of Wage Determination," NBER Working Paper No. 2271, June 1987(b).

Heywood, J. S., "Labor Quality and the Concentration-Earnings Hypothesis," *Review of Economics and Statistics,* Vol. 68, 1986.

Hodson, R., and England, P., "Industrial Structure and Sex Differences in Earnings," *Industrial Relations,* Vol. 25, 1986, pp. 16–32.

Holzer, Harry, Lawrence F. Katz, and Alan B. Krueger, "Job Queues and Wages: Some New Evidence on the Minimum Wage and Inter-industry Wage Structure," NBER Working Paper No. 2461, April 1988.

Kalachek, E., and Raines, F., "The Structure of Wage Differences Among Mature Male Workers," *Journal of Human Resources,* Vol. 11, 1976, pp. 484–506.

Katz, Lawrence F., "Efficiency Wage Theories: A Partial Evaluation," in Stanley Fischer (ed.), *NBER Macroeconomics Annual 1986,* MIT Press, Cambridge, MA, 1986.

Katz, Lawrence F., and Summers, Lawrence H., "Can Interindustry Wage Differentials Justify Strategic Trade Policy?" NBER Working Paper No. 2739, October 1988.

Keane, Michael P., "Individual Heterogeneity and Interindustry Wage Differentials," *Journal of Human Resources,* Vol. 28, No. 1, Winter 1993, pp. 134–161.

Krueger, Alan B., and Lawrence H. Summers, "Reflections on the Inter-industry Wage Structure," in K. Lang and J. Leonard, (eds.), *Unemployment and the Structure of Labor Markets,* Basil Blackwell, Oxford, 1987.

————, "Efficiency Wages and the Inter-industry Wage Structure," *Econometrica,* Vol. 56, March 1988, pp. 259–294.

Lawrence, C., and R. Lawrence, "Relative Wages in U.S. Manufacturing: An Endgame Interpretation," *Brookings Papers on Economic Activity,* 1985, pp. 47–106.

Lawson, Tony, "On the Stability of the Inter-industry Structure of Earnings in the U.K.: 1954–1978," *Cambridge Journal of Economics,* Vol. 6, No. 3, September 1982, pp. 249–266.

Levine, David I., "Can Wage Increases Pay for Themselves? Tests With a Production Function," *Economic Journal,* Vol. 102, September 1992, pp. 1102–1115.

Montgomery, E., and D. Stockton, "Evidence on Causes of the Rising Dispersion of Relative Wages," mimeo, April 1985.

Oi, Walter, "Heterogeneous Firms and the Organization of Production," *Economic Inquiry,* Vol. 21, April 1983, pp. 147–171.

Raff, Daniel M. G., and Lawrence H. Summers, "Did Henry Ford Pay Efficiency Wages?" *Journal of Labor Economics,* Vol. 5, No. 4, Part 2, October 1987, pp. 57–86.

Tarling, Roger, and Frank Wilkinson, "Changes in the Interindustry Structure of Earnings in the Post-War Period," *Cambridge Journal of Economics,* Vol. 6, No. 3, September 1982, pp. 231–248.

DISCUSSION QUESTIONS

1. Explain the role of industry concentration and industry profitability in the determination of industry wage differentials.
2. Discuss two reasons why larger firms might pay higher wages than smaller ones.
3. Briefly describe each of the four models developed by the efficiency wage theory to explain the benefits a firm gains from paying higher wages. Discuss how each relates to the empirical evidence on industry wage differentials.

4. Summarize the evidence on the relation between changes in the industrial composition of employment and the rise of earnings inequality in the 1980s in the United States.
5. Discuss three reasons why wage differentials between different skill levels of workers (or occupations) might change over time.

WEALTH AND SAVINGS

PART III

Chapter

10

HOUSEHOLD WEALTH

In Part 1 of the book, we saw how income inequality is high in the United States by world standards and has been growing in the United States as well as in many European countries. But income is only an annual flow of economic resources. Economists believe that wealth—the stock of economic resources—may be a better indicator of the long-term economic well-being of a household. As it turns out, the United States also has the most unequal distribution of wealth in the industrialized world, and wealth inequality has gotten more severe over the past dozen years or so. Why has wealth inequality been growing in the United States? Why is the U.S. wealth distribution more unequal than in other advanced countries?

In Part 3 of the book, we switch focus from household income to household wealth. Wealth represents a *stock* of accumulated assets; income represents a flow of current output. Families not only receive income over the course of a year but also save part of their income in the form of housing, savings accounts, stocks, bonds, and the like. Such accumulated savings are referred to as wealth. Wealth, like income, has an important bearing on the well-being of families and individuals. This chapter develops the concept of household wealth, discusses some of the problems inherent in its measurement, and presents statistics on changes in both average wealth holdings among households and the inequality of wealth holdings over time.

What determines the distribution of wealth? The principal way households accumulate wealth is through savings. Therefore, in order to understand why the distribution of wealth has changed over time or why wealth differs among households at any given time, we must understand savings behavior. In Chapter 10, we investigate the process of household wealth accumulation, or household savings. We consider different models of savings behavior and evaluate the available evidence.

The first part of this chapter, Section 10.1, develops the concept of household wealth and discusses several methodological issues involved in its definition and measurement. The household balance sheet for 1989 is also shown. Section 10.2 presents statistics showing historical change in both household wealth and its composition. Two issues are of particular interest. First, have average wealth holdings increased faster or slower than average income? Second, what are the major forms in which wealth is accumulated by households—such as housing, stocks, and bank deposits—and has their relative importance changed over time? Changes in homeownership rates are also shown.

In Section 10.3, we investigate changes in household wealth inequality in the United States. We begin with a discussion of some of the methodological issues involved in estimating the size distribution of household wealth. The next part shows long-term trends in U.S. wealth concentration covering the period from 1922 to 1989. The third part of Section 10.3 shows more detailed estimates of changes in wealth inequality for the period from 1962 to 1989. We also look at changes in average wealth over this period, differences in the composition of wealth by wealth and age class, and the relation between family income and family wealth.

Section 10.4 draws international comparisons of household wealth inequality. The first part of this section shows long-term time trends in household wealth inequality for Sweden, the United Kingdom, and the United States. Comparisons of more recent measures of household wealth inequality are presented for Canada, France, Sweden, the United Kingdom, and the United States. A summary of the chapter is provided in Section 10.5.

10.1 WHAT IS HOUSEHOLD WEALTH?

Wealth and Well-Being

Why are we interested in household wealth? Most studies use income as a measure of family well-being. Though certain forms of income are derived from wealth, such as interest from savings accounts and bonds, dividends from stock shares, and rent from real estate, income and wealth are by no means identical. Many kinds of income, such as wages and salaries and transfer payments, are not derived from household wealth, and many forms of wealth, such as owner-occupied housing, produce no corresponding income flow.

Moreover, family wealth by itself is also a source of well-being, independent of the direct financial income it provides. There are four reasons. First, some assets, particularly owner-occupied housing, provide services directly to their owner. This is also true for consumer durables, such as automobiles. Such assets can substitute for money income in satisfying economic needs.

Families with the same money income but differing amounts of housing and consumer durables will have different levels of welfare.

Second, wealth is a source of consumption, independent of the direct money income it provides. With the possible exception of consumer durables, assets can be converted directly into cash and thus provide for immediate consumption needs. This is also true for the equity in owner-occupied housing, because second mortgages and home equity loans are another source of credit.

Third, the availability of financial assets can provide liquidity to a family in times of economic stress (such as occasioned by unemployment, sickness, or family breakup). In this sense, wealth is a source of economic security for the family over and above the income that it directly provides.

Fourth, large fortunes can be a source of economic and social power that is not directly captured in annual income. Large accumulations of financial and business assets can confer special privileges to their holders. Such large fortunes are often transmitted to succeeding generations, thus creating family "dynasties."

Thus, wealth holdings provide another dimension to household welfare over and above income flows. As we shall see in Section 10.3, attempts have been made to create a more comprehensive measure of well-being that incorporates information on both family income and wealth.

Marketable Wealth

The conventional definition of household wealth includes assets and liabilities that have a current market value and that are directly or indirectly marketable. A typical list of assets includes owner-occupied housing and other real estate; consumer durables; cash, checking, and savings accounts; bonds and other financial instruments; corporate stock; equity in unincorporated businesses; and trust fund equity. We will refer to this measure as "marketable household wealth" (or simply "household wealth"), since it represents those assets over which the family or individual has control. This notion corresponds to wealth as a store of value and is used in conjunction with a standard national accounting framework.

Table 10.1 presents the **balance sheet** for the household sector in 1989, the latest year for which comprehensive data are available. The wealth accounts contain a fairly complicated array of entries. The full balance sheet is first divided into two major categories: assets and liabilities. Assets consist of items owned by households which have a positive value to them, while liabilities are debts, which by definition have a negative value. The difference between total assets and total liabilities is called **net worth** or, simply, wealth. In 1989, total household assets amounted to 23.5 trillion dollars, total liabilities were 3.2 trillion dollars, and household net worth was 20.2 trillion dollars.

Assets are divided into three main groups. The first, tangible assets, includes stocks of real goods that are both "reproducible," such as houses,

**Table 10.1 Balance Sheet of Total Household Wealth, 1989[a]
(billions of dollars)**

Panel A: Marketable Net Worth

	Value of Component	Percent of Total Asset
I. Total Assets	23,455	100
A. Tangible Assets	10,894	46
1. Owner-occupied housing	6,118	26
2. Other real estate and undeveloped land	2,842	12
3. Consumer durables	1,934	8
B. Financial Assets	4,916	21
1. Checking accounts, cash, and currency	493	2
2. Time deposits, money market funds, CDs, IRAs, Keogh plans, and other retirement accounts	2,834	12
3. Bonds and financial securities	1,238	5
4. Life insurance cash surrender value	351	1
C. Equities	6,645	28
1. Stocks and mutual funds	2,500	11
2. Unincorporated business equity	3,478	15
3. Trust equity	667	3
D. Miscellaneous Assets[b]	1,001	4
II. Liabilities	3,211	14
A. Mortgage Debt[c]	2,470	11
B. Other Debt[d]	742	3
III. Net Worth	20,244	86
Memo:		
A. Home Equity[e]	4,432	19
B. Pension Fund Reserves	2,857	12

(continued)

and "nonreproducible," such as land. In 1989, total tangible assets owned by households were worth 10.9 trillion dollars, which amounted to almost half of total household assets. The major tangible asset owned by households is owner-occupied housing (that is, houses that are lived in by their

Table 10.1   *(concluded)*

Panel B. Other Concepts of Household Wealth

Total Net Worth		Ratio to Marketable Net Worth
Marketable wealth	20,244	1.00
Fungible wealth	18,310	0.90
Financial wealth	13,878	0.69
Augmented wealth	31,686	1.57
A. Pension Wealth	3,540	0.17
B. Social Security Wealth	7,902	0.39

[a] Sources: 1989 Survey of Consumer Finances (tape); Federal Reserve Board (1990) Flow of Funds; and Wolff (1994).
[b] This includes amounts that the family business owes the family, gold, royalties, jewelry, furs, and loans to friends and relatives.
[c] This includes home equity loans, mortgages or notes outstanding on real estate already sold, and mortgages on other property.
[d] This includes credit card debt, consumer loans, the amount the family owes to its family business, margin account debt, and life insurance loans.
[e] Defined as gross value of owner-occupied housing less outstanding mortgage debt.

owner). This accounted for about 26 percent of total household assets. The second component consists of land, apartment buildings, other rental property, and other real estate held by households. This group made up 12 percent of all assets. The third category, called consumer durables, includes automobiles, washing machines and other appliances, furniture, and other long-lasting household equipment. Cars are the major component of household durables, and altogether durables comprised 8 percent of total assets.[1]

The second major group is referred to as financial assets. These are assets which function as money or are readily convertible to money. They include cash, demand deposits (checking accounts), and time and savings deposits, which function directly as a means of exchange (and together constitute "M2"). They also include bonds, notes, and financial securities issued mainly by corporations and the government. Such securities are "promissory notes," by which the borrower agrees to pay back the lender a certain amount of money (the principal plus interest), at a certain date. The fourth component in this group is the "cash surrender value" of life insurance funds. Certain life insurance plans (called "full-life insurance") allow individuals to contribute to a savings funds, and the amount the individual

---

[1] In some wealth accounts, another component, called household inventories, is also included in tangible assets. This is a catch-all group which consists of "semidurable" items kept in homes, such as food, clothing, and general housewares.

can withdraw from this savings fund is referred to as its cash surrender value.

In 1989, financial assets constituted 21 percent of household assets. Demand deposits and currency together amounted to only 2 percent of total assets, while time and savings deposits constituted 12 percent. Bonds and other securities amounted to 5 percent, while the cash surrender value of insurance plans was only 1 percent.

The third major group consists of equities or ownership rights. A corporate stock certificate issued by a company represents ownership of a certain percentage of the company's assets. Unincorporated business equity refers to small businesses (such as a farm or a store) owned directly by individuals, in contrast to corporations, which are owned through stock shares. A person's equity in an unincorporated business is the value of the business. The third item, trust fund equity, refers to bank deposits, securities, corporate stock, and other financial instruments, which are held in a special legal arrangement called a trust fund. In a typical trust, the actual assets are managed by a specially named administrator (often a bank), and the income earned from the assets in the trust is remitted to individual beneficiaries. Trust funds held for individuals are counted as part of household wealth.

As a group, equities comprised 28 percent of total household assets in 1989. Corporate stock shares made up 11 percent of total household assets, unincorporated business equity 15 percent, and trust fund equity 3 percent.

On the liability side, the major form of household debt is home mortgages. A mortgage is a loan issued normally by a bank and usually for a period of 15 to 30 years, which is used to finance the purchase of real property, particularly homes. In 1989, mortgage debt comprised 77 percent of total household debt. The remaining 23 percent consisted of other household debts, including automobile and other consumer loans and credit card debt. Together, total household debt amounted to 14 percent of the value of total household assets.

Two other entries are shown in the bottom of Table 10.1. The first of these is home equity, defined as the gross value of owner-occupied housing less outstanding mortgage debt. This represents the amount of money a family could net from the sale of the house (after paying off its outstanding mortgage balance). Home mortgages amounted to 28 percent of the value of owner-occupied housing. As a result, home equity made up a smaller proportion of total assets than the gross value of owner-occupied housing—19 versus 26 percent.

The last entry is the reserves (assets) of pension funds. These funds are accumulated mainly by corporations in order to pay pension benefits for their workers when they retire. In 1989, they amounted to 12 percent of total household assets. Technically speaking, these reserves are not part of marketable household wealth, since households have no control over the assets in these funds and cannot directly draw on these funds. On the other hand, these reserves are held for the benefit of individuals and therefore have some of the characteristics of a trust fund. We shall discuss the treatment of retirement wealth in the next section.

In sum, the principal household asset in 1989 was owner-occupied housing, which comprised 26 percent of total assets. However, net home equity amounted to only 19 percent of total assets. Financial assets as a group were 21 percent of total assets, while corporate stocks and unincorporated business equity were 25 percent. The other major component, other real estate, comprised 12 percent of total assets. The ratio of total debt to total assets was 14 percent.

Other Definitions of Household Wealth

A theme that regularly emerges in the literature on household wealth is that there is no unique concept or definition of wealth that is satisfactory for all purposes. Two concepts that are more narrow than marketable wealth are often used. The first of these is **fungible household wealth,** defined as marketable wealth less consumer durables. This definition includes only assets that can be readily converted to cash (that is, "fungible" ones). Although consumer durables provide consumption services directly to the household, they are not easily marketed. In fact, the resale value of these items typically far understates the value of their consumption services to the household. As shown in Panel B, total fungible household wealth amounted to 18.3 trillion dollars in 1989, which was 90 percent of total marketable wealth.

The second is **financial household wealth,** defined as fungible net worth minus net equity in owner-occupied housing, where net equity is defined as the difference between the value of the property and the outstanding mortgage debt on the property. Financial wealth is a more "liquid" concept than marketable wealth, since one's home is difficult to convert into cash in the short term. It thus reflects the resources that may be directly available for consumption or various forms of investments in the short term. As shown in Panel B, total household financial wealth was 13.9 trillion dollars in 1989, 69 percent of marketable wealth.

One of the major developments since the end of World War II has been the enormous growth in both public and private pension systems. Even though such pension funds are not in the direct control of individuals or families, they are a source of future income to families and thus may be perceived as a form of family wealth. Moreover, as Martin Feldstein (1974) has argued, insofar as families accumulate "traditional" wealth to provide for future consumption needs, the growth of such pension funds may have offset private savings and hence traditional wealth accumulation.

A wider definition of household wealth will thus add some valuation of pension rights, from both public and private sources, to marketable wealth. Such a measure provides a better gauge of potential future consumption. **Augmented household wealth** is defined as the sum of household marketable wealth, social security wealth, and pension wealth. **Social security wealth** is defined as the present discounted value of the stream of future social security benefits, and **pension wealth** is defined as the present discounted value of future pension benefits.[2] As is apparent from the definitions, these two forms of wealth are not fungible or marketable, since individuals cannot convert these assets into cash.[3]

What is the rationale for including these two forms of wealth? The main motivation is that from the standpoint of an individual, a future guaranteed flow of income is in many ways like owning a financial asset. Indeed, there are marketable assets called "annuities," which have precisely the characteristic of providing a steady stream of income after a certain time (or age) is reached. The anticipated social security (or pension) benefits that an individual will receive after retirement is comparable to such an annuity. From the individual's point of view, then, a guaranteed stream of future pension or social security benefits may be as much a form of wealth as money put into a savings account that will be drawn on after retirement.[4]

According to the author's estimates, total pension wealth in 1989 was $3.5 trillion, and total social security wealth was $7.9 trillion (see Panel B). Together, they amounted to 57 percent of marketable net worth. Social security wealth by itself was thus larger than any other component of household wealth, including owner-occupied housing and total bank accounts. As we shall see in Section 10.3, the large size of social security wealth has important implications for differences in the distribution of marketable household wealth and augmented household wealth.

10.2 Time-Series Data on Household Wealth and Its Composition

There are two major historical time series available on aggregate household wealth in the United States: (1) For the period 1900–1958, household balance sheet data are available in Raymond Goldsmith, Dorothy Brady, and Horst Mendershausen (1956) and Raymond Goldsmith, Robert Lipsey, and Morris Mendelsen (1963). (2) For the period 1946 to the present, complete balance sheet data are contained in the Flow of Funds Accounts of the Board of Governors of the Federal Reserve System (these are published annually).

Unfortunately, the wealth data contained in these two sources are not entirely consistent with each other, thus necessitating several adjustments to make them comparable. First, there are several differences in the categorization of assets between the various data sources. These differences do not

---

[2] Recall from Section 5.2 the procedure used to compute the present value of a stream of future income.

[3] The exceptions are certain forms of pension plans that allow workers to convert their accumulated pension contributions into cash at any point in time (their so-called "cash surrender value"), and IRA and Keogh plans, which are also currently convertible to cash. These forms of wealth are already included in marketable wealth.

[4] The imputation of both pension and social security wealth involves a large number of steps. These are presented in greater detail in the Appendix to Chapter 13.

affect the wealth totals, only the composition among asset categories. Second, there are some differences in the definition of household wealth. Third, there are methodological differences. For example, the two series treat trust fund equity and pensions differently. Fourth, for the overlapping period, 1946–1958, the data contained in the earlier two Goldsmith works have since been revised by the Federal Reserve Board. Complete details on the adjustments can be found in Edward Wolff (1989).

Trends in Average Wealth

The combined estimates are shown in Table 10.2 for selected years between 1900 and 1992 (see also Figure 10.1). The basic data have been converted to figures on average wealth per household in constant (1992) dollars. Between 1900 and 1992, average marketable wealth increased by a factor of 2.3, or by 0.9 percent per year. However, the growth was not uniform over the period. Between 1900 and 1929, it grew at a substantially higher rate, 1.4 percent per year. During the Depression and War years of 1929 to 1949, average household wealth actually declined in real terms, altogether by 7 percent. During the high-growth period of the 1950s and 1960s, its growth accelerated to 1.9 percent per year, its highest level of the century. Then,

Table 10.2 Mean Marketable Net Worth, Augmented Net Worth, GNP, and Personal Disposable Income per Household, 1900–1992[a] (1992 Dollars)

Year	Marketable Net Worth	Pension Wealth	Social Security Wealth	Augmented Net Worth	Personal Disposable Income	GNP
1900	92,609	0	0	92,609	16,065	24,064
1929	137,404	576	0	137,980	23,073	34,612
1949	127,921	3,570	33,411	164,903	25,773	37,936
1969	187,366	16,747	82,861	286,974	37,714	55,613
1989	224,751	43,789	96,120	364,659	44,399	62,658
1992	217,428	45,337	94,688	357,453	44,414	61,513
Annual Rate of Growth (in percent)						
1900–29	1.36			1.37	1.25	1.25
1929–49	−0.36	9.12		0.89	0.55	0.46
1949–69	1.91	7.73	4.54	2.77	1.90	1.91
1969–89	0.83	4.38	0.44	1.05	0.59	0.58
1989–92	−1.10	1.16	−0.50	−0.67	0.01	−0.61
1900–92	0.93			1.47	1.11	1.02

[a]Sources: Wolff (1989), Wolff (1994), *Economic Report of the President, 1994*, and author's computations from the 1989 Survey of Consumer Finances.

Figure 10.1   Marketable and Augmented Wealth, GNP, and Personal Disposable Income per Household, 1900–1992

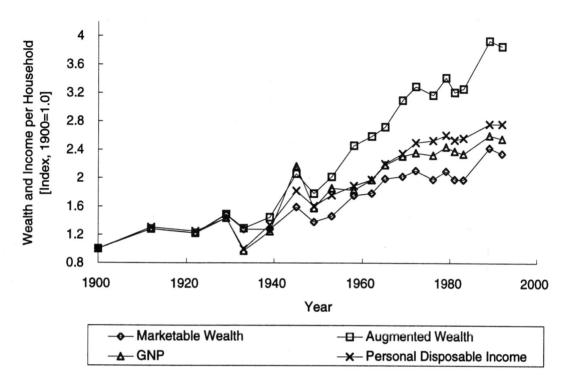

during the ensuing slow-growth period from 1969 to 1989, the growth in mean wealth per household slowed to 0.8 percent per year. Between 1989 and 1992, it again declined in real terms, by 1.1 percent per year.

In comparison, between 1900 and 1992, real GNP per household rose by a factor of 2.6, or 1.0 percent per year, faster than average wealth holdings. Personal disposable income per household grew slightly more, by 1.1 percent per year, over the same period. However, with the exception of the 1929–1949 and 1989–1992 periods, wealth has grown at the same rate or faster than personal disposable income and GNP. Between 1949 and 1969, all three increased at virtually the same rate. From 1969 to 1989, average household wealth rose by 0.8 percent per year, while disposable income and GNP per household increased by 0.6 percent per year.

Augmented household wealth grew considerably faster than personal disposable income or marketable wealth. Between 1900 and 1992, augmented wealth per household increased by a factor of 3.9, compared to a 2.3-fold increase in average marketable wealth and a 2.8-fold increase in average disposable income. Average pension wealth mushroomed from virtually zero in 1900 to over $45,000 in 1992, and average social security wealth from zero in 1937 (when the social security system started up) to over $94,000. Even in 1949, pension wealth amounted to only 3 percent of marketable wealth and social security wealth to 26 percent, compared to 21 percent and 44 percent, respectively, in 1992.

Insofar as the standard of living is reflected in both family income and family wealth holdings, differences in growth rates between the two will affect our measurement of changes in well-being. If wealth grows faster than income, then our usual income-based measures will understate the true growth in the standard of living. Such differences are particularly marked between personal disposable income and augmented net worth. Insofar as families are deferring more and more income to their retirement years, the growth in current income will increasingly understate the growth in well-being.

Changes in Wealth Composition

The portfolio composition of household wealth is important for several reasons. First, it shows the forms in which households save. Do households save for direct consumption, as, for example, in the form of housing and automobiles? Do families save for precautionary reasons, as, for example, in the form of demand deposits or time and savings deposits? Do they save for retirement, as in insurance plans, IRAs (Individual Retirement Accounts), etc.? Or do they save mainly for investment purposes, as in financial securities and corporate stock? This disposition of household wealth has implications for theories of household savings, as we shall discuss in the next chapter.

Second, this information indicates how much financial capital is available for investment purposes by the business sector of the economy. If households save mainly to finance their own consumption, particularly in housing, then only a relatively small proportion of total household savings will be available for new investment by the business sector. On the other hand, if savings takes mainly the form of financial instruments, then a considerable amount of capital will become available to the business community. Third, these data have a bearing on the theory of risk and portfolio selection (which assets are purchased) among families. Assets differ in both their expected yield and their attendant risk. A body of theory has been developed in economics to explain how families trade off expected returns on assets and risk.

Historical time trends on wealth composition are shown in Table 10.3 (see also Figure 10.2). The sources used to construct this table are the same as for Table 10.2.[5] The results show that there have been important changes in the composition of household wealth over the twentieth century. Consumer durables rose from 6 percent of total assets in 1900 to 9 percent in

---

[5]Note that the 1989 figures in this table differ slightly from those reported in Table 10.1, because of the need to make the accounting scheme consistent over time.

Part III   Wealth and Savings

Table 10.3 The Composition of Aggregate Marketable Household Wealth, 1900–1989[a] (Percent of Gross Assets)

Year	Consumer Durables	Gross House Value	Bank Deposits and Other Liquid Assets	Nonhome Real Estate and Unincorporated Business Equity	Corporate Stock and Financial Securities	Total Debt	Home Equity
1900	5.8	22.6	5.0	46.6	20.0	4.1	21.4
1929	6.8	16.8	7.9	29.5	38.9	6.8	15.4
1949	8.3	23.7	13.0	33.2	21.8	5.7	22.3
1969	9.1	25.0	13.4	23.5	29.0	11.7	18.4
1989	8.6	27.2	16.4	28.1	19.6	14.3	18.9

[a] Sources: Wolff (1989) and Wolff (1994). Miscellaneous assets are excluded from household wealth.
Key:
Gross house value—Gross value of owner-occupied housing.
Nonhome real estate and unincorporated business equity—Gross value of other real estate plus net equity in unincorporated farm and nonfarm businesses.
Deposits and other liquid assets—Cash, currency, demand deposits, time deposits, money market funds, cash surrender value of insurance and pension plans, and IRAs.
Corporate stock and financial securities—Corporate stock, including mutual funds; corporate bonds, government bonds, open-market paper, notes, and other fixed-interest financial securities; and net equity in personal trusts and estates.
Total debt—Mortgage, installment, consumer, and other debt.
Home equity—Gross value of owner-occupied housing less apportioned mortgage debt (split proportionally between owner-occupied housing and other real estate).

1989. Perhaps, somewhat surprisingly, (gross) owner-occupied housing increased only moderately as a proportion of gross assets, from 23 percent in 1900 to 27 percent in 1989. In fact, the increase was not continuous throughout the period. Between 1900 and 1912, owner-occupied housing fell from 23 to 18 percent of total assets and then remained at this level until 1945. Thereafter, the proportion rose almost continuously to 30 percent in 1979, and then fell off to 27 percent in 1989.

The trend in home equity (the difference between the gross value of owner-occupied housing and mortgage debt) was somewhat different. Home equity remained relatively constant as a proportion of total assets from 1912 to 1945, at about 17 percent, increased to 23 percent in 1953, and then fell off to 19 percent by 1989. What is particularly striking is the difference in trend between gross house value and net home equity. The two figures remained quite close from 1900 to 1949, indicating relatively little mortgage debt on homes. They diverged more and more thereafter, indicating a rising proportion of mortgage debt to home value. Home mort-

Figure 10.2 Composition of Household Wealth, 1900–1989

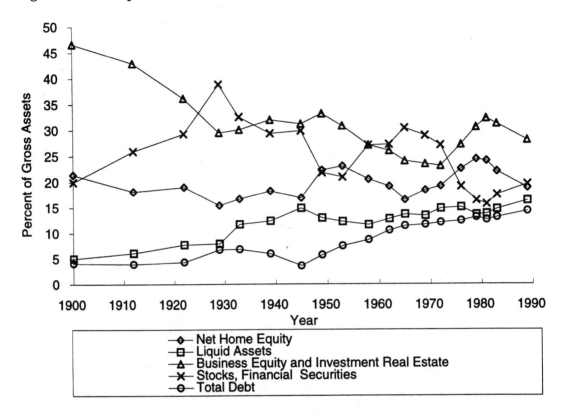

gage debt grew from 5 percent of the gross value of owner-occupied housing at the beginning of the century to 31 percent by 1989.

This tendency is also reflected in increasing total household debt. Total debt as a proportion of total assets remained at about 4 to 6 percent of total assets from 1900 to 1949 and then rose rather steadily over the postwar period, reaching 14 percent in 1989. The ratio of debt other than home mortgages to total assets grew from 2.9 percent in 1900 to 6.1 percent by 1989.

Bank deposits and other liquid assets showed relatively steady growth as a share of total assets, climbing from 5 percent in 1900 to 16 percent in 1989. In contrast, over the same period nonhome real estate and unincorporated business equity fell almost continuously as a proportion of assets, from 47 to 28 percent. Most of the decrease is accounted for by the declining importance of small owner-run farms in the U.S. economy. The share of unincorporated farm business equity in total assets alone fell from 27 percent in 1900 to 5 percent in 1989.

The most volatile element in the household portfolio is corporate stock and financial securities. Between 1900 and 1929, their share in total assets

Part III   Wealth and Savings

almost doubled, from 20 to 39 percent, then fell off to 22 percent in 1949, increased to 29 percent in 1969, and then declined to 16 percent in 1979 before rising again to 20 percent in 1989. The rise and fall of this component is largely explained by movements in the stock market, which had peaks in 1929, 1969, and 1989.

In sum, over the twentieth century, households have invested more of their wealth in consumer durables. Home equity has remained relatively constant as a share of total assets. Among investment type assets, households have substituted more liquid and less risky assets such as bank deposits and money market funds for risky, illiquid assets such as small business equity and nonhome real estate. Changes in the share of corporate stock and financial securities in the household portfolio tend to follow movements in the stock market. Finally, the rising ratio of liabilities to assets suggests the greater willingness of households to take on debt, as well as the greater accessibility of mortgages on real property and the greater availability of consumer credit.

Homeownership Rates

Table 10.4 shows statistics on the homeownership rate, the percentage of housing units that are owner occupied (that is, owned by their occupants). The data cover the years from 1920 to 1991. One of the more remarkable trends in the twentieth century has been the increasing proportion of American families owning their own homes. For the full population, the homeownership rate increased from 46 percent in 1920 to 48 percent in 1930, fell to 44 percent during the Great Depression, and then rose almost

Table 10.4 Homeownership Trends in the United States, 1920–1991[a] (Percent of Housing Units That Are Owner-Occupied)

Year	All Races	Whites	Nonwhites
1920	45.6	48.2	23.9
1930	47.8	50.2	25.2
1940	43.6	45.7	23.6
1950	55.0	57.0	34.9
1960	61.9	64.4	38.4
1970	62.9	65.4	42.1
1975	64.6	67.4	43.8
1980	64.4	67.8	44.2
1985	63.5	66.8	42.8
1991	64.2	67.9	43.2

[a] Sources: U.S. Bureau of the Census, *Statistical Abstract of the United States: 1989* (109th Edition), Washington, D.C., 1989; U.S. Bureau of the Census, *Statistical Abstract of the United States: 1994* (114th Edition), Washington, D.C., 1994.

continuously to 65 percent in 1975. However, since 1975, the homeowner-ship rate has remained relatively unchanged. It actually fell by a full percentage point between 1975 and 1985 but by 1991 was back to its 1975 level.

Table 10.4 also shows separate statistics by race. Time trends were quite similar for whites and nonwhites. Among nonwhite families, in fact, the homeownership rate almost doubled between 1920 and 1975. The home-ownership rate peaked for this group in 1980, at 44 percent, and fell to 43 percent in 1991. However, the homeownership rate among nonwhite families still remains considerably below that of white families.

Homeownership is often considered a key determinant of middle-class status. After increasing for many years, the percentage of American families owning their own home has been more or less unchanged since 1975. These results are the basis of the concern expressed in recent years about the greater difficulty of a family owning its own home and thus gaining entry to the middle class.

10.3 Wealth Inequality in the United States

There are now official estimates of the size distribution of household income in the United States today (as well as in most other industrialized countries). The United States Census Bureau conducts an annual survey in March, called the Current Population Survey, which provides detailed information on individual and household earnings and income. On the basis of these data, the U.S. Census Bureau constructs its estimates of both family and household income inequality. Moreover, the Current Population Surveys have been conducted in the United States since 1947. As a result, there exists a consistent time-series on household income distribution for the United States which covers almost five decades.

Unfortunately, comparable data do not exist on the size distribution of household wealth for the United States or, for that matter, for any other country in the world. There are no official household surveys conducted on an annual basis for this purpose. As a result, researchers in this field have had to make estimates of household wealth inequality from a variety of sources, which are sometimes inconsistent. Compounding this problem is the fact that household wealth is much more heavily concentrated in the upper percentiles of the distribution than income. Thus, unless surveys or data sources are especially designed to cover the top wealth groups in a country, it is quite easy to produce biased estimates of the size distribution of wealth which understate the true level of inequality. The net result is that estimates of household wealth distribution are more problematic than those of income distribution.

In this section, we shall first discuss the methods researchers have used to measure inequality in household wealth. We shall then look at long-term time trends in wealth concentration in the United States and then more recent changes.

Methods Used to Estimate Wealth Inequality

There have been four principal sources of data for developing household wealth estimates: (1) estate tax data, (2) household survey data, (3) wealth tax data, and (4) income capitalization techniques. Each has its characteristic advantages and disadvantages.

Estate Tax Data   Estate tax data was the first major source of data used for wealth analysis. When someone dies, the person's assets are said to comprise his or her estate, and estate tax records are actual tax returns filed for probate. Such data have a great degree of reliability, since they are subject to scrutiny and audit by the state. Their main limitation (in the United States, at least) is that the threshold for filing is relatively high, so only a small proportion of estates (typically, one percent or so) are required to file returns.[6]

Another difficulty with this data source is that the sample consists of decedents. Since most researchers are interested in the distribution of wealth among the *living* population, a technique based on "mortality multipliers" is used to infer the distribution of wealth among the actual population. If mortality rates were the same for each group, then the wealth of decedents would constitute a representative sample of the living population, and researchers could use the estate data directly. However, mortality rates are much greater for older people than younger ones, so different "weights" must be assigned to the estates filed by decedents of different ages. Mortality rates are also higher for men than for women (that is, women, on average, live longer than men). They are also higher for black individuals than whites. As a result, estates are assigned a weight based on the inverse of the group's mortality rate (one divided by the mortality rate), and these are then used to generate the size distribution of wealth in the living population.

Estimates of wealth inequality based on this technique are, as might be expected, quite sensitive to the precision of the mortality multipliers. The estimates can have a very large standard error, particularly for the young, since there are very few of them in the sample. This means that the results are very sensitive to who happens to die in a given year and may therefore not be very reliable for young adults. There are two other problems associated with this technique. First, insofar as mortality rates are inversely correlated with wealth (that is, the rich tend to live longer), the resulting multipliers can be biased.[7] Most studies do try to correct for this problem by using mortality rates for the wealthy that are lower than for the population as a whole, due to the longer expected life span of the wealthy.

---

[6] In Great Britain the threshold is considerably lower, so tax returns are filed on the majority of estates. This is also true for some states in the United States, as well as Washington, D.C., which have their own estate tax requirements.

[7] See Jianakoplos, Menchik, and Irvine (1989) for some recent evidence on the correlation between wealth and life expectancy.

Second, the distribution of wealth estimated by this technique is for individuals, rather than for families. Changing ownership patterns within families (for example, joint ownership of the family's house) can affect estimated wealth concentration. For example, as noted by Anthony Atkinson (1975) and Anthony Shorrocks (1987), marital customs and relations have changed over the century. Married women now inherit more wealth and have higher wealth levels than they did in 1900 or 1930. This reduces individual concentration even if household wealth inequality does not change. For example, between 1929 and 1953, Robert Lampman (1962) reported that the percentage of married women among top wealth holders increased from 9 to 18 percent. As a result, since most researchers are interested in the distribution of family wealth rather than individual wealth, additional imputations must be performed to infer family wealth from estimates of individual wealth holdings.[8]

Another problem with this data source is underreporting and nonfiling for tax avoidance. Though the returns are subject to audit, the value of cash on hand, jewelry, housewares, and business assets are difficult to ascertain. Their value is typically understated in order to reduce the tax liability of the estate. Moreover, **inter vivos transfers** (that is, transfers of wealth between living individuals), particularly in anticipation of death, can bias estimates of household wealth among the living. If older people pass on wealth to their children just before they die, then their estates would tend to underrepresent the wealth of comparably aged individuals still living.

Estate tax data have been extensively used by Anthony Atkinson and A. J. Harrison (1978) and Anthony Shorrocks (1987) for the United Kingdom, and Robert Lampman (1962), James Smith (1984, 1987), and Edward Wolff and Marcia Marley (1989) for the United States. The long-term time-series on wealth concentration for Britain and the United States are based on estate tax data (see the second part of Section 10.3).

Household Survey Data Household surveys are questionnaires that are given to a sample of households in a population. Their primary advantage is to provide considerable discretion to the interviewer about the information requested of respondents. Their major drawback is that information provided by the respondent is often inaccurate (response error), and in many cases, the information requested is not provided at all (nonresponse problems). Another problem is that because household wealth is extremely skewed, the very rich (the so-called "upper tail" of the distribution) are often considerably underrepresented in random samples. An alternative is to use stratified samples, based typically on income tax returns, which oversample the rich. However, studies indicate that response error and nonre-

---

[8]These typically involve making assumptions about marriage patterns—in particular, the correlation between the wealth holdings of spouses (whether, for example, rich husbands tend to be married to rich wives or poor wives).

sponse rates are considerably higher among the wealthy than among the middle class. Moreover, there are problems in "weighting" the sample in order to reflect the actual population distribution. Results based on three major wealth surveys for the United States, the 1962 Survey of Financial Characteristics of Consumers and the 1983 and 1989 Surveys of Consumer Finances, are presented in the third part of Section 10.3.

Income Capitalization Techniques The third source of wealth data is based on the "income capitalization" technique, which is usually applied to a sample of income tax returns.[9] In this procedure, certain income flows, such as dividends, rents, and interest, are converted into corresponding asset values based on the average asset yield. For example, dividends are capitalized into corporate stock holdings by dividing dividends reported in an income tax return by the average ratio of dividends to corporate stock in the economy as a whole. This technique when applied to a large sample of tax returns can provide an estimate of the size distribution of wealth.

This source also suffers from a number of problems. First, only assets with a corresponding income flow are covered in this procedure. Thus, owner-occupied housing, consumer durables, and idle land can not be directly captured. Also, in the United States, state and local bonds cannot be estimated, because this source of interest income is exempt from federal income taxes. Second, the estimation procedure rests heavily on the assumption that asset yields are uncorrelated with asset levels (that is, for example, that large stockholders will receive the same average return on their stock holdings as small stockholders). Any actual correlation between asset holdings and yields can produce biased estimates. Third, the observational unit is based on the tax return. Various assumptions must be made in order to construct family wealth estimates from tax unit wealth.

Wealth Tax Data A fourth source is wealth tax return data, which is available in a number of European countries such as Germany, Sweden, and Switzerland. These countries assess taxes not only on current income but also on the stock of household wealth. Though there is typically a threshold for paying wealth taxes, population coverage can be considerably greater than that of estate tax returns. However, the measurement problems are similar to that of estate tax data. The filer has a great incentive to understate the value of his or her assets, or even not to report them at all, for tax avoidance. Moreover, the assets subject to tax do not cover the full range of household assets (for example, consumer durables, pensions, and life insurance policies are often excluded). In addition, the observational unit is the tax return unit, which does not directly correspond to the family unit. Wealth tax data have been used extensively by Roland Spånt (1987) for an analysis of wealth trends in Sweden (see Section 10.4).

---

[9]The earliest use of this technique on U.S. data was a 1939 study by Stewart.

Long-Term Trends in Household Wealth Inequality in the United States

Data on the size distribution of household wealth in the United States are available principally from estate tax records and household surveys. A reasonably consistent series of estate tax records for the very wealthy, collected from national estate tax records, exists for selected years between 1922 and 1986. Estimates of household wealth inequality are also provided in four surveys conducted by the Federal Reserve Board, in 1962, 1983, 1986, and 1989. They are from a 1969 synthetic dataset constructed from income tax returns and information provided in the Census of Population and from the 1979 Income Survey and Development Program (ISDP), conducted by the U.S. Bureau of the Census.

The author put these data together to construct a time-series on wealth concentration in the United States (see the author's 1995 book for details on sources and methods). The resulting series is shown in Figure 10.3. The figures show a high concentration of wealth throughout the period from 1922 to 1989. A quarter or more of total wealth was owned by the top one percent in each of these years except 1976 and 1981. A comparison of the two end points reveals almost identical concentration figures: 37 percent in 1922 and 36 percent in 1989. However, this comparison hides important trends over the period.

Between 1922 and 1929 there was a substantial increase in wealth concentration, from 37 to 44 percent. Wealth inequality in 1929 was at its high-

Figure 10.3 Share of Wealth Owned by the Top One Percent of U.S. Households, 1922–1989

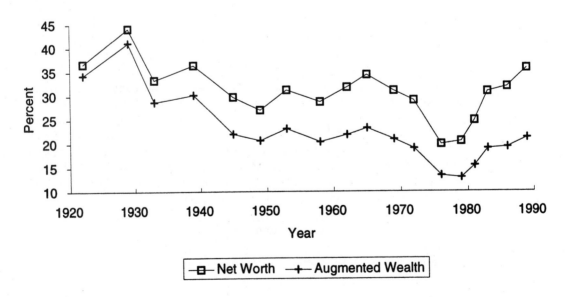

est point over the twentieth century. The Great Depression saw a sizable drop in inequality, with the share of the top percentile falling to 33 percent. By 1939, however, the concentration level was almost the same as it was in 1922. There followed a substantial drop in inequality between 1939 and 1945, a result of the leveling effects of World War II, and a more modest decline occurred between 1945 and 1949.

The share of wealth held by the richest one percent of households showed a gradual upward trend from 27 percent in 1949 to a peak of 34 percent in 1965. There followed a rather pronounced fall in wealth inequality lasting until 1979. Between 1965 and 1972, the share of the top percentile fell from 34 to 29 percent, and then from 29 to 20 percent between 1972 and 1976. The main reason for the decline in concentration over this four-year period is the sharp drop in the value of corporate stock held by the top wealth holders. The total value of corporate stock owned by the richest one percent fell from $491 billion in 1972 to $297 billion in 1976 (see Smith, 1987). Moreover, this decline appears to be attributable to the steep decline in share prices, rather than a divestiture of stock holdings.

Wealth inequality appears to have bottomed out some time during the late 1970s. A sharp increase in wealth concentration occurred between 1979 and 1981, from a 21 to a 25 percent share, again from 1981 to 1983, from a 24 to a 31 percent share, and then again between 1983 and 1989, from 31 to 36 percent. As with income inequality, a sharp rise in the concentration of household wealth is evident during the 1980s.

Figure 10.3 also shows the trend in the share of augmented household wealth owned by the top one percent of wealth holders as ranked by augmented wealth. The addition of pension and social security wealth has had a significant effect on measured wealth inequality. Because pension and social security wealth have grown in relation to marketable wealth, the gap between the marketable wealth and the augmented wealth series has widened over time, from two percentage points in 1922 to 13 percentage points in 1989. However, the time paths are almost identical. Wealth concentration based on augmented wealth shows a sharp increase between 1922 and 1929, a substantial decline from 1929 to 1933 followed by an increase between 1933 and 1939, a significant decrease between 1939 and 1945, a fairly flat trend from 1945 through 1972, a sharp decline from 1972 to 1976, and then a substantial rise between 1979 and 1989. The increase during the 1980s is more muted on the basis of augmented wealth, 8 percentage points, in comparison to marketable wealth, 15 percentage points.

Comparisons with Income Inequality Wealth inequality is today and has historically been extreme and substantially greater than income inequality. Indeed, the top one percent of wealth holders have typically held over one-quarter of household wealth, in comparison to an 8 or 9 percent share of income received by the top percentile of the income distribution.

Figure 10.4 shows the share of total family income held by the top five percent of families as ranked by income. The basic data source is the 1947

Figure 10.4   Wealth Inequality, Income Inequality, and the Ratio of Stock Prices to Housing Prices, 1922–1989

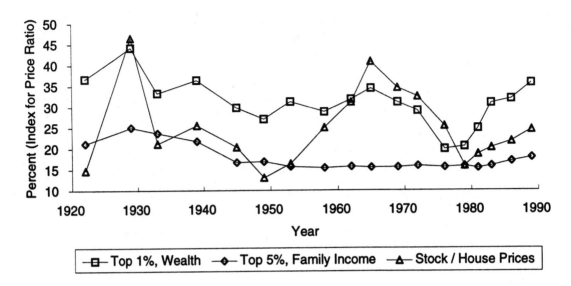

to 1989 Current Population Report series on shares of income held by families. The earlier data, from 1922 to 1949, are from Kuznets' (1953) series on the percentage share of total income received by the top percentiles of tax units. This series is benchmarked against the Census figure for 1949.

Though wealth inequality is more extreme than income inequality, has its historical course mirrored the time pattern of income inequality? Income inequality, as measured by the share of the top five percent, increased between 1922 and 1929, from 21 to 25 percent; declined rather steadily during the Depression years, reaching a 22 percent share in 1939; and then fell precipitously during World War II, bottoming out at 17 percent in 1945. There was a slight decline between 1945 and 1953, from 17 to 16 percent, but then income inequality remained virtually flat until 1981. Between 1981 and 1989, a fairly sharp rise in income inequality ensued, from a 15 to a 18 percent share.

A comparison of trends in income inequality and wealth inequality during the 1980s might prove illuminating at this point, particularly since the rise in the former has received so much attention in both professional economic journals and the mass media. There are several points of interest. First, the evidence presented above indicates that the level of wealth concentration was at a postwar high in 1989. The author's time series on income inequality indicates exactly the same result for the concentration of household income. Second, the rise in wealth inequality that characterized the 1980s was unprecedented in the twentieth century except for the 1920s. A similar finding can be reported for income inequality, which either declined or remained stable over the century except for the 1920s and 1980s.

It is hard to provide a direct comparison on the degree of increase in inequality for the two series, because of limitations on data availability and differences in the apparent timing of the rise of each. The Gini coefficient for wealth inequality shows an increase from 0.80 in 1983 to 0.84 in 1989, whereas, on the basis of the Current Population Report series, that for income inequality rose from 0.414 to 0.431 over the same period. The share of wealth held by the top five percent of wealth holders increased from 56 to 61 percent over these years, whereas the share of total income received by the top five percent of income recipients moved upward from 17.1 to 18.9 percent. Thus, over this period, the change in wealth inequality was more pronounced than that of income. Moreover, even if we move the clock backward to 1977, when income inequality began its recent ascent, we find that the Gini coefficient for income inequality increased by only 0.29, from 0.402 to 0.431, and the share of the top five percent by only 2.1 percentage points, from 16.8 to 18.9 percent.

As is apparent, the time paths of wealth inequality and income inequality have been similar but certainly not identical over the period from 1922 to 1989. Both showed a sharp rise from 1922 to 1929, followed by declines from 1929 through 1945 and increases from 1981 to 1989. However, income inequality was generally stable during the intervening years, while wealth inequality fell sharply during the 1970s. What can explain the discrepancy in these patterns?

Movements in Stock and Housing Prices   One variable that appears to explain much of the additional variation in movements in wealth inequality is the ratio of stock prices to housing prices. The rationale is that stocks are an asset held primarily by the upper-wealth classes, whereas housing is the major asset of the middle classes (see below). If stock prices increase relative to housing prices, the share of wealth held by the top wealth groups will rise, and conversely.

This price ratio (indexed to a value of 15 in 1922 in order to fit on Figure 10.4) shows a time path very similar to that of wealth inequality. The ratio more than trebled between 1922 and 1929, corresponding to the tremendous growth in wealth inequality. It fell by half between the 1929 "Crash" and 1933, as wealth inequality declined. Then it increased by about 20 percent between 1933 and 1939 as the stock market partially recovered, which helped cause a rise in wealth inequality. The price ratio then fell by almost half between 1939 and 1949, because of rapid inflation in housing prices, which, in turn, partly accounted for the pronounced decline in wealth inequality.

The ratio of stock to housing prices more than trebled between 1949 and 1965, fueled mainly by rapidly rising stock values, and this movement corresponded to a rise in wealth inequality. Between 1965 and 1979, this ratio fell by almost two-thirds, with most of the decline occurring after 1972.

Before 1972 the main culprit was rising house prices, but after 1972, the principal reason was a stagnating stock market. This period was, not surprisingly, characterized by a dramatic decline in wealth inequality. Between 1979 and 1989, the price ratio increased by more than half, as the stock market flourished, and a sharp increase in wealth inequality was also recorded over this decade.

Econometric analysis revealed that the dominant factor in explaining changes in wealth concentration is income inequality.[10] However, the movement in the ratio of stock to housing prices explains most of the increase in wealth inequality between 1949 and 1965 and the subsequent decline between 1965 and 1979 (particularly between 1972 and 1976). What about the 1980s? From the statistical results, almost half (49 percent) of the increase in wealth concentration between 1981 and 1989 is attributable to the increase in income inequality, and 21 percent is attributable to the increase of stock prices relative to housing prices (with the remainder unexplained).

Changes in Wealth Inequality, 1962–1989

Three household wealth surveys conducted by the Federal Reserve Board—the 1962 Survey of Financial Characteristics of Consumers (SFCC), the 1983 Survey of Consumer Finances (SCF), and the 1989 Survey of Consumer Finances (SCF)—provide the basis of a detailed comparison of household wealth inequality in those years. All three surveys use similar methodology. Each is stratified by income—that is, each oversamples high-income households. The original survey data from the 1962 SFCC and the 1983 and 1989 SCF were then adjusted, so the surveys are consistent in wealth concept and align to national balance sheet totals for that year (see Wolff, 1987a, and Wolff, 1994, for details on the adjustment procedures).

Changes in Average Wealth Holdings We begin the analysis with trends in real wealth over the period from 1962 to 1989 (all figures are reported in 1989 dollars). As shown in Table 10.5, average marketable wealth grew at an average annual rate of 1.8 percent between 1962 and 1983 and *almost doubled* at 3.4 percent between 1983 and 1989. By 1989, the average wealth of households was about $200,000, almost double that of 1962. Average financial wealth grew faster than marketable wealth in the 1983–1989 period (4.3 versus 3.4 percent per year), reflecting the increased importance of bank

---

[10] A regression was performed of a wealth inequality index, measured by the share of marketable wealth (HWX) held by the top one percent of households (WLTH) on income inequality, measured by the share of income received by the top five percent of families (INC), and the ratio of stock prices (the Standard and Poor's Index) to housing prices (RATIO), with 18 data points between 1922 and 1989 yields:

$$\text{WLTH} = 4.50 + 1.17 \text{ INC} + 1.04 \text{ RATIO}, \quad R^2 = 0.62, \quad N = 18,$$
$$\quad\quad (0.8) \quad (3.8) \quad\quad (2.3)$$

with t-ratios shown in parentheses. Both variables are statistically significant (INC at the one percent level and RATIO at the five percent level) and have the expected (positive) sign. Also, the fit is quite good, even for this simple model.

Table 10.5 Changes in Average and Median Real Household Wealth and Income, 1962–1989[a]

	Values, in 1989 Dollars			Annual Rate of Growth (%)		
	1962	1983	1989	1962–1983	1983–1989	1962–1989
Means						
Marketable net worth	110,409	161,732	198,639	1.82	3.43	2.18
Financial net worth	87,807	117,367	151,755	1.38	4.28	2.03
Income	26,179	35,711	41,889	1.48	2.66	1.74
Medians						
Marketable net worth	29,520	41,538	44,793	1.63	1.26	1.54
Financial net worth	7,969	8,971	10,423	0.56	2.50	0.99
Income	21,542	25,207	27,027	0.75	1.16	0.84

[a]Figures are calculated from the 1962 Survey of Financial Characteristics of Consumers and the 1983 and 1989 Survey of Consumer Finances. See Wolff (1994) for details.

deposits, financial assets, and equities in the overall household portfolio for this period. On the other hand, financial wealth grew more slowly than marketable wealth between 1962 and 1983, 1.4 versus 1.8 percent per year. Thus, the acceleration in the growth of financial wealth during the 1983–1989 period was even greater than marketable net worth.

Average household income also grew faster in the 1983–1989 period than the 1962–1983 period. Its annual growth accelerated from 1.5 percentage points to 2.7. However, in both periods, average income grew more slowly than average wealth, and the difference increased from 0.3 percentage points per year in 1962–1983 to 0.8 percentage points in 1983–1989.

The trend in median household wealth gives a contrasting picture to the growth of mean wealth. Median household wealth grew more slowly than mean household wealth in both periods, but the difference is much more marked for the later period, 2.2 percentage points, than for the 1962–1983 period, 0.2 percentage points. The result for the 1983–1989 period implies that the upper wealth classes enjoyed a disproportionate percentage of the total wealth increase over the period—a finding consistent with rising wealth inequality during this period. Median financial wealth also grew more slowly in both periods than mean financial wealth, but here too, the difference was considerably greater over the years 1983–1989. Median household income increased at a slower pace than mean income in both periods, but unlike wealth, the difference was slightly larger in the period between 1962 and 1983.

Trends in Wealth Inequality The results of Table 10.5 point to rising wealth inequality in the 1980s. This is confirmed in Table 10.6. The most telling

Table 10.6 Gini Coefficient and Percentage Shares of Total Wealth and Income By Percentile Group and Quintile, 1962, 1983, and 1989[a]

Year	Gini Coeff.	Top 0.5%	Next 0.5%	Next 4.0%	Next 5.0%	Next 10.0%	Bottom 80.0%	All
				Percentage Share of Wealth (Income) Held by:				
A. Marketable Net Worth								
1962	0.80	25.9	7.5	21.2	12.4	14.0	19.1	100.0
1983	0.80	26.2	7.5	22.3	12.1	13.1	18.7	100.0
1989	0.84	31.4	7.5	21.9	11.5	12.2	15.4	100.0
Percent of Total Net Worth Increase Accruing to Each Group[b]								
1962–1983		26.9	7.6	—	36.5	—	11.2	17.9	100.0
1983–1989		54.2	7.4	—	28.7	—	8.5	1.2	100.0
B. Financial Net Wealth								
1962	0.88	31.5	8.8	23.8	12.9	12.7	10.4	100.0
1983	0.89	34.0	8.9	25.1	12.3	11.0	8.7	100.0
1989	0.93	39.3	8.8	24.1	11.5	10.1	6.1	100.0
Percent of Total Financial Wealth Increase Accruing to Each Group[b]								
1962–1983		41.4	9.4	—	39.4	—	6.1	3.7	100.0
1983–1989		57.6	8.6	—	29.6	—	7.2	−3.0	100.0
C. Household Income								
1962	0.43	5.7	2.7	11.3	10.2	16.1	54.0	100.0
1983	0.48	9.2	3.7	13.3	10.3	15.5	48.1	100.0
1989	0.52	13.4	3.0	13.3	10.4	15.2	44.5	100.0
Percent of Total Income Increase Accruing to Each Group[b]								
1962–1983		18.8	6.4	—	29.1	—	13.7	32.1	100.0
1983–1989		38.2	−0.8	—	24.9	—	14.0	23.7	100.0
D. Augmented Wealth[c]		*Top 1%*						
1962	0.59	21.9		16.1				
1983	0.57	19.0		17.4				

(continued)

finding is that the share of marketable net worth of the top one-half of one percent (the "super-rich") increased by five percentage points over this period. In 1989, this group owned 31 percent of total household wealth, compared to 26 percent in 1983. The share of the next half of a percent (the "very rich") remained almost unchanged over the period, while the share

Table 10.6 *(concluded)*

Year	Top	Second	Third	Fourth	Bottom	All
	*Percentage Share of Wealth (Income) Held by Quintile*					

Year	Top	Second	Third	Fourth	Bottom	All
A. Net Worth						
1962	81.0	13.4	5.4	1.0	−0.7	100.0
1983	81.3	12.6	5.2	1.2	−0.3	100.0
1989	84.6	11.5	4.6	0.8	−1.4	100.0
B. Financial Net Wealth						
1962	89.6	9.6	2.1	−0.0	−1.4	100.0
1983	91.3	7.9	1.7	0.2	−1.0	100.0
1989	93.9	6.8	1.5	0.1	−2.3	100.0
C. Household Income						
1962	46.0	24.0	16.6	9.9	3.5	100.0
1983	51.9	21.6	14.1	8.6	3.7	100.0
1989	55.5	20.7	13.2	7.6	3.1	100.0
D. Augmented Wealth[c]						
1962	62.5	17.6	10.5	6.4	3.1	100.0
1983	61.7	17.4	10.8	6.7	3.3	100.0

[a] Sources: Computations from 1962 Survey of Financial Characteristics of Consumers and 1983 and 1989 Survey of Consumer Finances. See Wolff and Marley (1989) and Wolff (1994) for details.
[b] The computation was performed by dividing the total increase in wealth (income) of a given group by the total increase of wealth (income) for all households over the period, under the assumption that the number of households in each group remained unchanged over the period. It should be noted that the families found in each group (such as the top one half percent) may be *different* in each year.
[c] Augmented wealth is the sum of marketable net worth, pension wealth, and social security wealth. It is assumed in these calculations that average social security benefits will grow at 2 percent per year in real terms.

of the next nine percent (the "rich") declined somewhat. The share of the bottom 80 percent declined by over three percentage points, from 19 percent of total wealth to 15 percent.

An examination of the quintile shares reveals that while the top 20 percent increased their share of total wealth by 3.3 percentage points, the second quintile lost 0.9 percentage points, the middle lost 0.6, the fourth lost 0.4, and the bottom 0.9. The bottom quintile had a negative net worth on average (their debts outweighed their assets). This is true for both 1983 and 1989 (as well as 1962). Another indicator of overall inequality, the Gini coefficient, also shows a sizable increase over the period, from 0.80 to 0.84.

Data are also presented for 1962. The estimated inequality figures for 1962 and 1983 are very similar. The Gini coefficient is 0.80 for 1962 and 0.80 for 1983; the share of the top one percent of wealth holders was 33.4 percent in 1962 and 33.7 percent in 1983; and the share of the top 5 percent was 54.6 percent in 1962 and 55.6 percent in 1983.[11]

Another dimension is afforded by looking at the distribution of financial net worth, defined as net worth less the equity in owner-occupied housing. Financial wealth is distributed even more unequally than total household wealth. In 1989, the top one percent of families as ranked by financial wealth owned 48 percent of total financial wealth. In contrast, the top one percent of marketable wealth holders owned a 39 percent share of marketable net worth (also compare the Gini coefficients of 0.84 for total net worth and 0.93 for financial wealth in 1989). The top quintile (as ranked by financial wealth) accounted for 94 percent of total financial wealth, and the second quintile accounted for nearly all the remainder.

The concentration of financial wealth increased to the same degree as that of net worth between 1983 and 1989. The share of the top one-half of one percent of financial wealth holders increased by 5 percentage points, from 34 percent of total financial wealth to 39 percent, and the Gini coefficient rose from 0.89 to 0.93. The share of the bottom 80 percent of financial wealth holders fell from 8.7 percent to 6.1 percent. Interestingly, the concentration of financial net worth also increased modestly between 1962 and 1983, with the share of the top one percent rising from 40 to 43 percent and that of the top quintile from 90 to 91 percent, and the Gini coefficient nudging up from 0.88 to 0.89.

Comparable results on household income distribution are shown in Panel C, where families are ranked in terms of income to calculate the percentile shares. These data confirm that the concentration of income has also increased between 1983 and 1989. As with wealth shares, most of the relative income gain accrued to the top half of one percent of income recipients, whose share grew by 4.2 percentage points. Almost all the loss in income was sustained by the bottom 80 percent of the income distribution, with the loss fairly evenly spread over the bottom four quintiles. The Gini coefficient also showed a sharp increase, from 0.48 to 0.52.[12] There was also a large increase in income inequality between 1962 and 1983. The Gini coefficient rose from 0.43 to 0.48, and the share of the top one percent increased from 8 to 13 percent and that of the top quintile from 46 to 52

---

[11] This is not to say that there was no change in inequality between 1962 and 1983. Results reported in the second part of this section indicate that wealth concentration, while remaining relatively constant between 1962 and 1973, fell sharply between 1973 and the mid-1970s and then increased substantially between the late 1970s and 1983.

[12] The SCF data show a much higher degree of income inequality than does the CPS. According to the U.S. Bureau of the Census (1990a, p. 30), the Gini coefficient for all households was 0.43 and the share of the top quintile was 46.3 in 1988, compared to figures of 0.52 and 55.5 percent, respectively, from the SCF. The difference is to be expected, since the SCF has a high-income supplement and does not "top-code" income figures, as is done in the CPS.

Figure 10.5   Lorenz Curves for Family Income and Household Wealth, 1989

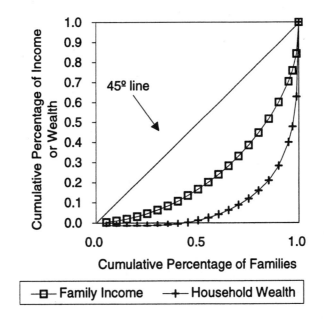

percent. According to Census data, almost all of this increase occurred after 1973.

It is also illuminating to contrast the relative level of income and wealth inequality. Wealth is distributed *much more unequally* than income. As shown in Figure 10.5, the Lorenz curve for family income in 1989 lies considerably inside the Lorenz curve for wealth. The share of the top one percent of wealth holders in 1989 was 39 percent, while that for the top one percent of income recipients was 16 percent. The top quintile of wealth holders owned almost 85 percent of total household wealth, while the top quintile of income recipients accounted for a little over half of total family income. The Gini coefficient for wealth in 1989 is 0.84, compared to 0.52 for income.

Another way of highlighting the changing distribution of wealth is to look at the proportion of the total increase in real household wealth accruing to each percentile group. This is calculated by computing the increase in total wealth of each percentile group and dividing this figure by the total increase in household wealth. If a group's wealth share remains constant over time, then the percentage of the total wealth growth received by that group will equal its share of total wealth. If a group's share of total wealth increases (decreases) over time, then it will receive a percentage of the total wealth gain greater (less) than its share in either year. However, it should be noted that in the calculations shown in Table 10.6, the households found in each group (say the top quintile) may be different in the two years.[13]

The calculations show that the top one percent of wealth holders together accounted for 62 percent of the growth of total household wealth between 1983 and 1989, and the top quintile for 99 percent of the total wealth gain. Only 1.6 percent of the total wealth growth accrued to the middle quintile, and the bottom two quintiles accounted collectively for a *loss* of 7.1 percent of the total wealth growth—a loss of about 300 billion dollars of wealth. In contrast, over the 1962–1983 period, each percentile and quintile group enjoyed some share of the overall wealth growth, and the gains were roughly in proportion to the share of wealth held by the group in 1962.

Gains in the overall growth in financial wealth were distributed even more unevenly than in marketable net worth. Two-thirds of the growth accrued to the top one percent, 103 percent to the top quintile, 3 percent to the second quintile, 0.8 percent to the middle quintile, and −6.8 percent to the bottom two quintiles. Results for 1962–1983 show that while gains in financial wealth were distributed more unevenly than those in marketable net worth over the period, they were distributed more equally than gains in financial wealth over the 1983–1989 period.

A similar calculation using the income data reveals that 37 percent of the total real income gain between 1983 and 1989 accrued to the top one percent of income recipients. This is still substantial, though considerably less than the proportional gain among the top one percent of wealth holders. Over three-fourths of income growth went to the top quintile of income recipients, 15 percent to the second quintile, 8 percent to the middle, 1.7 percent to the fourth, and −0.7 percent to the bottom, reflecting a decline in their average real income of 3.2 percent. The distribution of income gains was more equal over the 1962–1983 period, with the top quintile receiving 68 percent of the growth, the next to bottom quintile 5.0 percent, and the bottom quintile 4.3 percent.

The increase in wealth inequality recorded over the 1983–1989 period in the United States is almost unprecedented. The only other time during the twentieth century with a similar increase in the concentration of household wealth was during the period from 1922 to 1929. This latter increase in inequality was buoyed primarily by the excessive increase in stock values, which eventually precipitated the Great Depression of the 1930s.

Pension and social security wealth were also imputed to the household balance sheet in the 1962 and 1983 data. Pension wealth is defined as the

---

[13]This method of calculating the wealth gains by group is slightly distorted, since it reflects both the increase in the average wealth of a group and the increase in the number of households in that group. For example, a group whose average wealth shows no increase but whose number of households does increase will be accorded a positive share of the overall wealth growth over the period. Though there is no simple analytical way of separating out the effects of the growth in average wealth from that in the number of families, the same calculation can also be performed holding the number of households in each group constant over time. This method is used for the results presented in Table 10.6.

present value of discounted future pension benefits. Social security wealth is defined as the present value of the discounted stream of future social security benefits. Panel D shows results on the distribution of augmented household wealth, defined as the sum of marketable wealth plus pension and social security wealth. The addition of retirement wealth to traditional wealth causes a marked reduction in measured inequality. The Gini coefficient for augmented wealth is 0.57, and the share of the top one percent was 19 percent in 1983, compared to a Gini coefficient of 0.80 and a 34 percent share of the top one percent for marketable wealth in the same year.

A comparison of the 1962 SFCC and the 1983 SCF also reveal the growing importance of both social security and pension wealth. Without retirement wealth, measured wealth inequality is almost identical in the two years—with Gini coefficients of 0.80 and a share of the top percentile of about one-third. With social security and pension wealth included in the household portfolio, measured inequality is found to decline between the two years, from a Gini coefficient of 0.59 to 0.57 and with the share of the top percentile falling from 22 to 19 percent. The share of wealth of the top two quintiles also fell while the share of the bottom three rose.[14]

Portfolio Composition by Wealth and Age Class   There are also marked differences in the assets owned by different wealth classes. Some assets are more concentrated in the hands of the rich, and others are more dispersed among families of different wealth levels. Table 10.7 shows the proportion of total assets held by different wealth classes in the United States in 1989. We have divided the assets into two groups: those held primarily by the rich and those more dispersed in the population.

The super rich (the top one-half of one percent of wealth holders) held almost one-third of all outstanding stock owned by households, over 40 percent of financial securities, almost half the value of unincorporated business, and about one-third of total trust equity and nonhome real estate. The top 10 percent of households accounted for almost 90 percent of stock shares, bonds, trusts, and business equity, and 80 percent of nonhome real estate.

In contrast, owner-occupied housing, life insurance, and deposits were more evenly distributed among households. The bottom 90 percent of families accounted for almost two-thirds of the value of owner-occupied housing, over half of life insurance cash value, and over 40 percent of deposits. Debt was probably the most evenly distributed component of household wealth. The bottom 90 percent were responsible for 70 percent of the indebtedness of American households.

Table 10.8 presents a somewhat different slice of the same issue, showing the proportion of the total assets of each wealth class held in different asset types. Perhaps, somewhat surprisingly, 50 percent of the wealth of the top one-half of one percent in 1989 was in the form of unincorporated

---

[14]Similar calculations for the 1989 data are as yet unavailable.

Table 10.7 Selected Holdings of Assets by Family Wealth Level, 1989[a]
(percent of total assets held by each group)

Asset Type	Super Rich (Top 0.5%)	Very Rich (Next 0.5%)	Rich (90–99%)	Rest (0–90%)	Total
A. *Assets Held Primarily by the Wealthy*					
Stocks	30.5	15.7	43.1	10.7	100.0
Bonds	41.4	12.8	34.3	11.5	100.0
Trusts	38.1	15.5	35.4	11.0	100.0
Business equity	46.9	9.4	33.7	10.0	100.0
Nonhome real estate	30.7	9.6	39.6	20.0	100.0
B. *Assets and Liabilities Held Primarily by the Nonwealthy*					
Principal residence	4.4	3.0	26.3	66.3	100.0
Life insurance	12.6	4.2	27.7	55.4	100.0
Deposits[b]	13.2	7.8	37.8	41.2	100.0
Total debt	7.5	2.6	19.9	70.0	100.0

[a]Families are classified into wealth class on the basis of their net worth.
Source: Computations from the 1989 Survey of Consumer Finances.
[b]Includes cash, currency, demand deposits, savings and time deposits, money market funds, certificates of deposit, and IRA and Keogh accounts.

business equity and investment real estate, while only 30 percent took the form of stocks, financial securities, and trusts. This suggests that small businesses and real estate investment were the avenue to great fortunes during the 1980s, while stocks and securities (the holdings of the "rentier class") appear less important as a source of great wealth.

The importance of owner-occupied housing as a form of wealth increases as household wealth declines. Among the second (from the top) and middle quintiles (percentiles 40 to 80), gross housing value comprised over 60 percent of gross assets, and net home equity accounted for over 40 percent. For the bottom 40 percent, gross house value accounted for almost 60 percent of their total assets, but net home equity for only 27 percent—a reflection of their larger mortgage debt. Deposits and other liquid assets were also more important in the household portfolio of the lower- and middle-wealth classes than the rich.

Nonhome real estate and business equity, financial securities, and trusts and stocks all declined as a share of household assets in tandem with the wealth level of the household. For the second and middle quintiles, these assets comprised only 15 percent of gross assets, and among the bottom 40 percent, 19 percent.

Table 10.8 Composition of Household Wealth by Wealth and Age Class, 1989[a]

Group	Gross House Value	Other Real Estate & Business Equity	Liquid Assets[b]	Bonds	Trusts and Stocks	Total Debt	Net Home Equity	Ratio of Debt to: Net Worth	Ratio of Debt to: Family Income
			(Percent of Gross Assets)						
All	28.5	29.4	17.1	5.8	14.7	14.1	20.3	16.5	78.2
A. *Wealth Class (percentile level)*									
Top ½%	5.4	49.5	9.6	10.1	20.1	4.5	4.4	4.7	67.7
Next ½%	10.0	32.9	15.0	8.6	27.2	4.4	8.6	4.6	63.3
90–99%	21.8	31.0	18.3	5.7	17.7	8.2	17.1	8.9	77.0
80–90%	47.0	15.4	25.1	2.8	7.1	13.7	36.8	15.9	70.1
40–80%	62.4	10.0	19.7	1.5	3.5	27.2	41.2	37.4	80.8
Bottom 40%	57.3	15.2	19.8	1.4	2.7	73.2	27.6	−308.8	81.1
B. *Age Class*									
Under 35	41.0	29.9	12.4	1.4	9.3	31.8	17.3	46.7	84.3
35–44	36.8	29.2	16.0	3.1	9.4	28.1	20.4	39.1	106.7
45–54	28.4	36.6	15.2	3.6	11.5	14.1	21.3	16.5	76.2
55–64	25.2	30.6	19.1	5.6	15.1	9.1	20.7	10.0	69.8
65–74	20.6	28.5	17.9	8.6	19.9	3.2	19.3	3.3	32.1
75 & over	22.0	13.9	21.5	13.7	26.0	1.5	21.6	1.5	16.8
Under 65	31.3	31.9	16.3	3.8	11.7	18.7	20.4	23.0	87.2
65 & Over	21.1	23.2	19.2	10.5	22.1	2.6	20.1	2.6	26.9

[a]Families are classified into wealth class on the basis of their net worth and into age class on the basis of the age of the family head. Miscellaneous assets are excluded from this table.
Source: Computations from the 1989 Survey of Consumer Finances.
[b]Includes demand deposits, savings and time deposits, money market funds, certificates of deposit, life insurance cash surrender value, and IRA, Keogh, and other pension accounts.

Relative indebtedness is much greater among poorer households than richer ones. The debt-equity ratio (debt as a proportion of net worth) rose from 5 percent for the super-rich to 37 percent for the second and middle quintiles. For the bottom two quintiles, household debt exceeded the total value of assets. In fact, 18 percent of all U.S. households had zero or negative net worth, and 27 percent had zero or negative financial net worth. However, interestingly, debt as a proportion of family income shows much less variation by wealth class, ranging from 64 percent of total income among the second half of a percentile to 81 percent among the bottom two quintiles.

Age-class differences are also interesting (Panel B of Table 10.8). Gross owner-occupied housing was the most important asset among families under 35 years of age, comprising 41 percent of their gross assets. However, the proportion declined almost systematically with age, from 41 percent for the youngest age group to 22 percent for the oldest. On the other hand, net home equity as a proportion of gross assets shows little variation by age class, comprising 20 percent overall and about the same for each age group. Liquid assets accounted for a larger share of the assets of the elderly than the nonelderly (19 versus 16 percent), while the value of nonhome real estate and business equity was considerably more important for families under 65, accounting for 32 percent of their gross assets compared to 23 percent for the elderly.

Financial securities, stocks, and trust equity increased systematically with age. All together, these assets comprised 16 percent of the assets of families under 65 and 33 percent of those of the elderly. Debt shows the opposite pattern, declining in importance with age, from 32 percent of gross assets for the youngest group to 2 percent for the oldest. The debt-equity ratio was 23 percent for families under 65 and only 3 percent for the elderly. The debt-income ratio also declined with age (except for the second youngest age group). The ratio was 87 percent among nonelderly families and 27 percent among the elderly.

Relation Between Income and Wealth   It is often believed that income and wealth are almost interchangeable as measures of family well-being. That is to say, many believe that families with high income almost always (or, indeed, necessarily) have high wealth, and low-income families are low-wealth ones. However, this is not the case. Some tabulations prepared by Radner and Vaughan (1987) and shown in Table 10.9 show that the two distributions are not identical.

In Table 10.9, if income and wealth were perfectly correlated, then each element of the diagonal of the matrix would equal 20 percent and the off-diagonal terms would all be zero. There is generally a strong positive correlation between income and wealth. For example, in the bottom income quintile, 41 percent (8.1/20.0) of the households are in the bottom net worth quintile, while only 7 percent (1.3/20.0) are in the top net worth quintile. In the top income quintile, only 5 percent are in the bottom net worth quintile, while 45 percent fall in the top net worth quintile.

However, the correlation is far from perfect, and there is still a substantial amount of dispersion of wealth by income group. No net worth quintile contains more than 44 percent of the households in the corresponding income quintile. Moreover, in the three middle-income quintiles, each net worth quintile has at least 10 percent of the households in the income quintile. Thus, income and wealth, while positively correlated, are distributed rather differently among households. Wealth thus represents another dimension of well-being over and above income.

Table 10.9 **The Joint Distribution of Households Among Net Worth and Income Quintiles, 1979**[a] **(Percentage of Households in the Income and Net Worth Quintile)**

Income Quintile	Net Worth Quintile					
	1	*2*	*3*	*4*	*5*	*Total*
1	8.1	4.8	3.5	2.2	1.3	20.0
2	5.5	4.5	3.5	3.5	2.9	20.0
3	3.6	4.9	5.0	3.5	3.1	20.0
4	2.0	4.5	4.6	5.1	3.8	20.0
5	0.9	1.2	3.4	5.6	8.9	20.0
Total	20.0	20.0	20.0	20.0	20.0	100.0

[a] The source is Radner and Vaughan (1987), Table 5.6. The underlying data are from the 1979 Income Survey Development Program (ISDP) file.

There have been several attempts to combine the income and wealth dimension into a single index of household well-being. The most common technique is to convert the stock of wealth into a flow and add that flow to current income. In this approach, wealth is converted into a lifetime "annuity" for the expected remaining life of the family. The annuity is defined as a stream of annual payments which are equal over time and which will fully exhaust the stock of initial wealth. (This is like a fixed rate mortgage with constant payments, except in reverse!) This annuity is then added to obtain an "augmented" measure of family income.[15] The interesting issue is whether the distribution of augmented income is greater than or less than that of money income.

Three examples of this approach are presented in Table 10.10. The first, by Burton Weisbrod and Lee Hansen (1968), is based on the 1962 SFCC. The original data show that the share of the top two income classes was 5 percent of total money income in 1962, and that of the bottom income class was 20 percent. They then used both a 4 percent and a 10 percent annuity rate on household net worth. Their calculations showed that the share of the top two income classes increased from 5 percent to 8 percent at a 4 percent annuity rate and to 10 percent at a 10 percent rate, while the share of the bottom income class fell from 20 percent to 18 percent and 17 percent, respectively. The inclusion of a wealth annuity in income thus increases measured income inequality.

The second study, by Michael Taussig (1973), makes use of the 1967 Survey of Economic Opportunity (SEO) database. Taussig computed Gini

---

[15] Technically, property income is first subtracted from current money income so that there is no double counting of the returns from household wealth.

Table 10.10 The Distribution of Income Before and After the Inclusion of a Wealth Annuity

A. *Calculations from the 1962 Survey of Financial Characteristics of Consumers*[a]

	Income Class							
Income Class	Under $3,000	$3,000– $4,999	$5,000– $7,499	$7,500– $9,999	$10,000 $14,999	$15,000– $24,999	$25,000 & Over	All
Percentage Distribution								
Money Income	20	19	27	17	13	4	1	100
+ Annuity at 4%	18	17	25	17	15	6	2	100
+ Annuity at 10%	17	16	24	16	17	7	3	100

B. *Calculations from the 1967 Survey of Economic Opportunity*[b]

		Age Group					
	All	Under 25	25–34	35–44	45–54	55–64	65 & Over
Gini coefficient							
Money Income	0.36	0.32	0.26	0.28	0.32	0.39	0.45
+ Annuity at 6%	0.39	0.32	0.28	0.32	0.37	0.44	0.48

C. *Calculations from the 1989 Survey of Consumer Finances*[c]

		Age Group			
	All	18–34	35–54	55–69	70+
Gini coefficient					
Income	0.52	0.44	0.48	0.57	0.57
+ Annuity at 3%	0.54	0.45	0.50	0.60	0.60

[a] Source: Weisbrod and Hansen (1968).
[b] Source: Taussig (1973).
[c] Source: Calculations from the 1989 SCF file.

coefficients on the basis of money income and the sum of money income and a 6 percent annuity on household wealth. When the annuity is added to current money income, the measured Gini coefficient for all families rises from 0.36 to 0.39. Inequality also increases for all age groups, though the disequalizing effect is considerably stronger for older age groups.

A similar technique is used in Panel C, on the basis of the 1989 SCF. As in the Taussig results, the Gini coefficient increases for all families, from 0.52 to 0.54, when a wealth annuity is added to money income. Measured inequality rises for all age groups, though the increase is greater for older age groups.

All three studies thus find that the distribution of income becomes more unequal once the returns to wealth are included as part of total income. However, the disequalizing effects are not great. There are two reasons for this. First, though family income and wealth are positively correlated, they are not perfectly correlated. Hence, there are families with low income but high wealth, and also some with high income but low wealth. Second, the annuity payments are small relative to current money income, typically on the order of 10 percent on average. As a result, their inclusion in augmented income does not alter the overall distribution very much. Moreover, annuities are much smaller for younger families than older ones, both because younger ones have lower wealth and because they have a longer remaining life expectancy. As a result, wealth annuities have a more disequalizing effect for older households than younger ones.

10.4 INTERNATIONAL COMPARISONS OF HOUSEHOLD WEALTH DISTRIBUTION

The availability of comparable household wealth data in other countries is quite limited. Besides the United States, needed data to calculate measures of household wealth inequality are readily available only for Canada, France, Germany, Japan, Sweden, and the United Kingdom. With the exception of Sweden and the United Kingdom, these estimates are available only since 1970.

Comparisons of Long-Term Time Trends

There are two other countries besides the United States for which long-term time-series are available on household wealth inequality: the United Kingdom and Sweden. The most comprehensive data exist for the United Kingdom. The data are based on estate duty (tax) returns and use mortality multipliers to obtain estimates of the wealth of the living. Estimates are for the adult population (that is, individuals, not households). Figures are available on an almost continuous basis from 1923 to 1990.

The Swedish data are available on a rather intermittent basis from 1920 through 1990. The data are based on actual wealth tax returns. Tax return data are subject to error, like other sources of wealth data. The principal problem with tax return information is underreporting due to tax evasion and legal tax exemptions. However, some assets, such as housing and stock shares, are extremely well covered, because of legal registration requirements in Sweden. Also, the deductibility of interest payments from taxable income makes it likely that the debt information is very reliable. On the

Figure 10.6 Share of Marketable Net Worth Held by the Top 1 Percent of Wealthholders

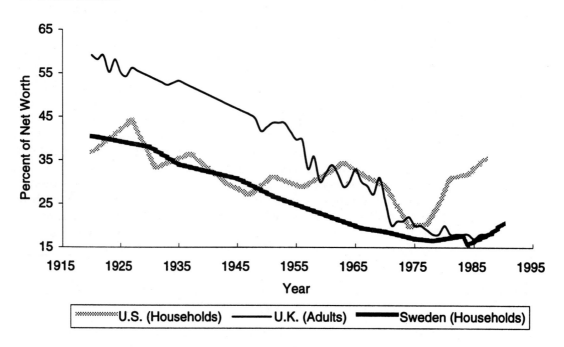

other hand, bank accounts and bonds are not subject to similar tax controls, and it is likely that their amounts are underreported.

Figure 10.6 shows comparative trends among the three countries.[16] For the United Kingdom, there was a dramatic decline in the degree of individual wealth inequality from 1923 to 1974 but little change thereafter. The share of the top one percent of wealthholders fell from 59 percent in 1923 to 20 percent in 1974. However, between 1974 and 1990, there was only a relatively minor reduction in the concentration of household wealth, from a 20 percent share of the top percentile to 18 percent.

In Sweden, as in the United Kingdom, there was a dramatic reduction in wealth inequality between 1920 and the mid-1970s. Based on the years for which data are available, the decline appears to be a continuous process between 1920 and 1975. Over this period, the share of the top percentile declined from 40 to 17 percent of total household wealth. Between 1975 and 1985, there was virtually no change in the concentration of wealth. However, between 1985 and 1990, there was a sharp increase in wealth in-

---

[16] The U.S. series, derived from Table 1, is based on marketable wealth for the household unit. Sources for the United Kingdom are: Shorrocks (1987) and *Inland Revenue Statistics, 1992*, Series C. Results are based on marketable wealth for adult individuals. Sources for Sweden are Spånt (1987) and Statistics Sweden (1992). The unit is the household, and wealth is valued at market prices.

equality, with the share of the top percentile increasing from 17 to 21 percent, a level similar to that of the early 1960s.

Comparisons among the three countries are rather striking. In all three countries, there was a fairly sizable reduction in wealth concentration between the early 1920s and the late 1970s, though the pattern appears much more cyclical in the United States than in the other two countries. However, during the 1980s, the United States showed an extremely sharp increase in wealth inequality, whereas the trend was almost flat in the United Kingdom. In Sweden, wealth inequality remained relatively constant between the late 1970s and mid-1980s and then showed a fairly substantial jump in the late 1980s.

Comparisons of Recent Trends

More recent trends in household wealth inequality are highlighted in Table 10.11. In addition to Sweden, the U.K., and the U.S., time-series data are also available for Canada and France. Again, it should be stressed that the data sources differ among the countries. To emphasize this point, the author has presented the time-series as an index, with the initial year of the series set to 100.

Table 10.11   Share of Marketable Net Worth Held by Top Percentiles of Wealth Holders and Gini Coefficients for the Household Wealth, Selected Countries, 1970–1990[a] (Index, Initial Year of Series = 100)

Year	U.S.	U.K.	Sweden	Canada	France
1970		100	100	100	
1972	100	107			
1975		72	91		100
1976	68	72			
1977		76		95	
1978		69	89		
1979	71	69			
1980		65			99
1981	85	62			
1983	106	69	95		
1984		62	84	96	
1985		62	89		
1986	110	62			100
1988		58	99		
1989	123	62			
1990		62	111		

[a] Source: Wolff (forthcoming).

Chapter 10   Household Wealth

The results rather dramatically point out the difference between the U.S. experience and that of the other countries. As noted above, in the United States there was a very substantial increase in wealth inequality dating from the late 1970s. The degree of wealth inequality appears to have almost doubled between 1976 and 1989 and was about a fourth higher in 1989 than in 1972. In the United Kingdom, wealth concentration shows a sizable decline between 1972 and 1975 (perhaps not unrelated to the similar decline in the United States), but it shows a further though more moderate decline between 1975 and 1981 and then stabilizes until 1990, the last date of the series. In Sweden, there was a downward trend from 1970 to 1985, which was followed by a relatively sharp increase in 1990. In 1990, the level of wealth concentration was about 10 percent greater than in 1970.

The Canadian data are derived from the (Canadian) Survey of Consumer Finances, administered by Statistics Canada. The survey estimates suggest that wealth inequality in Canada showed a modest decline between 1970 and 1977 and then remained virtually unchanged between 1977 and 1984. There is thus no evidence of rising wealth inequality in Canada between the 1970s and mid-1980s. The last column of Table 2 shows results for France for 1975, 1980, and 1986 based on household surveys. The results of the three surveys show virtually no difference in wealth inequality in the three years.

As noted in Section 10.3, one must be cautious in comparing household wealth data drawn from different data sources because wealth concentration estimates are sensitive to definitions of household wealth, sampling frames, and units of analysis. However, it is possible to make some bilateral comparisons when conformable accounting and sampling frameworks are carefully constructed.

In the case of France and the United States, a special study was undertaken to compare the size distribution of household wealth in the two countries (see Kessler and Wolff, 1991, for details). The main difficulty in the study was that survey data in the two countries cover different assets and liabilities (in fact, the French survey did not include any information on household debt). In order to compare the two distributions, it was necessary to create a "conformable" set of wealth or balance sheet accounts for the two countries.

Table 10.12 shows comparative data for the size distribution of household gross wealth in the two countries. The French data come from the 1986 Enquete sur les Actifs Financiers conducted by the Institut National de la Statistique et des Etudes Economiques (INSEE). For the United States, we use the 1983 Survey of Consumer Finances (SCF), conducted by the Federal Reserve Board. The U.S. survey data were then adjusted to conform to the coverage of the French survey data. Automobiles and other consumer durables were eliminated from the U.S. data, since these assets are not captured in the French data. Moreover, household debt is not covered in the French survey. As a result, statistics are shown for gross assets, instead of net worth (total assets less total debt).

Table 10.12 The Size Distribution of Household Wealth in Canada, France, Sweden, and the United States, Derived from Household Survey Data, 1983–1986[a]

	Gini Coeff.	Top 1%	Top 5%	Top Quintile	2nd Quintile	3rd Quintile	4th Quintile	Bottom Quintile
				Percent of Total Wealth Held by:				
I. Gross Assets								
A. France, 1986	.71	26	43	69	19	9	2	1
B. United States, 1983	.77	33	54	78	14	7	2	0
II. Net Worth								
A. United States, 1983	.78	33	55	80	13	6	2	0
B. Canada, 1984	.69	17	38	69	20	9	2	0
C. Sweden, 1985/1986		16.5	37	75				

[a] Source: Wolff (forthcoming).

On the basis of the French survey data, the Gini coefficient for gross assets is 0.71, the share of the top one percent is 26 percent of total household wealth, and that of the top quintile is 69 percent. On the basis of the U.S. data, the Gini coefficient is 0.77, considerably higher than the French coefficient. The share of the top 1, 5, and 20 percent are also considerably higher in the United States than France, whereas the share of the second quintile is substantially higher in France. The shares of the bottom three quintiles are quite similar in the two countries.

The results appear to indicate that wealth is more unequally distributed in the United States than in France. The differences are considerable. This result is also consistent with our finding that French households have a substantially higher proportion of their wealth in the form of owner-occupied housing, which is more equally distributed among the population than most other assets (particularly, bonds and corporate stock).

Panel II of Table 10.12 compares the Canadian data derived from the Statistics Canada Survey of Consumer Finances in 1984 and U.S. data derived from the 1983 Survey of Consumer Finances. Though the sample size for the Canadian SCF is about four times as large as that for the U.S. SCF, there is no special high-income supplement added to the Canadian SCF as there is for the U.S. SCF. As a result, as James Davies (1993) points out, there is reason to believe that estimates of the concentration of household wealth may be understated in Canada relative to the United States. He provided adjustments to the Canadian data. Wealth inequality in the United States was clearly greater than in Canada. On the basis of the original Canadian data, the share of the top percentile was 17 percent in Canada and 33 percent in the United States and the Gini coefficient is 0.69 for the

Canadian data and 0.78 for the U.S. survey. On the basis of the adjusted data, the share of the top 1 percent lies somewhere in the range of 22 to 27 percent of total household wealth. Though Canadian wealth concentration is greater as a result of these adjustments, it is still lower than in the United States.

The last set of estimates is shown for Sweden in 1985–1986. It is based on a household survey conducted by Statistics Sweden at the same time. The asset and liability coverage appears to be similar to that of the American and Canadian Surveys of Consumer Finances. However, there is no stratification of the survey by income or wealth level. The concentration of wealth appears to be significantly greater in the United States than in Sweden, which is consistent with the estate tax data comparisons. The original 1984 Canadian SCF data indicate about the same level of wealth concentration in Canada as in Sweden, though Davies' adjusted estimates show a somewhat higher concentration in Canada.

10.5 SUMMARY

Marketable household wealth (or net worth) is defined as the sum of the following less mortgage and other debt: owner-occupied housing and other real estate; consumer durables; cash, checking, time and other savings accounts; bonds and other financial instruments; corporate stock; equity in unincorporated businesses; and trust fund equity. In 1989, owner-occupied housing comprised 26 percent of total marketable assets, net home equity 19 percent, financial assets as a group 21 percent, corporate stocks and unincorporated business equity 25 percent, and nonhome real estate 12 percent. The ratio of total debt to total assets was 14 percent.

Three other concepts of household wealth were developed in the chapter. The first is fungible household wealth, defined as marketable wealth less consumer durables. The second is financial household wealth, defined as fungible net worth minus net equity in owner-occupied housing. The third is augmented household wealth, defined as the sum of household marketable wealth, social security wealth, and pension wealth. Fungible household wealth comprised 90 percent of marketable wealth, and financial wealth 69 percent, while augmented wealth was 57 percent greater than marketable wealth.

Between 1900 and 1992, real marketable wealth per household grew by 0.9 percent per year, while average household income increased by 1.1 percent per year. However, since 1969, average wealth has grown faster than average income. Augmented wealth per household has grown faster than either marketable wealth or income per household, averaging 1.5 percent per year between 1900 and 1992.

Over these years, households invested more of their marketable wealth in consumer durables. Though the homeownership rate increased from 46 percent in 1920 to 65 percent in 1991, home equity remained relatively constant as a share of total assets. Households also substituted liquid assets, such as bank deposits and money market funds, for business equity and non-home real estate. Changes in the share of corporate stock and financial securities in the household portfolio tended to follow movements in the stock market. The ratio of liabilities to total assets increased from 4 to 14 percent.

Four principal data sources have been used to develop measures of household wealth inequality: (1) estate tax data, (2) household survey data, (3) wealth tax data, and (4) income capitalization techniques. Each has its characteristic strengths and weaknesses.

Long-term trends in U.S. wealth concentration have been estimated from estate tax and household survey data. The share of marketable wealth owned by the top one percent of wealth holders shows a sharp increase between 1922 and 1929, a substantial decline from 1929 to 1933 followed by an increase between 1933 and 1939, a significant decrease between 1939 and 1945, a fairly flat trend from 1945 through 1972, a sharp decline from 1972 to 1976, and then a rise of 15 percentage points between 1976 and 1989. Two important factors in explaining trends in the concentration of wealth are changes in income inequality and movements in the ratio of stock prices to housing prices.

The share of augmented wealth owned by the top one percent has been lower than the comparable share of marketable wealth, and the gap has grown over time, from two percentage points in 1922 to 13 percentage points in 1989. However, time trends of the two are similar, though the increase in the share of augmented wealth between 1976 and 1989 is smaller on the basis of augmented wealth, 8 percentage points.

A comparison of the 1983 and 1989 Survey of Consumer Finances highlights the sharp increase in wealth inequality during the 1980s. Mean household wealth increased much more rapidly over these years than median household wealth. The share of the marketable net worth of the top one half of one percent increased by five percentage points over this period, while the share of the bottom 80 percent declined by over three percentage points. The top one percent of wealth holders together accounted for 62 percent of the growth of total household wealth between 1983 and 1989. The top quintile accounted for 99 percent of the total wealth gain, while the bottom two quintiles accounted collectively for a loss of about $300 billion of wealth. In 1989, the inequality of household wealth was at its highest point since 1929.

Wealth is distributed more unequally than income. The share of the top one percent of wealth holders in 1989 was 39 percent, while the share of the top one percent of income recipients was 16 percent. The Gini coefficient for wealth was 0.84, compared to 0.52 for income. Though household wealth and income are positively correlated, there is still a considerable amount of dispersion of wealth by income class. Adding an annuity value of wealth to income makes the distribution of income more unequal, particularly for older households, but the differences are not great.

There are considerable differences in the assets owned by different wealth classes. The top 10 percent of wealth holders accounted for almost

90 percent of stock shares, bonds, trusts, and business equity and 80 percent of nonhome real estate in 1989. The bottom 90 percent of families accounted for almost two-thirds of the value of owner-occupied housing, over 40 percent of deposits, and 70 percent of household debt. The debt-equity ratio was much greater among poorer households than richer ones and larger for younger families than older ones.

Comparisons of long-term wealth inequality trends among Sweden, the United Kingdom, and the United States shows a substantial reduction in wealth concentration in all three countries between the early 1920s and the late 1970s. During the 1980s, both the United States and Sweden showed a sharp increase in wealth inequality, whereas little change was apparent for the United Kingdom, Canada, and France. Wealth inequality appeared to be considerably greater in the United States during the 1980s than in Canada, France, Sweden, and the United Kingdom.

REFERENCES AND SUGGESTIONS FOR FURTHER READING

A. Aggregate Household Wealth

Board of Governors of the Federal Reserve System, Flow of Funds Section, *Balance Sheets For the U.S. Economy, 1946–1985,* Board of Governors of the Federal Reserve System, Washington D.C., 1986.

Curtin, Richard T., F. Thomas Juster, and James N. Morgan, "Survey Estimates of Wealth: An Assessment of Quality," in Robert E. Lipsey and Helen Tice (eds.), *The Measurement of Saving, Investment, and Wealth,* Studies of Income and Wealth, Vol. 52, Chicago University Press, Chicago, 1989.

Goldsmith, Raymond W., *Comparative National Balance Sheets,* University of Chicago Press, Chicago, 1985.

———, *National Wealth of the United States in the Postwar Period,* Princeton University Press, Princeton, N.J., 1962.

Goldsmith, Raymond W., Dorothy S. Brady, and Horst Mendershausen, *A Study of Saving in the United States,* Vol. III, Princeton University Press, Princeton, 1956.

Goldsmith, Raymond W., and Robert E. Lipsey, *Studies in the National Balance Sheet of the United States,* Vol. I, Princeton University Press, Princeton, N.J., 1963.

Goldsmith, Raymond, Robert E. Lipsey, and Morris Mendelson, *Studies in the National Balance Sheet of the United States,* Vol. II, Princeton University Press, Princeton, N.J., 1963.

Internal Revenue Service, *Statistics of Income—1972, Personal Wealth, United States,* Government Printing Office, Washington, D.C., 1976.

Kendrick, John W., Kyu Sik Lee, and Jean Lomask, *The National Wealth of the United States: By Major Sectors and Industry,* The Conference Board, New York, 1976.

Lampman, Robert J., *The Share of Top Wealth Holders in National Wealth, 1922–1956,* Princeton University Press, Princeton, N.J., 1962.

Musgrave, John C., "Fixed Reproducible Tangible Wealth in the United States; Revised Estimates," *Survey of Current Business,* Vol. 66, No.1, Jan. 1986, pp. 51–75.

Projector, Dorothy, and Gertrude Weiss, *Survey of Financial Characteristics of Consumers,* Federal Reserve Technical Papers, 1966.

Ruggles, Richard, and Nancy Ruggles, "Integrated Economic Accounts for the United States, 1947–1980," *Survey of Current Business,* Vol. 62, May 1982, pp. 1–53.

Wolff, Edward N., "Trends in Aggregate Household Wealth in the United States, 1900–1983," *Review of Income and Wealth,* Series 35, No. 1, March 1990, pp. 1–29.

B. The Distribution of Household Wealth

Atkinson, A. B., "The Distribution of Wealth in Britain in the 1960s—the Estate Duty Method Reexamined," in James D. Smith (ed.), *The Personal Distribution of Income and Wealth, NBER, Studies in Income and Wealth,* No. 39, Columbia University Press, New York, 1975.

——, and A.J. Harrison, *Distribution of Personal Wealth in Britain,* Cambridge University Press, Cambridge, 1978.

Avery, Robert B., Gregory E. Elliehausen, and Arthur B. Kennickell, "Measuring Wealth With Survey Data: An Evaluation of the 1983 Survey of Consumer Finances," *Review of Income and Wealth,* Series 34, No. 4, December 1988, pp. 339–371.

Avery, Robert B., and Arthur B. Kennickell, "Household Saving in the United States," *Review of Income and Wealth,* Series 37, No. 4, December 1991, pp. 409–432.

Avery, Robert B., and Arthur B. Kennickell, "U.S. Household Wealth: Changes from 1983 to 1986," in Edward N. Wolff (ed.), *Research in Economic Inequality,* Vol. 4, JAI Press, Greenwich, CT, 1994.

Board of Inland Revenue, *Inland Revenue Statistics, 1992,* HMSO, London, 1992.

Cartwright, William S., and Robert B. Friedland, "The President's Commission on Pension Policy Household Survey 1979: Net Wealth Distribution by Type and Age for the United States," *Review of Income and Wealth,* Series 31, No. 3, September 1985, pp. 285–308.

Davies, James B., "The Distribution of Wealth in Canada," in Edward N. Wolff (ed.), *Research in Economic Inequality,* Vol. 4, "Studies in the Distribution of Household Wealth," JAI Press, Greenwich, CT, 1993, pp. 159–180.

Feldstein, Martin, "Social Security, Induced Retirement, and Aggregate Capital Accumulation," *Journal of Political Economy,* 82, September/October 1974, pp. 905–926.

——, "Social Security and the Distribution of Wealth," *Journal of the American Statistical Association,* 71, December 1976, pp. 800–807.

Freidman, J., "Asset Accumulation and Depletion Among the Elderly," paper presented at the Brookings Institution Conference on Retirement and Aging, 1982.

Gallman, Robert E., "Trends in the Size Distribution of Wealth in the Nineteenth Century," in Lee Soltow (ed.), *Six Papers on the Size Distribution of Wealth and Income,* National Bureau of Economic Research, New York, 1969.

Greenwood, Daphne T., "An Estimation of U.S. Family Wealth and Its Distribution From Microdata, 1973," *Review of Income and Wealth,* Series 29, March 1983, pp. 23–43.

———, "Age, Income, and Household Size: Their Relation to Wealth Distribution in the United States," in E. Wolff (ed.), *International Comparisons of the Distribution of Household Wealth,* 1987.

———, and Edward N. Wolff, "Relative Wealth Holdings of the Young and Old: The United States, 1962–1983," in T. Smeeding, J. Palmer, and B. Torrey (eds.), *The Well-Being of Children and the Elderly,* 1989.

Harbury, C. D., and D. M. W. N. Hitchens, "The Influence of Relative Prices on the Distribution of Wealth and the Measurement of Inheritance," in E. Wolff (ed.), *International Comparisons of the Distribution of Household Wealth,* 1987.

Haveman, Robert, Barbara Wolfe, Ross Finnie, and Edward Wolff, "The Well-Being of Children and Disparities Among Them Over Two Decades: 1962–1983," in T. Smeeding, J. Palmer, and B. Torrey (eds.), *The Well-Being of Children and the Elderly,* 1989.

Jianakoplos, Nancy Ammon, Paul L. Menchik, and F. Owen Irvine, "Using Panel Data to Assess the Bias in Cross-Sectional Inferences of Life-Cycle Changes in the Level and Composition of Household Wealth," in Robert E. Lipsey and Helen Tice (eds.), *The Measurement of Saving, Investment, and Wealth,* Studies of Income and Wealth, Vol. 52, Chicago University Press, 1989.

Kennickell, A. B., and J. Shack-Marquez, "Changes in Family Finances from 1983 to 1989: Evidence From the Survey of Consumer Finances," *Federal Reserve Bulletin,* Board of Governors of the Federal Reserve System, Vol. 78, No. 1, 1992, pp. 1–18.

Kennickell, Arthur B., and R. Louise Woodburn, "Estimation of Household Net Worth Using Model-Based and Design-Based Weights: Evidence from the 1989 Survey of Consumer Finances," mimeo, Federal Reserve Board, April 1992.

Kessler, Denis, and Andre Masson, "Personal Wealth Distribution in France: Cross-sectional Evidence and Extensions," in E. Wolff (ed.), *International Comparisons of the Distribution of Household Wealth,* 1987.

———, and Edward N. Wolff, "A Comparative Analysis of Household Wealth Patterns in France and the United States," *Review of Income and Wealth,* Series 37, No. 3, September 1991, pp. 249–266.

Kuznets, Simon, *Shares of Upper Income Groups in Income and Savings,* (New York: National Bureau of Economic Research), 1953.

Lampman, Robert, *The Share of Top Wealth-Holders in National Wealth, 1922–1956*, Princeton University Press, Princeton, N.J., 1962.

Lansing, John B., and John Sonquist, "A Cohort Analysis of Changes in the Distribution of Wealth," in Lee Soltow (ed.), *Six Papers on the Size Distribution of Income and Wealth*, National Bureau of Economic Research, New York, 1969.

Lebergott, Stanley, *The American Economy*, Princeton University Press, Princeton, N.J., 1976.

Projector, Dorothy, and Gertrude Weiss, *Survey of Financial Characteristics of Consumers*, Federal Reserve Board Technical Papers, Washington, D.C., 1966.

Radner, Daniel B., and Denton R. Vaughan, "Wealth, Income, and the Economic Status of Aged Households," in E. Wolff (ed.), *International Comparisons of the Distribution of Household Wealth*, 1987.

Schwartz, Marvin, "Trends in Personal Wealth 1976–1981," *Statistics of Income Bulletin*, Vol. 3, Summer 1983, pp. 1–26.

———, "Preliminary Estimates of Personal Wealth, 1982: Composition of Assets," *Statistics of Income Bulletin*, Vol. 4, Winter 1984–1985, pp. 1–17.

Schwartz, Marvin, and Barry Johnson, "Estimates of Personal Wealth, 1986," *Statistics of Income Bulletin*, Vol. 9, Spring 1990, pp. 61–78.

Shorrocks, A. F., "The Age-Wealth Relationship: A Cross-Section and Cohort Analysis," *Review of Economics and Statistics*, Vol. 57, May 1975, pp. 155–163.

———, "United Kingdom Wealth Distribution: Current Evidence and Future Prospects," in E. Wolff (ed.), *International Comparisons of the Distribution of Household Wealth*, 1987.

Smith, James D., "The Concentration of Personal Wealth in America, 1969," *The Review of Income and Wealth*, Series 20, No. 2, June 1974.

———, "Trends in the Concentration of Personal Wealth in the United States, 1958–1976," *Review of Income and Wealth*, Series 30, December 1984, pp. 419–428.

———, "Recent Trends in the Distribution of Wealth in the United States: Data, Research Problems, and Prospects," in E. Wolff (ed.), *International Comparisons of the Distribution of Household Wealth*, 1987.

———, and Stephen Franklin, "The Concentration of Personal Wealth, 1922–1969," *American Economic Review*, Vol. 64, No. 2, May 1974, pp. 162–167.

Soltow, Lee, "Economic Inequality in the United States for the Period from 1860 to 1970," *Journal of Economic History*, 31 December 1971, pp. 822–839.

———, *Men and Wealth in the United States, 1850–1870*, Yale University Press, New Haven, Conn., 1975.

Spånt, Roland, "Wealth Distribution in Sweden: 1920–1983," in E. Wolff (ed.), *International Comparisons of the Distribution of Household Wealth*, 1987.

Statistics Sweden, *Income Distribution Survey in 1990,* SCB Publishing Unit, Orebro, Sweden, 1992.

Steuerle, C. Eugene, "Realized Income and Wealth for Owners of Closely Held Farms and Businesses: A Comparison," *Public Finance Quarterly,* Vol. 12, October 1984, pp. 407–424.

Stewart, Charles, "Income Capitalization as a Method of Estimating the Distribution of Wealth by Size Group," *Studies in Income and Wealth,* Vol. 3, National Bureau of Economic Research, New York, 1939.

Taussig, Michael K., *Alternative Measures of the Distribution of Economic Welfare,* Princeton University Industrial Relations Section Monograph, 1973.

Weisbrod, Burton A., and W. Lee Hansen, "An Income-Net Worth Approach to Measuring Economic Welfare," *American Economic Review,* Vol. 58, December 1968, pp. 1315–1329.

Williamson, Jeffrey G., and Peter H. Lindert, "Long-Term Trends in American Wealth Inequality," in James D. Smith (ed.), *Modeling the Distribution and Intergenerational Transmission of Wealth,* Chicago University Press, Chicago, 1980.

Wolff, Edward N., "The Distributional Effects of the 1969–1975 Inflation on Household Wealth Holdings in the United States," *The Review of Income and Wealth,* Series 25, No. 2, June 1979.

———, "Estimates of the 1969 Size Distribution of Household Wealth in the United States from a Synthetic Database," in James D. Smith, (ed.), *Modeling the Distribution and Intergenerational Transmission of Wealth,* Chicago University Press, Chicago, 1980.

———, "The Size Distribution of Household Disposable Wealth in the United States," *Review of Income and Wealth,* Series 29, June 1983, pp. 125–146.

———, [1987 a] "Estimates of Household Wealth Inequality in the United States, 1962–1983," *Review of Income and Wealth,* Series 33, September 1987, pp. 231–256.

———, [1987 b] "The Effects of Pensions and Social Security on the Distribution of Wealth in the United States," in E. Wolff (ed.), *International Comparisons of the Distribution of Household Wealth,* 1987.

———, "Trends in Aggregate Household Wealth in the United States, 1900–1983," *Review of Income and Wealth,* Series 35, No. 1, March 1989.

———, "Methodological Issues in the Estimation of the Size Distribution of Household Wealth," *Journal of Econometrics,* Vol. 43, No. 1/2, January/February 1990, pp. 179–195.

———, "Wealth Holdings and Poverty Status in the United States," *Review of Income and Wealth,* Series 36, No. 2, June 1990, pp. 141–165.

———, "Methodological Issues in the Estimation of Retirement Wealth," in Daniel J. Slottje (ed.), *Research in Economic Inequality,* Vol. 2, JAI Press, Greenwich, CT, 1992, pp. 31–56.

————, "Trends in Household Wealth in the United States, 1962–1983 and 1983–1989," *Review of Income and Wealth*, Series 40, No. 2, June 1994, pp. 143–174.

————, *Top Heavy: A Study of Increasing Inequality of Wealth in America*, The Twentieth Century Fund Press, 1995.

————, "International Comparisons of Personal Wealth Inequality," *Review of Income and Wealth*, forthcoming.

Wolff, Edward N. (ed.), *International Comparisons of the Distribution of Household Wealth*, Oxford University Press, New York, 1987.

Wolff, Edward N., and Marcia Marley, "Long-Term Trends in U.S. Wealth Inequality: Methodological Issues and Results," in Robert E. Lipsey and Helen Tice (eds.), *The Measurement of Saving, Investment, and Wealth*, Studies of Income and Wealth, Vol. 52, Chicago University Press, 1989.

Wolfson, Michael C., "Wealth and the Distribution of Income, Canada 1969–1970," *Review of Income and Wealth*, Series 25, June 1979, pp. 129–140.

————, "Lifetime Coverage: the Adequacy of Canada's Retirement Income System," in E. Wolff (ed.), *International Comparisons of the Distribution of Household Wealth*, 1987.

DISCUSSION QUESTIONS

1. Which is more equal, the distribution of wealth among individuals or the distribution of wealth among families? Why?

2. How is estate tax data used to obtain estimates of the concentration of household wealth? Briefly explain two problems associated with the use of estate tax data for this purpose.

3. Why might movements in stock prices relative to housing prices be associated with changes in wealth inequality?

4. Briefly describe trends since 1920 in wealth concentration in the United States on the basis of marketable wealth and augmented wealth. Why is inequality in marketable wealth greater than that of augmented wealth?

5. List the major components of household wealth. Which are more concentrated in the portfolios of the rich and which are more evenly dispersed among the general population?

11

THE LIFE CYCLE MODEL, INTERGENERATIONAL TRANSFERS, AND INTERGENERATIONAL EQUITY

Why do individuals save and what explains differences in wealth among individuals and families? These questions are relevant because they bear directly on the determinants of the inequality of wealth and equity in the distribution of household resources. One significant issue throughout this literature is the relative importance of life cycle savings—the tendency of individuals to build up assets as they grow older—versus inheritance in the accumulation of household wealth. If the former is the major determinant, then differences in household wealth can be viewed as the result of the "natural" process of aging and therefore not a major concern of public policy. However, if inheritances plays the major role, then issues of fairness and equity come to the fore.

The accumulation of household wealth depends not only on income but also on savings behavior, capital appreciation, and gifts and inheritances. Moreover, wealth is the direct source of property income, which is an important factor in accounting for disparities in family income. This chapter considers some of the factors that account for differences in wealth among families. The first of these is the role of age in explaining differences in wealth among households. Since individuals work only part of their life, they have a strong incentive to accumulate wealth for their retirement years. In this chapter, we explore the standard life cycle model that economists have developed to describe this behavior. Other factors, such as gifts and inheritances and capital appreciation, also play a role in wealth accumulation, and these too are treated in the chapter.

Section 11.1 begins with a presentation of the basic life cycle model. We then examine some of the evidence on the validity of the model, including age-wealth profiles (average wealth by age group), longitudinal analyses, simulation studies, and regression studies. There have been various attempts to expand the life cycle model. Section 11.2 discusses four extensions of the model: (1) introduction of uncertainty about length of life, (2) the role of retirement wealth, (3) the bequest motive, and (4) precautionary savings and liquidity constraints. Pertinent empirical studies are also reviewed.

Three topics on intergenerational equity are treated in Section 11.3. The first is the role the government plays, particularly through the social security system, in the distribution of public benefits across generations. We will see that the current system transfers considerable wealth from today's working population to today's retirees. The second is the role of private transfers—in particular, bequests and gifts. We will present evidence that, in many ways, private transfers offset the public transfer system by redistributing wealth from the elderly to the working population. The third topic, intergenerational mobility, examines whether children from poor families have the same likelihood of accumulating wealth as children of rich parents. The last part, Section 11.4, provides a summary, as well as an overall assessment.

11.1 THE BASIC LIFE CYCLE MODEL

The basic **life cycle model** (LCM), developed by Franco Modigliani and Richard Brumberg in a 1954 article, assumes that households save in order to spread out their consumption uniformly over their lifetime. Since individuals normally work until age 65 or so but live into their 70s and 80s, they will save during their working years to provide for consumption during retirement. This, in turn, implies that household wealth, defined as accumulated savings, will rise with age until retirement and then decline.

In the simplest form of the model, it is assumed that families earn the same amount in each year until retirement, that lifetime earnings are fully consumed over the lifetime, that age of retirement and longevity are known with certainty at the beginning of work life, and that the interest rate is zero. Under a certain class of utility functions, maximization of lifetime utility leads to a constant annual consumption over the lifetime. The savings pattern that results is a constant savings rate per year until retirement and a constant dissavings rate thereafter. The resulting age-wealth profile is an inverted "V" (see Figure 11.1). Net worth rises linearly with age until retirement and then declines with age in linear fashion.

In a later paper, Alpert Ando and Franco Modigliani (1963) relaxed the assumption of a zero interest rate and assumed that it is positive and unchanging over time. The resulting profile is an inverted "U," with net worth rising with age until around retirement age and declining thereafter (again, see Figure 11.1). In both cases, the "hump-shaped" profile implies that wealth will decline after retirement, an issue that has received extensive empirical investigation.

Figure 11.1   Life-Cycle Age-Wealth Profiles

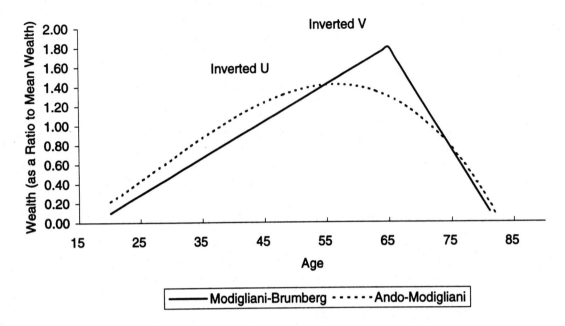

Age-Wealth Profiles

We begin our survey of empirical work on the LCM with a consideration of age-wealth profiles, which show average wealth by age group. It should be noted at the outset that the LCM is a longitudinal model—that is, it describes the path of wealth accumulation for a given household as it ages over time. On the other hand, age-wealth profiles are "cross-sectional"—that is, they describe the wealth holdings of households of different ages at a single point in time. There are two biases that may arise from the use of cross-sectional profiles as a test of the LCM.

First, because real income typically increases over time, the cross-sectional age-wealth profile may be hump-shaped even though the longitudinal profile rises over time (see Anthony Shorrocks, 1975). This stems from the fact that if real incomes rise over time, lifetime income may be higher for younger age cohorts than older ones. As a result, in the cross-section (at a given point in time, say 1995), we may observe that 60-year-olds have greater wealth than 70-year-olds, even though the 70-year-olds have greater wealth in 1995 than they had 10 years ago, when they were 60. As a result, accumulated wealth may peak among families in their 60s in the cross-section, even if each age cohort has continued to save money over time.

Second, as Anthony Shorrocks (1987) notes, a positive correlation between wealth and longevity exists, so people who live longer will generally be wealthier than those who have become deceased. In this case, the cross-sectional profile may slope upward, particularly among the older age cohorts, even though the longitudinal profiles are hump-shaped. The two biases are offsetting, but the net effect of the two is not known (see Douglas Bernheim, 1984, for an analysis).

The early work on age-wealth profiles provided mixed results on the issue of whether families dissave after retirement. H. Lydall (1955), analyzing wealth data for the United Kingdom in 1953, found almost no difference in mean wealth between families in ages 55–64 and those 65 and over. John Lansing and John Sonquist (1969) reported that in 1953 average wealth was slightly greater for 63-year-olds than 53-year-olds in the United States. In 1962 mean wealth among 62-year-olds exceeded that among 52-year-olds but was less than the average wealth of 72-year-olds. John Brittain (1978), using estate tax data for the United States, found wealth increasing with age among older Americans.

Table 11.1 shows age-wealth profiles based on more recent data for the United States. The wealth concept is marketable net worth. The first is computed from the 1962 Survey of Financial Characteristics of Consumers. It shows wealth rising steadily with age until age group 55–59, peaking at 1.7

Table 11.1 Age-Wealth Profiles for Marketable Net Worth, 1962, 1983, and 1989[a] (Mean Wealth by Age Group as Ratio to the Overall Mean)

Age Group	1962 SFCC[b]	1983 SCF[c]	1989 SCF[d]
Under 25	0.13	0.14	0.11
25–34	0.44	0.35	0.32
35–44	0.79	0.78	0.71
45–54	1.05	1.70	1.47
55–59	1.74	1.78	1.46
60–64	1.25	1.83	1.71
65–69	1.65	2.29	1.75
70–74	1.44	1.52	1.47
75–79	1.34	1.25	1.37
80 & over	1.01	0.93	1.30
Mean	1.00	1.00	1.00

[a] The statistics are for household wealth. Families are classified into age group according to the age of the head of household.
[b] Source: 1962 Survey of Financial Characteristics of Consumers, adjusted to align with national balance sheet totals. See Wolff (1987b) for details.
[c] Source: 1983 Survey of Consumer Finances, adjusted to align with national balance sheet totals. See Wolff (1987b) for details.
[d] Source: 1989 Survey of Consumer Finances, adjusted to align with national balance sheet totals. See Wolff (1994) for details.

Figure 11.2   Age-Wealth Profiles, 1983

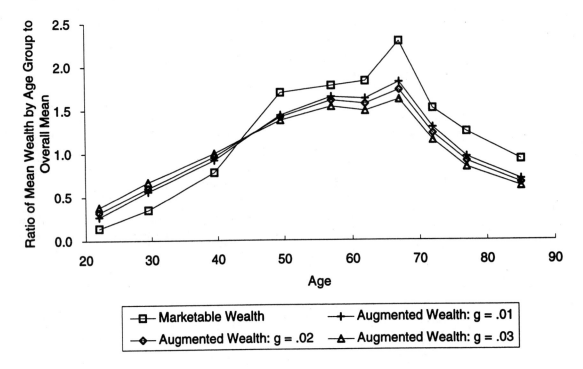

times the overall mean for this age cohort, and then generally declining with age thereafter.

The second set of results is based on the 1983 Survey of Consumer Finances (see also Figure 11.2). The profile shows mean wealth rising steadily with age and peaking in the 65–69 age group at 2.3 times the overall mean and then falling sharply among older age groups. The third set is drawn from the 1989 Survey of Consumer Finances. The results are quite similar to the 1983 data. Wealth rises with age until the 65–59 age group, where the peak is 1.8 times the mean, followed by a steady decline thereafter.

The age-wealth profiles do provide general support to the hump-shaped pattern predicted by the LCM. Wealth increases with age, peaks around age 65, and then declines with age. However, two anomalies do appear. First, though wealth does decline among older age groups, it does not appear to approach zero, even for households aged 80 and over. This result is consistent with earlier tests of the LCM (see J. Friedman, 1982, and Daniel Hammermesh, 1984, for example).

Second, the data show that the cross-sectional age wealth profiles have become more hump-shaped over the 1962–1983 period and have a higher mean wealth at the peak. However, the 1989 profile is flatter than the 1983 one and, indeed, is very close in shape to the 1962 profile. These results suggest that age-wealth profiles are not static but can change quite substantially over time.

Table 11.2 shows the effect of adding pension wealth (PW) and social security wealth (SSW) to marketable net worth on the shape of the age-

Table 11.2   Age-Wealth Profiles for Marketable and Augmented Household Wealth, 1962 and 1983[a] (Mean Wealth by Age Group as Ratio to the Overall Mean)

Age Group	Marketable Wealth	Augmented Household Wealth[b]		
		g = 0.01	g = 0.02	g = 0.03
A. 1962 SFCC[c]				
Under 25	0.13	0.23	0.28	0.37
25–34	0.44	0.50	0.54	0.61
35–44	0.79	0.81	0.83	0.86
45–54	1.05	1.09	1.09	1.09
55–59	1.74	1.63	1.59	1.54
60–64	1.25	1.31	1.28	1.23
65–69	1.65	1.61	1.56	1.49
70–74	1.44	1.35	1.29	1.22
75–79	1.34	1.13	1.07	1.01
80 & over	1.01	0.82	0.78	0.73
Mean	1.00	1.00	1.00	1.00
B. 1983 SCF[d]				
Under 25	0.14	0.27	0.32	0.38
25–34	0.35	0.56	0.60	0.67
35–44	0.78	0.92	0.96	1.00
45–54	1.70	1.44	1.42	1.38
55–59	1.78	1.65	1.61	1.54
60–64	1.83	1.63	1.57	1.49
65–69	2.29	1.82	1.73	1.62
70–74	1.52	1.30	1.23	1.15
75–79	1.25	0.96	0.91	0.84
80 & over	0.93	0.70	0.66	0.62
Mean	1.00	1.00	1.00	1.00

[a]The statistics are for household wealth. Households are classified by age group by age of the head of household in 1962 and age of respondent in 1983.
[b]g is the assumed rate of growth of social security benefits over time.
[c]Source: 1962 Survey of Financial Characteristics of Consumers, adjusted to align with national balance sheet totals. See Wolff (1987b) for details.
[d]Source: 1983 Survey of Consumer Finances, adjusted to align with national balance sheet totals. See Wolff (1987b) for details.

wealth profile (see also Figure 11.2). Pension wealth is defined as the present discounted value of future pension benefits. In a similar fashion, social security wealth is defined as the present discounted value of the stream of future social security benefits (see the author's 1993 paper for details on the estimation of PW and SSW).

In the previous chapter we talked at some length about the concept of augmented household wealth. From an individual's standpoint, a future guaranteed flow of income is in many ways like owning a financial asset. Indeed, there are marketable assets called "annuities," which have precisely the characteristic of providing a steady stream of income after a certain time (or age) is reached. The anticipated social security (or pension) benefits that an individual will receive after retirement is comparable to such an annuity (we will have more to say about this below). In the context of the life cycle model, the main motivation for saving is to guarantee a steady stream of income after retirement so that social security (or pension) wealth may *substitute* for marketable wealth. One implication of this, as we will discuss below, is that there may be a *trade-off* between the accumulation of marketable wealth and that of retirement wealth.

A look at the results will show that SSW (and PW) has been constructed to reflect conditional mortality rates. It contains a built-in bias for its mean value to decline with age, particularly after age 70. In other words, since a person's remaining life expectancy declines as the person ages, the total value of his or her remaining social security wealth is also going to decline. Despite this, the net effect of including retirement wealth is a flattening of the age-wealth profile (compare the first two columns of Table 11.2, for example). The younger-age cohorts gain relative to the older ones and peak wealth declines. Moreover, the greater the assumed rate of growth of future social security benefits (the parameter g), the more the younger groups gain and the more the peak flattens. However, all three measures of augmented wealth retain the basic hump shape of the LCM.

Longitudinal Analyses*

Though cross-sectional age-wealth profiles generally follow the basic inverted U-shape predicted by the LCM, this can not be taken as confirmation of the LCM. As noted above, Anthony Shorrocks (1975) demonstrated that if real income is growing over time, the cross-sectional age-wealth profile can be hump-shaped even though individuals continue to accumulate wealth over their lifetime (that is, the longitudinal age-wealth profile slopes upward). A hump-shaped, cross-sectional wealth profile is a necessary but not sufficient condition to ensure a hump-shaped wealth profile over the lifetime.

Thad Mirer (1979) used actual data on real earnings growth over time to adjust cross-sectional, age-wealth profiles for differences in cohort earnings. Using a cross-sectional sample of individuals over 65 in the United States and adjusting for actual differences in cohort earnings, he found no significant reduction in wealth with advancing age. In other words, even though age-wealth profiles were hump-shaped, the evidence indicated that elderly families did not dissave as they aged. In a follow-up piece, Mirer (1980) used a one-year panel from the 1963 and 1964 Federal Reserve Board Survey of Financial Characteristics of Consumers (the same families observed in the two years) and calculated a very small dissavings rate for the elderly—a median of 1.2 percent over the year—though it was not statistically significant.

Later work on the LCM used longitudinal (panel) data, which followed the same individuals over time. Peter Diamond and Jerry Hausman (1984), using the National Longitudinal Sample of older men, found that individuals accumulated wealth up to retirement and then depleted it, though very few individuals in their sample had actually retired. J. Friedman (1982), using the Retirement History Survey (RHS), which covered individuals from age 58 to 73 over a ten-year period, reported that individuals continued to save in the first four to six years after retirement and then dissaving began.

Daniel Hammermesh (1984) found from the RHS that spending on consumption items covered in this survey (food, housing, transportation, and health) declined in the first few years after retirement, a finding consistent with Friedman. This finding also confirmed the earlier work of Sheldon Danziger *et al.* (1982), based on the cross-sectional 1972–1973 Consumer Expenditure Survey. Danziger found that the average ratio of consumption expenditures to after-tax income declined with age after age 71. Alan Blinder, Roger Gordon, and Donald Weiss (1983), also using the RHS and introducing a variable for lifetime earnings, found that conventionally measured wealth showed no tendency to decline with age among older people.

However, Michael Hurd (1987, 1990), using evidence from the same source of data (the RHS), reached the opposite conclusion. In these papers, Hurd reported that the wealth of the elderly did decline over time, by 22 percent for singles and 2 percent for couples over the period 1969 to 1979. Later, Hurd (1992) concluded from the RHS that though family consumption declined after retirement as the family aged, so did its wealth.

Axel Borsch-Supan (1992) reached a striking conclusion regarding the savings patterns of elderly German families. He found that though wealth holdings declined between families aged 60 and 70, they increased after age 70. The very old (over age 80) had the highest savings rate among all age groups. He attributed this finding to two factors. First, the German social security system provides very generous annuities to aged pensioners, as well as complete health coverage. Second, consumption expenditures actually declined with age after age 70, presumably reflecting the lessening needs for items such as clothing, transportation and travel, and food. This is similar to the results reported for U.S. households by Hammermesh (1984).

All in all, econometric studies have generally confirmed the age-wealth profile predicted by the life cycle model, with only one or two exceptions. These findings provide further reinforcement to the cross-sectional studies, which have also largely found the inverted U-shape profile of the LCM.

Simulation and Regression Analysis*

Simulation and regression techniques have also been used to assess the explanatory power of the life cycle model. In simulation analysis, the researcher attempts to reproduce the actual characteristics of the wealth distribution on the basis of the LCM and the assumed or estimated parameters of the model.

Anthony Atkinson (1971) used a simulation experiment to account for the concentration of household wealth. He started with the actual distribution of labor earnings in the United Kingdom and assumed that all wealth accumulation was due to life cycle savings. He simulated that the basic LCM would predict that the top 10 percent of the population would hold only about 20 percent of total wealth, well below the actual concentration ratio of 60 to 70 percent. He then added the assumption that the top 10 percent of the distribution received equal inheritance shares. Even with this added assumption, he calculated that the top 10 percent would hold at most 30 percent of total wealth, still well below the actual share held by the top decile. He concluded that the simple LCM, even with the introduction of some inheritance effects, could not account for the actual concentration of household wealth.

N. Oulton (1976) generalized Atkinson's model to allow the age distribution, individual earnings functions, and the rate of return on assets to vary. Substituting the distribution of earnings estimated from the actual British data into his model and assuming no inheritance, Oulton computed a maximum coefficient of variation of wealth of 0.75, which was substantially less than the actual value of 3.98. He also concluded that the LCM could not by itself adequately explain inequality in individual wealth holdings.

Two American studies, Betsy White (1978) and Laurence Kotlikoff and Lawrence Summers (1981), used simulation to determine whether the LCM could account for the aggregate accumulation of wealth observed in the U.S. economy. Both found that the LCM could explain only a very small proportion of observed household wealth in the United States. Kotlikoff and Summers, for example, used actual age-earnings profiles (showing average earnings by age group) and consumption rates by age group in the United States. They calculated that life cycle savings accounted for only about 20 percent of observed U.S. household wealth in 1974. The remainder, by implication, was due to inheritance and intergenerational transfers.

The author (1981 and 1988) used regression analysis to explore the explanatory power of the life cycle model in accounting for differences in wealth holdings among households in the United States. The regressions were cross-sectional in nature, with observations on households of different ages at a given point in time. However, cohort effects were controlled for by the addition of a lifetime earnings variable. Results of the second paper are summarized in Table 11.3.

Various specifications were tried, including quadratic, cubic, and fourth-power functions of age, as well as piece-wise linear functions. The best fit in

Table 11.3 Life Cycle Regressions on Marketable and Augmented Wealth, Based on the 1983 Survey of Consumer Finances[a]

Independent Variables	Dependent Variable					
	HW	AHW	HW	AHW	HW	AHW
Constant	−49.3	−19.0	−37.8	−4.9	−20.7	−66.0*
(1,000s)	(1.91)	(0.69)	(1.43)	(0.18)	(1.81)	(2.03)
$AGE^2/100$	1.91**	2.15**	1.58**	1.76**	0.55**	1.44*
	(6.20)	(6.58)	(5.03)	(5.48)	(9.72)	(11.0)
AGE^3	−2.05**	−2.26**	−1.64**	−1.68**	−0.58**	−1.78
	(5.57)	(5.83)	(4.40)	(4.73)	(7.82)	(10.45)
LE			0.20**	0.21**	0.25**	0.33**
			(13.2)	(15.9)	(18.4)	(27.0)
R^2	0.012	0.015	0.037	0.051	0.122	0.198
Adj. R^2	0.012	0.015	0.036	0.050	0.120	0.192
F-Test	25.9**	32.7**	54.6**	76.1**	235.8**	324.3**
Sample	All HH	All HH	All HH	All HH	Bot 95%	Bot 95%
Sample Size	4,262	4,262	4,262	4,262	4,049	4,049

[a] t-ratios are shown in parentheses. Key: HW—marketable household wealth; AHW—augmented household wealth, the sum of HW, pension wealth, and social security wealth (it is assumed that the annual rate of growth of future social security benefits is 2 percent); AGE—age of respondent; LE—lifetime earnings (it is assumed that the future annual rate of growth of labor earnings is 1 percent). Source: Wolff (1988).
* Significant at 5 percent level (2-tail test for coefficients; 1-tail test for F value).
** Significant at 1 percent level (2-tail test for coefficients; 1-tail test for F value).

terms of the adjusted R^2 is the cubic form, shown in Table 11.3.[1] In the first regression, with marketable wealth (HW) as the dependent variable, the coefficients of the two age variables have the predicted signs (the coefficient of AGE^2 is positive and that of AGE^3 is negative) and both are significant at the one-percent level. However, the R-square (the measure of the goodness of fit or the explanatory power of the equation) is very low, with a value of 0.012 (only about one percent of the variation of household wealth is explained by age). Regression results are also shown for augmented household wealth, AHW (second column). The R-square for this regression form is 0.015.

As noted above, the use of cross-sectional data tends to produce a biased test of the (longitudinal) LCM if real earnings have been rising over time.

---

[1] The quadratic form produces a symmetric (parabolic) age-wealth profile with respect to age. However, a cubic or higher power form yields an asymmetrical profile, which corresponds more closely to the age-wealth profiles illustrated in Figures 11.1 and 11.2. After some experimentation, it was found that the best fit was provided by a cubic form which included only an AGE^2 and AGE^3 term.

The introduction of measures of lifetime earnings should control for this effect. Moreover, differences in lifetime earnings should also explain a substantial portion of the intra-cohort variation (differences among households of the same age) in household wealth.[2]

Results on the LCM with the inclusion of lifetime earnings (LE) are shown in the third and fourth columns of Table 11.3. The LE variable is highly significant, with t-statistics of 13.2 and 15.9. The inclusion of LE triples the goodness of fit of the model. Even so, the extended model explains only 4 to 5 percent of the variation of wealth holdings among households.

The same equations were then estimated on a subset of the original sample, in which the upper one percent of the wealth distribution is excluded (columns 5 and 6 of Table 11.3).[3] The significance level of all the independent variables—the age terms and lifetime earnings—increases markedly. Moreover, the explanatory power of the model increases substantially. The R-square increases from 0.037 to 0.122 for marketable wealth (HW) and from 0.051 to 0.198 for augmented wealth (AHW).

These results suggest that the explanatory power of the LCM in accounting for the variation of marketable wealth among all households is quite weak. This remains true even when we control for differences in lifetime earnings among households. When we expand the concept of household wealth to include both social security and pension wealth (or, together, retirement wealth), the goodness of fit of the regression improves. As noted above, the inclusion of retirement wealth in household wealth is more consistent with the LCM than the use of marketable household wealth alone. However, as before, the explanatory power of the model is still very low (at most 5 percent of the variation of wealth explained), even when lifetime earnings are introduced into the model.

Perhaps, the most telling result is that the explanatory power of the LCM (particularly with lifetime earnings) is substantially greater (by a factor of three or four) when the sample is restricted to the bottom 95 percent of the wealth distribution. This holds for all measures of household wealth. This suggests that, though the LCM predicts household savings behavior well for the vast majority of households, it is not successful in explaining the wealth accumulation motives of the top wealth classes, who also happen to hold the majority of household wealth. It appears that the difference is due

---

[2] The inclusion of lifetime earnings also implicitly controls for the other source of bias noted by Shorrocks (1987), the sample selection effect induced by the positive correlation between wealth and longevity. The reason for this is the high positive correlation between wealth and lifetime earnings and, correspondingly, between lifetime earnings and life expectancy. As a result, the fact that richer families are over-represented among the older age groups is controlled for by their higher lifetime earnings. See also Bernheim (1984), who found this sample selection bias relatively small in other tests of the LCM.

[3] Technically, the truncation of the sample on the top and the bottom (see below) introduces a sample selection bias, since the error term is now also truncated. To correct for this truncation bias, the author used the two-stage procedure developed by Heckman (1976, 1979). It entails, first, the estimation of a probit model for high wealth holders and, then, the inclusion of the inverse of the Mills' ratio in a second stage regression of wealth on age and lifetime earnings. See also King and Dicks-Mireaux (1982) for more details on this procedure.

to dissimilarities in the strength of the bequest motive. One inference drawn from these results is that the top wealth classes likely form a distinct social class in the sense that their motivation for wealth accumulation is for political and economic power and social status. It also appears that this class is interested in the expansion of family wealth over the generations.

11.2 Extensions of the Life Cycle Model

The general finding that individuals did not totally exhaust their wealth at time of death and that many older individuals did not dissave (reduce their wealth) as they aged raised some questions about the validity of the LCM. The response was to modify the basic model, by relaxing one or more of its assumptions. There are four directions that we shall review here: (1) uncertainty, particularly about length of life; (2) the role of social security and pension wealth; (3) the introduction of a bequest motive; and (4) precautionary savings and liquidity constraints. The first two topics are directly related, as we shall see.

The Role of Uncertainty About Death and Lifetime Annuities

In the basic LCM and the Ando-Modigliani version, it is assumed that length of life is known with certainty. However, individuals do not know when they will die. The introduction of uncertainty about length of life can affect the shape of the age-wealth profile, particularly the pattern of dissavings after retirement. Menaham Yaari (1965) was the first to analyze the effects of uncertainty on life cycle behavior. He demonstrated that uncertainty by itself could lead to increased savings and an (nonaltruistic) individual will always leave unintended bequests, since the individual will always have savings available for the possibility of living longer than expected.

Yaari then introduced annuities into his model. An annuity is a savings instrument that guarantees an individual a fixed annual income until death. At time of death, the value of this asset becomes zero. An example of this is a pension. Most pensions guarantee a retiree a fixed annual income until time of death (some will also continue the benefit for a surviving spouse). Such an asset removes most of the problems associated with uncertainty about death, since the pension provider assumes the risk about length of life. It thus has considerable advantages over a fixed-value asset such as a bond. Yaari demonstrated that if an annuity were available that was indexed for inflation, then the availability of such an indexed annuity would lead to reduced savings in other forms by older individuals and might lead to an exhaustion of wealth at death.

Following Yaari's line of reasoning, Laurence Kotlikoff and Avia Spivak (1981) estimated on the basis of certain parameter values that individuals could leave up to a quarter of their wealth at age 55 unintentionally—that is, without directly planning that it should be left as a bequest to their spouse or children. James Davies (1981) applied the same argument to explain the slow dissaving by individuals after retirement. In a life cycle model with uncertain longevity, he demonstrated that consumption during retirement would be smaller than in a regime of complete certainty. Using Canadian data, he simulated the post-retirement consumption and savings pattern of Canadian families. He found that savings would still be higher with uncertainty than with certainty about longevity, even with the availability of pensions (a form of annuity). He concluded that uncertainty about length of life could explain the slow dissaving of households after retirement. Using the same data, Mervyn King and Louis Dicks-Mireaux (1982) did find that household wealth decreased after retirement but at a rate much slower than predicted by the basic LCM. They attributed this discrepancy to uncertainty over lifetime and the bequest motive (see below).

The Role of Pension and
Social Security Wealth

The empirical work on household savings and social security dates from Martin Feldstein's 1974 article using aggregate time-series data for the United States. He argued that social security should reduce household savings, since the need to put away money for retirement would be lessened if the government was guaranteeing future retirement benefits. He also argued that the payment of social security benefits would reduce household disposable income and therefore decrease savings.[4] He estimated that social security may have reduced personal savings by as much as 50 percent.

This provocative paper generated considerable work on the effects of social security on household savings. Cross-sectional evidence has generally been mixed. Martin Feldstein and Anthony Pellechio (1979), using the 1963 Survey of Financial Characteristics of Consumers, found a very strong offset of social security wealth for private wealth. Blinder, Gordon, and Weiss (1983), using the Retirement History Survey (RHS), estimated that each dollar of social security wealth substituted for 39 cents of private wealth, though the estimated coefficient had a very large standard error and was quite unstable over alternative specifications. Diamond and Hausman (1984), using the National Longitudinal Survey of older men, estimated effects on private wealth from 30 to 50 cents per dollar of social security wealth. Kotlikoff (1979) found a significant negative tax effect of social security contributions on individual savings.

Dean Leimer and Selig Lesnoy (1982), using the same aggregate time-series data as Feldstein, found no negative effect of social security on private savings. However, Feldstein's (1982) reply reconfirmed his earlier results as did his 1983 study. Henry Aaron (1982), in a review of the literature, sur-

---

[4]Feldstein also argued that the availability of social security retirement income might induce workers to retire earlier than otherwise and this possibility might have a positive effect on private savings. No independent estimate of this effect on savings was provided.

mised that the wide variation in results on this subject made it difficult to reach any definitive conclusion of the impact of social security on savings.

Martin David and Paul Menchik (1981) employed a special sample of probate records (estate tax records with information on the individual's wealth) matched to income tax records for Wisconsin males born between 1890 and 1899. They investigated the effect of social security benefits on household wealth by comparing the actual age-wealth profile of males in the sample with what would have been predicted from the LCM augmented with social security wealth. They found no evidence that the availability of social security benefits affected the accumulation of marketable wealth over time. They concluded on the basis of this sample that social security does not depress or displace saving in traditional assets and that individuals do not deplete their marketable wealth in old age.

Glenn Hubbard (1983), using 1979 and 1980 survey data collected by the U.S. President's Commission on Pension Policy (1980) and controlling for permanent income, found that both social security wealth and pension wealth had statistically significant negative effects on private wealth. Social security wealth was estimated to have a 33 cents per dollar offset on private wealth, while private pensions had a 16 cents per dollar offset. However, as he noted, the substitution effects were considerably less than the dollar-for-dollar reduction predicted in a standard life cycle model.

Robert Avery, Gregory Elliehausen, and Thomas Gustafson (1985) provided similar estimates based on the 1983 Survey of Consumer Finances (SCF). Their analysis was confined to households headed by persons 50 years of age or older who were in the labor force. Their computation of net social security and pension wealth is based on the difference between the present value of expected benefits less that of anticipated contributions into the respective systems. Standard mortality rates were used to calculate present values. For pensions, expected benefits were based on respondent information, while for social security, expected benefits were calculated on the basis of current and future social security rates. Current family income was included as an independent variable, though a measure of lifetime earnings or permanent income was not. They reported a substantial substitution between pension and nonpension wealth. A dollar increase in pension wealth offset nonpension wealth by 66 cents. However, coefficients for social security wealth were small in size and statistically insignificant, indicating little substitution between social security wealth and marketable wealth.

Wolff (1988), relying on the same 1983 Survey of Consumer Finance data, reached different conclusions. This study included estimates of gross pension and social security wealth, along with a measure of lifetime earnings, in a standard life cycle regression, with marketable wealth as the dependent variable. No statistically significant substitution effect was found between marketable wealth and pension wealth. The substitution effect between social security wealth and marketable wealth was marginally significant for both the full sample and the bottom 95 percentiles, and the coefficient was less than half in both cases.

Another study of direct interest is that of Douglas Bernheim (1986). Using the RHS, he first divided his sample into retirees and nonretirees. He computed longitudinal age-wealth profiles for retirees and found significant dissaving in traditional wealth after retirement. He then argued that, with annuities such as social security available, the proper concept of wealth is the sum of traditional wealth and the simple discounted value of private pension and social security benefits.[5] He found that augmented wealth showed little tendency to decline with age after retirement.

Bequests

The LCM has also been generalized by introducing a bequest motive for households. If an individual wants to leave a bequest for children (or other heirs), the person will make sure that some wealth will be left at time of death. The bequest motive, like uncertain longevity, will therefore result in a nonzero net worth at time of death.

Modigliani and Brumberg recognized this possibility in their original paper. Later, Modigliani (1975) estimated that only somewhere between one-tenth and one-fifth of all (private) wealth could be traced to inheritances. This estimate was subsequently challenged—for example, by White (1978) and Kotlikoff and Summers (1981), who put the estimated share much higher (see above). There have also been theoretical attempts to incorporate the bequest motive into a life cycle model. For example, Menchik and David (1983) have introduced the notion of intergenerational "altruism" to account for the willingness of parents to leave part of their wealth to their children.

Survey evidence on the importance of bequests is fairly consistent. Dorothy Projector and Gertrude Weiss (1966), on the basis of the 1963 Survey of Financial Characteristics of Consumers, reported that only 17 percent of families had received any inheritance. This compares with a figure of 18 percent, reported by James Morgan, Martin David, William Cohen, and Harvey Brazer (1962). The Projector and Weiss study also found that only 5 percent of households had received a "substantial" proportion of their wealth from inheritance. However, this latter proportion did rise with household wealth; 34 percent of the families had a net worth exceeding half a million dollars, indicating a substantial bequest. Barlow, Brazer, and Morgan (1966) found from a 1964 Brookings study on the affluent, covering families with income of $10,000 or more, that only 7 percent of the sample mentioned gifts and inheritance alone as the source of most of their present assets. They estimated that about one-seventh of the total wealth of this group came from inheritance.

Menchik and David (1983) used probate records of men who died in Wisconsin between 1947 and 1978 to obtain an estimate of $20,000 (in

[5] As King and Dicks-Mireaux (1982) argued, the use of actuarial values to compute retirement wealth builds in a tendency for total wealth to decline rapidly after retirement, because conditional life expectancy decreases with age.

1967 dollars) for the mean bequest of all decedents in their sample. This figure includes not only intergenerational transfers but interspousal and other transfers as well. They also found no evidence that older individuals de-accumulated wealth. They attributed this to the presence of a bequest motive.

David and Menchik (1982) estimated that of this the average interspousal transfer was $15,800, with about one-half of all individuals dying while still married. Moreover, they computed that about 60 percent of all noninterspousal bequests went to children. Putting these figures together, we obtain the rough estimate that the average intergenerational bequest among decedents was $7,500 in 1967 dollars, which amounted to less than one-fifth of average household wealth in 1967 and about 10 percent of the average household wealth of families 65 or over in age.

Michael Hurd and Gabriella Mundaca (1989) analyzed data from both the 1964 Survey on the Economic Behavior of the Affluent and the 1983 Survey of Consumer Finances on the importance of gifts and inheritances in individual wealth holdings. Both surveys asked questions of the respondents about whether they had received gifts and inheritances and how much these transfers were worth. They found from the 1964 data that only 12 percent of households in the top 10 percent of the income distribution reported that more than half their wealth came from gifts or inheritances. The corresponding figure from the 1983 data was only 9 percent. They concluded that intergenerational transfers were not an important source of wealth, even for rich families.

A similar type of analysis was conducted on French data by Denis Kessler and Andre Masson (1979) (see also Kessler and Masson, 1989). In a 1975 survey of 2,000 French families, the respondent was asked whether the family had received any significant inheritance (above $4,000) or gifts (above $2,000). Of all the households in the sample, 36 percent reported that they had already received some inheritance. Of the total wealth of the population, Kessler and Masson estimated that 35 percent originated from inheritances or gifts. Among those who had reported receiving an intergenerational transfer (who were about $2^{1}/_{2}$ times richer than the average household), the corresponding proportion was 40 percent.

Blinder, Gordon, and Weiss (1983) also attempted a test of the importance of bequests, using the RHS. Their hypothesis was that if there is a strong bequest motive in accumulating wealth, it should imply that families with more children should have greater assets later in life than families with fewer children. Their results did not support this hypothesis, though it should be noted that *inter vivos* intergenerational transfers were not included. Hurd (1987), testing a similar hypothesis found that, in fact, families with more children have less wealth than smaller families and dissave the same fraction of wealth after retirement.

Hurd (1992) made an interesting test of the bequest motive. He argued that if families were motivated to accumulate in order to bequeath wealth, elderly couples who had children should show greater wealth and lower consumption (after controlling for income) than childless couples. On the basis of the RHS, he reported no significant difference in the consumption and wealth profiles between these two groups of elderly couples.

Though direct survey evidence and econometric tests on household survey data (or probate records) failed to show a significant effect of bequests on household wealth accumulation (except, perhaps, for the French studies), indirect tests have. One model developed by Davies (1982) augmented the standard life cycle model with a bequest motive. He began with the actual distribution of wealth in Canada in 1970. He then used actual data on the distribution of inheritances, mortality rates, and other factors to simulate the effects of inheritance on the distribution of wealth in Canada. He concluded that inheritances were a major source of wealth inequality in Canada.

In a follow-up paper, James Davies and France St-Hilaire (1987) used the same model to estimate the proportion of total wealth accumulation in Canada that could be traced to inheritances. Without cumulating interest on inheritances, they estimated that 35 percent of total household wealth was traceable to inheritances. With the interest on the inheritances added in, the proportion rose to 53 percent.

In another simulation analysis, Daphne Greenwood and Edward Wolff (1992) investigated the importance of four sources of household wealth accumulation: (1) savings, (2) capital appreciation on existing wealth holdings, (3) inheritances, and (4) *inter-vivos* transfers (gifts from living parents to their children). In the simulation, initial wealth holdings by age group, as reported in the 1962 SFCC, were updated annually until 1983 on the basis of savings rates computed from Consumer Expenditure Survey data and capital gains by individual asset type. On the basis of mortality rates by age cohort and age differences between generations, the study was able to simulate the transfer of inheritances between parents and children.

As shown in Table 11.4, it was estimated that 75 percent of the growth of overall household wealth between 1962 and 1983 arose from capital gains (appreciation) of existing wealth and the remaining 25 percent from savings (income less consumption expenditures). However, there are striking differences by age cohort. First, as to be expected, savings were relatively more important than capital appreciation for younger age groups than older ones. Second, inheritances (including the capital appreciation on the assets in the bequest) accounted for a substantial portion of the wealth accumulation for households under the age of 65 in 1983. The proportion ranged between 23 percent for age class 45–49 in 1983 to 49 percent for age class 50–54. For ages 40 to 64 as a whole, 34 percent of the wealth accumulated over this 21-year period (1962 to 1983) could be traced to inheritances.[6]

Third, even with inheritances included in the model, the simulations systematically fell short of explaining the wealth of younger age groups but

---

[6]Even this figure might be an understatement of the actual importance of inheritance, since there was no information available on the sources of wealth before the calendar year 1962.

Table 11.4   Sources of Wealth Accumulation by Birth Cohort, 1962–1983[a]

1983 Age Class	Net Worth[b] 1962	Net Worth[b] 1983	Savings[c]	Appreciation of Wealth[d]	Inheritance[e]	Remaining Gap
40–44	4.8	110.6	13	6	27	54
45–49	18.7	251.7	9	13	23	55
50–54	44.1	180.7	34	34	49	−16
55–59	60.8	230.0	34	41	38	−13
60–64	80.4	246.3	40	48	37	−25
65–69	93.6	339.0	32	39	21	8
70–74	101.6	203.5	44	76	22	−42
75–79	173.8	166.4	47	151	14	−112
80 & Over	131.3	133.2	38	160	6	−105
All	95.6	142.5	25	75	—	—

The header spans: *Sources of Wealth Change, 1962–1983 (percent)* over Savings, Appreciation of Wealth, Inheritance, and Remaining Gap.

[a] Calculations from simulations based on the 1962 SFCC and the 1983 SCF.
Source: Greenwood and Wolff (1992).
[b] Net worth in thousands, 1985 dollars, by birth cohort.
[c] Includes appreciation of assets accumulated in savings.
[d] Appreciation of initial wealth only.
[e] Includes appreciation of assets received in inheritance.

overstated that of older ones. For example, for age groups 40–44 and 45–49 (in 1983), we were able to account for only 45 percent of their total wealth accumulation, with 55 percent unaccounted for. On the other hand, for age groups over 69 years of age, their simulated wealth was much larger than their actual wealth holdings in 1983. What is the likely explanation? It appeared that *inter-vivos* transfers (gifts) was the missing factor. The wealth holdings of younger households in 1983 were much larger than that which could be explained by their savings, capital gains, and inheritances, while the wealth holdings of older households were much smaller than would have been the case if they kept all their wealth accumulation. The most reasonable explanation is that older parents have been transferring significant amounts of wealth to their (adult) children in the form of gifts. All told, it was estimated that inheritances and *inter-vivos* transfers together accounted for 40 percent of the wealth accumulation of age cohorts under the age of 65 between 1962 and 1983.

What accounts for this sizable discrepancy in results between the direct survey evidence (and regression analysis) and the simulation results in regard to the importance of intergenerational transfers in household wealth accumulation? The direct survey evidence suggests that no more than about 20 percent of household wealth is due to intergenerational transfers (though the figure is closer to one third for French households). In contrast, the simulation models suggest that life cycle savings explain only a small portion of total wealth accumulation. The Kotlikoff and Summers (1982) results suggest that only 20 percent of wealth accumulation is due to life cycle savings, with the remainder presumably the result of intergenerational transfers.

This subject was the source of a lively debate between Modigliani (1988a, 1988b) and Kotlikoff (1988) and Kotlikoff and Summers (1988), with commentary by Blinder (1988) and Kessler and Masson (1989). There are three major differences between the two approaches. First, direct survey evidence is hampered by recall bias and underreporting. It is hard for people to remember the amount of inheritances received 5, 10, or, certainly, 20 years ago. As a result, many respondents may understate the value of inheritances received, and this may bias downward the direct survey evidence on the importance of inheritances.

Second, the treatment of the appreciation of inheritances is a crucial factor. Suppose a house was inherited ten years ago and its value doubled over the decade. Should its contribution to current wealth be valued at its original value or at its now appreciated value? Modigliani appears to favor the former method, in which the appreciation of inherited assets is counted as savings, while Kotlikoff and Wolff include the appreciation on the inheritance as part of the contribution of inheritances to current wealth. This issue is definitional—it depends on the accounting framework one uses—but the difference in the assessment can be quite substantial.

Third, the role of *inter-vivos* transfers is often overlooked in direct tests of the bequest motive. When asked about in direct surveys, gifts are particularly subject to recall error, since, typically, there are no formal records made of these transfers. Moreover, as the Greenwood and Wolff simulations suggest, they may be a particularly important source of wealth for young households.

Precautionary Savings and Liquidity Constraints

Another way to modify the LCM is to introduce capital market imperfections into the model. These usually take one of two forms. The first is that the interest rate at which a consumer can borrow may differ from that at which he or she can lend (the borrowing rate is usually higher than the lending rate). A second is that due to credit market restrictions, a consumer can not borrow all that he or she may desire. These two cases are usually referred to as a "liquidity constraint." In both cases, the implication is that the consumer cannot carry out his or her optimal lifetime consumption plan, and at some stage, desired consumption will be constrained by current resources (in particular, by disposable income and the amount of financial assets). Moreover, since borrowing is constrained, the family will accumulate more wealth than a pure life cycle model would predict. James Tobin and Walter Dolde (1971a, 1971b) provided the early theoretical foundations for this approach

Several studies have suggested the importance of these liquidity constraints on wealth accumulation. Hubbard and Judd (1986a, 1986b) developed a 55-period simulation model in which young consumers are constrained in terms of borrowing for nine years (ages 20 to 29). They estimated that such liquidity constraints could increase aggregate savings by as much as one-third.

The age-wealth profiles shown in Section 11.1 indicate that even families under the age of 25 have, on average, accumulated positive net worth. As a result, only a fraction of young households may face a liquidity constraint. Emily Lawrence (1987) used such an approach and found a smaller effect on aggregate savings from liquidity constraints.

A related argument is that consumers will accumulate precautionary savings (that is, saving for a rainy day). Individual consumers will accumulate a stock of assets in order to allay the uncertainties associated with their future stream of labor earnings—for example, those related to layoffs, changing jobs, sickness, etc. In this sense, precautionary savings serve as insurance against potential earnings misfortunes. As a result, young families will accumulate more wealth than if their future income stream was known with certainty. This argument also leads to the hypothesis that consumers will accumulate more wealth than is strictly optimal from a pure life cycle perspective. This motive will also yield a hump-shaped, age-wealth profile even in the absence of the standard LCM retirement motive.

There is evidence that precautionary savings do explain a sizable fraction of the wealth accumulation observed among households. S. P. Zeldes (1986) modeled the uncertainty associated with future earnings. He argued that the fear of being liquidity constrained some time in the future (from a shortfall of income) may induce consumers to save more today. On the basis of simulation analysis, Zeldes found that the possibility of future liquidity constraints might raise total savings by as much as 25 percent. A similar analysis and result is reported by J.S. Skinner (1986).

Kotlikoff (1989, Chapter 6) explored the relation between household saving and uncertainty over future health expenses. He argued that in the absence of full health insurance, families will save as a hedge against uncertain future health expenses. Using simulation analysis, he found that the absence of complete health insurance could exert a substantial positive effect on personal savings.

Ricardo Caballero (1991) calculated from a simulation model that 60 percent of the observed wealth of U.S. households, net of the portion due to strictly life cycle savings, could be attributed to precautionary savings. Christopher Caroll and Andrew Samwick (1992) estimated that as much as 40 percent of aggregate financial (nonhousing, nonbusiness) wealth is held for precautionary motives.

11.3 INTERGENERATIONAL EQUITY

Part 5 of the textbook will provide a fuller account on issues of equity, but here we want to focus on one particular aspect of this issue—the distribution of resources across generations. The government plays an important role, as do private transfers. We have discussed above bequests and *inter-vivos* transfers in the context of the LCM. In this section, we treat the issue in terms of the intergenerational distribution of resources. We also consider how inheritances affect intergenerational wealth mobility

Social Security Annuity and Transfer Wealth

Several studies have examined the intergenerational effects of the social security system. In this work, social security wealth is divided into two components: an **annuity value** and a **transfer value**. The annuity portion is defined as the benefit level the worker would receive on the basis of his or her contributions into the social security system (OASI) if the system were *actuarially fair*. The calculation is based on the worker's earnings history and social security contributions. The contributions are accumulated over the worklife of the employee (with interest). The lump-sum amount is then converted into an annuity—that is, an annual stream of income based on the person's life expectancy. The transfer portion is the difference between the actual social security benefit the person receives or is expected to receive and the annuity value based on the person's contributions into the social security system.[7]

First, it is of interest to examine the relative size of social security transfers and annuities and to determine whether the ratio has changed over time. Four sets of estimates are available. The first two are from Wolff (1993), based on the a 1969 synthetic dataset on household wealth (called the MESP file) and the 1983 SCF. The third set is from Richard Burkhauser and Jennifer Warlick (1981), which is developed from the 1973 Social Security Exact Match file. Calculations are based on actual earnings and OASI histories. The fourth is from Michael Hurd and John Shoven (1985), based on the Retirement History Survey for 1969. Their calculations are based on actual earnings histories, though social security contributions are imputed.

As shown in Table 11.5, Burkhauser and Warlick calculated that overall, social security transfers amounted to 73 percent of total social security income for households 65 and over. The author's calculations yielded ratios of 0.85 for 1969 and 0.66 (treasury bill rate) and 0.61 (portfolio rate) for 1983, and Hurd and Shoven's estimate for 1969 is 0.80. Though the three methodologies differ, the results still strongly suggest that the transfer component of social security income has been declining over time (that is, the annuity portion has been rising).

---

[7] In effect, social security contributions are treated as if they are made into a "defined contribution" pension plan, the benefits from which are based directly on the contributions. See Burkhauser and Warlick (1981), Wolff (1987b), and Wolff (1993) for technical details on the imputation techniques used.

Table 11.5 Ratio of Social Security Transfers to Total Social Security Benefits for Households 65 and Over, 1969, 1973, and 1983

Year	Source	Ratio
1969	MESP dataset[a]	0.85
1969	Hurd-Shoven (1985)[b]	0.80
1973	Burkhauser-Warlick (1981)[c]	0.73
1983	SCF dataset (treasury bill rate)[d]	0.66
1983	SCF dataset (portfolio rate)[d]	0.61

[a] Source: Wolff (1993), on the basis of the 1969 MESP file. The treasury bill rate is used as the discount rate.
[b] Source: Hurd and Shoven (1985), on the basis of the Retirement History Survey for 1969.
[c] Source: Burkhauser and Warlick (1981), on the basis of the 1973 Social Security Exact Match file.
[d] Source: Wolff (1993), on the basis of the 1983 SCF file. The treasury bill rate is based on the yield of ten-year U.S. treasury bills. The portfolio rate is calculated at 3.28 percent per year (in real terms) on the basis of the average portfolio holdings of U.S. households over the period 1962–1983.

These results together also indicate that social security transfers comprise a rather large (perhaps, surprisingly large) proportion of social security income. In other words, the benefits received from the social security system have far outweighed the annuity value of the social security contributions. The average retiree in 1983, for example, received twice as much in social security benefits as he or she contributed into the system. Thus, most of the social security benefits received by people who retired during the 1960s, 1970s, and 1980s have been a pure government transfer, over and above the actual contributions made into the system by the retirees.

Table 11.6 shows results on the ratio of social security transfers to social security benefits by age group in 1983. The most striking result is that the ratio of social security transfers to social security benefits among households under 65 is slightly *negative*, −0.08. This means that, on average, those who were under 65 years of age in 1983 will contribute slightly more into the social security system than they will receive in benefits. The corresponding ratio among individuals who were retired in 1983 is 0.66. They have received (or will receive) about twice as much in benefits as they contributed in the form of social security taxes.

The results by age group are also dramatic. Because of increasing OASI (social security) tax rates since the start-up of the system in 1937, the transfer component as a percentage of the total social security benefit increases almost monotonically with age, from −0.52 for the 31–35 age group to 0.62 for the 61–65 age group. The latter ratio is almost identical to that for

Table 11.6 The Ratio of Social Security Transfers to Total Social Security Benefits by Age Group, 1983[a]

Age Group	Ratio
18–30	−0.05
31–35	−0.52
36–40	−0.39
41–45	−0.26
46–50	−0.09
51–55	0.33
56–60	0.36
61–65	0.62
65–69	0.63
70–74	0.65
75–79	0.68
80 and over	0.73
Under 65	−0.08
65 and Over	0.66

[a] Source: The author's calculations from the 1983 SCF file. Calculations assume that real social security benefits will grow at 2 percent per year and use the treasury bill rate to discount social security contributions and benefits.

retirees aged 65 to 69. Workers who were age 50 or younger in 1983 will be net losers in the social security system, contributing more into the system than they will get out. Workers over 50 will be net gainers, though the gains will be relatively small, except for those in age group 61 to 65. The ratio of social security transfers to social security benefits is also found to increase with age group among the elderly. The ratio ranges from 0.63 for those in age group 65–69 to 0.73 for those 80 and over.

These results highlight one important aspect of intergenerational equity. The social security system has provided today's elderly population with benefits far in excess of their contribution into the social security system. Indeed, the figures presented above *understate* the full value of the transfer component, since additional benefits from Medicare are not included in the calculation. Insofar as it is a "pay-as-you-go" system (the benefits of the retired population in any given year is financed by the social security contributions of the working population of that year), this represents a major *transfer* of income between the nonelderly and the elderly. In other words, today's working population is subsidizing their parents' generation via the social security system.

It is also clear that the transfer component of social security income has been declining over time (that is, the annuity portion has been rising).

There are two reasons for this. First, older beneficiaries paid into the social security system over a fewer number of years, since the system started up in 1937, and paid lower tax rates (OASI contribution rates for employees increased from 1 percent in 1937 to 4.8 percent in 1983). Second, Congress periodically increased OASI benefit levels for retirees over the last few decades.

In rather stark contrast, net social security transfers for today's working population are actually negative. Current workers will contribute more into the social security system than they will receive in the form of benefits. Under current law, today's working population will be net losers from the social security system.

Private Intergenerational Transfers

Whereas today's retirees are the net beneficiaries of intergenerational transfers through the social security system, older people also transfer wealth to younger people—primarily their children—through gifts and bequests.

Robert Barro has argued in a 1974 article that the two processes of intergenerational transfers are not independent. As we noted above, a deficit in the government budget implies that today's population is consuming more through government purchases than it is paying in the form of taxes. As a result, today's population is able to expand its public consumption over and above the amount it reduces its private consumption by paying taxes. Insofar as the government debt is transferred to future generations, the latter, in effect, are financing the consumption of today's population.

Barro (1974) argued that private transfers may, in fact, offset the burden of government debt on future generations. He argued that if families are *altruistic,* they would respond to today's government deficit by maintaining the same level of consumption that they would have had if they paid enough taxes to finance fully government expenditure and passing the full amount of this additional savings onto their children in the form of gifts and inheritances. These additional private transfers, in effect, enable their children's generations to pay for the added government debt. In this sense, private (intra-family) transfers should fully compensate for the public intergenerational transfers that flow from the children's generation to their parents'.

Several studies have tried to determine whether, in fact, families act "altruistically" toward their children. In several of these formulations, the parent is viewed to have a utility function, which includes not only their own well-being but that of their children. Direct tests of such a specification are difficult to conduct. However, indirect tests are feasible, since one can draw testable implications from models of altruism.

One set of implications concerns the division of estates among children. It is interesting to note that in some countries, such as France (and others that have adopted the Napoleonic code of law), equal division is prescribed by law (with a slight degree of leeway). However, in the United States and the United Kingdom (and other "common law" countries), the division of the estate is at the discretion of parents through their will. How do parents divide their estate?

According to the altruism model, the division of the estate should be "compensatory." This means that parents will leave less money to their more successful (richer) child and more money to their poorer offspring. Several studies have examined this issue. Nigel Tomes (1981), using questionnaire data taken from a survey in Cleveland, Ohio, found that most estates were *unequally* distributed among heirs. However, Menchik (1988) reexamined the same Cleveland data and concluded that the appearance of unequal division was simply the result of response error. Moreover, using probate records from Connecticut, Menchik (1980) reported that most parents divide their estate equally among their children. David Joulfaian (1992) used a specially prepared file of estate data for the United States in 1982, linked to income tax records of the heirs. He found that somewhat less than two-thirds of estates provide for equal division of bequests and the remaining third unequal division. Mark Wilhelm (1991) concluded from the same data source that there was no evidence that the division of bequests could be interpreted as compensating differences in income among children.

Another prediction of the altruism model is that members of an extended family (including parents and adult children living in separate households) should fully share resources in the sense that the consumption of members of the extended family should be equal, independently of their individual incomes. Joseph Altonji, Fumio Hayashi, and Laurence Kotlikoff (1992) provided a test of this model using the Panel Study of Income Dynamics, in which parents are linked to adult children living in separate households. They found "overwhelming" evidence that such sharing does *not* occur. Instead, they found that the consumption of adult children (as well as parents) is significantly related to their income levels and the other direct resources at their disposal. The wealth of the parents have at most a modest effect on the consumption of the adult children.

Whether or not parents leave inheritances for altruistic motives or to offset the large public transfers from younger generations to older ones is still a matter of debate. However, what is clear from the various studies reviewed in this chapter is that inheritances play a large role in the process of wealth accumulation. Whereas it is the case that public transfers of wealth from younger generations to the elderly are distributed rather equitably among the elderly population (see Wolff, 1993, for details), it is certainly not the case with private transfers. The children of wealthy parents will, on average, receive much larger inheritances than the offspring of poorer parents. Bequests and gifts are thus not distributed equitably among younger families.

How do bequests and gifts affect wealth inequality among younger households? It is hard to answer this question directly because little information on direct gifts and transfers is available. However, one can look at the question of intergenerational *mobility* in wealth. How likely is it that a child of poor parents will become wealthy over his or her lifetime?

Several economists have tried to examine this issue. Some have looked at the intergenerational correlation of wealth, between parents and children. Their studies are based on a "coefficient of immobility," whose value ranges from zero to one. A value of zero indicates that there is no intergenerational correlation of wealth (all individuals are equally likely to amass wealth, independently of their parent's wealth) and a value of one indicates a perfect correlation between parent and children wealth (wealthier children have wealthier parents). Menchik (1979) used probate records of men who died in Connecticut in the 1930s and 1940s, which were matched to probate records of their children. He calculated a coefficient of immobility of 0.7. In contrast, the corresponding figure for income immobility between generations was only 0.25. In a later study, using data from the National Longitudinal Surveys of Mature Men between 1966 and 1981, Nancy Jiankoplos and Paul Menchik (1993) calculated an immobility coefficient of 0.67.

C. D. Harbury and D. M. W. N. Hitchens (1979) and Anthony Atkinson, A. K. Maynard, and C. G. Trinder (1983) examined estate tax records of deceased males in 1973 from the United Kingdom. These records linked the estate of the deceased with that of his father (the study was conducted only for males). The two studies found both wealth and income immobility figures in the order of 0.5.

Harbury and Hitchens (1976), examining the same estate tax records of deceased males in 1973 linked to the estates of their father, found that 58 percent of the fathers of the wealthy in 1973 (which they defined as net worth in excess of 25,000 pounds sterling) were also wealthy. The other 42 percent of the wealthy in 1973 were what they called "self-made men," who started with little wealth and made their fortunes during their lifetime.

These figures appear to be about the same in the United States. A recent survey (1992) of the *Forbes 400*, for example, asked the 400 richest families in the United States the source of their wealth—whether it was inherited or accumulated during their lifetime. The survey results suggest that about half of great fortunes in the United States are inherited while the other half are accumulated during the person's lifetime.

These studies do indicate that individuals can accumulate significant wealth through savings and entrepreneurial activity. Yet, it is hardly a fair game, since children of the rich are much more heavily favored to win.

11.4 SUMMARY

This chapter has provided an overview of the major sources of saving and wealth accumulation. We began with the life cycle model (LCM). The LCM predicts that individuals will accumulate wealth over time until retirement age and then reduce their wealth holdings. Cross-sectional, age-wealth profiles conform to this prediction. However, longitudinal data (which follow the same individuals over their lifetime) provided mixed results. Some studies show the elderly dissaving, whereas others indicated little if any dissaving in older ages. One reason for this latter set of findings may be that the very old (over age 75) reduce their consumption expenditures as their needs decline. Moreover, there is no evidence that families draw down their wealth to near zero as they age.

How much does the LCM explain about the distribution of household wealth? Two simulation studies, based on data for the United Kingdom, concluded that the LCM could explain at most about one-quarter of the actual concentration of wealth of the top wealth holders in Britain.

Regression analysis was used to explore the explanatory power of the LCM in accounting for differences in wealth holdings in a sample of U.S. households. The results reported in this chapter indicate that the basic LCM does yield statistically significant age coefficients with the predicted signs but explains a very small part of the variation of household wealth (less than 2 percent). With the inclusion of lifetime earnings, the explanatory power of the model increases to at most 5 percent. However, when the sample is restricted to the bottom 95 percent of the wealth distribution (that is, the very wealthy are excluded), the explanatory power of the life cycle model increases by a factor of four. These results suggest that, though the LCM predicts household savings behavior well for the vast majority of households, it is not successful in explaining the wealth accumulation motives of the top wealth classes who hold the majority of household wealth. It appears likely that the difference is due to the strength of the bequest motive of the very rich.

These results also suggest that tests of the life cycle model depend very heavily on the sample used—particularly on how much of the upper tail of the distribution is captured in the sample. Analysis using data sources, such as the PSID, RHS, and SIPP, which focus almost exclusively on middle-income families, will give very different results than surveys like the SCF, which has a good representation of the very wealthy.

How much does the life cycle model explain about wealth accumulation? Two U.S. studies concluded that the LCM could account for only a small part of (in one study, only 20 percent) of the growth in household wealth over time.

Partly to overcome deficiencies in the predictive power of the basic life cycle model, subsequent theoretical and empirical work has extended the LCM by modifying one or more of its basic premises. Four modifications were reviewed in this chapter: (1) uncertainty about length of life, (2) the role of social security and pension wealth, (3) the introduction of a bequest motive, and (4) liquidity constraints and precautionary savings.

Estimates vary about the importance of each of these other factors. With regard to uncertainty about death, the theoretical work suggests that this factor might account for increased savings and, in particular, the nonexhaustion of wealth at death. One study found that up to a quarter of wealth could be explained by including this factor in the LCM.

Theoretical work indicates that the availability of social security and pension wealth should lead to a reduction in the accumulation of traditional (marketable) wealth. Several studies have found that social security and pension wealth has reduced traditional savings, but others have found no effect. In the former case, the estimated substitution effects were considerably less than the dollar-for-dollar reduction predicted in the standard life cycle model.

The desire to leave bequests is another explanation for the slow dissaving (or positive saving) of elderly families and the nonexhaustion of wealth at time of death. Studies differ drastically about the importance of bequests in household wealth accumulation. Direct questionnaire evidence suggests that no more than about 20 percent of household wealth in the United States is due to intergenerational transfers. In contrast, simulation studies suggest that life cycle savings explain only a small portion of total wealth accumulation (typically, 25 percent or less), with the remainder presumably the result of intergenerational transfers. The discrepancy in results can be traced to three factors: (1) recall error in direct surveys; (2) the accounting framework, particularly, the treatment of the capital appreciation of inheritances; and (3) the role of *inter-vivos* transfers.

The presence of liquidity (borrowing) constraints implies that a family will accumulate more wealth than a pure life cycle model would predict. Precautionary savings serve as a self-insurance device against potential earnings misfortunes, and, as a result, consumers will accumulate more wealth than if their future income stream is known with certainty. Some studies have estimated that liquidity constraints and precautionary saving could explain as much as one third of total household wealth.

Issues of intergenerational equity were also raised in this chapter. The social security system was examined. It was found that today's elderly population receive more in social security benefits (about twice as much) than they have paid into the system in the form of social security contributions. This represents a transfer of resources from younger Americans to older ones. In contrast, today's working population will fail to break even with respect to the social security system—that is, their expected benefits will not cover their contributions into the system.

In contrast, private transfers generally go in the opposite direction—from older people to their children. Robert Barro argued that if parents are "altruistic," their bequests and gifts to their children should fully compensate for the public intergenerational transfers that flow from the children's generation to their parents.' However, microdata tests of altruism models have generally proved negative.

Whether or not parents leave inheritances for altruistic motives, it is still the case that inheritances play a large role in the process of wealth accumulation. Moreover, intergenerational transfers are not distributed equitably among younger families. How do bequests and gifts affect intergenerational wealth mobility? Studies for the United States indicate that there is a very strong correlation between an individual's wealth and that of his or her parent's—in the order of 70 percent. Moreover, half of all large fortunes appear to be inherited. These results suggest that individuals can accumulate significant wealth over their lifetime through savings and entrepreneurial activity, but a person is much more likely to be rich if his or her parents are also rich.

REFERENCES AND SUGGESTIONS FOR FURTHER READING

Aaron, Henry J., *Economic Effects of Social Security*, Brookings Institution, Washington, D.C., 1982.

Abel, Andrew B., "Precautionary Saving and Accidental Bequests," *American Economic Review*, Vol. 75, No. 5, September 1985, pp. 777–791.

———, "Aggregate Savings in the Presence of Private and Social Insurance," in Rudiger Dornbusch, Stanley Fischer, and John Bossons (eds.), *Macroeconomics and Finance: Essays in Honor of Franco Modigliani*, 1987, pp. 131–157.

Alessie, Rob, Arie Kapteyn, and Bertrand Melenberg, "The Effects of Liquidity Constraints on Consumption: Estimation from Household Panel Data," *European Economic Review*, Vol. 33, No. 2/3, 1989, pp. 547–555.

Altonji, Joseph G., Fumio Hayashi, and Laurence J. Kotlikoff, "Is the Extended Family Altruistically Linked? Direct Tests Using Micro Data," *American Economic Review*, Vol. 82, No. 5, December 1992, pp. 1177–1198.

Ando, Alpert, and Franco Modigliani, "The Life Cycle Hypothesis of Saving: Aggregate Implications and Tests," *American Economic Review*, Vol. 53, March 1963, pp. 55–84.

Atkinson, A. B., "The Distribution of Wealth and the Individual Life Cycle," *Oxford Economic Papers*, Vol. 23, July 1971, pp. 239–254.

Atkinson, A. B., A. K. Maynard, and C. G. Trinder, *Parents and Children*, Heinemann, London, 1983.

Auerbach, Alan J., Jagadeesh Gokhale, and Laurence J. Kotlikoff, "Generational Accounting," in David Bradford (ed.), *Tax Policy and the Economy*, MIT Press for the National Bureau of Economic Research, Cambridge, Mass., 1991, pp. 55–110.

Avery, Robert B., Gregory E. Elliehausen, and Thomas A. Gustafson, "Pensions and Social Security in Household Portfolios: Evidence from the 1983 Survey of Consumer Finances," Federal Reserve Board Research Papers in Banking and Financial Economics, October 1985.

Barlow, R., H. E. Brazer, J. N. Morgan, *Economic Behavior of the Affluent*, The Brookings Institution, Washington, D.C., 1966.

Barro, Robert J., "Are Government Bonds Net Wealth?" *Journal of Political Economy*, Vol. 48, No. 6, 1974, pp. 1095–1118.

Bernheim, B. Douglas, "Life Cycle Annuity Valuation," NBER Working Paper No. 1511, December 1984.

———, "Dissaving After Retirement: Testing the Pure Life Cycle Hypothesis," in Z. Bodie, J. Shoven, and D. Wise, (eds.), *Issues in Pension Economies*, University of Chicago Press, Chicago, 1986.

Blinder, Alan S., "A Model of Inherited Wealth," *Quarterly Journal of Economics*, Vol. 87, No. 4, November 1973, pp. 608–626.

———, "Comments on Chapters 1 and 2," in Denis Kessler and Andre Masson (eds.), *Modeling the Accumulation and Distribution of Wealth*, Oxford University Press, Oxford, 1988, pp. 68–76.

———, Roger Gordon, and Donald Weiss, "Social Security Bequests and the Life-Cycle Theory of Savings: Cross-Sectional Tests," in Franco Modigliani and Richard Hemming (eds.), *Determinents of National Saving and Wealth*, St. Martin's Press, New York, 1983.

Borsch-Supan, Axel, "Saving and Consumption Patterns of the Elderly: The German Case," *Journal of Population Economics*, Vol. 5, 1992, pp. 289–303.

Brittain, John A., *Inheritance and the Inequality of Material Wealth*, Brookings Institution, Washington, D.C., 1978.

Burkhauser, Richard V., and Jennifer L. Warlick, "Disentangling the Annuity from the Redistributive Aspects of Social Security in the United States," *Review of Income and Wealth*, Series 27, No. 4, December 1981, pp. 401–421.

Caballero, Ricardo J., "Earnings Uncertainty and Aggregate Wealth Accumulation," *American Economic Review*, Vol. 81, No. 4, September 1991, pp. 859–871.

Carroll, Christopher D., and Andrew A. Samwick, "How Important Is Precautionary Saving?" mimeo, MIT, December 1992.

Danziger, Sheldon *et al.*, "The Life Cycle Hypothesis and the Consumption Behavior of the Elderly," *Journal of Post Keynesian Economics*, Vol. 5, No. 2, Winter 1982–1983, pp. 208–227.

David, Martin, and Paul L. Menchik, "The Effect of Social Security on Lifetime Wealth Accumulation and Bequests," Institute for Research on Poverty Discussion Paper No. 671–681, December 1981.

———, "Distribution of Estates and Its Relationship to Intergenerational Transfers," Statistics of Income and Related Administration Record Research: 1982, Department of the Treasury, Internal Revenue Service, Statistics of Income Division, October 1982.

Davies, James B., "Uncertain Lifetime, Consumption and Dissaving in Retirement," *Journal of Political Economy*, Vol. 89, June 1981, pp. 561–578.

———, "The Relative Impact of Inheritance and Other Factors on Economic Inequality," *Quarterly Journal of Economics*, August 1982, pp. 471–498.

———, and France St-Hilaire, "Reforming Capital Income Taxation in Canada," Minister of Supply and Services in Canada, Ottawa, 1987.

Diamond, Peter A., and Jerry A. Hausman, "Individual Retirement and Savings Behavior," *Journal of Public Economics*, Vol. 23, 1984, pp. 81–114.

Feldstein, Martin S., "Social Security, Induced Retirement, and Aggregate Capital Accumulation," *Journal of Political Economy*, Vol. 82, October 1974, pp. 905–926.

———, "Social Security and the Distribution of Wealth," *Journal of the American Statistical Association*, Vol. 71, December 1976, pp. 800–807.

———, "Social Security and Private Saving: Reply," *Journal of Political Economy*, Vol. 90, June 1982, pp. 630–641.

———, "Social Security Benefits and the Accumulation of Preretirement Wealth," in Richard Hemming and Franco Modigliani (eds.), *Determinants of National Saving and Wealth*, MacMillan Press, London, 1983.

———, and Anthony Pellechio, "Social Security and Household Wealth Accumulation: New Microeconomic Evidence," *Review of Economics and Statistics*, Vol. 61, August 1979, pp. 361–368.

Freidman, J., "Asset Accumulation and Depletion Among the Elderly," paper presented at the Brookings Institution Conference on Retirement and Aging, 1982.

Greenwood, Daphne, "Age, Income, and Household Size: Their Relation to Wealth Distribution in the United States," in E. Wolff, (ed.), *International Comparisons of the Distribution of Household Wealth*, 1987.

———, and Edward N. Wolff, "Changes in Wealth in the United States, 1962–1983: Savings, Capital Gains, Inheritance, and Lifetime Transfers," *Journal of Population Economics*, Vol. 5, No. 4, 1992, pp. 261–288.

Hammermesh, Daniel S., "Consumption During Retirement: The Missing Link In the Life Cycle," *Review of Economics and Statistics*, Vol. 66, No. 1, February 1984, pp. 1–7.

———, and Paul L. Menchik, "Planned and Unplanned Bequests," National Bureau of Economic Research Working Paper No. 1496, November 1984.

Harbury, C. D., and D. M. W. N. Hitchens, "The Inheritances of Top Wealth Leavers: Some Further Evidence," *The Economic Journal*, Vol. 86, June 1976, pp. 321–326.

———, *Inheritance and Wealth Inequality in Britain*, Allen and Unwin, London, 1979.

Heckman, J. J., "The Common Structure of Statistical Models of Truncation, Sample Selection and Limited Dependent Variables and a Simple Estimator for Such Models," *Annals of Economic and Social Measurement*, Vol. 5, 1976, pp. 475–492.

———, "Sample Selection Bias as a Specification Error," *Econometrica*, Vol. 47, 1979, pp. 153–162.

Hubbard, R. Glenn, "Uncertain Lifetimes and the Impact of Social Security on Individual Wealth Holding," mimeo, Harvard University, 1983.

———, "Uncertain Lifetimes, Pensions, and Individual Savings," in Z. Bodie, J. Shoven, and D. Wise, (eds.), *Issues in Pension Economies*, University of Chicago Press, Chicago, 1986.

———, "Do IRA's and Keoghs Increase Saving?" *National Tax Journal*, Vol. 37, 1984, pp. 43–54.

———, "Precautionary Saving Revisited: Social Security, Individual Welfare, and the Capital Stock," NBER Working Paper No. 1430, August 1984.

———, and Kenneth L. Judd, "Liquidity Constraints, Fiscal Policy, and Consumption," *Brookings Papers on Economic Activity*, 1:1986(a), pp. 1–59.

———, "Finite Lifetimes, Borrowing Constraints, and Short-Run Fiscal Policy," mimeo, Northwestern University, 1986(b).

Hubbard, R. Glenn, Jonathan Skinner, and Stephen P. Zeldes, "Precautionary Saving and Social Insurance," mimeo, Columbia University, April 1992.

Hurd, Michael D., "Savings of the Elderly and Desired Bequests," *American Economic Review*, Vol. 77, No. 2, 1987, pp. 298–312.

———, "Mortality, Risk, and Bequests," *Econometrica*, Vol. 57, No. 4, 1989, pp. 779–813.

———, "Research on the Elderly: Economic Status, Retirement, and Consumption and Saving," *Journal of Economic Literature*, Vol. 28, June 1990, pp. 565–637.

———, "Wealth Depletion and Life-Cycle Consumption," in David A. Wise (ed.), *Topics in the Economics of Aging*, University of Chicago Press for the National Bureau of Economic Research, Chicago, 1992, pp. 135–160.

———, and Gabriella Mundaca, "The Importance of Gifts and Inheritances among the Affluent," in Robert E. Lipsey and Helen Stone Tice (eds.), *The Measurement of Saving, Investment, and Wealth*, Studies of Income and Wealth, Vol. 52, Chicago University Press, Chicago, 1989, pp. 737–763.

Hurd, Michael D., and John B. Shoven, "The Distributional Impact of Social Security," in David A. Wise (ed.), *Pensions, Labor, and Individual Choice*, Chicago University Press, Chicago, 1985.

Jappelli, Tulio, and Marco Pagano, "Consumption and Capital Market Imperfections: An International Comparison," *American Economic Review*, Vol. 79, No. 5, December 1989, pp. 1088–1105.

Jiankoplos, Nancy A., and Paul L. Menchik, "Wealth Mobility," mimeo, 1993.

Joulfaian, David, "The Distribution and Division of Bequests in the United States: Evidence from the Collation Study," mimeo, January 1992.

Kessler, Denis, and Andre Masson, "Les transferts intergenerationales: l'aide, la donation, l'heritage," *C.N.R.S. Report*, Paris, 1979.

———, "Bequests and Wealth Accumulation: Are Some Pieces of the Puzzle Missing?" *Journal of Economic Perspectives*, Vol. 3, No. 3, Summer 1989, pp. 141–152.

King, Mervyn A., "The Economics of Saving: A Survey of Recent Contributions," in Kenneth J. Arrow (ed.), *Frontiers of Economics*, Basil Blackwell Ltd., Oxford, England, 1985, pp. 227–294.

King, Mervyn A., and Louis Dicks-Mireaux, "Asset Holdings and the Life Cycle," *Economic Journal*, Vol. 92, June 1982, pp. 247–267.

Kotlikoff, Laurence J., "Testing the Theory of Social Security and Life Cycle Accumulation," *American Economic Review*, Vol. 69, June 1979, pp. 396–410.

———, *What Determines Savings?* MIT Press, Cambridge, Mass., 1989.

———, "Intergenerational Transfers and Savings," *Journal of Economic Perspectives*, Vol. 2, No. 2, Spring 1988, pp. 41–58.

———, *Generational Accounting*, Macmillan, the Free Press, New York, 1992.

Kotlikoff, Laurence J., and Daniel E. Smith, *Pensions in the American Economy*, University of Chicago Press, Chicago, 1983.

Kotlikoff, Laurence J., and Avia Spivak, "The Family as an Incomplete Annuities Market," *Journal of Political Economy*, Vol. 89, April 1981, pp. 372–391.

Kotlikoff, Laurence J., Avia Spivak, and Lawrence H. Summers, "The Adequacy of Savings," *American Economic Review*, Vol. 72, No. 5, December 1982, pp. 1056–1069.

Kotlikoff, Laurence J., and Lawrence H. Summers, "The Role of Intergenerational Transfers in Aggregate Capital Accumulation," *Journal of Political Economy*, Vol. 90, August 1981, pp. 706–732.

——, "The Contribution of Intergenerational Transfers to Total Wealth: A Reply," in Denis Kessler and Andre Masson (eds.), *Modelling the Accumulation and Distribution of Wealth*, Oxford University Press, Oxford, 1988, pp. 53–67.

Lansing, John B., and John Sonquist, "A Cohort Analysis of Changes in the Distribution of Wealth," in Lee Soltow, (ed.), *Six Papers on the Size Distribution of Income and Wealth*, National Bureau of Economic Research, New York, 1969.

Lawrence, Emily C., "Transfers to the Poor and Long Run Savings," *Economic Inquiry*, Vol. 25, No. 3, July 1987, pp. 459–478.

Leimer, Dean R., and Selig D. Lesnoy, "Social Security and Private Saving: New Time-Series Evidence," *Journal of Political Economy*, Vol. 90, June 1982, pp. 606–621.

Lydall, H., "The Life Cycle, Income, Saving, and Asset Ownership," *Econometrica*, Vol. 46, 1955, pp. 985–1012.

Masson, Andre, "A Cohort Analysis of Age-Wealth Profiles Generated by a Simulation Model of France (1949–1975)," *Economic Journal*, Vol. 96, 1986, pp. 173–190.

——, "Age, Income, and the Distribution of Wealth: A Life Cycle Interpretation," *Annales d'Economie et de Statistique*, No. 9, Janvier/Mars, 1988.

Menchik, Paul L., "Inter-generational Transmission of Inequality: An Empirical Study of Wealth Mobility," *Economica*, Vol. 46, 1979, pp. 349–362.

——, "Primogeniture, Equal Sharing, and the U.S. Division of Wealth," *Quarterly Journal of Economics*, Vol. 94, 1980, pp. 299–316.

——, "Unequal Estate Division: Is it Altruism, Reverse Bequests, or Simply Noise?" in Denis Kessler and Andre Masson (eds.), *Modeling the Accumulation and Distribution of Wealth*, Oxford University Press, Oxford, 1988, pp. 105–116.

——, and Martin David, "Income Distribution, Lifetime Saving, and Bequests," *American Economic Review*, September 1983.

Mirer, Thad W., "The Wealth-Age Relationship Among the Aged," *American Economic Review*, Vol. 69, June 1979, pp. 435–443.

——, "The Dissaving Behavior of the Retired Elderly," *Southern Economic Journal*, Vol. 46, No. 4, April 1980, pp. 1197–1205.

Modigliani, Franco, "The Life Cycle Hypothesis of Saving, Twenty Years Later," in M. Parkin, (ed.), *Contemporary Issues in Economics*, Manchester University Press, Manchester, 1975, pp. 2–36.

——, "Measuring the Contribution of Intergenerational Transfers to Total Wealth: Conceptual Issues and Empirical Findings," in Denis Kessler and Andre Masson (eds.), *Modelling the Accumulation and Distribution of Wealth*, Oxford University Press, Oxford, 1988(a), pp. 21–52.

———, "The Role of Intergenerational Transfers and Life Cycle Savings in the Accumulation of Wealth," *Journal of Economic Perspectives*, Vol. 2, No. 2, Spring 1988(b), pp. 15–40.

———, and Richard Brumberg, "Utility Analysis and the Consumption Function: An Interpretation of Cross-section Data," in K. Kurihara, (ed.), *Post-Keynesian Economics*, Rutgers University Press, New Brunswick, N.J., 1954.

Morgan, J. N., M. H. David, W. J. Cohen, and H. E. Brazer, *Income and Welfare in the United States*, McGraw-Hill Book Company, Inc., New York, 1962.

Oulton, N., "Inheritance and the Distribution of Wealth," *Oxford Economic Papers*, Vol. 28, March 1976, pp. 86–101.

President's Commission on Pension Policy, "Preliminary Findings of a Nationwide Survey on Retirement Income Issues," mimeo, 1980b.

Projector, Dorothy, and Gertrude Weiss, "Survey of Financial Characteristics of Consumers," Federal Reserve Technical Papers, 1966.

Radner, Daniel B., and Denton R. Vaughan, "Wealth, Income, and the Economic Status of Aged Households," in E. Wolff, (ed.), *International Comparisons of the Distribution of Household Wealth*, 1987.

Sheshinski, Eytan, and Yorman Weiss, "Uncertainty and Optimal Social Security Systems," *Quarterly Journal of Economics*, Vol. 96, May 1981, pp. 189–206.

Shorrocks, A. F., "The Age-Wealth Relationship: A Cross-section and Cohort Analysis," *Review of Economics and Statistics*, Vol. 57, May 1975, pp. 155–163.

———, "U.K. Wealth Distribution: Current Evidence and Future Prospects," in E. Wolff, (ed.), *International Comparisons of the Distribution of Household Wealth*, 1987.

Skinner, J. S., "Risky Income, Life Cycle Consumption, and Precautionary Savings," mimeo, University of Virginia, 1986.

Tobin, James, and Walter Dolde, "Monetary and Fiscal Effects on Consumption," in *Consumer Spending and Monetary Policy: the Linkages*, Federal Reserve Bank of Boston Conference Series 5, Federal Reserve Bank of Boston, Boston, 1971(a).

———, "Wealth, Liquidity, and Consumption," in *Consumer Spending and Monetary Policy: the Linkages*, Federal Reserve Bank of Boston Conference Series 5, Federal Reserve Bank of Boston, Boston, 1971(b).

Tomes, Nigel, "The Family, Inheritance, and the Intergenerational Transmission of Inequality," *Journal of Political Economy*, Vol. 89, 1981, pp. 928–958.

White, Betsy B., "Empirical Tests of the Life-Cycle Hypothesis," *American Economic Review*, Vol. 68, September 1978, pp. 547–560.

Wilhelm, Mark O., "Bequest Behavior and the Effect of Heirs' Earnings: Testing the Altruistic Model of Bequests," mimeo, January 1991.

Wolff, Edward N., "The Accumulation of Household Wealth Over the Life-Cycle: A Microdata Analysis," *Review of Income and Wealth*, Series 27, June 1981, pp. 75–96.

———, "The Effects of Pensions and Social Security on the Distribution of Wealth in the United States," in *International Comparisons of Household Wealth Distribution*, E. Wolff (ed.), Oxford University Press, 1987(a).

———, "Estimates of Household Wealth Inequality in the United States, 1962–1983," *Review of Income and Wealth*, Series 33, September 1987(b), pp. 231–256.

———, "Social Security, Pensions, and the Life Cycle Accumulation of Wealth: Some Empirical Tests," *Annales d'Economie et de Statistique*, No. 9, Janvier/Mars, 1988.

———, "Methodological Issues in the Estimation of Retirement Wealth," in Daniel J. Slottje (ed.), *Research in Economic Inequality*, Vol. 2, JAI Press, Greenwich, Conn., 1992, pp. 31–56.

———, "The Distributional Implications of Social Security Annuities and Transfers on Household Wealth and Income," in E. Wolff (ed.), *Research in Economic Inequality*, Vol. 4, JAI Press, Greenwich, Conn., 1993, pp. 131–157.

———, "Trends in Household Wealth in the United States, 1962–1983 and 1983–1989," *Review of Income and Wealth*, Series 40, No. 2, June 1994, pp. 143–174.

Wolff, Edward N., (ed.), *International Comparisons of the Distribution of Household Wealth*, Oxford University Press, New York, 1987.

Yaari, Menaham E., "Uncertain Lifetime, Life Insurance, and the Theory of the Consumer," *Review of Economic Studies*, Vol. 32, April 1965, pp. 137–158.

Zeldes, S. P., "Optimal Consumption with Stochastic Income: Deviations from Certainty Equivalence," mimeo, University of Pennsylvania, 1986.

DISCUSSION QUESTIONS

1. Explain why a cross-sectional, age-wealth profile may give a biased picture of the longitudinal age-wealth profile.

2. Why would uncertainty about death or the existence of liquidity constraints lead to positive wealth at the time of death in the context of the life cycle model?

3. Discuss the arguments for why expected social security and pension benefits might displace private savings. What is the evidence on this issue? Why is this issue relevant to the determination of the inequality of household wealth?

4. Summarize the available evidence on the respective roles of the life cycle motive and the bequest motive in accounting for differences in household wealth among households.

5. Give three reasons why today's older generations have received much higher *net* benefits from the social security system than younger generations have received or are likely to receive.

DISCRIMINATION

PART IV

12

Discrimination: Meaning, Measurement, and Theory

In Part 2 of the book, we looked at the functioning of the labor market and how it was responsible for differences in earnings among workers. In Part 4, we consider another factor which causes earnings differences—discrimination. This has taken two predominant forms in the United States—racial and gender discrimination.

The terms *discrimination, prejudice,* and *racism* evoke considerable passions. Prejudice refers to attitudes, particularly unfavorable feelings that an individual has toward another group of people. Discrimination refers to actions or outcomes, which suggest that one group is treated unfairly compared to another. People who consciously believe that they are not prejudiced against a particular group may engage in actions that treat members of this group unfairly. Conversely, people who are prejudiced may consciously try to avoid treating another group unfavorably. In this and the next two chapters, we will focus mainly on discrimination, rather than on prejudice.

Racism is often used as a "loaded" term to encompass both prejudicial attitudes and discriminatory behavior. In its narrow usage, it refers to the overt behavior of individuals who engage in specific actions against another race—for example, racial taunts, assaults, and, in the extreme case, killings. The current usage refers to a set of attitudes and institutions that appear to produce unfavorable outcomes for a particular race. Some extremist black leaders, for example, blame the low incomes and high poverty among black families on white racism. Because *racism* is very hard to define or identify, we shall avoid this term in our treatment of discrimination.

Some suggestive statistics on discrimination are shown in Tables 12.1 and 12.2. In 1992, the average income of black households was only 62 percent that of white households. The ratio of median household income was even lower, 58 percent (recall that the median is the income of the household in the middle of the income distribution and the mean is the total income divided by the number of households). For families (two or more related individuals living in the same housing unit), the ratio in mean income was 60 percent and the ratio of median income 54 percent. In 1992, black families still lagged considerably behind whites in terms of income.

The table also shows that nonwhite households did gain on whites between 1947 and 1967 (there are no separate statistics available for black households over this period). In 1947, the median income of nonwhite

Table 12.1 Ratio of Household and Family Income Between Blacks and Whites, 1947–1992[a] (in percent)

Year	Ratio of	
	Means	Medians
1. Household Income: Ratio of Nonwhite Income to White Income[b]		
1947		51
1957		53
1967		62
2. Household Income: Ratio of Black Income to White Income[c]		
1967	63	58
1983	62	57
1989	63	59
1992	62	58
3. Family Income (Families Only): Ratio of Black Income to White Income[c]		
1967	62	59
1983	61	56
1989	61	56
1992	60	54

[a] Sources: U.S. Bureau of the Census, Current Population Reports, Series P-60, No. 167, *Trends in Income: by Selected Characteristics: 1947 to 1988*, U.S. Government Printing Office, Washington, D.C., 1990; U.S. Bureau of the Census, Current Population Reports, Series P-60, No. 168, *Money Income and Poverty Status in the United States: 1989*, U.S. Government Printing Office, Washington, D.C., 1990; and U.S. Bureau of the Census, Current Population Reports, Series P60–184, *Money Income of Households, Families, and Persons in the United States: 1992*, U.S. Government Printing Office, Washington, D.C., September 1993.
[b] Ratio is between nonwhites and whites; Hispanic households are included and may be of any race.
[c] Ratio is between blacks and whites; Hispanic households are excluded.

households was only 51 percent of white households; by 1967, the ratio had climbed to 62 percent. The data also indicate that the major gains were made between 1957 and 1967, a period that was characterized by a major civil rights movement (see the next chapter for more discussion of this point). However, between 1967 and 1989, there was virtually no change in the relative position of black families. In 1967, the ratio of mean household income between black and white families was 63 percent, slightly higher than in 1992, and the ratio of median incomes was 58 percent, the same as in 1992.

Table 12.2 shows the ratio of median wage and salary income for full-time workers (those working 35 hours per week or more) between females and males. In 1992, the average full-time female worker earned 70 percent that of male workers. However, female workers have made sizable gains on male workers. In 1967, the gender earnings gap was only 50 percent; in 1983, it closed to 63 percent; and it reached 66 percent by 1988 and 70 percent by 1992. Thus, female workers have made progress relative to male workers over the last 25 years but still remain behind.

These "raw" income ratios suggest the presence of both racial and gender discrimination but do not provide direct proof. In the first section of this chapter, we consider what discrimination means and how is it measured. The next seven sections present different views on the sources of labor market discrimination. A summary is provided in the last section. Chapter 13 focuses on racial discrimination. We consider whether minorities have gained on white families in terms of earnings, unemployment rates, labor force participation rates, education, family income, wealth, and poverty incidence over the last half century. We will also examine the effect of civil rights legislation on the progress of black families. Chapter 14 looks into gender discrimination. We will present further evidence that the gender wage gap has declined since the 1960s and that women have made gains in penetrating

Table 12.2   Ratio of Median Earnings of Full-Time Workers by Gender, Selected Years, 1967–1988[a] (in percent)

Year	Ratio of Medians
1967	50
1977	55
1983	63
1988	66
1992	70

[a] Sources: U.S. Bureau of the Census, Current Population Reports, Series P-60, No. 167, *Trends in Income by Selected Characteristics: 1947 to 1988,* U.S. Government Printing Office, Washington, D.C., 1990; and U.S. Bureau of the Census, Current Population Reports, Series P60–184, *Money Income of Households, Families, and Persons in the United States: 1992,* U.S. Government Printing Office, Washington, D.C., September 1993.

traditionally male occupations. We will also consider the role of equal-employment programs on the progress made by females since the 1960s.

12.1 THE MEANING OF DISCRIMINATION

The data in Tables 12.1 and 12.2 indicate that black families have historically had lower incomes than white families and that female workers have earned less than men. Though there have been some gains made by blacks relative to whites (principally between the mid-1950s and the late 1960s) and women relative to men (primarily since 1967), the racial income gap and the gender wage gap were still quite substantial in 1992. Do these figures constitute *prima facie* evidence for the existence of gender and race discrimination in the American labor market? The answer depends on what we mean by discrimination. As we have seen in previous chapters, there are many factors which explain why workers earn different amounts—schooling attainment, years of experience, ability, union status, industry of employment, occupation, and firm size. If one worker has more schooling than another, then it may be *justifiable* that the first earns more than the second. If white males have, on average, more schooling than black males, then part of the difference in their average earnings may be attributable to difference in productivity. The mere existence of earnings differentials between two groups of workers does not, by itself, constitute proof of discrimination.

Labor economists view discrimination as the "unexplained" difference in earnings between two groups of workers. Economists will differ in the variables they use to control for earning differences. Their selection of variables depends on the model or theoretical framework they use. However, almost all include schooling, experience, and ability as explanatory factors. Proof of discrimination would require evidence that one group earns less than another even after *controlling* or *standardizing* for pertinent explanatory variables.

Employment discrimination may take one of two forms. First, workers with the same human capital—schooling, experience, ability, and so on—may be assigned different jobs because they are members of different groups. Women equally qualified with men may be assigned jobs lower down the job ladder—for example, college-educated females may be given secretarial jobs while college-educated men are given executive jobs. Second, workers with essentially the same job may receive different pay because they are from different groups. For example, female prison guards may receive lower pay than male prison guards who perform essentially the same work.

Labor market discrimination may take two other forms besides differences in pay. First, the incidence of unemployment may vary between groups. As we saw in Chapter 5, black workers have historically experienced much higher unemployment rates than white workers. Both hiring and layoff decisions may reflect the prejudices of employers. Employers may give white workers preference in terms of hiring. Moreover, in times of economic downturns, black workers may be dismissed before white ones.

Second, labor force participation rates may differ between groups. As we discussed in Chapter 5, a person is classified as unemployed if he or she does not currently have a job but is actively looking for one. Persons who do not have a job and are not actively seeking one are classified as not in the labor force. Individuals who search for a job for a long time but do not find one may simply "drop out" of the labor force. This phenomenon is referred to as the discouraged worker effect. The evidence presented in Chapter 5 indicates that the labor force participation rate of black men has recently been lower than that of white men of the same age. This is particularly true among older men (ages 45 to 64). It may also reflect discrimination against black workers.

Prelabor Market Discrimination

In Part 4 of this book, we shall principally investigate forms of labor market discrimination. However, there are other forms of discrimination that affect the socioeconomic status of minorities and females. One of the most pernicious forms is housing segregation. U.S. Bureau of the Census data, based on the current population survey, indicate that in 1989, 71 percent of poor black families lived in urban areas classified as poverty neighborhoods by the Census Bureau. This compares to a figure of 70 percent in 1975.

Housing segregation has direct implications for access to quality schooling, as we shall see below. However, it also affects other aspects of economic success. Some social scientists see the increasing concentration of poor black families in inner-city ghettos as a primary reason for the high incidence of welfare dependency, dropping out of school, teenage pregnancy, almost permanent joblessness, the presence of families headed largely by females, drug trafficking, gang membership, and crime (see Wilson, 1987, for example). The lack of jobs and economic opportunity in inner-city ghettos often creates a sense of hopelessness, loss of self-esteem, and pessimism for the future among poor black families, which leads to complete withdrawal from the labor market.

There are several reasons for the persistence of housing segregation over time. First, up until the 1950s, there were explicit Jim Crow laws in the South which forbade blacks from living in white neighborhoods. Housing segregation in the South was not only *de facto* but *de jure* as well.[1] Second, from the 1940s through the 1960s, there was a massive migration of black families from the South to northern cities. During this period, blacks settled in mainly white cities, like Boston, New York, Philadelphia, Chicago, St. Louis, and Detroit. As more and more blacks settled in these cities, racial tensions often grew and many white families left the cities for the surrounding suburbs (so-called "white flight"). This has resulted in a large concentration of black families in inner-city areas in northern cities. The relatively

---

[1] Jim Crow practices also included prohibitions of blacks from working in certain trades, school segregation, and restrictions on the use of public facilities (for example, blacks were not allowed to drink water from "white" drinking fountains and blacks had to sit in the back of public buses).

low income of most black families prevented them from buying homes in the suburbs.

Third, though since the 1960s explicit laws prohibiting black families from settling in white neighborhoods have been declared unconstitutional, other means have been used. As incomes of black families grew and suburban housing became affordable to many of them, they often encountered an unwillingness on the part of white homeowners to sell to them. This was often due to an unofficial covenant among white homeowners in a area to exclude black families (and often other racial or ethnic minorities). Real estate brokers often colluded with white homeowners by "steering" prospective black home buyers away from all-white areas. Though this practice is illegal, it is very difficult to prove.

Fourth, zoning regulations adopted by wealthier white communities have also served to maintain housing segregation. These include restrictions on the minimum size of house lots, which keep housing prices high and out of reach of middle-class black families. Many suburban communities also exclude most public and private forms of low-income housing, which prevents many black families from living there.

Fifth, the federal government itself actually exacerbated housing segregation through its public housing programs. The Federal Public Housing Administration subsidized the construction of low-income rental apartments in inner cities throughout the country. To qualify for a lease, applicants were subjected to a maximum income level, which meant that black families were more apt to qualify than whites. Many of these inner-city housing projects were occupied almost exclusively by black families, which tended to reinforce existing patterns of housing segregation.

Another federal program, the Federal Housing Administration (FHA), was set up in 1938 to guarantee mortgage loans on residential housing. It helped to finance almost one-third of all new housing built during the postwar housing boom of the late 1940s and 1950s. Part of its original mandate was to ensure that properties in a community were occupied by the same racial and social groups (ostensibly to maintain social stability in a neighborhood). As a result, the FHA purposely helped retain existing patterns of housing segregation. Though President Kennedy issued an executive order in 1962 which outlawed the segregationist practices of the FHA, it was too late. The racial pattern of suburban housing had been fairly well established by then.

A sixth source of housing segregation occurs in the credit market. To purchase a house, families almost always have to take out a mortgage loan. There is considerable evidence that banks and other credit providers have typically discriminated against black families in providing such mortgages. White and black families with identical income and earnings histories are often treated differently by banks. This often helps to exclude black families from white neighborhoods.

A related practice is "redlining," which means that certain sections of a city or town are "lined in red pencil" to indicate that they are "off limits" for mortgage loans. These areas are typically occupied by black families or members of other minority groups. This practice does not reinforce housing segregation, but it does make it difficult for black and minority families to obtain better housing in their own (segregated) neighborhood. Discrimination may also apply to other forms of credit—such as car loans and credit cards. The availability of credit may affect a family's wealth. Evidence presented in the next chapter will show that black families have accumulated considerably less wealth than whites.

Prelabor market discrimination refers to inequality of opportunity in the acquisition of schooling and other forms of human capital. For example, blacks in the South, up until 1960 or so, were often served by inferior schools and had less access to higher education than Southern whites. Though the earnings of Southern black males in comparison to white males might be attributable to their lower level of schooling, the fact that they received less schooling or lower quality schooling might itself be due to discrimination in schooling.

Today, unequal access to the same quality schooling often results from housing segregation. Black families (and Hispanic families) are often concentrated in segregated neighborhoods. Since school enrollment is usually allocated on a neighborhood basis, school children are often segregated into different schools on the basis of race. This is referred to as *de facto* segregation.

School busing is one strategy that has been used over the past 35 years to achieve some measure of racial parity among schools. However, such efforts occasionally meet with resistance from local communities. Moreover, legally, it is more difficult to effect school busing across local jurisdictional lines, so wealthy white communities are often unreachable for inner-city black students.

To obtain an idea of the extent of school desegregation, a study was conducted by the (then) U.S. Department of Health, Education, and Welfare. It found that in 1976, 44 percent of minority students were enrolled in schools that were 80 percent or more minority, and another 23 percent in schools that were 50 to 80 percent minority. Only one-third of minority students were in schools that were less than 50 percent minority. Schools in 1976 were still largely segregated. Interestingly, the most segregated schools were found in the Northeast and the least segregated in the South and border states.

Conditions did not change much between 1976 and 1992. In the later year, according to statistics compiled by Gary Orfield (1993), 34 percent of black students were still found in schools that were 90 percent or more minority and another 32 percent in schools that were between 50 and 90 percent minority. As in 1976, only one-third of black students attended schools that were more than half nonminority. Segregation is even more marked for Hispanic students. In 1992, 34 percent were enrolled in schools 90 percent or more minority and another 39 percent in schools between 50 and

90 percent minority. Thus, only about one quarter of Hispanic students attended integrated schools.

Is school segregation in and of itself bad? There are three problems that result from school segregation. First, different schools within the same locality may be allocated different resources depending on the racial makeup of the school. This was particularly true in the South before 1960, where educational expenditures per pupil were lower for black schools, though it is less true today. Second, even today, schools in *different communities* spend very different amounts on education per pupil, depending on the wealth of the community. Insofar as white communities are generally richer than those occupied by minorities, their school expenditures will be higher.

Third, many studies have shown that the racial composition of a school affects the performance of minority children. Black students, in particular, are found to achieve better in schools that are racially mixed. One reason for this is that black students from poor neighborhoods often develop value systems that are quite different than the value systems of white students from affluent areas. The exposure of black pupils to more education-oriented values often helps improve their school performance.

It is interesting that most recent studies have failed to find much difference between white and black students in regard to input measures of education, such as expenditures per pupil, teacher-student ratios, and other indices of school resources. However, most studies find clear racial differences in "measured output" from schooling. One telling statistic is from a report issued by the National Center for Educational Statistics in 1979. It found that among nine-year-olds, black students scored 12 percent lower on a standardized math test and 11 percent lower in reading, while among high school graduates, the differentials had widened to a 20 percent gap in math scores and a 16 percent gap in reading comprehension. A second statistic is based on a study conducted by the Office of Education (see Congressional Budget Office, 1977). Using a reading test consisting of such items as street signs and telephone directories, which was given to 17-year-old high school students, it classified 42 percent of blacks in this group as functionally illiterate, compared to only 8 percent of the white students.

A third statistic is racial and ethnic differences in the educational attainment of persons 25 years or older. According to data from the U.S. Bureau of the Census (1994), 26 percent of white males 25 years or older completed 4 years of college or more in 1993, compared to 12 percent of black males and only 10 percent of Hispanic males in this age group. Comparable statistics on college completion rates among females 25 years or older are 20 percent for white women, 12 percent among black women, and only 9 percent among Hispanic women.

These differences in educational output cannot fail to affect the relative labor market performance of whites, blacks, and Hispanics. In the next chapter, we shall more closely examine the educational attainment of the black, white, and Hispanic population and how it has changed over time.

A more subtle form of prelabor market discrimination evolves from "sex stereotyping." As we shall see in Chapter 14, the main source of differences in earnings between men and women is that they tend to work in different occupations. This phenomenon is referred to as "occupational segregation." A large proportion of female workers have traditionally been found in teaching, nursing, secretarial jobs, and clerical jobs. The source of this pattern is not clearly understood. However, it appears to stem, at least in part, to different socialization patterns that boys and girls experience. Exposure to television and societal norms leads to different role models for boys and girls, and this in turn, may lead to different job preferences. We shall return to this issue in Chapter 14.[2]

12.2 THEORIES OF DISCRIMINATION: AN OVERVIEW

How do we explain both the existence and the apparent persistence of discrimination? If we consider the strictly constructed neoclassical model of the labor market (see Section 6.1), discrimination makes no sense. Suppose two male workers from different groups have exactly the same marginal productivity but the first is paid a wage equal to his marginal product and the latter is paid a lower wage. If there were perfect competition among employers, then a profit-maximizing firm would realize that it could increase its profits by paying the second worker slightly more than his current wage but still less than the person's marginal product. With perfect information, all employers would realize this and a bidding war would occur until the wage of the second worker was brought in line with that of the first. Thus, if all the assumptions of the neoclassical model held, discrimination could occur only in the short run, until the labor market was brought into equilibrium.

In this chapter, we consider six models that try to account for the existence of discrimination in the labor market. In each, one or more of the assumptions of the neoclassical model are changed. The first, developed by Gary Becker, assumes that employers may have a "taste" for discrimination—that is, gain utility from hiring one type of worker over another. In this model, employers maximize utility rather than monetary profits. This leads to wage differentials between the two groups, depending on how prejudiced employers are and the relative size of the minority population. The result is that white workers are paid more than equally productive black workers.

The second, the statistical theory of discrimination, assumes that employers do not have complete information about the true productive abilities of potential employees. Employers rely on past information or data (thus the term statistical discrimination) to form expectations about the

---

[2]See also D'Amico (1987) for an interesting discussion of labor market and prelabor market discrimination in the case of differences in success between black males born in the United States and those who immigrated to the United States from the West Indies.

likely productivity of job candidates. In so doing, they often group prospective employees according to their race or gender and screen on these characteristics (see Section 7.4 for a discussion of the screening model in its relation to education). On the basis of past performance, employers may view minority and female workers as less capable than white male workers with similar credentials and pay them less.

The third explanation derives from the job competition model developed by Lester Thurow. In this model, employers also screen potential employees on the basis of race and gender. It is assumed that there is a fixed distribution of jobs, which pay different amounts because they are of differing importance in the production scheme. New entrants to the labor force compete or "queue" for jobs along the job ladder. The employer's prime motivation in selecting a candidate for a job is to minimize training costs. Employers may select a white male over a minority or female candidate because they expect the training costs to be less.

The fourth model derives from the dual labor market model (see Section 8.2). It is assumed that a firm's labor force is roughly divided into two segments. The first, the primary labor force, consist of workers who are expected to be long-term employees of a company. The second, the secondary labor force, consist of more marginal employees whose tenure with the company is expected to be short-lived. Companies invest more heavily in and pay higher wages to their primary workers than to the secondary workers. Employers may be predisposed to believe that both minority and female workers are less likely to remain long-term employees and therefore track them into the lower-paying, secondary jobs.

The fifth is a Marxian model which argues that the division of the national product between the capitalists and the workers is a result of the class struggle. It is in the interests of the capitalist class to prevent the workers from forming a cohesive and unified political front. One means is a "divide and conquer" strategy, whereby capitalists strive to create divisions within the working class. One way is to segment workers within the workplace on the basis of race and gender. White male workers are assigned the elite positions, while minorities and females are shunted into the low-paying ones. This policy creates internal friction within the working class and prevents the formation of a united class.

The sixth is the over-crowding model, usually applied to gender discrimination. Either because of employer discrimination or gender differences in job preference, males and females are segregated into two groups of occupations. Though such segregation by itself need not cause gender differences in wages, pay differences may result if job opportunities in the female occupations are low relative to those in the male occupations.

12.3 TASTE FOR DISCRIMINATION

This model, developed by Gary Becker in a 1957 book (and later expanded in the second edition of the book in 1971), assumes that employers have a "taste for discrimination." Because of prejudice, some employers may prefer hiring one group of workers to another. This prejudice may take the form of desiring to maintain social distance from another race, or it may stem from a belief in what jobs constitute appropriate social roles for women.

In economic terms, prejudice means that an employer is willing to pay a premium for one type of worker over another with exactly the same productive capabilities. Formally, the model assumes that two groups of workers have the same skills and are perfect substitutes in the production process. Employers who harbor prejudice against a minority group will hire these workers only at a wage discount sufficient to compensate for the disutility of working with them.

Becker defines employer i's "discrimination coefficient" d_i for a minority worker as the percentage difference between the worker's marginal product and the "value" or utility of the worker to employer i. Suppose MP_m is the marginal product produced by a minority worker. Then the value of this worker to a particular employer i is given by $MP_m(1 + d_i)$, where $d_i \leq 0$, and this is also the wage employer i will pay the minority worker.[3]

It should be noted that discrimination coefficients d_i will generally differ among employers. If an employer is prejudiced against minority workers, then d_i would be negative for *this employer,* and this employer will pay less for a minority worker than a white worker of the same skills. If, for example, both workers have marginal product MP^*, then employer i will pay the white worker a wage $w^* = MP^*$ but the minority worker only $w^*(1 + d_i)$.[4] The more prejudiced an employer is, the more negative the value of d_i. However, some employers may not be prejudiced at all, and for them, d_i will be zero.

Because the degree of prejudice will generally differ among employers, the actual market degree of discrimination will depend on *both* the *distribution* of individual discrimination coefficients d_i and the *size of the minority population.* This can be seen with the aid of Diagram 12.1. The vertical axis shows the ratio of the wage paid to a minority worker to the wage paid to a white worker with the same productive capabilities, and the horizontal axis shows the employment level of minority workers. Let us first consider the demand curve for minority workers, indicated by the "kinked line" labeled D_m. The demand curve is formed by arranging wage offers made by employers in order of the size of the offer.[5] This is equivalent to ordering employers in reverse order of their discrimination coefficients d_i.

The left part of the line is horizontal, at a wage rate ratio of 1.0. This portion represents the employers who harbor no prejudice ($d_i = 0$ for them)

---

[3] It is assumed that there is a single wage for white workers and a single wage for minority workers.

[4] It is also equivalent to argue that the employer will pay a minority worker with marginal product MP^* the same wage as a less productive white worker, with marginal product $MP^* (1 + d_i)$.

[5] Technically, it is assumed that the total employment in a given type of work is fixed and that the equilibrium wage rate for white workers is fixed (and, in particular, is independent of the number of white workers employed).

Diagram 12.1   The Formation of an Equilibrium Wage Differential Between Minority and White Workers in Becker's Taste for Discrimination Model

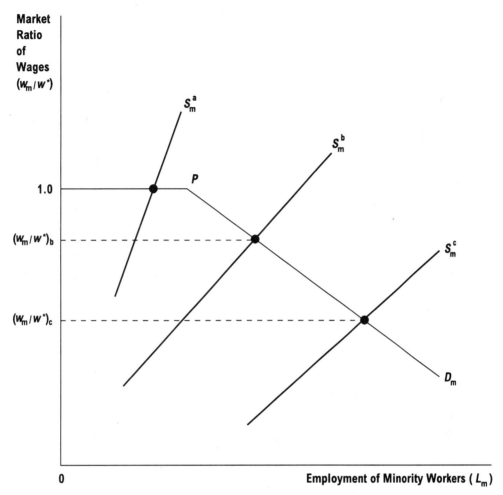

Key:
w_m— wage paid to minority worker
w^*— wage paid to white worker

and are willing to pay minority workers the same as white workers (of equal productivity). The demand curve then slopes downward (at point P), indicating that beyond this point, all other employers have some taste for discrimination (d_i is less than zero for them). Some of these are only mildly prejudiced and thus willing to hire minority workers at only a slight "discount." The further to the right along the demand curve, the more discriminatory the employer and the lower the wage the employer is willing to pay for a minority worker.

Three alternative supply curves for minority workers are shown in this diagram—S_m^a, S_m^b, and S_m^c. If the size of the minority workforce is small (S_m^a), then the supply curve may intersect the demand curve at its horizontal portion. In this case, the market equilibrium will be at 1.0—that is, minority workers will be paid exactly the same wage as white workers. This is true even though some (or even most) of the employers are prejudiced against minority workers. Despite this, there are a sufficient number of non-prejudiced employers (with zero values of d_i) willing to hire the total supply of minority workers at the same wage as white workers. This case may help account for why the relative wages of certain small minority groups, such as the Chinese or Japanese, are comparable to those of whites, even though some or many employers may be prejudiced against these groups.

If the supply curve for minority workers lies further to the right, as S_m^b, then it will intersect the demand curve in its downward slope. In this case, the equilibrium wage ratio between minority and white workers will be less than unity. Employers represented on the demand curve to the left of the supply curve will hire the minority workers, while those found to the right will not hire any minorities (only white workers). If the supply of the minority labor force is larger, as illustrated by S_m^c, then the equilibrium wage gap will be even greater. The wage ratio will be lower the larger the size of the minority labor force, because the value of d_i for the marginal employer whose wage offer will clear the market will be more negative and therefore the equilibrium wage w_m will be lower.

In this model, it is assumed that employers do not necessarily maximize money profits but rather their utility, where taste for discrimination is one of the parameters. Becker also argues that even if employers themselves are not discriminatory, profit-maximizing firms may engage in discriminatory behavior if customers or coworkers are prejudiced. Customers who are prejudiced against a minority group will be willing to buy products from them only at a discount (that is, a lower price). This type of prejudice can arise in retailing or service jobs. In this case, employers may be forced to pay their minority workers a lower wage.

If white employees are prejudiced, they may be willing to work with minority workers only if they are offered a premium by their employer to compensate for the disutility of having minority coworkers. In such a case, the expected outcome is complete racial segregation of firms, since an integrated firm would be more costly to run (because of the higher wages to white workers) than an all-white or all-minority company.

This model was criticized by Arrow (1973) because it fails to account for the long-term persistence of discrimination in the labor market under conditions of perfect competition. We illustrate the argument in Diagram 12.2. Consider the case of a competitive industry. The initial market demand curve for minority workers is given by D_m^1, with a kink at P, and the supply curve for minority workers is given by S_m. The initial equilibrium wage ratio

Diagram 12.2   The Movement Over Time of the Wage Differential Between Minority and White Workers Under Perfect Competition in Becker's Taste for Discrimination Model

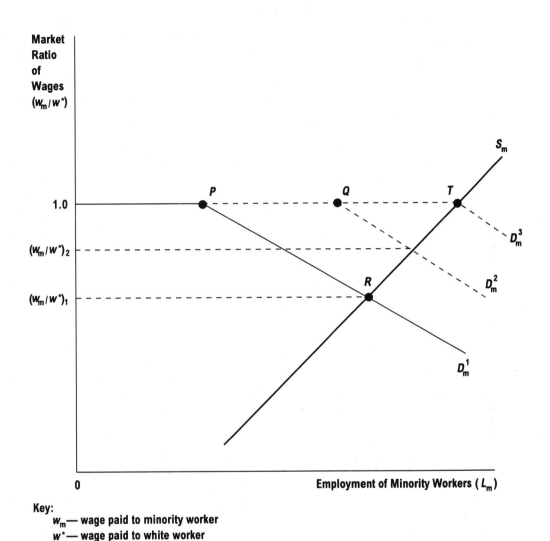

Key:
w_m— wage paid to minority worker
w^*— wage paid to white worker

is thus given by $(w_m/w^*)_1$. Firms which lie to the right of point R on the demand curve, D_m^1, will hire only white workers, and firms to the left will hire minority workers.

Since the less prejudiced employers (with a lower d_i) are willing to hire minority workers at their lower wage, their wage costs will be lower and their profits will therefore be greater than those employers who have a high d_i

and hire only white workers.[6] Firms which hire minority workers are at a competitive advantage and should expand faster than firms that hire only white workers. Over time, the demand curve for minority workers will shift to D_m^2 (with a kink at point Q), and the new equilibrium wage ratio will become $(w_m/w^*)_2$, higher than the previous level. Over the long run, the nondiscriminators should win out and dominate the industry, and the market wage ratio between minority and white workers should eventually approach unity (at point T).[7] In a sense, the market rewards the progressive employers—the ones who do not exhibit prejudice against minority groups.

Becker also argues that in a competitive industry, there would be forces that would reduce the level of discrimination over time. In a monopolistic industry, on the other hand, free entry is excluded and therefore discrimination against minorities may persist over time. Becker therefore predicted that the degree of wage discrimination against minorities would be higher in a monopolistic industry than a competitive one.

In his 1971 book, Becker presented some evidence to support his argument. While his model has a direct implication regarding the observed pay differential between white and minority workers, the use of pay differentials as a measure of discrimination is difficult, because of the influence of other factors such as schooling and experience on wages (see the next chapter for further discussion of this issue). However, this model also provides a hypothesis regarding the proportion of minority workers an industry will hire. In particular, less discriminatory employers should, *ceteris paribus,* hire a higher percentage of black workers than a discriminatory employer (since the required wage discount is higher for the latter). By implication, competitive industries should have a higher proportion of minority workers in a given type of job than monopolistic ones.

To analyze this proposition, Becker selected 38 industries in the South in 1940, ten of which he described as monopolistic and 28 as competitive. He divided employment into eight occupational groups and found that the relative number of black employees was greater in the competitive industries than the monopolistic ones in 7 out of 8 occupational groups. This result provided direct support to the Becker model. However, a paper by Franklin and Tanzer (1970) disputed this result. They showed that if the 38 industries were ordered by their degree of monopoly instead of being divided into two groups, there was no statistically significant correlation between the degree of monopolization and the percentage of black employees in the industry. This has cast some doubt on the validity of the Becker model of discrimination.

---

[6] Recall that, by assumption, minority workers are as productive as white workers. Since their wages are lower, a firm which hires minority workers will have a greater profit than those that hire only white workers.

[7] Assume that there are at least a few employers in the industry who do not discriminate. If there are not, then presumably with reasonably open and competitive capital markets, minority-owned businesses may be able to move into such an industry to take advantage of the profit potential associated with minority workers. This suggests, by the way, that promoting minority-owned businesses may be one way to alleviate unfair wage discrimination against minority workers.

12.4 Statistical Discrimination

A second model of discrimination, developed by Phelps (1972), Arrow (1972a, 1972b, and 1973), and Aigner and Cain (1977), relies on the role of imperfect information in employment decisions. Two key assumptions are introduced: first, employers cannot determine the true productivity of a prospective employee; second, employers have a preconceived notion of the relative productivity of two groups of workers, say whites and minorities. Suppose that employers believe minority workers to be less productive than white workers with other characteristics that are identical, such as education and experience. Then employers will screen job candidates on race, assign a lower probability of success to a minority applicant, and therefore be less likely to hire a minority employee or be willing to hire the person only at a lower wage. In either case, minority workers will receive, on average, lower earnings than comparably "qualified" white workers. The same argument can be used to explain lower earnings for female workers.

In contrast to the Becker model, employers are assumed to be profit-maximizers. Moreover, there is no reliance here on the formation of exogenous tastes. Instead, the model is based on subjective probabilities about how productive different kinds of workers are. But this begs the question of where such subjective evaluations or "stereotypes" come from in the first place.

Phelps (1972) provides an ingenuous solution. He argues that the current assessment of relative productive capability is likely to be based on past experience. Suppose that out of pure prejudice or because of existing social norms, employers in the past hired white workers for the more skilled jobs and minorities for the less skilled ones. White workers also received higher wages, enjoyed superior working conditions, and obtained more training than minority workers. As a consequence, minority workers might show slower growth of productivity over time due to limited training and might even become discouraged and leave the firm. Employers might then base their current assessment of the likely success of different groups of workers on their previous "statistical" experience with them. In this case, we have a self-fulfilling prophecy, whereby initially incorrect signals or evaluations lead to discriminatory actions, which actually result in creating productivity differences between races. Thus, reliance on past (incorrect) information leads to actions, which corroborate the past information.[8]

The statistical discrimination model does a better job than the Becker model in explaining why competition does not eventually eliminate discrimination. In Becker's model, those employers who are nondiscriminatory should eventually prevail over the employers who do discriminate. In the statistical discrimination model, discrimination is due to imperfect information, which can persist over long periods of time. If men believe that a

---

[8] See also Bergmann (1976) and Blau (1977) for related arguments of feedback effects on pay discrimination.

woman would never make a good president and a woman is never given the opportunity to become president and disprove this misconception, then there is no reason why this misconception should go away.

This is not, of course, to say that such erroneous ideas can never disappear. Sometimes, extraordinary events are necessary for this to happen. This often happens in tight labor markets (periods of low unemployment) when there are shortages of qualified white males and companies are forced to hire minority and female workers to fill skilled jobs normally reserved for white males. During World War II, for example, when there was a shortage of male workers for skilled factory jobs, many women were hired for these positions. "Rosie the Riveter" became a national symbol for the success of women in these traditionally male jobs. In this case, when World War II ended and the veterans returned from Europe and the Far East, these factory jobs were restored to the men, and women returned to their traditional role as homemaker.

Another famous example is the hiring of the black ball player Jackie Robinson by the (then) Brooklyn Dodgers in 1947. Major League baseball had until that time been a completely segregated sport. Many owners were afraid that fans would not come to the stadium to see black ball players. However, Robinson was an exceptional player and helped the Dodgers win several pennants during the early 1950s. Fans did come to see the Dodgers play because they were more interested in a winning team than in the color of the ball players. The success of the Brooklyn Dodgers and Jackie Robinson opened the way for the integration of professional baseball.

Smart employers will then hire minorities and females into the skilled jobs at their lower prevailing market wages, increase their profit, and expand more rapidly than their "ignorant" competitors. Over time, nondiscriminatory employers will eventually dominate the industry, and discriminatory differences in earnings should be eliminated.[9] Look at professional basketball where white players are now a distinct minority.

It may require extraordinary circumstances to break through statistical discrimination. This form of discrimination may thus provide a rationale for affirmative action—a government program designed to induce employers to hire more minorities and females into traditionally white male jobs (a program that we will discuss in more detail in the next chapter). In the context of this model, affirmative action may be seen as one way of breaking the vicious cycle of self-fulfilling prophecy based originally on prejudice and race and sex stereotypes. By providing minority and female workers with the same opportunity for decent wages, good working conditions, and adequate training as white males, this program may enable these groups to perform equally to white males in the workplace. Companies may, as a result, reassess

---

[9]There is an analogous argument with respect to insurers. If one group is thought to be a greater risk than another (female drivers as compared to male, perhaps) based on incorrect information, then a "smart" insurance company should eventually discover this and expand its profit by readjusting its rates. In long-run equilibrium, the rate structure should reflect the true relative risk of different classes of individuals.

their statistical evaluation of the relative likelihood of success of these groups and help end the use of race or gender as a screening device.[10]

12.5 JOB COMPETITION MODEL

Another explanation of discrimination derives from the job competition model, developed by Lester Thurow (1975). It is similar in spirit to the screening model, except that the emphasis here is on the relative training costs of prospective employees. The job competition model is characterized by the assumption that marginal productivity is attached to the job, not the individual, as in the human capital model. As a consequence, the wage rate is determined by the characteristics of the job, not those of the individual holding the job.

Individuals compete for jobs (thus the name *job competition model*). Workers enter the job market without possessing the skills needed for the job, as assumed in the human capital model. But prospective employees differ in terms of their trainability for a specific job. Jobs also differ in their training requirements. Employers try to minimize their job training costs by ranking available personnel according to their prospective training costs and choosing those at the top of the queue.

In searching for candidates for a particular job opening, employers will consider those characteristics which they consider most relevant in predicting success in a particular job. Schooling and previous job experience are considered key variables in selecting candidates for most jobs, since they indicate how successful the person has been in other forms of training. In general, a job candidate is classified into a certain group based on his or her observable characteristics and ranked according to how successful this *group* has been in performing a certain type of job, since, by assumption, the individual cannot be observed performing a particular job until he or she has received the training to do it. In other words, employers typically use statistical discrimination in screening employees, where an individual is judged on the basis of the past success of the *group* to which he or she belongs rather than upon his or her own personal characteristics. These judgments can be objective in the sense that the group actually has had such an *average* past performance, though they may incorrectly rate a particular individual.

Schooling and experience are typical characteristics used to group individuals, since different schooling and experience groups usually have different success rates at a particular type of job. However, race and gender could also be used by employers to group job applicants if they perceive differences in expected training costs or job success rates between different races or genders. In the case of minority workers, an employer may correctly ob-

---

[10] See the interesting discussion of the relation between statistical discrimination and affirmative action provided by Stephen Coate and Glenn Loury (1993), who suggest that affirmative action may induce employers to patronize minority workers which, in turn, may undercut their incentive to acquire additional skills.

serve that a minority member has received, on average, lower-quality schooling than the average white of comparable characteristics. Therefore the employer may believe that the white worker will have a lower training cost than a comparable minority worker. In the case of female workers, an employer may correctly observe that females have, on average, a greater tendency to drop out of the labor force than males because of child-bearing and child-rearing responsibilities and therefore assign a lower success rate to a female applicant than a comparable male applicant.

Thurow contends that his model can explain why discriminatory earnings differences persist over time with perfect competition. In this model, there is no loss of profit from discrimination. In the job competition model, the marginal product is characteristic of the job, not the worker, so an employer would not lose any revenue by selecting a white candidate over a minority one who was equally qualified and trainable for a particular job. Moreover, if the employer hires the minority applicant for an inferior job at a lower wage, there would be no incentive for another employer to bid away the minority worker at a higher wage, since, by assumption, the minority worker's marginal product would be no greater than his or her current wage. Therefore, discriminatory wage differentials could persist over a long period of time even if there were perfect competition.

Yet, in criticism, it should be noted that the employer gains no extra profit by hiring a white applicant over the equally gifted minority applicant. Moreover, if there were periods of tight labor markets and a shortage of qualified white applicants for a given job, then an employer who hired a qualified minority would gain relative to one who hired a less qualified white, since the former's training costs would likewise be less. If tight labor markets occurred frequently enough, then over the long term, employers would stop using race or gender as a screening category. They would realize that this characteristic was immaterial in predicting the success rate for employees. Discriminatory differences in earnings should then disappear over the long term.

12.6 DUAL LABOR MARKET MODEL

Developed by Doeringer and Piore (1971), the dual labor market model provides another explanation for the existence and persistence of labor market discrimination. The theory asserts that the labor market is generally divided into two pools of workers (see Section 8.2 for a more extended discussion of this model). The primary labor market has access to internal labor markets, which operate like self-contained labor markets within large firms and other organizations (such as a university). Entry into an internal labor market operates like an employment queue, where an employer ranks prospective employees by their characteristics, such as schooling, experience, other professional qualifications, gender, and race. The employer selects workers from the beginning of the queue until the job openings are filled.

Once inside an internal labor market, an employee is guaranteed a fairly well-established though rigid career path. Wages and salaries are attached to particular jobs, and there is little room for individual wage negotiations. There are also rigid promotional ladders, where seniority plays a major role in determining the order of promotion. The firm invests heavily in its primary labor force through extensive on-the-job training. The internal labor market is thus a relatively fixed job and wage structure intended for career and long-term employees of a company.

The secondary labor market consists of low-level jobs which are intended for relatively short-term employees. Most secondary jobs do not fit into a well-defined job cluster. Examples of these are blue-collar jobs in foundries and apparel plants and menial jobs in hospitals. Secondary employment is characterized by low wages and high turnover. Little or no training is provided by the firm.

Internal labor markets appear to benefit both the employer and the employee. From the point of view of the employer, the internal labor market reduces recruitment costs, screening costs, training costs, and termination costs by reducing labor turnover. The jobs in the internal labor market require a substantial investment in employees for the development of job-specific and firm-specific skills. From the standpoint of the employee, internal labor markets guarantee wage and job security. Moreover, the fact that firms invest in job-specific skills for employees increases their bargaining power and may result in higher earnings for the workers. A secondary labor market includes those jobs that require no or little employer investment so that the firm is willing to accept high turnover rates to gain the benefit of low wages.

In this context, then, race and sex discrimination may be a rational policy for both employer and primary employees. The primary work force views itself as having a form of monopoly over the internal allocation of jobs. For historical reasons, internal labor markets have been dominated by white male employees, while females and racial minorities have been generally segregated into the secondary labor market. Any attempt to change the distribution of jobs between races or genders may therefore be viewed by the incumbent primary work force as a threat to their monopolistic position. White employees may therefore resist attempts at integration, which they may see as an assault on their seniority and job security system. Employers, moreover, will be reluctant to change the distribution of jobs by race or gender, since such an alteration will, in general, impose extra recruitment, training, and screening costs on the firm.

The Doeringer and Piore model explains the persistence of discrimination over time. In this model, both employers and white male employees have an incentive for resisting any attempt to end discrimination—the former because it will lead to higher costs and the latter because it will threaten their job security and advancement possibilities. Unlike the Becker or Arrow-Phelps model, there is no long-run tendency for competition to eliminate discrimination. Moreover, there is benefit from maintaining a discriminatory job system in this model, in contrast to the job competition model, in which the firm is viewed to incur no cost but no extra benefit from discrimination.

The dual/internal labor market model has been criticized for its reliance on the assumption that internal labor markets are insulated from changes in the external labor market. In this framework, forces of competition between firms do not directly affect their internal labor markets. New firms, for example, taking advantage of the pool of qualified minorities and females may be able to produce more efficiently than the established discriminatory establishments, thereby forcing them out of business (see also Wachter, 1974, for further criticisms of this approach).

12.7 THE MARXIAN MODEL

A model of discrimination also derives from Marxian economic theory. The central assumption of Marxian thought is that there are two major classes in a capitalist society, the capitalists and the workers. The division of the national product between these two classes is a result of "class struggle." This battle takes both an economic form, as in collective bargaining and strikes, as well as a political form, as in the development of labor parties in many Western European countries and lobbying in the United States. It is generally in the best interests of the capitalist class to prevent the workers from forming a cohesive and unified political party or economic front. One way of accomplishing this is a divide and conquer strategy, whereby the capitalists try to create divisions within the working class. Such a strategy could weaken working class consciousness and solidarity and enable the capitalists to obtain a larger share of the national output.

As developed by Michael Reich (1977, 1978, 1981a, 1981b, and 1988), this line of argument continues that one effective way of fragmenting the work force is on the basis of race and gender. Occupational segregation therefore occurs when minorities and whites are given different jobs, as are males and females. Antagonism develops between groups of workers on the basis of visible differences of race and gender. White workers see minority workers as a threat to their jobs. The interest of white workers is to prevent minority workers from taking over their jobs. Minority workers see white workers as preventing them from advancing. The interest of minority workers is to occupy the jobs formerly reserved for white workers. The same sort of antagonism develops between male and female workers. The result is that workers see other groups of workers as their primary enemies instead of uniting against the capitalists. In consequence, workers' bargaining power against capitalists is reduced, and capitalists receive higher profits.[11]

This model, like the dual labor market model, is consistent with the persistence of discrimination over time. It is in the interest of the capitalists to maintain discriminatory pay differentials between races and genders. It is

---

[11] Some statistical evidence supporting this hypothesis is presented in Reich (1978).

also in the interests of the white male workers to maintain their hegemony. Both capitalists and white males benefit from continued racism and sexism. Moreover, by co-opting one segment of the working class, the capitalists have managed to maintain control over the economy.

But why don't workers "get smart" and realize that the work force as a whole would benefit from eliminating antagonisms along race and gender lines and presenting a united front to the capitalists? Marxian work has not provided a compelling argument as to why a more unified working class has failed to form in the United States, whereas it has formed in other advanced industrial economies.[12]

12.8 OVERCROWDING MODEL OF OCCUPATIONAL SEGREGATION

The overcrowding model of occupational segregation, originally developed by Bergmann (1974) and later extended by Stevenson (1975), Blau and Hendricks (1979), and Blau (1984b), is principally applicable to gender discrimination. It is assumed that there are separate male jobs and female jobs in the workplace. Occupational segregation by itself need not result in pay differentials between male and female workers. However, the model assumes that there are far fewer female occupations than male occupations. Women enter only the female occupations. This increases the supply of workers to the female sector and correspondingly lowers the supply of workers to the male sector. Since job opportunities in female occupations are small relative to the supply of female labor, wages in female jobs are artificially lowered. Likewise, the lower supply of workers in male jobs artificially raises wages in male occupations. As a result, females with the same qualifications as male workers will receive lower wages.[13]

This argument can be illustrated by means of Diagram 12.3. Two occupations are available to the labor force—secretaries (s) and truck drivers (t). We assume that the two occupations require identical human capital, so that the demand curve for each (D_s, D_t) is the same.[14] With no job discrimination, women and men can work freely in each job, so that the supply curves are identical (S_s, S_t). Under perfect competition, the wages for secretaries and truck drivers are the same, (w_c), and both males and females may be employed in each occupation.

---

[12]Another interesting issue is why individual employers do not break away from the pack and hire cheaper minority and female labor. An interesting game theoretic analysis is developed by Roemer (1978 and 1979). He shows that there are bargaining equilibria in which both white and minority workers are worse off and employers are better off than they would be without worker divisions. Moreover, the equilibria are stable over time, and because of the bargaining structure, market forces cannot overcome the discriminatory equilibrium wages.

[13]Another implication of the model is that employers will use more labor-intensive techniques for the female jobs and capital-intensive ones for male jobs. The lower female wages will then be associated with a lower marginal productivity of female workers. Male and female workers with the same human capital will generally have different pay and different productivity on the job.

[14]Moreover, we assume that the number of jobs available in each occupation is the same at a given wage rate.

Diagram 12.3   The Formation of Wage Equilibria for Male and Female Jobs in the Overcrowding Model

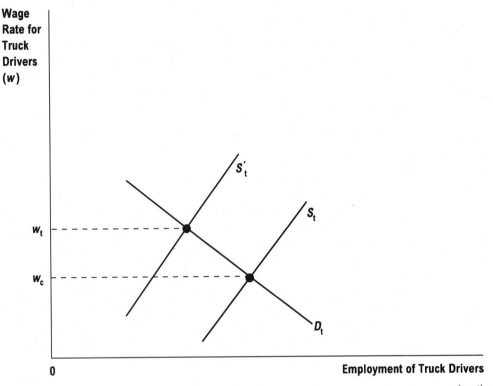

(continued)

Now, suppose that only females are allowed to work as secretaries, whereas male workers have a wide range of job opportunities. As a result, there are more females competing for secretarial jobs than males for truck driver positions. The supply curve for truck drivers therefore shifts to the left (S'_t) and that for secretaries shifts to the right (S'_s). The new equilibrium wage for truck drivers (w_t) is now higher than that for secretaries (w_s).[15]

This model raises a number of questions. First, what is the source of the occupational segregation? Bergmann in her 1974 article, following the work of Gary Becker, assumes that employer preference or preconceptions of "sex-appropriate" roles causes the segregation of male and female labor into separate occupations.

Job segregation may also reflect gender preferences. Family upbringing and general socialization processes may create sex-role models for different

---

[15]This model is quite similar in structure to the one used to explain the differential in pay between union and nonunion workers (See Section 8.1 for details).

Diagram 12.3 *(concluded)*

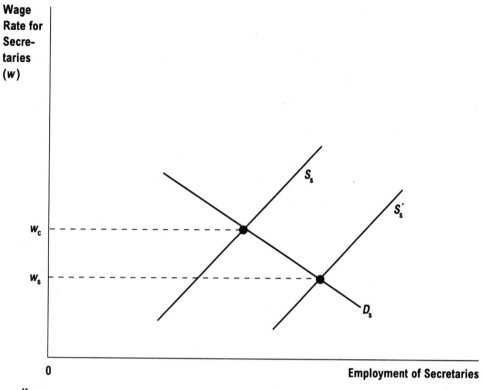

Key:
c — competitive equilibrium without discrimination
s — secretaries
t — truck drivers
D — demand curve
S — competitive supply curve
S'— supply curve with discrimination

types of occupations. Young women may voluntarily decide to develop skills and choose jobs that are consistent with traditional sex roles. The schooling system, starting even in primary school, may encourage boys to pursue certain career paths and girls to pursue others. In secondary school and college, this may take the form of encouraging males to take science and math and females to concentrate in the humanities.

Another important question is why "female" jobs tend to be overcrowded relative to male occupations. As we shall see in Chapter 14, female employment has historically been concentrated in six or seven occupations, whereas male workers are dispersed over a much wider range of jobs. It is not clear what historical mechanism funneled females into such a relatively small number of potential job opportunities.

Another issue is the long-term persistence of occupational segregation. Here, too, there is no clear explanation of the factors that maintain occupational segregation by gender in the face of competitive pressures. In the case of employer discrimination, there is always the potential that a "smart" employer will hire cheaper but equally productive female labor in traditionally male occupations and reap the extra profits. A more compelling argument for the persistence of sex segregation is that it emanates primarily from the early socialization process and sex stereotyping. However, as we shall see in Chapter 14, the 1980s have witnessed a large reduction in occupational segregation, with females making significant inroads into formerly male-dominated fields.

12.9 SUMMARY

Discrimination is another major factor that explains differences in earnings between groups in our country. In the United States, the two predominant forms have been racial and gender discrimination. In 1992, the income of black households averaged 62 percent that of white households; in 1992, female workers earned, on average, 70 percent that of male workers. However, black households did gain on white households, particularly during the late 1950s and the 1960s; and female earnings have increased relative to male earnings, particularly since the 1960s.

Differences in income between whites and minorities and between males and females do not of themselves constitute evidence of discrimination. Economists view discrimination as the "unexplained" difference in earnings between these groups. Though they may differ to some degree in what factors they consider relevant or "justifiable" in explaining earnings differences, almost all would include schooling and experience. Proof of discrimination would entail evidence that one group continues to earn less than another even after controlling or standardizing for pertinent explanatory variables.

This chapter considered several views of the sources of labor market discrimination. The Becker model derives from "tastes for discrimination" among employers. The equilibrium wage for minority workers is shown to depend on both the distribution of prejudicial preferences among employers and the size of the minority work force. The Arrow-Phelps statistical discrimination model is based on imperfect information and screening. On the basis of past "statistical" experience with minority or female workers, employers are led to believe that they are less productive or reliable than "comparable" white male employees. They pay the minority and female workers lower wages and provide them with less training than white male employees. This result leads to lower productivity gains for both minority and female workers and thus confirms the employers' original prejudices.

The Thurow job competition model, like the statistical discrimination model, is also based on screening, except that here the emphasis is placed on minimizing training costs for a particular job. In this model, marginal productivity resides in the job, not the individual, so that individuals compete for job openings. The employer's prime motivation in selecting a job candidate is to minimize the cost of training. Employers may select white male workers over minority or female candidates because they expect the training costs to be less.

The Doeringer and Piore dual labor market model maintains that employers expect workers hired into internal labor markets from the primary segment to be long-term employees of a company and therefore invest heavily in their training. Employers, on the other hand, pay lower wages and invest relatively little in their secondary labor force, because they do not expect these workers to remain very long with the company. White male workers who have historically dominated internal labor markets may resist attempts to introduce female and minority workers into their ranks, because they may feel that these changes will upset the status quo. Employers, who have invested heavily in their primary work force, may also not wish to incur the extra training costs from moving up minorities and females into this segment. Collusion between employers and primary workers helps to restrict minority and female workers to the lower-paying, secondary jobs.

The Marxian "divide and conquer" model is based on the view that capitalists attempt to create divisions within the working class. One way of accomplishing this objective is to segment workers on the basis of race and gender. White male workers are given the high-paying jobs, while minorities and females are consigned to low-paying ones. This stratagem creates internal friction within the working class, reduces class unity, and thereby increases the profits of the capitalist class.

The over-crowding model, usually applied to gender discrimination, rests on the assumption that male and female workers are typically segregated into male and female occupations. Because female opportunities are more limited than those of male workers, there is an oversupply of workers to the female occupations and a restricted supply to the male occupations. This raises the wages of male workers relative to females.

REFERENCES AND BIBLIOGRAPHY

Aigner, Dennis, and Cain, Glen G., "Statistical Theories of Discrimination in Labor Markets," *Industrial Labor Relations Review,* Vol. 30, January 1977, pp. 175–187.

Alexis, Marcus, "A Theory of Labor Market Discrimination with Interdependent Utilities," *American Economic Review,* Vol. 63, May 1973, pp. 296–302.

Arrow, Kenneth J., "Models of Job Discrimination," in A. H. Pascal (ed.), *Racial Discrimination in Economic Life*, D.C. Heath, Lexington, Mass., 1972(a), pp. 83–102.

———, "Some Mathematical Models of Race in the Labor Market," in A. H. Pascal (ed.), *Racial Discrimination in Economic Life*, D.C. Heath, Lexington, Mass., 1972(b), pp. 187–204.

———, "The Theory of Discrimination," in Orley Ashenfelter and Albert Rees, (eds.), *Discrimination in Labor Markets*, Princeton University Press, Princeton, N.J., 1973.

Becker, Gary S., *The Economics of Discrimination*, University of Chicago Press, Chicago, 2nd. ed., 1971.

Bergmann, Barbara P., "Occupational Segregation, Wages, and Profits When Employers Discriminate by Race or Sex," *Eastern Economic Journal*, April-July 1974, pp. 103–110.

———, "Reducing the Pervasiveness of Discrimination," in Eli Ginzberg (ed.), *Jobs for Americans*, Prentice-Hall, Englewood Cliffs, NJ, 1976, pp. 120–141.

Blau, Francine D., "Women's Place in the Labor Market," *American Economic Review*, Vol. 62, No. 2, May 1972, pp. 161–166.

———, *Equal Pay in the Office*, D.C. Heath and Company, Lexington, Mass., 1977.

———, "Discrimination Against Women: Theory and Evidence," in William Darity, Jr., (ed.), *Labor Economics: Modern View*, Kluwer-Hijhoff Publishing, Boston, Mass., 1984(a), pp. 53–89.

———, "Occupational Segregation and Labor Market Discrimination," in Barbara F. Reskin (ed.), *Sex Segregation in the Workplace: Trends, Explanations, Remedies*, National Academy Press, Washington, D.C., 1984(b).

——— and W.E. Hendricks, "Occupational Segregation by Sex: Trends and Prospects," *Journal of Human Resources*, Vol. 14, No. 2, Spring 1979, pp. 197–210.

Cain, Glen G., "The Economic Analysis of Labor Market Discrimination: A Survey," in Orley C. Ashenfelter and Richard Layard (eds.), *Handbook of Labor Economics*, Vol. 1, North-Holland Press, New York, 1986.

Coate, Stephen, and Glenn Loury, "Will Affirmative-Action Policies Eliminate Negative Stereotypes?" *American Economic Review*, Vol. 83, No. 5, December 1993, pp. 1220–1240.

Congressional Budget Office, *Inequalities in the Educational Experiences of Black and White Americans*, Government Printing Office, Washington, D.C., 1977.

Cymrot, Donald J., "Does Competition Lessen Discrimination: Some Evidence," *Journal of Human Resources*, Vol. 20, No. 4, Fall 1985, pp. 605–612.

D'Amico, Thomas, "The Conceit of Labor Market Discrimination," *American Economic Review*, Vol. 77, No. 2, May 1987, pp. 31–35.

Darity, William A., "The Human Capital Approach to Black-White Earnings Inequality: Some Unsettled Questions," *Journal of Human Resources*, Vol. 17, No. 1, Winter 1982, pp. 72–93.

Doeringer, Peter B., and Piore, Michael J., *Internal Labor Markets and Manpower Analysis,* Lexington Books, Lexington, Mass., 1971.

Franklin, Raymond, and Michael Tanzer, "Traditional Microeconomic Analysis of Racial Discrimination: A Critical View and Alternative Approach," in David Mermelstein (ed.), *Economics: Mainstream Readings and Critiques,* Random House, New York, 1970.

Gordon, David M., *Theories of Poverty and Underemployment,* Lexington Books, Lexington, Mass., 1972.

Hacker, Andrew, *Two Nations: Black and White, Separate, Hostile, Unequal,* Scribners, New York, 1992.

Kozol, Jonathan, *Savage Inequalities: Children in American Schools,* Crown, New York, 1991.

Krueger, Anne O., "The Economics of Discrimination," *Journal of Political Economies,* Vol. 71, October 1963, pp. 481–486.

Lloyd, Cynthia B. (ed.), *Sex, Discrimination, and the Division of Labor,* Columbia University Press, New York, 1975.

Lundahl, Mats, and Eskil Wadensjo, *Unequal Treatment: A Study in the Neo-Classical Theory of Discrimination,* New York University Press, New York, 1984.

Lundberg, Shelly J., and Richard Startz, "Private Discrimination and Social Intervention in Competitive Labor Markets," *American Economic Review,* Vol. 73, No. 3, June 1983, pp. 340–347.

Marshall, Ray, "The Economics of Racial Discrimination: A Survey," *Journal of Economic Literature,* Vol. 12, September 1974, pp. 849–871.

Massey, Douglas S., and Nancy A. Denton, *American Apartheid: Segregation and the Making of the Underclass,* Harvard University Press, Cambridge, Mass., 1993.

McCall, J. J., "The Simple Mathematics of Information, Job Search, and Prejudices," in A. H. Pascal (ed.), *Racial Discrimination in Economic Life,* D.C. Heath, Lexington, Mass., 1972.

National Center for Education Statistics, *The Condition of Education, 1978,* Government Printing Office, Washington, D.C., 1979.

Orfield, Gary, *The Growth of Segregation in American Schools,* National School Boards Association, Alexandria, Va., December 1993.

Phelps, Edmund S., "The Statistical Theory of Racism and Sexism," *American Economic Review,* Vol. 62, September 1972, pp. 659–661.

Piore, Michael J., "Manpower Policy," in S. Beer and R. Barringer (eds.), *The State and the Poor,* Cambridge, Mass., Winthrop, 1970.

———, "The Dual Labor Market: Theory and Implications," in David M. Gordon (ed.), *Problems in Political Economy,* 2nd. ed., D.C. Heath, Lexington, Mass., 1977.

Reder, Melvyn W., "Human Capital and Economic Discrimination," in I. Berg (ed.), *Human Resources and Economic Welfare,* Columbia University Press, New York, 1972.

Reich, Michael, "The Economics of Racism," in David M. Gordon (ed.), *Problems in Political Economy,* 2nd. ed., D.C. Heath, Lexington, Mass., 1977.

———, "Who Benefits from Racism? The Distribution Among Whites of Gains and Losses from Racial Inequality," *Journal of Human Resources,* Vol. 13, Fall 1978.

———, "Changes in the Distribution of Benefits from Racism in the 1960s," *Journal of Human Resources,* Vol. 16, No. 2, Spring 1981a, pp. 314–321.

———, *Racial Inequality,* Princeton University Press, Princeton, 1981b.

———, "Postwar Income Differences: Trends and Theories," in Garth Mangrum and Peter Phillips (eds.), *Three Worlds of Labor Economics,* M. E. Sharpe, White Plains, NY, 1988.

Roemer, John E., "Differentially Exploited Labor: A Marxian Theory of Discrimination," *Review of Radical Political Economics,* Vol. 10, No. 2, Summer 1978, pp. 43–53.

———, "Divide and Conquer: Microfoundations of a Marxian Theory of Wage Discrimination," *Bell Journal of Economics,* Vol. 10, No. 2, Autumn 1979, pp. 695–705.

Schwab, Stewart, "Is Statistical Discrimination Efficient?" *American Economic Review,* Vol. 76, No. 1, March 1986, pp. 228–234.

Stevenson, M. H., "Relative Wages and Sex Segregation by Occupation," in Cynthia B. Lloyd (ed.), *Sex, Discrimination, and the Division of Labor,* Columbia University Press, New York, 1975.

Stiglitz, Joseph E., "Approaches to the Economics of Discrimination," *American Economic Review,* Vol. 63, May 1973, pp. 287–295.

———, "Theories of Discrimination and Economic Policy," in G. M. von Furstenberg, A. R. Horowitz, and B. Harrison (eds.), *Patterns of Racial Discrimination,* Vol. II, Lexington Books, Lexington, Mass., 1974.

Thurow, Lester C., *Poverty and Discrimination,* Brookings, Washington, D.C., 1969.

———, *Generating Inequality,* Basic Books, New York, 1975.

U.S. Bureau of the Census, *Statistical Abstract of the United States, 1994,* U.S. Government Printing Office, Washington, D.C., 1994.

Wachter, Michael, "Primary and Secondary Labor Markets: A Critique of the Dual Approach," *Brookings Papers on Economic Activity,* No. 3, 1974, pp. 637–694.

Wilson, William Julius, *The Truly Disadvantaged: The Inner City, the Underclass, and Public Policy,* University of Chicago Press, Chicago, IL, 1987.

13

RACIAL DISCRIMINATION: PROGRESS AND REVERSAL FOR BLACK AMERICANS

In 1944, the Swedish economist Gunnar Myrdal published a major study of race relations in the United States, entitled *The American Dilemma: The Negro Problem and Modern Democracy*. In this book, he posed the "dilemma" between the alleged commitment to equal opportunity within the United States and actual discrimination against black Americans. Is such discrimination compatible with a democratic society?

Since the publication of this famous work, there have been many important changes in race relations and the economic status of black Americans. The story, as it unfolds, will show three decades of progress of blacks, from 1940 through 1970, followed by two decades of relative stagnation in both labor earnings and family incomes. Moreover, the last two decades have witnessed a sharp decline in the employment of black men, as well as rising inequality within the black community.

In Section 13.1, we review the basic evidence on the progress of black Americans. We begin with a comparison of the labor earnings of white and black Americans. We then look at changes over time in labor force participation patterns among blacks. Family incomes of blacks and whites are considered next, as well as differences in poverty incidence. Some comparative data are then presented on the wealth holdings of the two groups. Finally, since Hispanic Americans represent a large and growing minority in the United States, we also consider similar trends for this group.

The next four sections consider reasons for the advances made by black Americans in the two decades or so following World War II and the later

461

reversal of fortunes. One reason for their early gains was a massive migration out of the then low-wage South to the high-wage North, particularly since 1945 (Section 13.2). A second reason for their economic progress was steady gains in schooling attainment made by black Americans (Section 13.3). A third development has been the growth in the number of female-headed households in the black community, particularly since 1970, which has largely been responsible for the deterioration in incomes among black families (Section 13.4).

Public policy measures enacted to reduce racial discrimination have also made important contributions to progress among black families. Section 13.5 discusses the two major programs, the Civil Rights Act of 1964 and President Lyndon Johnson's 1965 Executive Order 11246. This section also presents evidence about the effectiveness of these programs. A summary is provided in the last section.

13.1 TRENDS AND STATUS REPORT ON RACIAL INEQUALITY

The Earnings Gap: Have Black Workers Made Gains on Whites?

We begin with a consideration of differences in wages and salaries between blacks and whites (Table 13.1). Earnings ratios are shown by age and schooling group for full-year, full-time employees in 1992. This enables us to *standardize* or control for differences in human capital between blacks and whites. A ratio of 1.0 would indicate identical earnings for blacks and whites.

The ratio in median earnings among all full-time, full-year male workers was 74 percent in 1992 (Panel A). When we standardize by education, the ratios are higher. Among males with less than nine years of schooling, black workers actually earned more than white workers. For those who attended high school but did not receive a degree, the ratio was 79 percent, while among high school graduates, the ratio was 78 percent. For those who attended college but did not receive a B.A., the ratio in earnings between blacks and white males was around 85 percent. Among those with a B.A. degree or more, the ratio was 74 percent. There is relatively little systematic difference in the earnings gap by age group.

Earnings ratios are also shown between black and white females who worked full-time, full-year (Panel B). Among all females, the ratio in median annual earnings was 0.91, compared to 0.74 among all males. The earnings differential was even noticeably less among women with eight years of schooling or less (no difference) and among those with a B.A. degree or better (only a three percent difference). There is little evidence of discrimination against black women, *at least in comparison to white women*. However, as we will see in the next chapter, both white and black females still earn less

Table 13.1 The Ratio of Median Annual Earnings Between Black and White Workers, Classified by Gender, Education, and Age, 1992[a]

	25–34	35–44	45–54	55–64	All Ages
A. Black Males/White Males					
Elementary 0–8	—	—	—	—	1.08
High school, no degree	0.83	0.71	0.77	0.83	0.79
High school graduate[b]	0.73	0.72	0.88	0.74	0.78
College 1–3	0.84	0.86	0.86	—	0.84
College, associate degree	1.01	0.85	—	—	0.86
College, B.A. or more	0.81	0.72	0.88	—	0.74
All schooling levels	0.78	0.72	0.76	0.75	0.74
B. Black Females/White Females					
Elementary 0–8	—	—	—	—	1.00
High school, no degree	0.96	0.88	0.84	—	0.86
High school graduate[b]	0.93	0.91	1.06	0.89	0.91
College 1–3	0.85	0.94	1.03	—	0.92
College, associate degree	0.92	0.86	—	—	0.93
College, B.A. or more	0.96	0.98	0.95	—	0.97
All schooling levels	0.87	0.89	0.94	0.86	0.91

[a] Source: U.S. Bureau of the Census, Current Population Reports, Series P60–184, *Money Income of Households, Families, and Persons in the United States: 1992*, 1993. Earnings data are for year-round (defined as those who worked 50 or more weeks), full-time (defined as those who work 35 or more hours per week) employees.
[b] Includes equivalency degrees.

than male workers. (See the next chapter also for more discussion of earnings differences between black and white women).

The results of Table 13.1 show that among full-time, full-year workers, black males earned about a quarter less than white males in 1992, after standardizing for human capital, while black females had almost reached parity with white females in terms of annual earnings. It is next of interest to see whether the racial earnings gap has widened or narrowed over time. Since part of the overall gains in earnings made by blacks is attributable to their increasing educational attainment (as we shall see in Section 13.3), it is again necessary to control for educational attainment when we make these earnings comparisons.

Table 13.2 shows the ratio of earnings between blacks and whites from 1939 to 1992 (also see Figures 13.1a and 13.1b). The results are quite dramatic. In 1939, black males typically earned about half that of white males.

Table 13.2 The Ratio of Mean Annual Earnings Between Black and White Workers, for Males and Females, Classified by Education, 1939–1992[a]

	1939	1949	1959	1969	1979	1984	1992
A. *Black Males/White Males*							
Elementary 0–8	0.48	0.56	0.60	0.70	0.78	0.86	0.81
High School 1–3	0.53	0.63	0.63	0.73	0.82	0.83	0.82
High School 4	0.57	0.60	0.61	0.71	0.71	0.66	0.72
College 1–3	0.50	0.53	0.62	0.75	0.75	0.77	0.75
College 4 or more	0.51	0.52	0.54	0.68	0.70	0.74	0.71
B. *Black Females/White Females*							
Elementary 0–8	0.43	0.54	0.54	0.67	0.95	1.08	0.94
High School 1–3	0.50	0.68	0.67	0.88	1.17	1.05	0.91
High School 4	0.53	0.69	0.73	0.92	1.03	0.99	0.97
College 1–3	0.56	0.72	0.85	1.15	1.09	1.06	0.94
College 4 or more	0.64	0.93	0.94	1.14	1.14	1.11	1.01

[a] Sources: Jaynes (1990); U.S. Bureau of the Census, *Current Population Reports, Series P60–184, Money Income of Households, Families, and Persons in the United States: 1992,* 1993.

Between 1939 and 1969, the earnings gap was steadily reduced, so that by 1969, the ratio of earnings between black and white males was about 70 percent. The earnings gap narrowed at all educational levels over this period.

After 1969, black males continued to make relative progress at some educational levels but not at others. The racial earnings gap continued to narrow among workers with no more than an elementary school education and those with one to three years of high school. By 1992, the earnings ratio between black and white males had increased to 0.81 for the former and 0.82 for the latter. Some relative advance was also made by black male college graduates, whose relative earnings increased from 68 to 74 percent of white male college graduates by 1984, though they declined to 71 percent in 1992. However, the relative earnings of black male high school graduates and those with one to three years of college remained essentially unchanged between 1969 to 1992.

The progress of black female workers relative to white female workers was even more dramatic than that of black males. Like black males, black females typically earned about half that of their white counterpart in 1939. However, unlike black males, their relative progress was steady throughout the period from 1939 to 1984, and by 1984, they had generally reached earnings parity with white females of the same educational level. Unfortu-

Figure 13.1a   Ratio of Annual Earnings Between Black and White Males, by Schooling Level, 1939–1992

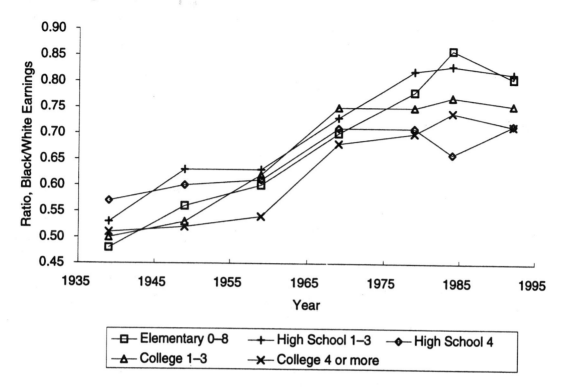

nately, from 1984 to 1992, the earnings ratio did decline, so that by 1992, black women were making about 5 percent less than white women with the same schooling.

Labor Force Participation and Unemployment

The previous part has documented the fact that black Americans have made considerable progress relative to white Americans in terms of labor earnings. For black males, most of the gains were made by 1969, though with some slow advances thereafter. Black females, on the other hand, had reached virtual parity with white females in terms of earnings by 1984, though they slipped backwards a bit in the early 1990s.

However, there is another aspect of this story—the proportion of working-age adults with jobs. This, in turn, has two dimensions, as we saw in Chapter 5: (1) the labor force participation rate—the percentage of working-age individuals who are in the labor force; and (2) the unemployment rate—the proportion of the labor force currently without a job but looking for

Figure 13.1b   Ratio of Annual Earnings Between Black and White Females, by Schooling Level, 1939–1992

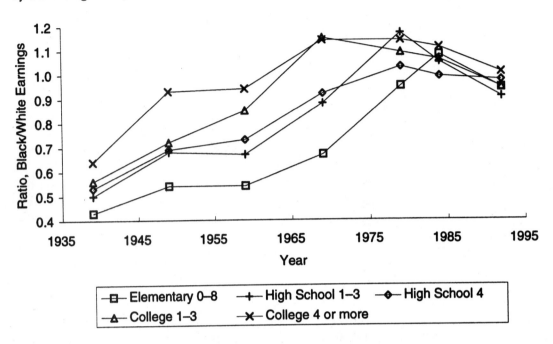

work. In both dimensions, black males have fared much more poorly than white males, particularly since 1970.[1]

Table 13.3 presents labor force participation rates (LFPR) by race. Let us first consider differences by educational attainment for men aged 25 to 34 (Panel A). In 1940, black and white males had almost identical levels of labor force participation. This remained generally true until the 1960s. After this, the LFPR of black men fell substantially below that of white men. This occurred at all levels of schooling, except among college graduates, and was particularly marked at lower educational attainment. In 1992, the LFPR of black males with no more than an elementary school education was 48 percent, compared to 85 percent for white males of the same schooling level—a difference of 37 percentage points. The difference was 17 percentage points (76 percent versus 93 percent) among high school graduates and 9 percentage points (86 versus 95 percent) among those who attended but did not complete four years of college.

Panel B shows LFPR by age group for black and white males from 1955 to 1992 (see also Figure 13.2a). The same trends are evident. In 1955, the overall LFPR of black and white males was identical, at 85 percent. Since

---

[1] There is also a third dimension, the portion of employed persons who hold part-time jobs as opposed to full-time ones. Black males have done comparatively worse than white males in this respect also—that is, a higher percentage of black males hold part-time jobs than white males.

Table 13.3 Labor Force Participation Rates by Race, Gender, Schooling, and Age[a]
(percent)

A. *Black and White Males by Educational Attainment, Ages 25–34*

	1940		1960		1980		1992	
Education	Blacks	Whites	Blacks	Whites	Blacks	Whites	Blacks	Whites
Elementary 0–8	95	95	92	91	66	76	48	82
High School 1–3	95	97	94	96	75	90	77	87
High School 4	97	98	95	98	86	95	76	93
College 1–3	93	95	91	94	89	94	86	95
College 4+	98	96	96	96	93	96	97	96

B. *Black and White Males by Age Group*

	1955		1970		1980		1992	
Age	Nonwhites	Whites	Nonwhites	Whites	Blacks	Whites	Blacks	Whites
25–34	96	98	94	97	91	96	86	94
35–44	96	98	93	97	89	96	86	94
45–54	94	97	88	95	83	92	79	90
55–64	83	88	79	83	62	73	55	66
All Ages	85	85	77	80	70	79	69	76

C. *Black and White Females by Age Group*

	1955		1970		1980		1992	
Age	Nonwhites	Whites	Nonwhites	Whites	Blacks	Whites	Blacks	Whites
25–34	51	33	58	43	71	65	72	75
35–44	56	40	60	50	68	65	76	78
45–54	55	43	60	54	61	60	71	75
55–64	41	32	47	43	45	41	45	49
All Ages	46	35	50	43	53	51	59	59

[a]Sources: Jaynes (1990); U.S. Bureau of Labor Statistics, *Handbook of Labor Statistics 1989*, 1990, Bulletin 2340; U.S. Bureau of the Census, Current Population Reports, Series P60–184, *Money Income of Households, Families, and Persons in the United States: 1992*, 1993; and worksheets provided by the U.S. Bureau of Labor Statistics. Note that before 1977, figures were provided for only nonwhites as a group.

that time, the LFPRs of both black and white males declined, but after 1970, they declined considerably faster for black men. Among white men, the LFPR fell from 85 percent in 1955 to 76 percent in 1992. The decline was particularly marked for white men aged 55 to 64, whose LFPR decreased from 88 to 66 percent. Among black men, the overall LFPR fell from 85

Figure 13.2a Labor Force Participation Rates of Black and White Males, by Age Group, 1954–1994

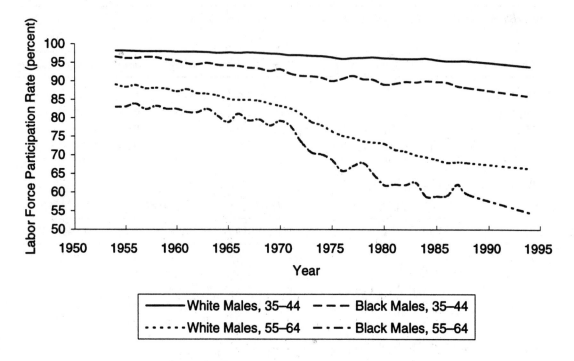

percent in 1955 to 69 percent in 1992—seven percentage points below the corresponding rate for white men. The decline occurred for all age groups, though it was particularly sharp among those 55 to 64 in age (down to 55 percent). By 1992, the LFPR of black men was lower than that of white men in *all age groups.*

The experience of women was opposite that of men (see Panel C of Table 13.3 and Figure 13.2b). Between 1955 and 1992, the overall LFPR of both black and white women increased—the former from 46 to 59 percent and the latter from 35 to 59 percent. The increase occurred for all age groups. The most telling difference is that a higher percentage of black women than white women have historically been in the labor force. In 1955, the LFPR of black females was 46 percent, compared to 35 percent for white females—a difference of 11 percentage points. However, the difference has narrowed over time, and by 1994, it completely disappeared.

Not all people in the labor force are employed at any given time, and there are also noticeable differences in the incidence of unemployment between black and white workers (see also Chapter 5). As shown in Table 13.4, the overall unemployment rate of black men has typically been about 2½ to 3 times that of white men. This relationship has not changed very much over the postwar period, as figures for 1955, 1975, and 1994 indicate. The unemployment incidence has been greater for black men in comparison to

Figure 13.2b Labor Force Participation Rates of Black and White Females, by Age Group, 1954–1994

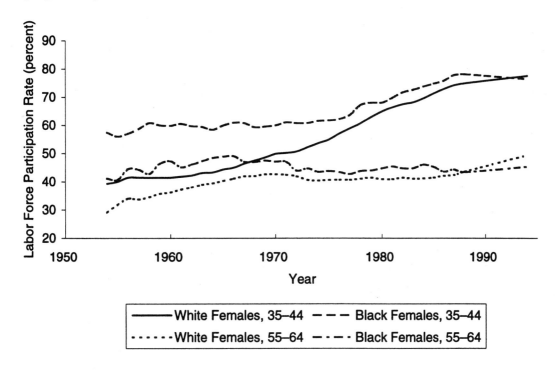

Table 13.4 Unemployment Rates by Race, Gender, and Age Group 1955, 1975, and 1994[a]

Age Group	1955		1975		1994	
	Nonwhites	Whites	Blacks	Whites	Blacks	Whites
A. *Black and White Males by Age Group*						
16–19 years	13.4	11.3	38.1	18.3	37.6	16.3
20 years & over	8.4	3.3	12.5	6.2	10.3	4.8
All	8.8	3.7	14.8	7.2	12.0	5.4
B. *Black and White Females by Age Group*						
16–19 years	19.2	9.1	41.0	17.4	32.6	13.8
20 years & over	7.7	3.9	12.2	7.5	9.8	4.6
All	8.5	4.3	14.8	8.6	11.0	5.2

[a] Source: Council of Economic Advisers, *Economic Report of the President, 1995*. Note that before 1972, figures were provided for only nonwhites as a group.

white men at every age level. However, recently (since the late 1970s), unemployment has been particularly high among young black males, under the age of 20.[2]

The picture is rather similar among females. Black females have also had substantially higher unemployment rates than white women, typically about double. This relationship has also remained relatively unchanged over the postwar period. As with black males, black females have experienced higher unemployment rates in every age group than white females. Here, too, differences are particularly marked among females under the age of 20.

One way of summarizing the differences in both LFPR and unemployment rates is to consider the number of persons of both races who earned zero labor income. According to calculations made by Jaynes (1990), in 1959, 5 percent of white men and 8 percent of black men aged 25 to 54 received no labor earnings. In 1984, the corresponding proportion for white men was still 5 percent but that for black men had risen to 16 percent. Results are even more striking for men aged 55 to 64. In 1959, the proportion of white men in this age group receiving no labor income was 14 percent and that of black men was 20 percent; by 1984, the respective proportions were 26 percent and *42 percent*. Thus, among black men in general, though particularly among older black men, there was a substantial decline in the percentage receiving income in the labor market.

Some economists, such as Butler and Heckman (1978), Heckman (1987), and Jaynes (1990), have argued that the relative progress made by black men in terms of earnings is related to the reduction in their employment rate (the number of employed divided by the population).[3] Their interpretation is based upon a *selectivity bias* in the population of black men with jobs. The argument is that low-skill workers have trouble finding jobs and, as a result, become discouraged and leave the labor force entirely. Since a higher proportion of black male workers are low skill in comparison to white male workers, the "discouraged worker effect" is greater for black males than white males. This, in turn, means that the distribution of wages observed for black workers is "truncated from below" to a much greater extent than for white workers. In other words, only a smaller proportion of black workers are "selected" for a job than white workers. The average labor earnings of black male workers thus appears higher than it would if all black workers (or if the same proportion of black workers as white workers) had a job.

One implication of this hypothesis is that gains made by black males since 1970 are *overstated* by using earnings data alone as the measure of labor market success. One way of showing the difference is to compare the

---

[2] See Leslie Stratton (1993) for a telling analysis of differences in unemployment propensities between white and black males.

[3] The employment rate is equal to one minus the unemployment rate multiplied by the labor force participation rate.

average weekly earnings of black males (with a job) to the average earnings of black males of working age (20 to 65), including those with a job and those without a job. According to calculations made by Jaynes (1990), the weekly earnings of black male workers relative to those of white male workers increased by 53 percent between 1939 and 1959 and by 24 percent from 1959 to 1979. The corresponding figures for earnings per black male of working age are much lower, 36 and 14 percent respectively. These results lead many to believe that gains made by black male workers are much more modest since 1960 than earnings data alone indicate. On the other hand, this argument does not apply to black women, since their employment rate is comparable to that of white women. A similar calculation shows almost no difference between the growth in the average weekly earnings of black women relative to white women and the growth in average earnings per female of working age.

Family Income, Poverty, and Wealth

The last two sections considered only the labor income of individuals. However, family income is the key concept for understanding changes in well-being or the standard of living. As we saw in Chapter 2, family income includes not only wages and salaries but also property income (such as interest, rent, and dividends) as well as transfer income (such as social security benefits, welfare payments, and unemployment insurance). Also, the family is a different unit of observation than the individual. A family may have more than one person working, or it may not have anyone working. Trends in family income may, as a result, be different than those for individual labor earnings.

What has happened to the income of black families relative to white families? Figure 13.3 shows the trends in the ratio of median family income between the two groups from 1947 to 1992.[4] In 1947, the ratio of median income was 51 percent. There was some increase in this ratio between 1947 and 1952, but by 1958, the ratio had returned to 51 percent. After that point, the trend was mostly upward, reaching a peak of 62 percent in 1975. However, since that time, the relative income of black families has generally declined, and by 1992, it had fallen to 54 percent, the same ratio as in 1962. Indeed, in absolute terms (constant dollars), the median income of black families was the same in 1992 as it was in 1969.

The trend in median family income seems at odds with changes over time in the wages and salaries of black workers, both male and female, which continued to gain on white workers during the late 1970s and into the 1980s, albeit rather slowly. There are two reasons for the difference. First, as we discussed above, there was also a large increase in the number of working-age black males who were without a job from 1970 onward. Second,

---

[4]Before 1967, data on median family income are available only for nonwhite families. This should not bias the graph too much, because in 1967, the median income of black families differed from that of all nonwhite families by only 4 percent.

Figure 13.3 Ratio of Median Family Income Between Black and White Families and Between Hispanic and non-Hispanic White Families, 1947–1992

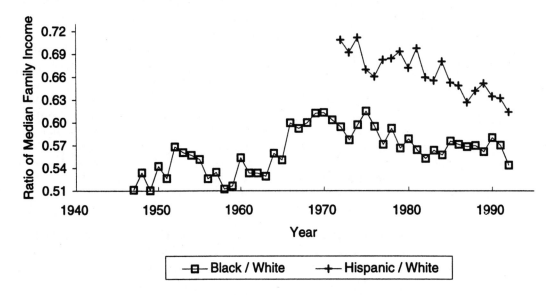

there was a significant change in the composition of black households, with a large increase in the number of families headed by females (with no husband present). We shall say more about this below.

Another equally disturbing trend is in the incidence of poverty among black Americans. As shown in Figure 13.4, black families have historically had a much higher poverty rate than white families. In 1959 (the earliest date for which such data are available), 55 percent of black families had incomes below the poverty line, compared to 18 percent of white families. Since that time, poverty has declined for both races. Among black families, the lowest poverty rate was reached in 1974, *at 30 percent.* By 1983, it had risen to 36 percent. It fell to 31 percent in 1989 but by 1993 had risen again to 33 percent.[5] In this dimension, too, we see that relatively little progress has been made by black families since the mid-1970s.

Another aspect of family well-being is its holdings of household wealth (see Table 13.5). Let us first consider the homeownership rate (the percentage of housing units that are owned by their occupant), which almost doubled among nonwhite families between 1940 (24 percent) and 1991 (43 percent). The ratio of homeownership rates between nonwhites and whites also increased, from 52 percent in 1940 to 64 percent in 1991, reaching parity with the relative income levels of that year. However, increases in nonwhite homeownership rates, in both relative and absolute terms, were confined to

---

[5] The relative poverty rate of black families (the ratio of poverty rates between blacks and whites) was as high as 3.7 in 1973 but has since fallen to 2.7 in 1993.

Part IV Discrimination

Figure 13.4 Poverty Rates by Race and Ethnicity, 1959–1993 (Percent of Persons Below Poverty Line)

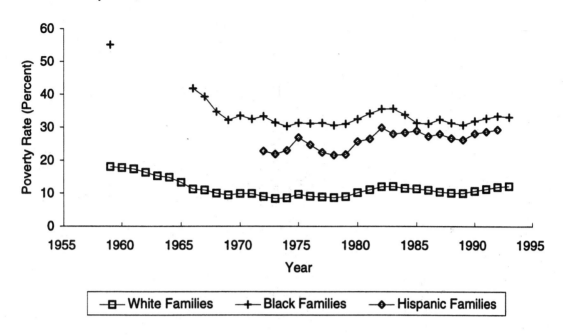

Table 13.5 Homeownership Rates by Race, 1920–1991[a]
(Percent of Housing Units That Are Owner-Occupied)

Year	All Races	Whites	Blacks and Others	Ratio Black/White
1920	45.6	48.2	23.9	0.50
1930	47.8	50.2	25.2	0.50
1940	43.6	45.7	23.6	0.52
1950	55.0	57.0	34.9	0.61
1960	61.9	64.4	38.4	0.60
1970	62.9	65.4	42.1	0.64
1980	64.4	67.8	44.2	0.65
1991	64.2	67.9	43.2	0.64

[a]Source: U.S. Bureau of the Census, *Statistical Abstract of the United States: 1994*, 114th Edition, 1994.

the 1940s and the 1960s. Since 1970, there has been virtually no increase in the homeownership rate among nonwhite families. Indeed, between 1980 and 1991, the homeownership rate among nonwhite families actually declined relative to white families. Racial differences in homeownership rates, besides reflecting racial disparities in family income, may also be caused by the discrimination in housing and mortgage lending that we discussed in the last chapter.

Nonwhite families also made substantial gains on whites in terms of net worth between the early 1960s and the early 1990s (see Table 13.6). Between 1962 and 1992, the ratio of mean wealth between nonwhite and white families grew from 12 percent to 37 percent, while the ratio of medians increased from 4 percent to 16 percent.

More disturbing is the fact that the wealth of nonwhite families averaged *only 37 percent* that of white families in 1992, compared to 60 percent for income; and the ratio of median net worth was *only 16 percent*, reflecting the large number of nonwhite families with zero or negative net worth. Why is the racial gap in wealth so much greater than that in income? One explanation emphasizes the role played by intergenerational transfers in household wealth accumulation. The argument is that inheritances and gifts play a crucial role in the accumulation of family wealth. Some economists estimate that up to 80 percent of the wealth owned by families today may have originated from such transfers (see Chapter 11 for more discussion).

Table 13.6   Ratio in Family Income and Wealth of Nonwhites to Whites, 1962–1992

	Ratio of	
Year	Means	Medians
I. *Family Income*[a]		
1967	0.62	0.59
1983	0.61	0.56
1989	0.61	0.56
1992	0.60	0.54
II. *Family Wealth*[b]		
1962	0.12	0.04
1983	0.22	0.10
1989	0.29	0.08
1992	0.37	0.16

[a]Sources: U.S. Bureau of the Census, Current Population Reports, Series P-60, No. 168, *Money Income and Poverty Status in the United States: 1989;* and U.S. Bureau of the Census, Current Population Reports, Series P60–184, *Money Income of Households, Families, and Persons in the United States: 1992.* Ratio is between black and white households; Hispanic households are excluded from this table.
[b]Sources: Author's calculations from the 1962 Survey of Financial Characteristics of Consumers and the 1983 and 1989 Survey of Consumer Finances and Kennickell and Starr-McCluer (1994). Hispanics are classified as nonwhites.

Some evidence of this is provided in two papers. The first, by Francine Blau and John Graham (1990), examined the sources of black-white differences in wealth holdings. Using econometric techniques on the National Longitudinal Survey, Blau and Graham were able to explain only about one-quarter of the difference in wealth holdings between black and white households on the basis of family income, age, and other demographic characteristics. They speculated that differences in inheritances may play an important role in explaining the rest of the discrepancy, because income differences between blacks and whites were much greater in older generations.

Paul Menchik and Nancy Jianakoplos (1995) were able to rigorously test this hypothesis, using data from a more recent version of the National Longitudinal Survey and the 1989 Survey of Consumer Finances. Both datasets contain information on inheritances received, as well as the income and wealth of respondents. They found that racial differences in inheritances accounted for between 10 and 20 percent of the black-white differences in average wealth holdings. Together with income and demographic differences, they were able to account for close to half of the interracial wealth gap.

If inheritances play an important role in wealth accumulation, then the much larger wealth of white families in comparison to nonwhites today may reflect differences in income and wealth of preceding generations. Though the wealth gap between nonwhite and white families has narrowed over the last 30 years, it remains higher than the income gap, because it reflects the larger racial income gap of the parents and grandparents of today's families. If this is so, then it may take several generations for the wealth gap between blacks and whites to narrow to the same level as the income gap.

Another troubling finding is that the inequality of income among black Americans is quite a bit higher than among whites. Calculations performed by the U.S. Bureau of the Census on the basis of 1992 Current Population Survey (U.S. Bureau of the Census, 1993) show that while the bottom 20 percent of white families accounted for 4.9 percent of all the income of the white community, the bottom quintile of black families received only 3.0 percent of the total income of the black community. Moreover, the top 20 percent of white families received 43.8 percent of the total income of white families, compared to a 48.8 percent share of the top quintile of black families.

In 1992, the Gini coefficient for family income among black families was 0.46, in comparison to a Gini coefficient of 0.39 among white families. Moreover, calculations performed by Jaynes (1990) indicate that the inequality in labor earnings among males has been rising much faster for blacks than whites. The Gini coefficient for white males increased from 0.37 in 1959 to 0.39 in 1984, while that for black males rose from 0.50 to 0.59.

Hispanics

Another important racial minority in the United States is Hispanics—those of mainly Caribbean or Latin American origin. Most of the Hispanic population in the United States originally came from Mexico, Puerto Rico, and

Cuba, although today there are also significant numbers from South America and Central America. The U.S. Bureau of the Census has provided separate statistics on Hispanics since 1972. There is some difficulty in classifying people of Hispanic origin, and the Census Bureau has typically used Spanish surnames as the basis of its classification. In most tabulations, Hispanics can be of any race—that is, white or black.

By most indices, Hispanic families have fared somewhat better than black families but significantly worse than white families. As shown in Figure 13.3, the median income of Hispanic families has been greater than that of black families, though it has been noticeably lower than that of whites. In 1992, the median family income of Hispanics was 13 percent greater than that of black families but only 61 percent the level of white families. Moreover, the ratio of median family income between Hispanic and white families has been declining steadily, from a peak of 71 percent in 1974.

The incidence of poverty has likewise been substantially greater for Hispanic families than whites, though somewhat lower than the poverty level for black families (see Figure 13.4). In 1992, the poverty rate for individuals of Hispanic origin was 29.3 percent, in comparison to 11.9 percent for whites and 33.4 percent for blacks. The poverty rate for Hispanics rose from 22 percent in 1973 to a peak of 30 percent in 1982, declined to 26 percent in 1989, but has since risen again to 29 percent in 1992.

Table 13.7 provides some comparative data on earnings of Hispanic and white males in 1992 by age and educational attainment. Hispanic males have earned lower wages and salaries than white males and have also fared somewhat worse than black males. Among full-time, full-year workers, His-

Table 13.7   The Ratio of Median Annual Earnings between Hispanic and White Male Workers, Classified by Education and Age, 1992[a]

	25–34	35–44	45–54	55–64	All Ages
Elementary 0–8	0.95	0.99	0.80	0.77	0.90
High school, no degree	0.79	0.91	—	—	0.78
High school graduate[b]	0.85	0.82	0.80	—	0.81
College 1–3	0.88	0.87	0.88	—	0.85
College, associate degree	0.94	—	—	—	0.84
College, B.A. or more	0.80	0.80	0.74	—	0.77
All schooling levels	0.69	0.68	0.66	0.72	0.67

[a]Source: U.S. Bureau of the Census, Current Population Reports, Series P60–184, *Money Income of Households, Families, and Persons in the United States: 1992*, 1993. Earnings data are for year-round (defined as those who worked 50 or more weeks), full-time (defined as those who work 35 or more hours per week) employees.
[b]Includes equivalency degrees.

panic males earned, on average, 67 percent the wages of white employees (compared to 74 percent for black male employees). However, when standardized by educational levels, the earnings ratios were noticeably higher, ranging from 77 to 90 percent across all age groups. This already indicates that a large part of the earnings gap between Hispanic and white workers is due to differences in educational attainment. Hispanic males also earned about the same as black males of the same educational attainment. Also, when standardized by schooling level, younger Hispanic males (ages 25 to 44) did slightly better relative to white workers of the same age group than older Hispanic workers (ages 45 to 64).

Table 13.8 shows both labor force participation rates (LFPR) and unemployment rates for Hispanic and white Americans. In both 1980 and 1988,

Table 13.8   Labor Force Participation Rates and Unemployment Rates for Hispanic and White Individuals by Age and Gender, 1977, 1980, and 1988[a] (in percent)

| | Labor Force Participation Rates | | | | Unemployment Rates | | | |
| | 1980 | | 1988 | | 1977 | | 1988 | |
Age Group	Hisp.	Whites	Hisp.	Whites	Hisp.	Whites	Hisp.	Whites
A. *Hispanic and White Males*								
16–17 years	45.2	53.6	38.6	49.3	24.4	17.6	29.5	16.1
18–19	74.8	74.1	70.1	71.0	18.2	13.0	19.5	12.4
20–24	88.0	87.2	89.4	86.6	12.2	9.3	9.2	7.4
25–34	93.3	95.9	93.4	95.2	8.2	5.0	7.0	4.6
35–44	93.8	96.2	93.8	95.4	4.9	3.1	5.9	3.4
45–54	91.7	92.1	88.5	91.8	5.4	3.0	6.1	3.2
55–64	73.6	73.1	68.8	67.9	6.8	3.3	6.7	3.3
65 and over	20.7	19.1	17.4	16.7	10.4	4.9	6.9	2.2
All, 16 & over	81.4	78.8	81.9	76.9	9.0	5.5	8.1	4.7
B. *Hispanic and White Females*								
16–17 years	29.9	47.2	32.4	47.7	31.0	18.2	24.5	14.4
18–19	50.4	65.1	55.5	66.3	23.0	14.2	18.9	10.8
20–24	57.0	70.6	62.3	74.9	12.3	9.3	10.7	6.7
25–34	54.0	64.8	60.9	73.0	9.7	6.7	7.2	4.5
35–44	55.3	65.0	62.1	74.9	7.9	5.3	6.2	3.7
45–54	54.5	59.6	57.9	69.2	10.7	5.0	5.9	3.1
55–64	34.7	40.9	41.5	43.6	10.2	4.4	4.6	2.5
65 and over	5.7	7.9	6.5	7.7	3.2	4.9	3.0	2.6
All, 16 & over	47.4	51.2	53.2	56.4	11.9	7.3	8.3	4.7

[a] Source: U.S. Bureau of Labor Statistics, *Handbook of Labor Statistics 1989*, Bulletin 2340, 1990.

Hispanic males had a higher overall LFPR than white males. However, when standardized by age, the LFPRs of the two groups are almost identical. (The higher overall LFPR of Hispanic men is due to the fact that a higher percentage of them fall within the prime working ages of 25 to 54 than white males.) Moreover, the LFPR of Hispanic males was noticeably higher than the LFPR of black males in both 1980 and 1988. For both these reasons, it seems unlikely that the type of selectivity bias discussed above in comparing the earnings of black and white men would affect the comparison of earnings between Hispanic and white males.

Though LFPRs were about equal between Hispanic and white males, unemployment rates of Hispanic males were about twice as great. This was true for almost every age group. The relative difference in unemployment rates was particularly high among older men (age 45 and over). However, unemployment among Hispanic males was less than that of black males (an overall rate of 8.1 percent in 1988 for the former in comparison to 11.7 percent for the latter).

Among females, the LFPR of Hispanics was lower than that of whites, though the differences narrowed somewhat between 1980 and 1988. This was true for every age group. Hispanic women also experienced a higher incidence of unemployment than white women. This pattern characterized every age group except women over age 65 in 1980. Interestingly, the unemployment rate among Hispanic women was almost the same as among Hispanic men in 1988.

13.2 Migration from the South

Work on racial discrimination has focused on the progress and eventual reversal of fortunes of black Americans. There are four factors that are predominantly responsible for changes in the economic status of black families: (1) migration from the South, (2) progress in schooling, (3) breakup of the black family unit and (4) public policy measures. In this section, we shall focus on the first issue.

At the time of the Civil War, and almost until 1900, 90 percent of black Americans lived in the South, mainly in rural areas. The preponderance of Southern blacks were employed in agriculture. By 1940, the proportion of blacks in the South had declined to 77 percent, in 1960 to 60 percent, and in 1980 to 53 percent, where it remained in 1990.[6] This change represents one of the greatest population migrations in the history of the United States.

Much of the change was driven by the prospects of higher wages in the North and, to some extent, the West. The shifting of the black population out of the low-wage South to the high-wage areas was one of the major factors accounting for their relative wage gains between 1940 and 1960.

---

[6]The sources for the data are: U.S. Bureau of the Census, *Statistical Abstract of the United States,* 1953, 1972, 1981, and 1994.

To see how this works, we will use a simple arithmetic example to illustrate the importance of *weighted averages*. Suppose the black/white earnings ratio is 0.4 in the South and 0.7 in the North and, for simplicity, that whites earn the same in the South as in the North. Also, suppose that about 80 percent of black employees worked in the South, as was the case in 1940. Then, the countrywide average ratio of black to white earnings would be 0.46 [0.8 × 0.4 + (1 − 0.8) × 0.7].

Suppose now that the proportion of blacks working in the South declines from 80 percent to 60 percent (as it did by 1960). Then, even if there were no change in the racial wage ratio in the South and the North, the new black/white earnings ratio would increase to 0.52 [0.6 × 0.4 + (1 − 0.6) × 0.7]. Thus, migration from the South to the North could be an important factor in explaining the relative wage gains made by black workers.

Actually, the explanation is a bit more complicated, because the wages of both white and black workers were initially higher in the North and there were regional changes of the wage gap over time. In fact, there are four separate effects involved, as these data suggest:

Black/White Earnings Ratios for Male Workers

	1940	1960
South	0.424	0.576
Non-South	0.669	0.740
Overall	0.489	0.637

(*Source:* O'Neill [1990, p. 30]. The data are for weekly wages.)

The first, as we just described, is the migration effect, resulting from the higher wages in the North than the South. The second is also a migration effect but derives from the fact that the ratio of earnings between black and white workers was higher in the non-South than the South. These two effects—the higher overall wage levels in the North and the lower racial wage gap in the North—gave an extra boost to black earnings from migrating to the North.

The third results from the gradual convergence in overall wage levels between the South and the North, which occurred between 1940 and 1980. Because a larger proportion of blacks continued to live in the South (despite their migration from it) than of whites, this tended to raise the average earnings of blacks relative to whites. Fourth, within each region (but particularly the South, as the numbers above indicate), the black-white earnings ratio rose. This also helped narrow the overall gap between black and white earnings.

A study by James Gwartney (1970b) analyzed the importance of the migration effect. He reported that in 1939 the income of nonwhite males 25 to

64 years of age residing in urban areas was 41 percent of the level of the equivalent group of white males in the South and 58 percent in the North. In 1959, the corresponding figures were 47 percent in the South and 64 percent in the North. He calculated that the migration of blacks from the South by itself raised the ratio of earnings between the two groups by 3 to 4 percentage points over this period.

Among females, Gwartney reported impressive gains for nonwhites relative to whites between 1949 and 1967, though there was very little gain during the 1940s. Earnings of nonwhite females relative to white females increased by 21 percent during the 1950s and 27 percent during the 1960s. He found that about a third of this gain was due to the migration of nonwhites to the North and the remainder was due to the increasing educational attainment and earnings by educational level of nonwhite females relative to white females.

13.3 PROGRESS IN EDUCATIONAL ATTAINMENT

Perhaps one of the most remarkable developments in the postwar period was the gradual convergence in educational attainment levels between black and white Americans. This, in turn, has been largely a result of the implementation of strong governmental programs to eliminate racial discrimination in this important social dimension.

In the antebellum South, the education of slaves was forbidden by law, so by 1865, the vast majority of Southern blacks were virtually illiterate. After the Civil War, schools for black children were established in the South. By 1880, about one-third of black children were enrolled in schools, compared to about two-thirds of white children, most of whom lived outside the South (see Smith, 1984, and O'Neill, 1990, for more discussion).

Systematic data on schooling attainment date from 1940. Table 13.9 shows the percent of adults (persons 25 years or older) who have completed high school and college. It is first instructive to see the tremendous gains in schooling made by black Americans. In 1940, only 7 percent of black male adults had completed high school, but by 1993, the percentage had risen to almost 70. In 1940, slightly more than one percent of all black male adults had graduated from college, whereas in 1993, the proportion stood at close to 12 percent. Similar gains were made by black women. The proportion who completed high school grew from 8 percent in 1940 to 71 percent in 1993, and the percentage who graduated from college increased from 1 to 12.

Schooling attainment was increasing for all Americans, so it is useful to consider the gains made by blacks in comparison to those made by whites. In 1940, while 7 percent of black male adults finished high school, 24 percent of white male adults graduated high school—more than a three-fold difference. By 1993, the respective proportions were 70 and 82 percent—only a 12 percentage point difference. Likewise, in 1940, 6 percent of white

Table 13.9 Educational Attainment of Persons 25 Years and Older by Race, Hispanic Origin, and Gender, 1940–1993[a]

| Year | Males | | | Females | | | All |
	White	Black[b]	Hispanic[c]	White	Black[b]	Hispanic[c]	
A. *Percent Who Have Completed Four Years of High School or More*							
1940	24.2	6.9		28.1	8.4		24.5
1947	33.2	12.7		36.7	14.5		33.1
1959	44.5	19.6		47.7	21.6		43.7
1970	57.2	32.4		57.6	34.8		55.2
1974	63.6	39.9	38.3	63.0	41.5	34.9	61.2
1980	71.0	51.1	46.4	70.1	51.3	44.1	68.6
1989	78.6	64.2	51.0	78.2	65.0	50.7	76.9
1993	81.8	69.6	52.9	81.3	71.1	53.2	80.5
B. *Percent Who Have Completed Four Years of College or More*							
1940	5.9	1.4		4.0	1.2		4.6
1947	6.6	2.4		4.9	2.6		5.4
1959	11.0	3.8		6.2	2.9		8.1
1970	15.0	4.6		8.6	4.4		11.0
1974	17.7	5.7	7.1	10.6	5.3	4.0	13.3
1980	22.1	7.7	9.7	14.0	8.1	6.2	17.0
1989	25.4	11.7	11.0	18.5	11.9	8.8	21.1
1993	25.7	11.9	9.8	19.7	12.4	8.7	24.8

[a]Source: U.S. Bureau of the Census, Current Population Reports, Series P-20, No. 451, *Educational Attainment in the United States: March 1989 and 1988*, 1991; and U.S. Bureau of the Census, *Statistical Abstract of the United States, 1994*, 1994.
[b]The data are for blacks and other races from 1940 to 1959, for blacks only from 1970 to 1989.
[c]Persons of Hispanic origin may be of any race.

male adults completed college, compared to 1.4 percent of black male adults—a four-fold difference. In 1993, the respective figures were 26 percent and 12 percent—still more than a two-fold difference. Similar trends are evident for black and white females.

Since educational attainment for all adults reflects the experience of different age cohorts over time, it is perhaps more telling to look at the educational performance of young adults. According to data from the 1992 Current Population Survey (see reference in Table 13.1), 85 percent of black males aged 25 to 34 graduated from high school, compared to 86 percent of white males in the same age group. The respective proportions for college graduates (bachelor's degree or better) in 1992 were 12 percent and 28 percent. Similar differences are evident between young black and white females.

Figure 13.5a   Median Years of Schooling, Males (Civilian Labor Force, 1959–1984)

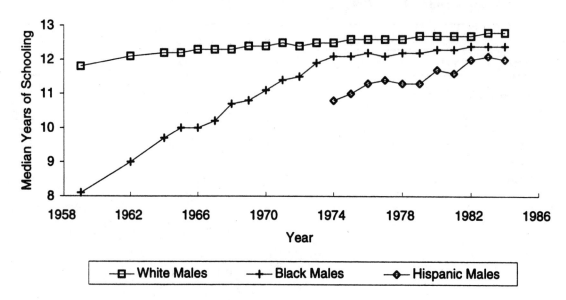

Median schooling levels of the civilian labor force (the schooling attainment of the person ranked in the middle of the distribution) tell a similar story (see Figures 13.5a and 13.5b). In 1959, the median years of schooling for black males who were in the civilian labor force stood at only 8.1 years, compared to 11.8 years for white males—a gap of 3.7 years.[7] By 1984 (the last date of this data series), median schooling of black males had increased to 12.4 years and that of white males to 12.8 years—a gap of only 0.4 year. The difference was even smaller between black and white females in 1984—0.2 year (12.6 and 12.8 years of schooling, respectively).

The schooling attainment of Americans of Hispanic origin also increased. The median years of schooling of Hispanic males in the civilian labor force grew from 10.8 years in 1974 to 12.0 years in 1984 and that of Hispanic females from 11.9 to 12.3. Moreover, according to the data in Table 13.9, both the percent of Hispanics who graduated both high school and college increased substantially between 1974 and 1993. Yet, even by 1993, there was a sizable difference between Hispanics and whites in the percent of adults who had graduated high school (53 percent for Hispanic males versus 81 percent for white males) and who had graduated college (10 percent and 26 percent, respectively).

Thus, from the end of World War II to the present, the educational attainment of black Americans has been catching up to that of white Ameri-

---

[7]The source is: Bureau of Labor Statistics, *Handbook of Labor Statistics*, BLS Bulletin 2217, June 1985.

Figure 13.5b Median Years of Schooling, Females (Civilian Labor Force, 1959–1984)

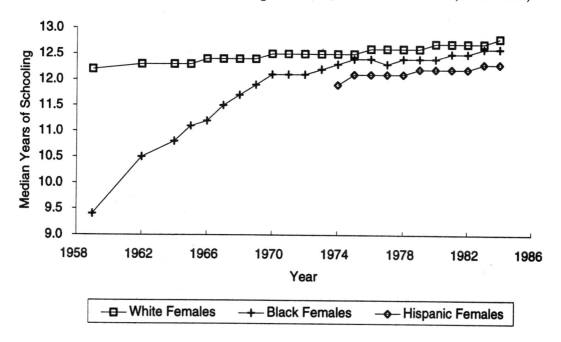

cans. This is particularly evident for median schooling and the percent who have graduated from high school. However, there is still a sizable gap in college graduation rates between whites and blacks. This difference was particularly important during the 1980s, since other evidence (see Chapter 9) suggests that demand patterns for workers have been favoring the college-educated relative to high school graduates. Moreover, Hispanic Americans still lagged behind white Americans in both high school graduation rates and college graduation rates.

The Role of Educational Gains on the Earnings Gap

Several studies have investigated the effects of the convergence of educational attainment between blacks and whites on the racial earnings gap. James Gwartney (1970a), using 1960 Census of Population data, reported that in 1959 the ratio of nonwhite to white median income was 58 percent for males living in urban areas. He estimated that differences in educational attainment accounted for 9 to 12 percentage points of the income difference, while differences in scholastic achievement accounted for another 12 to 18 percentage points. He concluded that in 1959 about half of the income disparity between nonwhite and white males was attributable to differences in educational attainment and achievement on scholastic aptitude tests.[8]

David Rasmussen (1970) analyzed the change in the relative income of nonwhite men over the period from 1939 to 1964. On the basis of Census of Population data, his figures indicated that the ratio of nonwhite to white incomes increased from 0.41 in 1939 to 0.54 in 1948 and then to 0.57 in 1964. On the basis of regression analysis on the 1948–1964 data, he found that, once cyclical fluctuations are removed,[9] the trend increase in the income ratio was about one percentage point every three years, or a gain of 0.052 over the 1948–1964 period. Of the 5.2 percentage point gain, 3.7 points could be attributed to rising educational attainment of nonwhite males relative to white males, with the remaining 1.5 percentage points the residual. Rasmussen concluded that the improvement in the relative position of nonwhite males over the 1948–1967 period was primarily due to their improved educational achievement. He also suggested that the reduction in the earnings gap was also partly attributable to a decline in discrimination against nonwhites (the unexplained residual).

A different conclusion was reached by Orley Ashenfelter (1970), who investigated the 1950–1966 period. He found little relative gain in the incomes of nonwhite males. For full-time employees, for example, the income ratio was 0.635 in 1955 and 0.632 in 1966. He estimated that over this period, the average quality of the nonwhite labor force, as estimated by its educational attainment, was growing at a rate of 0.6 to 0.7 percent per year, while that of the white labor force was growing at about 0.3 to 0.4 percent per year. Thus, in contradistinction to Rasmussen, Ashenfelter concluded that the relative increase in schooling for nonwhite males explained the total increase and more in the change in the earnings gap. Thus, he surmised that there was actually a slight increase in discrimination against nonwhite males over this period, which depressed their relative earnings between 0.1 and 0.4 percentage points per year.

On the other hand, among females, he found a significant reduction in the degree of discrimination. There was a substantial rise in the income of black women relative to white women. In 1955, for example, the ratio was 0.57 and in 1964 was 0.71. Moreover, though there were gains in the educational attainment of black women relative to white women, these gains accounted for only a small part of the closing of the earnings gap. He concluded that a secular decline in discrimination against black females ac-

---

[8]He also controlled for three other productivity-related factors: (1) age, (2) region of the country, and (3) city size. After controlling for these factors as well as educational attainment and scholastic achievement, he found that still unaccounted for was about one-third of the earnings gap. He inferred that this remaining earnings gap may be the result of employment discrimination.

[9]The cyclical adjustment was motivated by the finding that blacks do better relative to whites during periods of tight labor markets (low unemployment) and worse during periods of slack labor markets (high unemployment). The rationale is that when labor markets are slack, employers are more likely to screen good jobs on the basis of race and unions are likely to discriminate more to preserve their control over scarce jobs.

counted for a gain of 3.0 percentage points per year in the earnings ratio between nonwhite and white female workers.

Quality of Schooling

Not only do differences in schooling attainment affect relative earnings between blacks and whites but so do differences in schooling *quality*. Defining and measuring schooling quality is a difficult task, and economists have used resources devoted both to schooling (an "input" measure) and schooling achievement, as reflected in achievement test scores (an "output" measure), as indices of school quality.

As we noted above, by the latter part of the nineteenth century, school enrollment rates for blacks were about half the level of whites. Moreover, as June O'Neill (1990) reports, there was also a large difference in quality between schools attended by black and white children. Part of this was due to the fact that almost 90 percent of blacks lived in the South. The Civil War brought great destruction to the Southern economy, and the South could not devote much resources to schooling. In 1880, expenditures on schooling per person was *three* times as great in the North as in the South.

The other part was due to the fact that schooling systems were segregated in the South, with southern states devoting more resources to white schools than to black schools. Even in 1920 it was estimated that Southern black children had one-third fewer school days than Southern white children. Similar discrepancies existed in teacher salaries and student-teacher ratios.

However, by 1953, most of the disparity in resources devoted to black and white schools had disappeared. In that year, the length of school term for black Southern students was 96 percent that of white Southern students; the teacher-student ratios were almost equal in black and white schools; and teacher salaries in black schools stood at 90 percent of the corresponding white level.[10] By 1965, the Coleman Report (1966) reported that differences in resources devoted to black and white schools were negligible.

Although black-white differences in educational attainment have declined substantially over time, significant differences in education achievement remain. These are reflected in differentials in achievement test scores, which, in turn, are likely to be related to remaining differences in school quality and to differences in family background.

Data on achievement test results date from World War I and stem from the Armed Forces Qualifications Test (AFQT), administered by the military for testing recruits. The results of these tests indicate that the difference in test scores between white and Southern black draftees *of the same educational level* was very large around 1918. According to O'Neill (1990), among men

---

[10] In the following year, 1954, the famous Supreme Court case, *Brown v. Board of Education of Topeka, Kansas,* ruled that school desegregation was unlawful. See Section 13.5.

Chapter 13   Racial Discrimination: Progress and Reversal for Black Americans   485

who had attended four years of elementary school, Southern blacks scored, on average, only 36 percent the level of white men. On the other hand, the median score of Northern black draftees at the fourth grade level was 85 percent of the level scored by white males. Such differences likely reflect the very inferior schools attended by Southern blacks during the early part of the twentieth century and the better schools attended by Northern blacks.

The differentials in test scores did narrow for a time. During the mid-1950s, the ratio of mean test scores between (both Southern and Northern) black males and white males of the same schooling level who took the test had risen to about 50 percent. However, between the 1950s and the 1980s, there was relatively little additional gain on test scores by blacks over whites. This, of course, seems surprising in light of the other evidence presented above that school resources devoted to black students were quickly converging on those for white students.

We have no good explanation of why test scores of black males with the same educational attainment as white males have remained lower, even up to the present. Part of it may reflect the role of family background. White children have, on average, better educated parents than black children, and educational performance of students is positively related to the education of parents. (See Section 7.4 for a discussion of the role of family background on educational attainment.)

Returns to Schooling for Blacks and Whites*

Another way of characterizing differences in schooling quality and achievement is through the returns to education (see Chapters 6 and 7). As has been noted, the greater average educational attainment of white males relative to black males has been one major source of earnings inequality between the two groups. A related source is the lower *rate of return* to schooling for blacks—that is, the fact that black males receive less gain in earnings from additional years of schooling than white males. A number of studies have investigated this phenomenon. Three early studies—Giora Hanoch (1967), Lester Thurow (1969), and Randall Weiss (1970)—all found on the basis of 1960 Census of Population data that the returns to schooling for nonwhites were generally lower and considerably more erratic than those for whites.

Two later studies looked at the same issue with 1967 data for the United States, and some interesting changes were found. Leonard Weiss and Jeffrey Williamson (1972) discovered a significant shift in the earnings function for blacks between 1960 and 1967. In particular, schooling for black males in 1967 appeared to generate returns that were as large as those received by white males in that year. This increased payoff occurred at almost every educational level.

Finis Welch (1973a) reached somewhat different conclusions, though he also used the 1960 Census of Population data and the same 1967 data. His major finding was that black males who entered the work force in more recent periods fared better relative to white males than earlier entrants. Part of the reason for this was a convergence in educational level by race for younger workers. For example, black males in the labor force with 1 to 4 years of experience averaged 11.1 years of schooling, in comparison to a white average of 12.8, while for those with 13 to 25 years of experience, blacks averaged 8.8 years of schooling and whites 11.4. Moreover, there was a significant gain in the return to schooling for younger blacks in comparison to older blacks. In fact, in 1967, the rate of return to schooling was higher for young blacks than for young whites, while the rate of return to schooling for older blacks was significantly lower than for older whites.

In addition, the rate of return to schooling for the same cohort or "vintage" remained unchanged between 1960 and 1967.[11] Thus, the overall gains made by blacks in the payoffs to schooling between 1960 and 1967 were due to a "vintage effect"—namely, that younger blacks who had high rates of return to schooling were entering the labor force, while older blacks with very low returns to schooling were retiring from the labor force. Welch concluded that the reason for the gains in returns to schooling made by young blacks relative to young whites during the 1960s was most likely due to a decline in discrimination.

With the appearance of 1970 Census of Population data, several studies were conducted to ascertain whether blacks had improved their relative economic position over the decade of the 1960s. Richard Freeman (1973b) reported a continued narrowing of the income gap between whites and blacks. For females, the income ratio between blacks and whites rose from 0.57 in 1960 to 0.86 in 1970; for males, it rose from 0.58 to 0.64; and for males aged 20 to 24, it increased from 0.67 to 0.82. Among college graduates, rough equality in starting salaries between black and white males and between black and white females was attained by 1970. Moreover, he estimated that by 1970 the rate of return to a college education was actually somewhat greater for black graduates than for white graduates.

Joan Haworth, James Gwartney, and Charles Haworth (1975) found that the median earnings ratio between nonwhite and white males aged 25 to 64 increased from 0.57 to 0.66 between 1960 and 1970, or by 17 percent. They asked whether this gain was from the increased productivity of blacks during this period or reduced discrimination. They found three main contributory factors to the gain made by blacks during the 1960s. First, between 6 and 8 percentage points of this gain were attributable to the retirement from the labor force of older nonwhites with low productivity combined with the entry of younger better-prepared nonwhites (the "vintage effect"). Second, an additional 2 percentage points were due to relative gains made by nonwhites in schooling and experience levels. Third, the remaining 6 percentage points were attributable to a relative gain made by nonwhites in the *return* to schooling and other forms of human capital, and this gain, they concluded,

---

[11] That is to say, the rate of return for black males who were 30 years old in 1967 was the same as it was for the same group or cohort who were 23 years old in 1960.

was most likely due to a lessening of employment discrimination against blacks.

In a third study, James Smith and Finis Welch (1977a) also found that the relative income of black males significantly improved during the 1960s. All experience and schooling groups shared in these gains. However, though all black schooling and experience groups improved on average relative to their white counterparts, the largest gains were made by the most educated and the most recent entrants and the smallest by the least educated and the oldest cohorts. Significant gains were also made in the level of schooling completion of black males relative to white males.

Further evidence on the vintage effect was garnered by Greg Duncan and Saul Hoffman (1983) for the 1970s. Using the Panel Survey of Income Dynamics, they found that among males of ages 25 to 54, the ratio in mean hourly wages between blacks and whites increased from 64 percent in 1967 to 75 percent in 1978. For ages 25 to 34, the hourly wage ratio increased from 72 percent to 81 percent. They found that almost half of the relative earnings gain among all black workers was due to the departure from the labor market of older, lower-paid black workers and the improved relative earnings position of young black males entering the labor force.

Interestingly, they found little effect on relative earnings from the increased educational attainment of younger black males. The reason is that even though the black workers in entering cohorts were better educated than older black men, so also were entering cohorts of white males relative to older white males. As a result, the net contribution of increasing schooling among black males to relative earnings was negligible. However, the continuing improvement in the quality of schools attended by black males was likely responsible for the increasing relative earnings of the youngest black workers (relative to the youngest white workers) entering the labor force.

David Card and Alan Krueger (1992) concurred with these findings. Their focus was on the change in the quality of schooling in 18 segregated southern states between 1915 and 1966. They constructed various measures of schooling quality, including data on student-teacher ratios, annual teacher pay, and length of term for both white and black schools in these states. They found that schooling quality in the South increased substantially over this period, particularly after the 1954 Supreme Court school desegregation decision of *Brown v. Board of Education of Topeka, Kansas* (see Section 13.5). Card and Krueger estimated that about 20 percent of the narrowing of the black-white earnings gap between 1960 and 1980 could be ascribed to improvements in the quality of black schools in the South.

John Bound and Richard Freeman (1991) reported that advances made by black males, particularly younger ones, reversed during the 1980s. Their sample consisted of young males with less than 10 years of "potential experience" (workers in their twenties and early thirties).[12] They calculated that the percentage difference in earnings between blacks and whites in this

---

[12] Technically, this consists of workers who left school less than 10 years before the sample date.

sample, after controlling for differences in education and experience, increased from 6 percent in 1976 to 18 percent in 1989. In other words, the relative earnings of young black men declined substantially during the 1980s, even after controlling for changes in human capital. The authors do not feel that changes in school quality were responsible for the reversal. Rather, they put stress on changes in technology and resulting shifts in industrial and occupational demand patterns, particularly those emanating from the decline in the U.S. manufacturing base ("structural effects," as we discussed in Chapter 9).

June O'Neill (1990), using data from the National Longitudinal Survey of Youths, which has information on earnings, education, and AFQT scores, investigated the role of academic achievement in the earnings gap between black and white males. Her main result was that AFQT scores exerted a significant effect on earnings, even after holding schooling level constant. Moreover, the effect of AFQT scores was greater for black males than white males.[13]

O'Neill then analyzed the effects of differences in achievement test results on the black-white wage gap for males aged 22 to 29 in 1987. Before adjustment for any characteristics, the ratio in hourly wages between blacks and whites stood at 82.9 percent. When adjustments were made for different regions of residence, schooling levels, and potential work experience, the ratio increased to 87.7 percent. When AFQT test results were added, the wage ratio increased to 95.5 percent.

She concluded that difference in skills, as reflected in achievement test results, between black and white workers was a major source of the remaining wage gap between the two groups. Such skill differentials appeared to have become more important during the 1980s by the apparent shift in demand patterns favoring the more highly skilled workers. This change helps to account for the failure of the earnings of black men to gain on those of white men during the 1980s.[14]

Hispanic Americans*

Research on the economic status of Americans of Hispanic origin is more limited. This is partly because the Census Bureau introduced a separate category for this group only in 1972. The work has tended to focus on the role of English proficiency (or the lack thereof) on earnings differences between Hispanic Americans and white non-Hispanic Americans. Moreover, since Hispanics can be either white or black, these studies also control for racial differences.

Three studies that look at this issue are Cordelia Reimers (1983) and Walter McManus (1985 and 1990). They reach somewhat different

---

[13]Interestingly, measures of the quality of schools attended by the individuals in the sample, such as student-teacher ratios and the percent of school faculty with advanced degrees, had no significant effects on the individual's earnings.

[14]A similar conclusion was reached by Nan Maxwell (1994), using the same data source and the same measure of scholastic achievement.

conclusions. The first study used data from the 1976 Survey of Income and Education. The sample was large enough so that Reimers was able to divide the Hispanic population into five groups by country of origin: (1) Cuba, (2) Mexico, (3) Puerto Rico, (4) South and Central America, and (5) others. The purpose of the study was to determine what proportion of the lower wages received by Hispanic males relative to non-Hispanic white males was due to explainable differences in labor market characteristics, such as education, (potential) work experience, region of residence, U.S. military service, disability status, date of immigration to the United States, race, and fluency in English, and what portion was a residual and thus presumably due to discrimination.

Results varied by country of origin among the Hispanic population. For Hispanics of Cuban and Mexican origin, differences in labor market characteristics explained almost their entire wage gap relative to white, non-Hispanic males. Among Hispanics from Puerto Rico, Central and South America, and other places, differences in labor market characteristics accounted for, at most, half the difference in wages, with the remainder presumably due to discrimination. Interesting, the lack of English language skills was found to explain part of the Hispanic/non-Hispanic wage gap but not a very substantial part.

The second study, by McManus (1985), used the same data as Reimers and controlled for essentially the same labor market characteristics—education, work experience, region of residence, race, ethnicity, and place of birth. One interesting difference in McManus's specification is that he also included a variable measuring proficiency in Spanish, as well as proficiency in English. He found a much larger effect on the Hispanic/non-Hispanic wage gap from the lack of proficiency in English, which explained about one-third of the wage difference. He also calculated that almost all of the difference in wages usually associated with ethnicity, nativity, and time in the United States can be explained by the lack of English proficiency. Differences in labor market characteristics, as well as discrimination, accounted for the remaining gap. He also found that men who were proficient in both English and Spanish (bilingual proficiency) earned more than those who were proficient in English alone.

In a follow-up study, McManus (1990) found that the wage gap between Hispanics who are proficient in English and Hispanics who lack English-speaking skills was much lower if they lived in areas that were largely populated by Hispanics and much higher in other areas. The wage gap was 11 percent if they resided in areas that were at least 75 percent Hispanic and 26 percent if the areas were only 10 percent or less Hispanic.

More recent work has tended to look at the progress of Hispanic workers in terms of the economic effects of immigration. Some results compiled by George Borjas (1994) are rather startling. In 1970, immigrants from Mexico aged 25 to 34 who were newly arrived in the United States earned, on average, 27 percent less than Mexican-American natives. In 1990, the difference had expanded to 34 percent. For other Hispanic immigrants (in age group 25–34), the differential also widened, from 16 to 28 percent. One factor explaining this change is that the educational attainment of arriving Hispanic immigrants has been falling over time relative to that of native-born Hispanics.

13.4 CHANGES IN FAMILY STRUCTURE AMONG BLACK AMERICANS

Though there has been substantial catch-up between blacks and whites in terms of labor earnings for employed workers, buoyed largely by the rising educational levels of young black workers entering the labor market and rising returns to education, large differences persist between black and white family incomes. As we noted above, the ratio of median family incomes between blacks and whites peaked in 1975, at 62 percent, and declined thereafter, reaching 54 percent in 1993. One reason, as we discussed above, is the dropout of black male workers, particularly older ones, from the labor force. A second, and equally important, reason is the changing composition of the black family.

Table 13.10 highlights some of the changes in the structure of both black and white families since 1960. Because of the availability of Census data on which these tabulations are based, results are shown for both men and women in age group 15 to 44. There have been some dramatic changes in the living arrangements of black families since 1960. In 1960, over half of all black women (in age group 15 to 44) were married, but by 1988 the figure had fallen to under 30 percent. Trends are similar for black men: the proportion of this group that was married fell from 48 percent in 1960 to 31 percent. The most pronounced changes occurred during the 1970s, with changes during the 1980s relatively modest by comparison. The main reason for this change was that the percent of both black women and men who never married rose substantially: among black women, from 28 percent in 1960 to 52 percent in 1988, and among black men, from 40 to 58 percent. As a result, the proportion of female-headed households (with no husband present) rose from 31 percent of all family units in 1970 to 44 percent in 1988.

Such changes in the marital arrangements of black adults had similar implications for the living arrangements of black children. The most notable change is that the proportion of children living with two parents fell from two-thirds in 1960 to under 40 percent in 1988. Moreover, the proportion of black children living with a parent who had never married skyrocketed from 2 percent in 1960 to almost 30 percent in 1988. Over the same period, the proportion of black children born to a single mother rose from 23 percent to more than 60 percent.

When we compare family incomes between blacks and whites, the important issue is not so much the absolute change in the composition of black families but the change in black families relative to that of white families. There were similar trends in the living arrangements of white families,

Table 13.10 Composition of Families by Type and Race, 1960–1988[a] (percent)

	1960	1970	1980	1988
I. *Black Families*				
A. Percent of black women, 15–44				
1. Married, spouse present	51.4	44.4	31.2	29.1
2. Divorced, separated, widowed	20.3	18.1	20.9	18.7
3. Never married	28.3	37.5	47.9	52.2
B. Percent of black men, 15–44				
1. Married, spouse present	47.7	42.2	33.1	30.9
2. Divorced, separated, widowed	12.3	10.1	10.8	10.9
3. Never married	40.0	47.7	56.1	58.2
C. Percent of black children living with				
1. Married couple	67.0	58.5	42.2	38.6
2. Divorced, separated, or widowed parent	19.8	27.3	32.7	24.7
3. Never married parent	2.1	4.5	13.1	29.3
4. Not with a parent	11.1	9.7	12.0	7.4
D. Percent of black families who have				
1. Female householder, no husband present	—	30.5	41.7	43.5
2. All others	—	69.5	58.3	56.5
II. *White Families*				
A. Percent of white women, 15–44				
1. Married, spouse present	69.1	64.1	56.5	54.5
2. Divorced, separated, widowed	6.9	6.1	10.7	12.5
3. Never married	24.0	29.8	32.8	33.0
B. Percent of white men, 15–44				
1. Married, spouse present	61.8	58.6	50.9	48.5
2. Divorced, separated, widowed	4.5	3.6	6.8	9.0
3. Never married	33.7	37.8	42.3	42.5
C. Percent of white children living with				
1. Married couple	90.9	89.5	82.7	78.9
2. Divorced, separated, or widowed parent	7.1	8.5	14.0	15.5
3. Never married parent	0.1	0.2	1.1	3.4
4. Not with a parent	1.9	1.8	2.2	2.2
D. Percent of white families who have				
1. Female householder, no husband present	8.9	9.5	11.9	13.0
2. All others	91.1	90.5	88.1	87.0

[a] Sources: Ellwood and Crane (1990); U.S. Bureau of the Census, Current Population Reports, Series P-60, No. 168, *Money Income and Poverty Status in the United States: 1989*, 1990. The sum of percentages in each panel is 100 percent.

but the magnitude of these changes was not nearly as great. Between 1960 and 1988, the proportion of white women in age group 15 to 44 who were married fell from 69 to 55 percent, but the main reason was an increase in divorce and separation, not a decline in marriages. For them, also, the most dramatic change was during the 1970s. Similar trends are evident for white men. Still, in 1988, the percent of white women who were married was almost double the percentage of black women (54 percent versus 29 percent), and the percent of black female-headed households was over three times the proportion among white households (44 percent versus 13 percent).

Perhaps the most telling difference between black and white families is the living arrangements of children. The percent of white children living with two parents declined from 91 percent in 1960 to 79 percent in 1988. However, in 1988, the proportion of children living with two parents was more than double for white families (79 percent) than black families (39 percent). Moreover, the proportion of white children living with a never married parent was much lower (3 percent) than for black children (29 percent). Perhaps these changes more than anything else help explain why black family income has not kept up with white family income. (See Ellwood and Crane, 1990, for a more extended treatment of these changes.)

These implications are reflected in data both on poverty and family incomes. In 1989, the poverty rate (based on family count) among black female-headed households (no husband present) was 47 percent, compared to 12 percent among black married-couple families (almost a *four-fold* difference). The comparable statistics for white families are 25 percent for female-headed households and 5 percent for married-couple households.[15] Among black female-headed households with children, the poverty rate was an astounding 54 percent. Likewise, within the black population, the median income of female-headed households was much lower than the median income of married-couple households—$12,200 versus $30,800 in 1989. Within the white population, the difference in median incomes between the two household groups was smaller—$20,100 versus $39,300. As a result, the ratio of median family incomes between black and white families was higher among married-couple families, 78 percent, than among female-headed households, 64 percent.[16] Thus, among both black and white families, there is a close correspondence between incomes and poverty status and marital status. The lower overall median income and higher overall poverty rates for black families than white families are due, in large measure, to a higher percentage of female-headed households in the black population.

Three reasons have been advanced to help explain this large increase in the number of female-headed households in the black community. The first is the large increase in unemployment rates among black youths. As we can see in Table 13.4, the unemployment rate among black men under the age of 20 almost tripled between 1955 and 1975, from 13 to 38 percent, and has

[15] The source for these figures is: U.S. Bureau of the Census (1990a).
[16] The source for these figures is: U.S. Bureau of the Census (1990a).

remained at this level ever since. Second, the incarceration rate of young black men has also increased. In 1992, about half a million black males were serving time in jail or prison, and an approximately equal number were on parole. These two facts, taken together, suggest that the availability of marriageable black men who are capable of supporting a family is small relative to the number of black women who desire a family. The third is that blacks have a more matriarchal culture than whites, so that there is less social disapprobation attached to a single mother raising children on her own.[17]

13.5 PUBLIC POLICY AND DISCRIMINATION

Spurred in large measure by the Civil Rights movement of the 1950s and 1960s, the federal government has instituted several major programs to combat discrimination since 1960. In this section, we shall briefly describe some of these major efforts undertaken by the federal government, particularly as they relate to labor market discrimination. Then, we shall consider evidence about whether these programs have been effective in reducing discrimination against black Americans.

Public Policy Programs

Most of the cornerstone legislation and executive orders were put into place during the 1960s. However, the Supreme Court issued an important decision in 1954; it is considered to be a major stimulus to the subsequent programs enacted by the legislative and executive branches of the U.S. government.

Brown v. Board of Education of Topeka, Kansas, 1954   In this landmark case, the Supreme Court of the United States ruled that segregated schools are inherently unequal and therefore unconstitutional. As we discussed in Section 13.3, the evidence was ambiguous about whether, in fact, schools attended by black children were receiving fewer resources than those attended by white students. However, the Supreme Court argued that segregated schools were by their very nature *inherently* unequal, creating a feeling of inferiority among the black children who attended them. Even spending the same number of dollars per pupil in black schools as in white schools could never create equal educational opportunity for black children.[18]

The Supreme Court, in effect, took a psychological and sociological viewpoint on the issue of equality in educational opportunity. The mere act of segregation would create low esteem among black children, and as a result, they would likely perform more poorly and have lower expectations than white children.

---

[17] See Julius Wilson (1987) for more discussion of these points.

[18] Also, even if dollars spent per pupil on education were the same for whites and blacks, it may still not be the case that educational resources are the same. For example, inner-city schools may be forced to spend a much larger share of their budget on security measures and other nonclassroom functions than suburban or rural schools.

This decision led to major efforts to integrate schools around the nation, most notably (and most politically explosive) through school busing. The preponderance of subsequent evidence indicates that the *academic performance* of black children was enhanced by school integration (see, for example, the study of the Congressional Budget Office, 1977). Part of the improved performance of black children was from their exposure to white children, whose academic motivation was stronger and whose educational and employment goals were greater. Black students were more motivated in school by the belief that their opportunities were greater and that there was a payoff to success in school.

Executive Order 10925, 1961 Issued by President John Kennedy, this order was the first to require federal contractors (firms that receive procurement contracts from the federal government) to take affirmative action to alleviate discrimination and to provide specific penalties, including the termination of a contract, if the company failed to do so. Though the intent was notable, this order was not effectively enforced.

Equal Pay Act, 1963 A 1963 amendment was made to the Fair Labor Standards Act of 1938, which required that females receive the same pay as men for the same work. Known as the "Equal Pay Act," this amendment was designed to eliminate wage differentials based solely on gender. We shall discuss this act in more detail in the next chapter.

Civil Rights Act of 1964 The major piece of federal legislation prohibiting labor market discrimination was Title VII of the Civil Rights Act of 1964. Title VII states that it is illegal for an employer to discriminate against any individual on the basis of sex, race, color, religion, or national origin in regard to employment opportunities or compensation. The law originally applied to private businesses, labor unions, and employment agencies. In 1972, it was amended to apply to all levels of government and educational institutions and to all firms and unions with at least 15 members. This piece of legislation was one of the cornerstones of Lyndon Johnson's War on Poverty.

This law intended to end discriminatory hiring practices, as well as pay differentials based on race or sex. The Civil Rights Act set up the Equal Employment Opportunity Commission (EEOC) to administer and enforce the provisions of Title VII. The EEOC's original role was to seek voluntary compliance by employers on a case-by-case basis. Such voluntary compliance took the form of a consent agreement, where the employer agreed to refrain from further discrimination and to correct any underrepresentation of females or minorities. With a 1977 amendment, the EEOC was given the added power of taking court action on behalf of complainants. However, with its somewhat limited budget, the EEOC has usually suffered under an enormous backlog of cases.

Executive Order 11246, 1965 This Executive Order was issued by President Johnson and was designed to prevent discrimination by employers holding contracts with the federal government. This order forbids any federal contractor with a contract of $50,000 or more and 50 or more employees from discriminating on the basis of race, sex, religion, or national origin. It also requires them to take affirmative action to remedy any underrepresentation. The Office of Federal Contract Compliance (OFCC) of the Department of Labor was set up to enforce this order. In 1968, the OFCC established the requirement that the contractors must develop a written affirmative action plan containing target goals and a timetable to meet these goals to remedy deficiencies in equal opportunity employment. By 1972, standardization procedures were set up to identify underutilization of minorities and females in specified job categories and to issue progress reports on meeting goals.

The 1965 executive order, unlike its 1961 predecessor, has had considerable effect on the development of affirmative action plans by government contractors. Moreover, the requirement to develop a specific affirmative action plan has often led to the establishment of numerical goals for the hiring of minority workers into specific job categories. This, in turn, has led to the charge that *quotas* were being used to enforce the provisions of the order, and there is continuing controversy today over this charge. On the one hand, many have contended that unless specific numerical targets are issued and enforced, the executive order would lack teeth and be virtually unenforceable. On the other hand, the requirement of numerical standards for *equal opportunity* often leads to reliance on *equal results*, rather than equal opportunity. Indeed, some have contended that affirmative action plans tend to promote "reverse discrimination" (that is, preference for minority workers over white workers). Public policy makers are still unsure whether it is possible to enforce equality of opportunity except through the stipulation of numerical goals.

The OFCC has considerably more power than the EEOC. Under Title VII of the Civil Rights Act of 1964, affirmative action can be ordered only by a court and only after an employer has been found guilty of a legal violation. The OFCC, on the other hand, can order that an affirmative action plan be drawn up without the intervention of the court and can require the cancellation of all government contracts in the event of noncompliance. However, few government contracts have been canceled by the OFCC, and like the EEOC, the OFCC relies mainly on voluntary compliance by the offending employer.

The Effectiveness of the Antidiscrimination Programs

Title VII of the Civil Rights Act of 1964 and Executive Order 11246 are the two major legal instruments implemented to end employment discrimination. Since enforcement of both has and continues to be lax and reliance is made on voluntary compliance, one might think that its effect on reducing discrimination has also been slight. Yet, the preponderance of the evidence, though there are some dissenters, suggests just the opposite—namely, that employment discrimination against blacks has decreased since 1960, and this has been due, in part, to affirmative action programs.

Civil Rights Act of 1964 Richard Freeman (1981a and 1981b) examined the effects of the Civil Rights Act of 1964 on differences in racial earnings between 1964 and 1975. He concluded that significant gains were made by black workers after 1964. In the first of the two papers, he found that the ratio of mean annual earnings between black and white male workers increased from 0.59 in 1964 to 0.73 in 1975 and the ratio for year-round, full-time workers increased from 0.68 to 0.78. Younger workers made the most gain. By 1975, the ratio of median income between black and white year-round, full-time workers was 0.85 for those in the 20–24 age group, 0.81 for those aged 25–34, and 0.70 for those aged 45–54. Among females, virtual parity had been reached between black and whites by 1975. Moreover, among college graduates of both sexes, virtual parity in starting salaries between blacks and whites had been reached by 1970.

Freeman then separated out the influences of schooling, experience, home environment, and other productivity-related and background characteristics on the black-white earnings differential from the effect of labor market discrimination (the residual). He found a continuing reduction in the importance of labor market discrimination as an explanation of black-white earnings differences since 1964. Among the young, in particular, he calculated that background characteristics, such as parents' education, became a more important impediment to achieving black-white economic equality than labor market discrimination. Finally, he argued that, though blacks had made economic gains relative to whites prior to 1964, the rate of gain accelerated after 1964. He attributed this fact to the Civil Rights Act and other government antidiscrimination initiatives. In the follow-up study, Freemen (1981b) concluded that the relative gains made by blacks during the early 1970s were not dissipated during the sluggish economy of the late 1970s. Looking at 1979 data, he estimated that the relative earnings gains made by black workers between 1964 and 1975 were maintained through 1979, though no improvement was made beyond the 1975 level.

James Smith (1978) disputed the conclusions of the Freeman studies. He also found major advances made by black workers relative to white workers between 1960 and 1975. He presented two reasons for the gains made by blacks. The first is the vintage effect. Younger cohorts of black workers entered the labor market with larger stocks of human capital relative to white workers than older black cohorts did when they began work. This resulted in a convergence in the degree of educational attainment between black and white workers. A second factor is the narrowing of regional wage differentials between the non-South and the South, which has a large proportion of the black population. He concluded that the gains made by black workers were due to these two effects and the Civil Rights Act of 1964 did little to cause the improved position of blacks.

Charles Brown (1982), in an assessment of the conflicting evidence, asserted that most of the reported findings indicated that the economic position of blacks improved more rapidly since 1964 than would have been expected on the basis of past trends, general business conditions, or the increased educational attainment of blacks. However, the evidence does not demonstrate that this gain made by blacks was due to the work of the EEOC or the OFCC.

Two other studies argued that the Civil Rights Act had little effect on the relative gains made by black workers since the 1960s. Indeed, they both disputed that blacks had, in fact, made gains since 1964. The first, by Edward Lazear (1979), claimed that the finding that the wage differential between young black and white workers disappeared by 1972 is illusory. He argued that the full compensation a worker receives is the sum of the monetary wage plus the amount of on-the-job training (OJT) the worker receives. His results indicated that the Civil Rights Act led employers to give blacks higher monetary wages but lower OJT.

Computations made by Lazear showed that the total compensation differential between nonwhites and whites remained about constant between 1960 and 1974, while the wage differential narrowed. This meant that young black workers were effectively being shortchanged in the amount of OJT they received. As a result, as the cohort ages, the earnings of white workers will increase even more rapidly than in the past relative to black workers of the same age. He concluded that government antidiscrimination programs may have produced parity in starting salaries between black and white workers but have had no effect on differences in lifetime earnings.

Keith Hylton (1984), in a comment on the Lazear paper, disputed the results reported in the paper. Estimates of lifetime earnings depend on both the current wage of a person and the *slope* of the age-earnings profile (that is, the rate of growth of earnings with age) over the person's work life (see Section 7.1). He used the National Longitudinal Survey to reestimate the slope of the age-earnings profiles for both black and white workers. His main conclusion was that there was no statistical difference in the slope coefficients for black and white workers. As a result, he inferred that the gap in lifetime earnings between black and white workers did narrow after 1964.

The second argument is the censuring or dropout argument. Richard Butler and James Heckman (1978) argued that the observed relative increase in the earnings of black male workers is a statistical artifact, which essentially reflects a decrease in the labor force participation rate of black men (a decline that Freeman himself found puzzling in light of supposed increases in the demand for black workers resulting from the government antidiscrimination programs). They argued that along with government antidiscrimination programs came an expansion of welfare programs during the 1960s, which served to draw discouraged black male workers out of the labor force in large numbers (hence the decrease in their labor force participation rates). Since these discouraged workers were largely low-wage workers, their exodus from the work force resulted in a rise in the observed black to white average earnings ratio. They concluded that after controlling for such labor market dropouts, the apparent effect of government antidiscrimination programs in reducing the black-white earnings gap disappeared.

Several later papers reexamined the Butler-Heckman censuring argument. Charles Brown (1984) used cross-sectional data to recalculate the black-white earnings ratio, correcting for dropouts from the labor force. Even after this adjustment, the black-white ratio of median earnings still showed an increase after 1964, though the corrected trend was only half as large for black males as the uncorrected trend and somewhere between half and four-fifths as large for black females.

Wayne Vroman (1986), using the March 1978 Current Population Survey and earnings history records compiled by the Social Security Administration, also examined the labor market dropout effect over the 1964–1973 period. He drew three main conclusions from his study. First, although labor market reduction was greater among black males than white males, there was no acceleration of this trend after 1964, the period of improvement in the black-white earnings ratio. Second, both black and white men were receiving increased government transfers over this period, and no unusually large increase was observed for black men between 1964 and 1973. Third, the sample selection explanation based on increasing welfare availability for black men for the increased black-white earnings ratio over this period was not supported by the data.

What about the 1980s? As we discussed in Section 13.1, most studies found that the earnings of black workers, both male and female, had made substantial progress relative to white workers during the 1960s and 1970s. However, during the 1980s, further gains were slight, and indeed, for some educational groups, the relative earnings of black workers actually declined.

Some economists contended that the failure of black workers to make further progress during the 1980s was due to the lack of commitment on the part of the Reagan and Bush administrations to enforce Title VII of the Civil Rights Act. However, in a careful analysis of the data, James Smith (1993) found that the lack of further progress of black male workers could be explained almost entirely by labor market changes. First, during the 1980s, as we saw in Section 13.3, there was a slowdown in the narrowing of racial disparities in educational attainment. Second, there was a large increase in the return to education, particularly to a college degree (see Chapter 7). These two factors together explain most of the lack of further closure of the racial wage gap.

Affirmative Action Programs

A series of studies, carried out by Jonathan Leonard (1984a, 1984b, 1984c, 1985a, 1985b, 1986, 1990), examined the impact of affirmative action plans on the labor market success of minority workers. The focus was on the effectiveness of Executive Order 11246. Since this order applies only to federal contractors, one way of assessing its impact is to compare the progress of minority workers at firms with federal contracts with establishments that did not have affirmative action obligations. Leonard found that the share of both black male and black female employment in total employment rose significantly faster among federal contractors in comparison to noncontractors between 1974 and 1980. The difference remained statistically significant even after controlling for other factors such as establishment size, region of the country, industry, occupational structure, and corporate structure. He estimated that the difference in the employment growth of black males relative to white males was 0.82 percent per year faster among federal contractors than among noncontractors. Similar effects were also reported by Ashenfelter and Heckman (1976) and Heckman and Wolpin (1976).

Leonard also found that compliance reviews played a significant role in black employment growth over and above that required by an affirmative action plan. A compliance review consists of an actual audit of an employer's hiring record by the OFCC, with a timetable drawn up for remedying any underrepresentation of minority workers. Leonard found that employment growth for black males was twice that in firms undergoing compliance review than among federal contractors generally.

The earlier studies of both Ashenfelter and Heckman (1976) and Heckman and Wolpin (1976) indicated that while affirmative action increased the rate of growth of black employment, it did not increase the share of black employees in the skilled occupations before 1974. Leonard, working with later data, did find an increasing share of black employees in the skilled occupations among federal contractors from 1974 to 1980. The growth in skilled black employment was significantly greater among federal contractors than noncontractors.

Though affirmative action did spur employment growth among blacks during the 1970s, Leonard discovered that the picture changed in the 1980s. Examining data for the period between 1980 and 1984, he found that employment growth among black males was actually somewhat slower among federal contractors than among noncontractors. Differences were even more marked for black females. Leonard attributed this reversal in the effectiveness of affirmative action to a reduced commitment of the Reagan administration to push for compliance.

13.6 SUMMARY

Since 1940, black Americans made considerable progress relative to white Americans in terms of labor earnings. For black males, most of the gains were made by 1969, with some slow advances thereafter. Still, by 1992, black male workers earned, on average, only about three-fourths the incomes of white male workers. Moreover, the labor force participation rates (LFPR) of black men declined both in absolute terms, from 85 percent in 1955 to 69 percent in 1992, and relative to the LFPR of white males, which was

76 percent in 1992. Black males also suffered from unemployment rates $2\frac{1}{2}$ to 3 times as great as white males. As a result, the proportion of males of working age with zero labor earnings was three times as high among blacks (16 percent in 1984) as among whites (5 percent in the same year).

In contrast, black females had reached virtual parity with white females in terms of earnings by 1980, though their relative earnings declined slightly between 1980 and 1992. Moreover, a higher proportion of black women have historically been in the labor force than white women, though the difference disappeared by 1992 (59 percent for both groups). However, the unemployment rate among black women has typically been about twice the level as that for white women.

Though black workers, both males and females, have generally gained on whites in terms of labor earnings throughout the years since 1940, the same has not been true for family income. The ratio of median family income between black and white families increased from 51 percent in 1958 to 62 percent in 1975 but has subsequently fallen to 54 percent (as of 1993), the same ratio as in 1962. The poverty rate among black families reached its lowest point in 1974, at 30 percent; by 1983, it had risen to 36 percent. It fell to 31 percent in 1989 but by 1993 had increased again to 33 percent. Racial disparities in wealth holdings are even greater than income differences, though they have been narrowing since the 1960s.

What explains the progress of black families relative to white families from 1940 to the mid-1970s? There are five main factors. The first is the migration of black families from the low-wage South to the high-wage North. The second is the very significant catch-up in educational attainment between blacks and whites. By 1992, 85 percent of black males aged 25 to 34 were high school graduates, compared to 86 percent of white males in the same age group. The third was the improvement in the quality of schools attended by black children. Though this had been going on for some time, since the beginning of the twentieth century, the 1954 Supreme Court case of *Brown v. Board of Education of Topeka, Kansas,* appears to have given added impetus to the process.

The fourth is the vintage effect. Entry-level cohorts of black male workers made substantial gains on earnings of white males up until the late 1970s. Older black males did not. Part of their failure to gain on white males was due to their lower-quality education and their lower labor market experience, differences which reflected past discrimination against blacks. The retirement of older black males from the labor force and their replacement by young black males, with more and better education, is one factor that has reduced the black-white earnings differential.

The fifth was the enactment and implementation of several federal programs to combat discrimination. The two most important of these are the Civil Rights Act of 1964, which created the Equal Employment Opportunity Commission (EEOC), and Executive Order 11246, issued by President Johnson in 1965, which created the Office of Federal Contract Compliance (OFCC) and required the development of affirmative action plans. Despite the apparent anemic enforcement efforts of the EEOC and the OFCC, many studies have shown that blacks made gains in terms of both earnings and employment as a consequence of these programs from the mid-1960s through the 1970s. The likely reason is increased awareness of discrimination by employers and their sense of a moral imperative to lessen discrimination.

What explains the subsequent decline in the relative fortunes of black families since the mid-1970s? One factor is that academic achievement among black males, as measured by standardized achievement test scores, failed to advance on white males of the same educational level. This is also reflected in the fact that the returns to schooling for blacks, particularly young black workers, failed to increase during the 1980s, though they had increased during the 1960s and 1970s. This effect is compounded by structural shifts in the labor market favoring college graduates who have performed well in school and disfavoring low-skilled workers. Some researchers, in fact, attribute almost all of the remaining racial earnings gap to the difference in scholastic achievement between blacks and whites.

A second factor, as noted above, is the falling LFPR of black men, particularly after 1970 and particularly among older black men. The third is the substantial increase in the percentage of female-headed households (with no husband present) among the black population, particularly since 1970. The proportion of black children living with two parents fell from 59 percent in 1970 to 39 percent in 1988. The decline in the black-white ratio of median family income since the 1970s is closely correlated with the rising percentage of black female-headed families. The fourth is that the effectiveness of affirmative action appears to have dissipated during the 1980s, though some researchers disagree.

Hispanic families have fared somewhat better than black families but significantly worse than non-Hispanic white families according to most indices. In 1992, the median family income of Hispanics was 13 percent greater than that of black families but only 61 percent the level of white families. In the same year, the poverty rate for individuals of Hispanic origin was 29 percent, in comparison to 12 percent for whites and 33 percent for blacks. Moreover, the ratio of median family income between Hispanic and white families has been declining steadily, from a peak of 71 percent in 1974.

Among all full-time, full-year workers, Hispanic males earned, on average, 67 percent the wages of white employees. However, when standardized by age and educational levels, the earnings ratios were substantially higher, ranging from 77 to 90 percent. A large part of the earnings gap between Hispanic and non-Hispanic white workers is due to differences in educational attainment, which have not narrowed as much as between blacks and whites. The lack of fluency in English also appears to play an important role in explaining the relatively lower earnings of Hispanic men.

Has labor market discrimination against blacks and Hispanics ended? Probably not, but the preponderance of evidence does suggest that it has lessened considerably since the 1950s. This result, interestingly, is consistent with several of the models of discrimination discussed in the previous chapter, including Becker's taste for discrimination model and the Arrow-Phelps statistical discrimination model. There has also been substantial progress in providing equal educational resources to black children as those received by white children. A significant hurdle that still remains for achieving full racial equality between young blacks and whites stems from differences in parental resources. Insofar as parental background and income affect schooling performance, today's black students will continue be at a disadvantage relative to white students. Moreover, the larger wealth holdings of older whites relative to older black Americans will continue to place young black households at a disadvantage in the wealth accumulation process.

REFERENCES AND BIBLIOGRAPHY

Akin, John S., and Irv Garfinkel, "School Expenditures and the Economic Returns to Schooling," *Journal of Human Resources*, Vol. 12, Fall 1977, pp. 460–481.

———, "The Quality of Education and Cohort Variation in Black-White Earnings Differentials: Comment," *American Economic Review*, Vol. 70, Fall 1980, pp. 186–191.

Ashenfelter, Orley, "Changes in Labor Market Discrimination Over Time," *Journal of Human Resources*, Vol. 5, No. 4, Fall 1970, pp. 403–429.

———, "Comments," in M.D. Intriligator and D.A. Kendrick, (eds.), *Frontiers of Quantitative Economics*, Vol. II, American Elsevier, New York, 1974.

———, and James Heckman, "Measuring the Effect of an Antidiscrimination Program," in Orley Ashenfelter and James Blum (eds.), *Evaluating the Labor Market Effects of Social Programs*, Princeton University Press, Princeton, 1976.

Ashenfelter, Orley, and Albert Rees (ed.), *Discrimination in Labor Markets*, Princeton University Press, Princeton, N.J., 1973.

Bell, Duran, "Occupational Discrimination as a Source of Income Differences: Lessons of the 1960s," *American Economic Review*, Vol. 62, No. 2, May 1972, pp. 363–372.

Bergman, Barbara P., "The Effect on White Income of Discrimination in Employment," *Journal of Political Economy*, Vol. 79, March 1971.

Blau, Francine D., and John W. Graham, "Black-White Differences in Wealth and Asset Composition," *Quarterly Journal of Economics*, May 1990, pp. 321–339.

Bound, John, and Richard B. Freeman, "What Went Wrong? The Erosion of Relative Earnings and Employment Among Young Black Men in the 1980s," NBER Working Paper No. 3778, Cambridge, Mass., July 1991.

Borjas, George J., "The Economics of Immigration," *Journal of Economic Literature*, Vol. 32, No. 4, December 1994, pp. 1667–1717.

Brown, Charles, "Black/White Earnings Ratios Since the Civil Rights Act of 1964: The Importance of Labor Market Drop-Outs," *Quarterly Journal of Economics*, 1984, pp. 31–44.

Brown, Charles C., "The Federal Attack on Labor Market Discrimination: The Mouse that Roared?" in R. Ehrenberg (ed.), *Research in Labor Economics*, Vol. 5, JAI Press, New York, 1982, pp. 33–68.

Butcher, Kristin F., "Black Immigrants in the United States: A Comparison With Native Blacks and Other Immigrants," *Industrial and Labor Relations Review*, Vol. 47, No. 2, January 1994, pp. 265–284.

Butler, Richard, and James J. Heckman, "The Government's Impact on the Labor Market Status of Black Americans: A Critical Review," *Equal Rights and Industrial Relations* (1977 Industrial Relations Research Association Series), Wisconsin, 1978.

Card, David, and Alan B. Krueger, "School Quality and Black-White Relative Earnings: A Direct Assessment," *Quarterly Journal of Economics*, Vol. 107, No. 1, February 1992, pp. 151–200.

Card, David, and Thomas Lemieux, "Changing Wage Structure and Black-White Wage Differentials," *American Economic Review Papers and Proceedings*, Vol. 84, No. 2, May 1994, pp. 29–33.

Chiswick, Barry R., "Racial Discrimination in the Labor Market: A Test of Alternative Hypotheses," *Journal of Political Economy*, Vol. 81, No. 6, November/December 1973, pp. 1330–1352.

——, "The Effect of Americanization on the Earnings of Foreign-Born Men," *Journal of Political Economy*, Vol. 86, October 1978, pp. 897–921.

Coleman, James, *et al.*, *Equality of Educational Opportunity*, Government Printing Office, Washington, D.C., 1966.

Comanor, William, "Racial Discrimination in American Industry," *Economica*, Vol. 40, No. 160, November 1973, pp. 363–378.

Congressional Budget Office, *Inequalities in the Educational Experience of Black and White Americans*, Government Printing Office, Washington, D.C., 1977.

Duncan, D. D., "Inheritance of Poverty or Inheritance of Race?" in D. P. Moynihan (ed.), *On Understanding Poverty*, Basic Books, New York, 1968.

Duncan, Greg J., and Saul D. Hoffman, "A New Look at the Causes of the Improved Economic Status of Black Workers," *Journal of Human Resources*, Vol. 17, No. 2, Spring 1983, pp. 268–282.

Ellwood, David T., and Jonathan Crane, "Family Change Among Black Americans: What Do We Know?" *Journal of Economic Perspectives*, Vol. 4, No. 4, Fall 1990, pp. 65–84.

Flanagan, Robert J., "Actual Versus Potential Impact of Government Antidiscrimination Programs," *Industrial and Labor Relations Review*, Vol. 29, July 1976, pp. 486–507.

Fosu, Augustin Kwasi, "Occupational Mobility of Black Women, 1959–1981: The Impact of Post-1964 Antidiscrimination Measures," *Industrial and Labor Relations Review*, Vol. 45, No. 2, January 1992, pp. 281–294.

Freeman, Richard B., "Changes in the Labor Market for Black Americans, 1948–1972" *Brookings Papers*, Vol. 1, 1973a, pp. 67–120.

———, "Decline of Labor Market Discrimination and Economic Analysis," *American Economic Review*, Vol. 63, May 1973b, pp. 280–286.

———, "Labor Market Discrimination: Analysis, Findings, and Problems," in M. D. Intriligator and D. A. Kendrick (eds.), *Frontiers of Quantitative Economics*, Vol. II, American Elsevier, New York, 1974.

———, "Alternative Theories of Labor-Market Discrimination: Individual and Collective Behavior," in G. M. von Furstenberg, A. R. Horowitz, and B. Harrison (eds.), *Patterns of Racial Discrimination*, Vol. II, Lexington Books, Lexington, Mass., 1974.

———, "Overinvestment in College Training?" *Journal of Human Resources*, Vol. 10, Summer 1975, pp. 287–311.

———, "Time Series Evidence on Black Economic Progress: Shifts in Demand or in Supply?" unpublished paper, Harvard University, June 1978.

———, "Black Economic Progress After 1964: Who Has Gained and Why?" in Sherwin Rosen (ed.), *Studies in Labor Markets*, Number 31, University of Chicago Press, Chicago, 1981a.

———, "Have Black Labor Market Gains Post-1964 Been Permanent or Transitory?" National Bureau of Economic Research Working Paper No. 751, September 1981b.

Gottschalk, Peter, Sheldon Danziger, and John Engberg, "Decomposing Changes in the Black-White Earnings Gap: 1969 to 1979," *Research in Economic Inequality*, Vol. 1, JAI Press, Greenwich, Conn., pp. 311–326.

Grenier, Gilles, "The Effect of Language Characteristics on the Wages of Hispanic-American Males," *Journal of Human Resources*, Vol. 19, Winter 1984, pp. 25–52.

Gwartney, James D., "Discrimination and Income Differentials," *American Economic Review*, Vol. 60, June 1970a, pp. 396–408.

———, "Changes in the Nonwhite/White Income Ratio: 1939–1967," *American Economic Review*, Vol. 60, December 1970b, pp. 872–883.

———, and James E. Long, "The Relative Earnings of Blacks and Other Minorities," *Industrial and Labor Relations Review*, Vol. 31, April 1978, pp. 336–346.

Hacker, Andrew, *Two Nations: Black and White, Separate, Hostile, Unequal*, Scribner, New York, 1992.

Hanoch, Giora, "An Economic Analysis of Earnings and Schooling," *Journal of Human Resources*, Vol. 2, No. 3, Summer 1967, pp. 310–329.

Haworth, Joan G., James Gwartney, and Charles T. Haworth, "Earnings, Productivity, and Changes in Employment Discrimination During the 1960s," *American Economic Review*, Vol. 65, March 1975, pp. 158–168.

Heckman, James J., "The Impact of Government on the Economic Status of Black Americans," Department of Economics, University of Chicago, mimeo, 1987.

———, and Brook S. Payner, "Determining the Impact of Federal Antidiscrimination Policy on the Economic Status of Blacks: A Study of South

Carolina," *American Economic Review*, Vol. 79, No. 1, March 1989, pp. 138–177.

Heckman, James J., and Kenneth I. Wolpin, "Does the Contract Compliance Program Work? An Analysis of Chicago Data," *Industrial and Labor Relations Review*, Vol. 29, No. 4, July 1976, pp. 544–564.

Hirsch, Barry T., and Edward J. Schumacher, "Labor Earnings, Discrimination, and the Racial Composition of Jobs," *Journal of Human Resources*, Vol. 27, No. 4, Fall 1992, pp. 602–628.

Hoffman, Saul D., "Black-White Life Cycle Earnings Differences and the Vintage Hypothesis: A Longitudinal Analysis," *American Economic Review* Vol. 69, December 1979, pp. 855–867.

Hylton, Keith, "Illusory Wage Differentials: Comment," *American Economic Review*, Vol. 74, No. 5, December 1984, pp. 1124–1128.

Jaynes, Gerald D., "The Labor Market Status of Black Americans: 1939–1985," *Journal of Economic Perspectives*, Vol. 4, No. 4, Fall 1990, pp. 9–24.

Jaynes, Gerald David, and Robin M. Williams (eds.), *A Common Destiny: Blacks and American Society*, National Research Council, National Academy Press, Washington, D.C., 1989.

Jud, G. Donald, and James L. Walker, "Racial Differences in the Returns to Schooling and Experience Among Prime-Age Males, 1967–1975," *Journal of Human Resources*, Vol. 17, No. 4, Fall 1982, pp. 622–632.

Kennickell, Arthur, and Janice Shack-Marquez, "Changes in Family Finances From 1983 to 1989: Evidence From the Survey of Consumer Finances," *Federal Reserve Bulletin*, Vol. 78, No. 1, January 1992, pp. 1–18.

Kennickell, Arthur B., and Martha Starr-McCluer, "Changes in Family Finances From 1989 to 1992: Evidence From the Survey of Consumer Finances," *Federal Reserve Bulletin*, Vol. 80, October 1994, pp. 861–882.

Kneisser, Thomas J., A. H. Padilla, and Solomon W. Polachek, "The Rate of Return to Schooling and the Business Cycle," *Journal of Human Resources*, Vol. 13, Spring 1978, pp. 264–277.

Lazear, Edward, "The Narrowing of Black-White Wage Differentials Is Illusory," *American Economic Review*, Vol. 69, No. 4, September 1979, pp. 553–564.

Leonard, Jonathan S., "Employment and Occupational Advance Under Affirmative Action," *Review of Economics and Statistics*, August 1984a, pp. 377–385.

———, "The Impact of Affirmative Action on Employment," *Journal of Labor Economics*, Vol. 2, October 1984b, pp. 439–463.

———, "Antidiscrimination or Reverse Discrimination: The Impact of Changing Demographics, Title VII, and Affirmative Action on Productivity," *Journal of Human Resources*, Vol. 19, No. 2, Spring 1984c, pp. 146–174.

———, "Affirmative Action As Earnings Redistribution: The Targeting of Compliance Reviews," *Journal of Labor Economics*, Vol. 3, July 1985a, pp. 363–384.

———, "What Promises Are Worth: the Impact of Affirmative Action Goals," *Journal of Human Resources*, Vol. 20, Winter 1985b, pp. 3–20.

———, "What Was Affirmative Action?" *American Economic Review*, Vol. 76, No. 2, May 1986, pp. 359–363.

———, "The Impact of Affirmative Action and Equal Employment Law on Black Employment," *Journal of Economic Perspectives*, Vol. 4, No. 4, Fall 1990, pp. 47–63.

Link, Charles, "Black, Education, Earnings, and Interregional Migration: A Comment and Some New Evidence," *American Economic Review*, Vol. 65, March 1975, pp. 236–240.

———, and Edward Ratledge, "The Influence of the Quantity and Quality of Education on Black-White Earnings Differentials: Some New Evidence," *Review of Economics and Statistics*, Vol. 57, August 1975a, pp. 346–350.

———, "Social Returns to Quality and Quantity of Education: A Further Statement," *Journal of Human Resources*, Vol. 10, Winter 1975b, pp. 78–89.

———, and Kenneth Lewis, "Black-White Differences in Returns to Schooling: Some New Evidence," *American Economic Review*, Vol. 66, March 1976, pp. 221–223.

———, "The Quality of Education and Cohort Variation in Black-White Earnings Differentials: Reply," *American Economic Review*, Vol. 70, March 1980, pp. 196–203.

Masters, S. H., *Black and White Income Differentials*, Academic Press, New York, 1975.

Maxwell, Nan, "White-Nonwhite Income Inequality: Between-Race and Within-Race Changes, 1947–1985," *Research In Economic Inequality*, Vol. 2, JAI Press, Greenwich, Conn., pp. 45–87.

———, "The Effect on Black-White Wage Differences of Differences in the Quantity and Quality of Education," *Industrial and Labor Relations Review*, Vol. 47, No. 2, January 1994, pp. 249–264.

McCall, J. J., *Income Mobility, Racial Discrimination, and Economic Growth*, Lexington Books, Lexington, Mass., 1972.

McManus, Walter S., "Labor Market Costs of Language Disparity: An Interpretation of Hispanic Earnings Differences," *American Economic Review*, Vol. 75, No. 4, September 1985, pp. 818–827.

———, "Labor Market Effects of Language Enclaves: Hispanic Men in the United States," *Journal of Human Resources*, Vol. 25, No. 2, Spring 1990, pp. 228–252.

———, William Gould, and Finis Welch, "Earnings of Hispanic Men: The Role of Proficiency in the English Language," *Journal of Labor Economics*, Vol. 1, April 1983, pp. 110–130.

Menchik, Paul L., and Nancy Ammon Jianakoplos, "Black-White Wealth Inequality: Is Inheritance the Reason?" mimeo, August 1995.

Michelson, S., *Incomes of Racial Minorities*, Brookings, Washington, D.C., 1968.

Mooney, J. D. "Housing Segregation, Negro Employment and Metropolitan Decentralization," *Quarterly Journal of Economics*, Vol. 83, May 1969.

Moss, Philip, and Chris Tilly, *Why Black Men Are Doing Worse in the Labor Market: A Review of Supply-Side and Demand-Side Explanations*, Social Science Research Council, New York, August 1991.

Myrdal, Gunnar, *The American Dilemma: The Negro Problem and Modern Democracy*, Harper & Row, New York, 1944.

Neumark, David, "Employers' Discriminatory Behavior and the Estimation of Wage Discrimination," *Journal of Human Resources*, Vol. 23, No. 3, Summer 1988, pp. 279–295.

O'Neill, June, "The Role of Human Capital in Earnings Differences Between Black and White Men," *Journal of Economic Perspectives*, Vol. 4, No. 4, Fall 1990, pp. 25–45.

Orazem, Peter F., "Black-White Differences in Schooling Investment and Human Capital Production in Segregated Schools," *American Economic Review*, Vol. 77, No. 4, September 1987, pp. 714–723.

Rasmussen, David W., "A Note on the Relative Income of Nonwhite Men, 1948–1964," *Quarterly Journal of Economics*, Vol. 84, No. 1, February 1970, pp. 168–172.

Reich, Michael, *Racial Inequality*, Princeton University Press, Princeton, 1981.

Reimers, Cordelia, "Labor Market Discrimination Against Hispanic and Black Men," *Review of Economics and Statistics*, Vol. 65, 1983, pp. 570–579.

———, "Sources of the Family Income Differentials Among Hispanics, Blacks, and White Non-Hispanic Whites," *American Journal of Sociology*, Vol. 89, No. 4, January 1984, pp. 889–903.

Schwartz, Saul, "Earnings Capacity and the Trend in Earnings Among Black Men," *Journal of Human Resources*, Vol. 21, 1986, pp. 44–63.

Smith, James P., "The Improving Economic Status of Black Americans," *American Economic Review*, Vol. 68, No. 2, May 1978, pp. 171–178.

———, "Race and Human Capital," *American Economic Review*, Vol. 74, No. 4, September 1984, pp. 685–698.

———, "Affirmative Action and the Racial Wage Gap," *American Economic Review*, Vol. 83, No. 2, May 1993, pp. 79–84.

———, and Finis R. Welch, "Black-White Male Wage Ratios: 1960–1970," *American Economic Review*, Vol. 67, June 1977a, pp. 323–338.

———, "Black/White Male Earnings and Employment: 1960–1970," in F. Thomas Juster (ed.), *The Distribution of Economic Well-Being*, National Bureau of Economic Research, Ballinger, Cambridge, Mass., 1977b.

———, "Race Differences in Earnings: A Survey and New Evidence," in P. Mieskowski and M. Straszheim (eds.), *Current Issues in Urban Economics*, Johns Hopkins University Press, Baltimore, 1979.

———, "Affirmative Action and Labor Markets," *Journal of Labor Economics*, Vol. 2, No. 3, April 1984, pp. 269–301.

———, "Black Economic Progress After Myrdal," *Journal of Economic Literature*, Vol. 27, No. 2, June 1989, pp. 519–564.

Stratton, Leslie S., "Racial Differences in Men's Unemployment," *Industrial and Labor Relations Review*, Vol. 46, No. 3, April 1993, pp. 451–463.

Strauss, Robert F., and Francis W. Horvath, "Wage Rate Differences by Race and Sex in the U.S. Labor Market: 1960–1970," *Economica*, Vol. 43, August 1976, pp. 287–298.

Taylor, Daniel E., "Education, On-the-Job Training, and the Black-White Earnings Gap," *Monthly Labor Review*, Vol. 104, April 1981, pp. 28–34.

Thurow, Lester, *Poverty and Discrimination*, Brookings Institution, Washington, D.C., 1969.

U.S. Bureau of the Census, Current Population Reports, Series P-60, No. 168, *Money Income and Poverty Status in the United States: 1989*, U.S. Government Printing Office, Washington, D.C., 1990(a).

U.S. Bureau of the Census, Current Population Reports, Series P-60, No. 167, *Trends in Income: by Selected Characteristics: 1947 to 1988*, U.S. Government Printing Office, Washington, D.C., 1990(b).

U.S. Bureau of the Census, Current Population Reports, Series P60–184, *Money Income of Households, Families, and Persons in the United States: 1992*, U.S. Government Printing Office, Washington, D.C., 1993.

Vroman, Wayne, "Changes in Black Workers' Relative Earnings: Evidence from the 1960s," in G. M. von Furstenberg, A. R. Horowitz, and B. Harrison (eds.), *Patterns of Racial Discrimination*, Vol. II, Lexington Books, Lexington, Mass., 1974.

———, "Transfer Payments, Sample Selection, and Male Black-White Earnings Differences," *American Economic Review*, Vol. 76, No. 2, May 1986, pp. 351–354.

Weiss, Leonard, and Jeffrey Williamson, "Black Education, Earnings, and Interregional Migration: Some New Evidence," *American Economic Review*, Vol. 62, June 1972, pp. 372–383.

———, "Black Education, Earnings, and Interregional Migration: Even Newer Evidence," *American Economic Review*, Vol. 65, March 1975, pp. 241–244.

Weiss, Randall D., "The Effect of Education on the Earnings of Blacks and Whites," *Review of Economics and Statistics*, Vol. 52, May 1970, pp. 150–159.

Welch, Finis R., "Labor Market Discrimination: An Interpretation of Income Differences in the Rural South," *Journal of Political Economy*, Vol. 75, June 1967, pp. 225–240.

———, "Black-White Differences in Returns to Schooling," *American Economic Review*, Vol. 63, December 1973a, pp. 893–907.

———, "Education and Racial Discrimination," in O. Ashenfelter and A. Rees (eds.), *Discrimination in Labor Markets*, Princeton University Press, Princeton, N.J., 1973b.

———, "Human Capital Theory: Education, Discrimination, and Life Cycles," *American Economic Review*, Vol. 65, May 1975, pp. 63–73.

———, "The Quality of Education and Cohort Variation in Black-White Earnings Differentials: Reply," *American Economic Review*, Vol. 70, March 1980, pp. 192–195.

Wilson, William Julius, *The Declining Significance of Race: Blacks and Changing American Institutions*, University of Chicago Press, Chicago, 1978.

————, *The Truly Disadvantaged: The Inner City, the Underclass, and Public Policy*, University of Chicago Press, Chicago, 1987.

DISCUSSION QUESTIONS

1. Describe the gains made by black men relative to white men in terms of labor market earnings. Some researchers have argued that these gains are overstated because of the reduction in the employment rate of black men. Explain this argument.
2. Discuss three reasons why migration from the South may have led to improvements in the economic status of black families.
3. Though blacks have made gains relative to whites in terms of labor earnings, relative gains have been much smaller in terms of median family income and poverty rates. How have changes in family structure in the black community accounted for this difference?
4. Explain the provisions of the Civil Rights Act of 1964. Was this legislation effective in reducing racial discrimination? Discuss the evidence which supports the effectiveness of this Act. What are the three arguments and supporting evidence for why the Civil Rights Act of 1964 was not effective?
5. Describe the origins of affirmative action plans. Evaluate the evidence with regard to the effectiveness of affirmative action.

Chapter

14

The Gender Wage Gap and Occupational Segregation

The last chapter revealed that black families made substantial progress relative to whites from 1940 to 1970. However, since 1970, they experienced only modest relative gains in labor earnings and no gains in family incomes, and indeed, black males suffered a sharp decrease in employment. Curiously, the story is almost the reverse for females. We find that the economic status of females actually deteriorated somewhat from the end of World War II to 1970, but it then showed significant improvement after 1970, particularly from 1980 to the present.

In Section 14.1, we present the basic evidence on the progress of female workers in the United States, in terms of both earnings and labor force participation rates. Section 14.2 raises the question of why females failed to make progress before 1970 and then showed significant gains thereafter. One reason is that women, particularly married women, have historically had interrupted work careers, especially during childbearing and childrearing ages. The first part of this section considers the effects of experience differences on the earnings differentials between females and males. Occupational segregation is a second reason for the lower earnings of females, and the second part of this section looks at changes in indices of occupational segregation, as well as other factors that may have played a role in changing the male-female wage gap.

Section 14.3 considers the role of civil rights programs that have been established to combat gender-based job discrimination. The principal program is the Equal Pay Act of 1963, which was designed to eliminate wage differentials based solely on gender. Recent efforts have taken the form of comparable worth programs, which aim at creating pay parity between male and female jobs.

In Section 14.4, we look at an important issue regarding the effects of wives' earnings on the distribution of *family income*. Have the earnings of wives led to greater equality in the distribution of family income or have they been disequalizing in effect? In this section, we also consider a new development in gender disparities, referred to as the "feminization of poverty." This is principally related to changes in the structure of the American family. Some international comparisons are also presented in this section. A summary is provided in the last section of the chapter.

14.1 THE WAGE GAP AND LABOR FORCE PARTICIPATION TRENDS

We first look at the earnings or wage gap between female and male workers. Table 14.1 shows the ratio in annual earnings between male and female workers in 1992 by age and education group. The data are only for employees who worked full-time (35 or more hours per week) for the full year (50 or more weeks). The ratios are shown by racial group. Among all white persons who were full-time, full-year workers, women made, on average, only 70 percent the annual earnings of male workers.

Younger females did better than older ones. The average earnings of white females aged 25 to 34 was 82 percent that of males, whereas older white females (ages 35 to 64) earned only about two-thirds the amount of males in the same age group. Part of the explanation is that older females have had less continuous work experience than older males. In the past, at least, many married women typically worked until the birth of their first child, dropped out of the labor force, and then reentered the labor force when their children left home. As a result, the work experience of older women has typically been interrupted, and they have had fewer years of actual work experience than men of the same age. We shall return to this point in Section 14.2.

The earnings ratio shows relatively little variation by educational status. Among younger workers (under 35), the female-male earnings ratio was slightly greater among college-educated workers with professional degrees than other educational groups. Among workers 45 and over, the earnings ratio was somewhat higher among college graduates with an M.A. degree than among other workers.

The earnings gap between black females and males was smaller than that between white females and males. Black females earned, on average, 14 percent less than black males (an earnings ratio of 0.86). As with white workers, younger black females did better relative to younger black males than did older black females, relative to older black males. The earnings ratio between black females and males in age group 25–34 was 0.91, compared to a ratio of 0.77 for black females and males in age group 55–64.

Table 14.1   The Ratio of Median Annual Earnings between Male and Female Workers, Classified by Race, Education, and Age, 1992[a]

	25–34	35–44	45–54	55–64	All Ages
A. *White Females/White Males*					
Elementary 0–8	0.79	0.79	0.68	0.56	0.72
High school, no degree	0.74	0.60	0.61	0.59	0.65
High school graduate[b]	0.76	0.65	0.61	0.67	0.69
College, no degree	0.80	0.65	0.66	0.74	0.70
College, associate degree[c]	0.81	0.76	0.66	0.69	0.76
College, B.A. degree	0.76	0.70	0.68	0.66	0.72
College, M.A. degree	0.78	0.69	0.70	0.84	0.73
College, professional degree	0.83	0.57	—	—	0.59
College, Ph.D.	—	—	—	—	0.74
All Schooling Levels	0.82	0.66	0.63	0.67	0.70
B. *Black Females/Black Males*					
Elementary 0–8	—	—	—	—	0.67
High school, no degree	0.86	0.74	0.67	—	0.71
High school graduate[b]	0.96	0.82	0.73	0.80	0.81
College, no degree	0.82	0.71	0.80	—	0.76
College, associate degree[c]	0.74	0.78	—	—	0.82
College, B.A. or more	0.92	0.91	0.74	—	0.91
All Schooling Levels	0.91	0.82	0.78	0.77	0.86
C. *Hispanic Females/Hispanic Males*					
Elementary 0–8	—	0.77	0.78	—	0.78
High school, no degree	—	—	—	—	0.71
High school graduate[b]	0.87	0.71	0.77	—	0.80
College, no degree	0.88	0.81	—	—	0.82
College, associate degree[c]	—	—	—	—	0.91
College, B.A. or more	0.91	0.81	—	—	0.90
All Schooling Levels	0.99	0.77	0.75	0.60	0.84

[a] Source: U.S. Bureau of the Census, Current Population Reports, Series P60–184, *Money Income of Households, Families, and Persons in the United States: 1992*, 1993. Earnings data are for year-round (defined as those who worked 50 or more weeks), full-time (defined as those who work 35 or more hours per week) employees.
[b] Includes equivalency degrees.
[c] Community college degrees.

There is again very little systematic variation in the earnings ratio by educational group. However, more educated black females tended to do slightly better relative to males than less educated black females.

The smaller gender wage gap among black workers in comparison to white workers is *not* due to the higher earnings of black women relative to white women but rather to the lower earnings of black men relative to white men. Indeed, as we saw in the last chapter, white women and black women are virtually at parity in terms of earnings. In a sense, the results suggest that black women are discriminated against solely for being women, rather than for being black. The reasons why black women are not subjected to racial discrimination in addition to gender discrimination may arise from the fact that black women have historically had more continuous participation in the labor force than white women (see below).

The earnings ratio between Hispanic females and males was 0.84 in 1992, slightly lower than among blacks but higher than among whites. Here, also, younger Hispanic females fared better in relative terms than did older ones. More educated Hispanic females did better than less educated ones relative to Hispanic males in the same age group.

Time Trends

Has the female-male wage gap declined since the end of World War II? Table 14.2 presents data on the earnings gap by age group from 1947 to 1992. The results here are based on total annual income instead of labor earnings. Moreover, all men and women are included in the tabulation (as opposed to workers). Nonetheless, the results are quite dramatic. Among all age groups,

Table 14.2 The Ratio of Median Annual Income between Females and Males, By Age Group, 1947–1992[a]

	Age Group			
Year	*25–34*	*35–44*	*45–54*	*55–64*
1947	0.50	0.47	0.48	0.41
1957	0.39	0.38	0.40	0.36
1967	0.38	0.37	0.42	0.38
1970	0.39	0.36	0.40	0.38
1975	0.46	0.35	0.38	0.37
1980	0.45	0.32	0.32	0.31
1985	0.53	0.41	0.38	0.35
1988	0.56	0.44	0.41	0.37
1992	0.63	0.52	0.49	0.40

[a] Source: U.S. Bureau of the Census, Current Population Reports, Series P60–184, *Money Income of Households, Families, and Persons in the United States: 1992*, 1993.

Table 14.3   The Ratio of Median Annual Income Between Females and Males, Classified by Education, 1967–1992[a]

Year	Elementary 8 or less	High School 1 to 3	High School 4 years	College 1 to 3	College 4 years	College 5 or more	All
1967	0.33	0.33	0.40	0.38	0.44	0.60	0.33
1970	0.35	0.33	0.39	0.38	0.44	0.59	0.33
1975	0.44	0.37	0.38	0.41	0.48	0.58	0.36
1980	0.47	0.37	0.36	0.42	0.44	0.55	0.35
1985	0.54	0.44	0.43	0.49	0.51	0.59	0.41
1988	0.52	0.45	0.46	0.53	0.57	0.59	0.46
1992	0.61	0.51	0.50	0.56	0.61	0.62	0.50

[a] Source: U.S. Bureau of the Census, Current Population Reports, Series P-60, No. 167, *Trends in Income: by Selected Characteristics: 1947 to 1988*, and U.S. Bureau of the Census, Current Population Reports, Series P60–184, *Money Income of Households, Families, and Persons in the United States: 1992*, 1993. The computations include only persons age 25 and older.

the ratio of female to male income declined between 1947 and 1970. Among the youngest age group, the female-male ratio increased between 1970 and 1992, from 39 to 63 percent. Among the older three age groups, the female-male income ratio started to increase in 1980, rising from 0.32 in that year to 0.52 in 1992 for age group 35 to 44, from 0.32 to 0.49 for ages 45–54, and from 0.31 to 0.40 for age group 55–64.

Results using the same income concept by educational group reveal similar trends (Table 14.3). The gender earnings ratio increased at all schooling levels between 1967 and 1992, though the gains were more marked at the lower levels. Among those with 8 years of schooling or less, the ratio rose from 0.33 to 0.61; among high school graduates, from 0.40 to 0.50; and among college graduates, from 0.44 to 0.61. Among those with more than a B.A. degree, there was relatively little change in the wage gap.

Figure 14.1 shows the trend in the ratio of median annual labor earnings between female and male workers. Results are shown for all full-time, full-year workers and for all workers, including those who worked part-time and those who worked only part of the year. Among all workers, the earnings ratio rose almost steadily from 1973 (a ratio of 0.38) to 1992 (a ratio of 0.62). Part of these gains were due to the fact that female employees were working more hours per year after 1973 (see below). When we consider only full-time, full-year workers, the gender earnings ratio changed very little between 1967 and 1980 but then increased from 0.60 in 1980 to 0.71 in 1992.

Labor Force Participation Patterns

Another major change in the postwar period is the **labor force participation rate** of females, which has been steadily rising. We have already commented

Figure 14.1   Ratio of Median Annual Earnings Between Females and Males, 1967–1992

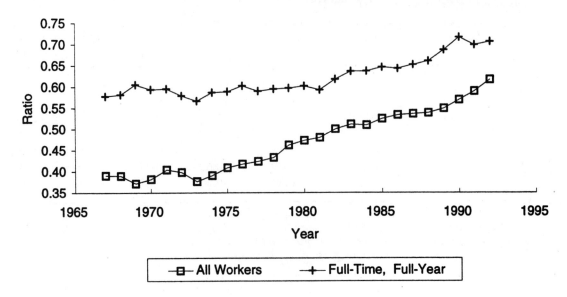

on this trend in Chapters 5 and 13. Table 14.4 highlights some of the changes. In 1947, 32 percent of all females (age 16 and over) were in the labor force (either employed or looking for work). This proportion increased gradually but continuously over the postwar period, and by 1992, 58 percent of women were in the labor force. In contrast, the labor force participation rate (LFPR) of men declined from 87 percent in 1947 to 76 percent in 1992.

The LFPR increased for both unmarried and married women. For single (never married) women, the LFPR declined from 51 percent in 1947 to 41 percent in 1965 but then increased continuously to 65 percent in 1992. The most dramatic change was among married women (living with their husbands). Their LFPR was only 20 percent in 1947, but it more than doubled to 40 percent in 1970 and increased even further to 59 percent in 1992. The LFPR of widowed, divorced, and separated women also rose, but the increase was fairly modest, from 37 percent in 1947 to 47 percent in 1992.

What is perhaps even more telling is the increase in the LFPR of women with children. The LFPR of women with school-age children (6 to 17) was 55 percent in 1975 but increased sharply to 76 percent by 1992. A similar change occurred for mothers with young children under the age of six. Their LFPR rose from 39 to 58 percent over the same years.

Another important development was that the proportion of working women who were employed full-time and full-year was also on the rise. In 1950, only 37 percent of working women worked full-time, full-year. By 1992, this figure had risen to 54 percent.

Table 14.4 Labor Force Participation Rates for Females by Marital Status, 1947–1992[a]

Year	All Males	All Females	Never Married	Married, Spouse Present	Widowed, Divorced, Separated	6–17	Under 6	FT–FY[b]
			Females Who Are			*Females with Children in Age Group*		*Percent of Female Employees Who Work*
1947	86.4	31.8	51.2	20.0	37.4			
1950	86.4	33.9	50.5	23.8	37.8			36.8
1955	85.4	35.7	46.4	27.7	39.6			37.9
1960	83.3	38.1	44.1	30.5	40.0			36.9
1965	80.7	40.3	40.5	34.7	38.9			38.8
1970	79.7	43.4	53.0	40.8	39.1			40.7
1975	77.9	46.3	57.0	44.4	40.8	54.9	39.0	41.4
1980	77.4	51.5	61.5	50.1	44.0	64.3	46.8	44.7
1985	76.3	54.5	65.2	54.2	45.6	69.9	53.5	48.9
1988	76.2	56.6	65.2	56.5	46.1	73.3	56.1	50.7
1992	75.6	57.9	65.0	59.2	47.0	75.9	58.1	53.5

[a] Source: *Handbook of Labor Statistics 1989*, U.S. Department of Labor, Bureau of Labor Statistics, 1990, Bulletin 2340, and U.S. Bureau of the Census, *Statistical Abstract of the United States, 1994*, 1994. Statistics refer to population age 16 and over.
[b] FT-FY: full-time (35 hours or more per week), full-year (50 or more weeks per year).

There are two questions of immediate interest. First, why have females, particularly married women, historically had lower labor force participation rates than men? Second, why has the LFPR of women been steadily increasing over the postwar period?

The human capital model, as developed by Gilbert Ghez and Gary Becker (1975), Gary Becker (1981), and Jacob Mincer (1962a, 1962b), provides a framework to treat both of these questions. The new household economics developed by these economists emphasizes the allocation of time within the household unit. According to this model, the market wage influences not only the allocation of time between market work and leisure but also that between market work and work in the home. An increase in the market wage relative to the wife's "household wage" would induce a substitution of market work (in the labor market) for household work. The strength of the effect would depend on the degree of substitutability between goods produced in the home and market goods. An increase in the husband's earnings or in family income generally would induce a substitution of leisure for total time worked. The degree to which hours of work in the labor market declined would depend on the income elasticity of market goods relative to that for goods produced in the home.

Another factor derives from the demand for children. Victor Fuchs (1989) suggests the hypothesis that women have a stronger demand for children than do men and have a greater interest in children after they are born. Biological constraints on the age of childrearing for women may help account for this difference. Differences in the pattern of socialization may also help explain these differences in preference. According to this argument, both the lower wage of females relative to males in the labor market and the greater preference for childrearing of women may account for the lower rate of labor force participation of women than men.

Several studies have applied this framework to explain the rising LFPR of women, particularly married women. Jacob Mincer (1962b) investigated the variation of the LFPR of married women among 57 large SMSAs (standard metropolitan statistical areas) on the basis of the 1950 Census of Population data. He found that wives' wages had a strong positive effect on their LFPR, while husbands' earnings exerted a negative, but weaker, influence. The combination of wives' wages and husbands' income explained about half of the variation in the labor supply of wives. Another factor that appeared important was the overall unemployment rate of the SMSA, which had a negative effect on the LFPR of married women. Mincer estimated that the change in women's earnings and family income could explain about 70 percent of the rise in the labor force participation rate of married women from 1920 to 1960.

Later studies by Glenn Cain (1966) and William Bowen and T. Aldrich Finegan (1969) on the basis of 1960 Census of Population data generally confirmed Mincer's findings, though the effects were smaller in magnitude. Judith Fields (1976) found still weaker effects using the 1970 Census of Population data. Fields suggested that the weakening of the wage and income effects over time could reflect a change in the labor supply function of wives, as women were substantially changing their work-role orientation. Glenn Cain and M. D. Dooley (1976) also incorporated the fertility rate (the number of births per 1,000 females) in their analysis and found that once this effect was included, the wife's wage and husband's income effects for the 1970 data were as strong as estimated by Mincer on the basis of the 1950 Census data. The Cain and Dooley results, as analyzed by O'Neill (1981), explained 86 percent of the increase in the LFPR of married women over the period 1947–1957, 63 percent over the 1957–1967 period, and more than 100 percent of the change from 1967 to 1977.

Using time-series data from 1948 to 1978, June O'Neill (1981) reestimated the effects of both wives' wages and family income on the LFPR of married women. Her analysis included, besides women's wage rates and men's income, the unemployment rate, an index of industrial composition, the divorce rate (which she explained as a proxy for the risk of losing the "job" of housewife), and the fertility rate (the number of children ever born per woman). She found that the female wage and male income were important and statistically significant. The unemployment rate had the expected sign but was not generally statistically significant. The divorce rate was significant and had a positive effect on women's LFPR. Past fertility was found to be quite significant, and it exerted a positive effect on the labor force participation of older females. She concluded that the rising LFPR of married women during the 1950s and 1960s was driven mainly by their rising wage earnings. However, during the 1970s, it was largely due to the slowdown in the growth of husband's total income.

James Smith and Michael Ward (1985) also investigated time-series changes in the labor force participation of females. Their analysis covered the period from 1900 to 1981. They concluded that rising real wages accounted for 58 percent of the overall growth of the female labor force. Of this 58 percent, almost half can be traced to the reduction in childbirth, which stemmed from the rise in female wages.

14.2 EXPLANATIONS OF THE WAGE GAP

The evidence so far indicates that the earnings gap between females and males has historically been quite large in the United States. Females have typically earned about 60 percent that of males. However, the earnings gap has not been unchanged over time. After widening between the end of World War II and the early 1950s, it remained almost unchanged for 20 years. Beginning in the early 1970s, female earnings started to gain on male workers, and this process has accelerated since 1980. Moreover, throughout the postwar period, the proportion of women in the labor force has been increasing dramatically. This has been true for all groups of women—single and married, those with and without children. In addition, of those women working, the percentage working full-time and full-year has also been on the rise.

Human Capital Differences

Differences in Experience Many economists have emphasized the experience differential between men and women as an explanation of the gender earnings gap. Women typically have fewer years of work experience than men of the same age and educational attainment. The reason is that, while men usually work continuously from the end of schooling, the labor force experience of women has historically been interrupted during childbearing and childrearing years. Though this pattern has changed recently, particularly among younger women who have entered the labor force since 1980, the experience differential will still exist between older men and women even today.

Evidence compiled by June O'Neill (1985) illustrates the magnitude of the differences in work experience. Unfortunately, there are no comprehensive data available on total work experience for men and women of different ages. However, there is information available on the number of years worked with the same employer. These data are shown in Table 14.5. There are three patterns that are evident from these figures. First, men have had,

Table 14.5   Median Years of Work Experience With Current Employer, for Women and Men by Age Group, 1951–1981[a]

	1951	1963	1973	1981
All, 16 years and over				
Men	3.9	5.7	4.6	4.0
Women	2.2	3.0	2.8	2.5
Difference	1.7	2.7	1.8	1.5
25–34 years				
Men	2.8	3.5	3.2	2.9
Women	1.8	2.0	2.2	2.0
Difference	1.0	1.5	1.0	0.9
35–44 years				
Men	4.5	7.6	6.7	6.6
Women	3.1	3.6	3.6	3.5
Difference	1.4	4.0	3.1	3.1
45–54 years				
Men	7.6	11.4	11.5	11.0
Women	4.0	6.1	5.9	5.9
Difference	3.6	5.3	5.6	5.1

[a]Source: June O'Neill (1985).

on average, greater work experience than women of the same age. This has been true for all years between 1951 and 1981. Second, the gender difference in work tenure increased rather sharply between 1951 and 1963 and then fell in all cases except one (for individuals ages 45 to 54). Third, the difference in work experience was greater among older workers. In 1981, men in age group 25–34 had, on average, 0.9 year more of work tenure with the same employer than women in the same age group; the difference was 3.1 years among workers in the 35–44 age group and 5.1 years for workers 45 to 54 years of age.

O'Neill also provides some estimates of the average number of years worked by age group for a more limited sample of female workers, based on the National Longitudinal Survey (NLS). These data also show that the work experience of women has been generally rising over time. The average number of years worked by white female employees in age group 25–29 increased from 5.2 years in 1973 to 6.1 years in 1978; while for those in the 30–34 age bracket, it fell slightly from 8.9 years in 1967 to 8.4 years in 1978. For women 35 to 39, average work experience increased from 11.6 years in 1967 to 12.1 years in 1972; among women 40–44, it rose from 14.1 years in

Table 14.6 Average Number of Years of Women's Labor Market Experience for Employed Women by Age Group, 1920–1990[a]

	1920	1950	1980	1986	1990
Working women, age 25	5.6	5.9	6.2	6.5	
Working women, age 30	8.7	8.0	9.5	10.5	10.4
Working women, age 40		14.0	14.4	15.5	17.0
Working women, age 50		19.3	20.6	21.5	22.5

[a] Source: Smith and Ward (1989).

1967 to 14.9 years in 1977; and for those 45–49, from 17.3 years in 1972 to 17.9 years in 1977.

Estimates provided by Smith and Ward (1989) show a similar pattern (see Table 14.6). The average years of work experience of working women aged 25 increased from 5.6 years in 1920 to 6.5 years in 1986. For women of age 30, the increase was from 8.7 years in 1920 to 10.4 years in 1990. Forty-year-old women saw their work experience rise from 14.0 years in 1950 to 17.0 years in 1990; for fifty-year-old women, it rose from 19.3 years in 1950 to 22.5 years in 1990. Thus, by their calculations, gains in work experience occurred for working women in all age groups, but the magnitude of the change since 1920 has been relatively small.

Though the results of O'Neill (1985) and Smith and Ward (1989) generally show rising work experience of women over time, the trends are rather modest. This might seem surprising, particularly in light of the dramatic increase in the labor force participation rates of women over time. Yet, the relation between rising LFPR and the average experience level of women is rather complicated. As O'Neill and Smith and Ward have argued, while an increase in the labor force participation of women does result in an increase in the average work experience *among all women* (working and not working), it does not necessarily result in an increase in the average work experience among *employed* women. Consider two cases. In the first case, suppose that female workers in the labor force have a high propensity to continue working over time. Then an increase in the overall LFPR of women must result from the fact that there are continually new female entrants into the labor force. Since the new entrants into the labor force have considerably less work experience than those women who are continuing to work, the *average* work experience of *working women* might actually go down.

In the second case, suppose that the female labor force is characterized by high turnover in employment. Then the work experience of both women in the labor force and those not in the labor force would tend to be equal. An increase in the overall labor force participation rate of women would then result from the *reentry* of women into the labor force who have already accumulated some work experience (but whose work experience had been interrupted). In this case, an increase in the LFPR of women would be associated with an increase in the average work experience of employed women.

The results of both O'Neill and Smith and Ward do show rising average work experience among employed women and seem to support the second case. Also, calculations made by Smith and Ward do indicate that the average work experience among *all women* (both employed and not employed) increases much faster than the average experience of employed women. For example, the average experience of working women of age 50 increased by 3.2 years between 1950 and 1990 (from 19.3 to 22.5 years), while that of all women increased by 7.0 years (from 10.9 to 17.9 years). This difference held for every age group.

Schooling Differences   Another surprising finding is that male workers have typically had fewer years of schooling than female workers. However, this difference has gradually eroded over time. Table 14.7 shows median years of schooling for male and female workers by age group from 1952 to 1983. In 1952, the average female worker had 12.0 years of schooling (a high school graduate). We discussed in the last chapter how average schooling levels in the workforce have been rising. This was true for both male and female workers, but the rate of increase was actually greater for men than for women. By 1969, the differential in favor of female workers had almost disappeared. Indeed, by 1983, the average male worker and the average female worker had completed 12.7 years of education. The results are similar by age group.

Why did men's schooling increase faster than women's? There are two reasons, according to O'Neill. First, during the 1950s, men entered college at a higher rate than women, aided in part by the educational benefits of the "GI bill," passed after World War II to provide benefits for veterans of the war. Second, the labor force participation of older, less educated females increased faster than younger, more educated women, thus reducing the *average* educational attainment among all female workers.

Effects of Human Capital Differences on the Gender Wage Gap*   How much do differences in schooling and work experience help account for the earnings gap between men and women? As in the case of racial disparities in earnings, there have been numerous studies on the sources of the wage gap between men and women. These have usually taken the form of regression analysis, in which the individual wages of men and women are regressed on (that is, related to) the schooling and work experience of that individual, as well as other relevant labor market characteristics. In these studies, the unexplained difference (the "residual") is usually attributed to the presence of discrimination.

As noted in Section 14.1, the gender wage gap has gone through three phases. In the early part of the postwar period, from the end of World War II to the early 1950s, the wage gap actually widened. Then, from the early 1950s to the early 1970s, the wage gap remained more or less stable. Finally,

Table 14.7 Median Years of Schooling for Male and Female Workers by Age Group, 1952–1983[a]

	1952	1959	1969	1979	1983
All, 18 years and over					
Women	12.0	12.2	12.4	12.6	12.7
Men	10.4	11.5	12.3	12.6	12.7
Difference	1.6	0.7	0.1	0.0	0.0
25–34 years					
Women	12.2	12.3	12.5	12.9	13.0
Men	12.1	12.3	12.6	13.1	13.0
Difference	0.1	0.0	−0.1	−0.2	0.0
35–44 years					
Women	11.9	12.2	12.4	12.6	12.8
Men	11.2	12.1	12.4	12.8	12.9
Difference	0.7	0.1	0.0	−0.2	−0.1
45–54 years					
Women		11.7	12.3	12.5	12.6
Men		10.4	12.2	12.5	12.7
Difference		1.3	0.1	0.0	−0.1
55–64 years					
Women		10.0	12.1	12.4	12.5
Men		8.8	10.9	12.4	12.5
Difference		1.2	1.2	0.0	0.0

[a] Source: June O'Neill (1985).

from the early 1970s to the present, female wages have been increasing faster than male wages. The various studies summarized below tend to concentrate on different phases of the wage gap trend.

Using U.S. Census of Population data, James Gwartney and Richard Stroup (1973) reported that the ratio of median income between females and males fell from 0.40 in 1949 to 0.32 in 1969 among all adults, and the ratio of median labor earnings declined from 0.58 to 0.47 among working adults. A large part of the gender difference in labor earnings was accounted for by differences in the amount of time worked. For example, in 1959, the ratio of annual earnings between females and males (including both full-time and part-time workers) was 0.49, but the ratio in hourly earnings (annual earnings divided by the number of hours worked) was 0.61. In 1969, the ratio in annual earnings for all workers was 0.47, but for full-time, year-round workers alone, it was 0.56. They found that age and education explained very little of the remaining gender gap in earnings. In fact, female workers had, on average, greater schooling than male workers in 1949 and 1959 and about the same level of schooling in 1969. Thus about 40 percent of the difference in earnings between females and males in those years was left unexplained after controlling for human capital factors.

On further analysis, the authors found that the earnings gap between single males and females was substantially less than that between married males and females. In 1959, after adjustments for age, education, and time worked, the female-male median income ratio was estimated to be between 0.91 and 0.96 for singles and to be 0.50 for those married. Gwartney and Stroup suggested that the large earnings gap between females and males may not necessarily reflect employer discrimination. It may instead reflect the preference of married females for low-responsibility jobs, which also carry with them lower pay.

Victor Fuchs (1971), also analyzing 1960 Census of Population data, calculated an average hourly earnings ratio between nonfarm females and males of 0.60. He then adjusted the earnings data for differences in schooling, age, race, and city size and found that the resulting gender earnings ratio increased to only 0.61. After further adjustments for differences in marital status, class of worker (whether self-employed, employed in private industry, or employed in the government), and commuting time,[1] the earnings ratio rose to 0.66. Thus, about 34 percent of the earnings gap was still left unaccounted for after controlling for productivity-related factors.

Fuchs also found that a large part of the earnings gap was due to gender differences in occupation of employment and, in particular, to the fact that women tended to be concentrated in the low-paying service occupations. Fuchs suggested that a large part of the earnings gap was due to gender differences in social roles. Role differentiation affected the choice of occupation, hours of work, and other variables that influence earnings. He speculated that role differences may themselves be a product of discrimination.

In a later paper, Fuchs (1974) compared the male-female earnings ratio using Census data over the decade between 1960 and 1970. In contrast to Gwartney and Stroup, he did find some relative gains made by females. The ratio of female to male hourly earnings, adjusted for age and schooling, increased from 0.61 to 0.64 over this decade, or by 5 percent. For some groups of females, the gain was even larger. For college-educated females, the earnings ratio increased from 0.59 to 0.66 relative to college-educated men, or by 11 percent. For self-employed females, the ratio (relative to self-employed males) increased by 11 percent from 0.51 to 0.57. He also found that the earnings gap was smaller among workers under 35 years of age than older workers, considerably smaller for singles than married individuals (as

---

[1] Commuting time was included as a variable, because married females might have a preference for jobs close to home even if they are low-paying.

Gwartney and Stroup had found), and smaller for government employees than nongovernment workers.

Ronald Oaxaca (1973) found substantial evidence of sex discrimination on the basis of the 1967 Survey of Economic Opportunity. Of the gross wage differential between white females and males of 0.54, he estimated that 0.40 points or 74 percent was due to discrimination. Of the gross wage differential between black females and males of 0.49, he estimated that 0.45 points or 92 percent was due to discrimination. In the absence of sex discrimination, he estimated that the average white female wage would have been 88 percent of the white male wage instead of the actual ratio of 54 percent. He also estimated that the average black female wage would have been 96 percent of the black male wage instead of the actual ratio of 67 percent.

In a follow-up study, Oaxaca (1977) found that the earnings ratio between year-round female and male workers actually fell between the mid-1950s and 1970s for whites, though it increased for blacks. He concluded that it was an increase in sex discrimination among white workers that accounted for the relative decline in the economic position of white female workers and a reduction in sex discrimination among black workers that accounted for the relative gain of black female workers.

June O'Neill (1985) examined changes in the overall wage gap between males and females over the period from 1955 to 1982. She found a U-shaped pattern, with the gender pay gap (defined as one minus the ratio of female to male annual earnings adjusted for hours worked) first widening from 0.31 in 1955 to 0.37 in the early 1970s but subsequently narrowing to 0.33 in 1983. On net, there was very little change in the wage gap over the entire period.

O'Neill's analysis indicated that changes in productivity-related characteristics were primarily responsible for movements in the gender wage gap. Male workers gained on females in educational attainment, from a difference of 1.6 years of schooling in favor of employed females in the 1950s to virtual parity in 1979. The rise in female labor force participation over the period tended to offset any increases in the average work experience of employed females. The work experience differential between women and men widened between 1952 and 1963 and then narrowed from 1963 to 1981. On net, there was little change in the experience differential between the early 1950s and the early 1980s. If anything, human capital of male workers increased relative to female workers between the 1950s and the 1980s. These changes should have resulted in an *increase* in the overall gender wage gap, so the fact that the overall wage gap did not increase may have reflected *reduced* labor market discrimination against females.

In a later study examining the gains made by females over the 1980s, June O'Neill and Solomon Polachek concluded that increases in female human capital were the primary reason for the narrowing of the wage gap. Using data from the Panel Study of Income Dynamics and the National Longitudinal Survey, they reported that the hourly wage gap between female and male workers declined by about one percent per year between 1976 and 1989. The two panel surveys allowed them to obtain good estimates of work experience for females, and they found that there was a significant increase in women's years of work experience over this period. Moreover, the return to female work experience (that is, the extra pay per year of experience) also rose over these years, presumably because of greater investment in on-the-job training. This latter effect may be due to increased effort on the part of female workers to obtain training, employer response to women's increased work attachment, or a decline in discrimination. O'Neill and Polachek also found that while the return to schooling increased for both men and women over this period, it increased faster for women and this also contributed to the narrowing of the wage gap.

Francine Blau and Andrea Beller (1988) examined changes in the gender wage gap between 1971 and 1981 on the basis of the Current Population Survey. They first analyzed changes in the gender wage gap. They found that the usual measure of the gender wage gap, the ratio in median earnings between full-time, year-round female and male workers, showed little change over this period—a 3 percent increase for whites and a 1 percent decline for blacks. However, when the earnings of all workers were adjusted for hours worked, the ratio in hourly wages between female and male workers increased by 9 percent for whites and 11 percent for blacks.

Blau and Beller then analyzed some of the factors contributing to the narrowing of the gender wage gap over this period. They found that declining gender role specialization (as reflected in the occupational composition of employment) and declining discrimination explained a large part of the narrowing. They also found that the "marriage penalty" on female wages—the proclivity of employers to pay lower wages to married women than single women with the same human capital—declined over this period.

Joni Hersch (1991) used the 1986 Quality of Employment Survey to analyze the effects of marital status, the number of dependents, and housework responsibilities on female wages in the labor market. She found that household responsibilities (as measured by the amount of time spent in work at home) had a negative effect on female wages but little effect on male wages. For women, household responsibilities appeared to reduce the amount of their human capital investments (particularly in firm training) and also to reduce the amount of effort available for market work. On the basis of the Michigan Panel Study of Income Dynamics, Hersch (1995) reported the striking result that time spent in housework not only depressed female wages by reducing the time available for human capital investment but also had a direct negative effect on wages. This latter effect may reflect a lack of complete commitment to market work, which women experience when they face burdensome household responsibilities in addition.

Elaine Sorensen (1991) examined changes in the gender wage gap over the 1980s. She first reported that women made tremendous gains relative to men over this period. Among full-time workers, the ratio of earnings between women and men increased from 61 percent in 1978 to 72 percent in

1990. Using the Panel Study of Income Dynamics, she estimated earnings equations for both males and females in 1979 and 1985 to analyze the sources of the narrowing of the wage gap. Her main conclusion was that most of the narrowing (77 percent among whites and 61 percent among blacks) was due to the unexplained residual, which she interpreted as a reduction in discrimination against females. There were three other contributing factors, whose effects were relatively small: (1) a modest convergence in the human capital of female and male workers; (2) growing similarity in the occupational distributions of female and male workers; and (3) industrial shifts in employment, in favor of the female-dominated service sectors and away from the male-dominated and heavily unionized goods-producing industries.

Another important dimension to labor market compensation is the value of fringe benefits. Two studies have examined gender differences in benefit coverage. Janet Currie (1993) used the May 1988 Current Population Survey's Survey of Employee Benefits to examine differences in benefit structure. She reported that in 1988, pensions accounted for 5 percent of employee payrolls, health insurance and related expenditures for 8.1 percent, and sick leave and disability together for 1.9 percent. The preponderance of fringe benefits takes the form of pensions and health insurance. Using regression analysis, she concluded that after controlling for age, education, marital status, and number of children, male employees were more likely to have pensions, health coverage, and disability than women, though women were more likely to have paid sick leave. These differences were statistically significant. However, after controlling for wages, differences in benefit coverage disappeared, suggesting that much of the difference in benefit coverage between males and females was due to the fact that women, on average, were employed in jobs which paid lower wages.

A similar analysis was conducted by Janet Currie and Richard Chaykowski (1992) for Canada. Using establishment-level data for union contracts in Ontario over the period from 1980 to 1990 and individual data from the 1986 Canadian Labour Market Activities Survey, they found that, after controlling for job tenure, female workers were less likely to be covered by pension plans. This difference persisted even after wages were controlled for. On the other hand, among unionized workers, female workers had more generous leave provisions than male workers.

Effects of Work Interruption on Earnings A related but somewhat different concern is the impact of work disruptions on the relative earnings of females. The work surveyed in the preceding section generally sought to use years of experience as an explanatory variable in accounting for wage differences between men and women. However, the fact that women have experienced more interruptions in their work history may have an added effect on their labor earnings.

There are three reasons why the continuity or discontinuity of work experience may affect earnings. First, as Jacob Mincer and Solomon Polachek

(1974) argued, the fact that women may expect discontinuous labor market participation and fewer total years at work than men provides less incentive for women to undertake human capital investments than men. This is particularly so for firm-specific training, since they will reap the rewards of such investment over fewer years. Second, employers will also have less incentive to train female workers, since the period for recapturing their investment is shorter. Third, withdrawals from the labor market may lead to depreciation of human capital, since the skills acquired may become obsolete.

Several studies have attempted to estimate the importance of work interruption on differences in earnings between males and females. Duncan and Hoffman (1979) were able to obtain direct measures of on-the-job training from the 1976 wave of the Panel Study of Income Dynamics. They found that men and women obtained the same return from on-the-job training. However, women systematically received less training than men with the same amount of past work experience. They noted that these results are consistent with the hypothesis that firms have different training and promotion policies for male and female employees. They concluded that the lower payoffs to experience observed for women may reflect, in part, discrimination on the part of employers in providing job training.

James Ragan and Sharon Smith (1981) pooled industry data on quit rates with 1970 Census of Population data on individual earnings and worker characteristics (including industry of employment) to estimate the effects of the likelihood of quitting on male-female wage differences. They argued that because of hiring and training costs, firms prefer, *ceteris paribus*, workers whose probability of leaving the firm is low. If an employer believes that the likelihood that a female will leave the company is greater than that of a male employee, the firm may hire female employees only if they accept a lower wage. They found that high quit probabilities are associated with lower wages, and in fact, the wage discount for female employees is greater than for male employees with the same quit rate. They concluded that differences in quit rates between males and females, together with other worker characteristics (schooling, experience, and socioeconomic characteristics), explained about half the wage gap between male and female workers in 1970.

The results reported so far suggest that the greater likelihood of female withdrawal from the labor force (or, at least, employer *perception* of a greater likelihood) is associated with less firm investment in female employees than male and thus a lower rate of return to female work experience than male work experience. A related issue is whether females are permanently penalized for labor market withdrawal when they reenter the labor force, due to the depreciation of their human capital while they are out of work. Several papers have analyzed the so-called "rebound effect." Jacob Mincer and Haim Ofek (1982) argued that the restoration of past occupational skills is more efficient than the acquisition of new skills. As a result, one should expect to find that wages are low during the first year following a labor market interruption but that wages should quickly recover after several years of

Part IV Discrimination

continuous work. Using data from the National Longitudinal Surveys for years 1966–1974, they found precisely this pattern: wages of female workers who had been out of the labor force for a period of time were lower on reentry than when they had last worked, but they soon recovered to their previous level.

Mary Corcoran, Greg Duncan, and Michael Ponza (1983) used data covering the period 1967–1979 from the Panel Study of Income Dynamics to analyze the effects of female labor market withdrawals on future wages. They found the same pattern as Mincer and Ofek and concluded that the net loss in earnings from labor market dropout was small for females. However, they proposed a different explanation from the one advanced by Mincer and Ofek—namely that on reentry there is often a mismatch between worker skills and jobs. After a work interruption, women workers often lack complete information about job opportunities, and employers often lack complete information about the skills of the new worker. One common mechanism for this sorting process is to assign new workers to low-wage jobs on hiring and then to promote them as their skills become known.

Joyce Jacobsen and Lawrence Levin (1992) reached a somewhat different conclusion on the basis of data from the 1984 wave of the Survey of Income and Program Participation. Like Mincer and Ofek (1982) and Corcoran, Duncan, and Ponza (1983), they found that when women reenter the labor force after a period of nonparticipation, their earnings are much lower than a comparable group of women with continuous labor market experience. Over time, the gap diminished between what they called the "gappers" and "nongappers" because of the rebound effect. However, even after 20 years, the gap did not entirely disappear. Moreover, the effect of a gap on women's lifetime earnings was significantly greater than their foregone earnings alone during the period of nonparticipation.

Nan Maxwell and Ronald D'Amico (1986), using data from the National Longitudinal Surveys over the period 1966–1983, looked at relative unemployment rates for males and females returning to the labor market. They found that unemployment rates among females who were reentering the labor force after a prolonged interruption were $2^{1}/_{2}$ times greater than men reentering the labor market after a similar period of interruption. They concluded that women fare considerably worse than men after job interruption.

Occupational Segregation

Another important factor accounting for differences in female and male earnings is that female workers tend to be concentrated in the relatively low-paying occupations. This phenomenon is often referred to as "occupational segregation." We have alluded to this factor before (in Section 12.8) in our discussion of the overcrowding model.

There are four questions of interest. First, what is the extent of occupational segregation between males and females? Second, how much does occupational segregation contribute to the female-male wage gap? Third, has occupational segregation lessened over time? Fourth, if so, how much has the abatement in occupational segregation contributed to the narrowing of the gender wage gap?

We show some figures on the composition of female employment by major occupational group over the period from 1900 to 1993 in Table 14.8. Panel A shows the distribution of total female employment among occupational groups. In 1993, the largest concentration of female employees was in clerical jobs (27 percent); professional and technical positions (20 percent); and service jobs, excluding domestic servants (16 percent). Indeed, even as late as 1983, one-third of all female employees were found in only nine detailed occupations: secretaries (8.7 percent), bookkeepers and accounting clerks (5.0 percent), teachers, excluding college (5.4 percent), registered nurses (3.0 percent), waitresses (2.7 percent), information clerks (2.4 percent), health technicians (2.1 percent), private household workers (2.1 percent), and typists (2.0 percent).[2]

However, there have been significant changes over the twentieth century. The proportion of female workers employed in professional and technical occupations rose rather steadily, from 8 percent in 1900 to 20 percent in 1993. The proportion in managerial and administrative positions increased from only *one* percent in 1900 to 12 percent in 1993, with almost half of the increase occurring after 1977. The percentage in clerical jobs grew from 4 in 1900 to 34 in 1977 but then declined to 27 in 1993, while the percent of females working in sales jobs increased from 4 to 13, with the bulk of the change occurring between 1977 and 1988. The share of women employed in service jobs (excluding domestic servants) also grew, from 7 percent in 1900 to 16 percent in 1993. In contrast, the proportion of women working as operatives (mainly machine operators) declined from 24 percent in 1900 to 6 percent in 1993, the proportion working in private households from 29 percent to 2 percent, and the proportion in farming from 19 to 1 percent. The proportion working in craft and kindred jobs remained almost unchanged, at 1 percent in 1900 and 2 percent in 1993.

Panel B presents figures on female employment in a particular occupational group as a percent of the total employment in that occupation. In 1993, females comprised 46 percent of overall employment but 95 percent of private household workers, 79 percent of clerical workers, 57 percent of service workers (excluding domestic servants), 53 percent of professional and technical employees, and 48 percent of sales workers. They made up only 9 percent of craft workers, 18 percent of nonfarm laborers, 15 percent

---

[2] Harriet Zellner (1972) reported that in 1960, 50 percent of employed women were concentrated in occupations where they represented 80 percent or more of the total employment in the occupation, whereas only 2 percent of total male employees were in these occupations. On the other hand, only 20 percent of female workers were employed in occupations where they represented a third or less of total employment in the occupation, whereas 90 percent of employed men were in these occupations. Indeed, Francine Blau (1972) found that in *1900*, 30 percent of the female labor force was employed in just one occupational category, that of private household workers, while 4 of the detailed Census occupations in that year accounted for 46 percent of the female labor force.

Table 14.8 The Percentage Composition of Female Employment by Occupation, 1900–1993[a]

	1900	1920	1940	1960	1970	1977	1988	1993
A. Female Employment by Occupation as a Percent of Total Female Employment								
Professional and technical	8	12	13	12	14	15	18	20
Managers (except farm)	1	2	3	5	4	6	11	12
Clerical workers	4	19	22	30	34	34	28	27
Sales workers	4	6	7	8	7	7	13	13
Craft and kindred	1	1	1	1	1	2	2	2
Operatives	24	20	20	16	15	12	7	6
Laborers (nonfarm)	3	2	1	0	1	1	2	2
Private household	29	16	18	10	5	5	2	2
Service (except household)	7	8	11	15	17	18	16	16
Farmers, farm managers, and farm laborers	19	14	4	4	2	1	1	1
Total	100	100	100	100	100	100	100	100
B. Female Occupational Employment as a Percent of Total Occupational Employment								
Professional and technical	35	45	41	36	38	43	49	53
Managers (except farm)	4	7	11	16	16	22	39	42
Clerical workers	24	48	54	68	74	79	80	79
Sales workers	17	26	27	39	43	44	49	48
Craft and kindred	2	2	2	3	3	5	9	9
Operatives	34	27	26	28	32	32	29	27
Laborers (nonfarm)	4	4	3	2	4	4	17	18
Private household	97	98	95	98	97	97	93	95
Service (except household)	34	37	39	53	60	58	58	57
Farmers, farm managers	5	4	3	4	5	5]	17	15
Farm laborers	14	18	10	33	32	29]		
Total	18	20	24	33	38	41	45	46
C. DD Index	52	49	49	44	44	44	36	34

[a] Sources: U.S. Department of Commerce, Bureau of the Census, *Historical Statistics of the United States: Colonial Times to 1970*, Bicentennial Edition, Part 2; U.S. Department of Labor, Bureau of Labor Statistics, *Handbook of Labor Statistics 1978*, Bulletin 2000, 1979; U.S. Department of Labor, Bureau of Labor Statistics, *Handbook of Labor Statistics 1989*, Bulletin 2340, 1990; and U.S. Bureau of the Census, *Statistical Abstract of the United States, 1994*, 1994.

of farm workers, 27 percent of operatives, and 42 percent of managers and administrators.

Even though this aggregated classification shows substantial differences in the occupational employment patterns of female and male workers,

Table 14.9 Female Occupational Employment as a Percent of Total Occupational Employment for Selected Detailed Occupations, 1979, 1986, and 1993[a]

Occupation	1979	1986	1993
Secretaries	98.8	99.2	98.9
Registered nurses	94.6	92.7	94.4
Bookkeepers, accounting and auditing clerks	88.1	93.0	90.9
Nursing aides, orderlies, and attendants	85.1	88.3	87.9
Cashiers	77.7	79.8	—
Computer operators	56.6	63.8	61.9
Assemblers	47.2	42.1	32.7
Accountants and auditors	34.0	44.7	49.2
Computer programmers	28.0	39.7	31.5
Supervisors and proprietors, sales occupations	22.4	26.6	36.4
Computer systems analysts	20.4	29.7	—
Janitors and cleaners	15.3	21.0	30.7
Lawyers	10.4	15.2	22.9
Sales representatives, mining, manufacturing, wholesale	10.1	13.4	21.0
Electrical and electronic engineers	4.4	9.4	7.6
Truck drivers, heavy	1.5	1.5	—
Carpenters, except apprentices	1.1	0.5	0.9
Automotive mechanics, except apprentices	0.9	0.6	0.6

[a] Source: U.S. Bureau of the Census, Current Population Reports, Series P-70, No. 10, *Male-Female Differences in Work Experience, Occupations and Earnings: 1984*, August 1987; and U.S. Bureau of the Census, *Statistical Abstract of the United States, 1994*, 1994. 1979 and 1986 figures are for full-time workers.

employment data by detailed occupations show an even more extreme pattern of occupational segregation. As shown in Table 14.9, in 1993, females accounted for 99 percent of all secretaries, 94 percent of registered nurses, 91 percent of bookkeepers, 88 percent of nursing aides, and 80 percent of cashiers (in 1986), while they accounted for less than 1 percent of automotive mechanics and carpenters, 2 percent of drivers of heavy trucks (in 1986), and 8 percent of electrical and electronic engineers.

Despite the evidence of substantial occupational segregation in the 1980s, there have been dramatic gains over time. Females comprised only 4 percent of managerial and administrative positions in 1900 but 42 percent in 1993, with most of the change occurring after 1977 (Table 14.8). They comprised 24 percent of clerical positions in 1900 and 79 percent in 1993; 17 percent of sales jobs in 1900 and almost half in 1993; and 34 percent of service jobs in 1900 and 57 percent in 1993.

Even since 1979, women have made substantial inroads into traditional male occupations. Their share among accountants and auditors increased from 34 to 49 percent between 1979 and 1993 (Table 14.9); among computer systems analysts from 20 to 30 percent (in 1986); among lawyers from 10 to 23 percent; and among electrical and electronic engineers from 4 to 8 percent.

Duncan and Duncan Index　A standard measure of occupational segregation is the Duncan and Duncan (DD) index, developed by Otis Dudley Duncan and Beverly Duncan in 1955. It is defined as follows:

$$DD = \Sigma_i \left| m_i - f_i \right| / 2 \tag{14.1}$$

where m_i is the percent of total male employees working in occupation i, f_i is the percent of total females employees working in occupation i, and "|" is the sign for the absolute value of the difference. The index ranges from zero, if the occupational distributions of male and female workers are exactly the same (the same proportion of male and female employees in each occupation), to 100, if male and female workers do not overlap in any occupation (that is, there is complete occupational segregation).[3]

DD indices computed on the basis of the 11 occupational groups are shown in the last line of Table 14.8. Over the entire period from 1900 to 1993, the degree of occupational segregation declined by a third, from a DD index of 52 to 34. However, there was almost no change in the degree of occupational segregation between 1900 to 1940; a noticeable reduction between 1940 and 1950, the effects of World War II on female employment;[4] almost no change between 1950 and 1977; and then a considerable decline between 1977 and 1993.

The DD indices calculated in Table 14.8 are based on a very aggregated occupational classification. Computations based on detailed occupations do show more change in the degree of occupational segregation. Andrea Beller (1985) calculated from Census of Population data that the DD index declined from 68.7 in 1960 to 65.9 in 1970, or by 2.8 points. Three studies were carried out for the 1970–1980 period on the basis of the 1970 and 1980 Census of Population data. Beller (1984) calculated a 4.2 point decline in the DD index over this period (65.9 to 61.7). Barbara Reskin and Heidi Hartmann (1988) calculated a 8.4 point decline (67.7 to 59.3), and Judith Fields and Edward Wolff (1991) a 8.3 point decline (from 66.8 to 58.5). Blau (1989), using data from the Current Population Survey, calculated only a 2.4 point decline (59.1 to 56.7) in the DD index between 1983 and 1987.

---

[3]As might be apparent, the magnitude of DD is very sensitive to the number of occupations used in the analysis. The measure is almost higher the more occupational classifications that are used. In time-series comparisons, the analyst tries to use the same number of occupations in each year.

[4]See Claudia Goldin (1991) for an interesting analysis of the effects of wartime employment (World War II) on the structure of female employment.

Table 14.10 shows calculations of the DD indices in 1960 and 1980 performed by Victor Fuchs (1989) on the basis of very detailed occupational categories for different demographic groups.[5] In 1980, the DD index stood at 57 among both whites and blacks. As Fuchs noted, a DD index of 57 suggests pervasive occupational segregation by gender, particularly when it is compared to the corresponding DD index by race—only 28 for black women versus white women and 33 for black men versus white men.

There was some reduction in occupational segregation by gender between 1960 and 1980. Among whites, the DD index declined by 5 percent (62 to 57) and among blacks by 14 percent (71 to 57).[6] The biggest reduction occurred among young adults, ages 25 to 34, for whom the DD index

Table 14.10   Duncan and Duncan Indexes of Occupational Segregation by Gender, 1960 and 1980[a]

	1960	1980	Change from 1960 to 1980
All		57	
Race			
Whites	62	57	−5
Blacks	71	57	−14
Age			
25–34	67	55	−12
35–44	63	58	−5
45–54	63	60	−3
55–64	65	61	−4
Schooling			
Elementary School or Less	66	60	−6
High School 1–3	64	61	−3
High School Graduate	66	62	−4
College Degree	66	50	−16
Graduate Degree	56	43	−13

[a] Source: Fuchs (1989). The 1960 calculations are based on 291 occupations from the 1960 Census of Population 1 in 100 Public Use Sample, and the 1980 calculations are based on 503 occupations from the 1980 Census of Population 1 in 100 Public Use Sample. Both samples are restricted to full-time, full-year employees.

[5] There were 503 occupations used for the 1980 computations but only 291 occupations for the 1960. Since the DD index usually rises as the number of occupations increases, the results are biased towards showing greater occupational segregation (a higher value of DD) in 1980 than in 1960.

[6] However, as Fuchs reported, there was an even greater reduction in occupational segregation by race. Between black women and white women, the DD index declined by 50 percent (from 56 to 28), and between black men and white men, the DD index declined by 34 percent (from 50 to 33).

fell by 12 percent (from 67 to 55), and among college-educated workers (16 percent for those with a college degree and 13 percent for those with a graduate degree). Thus, younger and more educated female workers were penetrating traditionally male occupations, whereas there was relatively little change for older and less educated females.

Occupational Segregation and the Change in the Gender Wage Gap Several studies have focused on the role of occupational segregation in explaining the gender wage gap and its change over time. In this literature, there are two sources that account for the overall gender wage gap. First, men and women are distributed differently among occupations, with women tending to be concentrated in the low-paying ones. Second, within occupations, women receive, on average, lower earnings than men. These studies have decomposed the overall gender wage gap into these two effects.

The author (1976) calculated, on the basis of 33 occupational groups drawn from the 1960 and 1970 Census of Population, that in 1960, 74 percent of the overall gender wage gap was due to the lower earnings of females within occupation and 26 percent was due to differences in their occupational distribution of employment. In 1970, the corresponding proportions were 69 percent and 31 percent. Using Current Population Surveys from 1967 to 1986, Peter Orazem, J. Peter Mattila, and Ruoh Chiann Yu (1990) found that all of the narrowing of the male-female wage gap was due to increases in relative female wages within occupation and none to shifts in female occupational patterns. In these two studies, gender differences in pay within occupation were found to be more important than gender differences in the pattern of occupational employment in explaining both the overall gender wage gap and its change over time.[7]

Explanations of Occupational Segregation Several arguments have been proposed to account for occupational segregation. First, Solomon Polachek (1981) argued that because women generally anticipate less continuous and shorter work lives than men, they will prefer "female occupations," which require smaller human capital investment and provide lower penalties for dropping out of the labor market. In this regard, women may also select occupations that are more compatible with their household responsibilities. Indeed, time budget studies have shown that women continue to perform the majority of household tasks even when they are working in the labor market (see Francine Blau and Marianne Ferber, 1986, for an example).

However, results reported by Paula England (1982) on the basis of the 1967 National Longitudinal Sample seemed to contradict this interpretation. She found that the penalty faced by women for time spent out of the

---

[7]A related point is that there may be a systematic relation between the male-female wage gap within occupation and the proportion of females employed within that occupation. Nancy Rytina (1981) found on the basis of the 1976 Survey of Income and Education that the occupational female-male wage gap was negatively related to the percent of females in that occupation (that is, the wage gap was smaller in occupations with a higher percentage of females).

labor force was no smaller if they worked in female occupations than if they worked in mixed or predominantly male occupations. There was no evidence that anticipation of intermittent employment made the choice of a traditionally female occupation economically rational. In fact, after controlling for time worked in the labor market, women had higher wages if they were employed in an occupation containing mainly males. Moreover, women with more intermittent labor market experience were not more apt to be in a predominantly female occupation than women with more continuous work experience.

A second explanation hinges on differences in tastes between male and female workers. Mark Killingsworth (1987) argued that differences in returns to job characteristics can arise in a nondiscriminatory manner if tastes for job attributes differ between males and females. Randall Filer (1983) obtained personnel records from a management consulting firm, which had unique data on the tastes of their employees with regard to work attitudes. Individuals in the firm were asked to rank eleven factors in order of importance: job satisfaction, security, power, occupational prestige, social prestige, income, family life, religious activities, community activities, freedom for travel and recreation, and contribution of job to society. Using regression analysis, Filer found that a significant portion of the gender earnings difference could be attributed to differences in job preferences, though there was still a large portion of the difference unexplained.

A third explanation rests on differences in socialization patterns. Victor Fuchs (1989) argued that women's greater role in reproduction and smaller upper body strength probably played a large role in gender segregation in preindustrial societies, but in modern society these differences have been amplified through socialization. The experiences of girls and boys in schools and families and their exposure to the media significantly affect their behavior as adults. These show up in the choice of school subjects and extracurricular activities and the goals they set with respect to family and career. If boys and girls are exposed to different influences, training, and role models, it is likely that they will enter the labor market with different aptitudes, interests, and aspirations. Traditionally, socialization has tended to direct females to the role of wife, mother, and homemaker and men to the role of husband, father, and provider. Jobs taken by both men and women have historically been more compatible with their traditional role models.

These arguments suggest that the difference in the occupational distribution of male and female employment results from differences in tastes or choices—either because women prefer jobs with less training and responsibility due to household or child care obligations or because they are socialized differently than men. An alternative view is that occupational segregation may result from unequal opportunities in the labor market—that is, discrimination. The model of statistical discrimination presented in Section 12.4 provides such a rationale.

It is rather difficult to distinguish empirically between choice on the one hand and discrimination on the other as the root cause of occupational segregation. Indeed, the two may reinforce each other if socialization leads women to prefer jobs that have traditionally been assigned to females because of discrimination. A study by Judith Fields and the author (1991), based on Census of Population data for detailed occupations over the 1970–1980 period, does suggest that discrimination may be an important factor. They found clear evidence that high employment growth within an occupation was associated with declines in segregation within that occupation. They concluded that job barriers against women tended to be lower in sectors where labor demand was strong.[8] This result is consistent with the model of statistical discrimination, from which it can be inferred that discriminatory barriers against minorities and females will lessen when labor market shortages exist for white males.

14.3 THE ROLE OF PUBLIC POLICY

There are three major policy instruments which prohibit gender discrimination. The first is the Equal Pay Act of 1963. A 1963 amendment to the Fair Labor Standards Act of 1938 required that females receive the same pay as men for the same work. Known as the "Equal Pay Act," this amendment was designed to eliminate wage differentials based on gender. However, this act did allow for differences in pay for the same work if it was based on seniority, merit, or some type of incentive plan. This act is enforced by the Wage-Hour and Public Contracts Division of the Department of Labor.

Operationally, it is often difficult to determine whether equal work is being performed by a male and female worker, particularly if different job titles are used. Moreover, this act does not address the critical problem of occupational segregation. Despite such difficulties, the division has investigated thousands of complaints, sought voluntary compliance from employers, and, where this has failed, helped complainants bring cases to court.

As discussed in the last chapter (see Section 13.5), the two other major antidiscrimination regulations are the 1964 Civil Rights Act and Executive Order 11246. Title VII of the Civil Rights Act of 1964 prohibits employers from discriminating on the basis of sex in hiring or firing, compensation, terms and conditions of employment, and employer-provided training. The 1964 Civil Rights Act also set up the Equal Employment Opportunity Commission (EEOC) to enforce the provisions of Title VII. Executive Order 11246, originally issued in 1965 to prohibit race discrimination, was extended in 1968 to prohibit gender discrimination by federal contractors. Executive Order 11246 also required federal contractors to take affirmative action to remedy any underrepresentation, and it established the Office of Federal Contract Compliance (OFCC) to enforce this order.

---

[8] They also found that declines in industry segregation within occupation were associated with improvements in relative female earnings (independently of other factors which affect relative pay) and that high employment growth was associated with improvements in relative female earnings, independently of its effect on occupational segregation.

Effectiveness of the Antidiscrimination Programs

The Equal Pay Act, Title VII of the Civil Rights Act of 1964, and Executive Order 11246 are the three major legal instruments implemented to combat employment discrimination. How effective have they been? A number of studies have been carried out to answer this question. As with studies on racial discrimination, they have generally been of two types. First, some have used time-series data to determine whether the passage of Title VII in 1964 has affected the trends in the relative earnings of females—in particular, whether there has been a statistically significant break in the series after 1964. As Francine Blau (1984) noted, the main problem with time-series analysis is the difficulty of including enough control variables so that one can be sure that the results isolate the effect of Title VII alone on the post–1964 trends. Second, other studies have used cross-sectional data to compare the progress of women in firms or industries covered by Executive Order 11246 (federal contractors) with those in sectors not covered. As Blau argues, the difficulty here is to identify correctly the covered and uncovered sectors.

Different studies have concentrated on different aspects of gender discrimination (see Morley Gunderson, 1989, for a detailed review). Andrea Beller (1976, 1979, and 1980) used Current Population Surveys over the period from 1967 to 1975 to estimate the effects of the EEOC enforcements provisions on the female-male wage gap. She included measures of both the probability of an EEOC investigation and the probability of a successful settlement from an EEOC investigation in her analysis of the change in male and female earnings. She found that the female-male wage gap declined by almost 10 percent between 1967 and 1974 and that the rate of increase was faster after 1972, the date of the amendment to Title VII, which provided for more effective enforcement. A higher probability of an investigation was found to be more important than a higher probability of a settlement in accounting for the increased earnings of female workers. She concluded that stricter enforcement of EEOC played an important role in the earnings gains made by females over this period.

In a later article, Andrea Beller (1982) used the same data to analyze the probability of a female worker entering a predominantly male occupation (defined as one in which at least two-thirds of the employees are males). She calculated that the probability of a female being employed in a male occupation relative to the probability of a male worker being found in such an occupation increased by 6.2 percent between 1967 and 1974. She found that both Title VII of the 1964 Civil Rights Act and the federal contract compliance program helped explain the inroads made by females into male-dominated occupations over this period. In this case, a higher probability of a settlement was found to be more important than a higher probability of an investigation in accounting for these gains.

Two other studies found no statistically significant effect of Title VII on the relative economic gains made by females after 1964. Jonathan Leonard (1984c) used data on employment by manufacturing industry over the period between 1966 and 1978 to determine whether there was any significant connection between the proportion of females employed within an industry and the degree of Title VII compliance (as measured by the number of class action lawsuits). He failed to find a significant relation. Ronald Oaxaca (1977) used Census of Population data for 1960 and 1970 and Current Population Report figures over the period 1955–1971 to estimate whether the Civil Rights Act of 1964 had any significant effect on relative female earnings gains over these periods. He reported no statistically significant change in the discrimination (that is, unexplained) component of the gender earnings gap before and after 1964.

The studies on the effects of affirmative action on the economic position of females are generally more positive. As noted above, Beller (1982), using Current Population Survey data, found that affirmative action efforts from the federal contract compliance program had a significant effect on the proportion of females entering male occupations over the 1967–1974 period. Osterman (1982), using data from the Panel Study of Income Dynamics in 1978 and 1979, found that the implementation of affirmative action plans significantly reduced the probability that female workers quit their jobs and that compliance reviews lowered the probability even more.

Four studies used EEO reports from individual establishments to assess the effects of affirmative action on female gains. James Smith and Michael Ward (1984) found that affirmative action had a positive effect on the employment of females, and the effect was quite large for black females, though relatively small for white females. Jonathan Leonard (1984a) constructed an index of occupational advance and found that affirmative action had a significant positive effect on this index and that compliance reviews had an even larger effect. Leonard (1984b) also reported that affirmative action spurred female employment growth, though compliance reviews did not augment these gains. In a 1985 article, Leonard further found that the establishment of targets by the OFCC exerted a separate effect in enhancing the employment growth of female employees.

As we noted in Chapter 13, the 1980s saw a diminution in the enforcement of antidiscrimination programs by the federal government. Jonathan Leonard (1990) pointed to a decrease in the federal budget devoted to affirmative action enforcement activity and the elimination of contract cancellation as a penalty for the failure to attain affirmative action goals. Moreover, both the executive branch of the federal government and the Supreme Court increased the requirements for plaintiffs to prove discrimination in Civil Rights Act lawsuits, and there was a decline in the number of class action lawsuits for employment discrimination during the 1980s. Leonard found in his study that the growth of female employment grew more slowly among federal contractors than noncontractors during the early 1980s, exactly the opposite of what occurred during the 1970s.

Comparable Worth

Though federal antidiscrimination policy appears to have had some effect in reducing occupational segregation by gender, such segregation remains strong even today and still exerts a major influence on the male-female wage gap. One reason seems to be that women have been much more likely to file for grievances if they are paid less than men for doing the same work at the same place than if they are not hired for a particular job in the first place. As a result, women have tended to avail themselves more of the Equal Pay Act and of the equal compensation provisions of Title VII than of the equal employment opportunities of the latter. Since the primary source of earnings differences between males and females is still differences in occupation of employment, an emphasis on equal pay for the same work will not by itself do much to bring about earnings equality between the sexes. Affirmative action plans may, however, still result in some progress in breaking down occupational barriers and reducing occupational segregation. But insofar as occupational segregation is due to role selection and role stereotyping that is deeply embedded in the social fabric of our society, ending employment discrimination may not result in earnings equality between the sexes unless prelabor market discrimination is reduced.

As a result, many economists and policy makers have advocated a policy of "comparable worth" or the principle of equal pay for jobs that are determined to be of equal "value" to the employer. Unlike the provisions of the Equal Pay Act of 1963 or the equal compensation clause of the Civil Rights Act of 1964, which prohibit unequal pay for the *same* job, comparable worth allows comparisons among otherwise dissimilar jobs or occupations. These ratings are usually based on direct job evaluation procedures.

The rationale for comparable worth comes from the overcrowding model of occupational segregation, which we discussed in Section 12.8. The model assumes that there are separate male jobs and female jobs in the workplace and that there are fewer female occupations than male occupations. The difference in the number of suitable occupations artificially raises the supply of workers to the female sector and correspondingly lowers the supply of workers to the male sector. The greater supply of workers to female occupations lowers the wages in female jobs, and the lower supply of workers in male jobs raises wages in male occupations. As a result, females with the same qualifications as male workers receive lower wages.

There are usually four steps involved in the development of a comparable worth program. First, jobs within an establishment are classified as either predominantly male or predominantly female (a cutoff of 70 percent of one gender is often used). Second, job evaluation experts assign job evaluation scores to each job based on various attributes of the work, such as educational requirements, skill, responsibility, effort, and working conditions. The point scores for each factor are then totaled to obtain the composite score for that job. Third, the total point scores are then compared to wages for each of the predominantly male jobs, and the same comparison is made for female jobs. The fourth step is to adjust female wages for a particular job to male wages of jobs that have the same point value.

As Morley Gunderson (1989) noted, a number of criticisms have been made of the comparable worth procedure. First, the assignment of points is to some extent arbitrary, and a gender bias can still exist if a higher range of points is allocated for jobs that are performed more often by men than by women. A gender bias can also exist if compensating points are awarded for undesirable working conditions (noise, dirt, etc.), which are normally associated with male work as opposed to female jobs. Second, job evaluation systems in most establishments were designed to provide only an ordinal ranking of jobs, not a cardinal number on which to base an actual dollar value. Also, because of difficulties in comparability for different occupational groups, separate evaluation systems were traditionally designed for white-collar and blue-collar employment.

Third, for certain "benchmark jobs," market forces were often taken into account in the assignment of job evaluation scores, and these jobs were pegged at the market wage. The wages of other jobs were then set relative to that of the benchmark job. The evaluation system in many companies was also adjusted if the job evaluation scores suggested a wage that was out of line with the corresponding market wage.

Fourth, difficulties occur in the appropriate adjustment of the wages of the female jobs. Should they be set to the wages of the corresponding male jobs in terms of evaluation points or to the average wage of jobs (both male and female) with the same number of points? What if there are no male jobs that have the same score as a given female job? Fifth, according to the standard neoclassical model of wage determination, wages are set at the *margin*, according to the market supply and demand for a given factor, not according to the average value of the inputs required for the job. If the wage for a job is artificially set above its market value, then employment in that job will fall and there will be an excess supply of labor seeking that job.

So far, in the United States, comparable worth has been applied only to public sector jobs.[9] According to Gunderson (1989), as of 1984, 25 states had legislation relating to comparable worth, and 10 states had implemented or were planning to implement comparable worth programs. Also, as of 1987, 20 states had allocated money to use in adjusting female salaries for state government employees according to comparable worth principles (see Blau and Kahn, 1992b). Minnesota, Iowa, and Washington (State) have to date the most developed systems of comparable worth for their state government employees.

---

[9]Australia has probably the most comprehensive system of comparable worth, covering the vast majority of both public and private workers. Canada and the United Kingdom have also instituted comparable worth programs to some extent. See Gunderson (1989) for more details.

Several studies have been made to test the effectiveness of the comparable worth programs in effect. Mark Killingsworth (1990) looked at the effects of comparable worth in both Minnesota and the city of San Jose and found that comparable worth adjustments lowered the male-female wage gap by between 6 and 10 percentage points but at the same time lowered female employment by 4 to 7 percentage points. June O'Neill, Michael Brien, and James Cunningham (1989) did a similar study for Washington State and reached similar conclusions: relative female wages gained but female employment declined. Peter Orazem and Peter Mattila (1990) found that for the state of Iowa, comparable worth had the potential of closing the male-female wage gap by 9 percentage points but in actuality narrowed it by only 1.4 percentage points.

14.4 OTHER ISSUES

Effects of Wives' Earnings on Family Income Inequality

As we discussed in Section 14.1, one of the most dramatic changes in the postwar American economy has been the increasing labor force participation of women. This is particularly true for wives, whose labor force participation rate increased from 20 percent in 1947 to 57 percent in 1988. In this section, we examine the effects of the increasing LFPR of wives on family income.

Figure 14.2 shows the median income of families in 1992 dollars over the period from 1967 to 1992. We have divided families into four types: (1) married couples, with wife working; (2) married couples, with wife not working; (3) male householders; and (4) female householders. It is helpful to consider two subperiods: 1967–1973 and 1973–1992. During the 1967–1973 period, all four groups experienced an increase in their real family income. Median income grew by 18 percent for married couples with wives at work, 15 percent for married couples with wives not working, 21 percent for single males, and 4 percent for single females.

However, the situation changed radically over the 1973–1992 period. Over this time period, married couples with wives at work experienced by far the highest increase in real income—a 10 percent growth. Single females (mainly elderly ones) had no change in their income. In contrast, married couples with wives not working saw their family income fall by 11 percent and single males by 13 percent. Also, between 1979 and 1992, the only group which experienced any increase in real income was married couples with wives at work—a 6 percent real growth.

How has the increased LFPR of wives affected the *inequality* of family income? There are two parts to this question. The first concerns its effect on the distribution of family income among married couples alone. Some have speculated that wives' earnings are disequalizing. This presumption is de-

Figure 14.2   Median Income of Families, 1992 Dollars, by Type of Family, 1967–1992

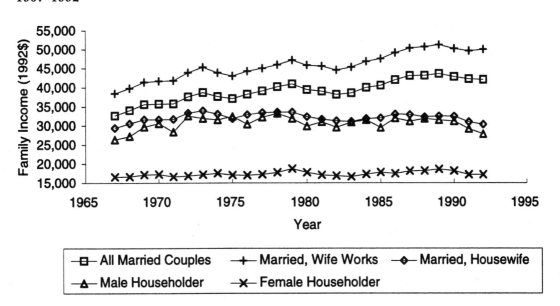

rived, at least in part, from the popular stereotype of "yuppie" couples in which both husband and wife are professionals earning high incomes. Two studies have shown that this is generally not the case. Indeed, such a phenomenon remains quite rare, so it has not had a major impact on the trend of family income inequality in recent years.

McKinley Blackburn and David Bloom (1989) calculated the Gini coefficient for the distribution of family income among married couples over the period between 1967 and 1985. Then they recalculated the Gini coefficient under the hypothetical assumption that wives had zero labor earnings. They found that the actual level of income inequality was uniformly less than the one estimated under the assumption that there were no working wives. In 1967, the Gini coefficient was 0.328 for the actual income distribution among married couples and 0.343 for the hypothetical one; in 1985, the corresponding Gini coefficients were 0.351 and 0.375. The explanation is a negative correlation between the hours worked by wives and the earnings of the husband—that is, wives are more apt to have a job and work more hours the less their husband earns.

Blackburn and Bloom also found that the equalizing effect of wives' earnings *increased* between 1967 and 1985.[10] In 1967, wives' earnings reduced the Gini coefficient by 0.015 points (from 0.343 to 0.328), and in 1985, by 0.024 points (from 0.375 to 0.351). Maria Cancian, Sheldon Danziger, and Peter Gottschalk (1993) reported a similar result. They found that

---

[10] Betson and van der Gaag (1984) reported the same trend for the 1968–1980 period.

wives' earnings had a greater equalizing effect on the distribution of income of married couples in 1988 than in 1968. This was true despite the growing similarity of labor force participation rates of wives with husbands who spanned the earnings spectrum. This finding was attributed to two factors: (1) wives' earnings were gaining ground on their husbands', and (2) the distribution of earnings among wives was becoming more equal, partly because of a decline in the number of nonworking wives.

The second issue is the effect of wives' earnings on the distribution of income among *all* family units. Blackburn and Bloom, using the same comparisons between the actual distribution of family income and a hypothetical one, under the assumption that wives did not work, calculated that the effect of wives' earnings was neutral. In 1967, the Gini coefficient was 0.395 for the actual distribution of family income (among all families) and 0.397 for the hypothetical one; in 1985, the corresponding coefficients were 0.426 and 0.424. They concluded that wives' earnings tend to equalize the distribution of income among married couples but have little effect on the distribution of income among all families.

Cancian, Danziger, and Gottschalk also found that growing labor earnings among wives substituted for general economic growth during the 1980s as the major source of gain in real family income (which, as we saw, did increase for two-earner families). It also prevented family income inequality from climbing to an even greater degree. But, as the authors indicate, such a trend is not sustainable in the long run for two reasons: (1) the proportion of adults living in married couple households has been falling, and (2) the labor force participation rate of women is bound to level off, given its dramatic rise in recent decades.

The Feminization of Poverty

The evidence presented in the chapter indicates steady labor market progress for women in terms of access to the labor market and gains in earnings relative to male workers, particularly during the 1980s. However, the well-being of women in the whole population depends both on labor market activity *and* the structure of the family. Labor earnings by themselves do not directly indicate how well off people are. In intact families (husband and wife present), incomes are typically pooled among all family members so that all members share the common fortunes of the family. Wives may thus enjoy a high standard of living even if they are not employed in the labor market (and conversely for nonworking husbands). However, such is not the case for unmarried adults, who must generally rely only on themselves for their income. The growth in the number of female-headed households since 1970, which we also discussed in the last chapter, thus has direct implications for poverty among women.

Table 14.11 highlights some of these trends in poverty rates. At the outset, it should be emphasized that poverty rates declined substantially for both females and males between 1940 and 1970, from 34 to 11 percent for

Table 14.11   Poverty Rates for Adults by Gender, 1940–1989[a]

	1940	1950	1960	1970	1980	1989	1993[b]
				Year			
A. *Poverty Rate by Gender*							
Women	34	23	15	11	11	13	15
Men	34	22	13	8	7	8	10
B. *Percentage Composition of the Poor*							
Women	50	51	55	60	62	63	62
Men	50	49	45	40	38	37	38
Total	100	100	100	100	100	100	100

[a]Sources: 1940–1980: Smith and Ward (1989). 1989: U.S. Bureau of the Census, Current Population Reports, Series P-60, No. 168, *Money Income and Poverty Status in the United States: 1989*; 1993: U.S. Bureau of the Census, Current Population Reports, Series P60–188, *Income, Poverty, and Valuation of Noncash Benefits: 1993*. *Adults* refers to individuals 16 years of age or older.
[b]Individuals 18 years of age or older.

the former and from 34 to 8 percent for the latter. Still, it is apparent that in 1940, poverty was gender-neutral. The poverty rates were the same for both adult males and females, and half the poor (adults) were female and half were male. It is perhaps not coincidental that in 1940 over 90 percent of all families included both a husband and wife (see Smith and Ward [1989], p. 19).

After 1940, particularly 1970 and after, poverty rates began to diverge between adult females and males. By 1993, the poverty rate among adult females was 15 percent and that among adult males only 10 percent. Moreover, by 1993, females comprised 62 percent of the adult poor, while men made up the other 38 percent. The growing feminization of poverty tracks almost exactly with the rising share of female-headed households in the population. By 1988, 13 percent of white families were headed by a female (up from 9 percent in 1960) and 44 percent of black families (up from 31 percent in 1970). James Smith and Michael Ward (1989) argued that the relative growth of poverty among females "has its origins exclusively in the growth of female-headed families" (p. 20). As long as families remained intact, the lower earnings capacity of females had no direct effect on the incidence of poverty by gender. However, with the breakup of the family, the relatively lower wages of females along with the presence of children in one-parent families made poverty far more likely for women than for men. The irony is that the feminization of poverty was occurring while labor market opportunities were improving for women.

International Comparisons

Though differences in male and female earnings continue to remain large in the United States, it is of interest to see how they compare to those of other countries. Some comparisons are shown in Table 14.12. In terms of male-female earnings inequality, the United States ranks in the middle of the pack among industrialized countries. In 1980, according to the Gunderson (1989) data, Japan had by far the largest male-female wage gap, a ratio of 0.54, and Sweden the narrowest, a ratio of 0.90. The female-male earnings ratio in the United States, according to these data, was 0.66. Interestingly, in the U.S.S.R., the earnings ratio was 0.70. Also, according to the Blau and Kahn (1992a) data, the female-male earnings ratio, adjusted for hours worked, in the mid-1980s ranged from a low of 0.62 in Switzerland and 0.63 in the United Kingdom to a high of 0.77 in Sweden. The corresponding earnings ratio in the United States was 0.68.

The Gunderson data also show changes in the earnings ratio between 1960 and 1980. According to these figures, all countries experienced a narrowing of the gender wage gap, except the United States and the U.S.S.R., which had no change. Thus, it appears that most industrialized countries had made more progress than the United States in closing the gender wage gap, at least over the period from 1960 to 1980.

Table 14.12 The Ratio of Female to Male Labor Earnings for Selected Industrialized Countries and Years

	Year		
	1960[a]	*1980[a]*	*mid-1980s[b]*
Australia	0.59	0.75	0.75
Austria			0.73
United Kingdom	0.61	0.79	0.63
Canada	0.59	0.64	
France	0.64	0.71	
Germany	0.65	0.72	0.69
Italy	0.73	0.83	
Japan	0.46	0.54	
Norway			0.73
Sweden	0.72	0.90	0.77
Switzerland			0.62
United States	0.66	0.66	0.68
U.S.S.R.	0.70	0.70	

[a] Source: Gunderson (1989).
[b] Source: Blau and Kahn (1992a). Earnings differentials are adjusted for hours worked.

14.5 SUMMARY

The gender wage gap, the most direct measure of inequality between males and females in the labor market, shows a U-shaped trajectory between the end of World War II and the 1990s. It first widened between the late 1940s and the early 1950s, remained relatively unchanged between the early 1950s and the early 1970s, and has since been narrowing, particularly from 1980.

Over the same time, the labor force participation of females has been steadily rising. The LFPR of all females increased from 32 percent in 1947 to 58 percent in 1993, while the LFPR of wives grew from 20 to 59 percent. For wives, the principal reasons for their increased participation rate has been rising real earnings for women, a slowdown of income growth for men (particularly after 1970), and a reduced fertility rate. Moreover, the proportion of females working full-time, full-year increased from 37 percent in 1950 to 54 percent in 1992.

Many studies have sought to explain the wage gap between male and female workers. Some have focused on differences in human capital. Women typically have fewer years of work experience than men of the same age and educational attainment because of interrupted work careers. However, the average experience level of women of almost every age group has risen between 1950 and today. In contrast, in 1950, female workers have had, on average, more years of schooling than male workers, but by 1969, the schooling differential had all but disappeared.

There may also be a separate effect on earnings from career interruptions. Some economists have argued that women will typically receive less on-the-job training than men of the same age because employers will have less incentive to invest in female employees. Several studies have confirmed that women, on average, receive less training than men with the same number of years of experience and that the return to experience is smaller for women than for men.

The overall wage gap can be decomposed into one component due to differences in human capital and an "unexplained" residual, usually interpreted as a measure of discrimination. Because male schooling levels have converged to female levels and differences in experience levels have narrowed between males and females, there was relatively little change in the relative quantities of human capital between working men and women from 1960 to 1990. As a result, many studies have concluded that the decline in the gender wage gap, particularly since 1980, has been primarily due to a lessening of sex discrimination.

However, other studies have found that while the return to schooling and experience increased for both male and female workers during the 1980s, it grew more for females than males. The rising payoff for experience to women, in particular, presumably reflects more intensive job training. These studies attributed a large part of the declining wage gap during the

1980s to the fact that returns to human capital increased more for women than men over these years.

Another factor accounting for lower female pay is occupational segregation. Women tend to be concentrated in low-paying occupations. However, the degree of occupational segregation has lessened over the postwar period, particularly after 1980, as female workers have penetrated traditionally male occupations. Despite this, several studies have documented that the lower overall pay of female workers relative to male workers is due much more to the lower pay received by female workers than male workers in the same occupation than to the difference in their occupational distributions. Moreover, the narrowing of the gender wage gap, particularly after 1980, was due almost exclusively to the increase in relative female wages within occupation, not to shifts in female occupational patterns.

Statistical analyses have also suggested that governmental antidiscrimination programs may have played an important role in the improving economic status of female workers. The three major legal instruments are the Equal Pay Act of 1963, Title VII of the 1964 Civil Rights Act, and the 1965 Executive Order 11246. Results on the effectiveness of Title VII have been mixed. However, there is strong evidence that affirmative action programs have increased the proportion of females entering male occupations, the growth of female employment in general, and the occupational advance of female workers. These effects were much stronger in the 1970s than the 1980s, which saw a diminution in the enforcement of antidiscrimination programs by the federal government.

Another type of antidiscrimination initiative, comparable worth, has been undertaken at the state and local government level. Comparable worth programs aim at providing equal pay to jobs of equal "value." To date these programs have been directed exclusively at public employees. Studies have shown that such efforts have been successful in increasing relative female earnings but they have also been responsible for a loss of female employment.

Several other findings are worthy of note. First, the earnings of wives have tended to equalize the distribution of family income among married couples, and their equalizing effect has increased between the late 1960s and the late 1980s. Moreover, the only family type that experienced any growth in real family income over the 1980s is married couples with working wives.

Second, there has been a growing "feminization of poverty" in the United States. In 1950, half the adult poor were females, but by 1989, this fraction had grown to almost two-thirds. The growth in female poverty tracks almost exactly with the rising share of female-headed households in the population.

Third, from an international perspective, the United States tends to rank in the middle in terms of gender inequality in earnings. However, whereas most other industrialized countries have seen a sharp reduction in the gender wage gap, this has not been the case in the United States.

REFERENCES AND BIBLIOGRAPHY

Aldrich, Mark, and Robert Buchele, *The Economics of Comparable Worth*, Harper & Row, Ballinger, Cambridge, Mass., 1986.

Barbezat, Debra A., James W. Hughes, and Peter Kuhn, "Sex Discrimination in Labor Markets: The Role of Statistical Evidence: Comment," *American Economic Review*, Vol. 80, No. 1, March 1990, pp. 277–286.

Barnes, William F., and Ethel B. Jones, "Differences in Male and Female Quitting," *Journal of Human Resources*, Vol. 9, Winter 1974, pp. 439–453.

Barron, John M., Dan A. Black, and Mark A. Lowenstein, "Gender Differences in Training, Capital, and Wages," *Journal of Human Resources*, Vol. 28, No. 2, Spring 1993, pp. 343–364.

Bartlett, Robin L., and Timothy I. Miller, "Executive Compensation: Female Executives and Networking," *American Economic Review*, Vol. 75, No. 2, May 1985, pp. 266–270.

Becker, Gary S., *A Treatise on the Family*, Harvard University Press, Cambridge, Mass., 1981.

———, "Human Capital, Effort, and the Sexual Division of Labor," *Journal of Labor Economics*, Vol. 3, January 1985, pp. S33–S58.

Beller, Andrea H., "EEO Laws and the Earnings of Women," *Industrial Relations Research Association Proceedings*, University of Wisconsin Press, Madison, Wis., 1976, pp. 190–198.

———, "The Impact of Equal Employment Opportunity Laws on the Male-Female Earnings Differential," in Cynthia B. Lloyd, Emily S. Andrews, and Curtis L. Gilroy (eds.), *Women in the Labor Market*, Columbia University Press, New York, 1979, pp. 304–330.

———, "The Effect of Economic Conditions on the Success of Equal Employment Opportunity Laws: An Application to the Sex Differential in Earnings," *Review of Economics and Statistics*, Vol. 62, No. 3, August 1980, pp. 370–387.

———, "Occupational Segregation By Sex: Determinants and Changes," *Journal of Human Resources*, Summer 1982, Vol. 17, pp. 371–392.

———, "Trends in Occupational Segregation by Sex and Race, 1960–1981," in Barbara F. Reskin (ed.), *Sex Segregation In The Workplace*, National Academy Press, Washington, D.C., 1984.

———, "Changes in the Sex Composition of U.S. Occupations, 1960–1981," *Journal of Human Resources*, Vol. 20, No. 2, Summer 1985, pp. 235–250.

Betson, David, and Jacques van der Gaag, "Working Married Women and the Distribution of Income," *Journal of Human Resources*, Vol. 19, No. 4, Fall 1984, pp. 532–543.

Bielby, William T., and James N. Baron, "Sex Segregation Within Occupations," *American Economic Review Papers and Proceedings*, Vol. 76, May 1986, pp. 43–47.

Blackburn, McKinley L., and David E. Bloom, "Income Inequality, Business Cycles, and Female Labor Supply," *Research in Economic Inequality*, Vol. 1, JAI Press, Greenwich, Conn., 1989.

Blau, Francine D., "Women's Place in the Labor Market," *American Economic Review Papers and Proceedings*, Vol. 62, May 1972, pp. 161–166.

————, *Equal Pay in the Office*, D.C. Heath and Co., Lexington, Mass., 1977.

————, "Discrimination Against Women: Theory and Evidence," in William Darity, Jr., (ed.), *Labor Economics: Modern View*, Kluwer-Hijhoff Publishing, Boston, MA, 1984, pp. 53–89.

————, "Occupational Segregation by Gender: A Look at the 1980s," University of Illinois at Urbana-Champaign, mimeo, January 1989.

————, and Andrea Beller, "Trends in Earnings Differentials by Gender, 1971–1981," *Industrial and Labor Relations Review*, Vol. 41, No. 4, July 1988, pp. 513–529.

————, and Marianne A. Ferber, *The Economics of Women, Men, and Work*, Prentice-Hall, Englewood Cliffs, NJ, 1986.

————, "Discrimination: Empirical Evidence From the United States," *American Economic Review Papers and Proceedings*, Vol. 77, May 1987, pp. 246–250.

————, "Career Plans and Expectations of Young Women and Men," *Journal of Human Resources*, Vol. 26, No. 4, Fall 1991, pp. 581–607.

Blau, Francine D., and W. E. Hendricks, "Occupational Segregation by Sex: Trends and Prospects," *Journal of Human Resources*, Vol. 14, No. 2, Spring 1979, pp. 197–210.

Blau, Francine D., and Lawrence M. Kahn, "The Gender Earnings Gap: Learning from International Comparisons," *American Economic Review Papers and Proceedings*, Vol. 82, May 1992a, pp. 533–538.

————, "Race and Gender Pay Differentials," NBER Working Paper No. 4120, July 1992b.

————, "The Gender Earnings Gap: Some International Evidence," NBER Working Paper No. 4224, December 1992c.

————, "Rising Wage Inequality and the U.S. Gender Wage Gap," *American Economic Review Papers and Proceedings*, Vol. 84, No. 2, May 1994, pp. 23–28.

Bowen, William G., and T. Aldrich Finegan, *The Economics of Labor Force Participation*, Princeton University Press, Princeton, NJ, 1969.

Brown, Clair, and Joseph A. Pechman (ed.), *Gender in the Workplace*, Brookings Institution, Washington, D.C., 1987.

Brown, Randall S., Marilyn Moon, and Barbara S. Zoloth, "Incorporating Occupational Attainment in Studies of Male-Female Earnings Differentials," *Journal of Human Resources*, Vol. 15, No. 1, Spring 1980, p. 28.

Cain, Glenn C., *Married Women in the Labor Force: An Economic Analysis*, University of Chicago Press, Chicago, 1966.

————, and M. D. Dooley, "Estimation of a Model of Labor Supply, Fertility and Wages of Married Women," *Journal of Political Economy*, Vol. 84, August 1976, pp. S177–S199.

Cancian, Maria, Sheldon Danziger, and Peter Gottschalk, "The Changing Contributions of Men and Women to the Level and Distribution of Family Income, 1968–1988" in Dimitri B. Papadimitriou and Edward N. Wolff (eds.), *Poverty and Prosperity in the USA in the Late Twentieth Century*, Macmillan Publishers, London, 1993.

Carlson, Leonard A., and Caroline Swartz, "The Earnings of Women and Ethnic Minorities," *Industrial and Labor Relations Review*, Vol. 41, No. 4, July 1988, pp. 530–546.

Coleman, Mary, and John Pencavel, "Trends in Market Work Behavior of Women Since 1940," *Industrial and Labor Relations Review*, Vol. 46, No. 4, July 1993, pp. 653–679.

Corcoran, Mary, "The Structure of Female Wages," *American Economic Review*, Vol. 68, No. 2, May 1978, pp. 165–170.

———, "Work Experience, Labor Force Withdrawals, and Women's Wages: Empirical Results Using the 1976 Panel of Income Dynamics," in Cynthia B. Lloyd, Emily S. Andrews, and Curtis L. Gilroy (eds.), *Women in the Labor Market*, Columbia University Press, New York, 1979.

———, and Paul N. Courant, "Sex Role Socialization and Labor Market Outcomes," *American Economic Review Papers and Proceedings*, Vol. 75, No. 2, May 1985, pp. 275–278.

Corcoran, Mary, and Greg J. Duncan, "Work History, Labor Force Attachment, and Earnings Differences Between the Races and Sexes," *Journal of Human Resources*, Vol. 14, Winter 1979, pp. 3–20.

———, and Michael Ponza, "A Longitudinal Analysis of White Women's Wages", *Journal of Human Resources*, Vol. 18, Fall 1983, pp. 497–520.

Cox, Donald, "Inequality in the Lifetime Earnings of Women," *Review of Economics and Statistics*, Vol. 64, No. 3, August 1982, pp. 501–504.

Currie, Janet, "Gender Gaps in Benefits Coverage," NBER Working Paper No. 4265, January 1993.

———, and Richard Chaykowski, "Male Jobs, Females Jobs, and Gender Gaps in Benefits Coverage in Canada," MIT, mimeo, November 1992.

Dean, Joyce, "Sex-Segregated Employment, Wage Inequality and Labor-Intensive Production," *Review of Radical Political Economy*, Vol. 23, No. 3 & 4, 1991, pp. 244–268.

Duncan, Greg J., and Saul Hoffman, "On-the-Job Training and Earnings Differences by Race and Sex," *Review of Economics and Statistics*, Vol. 61, No. 4, November 1979, pp. 594–603.

Duncan, Otis Dudley, and Beverly Duncan, "A Methodological Analysis of Segregation Indexes," *American Sociological Review*, Vol. 20, April 1955, pp. 210–217.

England, Paula, "The Failure of Human Capital Theory to Explain Occupational Segregation," *Journal of Human Resources*, Vol. 17, No. 3, Summer 1982, pp. 358–370.

Even, William E., "Sex Discrimination in Labor Markets: The Role of Statistical Evidence: Comment," *American Economic Review*, Vol. 80, No. 1, March 1990, pp. 287–289.

Even, William, and David Macpherson, "The Gender Gap in Pensions and Wages," *Review of Economics and Statistics*, Vol. 72, May 1990, pp. 259–265.

———, "The Decline in Private-Sector Unionism and the Gender Wage Gap," *Journal of Human Resources*, Vol. 38, No. 2, Spring 1993, pp. 279–296.

Fields, Judith, "A Comparison of Intercity Differences in the Labor Force Participation of Married Women in 1970 with 1940, 1950, and 1960," *Journal of Human Resources*, Vol. 11, Fall 1976, pp. 568–577.

———, and Edward N. Wolff, "The Decline of Sex Segregation and the Wage Gap, 1970–1980," *Journal of Human Resources*, Vol. 26, No. 4, Fall 1991, pp. 608–622.

———, "Industry Wage Differentials and the Gender Wage Gap," New York University, mimeo, February 1993.

Filer, Randall K., "Sexual Differences in Earnings: The Role of Individual Personalities and Tastes," *Journal of Human Resources*, Vol. 18, Winter 1983, pp. 82–99.

———, "Male-Female Wage Differentials: The Importance of Compensating Differentials," *Industrial and Labor Relations Review*, Vol. 38, No. 3, April 1985, pp. 426–437.

Frank, Robert H., "Why Women Earn Less: The Theory and Estimation of Differential Overqualifications," *American Economic Review*, Vol. 68, June 1978, pp. 360–373.

Fuchs, Victor, "Differences in Hourly Earnings Between Men and Women," *Monthly Labor Review*, Vol. 94, No. 5, May 1971, pp. 9–15.

———, "Recent Trends and Long-Run Prospects for Female Earnings," *American Economic Review*, Vol. 64, No. 2, May 1974, pp. 236–242.

———, "His and Hers: Gender Differences in Work and Income," *Journal of Labor Economics*, Vol. 4, No. 3, July 1986, pp. S245–S272.

———, "Women's Quest for Economic Equality," *Journal of Economic Perspectives*, Vol. 3, No. 1, Winter 1989, pp. 25–41.

———, *Women's Quest for Economic Equality*, Harvard University Press, Cambridge, Mass., 1988.

Ghez, Gilbert, and Gary Becker, *The Allocation of Goods and Time Over the Life Cycle*, Columbia University Press, New York, 1975.

Goldfarb, Robert S., and James R. Hosek, "Explaining Male-Female Wage Differentials for the 'Same Job,'" *Journal of Human Resources*, Vol. 11, Winter 1976, pp. 98–107.

Goldin, Claudia, "Monitoring Costs and Occupational Segregation by Sex," *Journal of Labor Economics*, Vol. 4, No. 1, 1986, pp. 1–27.

———, "Life-Cycle Labor Force Participation of Married Women: Historical Evidence and Implications," *Journal of Labor Economics*, Vol. 7, January 1989, pp. 20–47.

———, *Understanding the Gender Gap: An Economic History of American Women*, Oxford University Press, New York, 1990.

———, "The Role of World War II in the Rise of Women's Employment," *American Economic Review*, Vol. 81, No. 4, September 1991, pp. 741–756.

————, and Solomon Polachek, "Residual Differences by Sex: Perspectives on the Gender Gap in Earnings," *American Economic Review Papers and Proceedings*, Vol. 77, No. 2, May 1987, pp. 143–151.

Gronau, Reuben, "Sex-Related Differentials and Women's Interrupted Labor Careers—the Chicken or the Egg," *Journal of Labor Economics*, Vol. 6, No. 3, 1988, pp. 277–301.

Groshen, Erica L., "The Structure of the Female-Male Wage Differential," *Journal of Human Resources*, Vol. 26, No. 3, Summer 1991, pp. 457–472.

Gunderson, Morely, "Male-Female Wage Differentials and Policy Responses," *Journal of Economic Literature*, Vol. 27, March 1989, pp. 46–72.

Gwartney, James D., and Richard Stroup, "Measurement of Employment Discrimination According to Sex," *Southern Economic Journal*, Vol. 39, No. 4, April 1973, pp. 575–587.

Hartmann, Heidi, (ed.), *Comparable Worth: New Directions for Research*, National Academy of Sciences, Washington, D.C., 1985.

Heckman, James J., and Thomas E. MaCurdy, "A Life-Cycle Model of Female Labor Supply," *Review of Economic Studies*, Vol. 47, January 1980, pp. 47–74.

Hersch, Joni, "Male-Female Differences in Hourly Wages: The Role of Human Capital, Working Conditions, and Housework," *Industrial and Labor Relations Review*, Vol. 44, No. 4, July 1991, pp. 746–759.

————, "EEO Law and Firm Profitability," *Journal of Human Resources*, Vol. 26, No. 1, Winter 1991, pp. 139–153.

————, "The Impact of Nonmarket Work on Market Wages," *American Economic Review Papers and Proceedings*, Vol. 81, No. 2, May 1991, pp. 157–160.

————, "Housework, Wages, and the Division of Housework Time for Employed Spouses," *American Economic Review Papers and Proceedings*, Vol. 84, No. 2, May 1995, pp. 120–125.

Hill, Martha S., "The Wage Effect of Marital Status and Children," *Journal of Human Resources*, Vol. 14, No. 4, 1979, pp. 579–594.

Hodson, Randy, and Paula England, "Industrial Structure and Sex Differences in Earnings," *Industrial Relations*, Winter 1986, pp. 16–32.

Hundley, Greg, "The Effects of Comparable Worth in the Public Sector on Public/Private Occupational Relative Wages," *Journal of Human Resources*, Vol. 28, No. 2, 1993, pp. 318–342.

Jacobs, Jerry A., "The Sex Segregation of Occupations and Women's Career Patterns," doctoral dissertation, Department of Sociology, Harvard University, 1983.

Jacobsen, Joyce P., and Laurence M. Levin, "The Effects of Intermittent Labor Force Attachment on Female Earnings," paper presented at the 1992 American Economics Association Conference, New Orleans, Jan. 3–5, 1992.

Johnson, George, and Frank Stafford, "The Earnings and Promotion of Women Faculty," *American Economic Review*, Vol. 64, No. 6, December 1974, pp. 888–903.

Killingsworth, Mark R., "Heterogeneous Preferences, Compensating Wage Differentials, and Comparable Worth," *Quarterly Journal of Economics*, Vol. 102, No. 4, 1987, pp. 727–742.

————, *The Economics of Comparable Worth*, W. E. Upjohn Institute for Employment Research, Kalamazoo, Mich., 1990.

Kuhn, Peter, "Sex Discrimination in Labor Markets: The Role of Statistical Evidence," *American Economic Review*, Vol. 77, No. 4, September 1987, pp. 567–583.

Leibowitz, Arleen, "Education and Allocation of Women's Time," in F. Thomas Juster, (ed.), *The Distribution of Economic Well-Being*, Ballinger Publishing Co., Cambridge, Mass., 1977.

Leonard, Jonathan S., "Employment and Occupational Advance Under Affirmative Action," *Review of Economics and Statistics*, August 1984a, pp. 377–385.

————, "The Impact of Affirmative Action on Employment," *Journal of Labor Economics*, Vol. 2, October 1984b, pp. 439–463.

————, "Antidiscrimination or Reverse Discrimination: The Impact of Changing Demographics, Title VII, and Affirmative Action on Productivity," *Journal of Human Resources*, Vol. 19, No. 2, Spring 1984c, pp. 146–174.

————, "Affirmative Action as Earnings Redistribution: The Targeting of Compliance Reviews," *Journal of Labor Economics*, Vol. 3, July 1985, pp. 363–384.

————, "The Impact of Affirmative Action Regulation and Equal Employment Law on Black Employment," *Journal of Economic Perspectives*, Vol. 4, Fall 1990, pp. 47–63.

Levy, Frank, and Richard Murnane, "Earnings Levels and Earnings Inequality," *Journal of Economic Literature*, Vol. 30, No. 3, September 1992, pp. 1331–1381.

Lloyd, Cynthia B. (ed.), *Sex, Discrimination, and the Division of Labor*, Columbia University Press, New York, 1975.

Lloyd, Cynthia B., Emily S. Andrews, and Curtis L. Gilroy (eds.), *Women in the Labor Market*, Columbia University Press, New York, 1979.

MaCurdy, Thomas E., "An Empirical Model of Labor Supply in a Life-Cycle Setting," *Journal of Political Economy*, Vol. 89, No. 6, December 1981, pp. 1059–1085.

Madden, Janice, "The Persistence of Pay Differentials: The Economics of Sex Discrimination," *Women and Work*, Vol. 1, 1985, pp. 76–114.

Malkiel, B., and J. Malkiel, "Male-Female Pay Differentials in Professional Employment," *American Economic Review*, Vol. 63, No. 4, September 1973, pp. 693–705.

Maxwell, Nan L., and Ronald J. D'Amico, "Employment and Wage Effects of Involuntary Job Separation: Male-Female Differences," *American Economic Review Papers and Proceedings*, Vol. 76, No. 2, May 1986, pp. 373–377.

Mincer, Jacob, "On the Job Training, Costs, Returns, and Some Implications," *Journal of Political Economy*, supplement, Vol. 70, October 1962(a), pp. 50–79.

———, "Labor Force Participation of Married Women," in Gregg Lewis (ed.), *Aspects of Labor Economics*, Universities-National Bureau Conference Series, No. 14, Arno Press, Princeton, 1962(b).

———, and Haim Ofek, "Interrupted Work Careers: Depreciation and Restoration of Human Capital," *Journal of Human Resources*, Vol. 17, Winter 1982, pp. 3–24.

———, and Solomon Polachek, "Family Investments in Human Capital: Earnings of Women," *Journal of Political Economy*, Vol. 82, No. 2, Part II, March–April 1974, pp. S76–S108.

———, "Women's Earnings Reexamined," *Journal of Human Resources*, Vol. 13, Winter 1978, pp. 118–133.

Oaxaca, Ronald, "Sex Discrimination in Wages," in Orley Ashenfelter and Albert Rees (eds.), *Discrimination in Labor Markets*, Princeton University Press, Princeton, N.J., 1973.

———, "The Persistence of Male-Female Earnings Differentials," in F. Thomas Juster, (ed.), *The Distribution of Economic Well-Being*, Ballinger Publishing Co., Cambridge, Mass., 1977.

O'Neill, June, "A Time-Series Analysis of Women's Labor Force Participation," *American Economic Review Papers and Proceedings*, Vol. 71, No. 2, May 1981, pp. 76–81.

———, "The Trend in the Male-Female Wage Gap in the United States," *Journal of Labor Economics*, Vol. 3, No. 1, Part 2, January 1985, pp. S91–S116.

———, Michael Brien, and James Cunningham, "Effects of Comparable Worth Policy: Evidence from Washington State," *American Economic Review Papers and Proceedings*, Vol. 79, May 1989, pp. 305–309.

O'Neill, June, and Solomon Polachek, "Why the Gender Gap in Wages Narrowed in the 1980s," *Journal of Labor Economics*, Vol. 11, No. 1, pt. 1, 1993, pp. 205–228.

Orazem, Peter F., and J. Peter Mattila, "The Implementation Process of Comparable Worth: Winners and Losers," *Journal of Political Economy*, Vol. 98, February 1990, pp. 134–152.

———, and Ruoh Chiann Yu, "An Index Number Approach to the Measurement of Wage Differentials by Sex," *Journal of Human Resources*, Vol. 25, No. 1, Winter 1990, pp. 125–136.

Osterman, Paul, "Affirmative Action and Opportunity," *Review of Economics and Statistics*, Vol. 64, No. 4, 1982, pp. 604–612.

Polachek, Solomon, "Differences in Expected Post-School Investment as a Determinant of Market Wage Differentials," *International Economic Review*, Vol. 16, June 1975(a), pp. 451–470.

———, "Potential Biases in Measuring Male-Female Discrimination," *Journal of Human Resources*, Vol. 10, No. 2, Spring 1975, pp. 205–229.

———, "Occupational Self-Selection: A Human Capital Approach to Sex Differences in Occupational Structure," *Review of Economics and Statistics*, Vol. 63, February 1981, pp. 60–69.

Ragan, James F., and Sharon P. Smith, "The Impact of Differences in Turnover Rates on Male/Female Pay Differentials," *Journal of Human Resources*, Vol. 16, No. 3, Summer 1981, pp. 343–365.

Reskin, Barbara F., and Heidi I. Hartmann, (eds.), *Women's Work, Men's Work: Sex Segregation on the Job*, National Academy Press, Washington D.C., 1986.

Reubens, Beatrice G., and Edwin P. Reubens, "Women Workers, Nontraditional Occupations and Full Employment," in Ann F. Cahn (ed.), *Women in the U.S. Labor Force*, Praeger, New York, 1979.

Roos, Patricia A., "Sex Stratification in the Workplace, Male-Female Differences in Returns to Occupation," *Social Sciences Research*, Vol. 10, No. 3, October 1981, pp. 195–224.

Rytina, Nancy F., "Occupational Segregation and Earnings Differences by Sex," *Monthly Labor Review*, Vol. 104, No. 1, January 1981, pp. 49–53.

———, and Susan M. Bianchi, "Occupational Reclassification and Changes in Distribution by Gender," *Monthly Labor Review*, Vol. 107, March 1984, pp. 11–17.

Schumann, Paul L., Dennis A. Ahlburg, and Christine Brown Mahoney, "The Effects of Human Capital and Job Characteristics on Pay," *Journal of Human Resources*, Vol. 29, No. 2, Spring 1994, pp. 481–503.

Shackett, Joyce R., and John M. Trapani, "Earnings Differentials and Market Structure," *Journal of Human Resources*, Vol. 22, No. 4, Fall 1987, pp. 518–531.

Sorensen, Elaine, "The Crowding Hypothesis and Comparable Worth," *Journal of Human Resources*, Vol. 25, No. 1, 1990, pp. 55–89.

———, "Exploring the Reasons Behind the Narrowing Gender Gap in Earnings," Urban Institute Report 91–2, Washington, D.C., 1991.

Smith, James P., and Michael P. Ward, *Women's Wages and Work in the Twentieth Century*, Rand Corporation, Santa Monica, CA, 1984.

———, "Time-Series Growth in the Female Labor Force," *Journal of Labor Economics*, Vol. 3, No. 1, Part 2, January 1985, pp. S59–S90.

———, "Women in the Labor Market and in the Family," *Journal of Economic Perspectives*, Vol. 3, No. 1, Winter 1989, pp. 9–23.

Terrell, Katherine, "Female-Male Earnings Differentials and Occupational Structure," *International Labour Review*, Vol. 131, No. 4–5, 1992, pp. 387–404.

Treiman, Donald J., and Heidi I. Hartmann, (eds.), *Women, Work, and Wages: Equal Pay for Jobs of Equal Value*, National Academy Press, Washington, D.C., 1981.

Treiman, Donald J., and Kermit Terrell, "Women, Work, and Wages—Trends in the Female Occupational Structure Since 1940," in Kenneth C. Land and Seymour Spillerman (eds.), *Social Indicator Models*, Russell Sage Foundation, New York, 1975, pp. 157–200.

Weiss, Yoram, and Reuben Gronau, "Expected Interruptions in Labor Force Participation and Sex-Related Differences in Earnings Growth," *Review of Economic Studies*, Vol. 48, No. 4, 1981, pp. 607–619.

Wellington, Alison J., "Changes in the Male/Female Wage Gap, 1976–1985," *Journal of Human Resources*, Vol. 28, No. 2, Spring 1993, pp. 383–411.

Wolff, Edward N., "Occupational Earnings Behavior and the Inequality of Earnings by Sex and Race in the United States," *Review of Income and Wealth*, Series 22, No. 2, June 1976, pp. 151–166.

Wooley, F. R., "The Feminist Challenge to Neoclassical Economics," Carleton University, Ottawa, Canada, mimeo, October 1992.

Wright, Gavin, "Understanding the Gender Gap: A Review Article," *Journal of Economic Literature*, Vol. 39, September 1991, pp. 1153–1163.

Zellner, Harriet, "Discrimination Against Women, Occupational Segregation, and the Relative Wage," *American Economic Review*, Vol. 62, No. 2, May 1972, pp. 157–160.

DISCUSSION QUESTIONS

1. Describe the trend in the labor force participation rate of wives over the postwar period. Explain how changes in female earnings and male earnings helped account for the trend in their LFPR.

2. What has happened to the gender wage gap in the United States since 1970? Explain the effect of changes in women's schooling and experience on the change in the gender wage gap.

3. Explain why the Duncan and Duncan index is a useful measure of occupational segregation. What do changes in the Duncan and Duncan index for female workers in the U.S. economy indicate about trends in occupational segregation over the postwar period?

4. Evaluate three explanations for the existence of occupational segregation in the U.S. labor force.

5. Summarize the evidence on the effects of affirmative action on the economic position of women in the labor force.

6. Discuss and evaluate the economic rationale for comparable worth initiatives.

7.* Some economists have argued that total experience by itself might not be a good predictor of a woman's earnings because of the adverse effects of work interruption on human capital. Discuss the evidence that work interruptions might affect female earnings.

THE ROLE OF PUBLIC POLICY ON INEQUALITY

PART V

15

PUBLIC POLICY
AND POVERTY

The last two chapters of the book investigate the impact of public policy on poverty and income inequality. This chapter focuses on the government transfer system and other programs aimed at alleviating poverty. The next chapter analyzes the effect of government taxes and expenditures on the overall distribution of income.

This chapter begins with a brief recapitulation of the composition of the poverty population by age, sex of the household head, race, family size, work experience, and residence (Section 15.1). The next section presents a brief history of the development of the income maintenance system in the United States (Section 15.2).

We then look with more detail into three of the major income support systems in the United States today: (1) unemployment insurance (Section 15.3), (2) the social security system (Section 15.4), and (3) the welfare system, particularly, Aid to Families with Dependent Children and related manpower programs (Section 15.5). We describe the structure of each program, evaluate its effectiveness, and consider some of its incentive effects. Section 15.6 discusses another government program that directly affects the low-income population, the minimum wage.

The chapter ends with an overall assessment of these programs particularly with regard to the effectiveness of the various support systems in alleviating poverty (Section 15.7).

15.1 CHARACTERISTICS OF THE POOR

As we shall see in the next section, the welfare system has developed in a rather piecemeal fashion over the years. As a result, its effectiveness depends in large measure on which groups make up the poverty population and how the composition of the poor has changed over time. Programs designed at one point in time to meet the needs of one population of the poor may become less effective over time if the structure of poverty changes.

Let us first consider poverty by age group. The poverty rate for elderly families (age 65 and over) has declined dramatically, from 30 percent in 1959 to 7 percent in 1989 (see Table 15.1).[1] In 1959, the incidence of poverty among elderly persons (not families) was more than twice as great as among nonelderly adults (35 percent of elderly persons were poor versus 17 percent of the nonelderly). By 1989, poverty incidence among elderly individuals was only slightly higher than among adults aged 18 to 64 (11.4 versus 10.2 percent). In 1959, elderly families made up over one-fifth of the poverty population, but by 1989, only about 10 percent. In contrast, poverty rates among young households (under the age of 25) have risen since 1959. In 1989, their poverty rate was about five times that of the elderly.

The poverty rate among children (under 18) has been consistently higher than among adults. Moreover, the incidence of poverty has been increasing much more rapidly among children than among adults over the last two decades or so. Between 1973 and 1989, the poverty rate for children

Table 15.1 Poverty Rates for Families Categorized by Demographic Characteristics, Employment Status, and Residence, 1959 and 1989[a]

Family Characteristic	Poverty Rate for Group (in percent)		The Number of Poor as a Percent of Total Poor[b]	
	1959	1989	1959	1989
1. All Families	18.5	10.3	100.0	100.0
2. Age of Household Head				
a. 14–24	26.9	30.4	7.5	12.8
b. 25–44	16.5	12.0	39.8	55.8
c. 45–54	15.0	6.3	17.3	10.9
d. 55–64	15.9	7.4	13.1	10.2
e. 65 & Over	30.0	6.6	22.4	10.4
Children (pop. ct.)	27.3	19.6	43.6[c]	39.4[c]

(continued)

---

[1]Please note that after 1989, poverty statistics by demographic group are available only for persons (not families) and are therefore not strictly comparable with the 1959 figures.

Table 15.1 *(concluded)*

Family Characteristic	Poverty Rate for Group (in percent)		The Number of Poor as a Percent of Total Poor[b]	
	1959	1989	1959	1989
3. Sex of Household Head				
a. Male	15.8	5.9	77.0	48.3
b. Female	42.6	32.2	23.0	51.7
4. Race				
a. White	15.2	7.8	74.3	65.0
b. Nonwhite	50.4	25.0	25.7	35.0
5. Size of Family				
a. 2 persons	19.6	8.2	34.3	33.4
b. 3 persons	12.8	9.8	15.1	22.2
c. 4 persons	12.7	10.1	14.0	20.9
d. 5 persons	18.3	13.5	13.1	11.8
e. 6 persons	24.2	12.1	8.5	6.2
f. 7 or more persons	45.6	32.3	15.1	5.6
6. Work Experience of Head				
a. Did not work	45.2	23.4	30.5	50.8
b. Part of the year	26.9	19.0	31.0	28.0
c. Whole year	10.6	3.5	36.6	20.9
7. Educational Attainment of Head[d]				
a. No years of schooling		45.6		1.8
b. Elementary: less than 8		25.5		14.1
c. Elementary: 8 years		15.9		7.0
d. High School: 1–3 years		19.2		20.2
e. High School: 4 years		8.9		30.5
f. College: 1 or more years		3.6		13.6
8. Residence				
a. Central cities	13.7	14.9	25.2	41.8
b. Suburbs	9.6	6.4	16.7	29.7
c. Rural	28.2	12.5	58.1	28.5

[a] Sources. 1959: U.S. Bureau of the Census, Current Population Reports, Series P-60, No. 124, *Characteristics of the Population Below the Poverty Level: 1978*, U.S. Government Printing Office, Washington, D.C., July 1980; 1989: Source: U.S. Bureau of the Census, Current Population Reports, Series P-60, No. 166, *Money Income and Poverty Status in the United States: 1989*, U.S. Government Printing Office, Washington, D.C., September 1990.

[b] Note that the distribution shares do not sum to unity for some groupings, because of the exclusion of certain subgroups.

[c] Percent of all poor persons.

[d] Includes only families with household heads 25 and over.

increased from 14 to 20 percent, whereas the overall poverty rate (for individuals) increased from 11.1 to 12.8 percent. Indeed, between 1981 and 1989, the poverty rate for children was close to or greater than one-fifth. Moreover, in 1959, the incidence of poverty among children was less than among the elderly, but by 1989 it was considerably higher.

The poverty rate for female-headed families has historically been much higher than that among male heads. This is primarily due to the fact that the former are largely single-parent families and the mothers are unable to work due to child care responsibilities. By 1989, female-headed families constituted over *half* of all poor families, compared to less than a fourth in 1959. The reason for this is the rapid growth in the number of female-headed households in the population since 1960 (see Chapter 13).

Poverty rates have also been between three to four times higher among nonwhite than white families, though poverty has declined for both groups since 1959. However, in 1989, almost two-thirds of the poor were white families, because they constitute about 85 percent of the population.

In 1989, poverty incidence increased almost directly with family size (even though the poverty line is adjusted for family size). Very large families (seven or more persons) have had particularly high poverty rates (32 percent in 1989). The major change since 1959 is the substantial decline in poverty for two-person families. This primarily reflects the sharp drop in poverty among the elderly who constitute a high proportion of this group.

Poverty incidence also depends on work experience. In 1989, the poverty rate was 3.5 percent among families whose household head worked the whole year but 19 percent for part-year workers and 23 percent for those who did not work. In 1989, nonworkers made up half of poor families, compared to 31 percent in 1959. Part-year workers constituted 28 percent in 1989, slightly greater than in 1959, and full-year workers 21 percent, compared to 37 percent in 1959.

Not surprisingly, poverty rates varied inversely with the level of education of the household head. Despite this, about half the poor in 1989 consisted of families whose household head had attended high school (but not beyond) and 31 percent of those whose head had graduated high school (but did not attend college).

In 1959, the poverty rate in rural areas was much higher than in the central cities or suburban areas. However, in 1989, the highest poverty rates were to be found in the central city. While the proportion of poor families living in rural areas declined from 58 to 29 percent, the proportion living in urban areas (central cities) increased from 25 to 42 percent.

In summary, the most striking change in the composition of poverty is the increasing proportion of female-headed families in the poverty population. Households headed by women have always had a very high incidence of poverty. Because their relative number has grown, they now constitute over half of poor families. One important reason for their high poverty rate is that the demands of child care often make the mother unavailable for work.

Children also have a very high poverty incidence. Many of them live in single-parent households. Also, the mere fact that a family has many children means that the same income must be spread over more people. That is why the incidence of poverty is higher among large families than smaller ones. The elderly population, on the other hand, has experienced a very sharp decline in their poverty rate

Poverty incidence is also closely linked to employment status. For those not at work, the poverty rate is very high. Failure to work is due to either nonparticipation in the labor force or unemployment (see Chapter 5). The former may result from sickness, disability, old age, or child care responsibilities. Unemployment may be due to a business cycle downturn, structural changes in the labor force, a lack of adequate skills or education, search time, and the like.

However, even in 1989, half of the poverty population consisted of the "working poor." One reason for this is part-time or part-year work. Another reason is low wages. The incidence of low-wage jobs is particularly high among workers with minimal skills and low education, unattached individuals, women, minorities, and employees in seasonal or service industries.

15.2 A Brief History of Income Maintenance Programs

The development of our social welfare system has generally been dominated by two principles. The first is that work is the basis of income. The second is that the nuclear family is the principal unit in society. American society has traditionally believed that all able-bodied men should work and support their wives and children.

The development of our income maintenance (transfer) programs has generally followed from these two ideas. This has led to two types of programs. The first is public assistance or welfare for unfortunate people who cannot provide for themselves. In this regard, the state is viewed as a charitable organization.

The second is social insurance for the working population. Workers are viewed as taking out insurance in order to protect themselves in the event they are out of work.[2] The state is viewed as the insuring agency, and workers pay into various policies in the form of payroll taxes (such as social security or unemployment insurance).

Early Developments

Several states and cities began implementing charitable assistance programs for their indigent population in the nineteenth century, particularly in light of mounting poverty in the cities. Despite the growth of federal programs

---

[2]This concept of insurance is similar to property or automobile insurance. Individuals pay a premium for a policy which protects them against unforeseen and undesirable occurrences (fire, burglary, a car accident, etc.).

that provide assistance to the poor, many states and localities continue to administer their own welfare programs, which are referred to as **general assistance.**

The federal government's entry into welfare occurred in 1908 with the passage of **worker's compensation.** This program was developed to assist workers injured on the job. This law was designed to protect workers' families from lost income due to injury, both permanent and temporary, and also due to death. Though in theory an employee could sue his or her employer for an injury on the job, the tort system in this country was not easily used for this purpose, and judges were usually more sympathetic to the employers than the workers.

This is the earliest example of social insurance on the federal level. The justification for worker's compensation was that employment is the basis of income and the government should insure this source of income, at least from occupational hazards. If a person became disabled from a work-related injury, the government should provide at least some minimal income support until the person could get back on his or her feet and resume work. It is interesting that the scope of the intervention was limited to work interruptions resulting from injuries on the job. It would be another quarter century before the idea of social insurance was extended to work interruptions due to job loss.

A second entry into the income support system came with the passage of **veteran's disability** in 1918. This act effectively extended worker's compensation to soldiers and sailors disabled during World War I. The rationale was that men who served in World War I should normally return to work as soon as they were discharged from service. However, if they were injured during service and could not return to work, this occurrence was similar to injury on the job and the government should step in and provide these veterans with basic income support. This act extended the notion of social insurance to a new group, the armed forces.

The New Deal

The Great Depression began with the stock market crash in October of 1929. By the early 1930s, the unemployment rate had soared to 25 percent. There was very little action taken by President Hoover to combat the effects of the Depression, and partly as a result, Franklin Roosevelt was elected to office in 1932. He put together the first systematic attempt to provide a broad-based system of income support, called **The New Deal.** Three principal programs were formed: (1) unemployment insurance, (2) the social security system, and (3) Aid to Families with Dependent Children. All three programs were set up under the Social Security Act of 1935, and they still form the center of our welfare system. These three programs were each established under the assumptions that (1) the basic family unit is the nuclear family, a married couple with children, and (2) the husband is the primary earner (if not the sole earner) in the family.

Unemployment insurance extended the notion of social insurance already embodied in worker's compensation and the veteran disability programs to a new class of individuals. Whereas the two older programs insured workers against the loss of jobs resulting from injuries sustained on the job (or in war), this new program extended it to loss of work resulting from unemployment. Employers were required to pay a special payroll tax on wages into an unemployment insurance fund. A worker who was laid off could collect a payment from the government, which was set at a fixed proportion of his or her wage. The program was intended to provide basic income support to unemployed workers while they were searching for a new job (or waiting to be recalled to their old job).

The social security system is technically referred to as the "old age, survivors, disability, and health insurance program, or **OASDHI** ("OA" for old age, "S" for survivors, "D" for disability, "H" for health, and "I" for insurance). In 1935, the system provided only old age (retirement) benefits. This was supplemented in 1939 by survivor's benefits (in the event that the husband died, the wife would still receive some income support); in 1957 by disability benefits (for injuries not sustained on the job, since these were already covered by worker's compensation); and in 1966 by medical benefits for persons 65 and over (Medicare). The social security system is financed by a payroll tax paid in equal amounts by employees and employers. There is a cap on the wage base.

The hallmark feature of the system is that retirees who have paid into the system receive an income payment when they retire. The benefit structure is primarily based on the person's earnings history. However, the benefit levels are subject to legislative fiat and have been raised periodically by Congress.

The social security system has a dual character, both as a form of social insurance and as a pension plan. Poverty rates were very high among the elderly in the early 1930s; specific estimates are hard to come by, since there was no official government estimate of the poverty rate. However, as we saw above, even in 1959, the incidence of poverty among the elderly was much higher than that among the general population. The labor market is not a good solution to the problem of elderly poverty for two reasons. First, many older people are unable to work due to physical limitations or health problems. Second, many firms are unwilling to hire older workers, because they do not feel that the worker's longevity in the firm would warrant making an investment in the person's training. Moreover, most firms have historically had mandatory retirement ages, and though mandatory retirement is no longer legal today, firms still provide very strong incentives to induce older workers to retire.

Before the advent of the social security system, retirees were generally forced to rely on the generosity of their children to maintain them in old age. There were some exceptions—people who had saved substantial sums and those with private pension plans—but this group was relatively small and tended to be limited to the wealthiest Americans. With the massive unemployment of the 1930s, it was very difficult for workers to support their parents—workers were having a hard enough time making ends meet on their own.

The social security system was established as a form of social insurance—to insure workers against the loss of income in old age. The system establishes a minimum benefit level, to which all workers who contributed into the system are entitled, regardless of the total amount of their contributions. This level is intended to provide elderly couples with the basic necessities. The system also provides higher benefits to workers with greater contributions, which is analogous to a pension scheme. However, the benefit level does not increase in proportion to contributions as it would in a normal pension plan. Benefits of low-income workers are set at a higher percentage of their contributions than high-income ones. In this way, the social security system redistributes income from higher to lower earners.

The third prong of the social safety net was **Aid to Families with Dependent Children (AFDC)**. Eligibility is restricted to families with children under the age of 18 living at home and with income and assets below prespecified levels. The thresholds are set by each state according to general federal guidelines. Benefits are based on a schedule set by each state that provides a guaranteed amount, depending on the number of children in the family. The benefit level is reduced as family income rises above the threshold level.

AFDC was intended for families that fell "between the cracks" of the first two programs. The unemployment insurance system was designed to take care of families whose husbands were temporarily out of work. The social security system was set up to take care of the elderly. AFDC was supposed to provide basic support for nonelderly families with children who could not do so on their own. Who were these families? They were female-headed households, since it was assumed that husbands would all be at work or collecting unemployment insurance while looking for work. In 1935, female-headed households were an unusual occurrence, because both divorce and the birth of children to unmarried mothers were uncommon. As a result, the program was oriented toward widows and thought of as a form of social insurance to provide financial help in the event of the death of the primary wage earner—the husband. Viewing the nuclear family as the basic unit of society, the architects of this program could not have foreseen the huge increase in the number of female-headed households resulting from divorce and "out-of-wedlock" births (see Chapter 13).

Postwar Developments

The New Deal was the first period of major social legislation. The second was the Great Society program of the mid-1960s. The reason for this is not altogether clear, since this was a period of general prosperity and rapid economic growth. However, it was also the period when poverty was "rediscovered"—partly as a result of the publication of Michael Harrington's 1962 book, *The Other America.* It may also have resulted from the civil rights movement of the 1950s and early 1960s, which as we saw in Chapter 13, provided impetus to the civil rights legislation of the 1960s. President Kennedy provided the initiative for much of the social legislation of the period. After his assassination in 1963, President Johnson's adept political maneuverings resulted in the enactment of three new programs: (1) food stamps (1964), (2) Medicaid (1965), and (3) Medicare (1966).

The Food Stamp program was designed to provide eligible low-income families with a nutritionally adequate low-cost diet. The program provides vouchers for qualifying families that can be used for the purchase of only foodstuffs (alcohol and tobacco products, for example, are excluded). Eligibility is limited to families whose income and assets fall below prespecified levels. Since this is a federal program, the guidelines are set by the federal government and do not vary across states. In fact, almost all AFDC recipients are eligible for food stamps, as well as those covered by Supplemental Social Insurance (see below). The program is open to families with and without children, as long as they meet the income threshold. In 1994, the monthly income limit was set at $756 for a single-person household, $1,022 for a two-person household, and $1,555 for a four-person household.

The benefit level is determined by assuming that low-income families spend 30 percent of their cash income on food. The value of food stamps then makes up the difference between the cost of a nutritionally adequate low-cost diet (given the size of the family) estimated by the Department of Agriculture and 30 percent of the family's cash income. In 1994, the maximum monthly food stamp grant (for a family with no income) was $112 for a single-person household, $206 for a two-person household, and $375 for a four-person household. The food stamp allotment is reduced by $0.30 for each dollar of income earned.

Medicaid was established as an adjunct to AFDC. All families which qualify for AFDC and Supplemental Social Insurance (SSI) automatically qualify for Medicaid. The program also covers low-income pregnant women and children in low-income families who may not be covered by AFDC or SSI.

Like AFDC, Medicaid is administered by the individual states under federal guidelines. The federal government establishes a minimal level of medical coverage for eligible families. These include basic inpatient and outpatient hospital services, laboratory and X-ray services, and some doctor office visits. The states must meet these minimal requirements but may also include additional medical services. The federal government reimburses each state for Medicaid expenses (reimbursement rates vary inversely to the level of per capita income of the state and typically range between 50 and 80 percent).

Medicare was enacted as an adjunct to the social security system (it forms the "H" in OASDHI). Anyone aged 65 or older who is receiving social security ("old age") benefits is automatically eligible for Medicare. Persons under the age of 65 who receive social security disability benefits can also qualify for this program. The Medicare program pays all "reasonable" expenses for inpatient hospital care minus a small deductible.[3] The program also pays for 80 percent of the reasonable charges for doctor services, though certain types of procedures are excluded and there is a nominal deductible per year. Hospitals and doctors who subscribe to this program usually agree to accept the reimbursement rates set by Medicare.

These three new programs—food stamps, Medicaid, and Medicare—represent extensions of the basic income maintenance system put into place during the New Deal. The major change in philosophy is a movement away from cash income support to in-kind transfers of basic necessities. This may have reflected a paternalistic attitude on the part of the government to ensure that welfare benefits were used for "appropriate purposes." These programs provide low-income families directly with two of life's necessities, rather than with an additional cash allowance, so that they can purchase these items. Together with direct housing assistance (see below), these programs provide the basic necessities of life—food, shelter, and medical care.

Since the 1960s, the only significant addition to the income support system was **Supplemental Social Insurance (SSI),** enacted in 1972, during the Nixon administration. SSI provides cash payments to needy elderly, blind, and disabled persons. The guidelines are set by the federal government and are uniform across states. Elderly individuals (age 65 or over) who do not qualify for social security, as well as blind and disabled persons who meet the income and asset thresholds of this program, are eligible for benefits.

During 1994, the Clinton administration attempted to develop some form of universal health care. Most workers and their families receive health insurance from their employer. Medicare provides health coverage to the elderly and Medicaid to the poor. In addition, health coverage is available through private health insurance plans for families rich enough to afford the premiums. However, that still leaves about 15 percent of American families with no health coverage. These are mainly low-income working families employed in jobs which do not provide health insurance. Clinton's plan required employers to provide health insurance to all their employees, including low-wage workers. In August of 1994, this attempt was defeated in Congress.

Housing Assistance

Federal housing assistance programs have developed over the years, in a somewhat *ad hoc* fashion. The objective of these programs is to reduce housing costs for low-income families and to improve the quality of housing they receive.

The earliest programs, dating from 1937, provided rental assistance to low-income families. These have been (and still are) of two forms. The first has been through the construction of special housing projects reserved for

---

[3] This is the case for the first 60 days of hospital care. After that, the patient must pay a small coinsurance amount.

low-income families. Eligible families may qualify for an apartment in one of these housing units. The second is through household-based subsidies. Qualifying low-income families who rent standard apartments in the private housing market receive a rental subsidy from the federal government. In both cases (public housing and the private housing market), qualifying families are required to pay no more than a fixed percentage (generally 30 percent) of their income on rent. In the case of public housing, the rent is limited to this amount. In the case of the private housing market, the government pays directly to the landlord the difference between the market rent and the rental limit computed from the family income.

Besides rental assistance, the federal government also provides assistance to qualifying low- and moderate-income families to purchase homes. This usually takes the form of a long-term commitment to reduce the interest payments of the mortgage loan. The federal government has also recently (since 1991) started making block grants to state and local governments to build more public housing for low-income families. In addition, state and local governments finance and administer public housing projects for their low-income populations.

Public Expenditures on Major Federal Programs

Table 15.2 highlights trends in spending of the principal federal income transfer programs. The programs are separated into two groups, corresponding to the two principles of social welfare spending. The first consists of social insurance programs, which were set up to protect workers against job loss due to unemployment, disability, and old age. These programs are funded mainly through payroll taxes. The second group, referred to as public assistance or welfare, are intended to provide for families and individuals in need—irrespective of the circumstances that caused their poverty.

It is interesting to look at the 1993 figures first. The largest program in dollar terms was, by far, the social security system (OASDI). Government outlays on this program alone amounted to $302 billion, 42 percent of the total expenditures of the income transfer programs included in the table. Social security spending was almost exactly equal to defense spending in that year. Medicare was the second largest program in dollar terms, at $143 billion. Public spending on the elderly from OASDHI (social security plus Medicare) summed to $445 billion, or 62 percent of the total for these income support programs.

Expenditures on the other social insurance programs are much smaller. Outlays on unemployment insurance were 5 percent of the total, workers' compensation was 6 percent, and veteran's disability compensation 2 percent. Spending on public assistance programs amounted to a quarter of total federal social welfare spending. AFDC outlays were $25 billion in 1993, less than 10 percent of social security spending. SSI, food stamps, and housing assistance each cost about the same as AFDC. The largest public assis-

Table 15.2 Public Expenditures (Outlays) on Major Federal Income Transfer Programs, 1960–1993[a] (Billions of 1993 Dollars)

	Date Enacted	Year 1960	1970	1980	1990	1993	Annual Percent Rate of Growth, 1970–1993
A. Social Insurance							
Cash benefits							
Social security (OASDI)	1935	51.2	110.2	207.1	272.5	302.0	4.38
Unemployment insurance	1935	14.7	16.3	29.6	19.3	35.4	3.37
Workers' compensation	1908	6.3	11.4	23.6	40.7	45.6	6.36
Veterans' disability compensation	1917	0.0	25.3	20.5	16.9	17.8	−1.54
In-kind benefits							
Medicare	1965	0.0	25.3	59.6	118.7	143.2	7.53
B. Public Assistance (Welfare)							
Cash benefits							
Aid to Families With Dependent Children (AFDC)	1935	4.9	18.1	23.6	23.4	25.2	1.46
Supplemental Social Insurance (SSI)[b]	1972	0.0	0.0	10.0	12.7	21.2	5.78[c]
In-kind benefits							
Medicaid	1965	0.0	10.1	24.6	45.4	75.8	8.78
Food stamps	1964	0.0	1.9	15.9	17.6	24.6	11.07
Housing assistance	1937	0.0	1.8	12.6	23.3	27.5	11.97
Total expenditures		77.2	220.4	427.2	590.6	718.3	5.14
Total expenditures as a percentage of GDP		3.1	5.9	9.0	9.6	11.3	
Memo:							
National defense expenditures		221.1	286.0	250.2	347.2	303.6	0.26

[a]Benefits plus administrative expenses. Sources: U.S. House of Representatives, Committee on Ways and Means, *1994 Green Book*; Council of Economic Advisers, *Economic Report of the President, 1994*.
[b]Aid to the Blind, to the Permanently Disabled and Totally Disabled, and Old Age Assistance in 1965.
[c]Growth rate is for 1980–1993.

tance program is Medicaid, which amounted to $76 billion, or 11 percent of total income transfers.

Time trends are also striking. Social welfare spending increased from 3 percent of GDP in 1960 to 11 percent in 1993. In 1960, almost three times as much money was spent on national defense as on these programs. By 1993, income transfers were double national defense spending.

Spending on income transfer programs grew by 5.1 percent per year in real terms between 1970 and 1993. The annual growth in housing assistance topped the list, at 12 percent, followed by food stamps (11 percent), Medicaid (8.8 percent), and Medicare (7.5 percent). Social security (OASDI) expenditures grew at 4.4 percent per year, unemployment insurance at 3.4 percent per year, and workers' compensation at 6.4 percent per year. AFDC expenditures in real terms increased very slowly from 1970 to 1993, at 1.5 percent per year, and between 1980 and 1993, there was virtually no change. Spending on SSI grew much more rapidly, at 5.8 percent per year from 1980 to 1993. Spending on in-kind welfare benefits (food, medical, and housing benefits) has grown much faster than cash benefits over the last quarter century.

15.3 UNEMPLOYMENT INSURANCE

The Social Security Act of 1935 created a combined federal/state system of **Unemployment Insurance (UI).** The federal legislation provided strong incentives for each state to set up its own system of unemployment insurance. Each state administers its own system and sets the important regulations of the system, such as minimum and maximum benefits, the rules for eligibility, and the unemployment insurance tax rates. Originally, only workers in large companies in certain industries were covered by the system. However, federal legislation over the years, such as the Employment Security Act of 1970, has extended coverage of the system. In 1991, 97 percent of all wage and salary workers were covered by the UI system and about 88 percent of all employed persons.[4]

The stated objective of the 1935 Social Security Act was to provide temporary and partial wage replacement to involuntarily unemployed workers who were recently employed. There are a number of key elements to this statement. First, the worker had to be involuntarily unemployed. This means that unemployment must have occurred through job loss rather than discharge for cause (for example, being fired for lateness or absenteeism) or for voluntarily quitting. The most common cause of job loss is layoffs associated with a recession. Second, the worker must have been previously employed to qualify for UI. New workers, just entering the labor force, or reentrants, who have been out for an extended period of time, are not eligible. Third, the UI system guarantees only partial replacement of wages, not the level the worker earned before losing the job. Fourth, the relief is temporary so that UI benefits are provided for only a limited period of time, during which the worker is expected to search actively for another job.

---

[4]The source is: U.S. House of Representatives, Ways and Means Committee, *1994 Green Book,* p. 481.

Employers pay a payroll tax on wages and salaries into the unemployment insurance fund. The rate is set by the federal government (it has recently been of the order of 0.8 percent). There is a rather low cap on the wage base (recently $7,000 to $8,000), and the UI tax is levied only on wages up to this level. As a result, the effective UI tax on wages (the ratio of UI taxes to total covered wages) has been about 0.2 to 0.3 percent since the 1960s.

A Brief Description of the UI System

Though the details of the system vary across states, the basic structure is very similar. The program provides workers who become unemployed a certain level of benefits depending on the reason for their joblessness and their previous weekly earnings. In most states, a worker must have previously worked two quarters (6 months) and have been laid off from his or her job (not fired or voluntarily quit) to be eligible for UI benefits. In Rhode Island and New York, strikers are also eligible for benefits, and in some states, those who voluntarily leave a job are also entitled to benefits. Those newly joining or returning to the labor force do not qualify for benefits.

In all states, there is a minimum weekly UI benefit (UI_1) and a maximum benefit (UI_2) for those who are eligible. The minimum and maximum vary considerably across states. The actual UI benefit depends on the worker's previous earnings, which in some states is based on the earnings of the last full week worked, in others on the worker's earnings over the last year, and in still others on the individual's earnings during his or her best quarter over the last year. There is a minimum level of previous weekly earnings, W_1, needed to qualify for benefits. At W_1, the benefit is set at UI_1. Above W_1, the UI benefit increases in proportion to previous earnings W, though the rate is less than unity and typically about 50 percent (an additional dollar of benefit per two dollars of earnings). Benefits are capped at UI_2, corresponding to wage level W_2.

The replacement rate structure is shown in Figure 15.1, where the replacement rate is defined as the ratio of the individual's weekly UI benefit to previous weekly earnings W. At W_1, the replacement rate is equal to UI_1/W_1. From W_1 to W_2, the replacement rate remains at UI_1/W_1 (which, in turn, equals UI_2/W_2). Above W_2, the replacement rate declines inversely with W, since the benefit level is fixed at UI_2.

UI benefits generally last for a maximum of 26 weeks, as long as the individual shows evidence of actively looking for new work. During periods when the aggregate unemployment rate is particularly high, Congress has often enacted special legislation, which extends the maximum number of weeks an individual can collect UI benefits (typically an extra 13 weeks). Up until 1978, UI benefits were not subject to federal income taxes. Since 1978, UI benefits have been treated as taxable income only if total family income exceeds a prespecified maximum ($12,000 for single taxpayers and $18,000 for married couples).

Figure 15.1   The Replacement Rate Structure of the Unemployment Insurance System

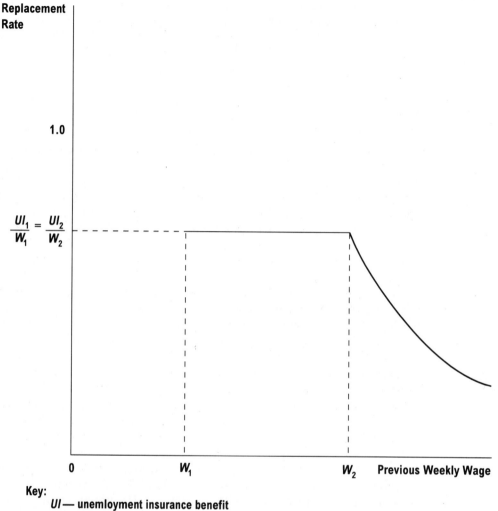

Key:
UI— unemloyment insurance benefit
W— previous weekly wage

Like social security, UI benefits are financed by a payroll tax, paid by the employer. An employer's UI tax rate is based on the employer's "experience rating." The rationale is that firms that lay off workers more frequently than others should pay a higher tax rate, since they place heavier demands on the UI system's finances. Like the benefit structure, there is both a minimum and a maximum UI tax rate that is assessed on the firm's total payroll. Firms that rarely lay off workers will pay the minimum rate. Firms that lay off workers frequently and for relatively long duration will pay the maximum rate. In between, the payroll tax rate is a step function of the firm's layoff record. Because of the structure of the system, firms that rarely lay off workers pay a greater amount into the system than the actual costs the system incurs from the firm (that is, the benefits the UI system pays to workers laid off by these firms). Conversely, firms that frequently lay off workers will pay less into the UI system than the system pays out in UI benefits to the firm's employees.

Table 15.3 shows relevant statistics on both eligibility requirements and benefit structure for a number of states in 1994. It is at once apparent that provisions vary considerably among states. The first column shows the minimum wage base, W_1, for eligibility. The minimum among these nine states varies from a low of $400 for Florida to $2,460 for New Jersey (the lowest minimum among the 50 states is $130 in Hawaii, and the highest is $5,400 in Montana). The maximum wage base, W_2, ranges from a low of $9,065 in Texas to a high of $13,080 in Pennsylvania (among the 50 states, from $4,650 in Nebraska to $27,144 in Colorado).

The minimum weekly UI benefit level, UI_1, corresponding to earnings level W_1, and the maximum benefit level, UI_2, corresponding to W_2, are shown in the third and fourth columns. Both minimum and maximum benefit levels differ considerably among the states (the minimum level from $5 in Hawaii to $73 in Washington State and the maximum from $154 in Nebraska to $487 in Massachusetts). The actual average weekly benefit paid to

Table 15.3 Eligibility Requirements and Benefits for Unemployment Insurance in Selected States, 1994[a]

	Required Total Earnings in Base Year for:		Weekly Benefit Amount		Average Weekly Benefit in 1993	Potential Duration in Weeks		Average Duration of Benefits (Weeks) in 1993
	Minimum Benefit	Maximum Benefit	Minimum	Maximum		Minimum	Maximum	
California	$1,125	$ 9,542	$40	$230	$152	14	26	18
Florida	400	10,000	10	250	165	10	26	15
Illinois	1,600	12,285	51	311	194	26	26	18
Michigan	1,340	11,320	42	293	210	15	26	12
New Jersey	2,460	11,567	69	347	228	15	26	18
New York	1,600	11,980	40	300	188	13	26	11
Ohio	1,702	9,520	42	319	180	20	26	15
Pennsylvania	1,320	13,080	35	337	197	16	26	17
Texas	1,480	9,065	41	245	177	9	26	16

[a] Source: U.S. House of Representatives, Committee on Ways and Means, *1994 Green Book.*

UI recipients in 1993 varied from $126 in Alabama to $247 in Hawaii—almost a two-fold difference.

Almost all states provide that an unemployed person can collect UI benefits for a maximum of 26 weeks (the exceptions are Massachusetts and Washington, which have a 30-week maximum). The actual number of weeks of eligibility is based on the person's previous earnings. New Yorkers, for example, who just meet the New York earnings requirement would be able to collect benefits for at most 13 weeks. The minimum potential duration varies from a low of 5 weeks in Oregon to 26 weeks in several states. The average number of weeks during which UI benefits were collected in 1993 ranged from 9 in Alabama to 18 in three states.

Time Trends in UI Benefits

Though almost all wage and salary workers are covered by the UI system, the actual percentage of unemployed workers receiving UI benefits has typically ranged from 30 to 70 percent. As we discussed above, there are two reasons for this. The first is that there are eligibility requirements for an unemployed person to receive UI benefits. These are of two forms: (1) a worker must have worked a certain number of weeks continuously or worked in a certain number of quarters before losing the job to qualify, and (2) a worker is required to have earned a certain minimum level of wages to qualify. The second is that unemployment benefits are exhausted after a certain number of weeks (usually 26 weeks). At this point, the worker is no longer eligible for UI benefits.

Table 15.4 highlights these trends (see also Figure 15.2). The insured coverage rate, defined as the number of unemployed workers receiving benefits at a percentage of total unemployment, has been as high as 76 percent (in 1975) and as low as 32 percent (1987 and 1988). Generally speaking, coverage rates declined rather sharply between the mid-1970s and the mid- to late-1980s but increased during the 1990s. It is also interesting to note that there is no clear connection between the overall civilian unemployment rate (shown in the first column of Table 15.2) and the coverage rate. The reason is that during recessionary periods, when unemployment has been high, Congress has frequently added auxiliary UI benefits by increasing the number of weeks of eligibility.

The average weekly UI benefit check, in 1987 dollars, increased from $130 in 1962 to a peak of $154 in 1972. However, by 1982, the average benefit had fallen to about $140, and it has more or less remained at this level ever since. Average real benefits from the UI system were lower in 1993 than 20 years prior.

A more revealing statistic is the replacement rate, which is the ratio of the UI benefit to the earnings the worker received just before he or she became unemployed. Unfortunately, information on this statistic is relatively spotty. However, we do have reliable data on the ratio of the average UI benefit to the average wage of the total private work force. Insofar as

Table 15.4 Unemployment Insurance (UI) Coverage and Benefit Rates, Selected Years, 1967–1993

Year	Civilian Unemployment Rate[a] [percent]	Insured Coverage Rate[b] [percent]	Average Weekly UI Benefit[c] [1987 $]	Ratio of UI Benefit to Average Wage[d]
1962	5.5		130	0.40
1967	3.8	43	140	0.41
1970	4.9	48	147	0.42
1975	8.5	76	148	0.43
1980	7.1	50	136	0.42
1985	7.2	34	135	0.43
1990	5.5	37	140	0.47
1993	6.8	48	141	0.48

[a]Source: Council of Economic Advisers, *Economic Report of the President, 1994*.
[b]Insured unemployment as a percent of total unemployment, average for year. Source: U.S. House of Representatives, Committee on Ways and Means, *1994 Green Book*.
[c]Source: Council of Economic Advisers, *Economic Report of the President, 1994*.
[e]The average weekly wage is for the total private work force. The source is: Council of Economic Advisers, *Economic Report of the President, 1994*.

Figure 15.2 The Overall Unemployment Rate and the UI Coverage and Replacement Rates, 1967–1993

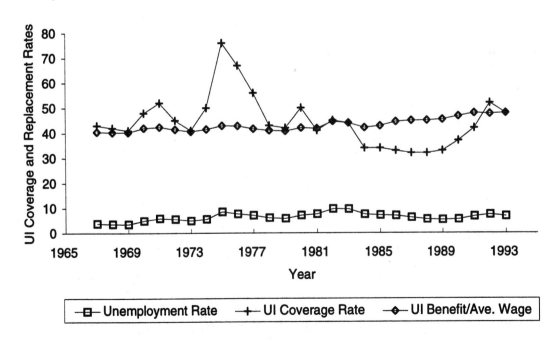

unemployed workers are a reasonably representative sample of the work force, this ratio is a good proxy of the actual replacement rate. The ratio of the average UI benefit to the average wage has been increasing rather steadily since the early 1960s, from 0.40 in 1962 to 0.48 in 1993. The reason for this is *not* that UI benefits have grown in real terms but rather that real earnings have declined.

Incentive Effects of the UI System

The UI system by its very nature may have an important effect on both the level of unemployment and its duration. In particular, by reducing the cost to an individual of being jobless, the UI system may actually prolong the duration of unemployment for many workers (see, for example, Feldstein, 1974). The original architects of the UI system explicitly recognized this and argued, in fact, that the added security individuals had while unemployed would enable them to select a job more compatible with their skills and interests. Rather than settling on the first position offered, an unemployed person could continue his or her job search until a better match and higher wages were provided. This, in turn, would prove socially beneficial, since better job matches should increase the national output by improving efficiency in the allocation of labor resources (see Haber and Murray [1966] for related arguments).

The type of unemployment occasioned by the job search process is called **search unemployment,** which is a form of frictional unemployment (see Chapter 5). Since the UI system reduces the costs of remaining unemployed, the reservation wage—the minimum wage a person is willing to accept—for those searching for a new job will be higher on average than without UI benefits and, as a result, so will be their average duration of unemployment. The higher the UI benefits, the longer will be the average unemployment spell. Most empirical studies have confirmed a positive relation between the UI replacement rate and the average duration of unemployment. Typically, an increase in the replacement rate of 0.1 is associated with a half week to week increase in the average duration of unemployment. All told, the UI system may cause covered workers to remain unemployed 16 to 31 percent longer than those not covered.[5]

The UI system itself may also directly affect the layoff policies of firms. This is due to two features of the UI system. First, until 1978, UI benefits were not subject to federal income tax and, after 1978, only if family income was above a certain critical level. As a result, if the (before-tax) UI replacement rate was 0.5, the after-tax replacement (the ratio of UI benefits to after-tax wages) would be higher. Feldstein (1974) estimated that in those states with higher UI benefits, the after-tax replacement rate could be as high as 80 percent for male workers and actually over 100 percent for some

---

[5] See Marston (1975), Ehrenberg and Oaxaca (1976), Classen (1979), Solon (1979), Barron and Mellow (1981), Moffitt and Nicholson (1982), Feldstein and Poterba (1984), and Meyer (1990).

female workers. The loss of pay to many workers from being unemployed for short periods is relatively small. Indeed, since the probability of being recalled from temporary layoffs may be very high and since many workers on temporary layoffs treat this time as a vacation period, collective bargaining contracts may have "inverse seniority" provisions, whereby the most senior workers are laid off first and rehired last (see Feldstein, 1978). As a result, some workers not only do not oppose temporary layoffs but even welcome them.

Second, because a firm's contribution to the UI system does not fully reflect the added costs to the system from laying off workers, a firm is not heavily penalized for temporarily laying off workers. Indeed, the added UI taxes it must pay from temporary layoffs may be quite minimal. As a result, firms also do not have much of a disincentive for laying off workers as a response to a decline in demand. In consequence, Feldstein and others argued that the UI system itself promotes a demand-deficient type of unemployment, since it discourages both firms and employees from reacting to declines in demand by wage reductions instead of layoffs. Topel (1983) estimated that more than one-fourth of layoffs and Anderson and Meyer (1994) estimated that about 20 percent of layoffs could be ascribed to the implicit subsidy of the UI system on layoff unemployment.

The UI system has also been shown to lead to increased seasonal unemployment. A study by Chiswick (1976) found that the extension of the coverage of the UI system to agricultural workers during the 1970s accounted for a sizable increase in the level of seasonal unemployment in that industry.

15.4 The Social Security System

The old-age and survivors insurance (OASI) program provides benefits to retired workers and their dependents and to survivors of insured workers. The original Social Security Act of 1935 provided benefits to retired workers, and a 1939 amendment to the Act added benefits for dependents and survivors.

Workers become eligible for OASI benefits by working in covered employment (that is, in industries or occupations that are included within the social security system). In 1994, about 96 percent of the paid labor force was covered by the social security system. Contributions to the social security system are made under the Federal Insurance Contributions Act (FICA, for short). In 1994, employees contributed 7.65 percent of their wages and salaries to the social security fund up to a maximum taxable wage base of $60,600. This is matched with an identical contribution from the employer, so the effective social security tax rate on wages and salaries is 15.30 percent (see the next chapter for more details on the tax side).

When a person who is covered by the social security system retires, he or she is usually eligible to receive a monthly social security benefit. Under current rules, the person must have received covered earnings in at least six quarters to receive social security benefits. In 1994, the person must have

Table 15.5   OASI Cash Benefits to All Recipients and New Awards, 1993[a]

Recipient Class	All Beneficiaries		New Awards in 1993	
	Number of Beneficiaries (1,000s)	Average Monthly Benefit	Number of Beneficiaries (1,000s)	Average Monthly Benefit
All beneficiaries	42,246	$607	4,001	$530
Retired workers	26,104	$674	1,661	$647
Spouses of retired workers	3,094	$347	291	$315
Children of retired workers	436	$297	107	$277
Disabled workers	3,726	$642	635	$638
Widowed mothers and fathers	289	$448	56	$435
Widows and widowers	5,077	$630	434	$624
Surviving children	1,836	$443	311	$436

[a]Figures do not sum to totals for all beneficiaries because of excluded groups. Source: U.S. House of Representatives, Committee on Ways and Means, *1994 Green Book.*

earned at least $620 during the quarter for it to qualify as a covered quarter. If a covered worker dies before retirement, the worker's spouse and/or children may also be entitled to receive social security benefits. In both cases, the award is based on the worker's earnings history.

Table 15.5 shows average OASI payments to various groups of beneficiaries in 1993. Over 42 million persons collected social security benefits of one form or another. The average monthly benefit was $607. Over 26 million retired workers received benefits in 1993, with an average monthly award of $674. Of this number, 1.66 million retired during 1993, and their average monthly benefit was $647. There were a total of 3.7 million disabled workers who were on the social security rolls, and their average benefit was $642. Widows and widowers collecting benefits amounted to a little over 5 million, and their average award was $630.

Determination of the Social Security Benefit

The OASI benefit is calculated as follows. A worker's earnings history is first converted into an **average indexed monthly earnings (AIME)** figure. This is the average monthly wage of the worker, adjusted for changes in the average wages of the total labor force. In effect, the indexing adjusts for both changes in the price level (inflation) and changes in real earnings. The computation of the AIME also reflects the number of quarters the person works in covered employment. A person must work (and receive a minimum amount of earnings) in at least 6 quarters to qualify for social security benefits. The maximum benefit is achieved at 40 quarters of covered work. If fewer than 40 quarters are worked in covered employment, the AIME is reduced in proportion to the shortfall in the number of quarters (for example, the AIME for a person who works 30 quarters will be three-fourths of the AIME of a person who works 40 quarters or more with the same average index earnings).

The AIME is then used to compute the monthly retirement benefit payable at the worker's normal retirement age. This is based on a progressive benefit formula to arrive at the **primary insurance amount (PIA)**. The PIA is subject to both a minimum and maximum level.

The actual benefit received is a fixed proportion of the PIA. If the person retires at the normal retirement age of 65, the retiree receives the full amount of the PIA.[6] If the person retires at age 62 (the earliest retirement age covered by the social security system), the person receives only 80 percent of the PIA. If the person retires at age 67, the benefit is set at 110 percent of the PIA, and at age 70, 125 percent of the PIA.

The different percentages are intended to make the benefits "actuarially fair." According to this formula, the discounted present value of the total social security benefit stream will be about equal for workers retiring at different ages. Since someone who retires at age 62 will, on average, collect social security benefits for three more years than someone retiring at age 65, the average monthly benefit is correspondingly reduced. Conversely, since someone retiring at age 70 will, on average, receive benefits for five fewer years than a worker retiring at 65, the average monthly benefits are higher.

Relative to the AIME, the PIA is redistributive. In other words, the system pays higher benefits relative to total social security contributions for lower-income families than higher-income ones. Computations shown below indicate that low-income workers have a higher PIA relative to their AIME than middle- or high-income workers do:

Ratio of Primary Insurance Amount (PIA) to Average Indexed Monthly Earnings (AIME) for Hypothetical Low-, Middle-, and High-Income Workers, 1993

	AIME	PIA	Ratio of PIA/AIME
Low-Income Worker	$ 926.00	$ 542.60	0.59
Middle-Income Worker	1,820.00	836.00	0.46
High-Income Worker	3,154.00	1,146.00	0.36

Source: U.S. House of Representatives, Ways and Means Committee, *1994 Green Book.*

---

[6] Under current legislation, the normal retirement age will be gradually raised to age 67 by the year 2022.

A low-income worker, defined here as one earning the minimum wage throughout his or her work life, who retired at age 65 would receive a monthly benefit of $542.60, or 59 percent of the person's AIME. This is, roughly speaking, the person's average monthly earnings. A middle-income worker, defined as someone receiving the national average wage in each year, who retired at 65 would receive a benefit of $836.00, 46 percent of the person's AIME. A high-income worker, defined as someone who earned the maximum amount of wages that can be credited to the person's social security record, who retired at 65 would receive a benefit equal to only 36 percent of the person's AIME.

Another way of looking at social security benefits is in terms of what percentage of the person's preretirement earnings the social security benefits represent or replace. Replacement rates are shown in Table 15.6 for retirement years 1940–1990, with projections made to the year 2040. It is again clear from this table that the social security benefit formula is redistributive in favor of low-income workers. Among persons retiring at age 65 in 1990, the social security benefit was equal to 58 percent of previous earn-

Table 15.6   Social Security Replacement Rates, 1940–2040[a]

Year of Birth	Year Attaining Normal Retirement Age	Replacement Rates		
		Low Earner[b]	Average Earner[c]	Maximum Earner[d]
1875	1940	39.4	26.2	16.5
1885	1950	33.2	19.7	21.2
1895	1960	49.1	33.3	29.8
1900	1965	45.6	31.4	32.9
1905	1970	48.5	34.3	30.1
1910	1975	59.9	42.3	30.1
1915	1980	68.1	51.1	32.5
1920	1985	61.1	40.9	22.8
1925	1990	58.2	43.2	24.5
1944	2010[e]	56.0	41.7	27.1
1954	2020[e]	56.0	41.7	27.8
1963	2030[e]	55.7	41.5	27.6
1973	2040[e]	55.7	41.5	27.5

[a]The replacement rate is defined as the social security benefit received at year of retirement as a percent of earnings in the year prior to retirement. Source: U.S. House of Representatives, Committee on Ways and Means, *1994 Green Book.*
[b]A worker earning 45 percent of the national average wage in each year.
[c]A worker earning the average national wage in each year.
[d]A worker earning the maximum taxable wage base in each year.
[e]Projected by the Social Security Administration.

ings for low-income workers, 43 percent for middle-income ones, and only 25 percent for the high earners. The social security system thus redistributes benefits in favor of the poor, relative both to lifetime earnings and, as we saw in Section 11.3, relative to the social security contributions paid into the system.

Replacement rates have increased over time from the inception of the social security system through 1980. For the average retiree, the replacement rate rose from 26 percent in 1940 to 51 percent in 1980. However, replacement rates fell between 1980 and 1990—for the average earner, from 51 to 43 percent. After 1990 and until the year 2040 at least, replacement rates are projected to stabilize at about 56 percent for low-income earners, 42 percent for average earners, and 28 percent for the high earners.

Since 1975, social security benefits have been automatically increased each year with changes in the cost of living.[7] This **automatic cost-of-living adjustment,** or **COLA,** is based on changes in the **Consumer Price Index (CPI).** Interestingly, since social security benefits are adjusted to keep up with inflation and real wages have been declining (see Chapter 2), social security benefits have been rising relative to real earnings. Since 1970, for example, while real earnings have fallen by 16 percent, social security benefits have been indexed upward through the COLA by 20 percent. This difference has had the effect of redistributing income from the working population to retirees. Moreover, it has had the somewhat perverse effect of making retirement more attractive relative to working, since retirement income is protected against inflation whereas wages are not, and it may induce people to retire at an earlier age.

Another provision of the social security laws is that benefits may be reduced if the retiree is still earning income at a job. The original architects of the social security law were concerned that social security benefits might not be sufficient to allow a family to attain a minimally desirable standard of living. As a result, they allowed retirees to earn outside income, usually at a part-time job, as long as the earnings did not exceed a prespecified maximum. This is referred to as the "earnings test."

In 1994, the exempt amount was $8,040 for retirees under the age of 65 and $11,600 for retirees between 65 and 69. There is no restriction on the earnings of retirees over the age of 69. If earnings exceed the maximum, then social security benefits are reduced in proportion to the earnings above the maximum. For retirees between 62 and 64, their benefit level is reduced by one dollar for each two dollars of earnings over the exempt amount, while for retirees between 65 and 69 of age, the benefits are reduced by one dollar for every three dollars of earnings over the exemption.

Before 1984, social security benefits were fully exempt from federal income taxation. However, beginning in 1984, a portion of the benefits be-

---

[7]Prior to 1975, social security benefits were periodically raised by the U.S. Congress. These upward adjustments were usually greater than the inflation rate.

came subject to taxation for high-income families. In 1984, half of the social security benefits were added to taxable income for individual taxpayers with an income of $25,000 or more and for married couples with an income of $32,000 or more. In 1994, the rules were changed so that 85 percent of social security benefits were included in taxable income for individual taxpayers with incomes of $34,000 or more and for married couples with incomes of $44,000 or more.

Incentive Effects on Labor Supply

As might be expected, the availability of social security benefits starting at age 62 has had an important effect on the retirement behavior of older workers. A host of studies have tried to estimate the labor participation effects of various aspects of the social security system. Almost all studies have found a significant negative effect of the system as a whole on work effort.

Particular attention has focused on two aspects of the system. First, as we saw in Chapter 11, the future flow of social security benefits can be viewed as a form of wealth. Likewise, the future flow of social security contributions, in the form of a tax on future earnings, can be viewed as a liability to the worker. The difference between these two flows, is the *net* value of social security wealth. In general, as a worker ages, his or her net social security wealth increases. At some point, this **wealth effect** may discourage additional work. See, for example, the papers by Boskin (1977), Quinn (1977), Boskin and Hurd (1978), Reimers (1977), Burkhauser and Quinn (1980), Gordon and Blinder (1980), and Clark and Johnson (1980).

Danziger, Haveman, and Plotnick (1981) concluded that the social security system did induce earlier retirement and probably accounted for a 12 percentage point decline in the labor force participation of men aged 65 and older between 1950 and 1980. Since, as we saw in Chapter 5, the labor force participation rate of this group fell by 25 percentage points over the period, rising social security eligibility and benefits would account for about half of this decline.

Second, as we described above, there is an earnings test applied to wages and salaries received by retired workers collecting social security benefits. Once the threshold is passed, wages above this level will reduce social security benefits. This may be viewed as an additional tax on labor earnings above the threshold, and this "tax" may also discourage work effort.[8] The existence of an earnings test appears to reduce the work effort of workers

---

[8] However, there is a subtle offset to the tax effect. The calculation of the AIME is based on the best 35 years of earnings. If an elderly person has a job that pays more than the lowest year of earnings used to calculate the person's AIME, then continuing to work at the job will allow a substitution of the new year of earnings for the lowest. The worker's AIME will then be recalculated, and his or her prospective social security benefit thereby increased. See Blinder, Gordon, and Wise (1980) for more details.

aged 62 to 70 by about 10 percent. See, for example, the work of Pellechio (1978).

15.5 AID TO FAMILIES WITH DEPENDENT CHILDREN

Perhaps the most controversial and politically sensitive of the government transfer programs is Aid to Families with Dependent Children (AFDC), which is often referred to as "government welfare." Established in 1935, along with social security and unemployment insurance programs, it is now at about the same magnitude (as measured by actual expenditures) as unemployment insurance but considerably smaller than social security. Yet, despite its relatively small size, AFDC has often been singled out as a political target.

The Workings of AFDC

The key feature of AFDC is to provide cash assistance to children who are needy, because their father or mother is absent from the home, disabled, deceased, or unemployed. Eligibility in AFDC ends when the child reaches the age of 18. The program is run by the individual states, which set benefit levels and establish eligibility criteria within federal guidelines. Federal funds pay for a little over half of the costs of the program, with the rest contributed by the states.

The hallmark of AFDC and related programs such as food stamps is that they are **means-tested.** A family is eligible for AFDC benefits only if its income and assets fall below a predetermined threshold. The threshold is based on a "need standard." Each state is required to determine the amount of monthly income that is required to satisfy the basic needs of families of different sizes. Only families with incomes below this level can qualify for AFDC benefits.[9]

Table 15.7 shows monthly income limits for selected states in 1994. There is considerable variation in the income limitations. Monthly income thresholds varied from a low of $320 in Indiana to $1,648 in New Hampshire in 1994 (the lower the threshold, the fewer the number of families who can qualify for AFDC benefits). The median income limit among the 50 states was $579.

The asset limitation is based on the total value of all assets, excluding, in most states, the value of the home and one automobile, less the value of outstanding debt. There is relatively little variation in the asset test among states, and the threshold is typically $1,000.

---

[9] Technically, this is true for most states. However, in some, the income limitation may actually be below the need standard.

Table 15.7 Eligibility Requirements and Benefits for AFDC, in Selected States, 1994[a]

A. *One-Parent Family of Three Persons*

	Monthly Income Limit	Maximum AFDC Grant	Food Stamp Benefit	Combined Benefits	AFDC Benefit as % of 1993 Poverty Line	Combined Benefits as % of 1993 Poverty Line
Alabama	$673	$164	$295	$ 459	17	48
Alaska	975	923	285	1,208	77	101
California	715	607	214	821	63	86
Connecticut	680	680	192	872	71	91
Florida	991	303	295	598	32	62
Illinois	890	367	291	658	38	69
Indiana	320	288	295	583	30	61
Michigan	587	489	249	738	51	77
New Jersey	985	424	276	700	44	73
New York[b]	577	577	239	816	60	85
Ohio	879	341	295	636	36	66
Pennsylvania	614	421	270	691	44	72
Texas	574	184	295	479	19	50
Washington	1,158	546	258	804	57	84
Median, all states	579	366	295	661	38	69

B. *Maximum AFDC Monthly Benefit by Family Size, 1994*

	1-Person Family	2-Person Family	3-Person Family	4-Person Family	5-Person Family	6-Person Family
Median, all states	$212	$294	$366	$435	$511	$577

[a] Source: U.S. House of Representatives, Committee on Ways and Means, *1994 Green Book.*
[b] New York City. Rules vary across counties.

The AFDC benefit awarded to a qualifying family (one that meets both the income and asset limits) depends on the family size. Each state sets a maximum benefit amount for each family size. A family with no reported income receives the maximum benefit. The award is decreased as income rises, though by less than a dollar-for-dollar basis. For example, in the case of Pennsylvania in 1994, the award structure looked as follows:

AFDC Benefit for a Mother with Two Children by Income Level, Pennsylvania in 1994

Annual Family Income	Annual AFDC Benefit
0	$5,052
$2,000	4,892
$4,000	3,292
$5,000	2,492
$6,000	1,692
$7,000	892
$8,000	0

Source: U.S. House of Representatives, Committee on Ways and Means, *1994 Green Book.*

Annual AFDC benefits are reduced by $200 on the first $2,000 of income. Between $2,000 and $8,000, the award is decreased by 80 cents for each additional dollar of income earned. Above $8,000 of income, there is no benefit.

There is also a very large variation in benefit levels among states. Table 15.7 shows the maximum AFDC benefits for a family of three with no income at all. In 1994, this varied from a low of $164 per month in Alabama to a high of $923 in Alaska (the high among the "Lower 48" was $680 in Connecticut). The median maximum benefit among the 50 states was $366. It is interesting to note that the maximum benefit in almost all states is below the monthly income limit, which is supposed to represent the income required to meet the basic needs of families.

When the AFDC benefit is compared to the 1993 poverty line for a family of three (fifth column), it is clear that no state provides an AFDC grant sufficient to bring the family above the poverty threshold. On average, the AFDC benefit was only 38 percent of the poverty threshold. This ratio ranged from a low of 17 percent in Alabama to a high of 77 percent in Alaska (71 percent in Connecticut among the "Lower 48").

Families receiving AFDC are also automatically eligible for Medicaid, and most are eligible for food stamps. Table 15.7 also shows the value of food stamps for families who receive AFDC. The median value of food stamp benefits for these families among the 50 states was $295 in 1994. There is relatively little variation in the benefit among states.[10]

---

[10] Food stamp benefits differ among states because the benefit is computed on the basis of an income concept that includes wages and salaries, other income, and AFDC. Families who otherwise have no reported income and live in states that have a high AFDC benefit (like Connecticut) will receive a relatively low food stamp benefit. The converse is true for a state like Alabama, which pays a very low AFDC benefit. There is also some variation in food stamp benefits across states due to state rules.

The fourth column shows the combined value of AFDC and food stamps. This combined benefit ranged from a low of $459 in Alabama to highs of $872 in Connecticut and $1,208 in Alaska. If we count food stamps as part of family income when computing the poverty rate,[11] the combined value of AFDC and food stamps in 1994 was still not sufficient to bring families over the poverty threshold in any state except Alaska (column 6). It averaged $661, 69 percent of the poverty threshold for a family of three in 1993.

Benefit levels also vary by family size to reflect different needs. As shown in Panel B of Table 15.7, the average monthly AFDC benefit level in 1994 varied from $212 for a one-person family to $577 for a six-person family. The monthly benefit increased by about $70 for each additional family member.

Time trends are shown in Table 15.8. In 1993, about 5 million families (14 million individuals) were receiving AFDC benefits. Between 1970 and 1975, the number of families on welfare increased by 1.36 million. From 1975 to 1990, only 0.71 million additional families were added to the welfare rolls, though the figure increased by another million between 1990 and 1993 (partly as a result of the 1992 recession).

The most striking statistic is the change in the average monthly benefit level of welfare families. Though the average benefit level doubled in nominal terms between 1970 and 1993, it declined in real terms by 45 percent. From 1990 to 1993, it also declined in nominal terms, from $389 to $373 per month. The average AFDC benefit in 1993 was $4,476 per year—a figure considerably below the poverty line for a single individual.

Another interesting statistic is provided by the average family size of families on AFDC. This declined from 4.0 to 2.9 persons between 1970 and

Table 15.8 Number of Beneficiaries and Average Monthly Benefits per Family from the AFDC Program, 1970–1993[a]

Year	Number of Families (1,000s)	Number of Recipients (1,000s)	Average Family Size	Average Monthly Benefit per Family (Current $)	(1993 $)
1970	1,909	7,429	4.0	178	676
1975	3,269	11,067	3.2	208	576
1980	3,574	10,597	3.0	269	483
1985	3,692	10,813	3.0	329	443
1990	3,974	11,460	2.9	389	434
1993	4,981	14,144	2.9	373	373

[a] Source: U.S. House of Representatives, Committee on Ways and Means, *1994 Green Book*.

---

[11] Recall from Chapter 4 that food stamps and other noncash government benefits are not included in family income when calculating the official poverty rate.

1993. This trend will be relevant when we discuss the effects of AFDC on childbearing behavior.

Incentive Effects of the Welfare System

As noted above, the welfare system has been subject to much criticism by economists, sociologists, political scientists, the media, and public officials. A major controversy was ignited by Charles Murray in a provocative book entitled *Losing Ground,* published in 1984. He argued that the structure of the welfare system itself is in large measure responsible for the persistence of poverty in this country. Murray claimed that it has led to the development of "welfare dependency" by creating strong disincentives against working and causing a large rise in the number of female-headed households.

Labor Supply Effects   Even before the appearance of Murray's book, considerable research had been devoted to analyzing the incentive effects of the welfare system. Much of the early work looked at the effects of the benefit structure of AFDC on labor supply. As the example for Pennsylvania illustrated above demonstrates, AFDC benefits are reduced for each additional dollar earned from wages and salaries. This is equivalent to an implicit "tax" on earnings, or "benefit reduction rate," which can be quite substantial. In order to increase net family income by a dollar, the parent may have to earn anywhere from $1.40 to $1.80. This effect becomes magnified even more when the value of food stamps and Medicaid are included in the welfare benefit. Indeed, if additional earnings cause total family income to pass the Medicaid threshold so that the family loses that benefit, the implicit tax rate may be in excess of 100 percent.

Needless to say, almost all empirical studies have found a significant negative effect of both the AFDC benefit level and of the benefit reduction rate on labor supply (both hours of work and the labor force participation rate). However, estimates of the magnitude of these effects do vary among studies. Danziger, Haveman, and Plotnick (1981), after surveying several major studies on the question,[12] concluded that the AFDC system probably reduces work effort among AFDC recipients by about 5 hours per week. Since AFDC recipients work about 9 hours per week, on average, this implies about a 30 percent reduction in their work effort. Or, to put it another way, if the recipients earned the minimum wage, the extra five hours per week would translate into an additional $1,000 per year (see Moffitt, 1992). This amount would enable only a small proportion of the AFDC families to escape poverty.

Another important implication of this literature, as reported by Moffitt (1992), is that the work disincentives of the AFDC program have had very little effect on the size of the welfare population. The empirical estimates indicate that only about 5 percent of AFDC recipients would leave the wel-

---

[12]See, for example, Garfinkel and Orr (1974), Williams (1975), Saks (1975), Masters and Garfinkel (1977), Levy (1979), Hausman (1981), and Moffitt (1983).

fare rolls if the implicit tax on earnings were eliminated from the program. As Moffitt (p. 17) concludes: "Thus, the problem of 'welfare dependency' (i.e., participation in AFDC) cannot be ascribed to the work disincentives of the program."

AFDC Participation Rates   A related issue is the effects of the AFDC benefit structure on both entry into and exit from the welfare rolls. Virtually all studies have found that higher AFDC benefits lead to higher participation rates in AFDC and lower exit rates (see, for example, Willis, 1980; Plotnick, 1983; Ellwood, 1986; Moffitt, 1986; and Blank, 1989).

One interesting tabulation of spell durations is provided by Ellwood (1986) and shown in Table 15.9. The first column of this table is based on the amount of time spent on AFDC from the time of entry to the time of first exit. This is referred to as the "duration of a single spell" of AFDC participation. The figures in the column show the percentage of total AFDC recipients classified according to the duration of their spell. The numbers indicate that 27 percent of AFDC recipients leave the AFDC rolls within one year, 47 percent leave within two years, and 70 percent leave within four years. However, 10 percent of AFDC recipients remain on the rolls for 10 or more years.

Since a person can leave the AFDC rolls and then return, the second column shows the total time spent by AFDC recipients over a fixed time length—in this case, 25 years. Here, it is clear that many families leave AFDC

Table 15.9   Percentage Distribution of AFDC Recipients by Amount of Time Spent on AFDC[a]

	Duration of Single Spell	Total Time Spent on AFDC Over a 25-Year Period[b]
1 year	27.0	15.7
2 years	20.4	14.1
3 years	10.0	9.4
4 years	12.3	10.9
5 years	2.4	5.1
6 years	8.9	8.3
7 years	4.9	5.9
8 years	2.1	3.8
9 years	1.8	3.3
10 or more years	10.2	23.5
Total	100.0	100.0

[a]Source: Ellwood (1986). Calculations are made for women who entered the AFDC rolls during the period 1971–1982.
[b]Includes all spells of AFDC participation over the period.

only to return at a later date (this is also referred to as "recidivism"). The figures indicate that 16 percent of AFDC recipients are on the welfare rolls for less than one year over this 25-year period, and half are on welfare for four years or less. However, the disturbing finding is that almost one-quarter (23.5 percent) spent at least 10 of the 25 years on welfare.[13]

These figures indicate that the exit rate falls the longer the length of time spent on AFDC. In other words, the probability of leaving welfare decreases the more time a person is on the AFDC rolls. This phenomenon may arise from the fact that spending time on AFDC itself causes them to lose their incentive to leave the welfare system. However, it may also arise because an individual's human capital may deteriorate while they are not working (see Chapter 7) or because employers are less likely to hire someone who has spent considerable time on AFDC.[14]

Marital Status and Child-Bearing Perhaps, the most controversial indictment of the welfare system is that it induces single women to have babies, unmarried mothers to remain unmarried, and mothers on the welfare rolls to have more children.

However, the basic time-series evidence on female headship would appear to contradict this hypothesis. As we saw in Chapter 13, there has been a steady growth in the percent of families headed by a female since 1960. However, while real welfare benefits grew from 1960 to the mid-1970s, there has been a steady deterioration of the real value of these benefits since the mid-1970s. Despite this, the rate of increase of female-headed families, if anything, accelerated after the mid-1970s rather than slowed down. The same is true for the illegitimacy rate, particularly among nonwhites. The percent of children born to unmarried black women actually increased faster after 1975 than before. The surface evidence does not appear to support this particular criticism of the welfare system.

The econometric studies generally find some evidence that both participation in AFDC and higher welfare benefits increase the probability of female headship and lower the probability of marriage or remarriage (see, for example, Ellwood and Bane, 1985; Hoffman and Duncan, 1988; Hutchens, Jakubson, and Schwartz, 1989; or Moffitt, 1990). However, the effects are

---

[13]There is a technical problem with these calculations that may lead to an overestimation of both spell duration and total time spent on AFDC. Because of data limitations, it was necessary to define a year of "AFDC receipt" as receiving at least one month of benefits sometime over the year. However, an examination of monthly data indicates that many families are on welfare for only part of a year (see Fitzgerald, 1991, for example), so that both spell durations and total time spent on AFDC may be less than the figures in Table 15.9 suggest.

[14]Another explanation is based on a spurious statistical correlation arising from "unobserved heterogeneity" in the AFDC population. The argument is that the AFDC population will differ in their level of human capital and hence their likely employability. In particular, those with lower human capital will likely remain on the welfare rolls longer than those with greater skills and education. Thus, the finding that the exit rate increases as duration on AFDC rises may be due to the fact that the more skilled AFDC recipients leave the welfare rolls faster than the less skilled, even though exit rates for each group remain constant over time. See Moffitt (1992) for more details.

not large enough to explain more than a small part of the growth in the number of female-headed families. AFDC seems to have little effect on the likelihood that a married women will become divorced in order to collect benefits (see Hoffman and Duncan, 1995). The evidence of the effects of the welfare system on the illegitimacy rate is very mixed (see, for example, Plotnick, 1990, and Lundberg and Plotnick, 1990).

Other Issues Another controversial issue is that because of the wide variation of welfare benefits across states (even after adjusting for differences in the cost of living), the welfare system induces poor people to migrate to states which pay the best benefits. As might be expected, the argument would be based on the difference in welfare benefits between the current state of residence and prospective states. Thus, poor people from Alabama would be more likely to migrate to the North than poor people from Florida (see Table 15.7).

The statistical work has confirmed the effects of welfare benefits on both residential location and migration patterns for low-income families. Female-headed households were found to have higher mobility rates from low-benefit states to high-benefit states rather than the reverse (Gramlich and Laren, 1984). They were more likely to move to a high-benefit state (Blank, 1988), and out of a low-benefit state (Clark, 1990). However, here again, the effects were not very large in relation to the overall change in welfare rolls by state.

Another concern expressed by critics of the welfare system is that it may induce welfare dependency across generations. In particular, daughters of mothers on welfare may be more likely than daughters of nonwelfare mothers to wind up on welfare when they are of age. The studies that have examined this issue have used panel data (that is, a dataset that has followed a sample of families over time and that shows the connections between adults in one family unit and their parents in another family unit). These studies have correlated the incidence of welfare recipiency in the parental unit with the later welfare incidence of the children in the family.

The results show consistent evidence that daughters from welfare families are much more likely to receive welfare themselves at a later date than those of nonwelfare parents, though sons are not (see, for example, McLanahan, 1988; Antel, 1988; and Gottschalk, 1990). Unfortunately, as Moffitt (1992) notes, these studies have not systematically controlled for other characteristics that might affect the poverty status of the daughters, such as the educational attainment of the parents. As a result, it is not clear that the welfare status of the parents is causally related to the welfare status of the daughter.

Work Programs

Current proposals for welfare reform have almost unanimously recommended the creation of training and work programs for the recipients of

AFDC. One such proposal, for example, is to change "welfare" to "work-fare"—that is, to require all able-bodied welfare participants to obtain a job, to work in a government program, or to obtain training. Some proposals would further limit AFDC eligibility to a maximum of two or so years in order to induce AFDC recipients to engage in these programs.

Despite the apparent novelty of this approach, there has been a long history of job and training programs attached to the AFDC system. The first major effort was the creation of a public jobs program called the **Works Progress Administration (WPA)** in 1935. This grew out of the unemployment crisis of the Great Depression and was instituted in order to alleviate unemployment. It was a massive job creation program, and during its peak year, 1936, it employed more than three million workers. This program ended in 1943.

For the next 20 years or so, there were no new formal programs enacted by the government to intervene directly in the labor market. However, in 1962, the **Manpower Development and Training Act (MDTA)** was created to provide vocational and on-the-job training for workers displaced by technological change. This program was principally targeted at unemployed male heads of household.

During the mid-1960s, a host of new job employment and training programs were created by the federal government in connection with the War on Poverty. These included the Job Corps, Neighborhood Youth Corps, Concentrated Employment Program, and Work Incentive Program, and they were targeted at welfare recipients, low-income youths, minorities, the elderly, and other disadvantaged groups. Motivated largely by the human capital theory, their principal objective was to provide training (both on-the-job and in the classroom) and work experience with the stated intention of increasing the long-term employability and earnings of these groups.

In 1973, the **Comprehensive Employment and Training Act (CETA)** was passed, which consolidated many of the disparate programs of the 1960s. Its principal objective was also to provide training and work experience for disadvantaged groups. In addition, it provided public service jobs for depressed areas of the country. This program was well funded and also provided considerable experimentation with different forms of labor market intervention. In 1982, CETA was effectively replaced by the **Job Training Partnership Act (JTPA).** This program discontinued public service jobs and emphasized, instead, training for the disadvantaged population.

Several job programs have been targeted directly at welfare recipients. The first of these programs was the **Work Incentive program (WIN)** for AFDC recipients, established in 1968. Under this program, welfare recipients were referred by their welfare office to training or work programs operated by the state. The WIN program provided for on-the-job training, institutional and work experience training, and publicly provided work projects.

The passage of the Family Support Act of 1988 created the job opportunities and basic skills training **(JOBS) program,** which supplanted the WIN program. Every state is required to have a JOBS program. The JOBS program requires parents on AFDC whose youngest child is 3 years or older to enroll in a training or educational program. The purpose of the program is to provide welfare recipients with the tools to eventually leave the welfare rolls. The Family Support Act also requires that states provide child care if it is decided that it is necessary for an individual's employment or participation in the JOBS program. However, despite these provisions, the JOBS program covered only a small percentage of the welfare caseload.

Effectiveness of the Jobs Programs There are several underlying rationales for the various jobs programs that have been instituted. First, the training and educational programs have been geared to increasing the human capital of the participants. In principle, this should lead to long-term improvement in both their employability and their lifetime earnings. Second, public employment programs such as the WPA were implemented as a counter-cyclical measure to provide jobs to unemployed workers and keep them off the unemployment rolls. Third, the public service jobs programs were also designed, in part, with the belief that giving out-of-work individuals work experience would increase their attractiveness to private-sector employers and thus provide them with more permanent jobs.

Fourth, requirements on welfare recipients to participate in a jobs program were implemented, in part, in order to reduce the welfare caseload. In this regard, as Moffitt (1992) notes, there are two offsetting effects. On the one hand, it is true that providing training and job experience to welfare recipients will increase their future employability and thus tend to reduce their time on the welfare rolls. On the other hand, however, the availability of a training or employment program attached to AFDC will make AFDC more attractive and thus may draw more women onto the welfare rolls. A priori, it is not possible to say which effect will dominate.

Most of the statistical work on jobs programs has concentrated on their effect on the long-term earnings of their participants. These studies have attempted to compare the labor market success of individuals who "graduate" from these programs with a comparable group of individuals who were not enrolled in the programs. As Moffitt (1992) notes, there is a danger in this procedure that it may not be possible to find such a comparable control group. For example, participants in a program may be selected on the basis of their future employability in the first place. It is likely that the more able members of the eligible pool enroll in training programs, so the effectiveness of these programs can be overstated.

Even with this caution in mind, the evidence seems to support overwhelmingly the success of these various training programs. A study by Ketron (1980) found that participants in WIN in 1974–1975 had higher earnings after two years than comparable nonparticipants. Similar results were reported by Bassi (1983) and Bassi et al. (1984) for AFDC recipients who were enrolled in CETA between 1976 and 1979; and by Hollister, Kemper, and Maynard (1984) and Grossman, Maynard, and Roberts (1985) for AFDC recipients who participated in various Work Support (WS) programs between 1977 and 1981. Similar effects were found for other governmental jobs programs (see, Moffitt, 1992, for more details).

These results might come as some surprise to the student, since the conventional wisdom has been that job training and employment programs have been notably ineffective in increasing employment or earnings. The evidence shows the opposite. However, the magnitude of the effect is not that large. Most results show that annual earnings rise by between $500 and $1,000 from participation in these programs. This amount is not nearly enough to have much effect on the poverty rate and AFDC participation rate among female heads.

15.6 THE MINIMUM WAGE

Another important piece of legislation that impacts directly on the low-income population is the **minimum wage.** The federal minimum wage was set up by the Fair Labor Standards Act of 1938.[15] Its purpose was to ensure that workers were paid a "living wage." The legislators of that time felt that market forces alone might not be sufficient to cause the market wage to reach a level such that would provide a minimal subsistence standard of living to workers.

Figure 15.3 illustrates why this might be so. We have used the standard supply and demand schedules for labor derived for competitive products and labor markets. Without a minimum wage, the equilibrium employment for unskilled labor is L_e and the corresponding equilibrium wage is w_e. Suppose now that we impose a minimum wage of w_m, which is greater than the prevailing market wage. The equilibrium point now moves from A to B. The effect is to raise the wage of the unskilled workers to w_m. However, their employment also changes, falling to L_m. At the minimum wage w_m, there is now a surplus of unskilled workers, measured by the horizontal distance between points B and C. The minimum wage has thereby induced unemployment of workers to occur.

In contrast, if the minimum wage is set at w_m', below the prevailing wage w_e, there is no effect on the labor market. The equilibrium wage remains at w_e, while equilibrium employment remains at L_e.

Most of the literature on the minimum wage has been concerned with its effects on employment and unemployment. The principal argument against the minimum wage is that it reduces the number of job opportunities and thereby decreases employment. Unskilled workers who remain at work do see their earnings increase, but this occurs at the expense of other unskilled workers who become unemployed. It is this trade-off that has occupied most of the policy discussion of the minimum wage.

---

[15] Actually, some states had enacted a minimum wage standard before 1938. The earliest was Massachusetts in 1912.

Figure 15.3   Supply and Demand Curves for Labor in Competitive Product and Labor Markets With a Minimum Wage

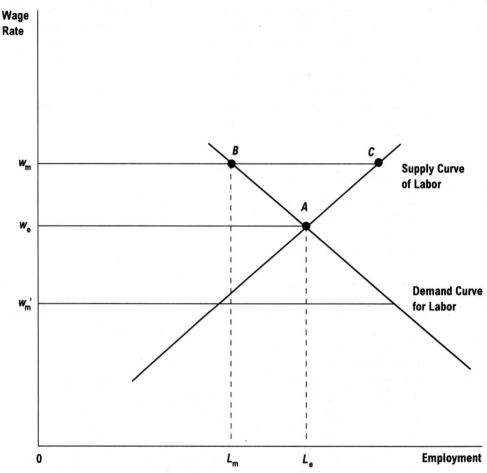

Key:

w_e— equilibrium wage in a free market
w_m— minimum wage (first alternative)
w_m'— minimum wage (second alternative)
L_e— equilibrium employment in a free market
L_m— employment level with minimum wage w_m

As shown in Table 15.10, the minimum wage was set at $0.25 per hour in 1938, which was 40 percent of the average hourly earnings of production workers in that year. The federal law covered only workers engaged in interstate commerce or in the production of goods for interstate commerce. In essence, the law applied mainly to manufacturing and mining at its inception and covered less than half of all nonsupervisory workers.

Table 15.10 **Minimum Wage in Current and Constant Prices and Ratio of Minimum Wage to Average Hourly Earnings, 1938–1993**[a]

	Minimum Wage (Current $)	Minimum Wage (1983 $)	Ratio of Minimum Wage to Average Hourly Earnings[b]
1938	0.25	1.77	0.40
1939	0.30	2.16	0.48
1945	0.40	2.22	0.39
1950	0.75	3.11	0.52
1956	1.00	3.68	0.51
1961	1.15	3.85	0.50
1963	1.25	4.08	0.51
1967	1.40	4.19	0.49
1968	1.60	4.60	0.53
1974	2.00	4.06	0.45
1975	2.10	3.90	0.43
1976	2.30	4.04	0.44
1978	2.65	4.06	0.43
1979	2.90	3.99	0.43
1980	3.10	3.76	0.43
1981	3.55	3.91	0.44
1987	3.55	3.13	0.36
1991	4.25	3.12	0.38
1993	4.25	2.94	0.36

[a] Source: *Social Security Bulletin*, Annual Statistical Supplement, 1994.
[b] Earnings are for production workers in manufacturing.

Over time, the minimum wage has been gradually increased, and the coverage of the law extended to more and more workers. Table 15.10 shows the years in which the minimum was changed (1993 is also shown for comparative reasons). The minimum wage has been raised over time on a rather sporadic basis. In real terms, the minimum increased over time between 1938 and 1968, when it peaked at $4.60 in 1983 dollars, almost three times its original level in 1938. However, since that time, the minimum wage has eroded in real terms, particularly since 1981. In 1991 (the last time it was changed), it was raised again to $4.25, but this was almost identical to the 1987 level in real terms. By 1993, the real minimum wage was at its lowest point since the late 1940s. The "collapse" of the minimum wage is one factor often cited in explaining the decline in the average real wage and the rise in poverty among working families.

Another way of looking at the minimum wage is in relation to the average hourly earnings of production workers. In 1938, it was set at 40 percent of average hourly earnings, and this gradually increased over time to 53 percent by 1968. Since that time, this ratio has also fallen, particularly since 1981. In 1987, the minimum wage stood at 36 percent of average earnings. In 1991, when the minimum wage was last increased, the ratio rose slightly to 38 percent, but by 1993 it had fallen back to 36 percent.

Coverage of workers has also widened over time. In 1961, the minimum wage was extended to employees in large retail and service trades, as well as local transit, construction, and gasoline stations. The 1966 amendments to the Fair Labor Standards Act further extended coverage to state and local government employees, small service establishments, such as restaurants and hotels, and, most notably, to agriculture. By 1993, about 80 percent of nonsupervisory workers were covered by the minimum wage.

Most of the empirical literature on the subject has failed to find much of an effect of the minimum wage on employment. As summarized in a lengthy review article by Brown, Gilroy, and Kohen (1982), the major effect of the minimum wage is on teenage employment. However, studies typically find that an increase in the minimum wage of 10 percent will reduce teenage employment by one to three percent (see also Brown, 1988; Katz and Krueger, 1992; Card, 1992a; and Card, 1992b). The effect of the minimum wage on young adults (ages 20 to 24) is also negative but even smaller in magnitude than for teenagers (see also Neumark and Wascher, 1992). Very little effect of changes in the minimum wage has been found on adult employment overall, though in a few low-wage industries such as clothing and textiles, the effects were negative but still relatively small. However, it should be noted that most of these studies considered only relatively small changes in the minimum wage. A large change might induce considerable unemployment of low-skill workers.

Interestingly, there is little evidence that changes in the minimum wage have affected overall family income inequality. The reason is that there is a weak relationship between low-wage workers and membership in low-income families, because many of the low-wage workers are teenagers or wives who work at secondary jobs in order to augment the income of the primary earner in the family (see Gramlich, 1976). A simulation analysis conducted by Johnson and Browning (1983) reached a similar conclusion. They simulated the effects of a 22 percent increase in the minimum wage under the (favorable) assumption that there was no loss of employment from the increase and computed that the average income of the bottom fifth of the income distribution would increase by only one percent. As a result, changes in the minimum wage have relatively little effect on the inequality of overall family income.

15.7 CONCLUSION AND OVERALL ASSESSMENT OF GOVERNMENT PROGRAMS

Today, over half of the poor are found in female-headed households. Children also have a very high poverty incidence, because many of them live in single-parent households. The elderly population, on the other hand, has experienced a very sharp decline in their poverty rate. Poverty rates are also very high among nonworking families. However, almost half of poor families consist of the working poor. One reason is that members of the household may work only part-time or part-year. However, another reason is that family members may be earning low wages, because they have minimal skills and low education, experience discrimination, or are employed in seasonal or service industries.

Spending on the major federal income transfer programs increased from 3 percent of GDP in 1960 to 11 percent in 1993. Outlays on these programs grew by 5.1 percent per year in real terms between 1970 and 1993. In 1993, public outlays on the major federal income transfer programs amounted to $718 billion, or 11 percent of GDP. The major program in 1993 was, by far, the social security system (OASDI), with outlays of $302 billion. Medicare was the second largest, at $143 billion. Thus, public spending on the elderly from OASDHI amounted to $445 billion, or 62 percent of the total for the major federal income support programs. The other social insurance programs are, correspondingly, much smaller in value—unemployment insurance at 5 percent, workers' compensation at 6 percent, and veteran's disability compensation at 2 percent.

Public spending on the public assistance programs amounted to only a quarter of total social welfare spending in 1993. Much more money was spent on in-kind welfare benefits than cash benefits. Outlays on Medicaid, food stamps, and housing assistance amounted to $128 billion, 18 percent of the total for the major federal income support programs. Spending on the two cash benefit programs, AFDC and SSI, was $46 billion, 6 percent of the total.

Effects on Poverty

How effective has the government income support system been? One way of assessing this issue is to determine the extent to which the income transfer system has alleviated poverty. It should be noted at the outset that these estimates are based on computing family income with and without transfer income. There are no behavioral assumptions built into the analysis—for example, modeling how the family might change its labor market behavior in the absence of transfer payments. As a result, some caution must be used in interpreting these figures.

Panel A of Table 15.11 reports estimates that were prepared by Robert Haveman (1988) on the effects of transfer income on the poverty rate. The first column provides the actual poverty rate for individuals in selected years between 1949 and 1983. For the second column, Haveman excluded reported transfer income from family income and recomputed the poverty rate on the basis of this new (smaller) family income. The difference between the two poverty rates gives an indication of the effect of transfer payments on poverty.

Table 15.11 Effects of the Government Transfer System on Poverty

A. *Effects on Poverty, 1949–1983*[a]

Year	*Actual Poverty Rate (percent)*	*Pretransfer Poverty Rate (percent)*	*Percentage Point Reduction in Poverty Due to Government Transfers*
1949	41	44	3
1959	22	27	5
1969	12	18	6
1979	12	21	9
1983	15	24	9

B. *Effects on Poverty, 1979–1992*[b]

	Year		
	1979	*1989*	*1992*
Poverty Rate (in percent)			
Actual poverty rate	11.7	12.8	14.5
Cash income before transfers	19.2	19.9	22.5
Plus social insurance (other than social security)	18.3	19.3	21.4
Plus social security	12.8	13.8	15.6
Plus means-tested cash transfers	11.7	12.8	14.5
Plus food and housing benefits	9.7	11.2	12.9
Less federal taxes	10.0	11.8	13.0
Total reduction in the poverty rate	9.2	9.2	9.5

[a] Source: Haveman (1988). Transfers include only government cash benefits.
[b] Source: U.S. House of Representatives, Committee on Ways and Means, *1994 Green Book.*

In 1949, the poverty rate was (a shocking!) 41 percent. If transfer income were excluded (that is, if we use pretransfer income), the poverty rate would have been 44 percent—still very high but not much higher than the actual rate. In 1949, government transfers were still quite small. By 1959, pretransfer poverty had fallen to 27 percent. If we include transfer income, the poverty rate falls still more, to 22 percent, or a 5 percentage point reduction. This larger reduction in the poverty rate reflects the growth in transfer payments during the 1950s.

A slightly larger reduction in the poverty rate from transfer payments is evident in 1969, a reflection of the beginnings of the War on Poverty. In this year, transfer income reduced the poverty rate by 6 percentage points. During the 1970s, pretransfer poverty rose, from 18 to 21 percent. This reflected, in part, the growth in income inequality and the changing composition of poverty toward female-headed households, who have a much weaker labor force attachment than married couples. Yet, the post-transfer (actual) poverty rate remained unchanged at 12 percent. Indeed, in 1979, transfer income reduced the poverty rate by 9 percentage points. This was due to the continued growth in the transfer programs during the 1970s.

Pretransfer poverty continued to rise during the early 1980s, from 21 percent in 1979 to 24 percent in 1983. However, the poverty-reducing effects of the transfer system remained unchanged, causing the poverty rate to fall by 9 percentage points again in 1983.

Panel B of Table 15.11 shows a similar set of statistics for 1979, 1989, and 1992. In addition, the effects of each of the major transfer programs on poverty have been isolated. In 1992, the actual (official) poverty rate among all individuals was 14.5 percent. Without any income transfers, the poverty rate would have been much higher, 22.5 percent. If we add in the cash benefits of unemployment insurance, workers' compensation, and other social insurance programs except social security, the poverty rate would fall only slightly, to 21.4 percent. If we next include social security benefits, the poverty rate falls quite considerably, to 15.6 percent. Adding means-tested cash transfers such as SSI and AFDC causes only a modest drop in the poverty rate, to 14.5 percent (the official rate). If we next add in the value of food stamps and housing assistance to total family money income, the poverty rate would decline even further, to 12.9 percent. Finally, subtracting federal taxes from family income would have resulted in a very slight increase in the poverty rate, to 13.0 percent.

All told, the transfer programs (including the negative effects of federal taxes) caused a 9.5 percentage point drop in the poverty rate in 1992. The largest effect comes from the social security system, which by itself reduced the poverty rate by 5.8 percentage points (61 percent of the total reduction). Public assistance (both cash transfers, food benefits, and housing assistance) results in another 2.7 percentage point decline (28 percent of the total reduction). The antipoverty effect of the government transfer system was virtually unchanged between 1979 and 1992. The overall reduction in poverty from these programs was 9.2 percentage points in both 1979 and 1989 and 9.5 percentage points in 1992 (the slight increase is mainly due to changes in federal income taxes).

How effective has the income transfer system been in reducing poverty? Without this "safety net," poverty rates would have been 50 to 70 percent higher during the 1980s and early 1990s. For the elderly, in particular, the poverty rate would have been *four to five times higher* without the income transfers (in 1992, for example, the pretransfer poverty rate was 57.0 percent, compared to an actual poverty rate of 12.9 percent). For female-headed households, poverty rates would have been about 12 to 13 percentage points higher.

Unfortunately, given the continued growth of income transfers during the 1980s and 1990s, both in real terms and as a percent of GDP, it is somewhat disappointing that their antipoverty effects have not increased. As noted above, their poverty reduction effect has remained virtually unchanged between 1979 and 1992. This is in large part due to the shift in the composition of the poor toward female-headed households, who rely heavily on AFDC and other forms of public assistance. This group has been particularly hurt by the fact that average AFDC monthly benefits have been declining in real terms since the late 1970s.

Proposals for Reform

The main problem with the Unemployment Insurance program is that coverage rates (the percentage of unemployed persons receiving UI benefits) have remained quite low since 1980. The coverage rate has been as low as one-third, though, as of 1993, it had recovered to about half. The main reason for this decline in coverage is an increase in the average duration of unemployment, so that a higher percent of the unemployed exhaust their benefits after 26 weeks. Another problem is that new entrants into the labor force, who are not covered by UI, have also been experiencing longer spells of unemployment before finding a job. A common proposal for reform is to extend UI coverage to a full year for workers who have lost a job and provide limited UI coverage for new entrants to the labor force. It should be noted that many European countries provide full unemployment benefits to new entrants.

Social security reform has focused on the likely shortfall in social security revenue to cover the benefits of "baby boom" workers who will begin to retire in the year 2010. By the year 2025, the number of retired persons per worker will be greatly increased from its current level. Another problem with the social security system is that it is an uncomfortable mixture of a pension system and an entitlement program. Should it function as a pension system, providing higher benefits to those who contribute more into the system, or should it remain largely an entitlement program, providing retirement benefits mainly in proportion to need? Both problems are related.

Most proposals for reform have focused on the benefit structure, since social security tax rates were already substantially increased during the 1970s and 1980s (see the next chapter). One proposal, currently in effect, is to extend the normal retirement age from 65 to 67. At age 67, the individual would receive 100 percent of his or her PIA, instead of at age 65, as the rules are currently structured. According to current legislation, the normal retirement age will increase to 67 by the year 2022. Proposals call for accelerating this change.

Another set of proposals call for social security benefits to be treated as a means tested benefit. Currently, both high-income and low-income retirees collect social security benefits, and the formula for the benefit depends only on their earnings history. As of 1994, the only difference in the treatment of high-income retirees is that 85 percent of their social security income is treated as taxable income and hence subject to income tax. Some have proposed that the social security benefit should also depend on the retiree's other income, such as private pension income and property income and that the benefit be reduced in stepwise fashion with the person's total income (in much the same way as AFDC benefits are determined). This method would significantly reduce the total benefits paid out by the social security system. However, it would represent a major change in the rationale for the social security system, in that it would be viewed as a public assistance program rather than as a pension scheme.

Perhaps the most volatile focus of reform is the welfare system. Some have adopted the extreme position that the welfare system should be entirely dismantled. However, as noted above, the primary objective of welfare programs such as AFDC is to ensure the well-being of children, irrespective of the merits of providing income support to "unworthy" parents.

In 1994, the Clinton administration proposed that greater resources be put into expanding the training, educational, and work programs for AFDC parents. The proposal would increase the amount of child care available for single parents to better enable them to participate in the training or work programs. The benefit structure would be modified to reduce the "earnings tax" on welfare benefits from increased labor earnings. Moreover, Medicaid benefits would be continued even if total family income exceeds the legal minimum.

The Republicans, in contrast, have proposed imposing a limit on the length of time on welfare—two years in most cases. Welfare recipients would be required to enroll in training programs or have a job. Some extreme proposals call for eliminating AFDC payments to unmarried teenage mothers and disallowing extra payments for additional births to mothers currently on welfare.

With regard to single mothers on welfare, both the Democrats and the Republicans have put increasing emphasis on the role of the absentee father. Many of these single-parent households do not receive any financial assistance from the absent parent, which greatly increases the likelihood that the family will fall into poverty. The Family Support Act of 1988 now requires welfare applicants to reveal the name of the absent parent in order to qualify for government assistance. The aim is to shift part of the financial responsibilities for childrearing back to the absent parent and thus reduce government transfers. So far, these new requirements have failed to make much of a dent in the welfare rolls. Both political parties now propose that greater enforcement be used to increase the amount of child support provided by the father. For example, fathers who fail to make child support payments would have a portion of their earnings withheld by the federal government. However, these provisions are limited by the earnings capacity of the absentee fathers—many of whom are out of work or receive wages that are too low to provide much in the way of child support.

The minimum wage is another policy issue that has received renewed attention from the Clinton administration. Their main concern is that the minimum wage has dramatically declined in real terms, particularly since the late 1970s. Among other effects, this has greatly increased the number of full-time working families with incomes below the poverty line. One proposal is to keep the minimum wage constant in real terms (that is, indexed for inflation); another is to peg the minimum wage as a fixed percentage of the average hourly earnings of production workers. Both proposals would maintain the real earnings of low-income workers. However, such an increase of the minimum wage in 1994 (of the order of 50 percent!) might have serious dislocation consequences for the employment of low-skill workers.

On the other side of the spectrum, some economists have argued that the minimum wage should be completely abolished. Their argument is that the minimum wage may make it more difficult for a person with relatively little education or training to find a job and gain experience and human capital through on-the-job training and eventually escape poverty. This issue may be particularly germane to welfare mothers who lack work experience. One compromise is to have a subminimum wage for teenagers (set at, perhaps, 60 or 80 percent of the adult level). This might, at least, give young workers a better opportunity to acquire the necessary workplace skills to eventually move into well-paying jobs in the primary labor market.

REFERENCES

A. General

Barr, Nicholas, "Economic Theory and the Welfare State: A Survey and Interpretation," *Journal of Economic Literature*, Vol. 30, June 1992, pp. 741–803.

Danziger, Sheldon, and Robert Plotnick, "Demographic Change, Government Transfers, and Income Distribution," *Monthly Labor Review*, Vol. 51, No. 1, March 1977, pp. 7–11.

Danziger, Sheldon, Robert Haveman, and Robert Plotnick, "How Income Transfer Programs Affect Work, Savings, and the Income Distribution: A Critical Review," *Journal of Economic Literature*, Vol. 19, September 1981, pp. 975–1028.

Gottschalk, Peter, and Sheldon Danziger, "A Framework for Evaluating the Effects of Economic Growth and Transfers on Poverty," *American Economic Review*, Vol. 75, No. 1, March 1985, pp. 153–161.

Harrington, Michael, *The Other America*, revised edition, Macmillan, New York, 1962.

Haveman, Robert, *Starting Even: An Equal Opportunity Program to Combat the Nation's New Poverty*, Simon and Schuster, New York, 1988.

———, *Poverty Policy and Poverty Research: The Great Society and the Social Sciences*, University of Wisconsin Press, Madison, Wis., 1987.

Jencks, Christopher, *Rethinking Social Policy: Race, Poverty, and the Underclass*, Harvard University Press, Cambridge, Mass., 1992.

Lampman, Robert J., *Social Welfare Spending*, Academic Press, New York, 1984.

Mead, Lawrence M., *The New Politics of Poverty: The Nonworking Poor in America*, Basic Books, New York, 1992.

Murray, Charles, *Losing Ground: American Social Policy 1950–1980*, Basic Books, New York, 1984.

U.S. House of Representatives, Committee on Ways and Means, *Overview of Entitlement Programs: 1994 Green Book*, U.S. Government Printing Office, Washington, D.C., July 15, 1994.

B. Unemployment Insurance

Anderson, Patricia M., and Bruce D. Meyer, "The Effects of Unemployment Insurance Taxes and Benefits on Layoffs Using Firm and Individual Data," NBER Working Paper No. 4960, December 1994.

Barron, John M., and Wesley Mellow, "Unemployment Insurance: The Recipients and Its Impact," *Southern Economic Journal*, Vol. 47, No. 3, January 1981, pp. 606–616.

Brechling, Frank, "Layoffs and Unemployment Insurance," in Sherwin Rosen, (ed.), *Studies in Labor Markets*, University of Chicago Press, Chicago, 1981.

Chiswick, Barry, "The Effect of Unemployment Compensation on a Seasonal Industry: Agriculture," *Journal of Political Economy*, Vol. 84, June 1976, pp. 591–602.

Classen, Kathleen P., "Unemployment Insurance and Job Search," in Steven A. Lippman and John J. McCall (eds.), *Studies in the Economics of Search*, North-Holland, Amsterdam, 1979, pp. 191–219.

Ehrenberg, Ronald G., and Ronald Oaxaca, "Unemployment Insurance, Duration of Unemployment, and Subsequent Wage Gains," *American Economic Overview*, Vol. 66, December 1976, pp. 754–766.

Feldstein, Martin, "Unemployment Compensation: Adverse Incentives and Distributional Anomalies," *National Tax Journal*, Vol. 27, June 1974, pp. 231–244.

———, "The Effect of Unemployment Insurance on Temporary Layoffs," *American Economic Review*, Vol. 68, December 1978, pp. 834–840.

———, and James Poterba, "Unemployment Insurance and Reservation Wages," *Journal of Public Economics*, Vol. 23, 1984, pp. 141–167.

Gustman, Alan, "Analyzing the Relation of Unemployment Insurance to Unemployment," *Research in Labor Economics*, Vol. 5, 1982, pp. 69–114.

Haber, William, and Merill Murray, *Unemployment Insurance in the American Economy*, Irwin, Homewood, Ill., 1966.

Halpin, Terrence, "The Effect of Unemployment Insurance on Seasonal Fluctuations in Employment," *Industrial and Labor Relations Review*, Vol. 32, 1979, pp. 353–362.

Katz, Lawrence F., and Bruce D. Meyer, "Unemployment Insurance, Recall Expectations, and Unemployment Outcomes," *Quarterly Journal of Economics*, Vol. 19, 1984, pp. 118–126.

Marston, Steven T., "The Impact of Unemployment Insurance on Job Search," *Brookings Paper on Economic Activity*, No. 1, 1975, pp. 13–48.

Meyer, Bruce D., "Unemployment Insurance and Unemployment Spells," *Econometrica*, Vol. 58, No. 4, July 1990, pp. 757–782.

Moffitt, Robert, and Walter Nicholson, "The Effects of Unemployment Insurance on Unemployment: The Case of Federal Supplemental Benefits," *Review of Economics and Statistics*, Vol. 64, No. 1, 1982, pp. 1–11.

Solon, Gary, "Labor Supply Effects of Extended Unemployment Benefits," *Journal of Human Resources*, Vol. 14, No. 2, Spring 1979, pp. 247–255.

Topel, Robert H., "On Layoffs and Unemployment Insurance," *American Economic Review*, Vol. 73, No. 3, September 1983, pp. 541–559.

C. Social Security System

Blinder, Alan S., Roger H. Gordon, and Donald E. Wise, "Reconsidering the Work Disincentive Effects of Social Security," *National Tax Journal*, Vol. 33, No. 4, December 1980, pp. 431–442.

Boskin, Michael J., "Social Security and Retirement Decisions," *Economic Inquiry*, Vol. 15, No. 1, 1977, pp. 1–25.

————, and Michael D. Hurd, "The Effect of Social Security on Early Retirement," *Journal of Public Economics*, Vol. 10, No. 3, December 1978, pp. 361–377.

Burkhauser, Richard V., and Joseph Quinn, "The Effects of Changes in Mandatory Retirement Rules on the Labor Supply of Older Workers," presented at NBER Conference on the Economics of Compensation, Cambridge, Mass., November 1980.

Clark, Robert, and Thomas Johnson, *Retirement in the Dual Career Family*, Final Report for the U.S. Social Security Administration, North Carolina State University, Raleigh, NC, 1980.

Gordon, Roger H., and Alan S. Blinder, "Market Wages, Reservation Wages, and Retirement Decisions," *Journal of Public Economics*, Vol. 14, No. 2, October 1980, pp. 277–308.

Pellechio, Anthony, "The Social Security Earnings Test, Labor Supply Distortions, and Foregone Payroll Tax Revenue," National Bureau of Economic Research Working Paper No. 272, August 1978.

Quinn, Joseph F., "Microeconomic Determinants of Early Retirement: A Cross-Sectional View of White, Married Men," *Journal of Human Resources*, Vol. 12, No. 3, Summer 1977, pp. 329–346.

Reimers, Cordelia K. W., *The Timing of Retirement of American Men*, Ph.D. Dissertation, Columbia University, New York, 1977.

D. The Welfare System

Antel, John, "Mother's Welfare Dependency Effects on Daughter's Early Fertility and Fertility Out of Wedlock," mimeo, University of Houston, 1988.

Bassi, Laurie J., "The Effect of CETA on the Postprogram Earnings of Participants," *Journal of Human Resources*, Vol. 18, No. 4, Fall 1983, pp. 539–556.

———, *et al.*, "Measuring the Effect of CETA on Youth and the Economically Disadvantaged," Urban Institute, Washington, D.C., 1984.

Bell, Stephen L., and Larry L. Orr, "Is Subsidized Employment Cost Effective for Welfare Recipients?" *Journal of Human Resources*, Vol. 29, No. 1, Winter 1994, pp. 42–61.

Besley, Timothy, and Stephen Coate, "Workfare Versus Welfare: Incentive Arguments for Work Requirements in Poverty-Alleviation Programs," *American Economic Review*, Vol. 82, No. 1, March 1992, pp. 249–261.

Blank, Rebecca, "The Effect of Welfare and Wage Levels on the Location Decisions of Female-Headed Households," *Journal of Urban Economics*, Vol. 24, No. 2, September 1988, pp. 186–211.

———, "Analyzing the Length of Welfare Spells," *Journal of Public Economics*, Vol. 39, No. 3, August 1989, pp. 245–273.

Burtless, Gary, "The Economists' Lament: Public Assistance in America," *Journal of Economic Perspectives*, Vol. 4, No. 1, Winter 1990, pp. 57–78.

Clark, Rebecca, "Does Welfare Affect Migration?" mimeo, The Urban Institute, Washington, D.C., 1990.

Danziger, Sheldon H., and Daniel H. Weinberg, *Fighting Poverty: What Works and What Doesn't*, Harvard University Press, Cambridge, Mass., 1986.

Danziger, Sheldon, and Peter Gottschalk, "Do Rising Tides Lift All Boats?" *American Economic Review*, Vol. 76, No. 2, May 1986, pp. 405–410.

Ellwood, David, "Targeting 'Would-Be' Long-Term Recipients of AFDC," Mathematica Policy Research, Princeton, N.J., 1986.

Ellwood, David T., *Poor Support: Poverty in the American Family*, Basic Books, New York, 1988.

Ellwood, David, and Mary-Jo Bane, "The Impact of AFDC on Family Structure and Living Arrangements," in Ronald Ehrenberg (ed.), *Research in Labor Economics*, Vol. 7, JAI Press, Greenwich, Conn., 1985.

Fitzgerald, John, "Welfare Durations and the Marriage Market: Evidence From the Survey of Income and Program Participation," *Journal of Human Resources*, Vol. 26, No. 3, Summer 1991, pp. 545–561.

Garfinkel, Irwin, and Larry L. Orr, "Welfare Policy and Employment Rate of AFDC Mothers," *National Tax Journal*, Vol. 27, No. 2, June 1974, pp. 275–284.

Gottschalk, Peter, "AFDC Participation Across Generations," *American Economic Review*, Vol. 80, No. 21, May 1990, pp. 367–371.

———, and Robert A. Moffitt, "Welfare Dependence: Concepts, Measures, and Trends," *American Economic Review*, Vol. 84, No. 2, May 1994, pp. 38–53.

Gramlich, Edward, and Deborah Laren, "Migration and Income Redistribution Responsibilities," *Journal of Human Resources*, Vol. 19, No. 4, Fall 1984, pp. 489–511.

Grossman, Jean, Rebecca Maynard, and Judith Roberts, "Reanalysis of the Effects of Selected Employment and Training Programs for Welfare Recipients," Mathematica Policy Research, Princeton, N.J., 1985.

Gueron, Judith M., "Work and Welfare: Lessons on Employment Programs," *Journal of Economic Perspectives*, Vol. 4, No. 1, Winter 1990, pp. 79–98.

Hausman, Jerry A., "Labor Supply," in Henry J. Aaron and Joseph A. Pechman (eds.), *How Taxes Affect Economic Behavior*, Brookings Institution, Washington, D.C., 1981, pp. 27–72.

Hoffman, Saul, and Greg Duncan, "A Comparison of Choice-Based Multinomial and Nested Logit Models: The Family Structure and Welfare Use of Decisions of Divorced or Separated Women," *Journal of Human Resources*, Vol. 23, No. 4, Fall 1988, pp. 550–562.

Hoffman, Saul D., and Greg J. Duncan, "The Effect of Incomes, Wages, and AFDC Benefits on Marital Disruption," *Journal of Human Resources*, Vol. 30, No. 1, Winter 1995, pp. 19–41.

Hollister, Robinson G., Peter Kemper, and Rebecca A. Maynard, *The National Supported Work Demonstration*, University of Wisconsin Press, Madison, Wis., 1984.

Hutchens, Robert M., George Jakubson, and Saul Schwartz, "AFDC and the Formation of Subfamilies," *Journal of Human Resources*, Vol. 24, No. 4, Fall 1989, pp. 599–628.

Ketron Inc., "The Long-Term Impact of WIN II: A Longitudinal Evaluation of the Employment Experiences of Participants in the Work Incentive Program," Wayne, PA, 1980.

Levy, Frank, "The Labor Supply of Female Household Heads, or AFDC Work Incentives Don't Work Too Well," *Journal of Human Resources*, Vol. 14, No. 1, Winter 1979, pp. 76–97.

Levy, Frank S., "Work for Welfare: How Much Good Will It Do?" *American Economic Review*, Vol. 76, No. 2, May 1986, pp. 399–404.

Lundberg, Shelley, and Robert Plotnick, "Testing the Opportunity Cost Hypothesis of Adolescent Premarital Childbearing," mimeo, paper presented at meetings of Population Association of America, Toronto, 1990.

Masters, Stanley H., and Irwin Garfinkel, *Estimating the Labor Supply Effects of Income Maintenance Alternatives*, Academic Press, New York, 1977.

McLanahan, Sarah, "Family Structure and Dependency: Early Transitions to Female Household Headship," *Demography*, Vol. 25, No. 1, February 1988, pp. 1–16.

Moffitt, Robert, "An Economic Model of Welfare Stigma," *American Economic Review*, Vol. 73, No. 5, 1983, pp. 1036–1052.

———, "Work Incentives in Transfer Programs (revisited): A Study of the AFDC Program," in Ronald Ehrenberg (ed.), *Research in Labor Economics*, Vol. 8, JAI Press, Greenwich, Conn., 1986, pp. 389–439.

———, "The Effect of the U.S. Welfare System on Marital Status," *Journal of Public Economics,* Vol. 41, No. 1, February 1990, pp. 101–124.

———, "Incentive Effects of the U.S. Welfare System: A Review," *Journal of Economic Literature,* Vol. 30, March 1992, pp. 1–61.

Plotnick, Robert, "Turnover in the AFDC Population: An Event History Analysis," *Journal of Human Resources,* Vol. 18, No. 1, Winter 1983, pp. 65–81.

———, "Welfare and Out-of-Wedlock Childbearing: Evidence from the 1980s," *Journal of Marriage and the Family,* Vol. 52, August 1990, pp. 735–746.

Saks, Daniel H., *Public Assistance for Mothers in an Urban Labor Market,* Industrial Relations Section, Princeton University, Princeton, N.J., 1975.

Weinberg, Daniel H., "Filling the Poverty 'Gap': Multiple Transfer Program Participation," *Journal of Human Resources,* Vol. 20, No. 1, Winter 1985, pp. 64–97.

Williams, Robert, *Public Assistance and Work Effort,* Industrial Relations Section, Princeton University, Princeton, N.J., 1975.

Willis, Patricia, "Participation Rages in the Aid to Families with Dependent Children Program, Part III," Working Paper 1387–1304, Urban Institute, Washington, D.C., 1980.

E. The Minimum Wage

Brown, Charles, "Minimum Wage Laws: Are They Overrated?," *Journal of Economic Perspectives,* Vol. 2, No. 3, Fall 1988, pp. 133–146.

———, Curtis Gilroy, and Andrew Kohen, "The Effect of the Minimum Wage on Employment and Unemployment," *Journal of Economic Literature,* Vol. 20, No. 2, June 1982, pp. 487–528.

———, "Time-Series Evidence of the Effect of the Minimum Wage on Youth Employment and Unemployment," *Journal of Human Resources,* Vol. 18, No. 1, Winter 1983, pp. 3–31.

Card, David, "Using Regional Variation in Wages to Measure the Effects of the Federal Minimum Wage," *Industrial and Labor Relations Review,* Vol. 46, No. 1, October 1992(a), pp. 22–37.

———, "Do Minimum Wages Reduce Employment? A Case Study of California, 1987–1989," *Industrial and Labor Relations Review,* Vol. 46, No. 1, October 1992(b), pp. 38–54.

Ehrenberg, Ronald G., "New Minimum Wage Research: Symposium Introduction," *Industrial and Labor Relations Review,* Vol. 46, No. 1, October 1992, pp. 3–5.

Gramlich, Edward M., "Impact of Minimum Wages on Other Wages, Employment, and Family Incomes," *Brookings Papers on Economic Activity,* No. 2, 1976, pp. 409–461.

Hammermesh, Daniel S., "Minimum Wages and the Demand for Labor," *Economic Inquiry,* Vol. 20, July 1982, pp. 365–380.

Hashimoto, Massanori, "Minimum Wage Effects of Training on the Job," *American Economic Review,* Vol. 72, No. 5, December 1982, pp. 1070–1087.

Johnson, William R., and Edgar K. Browning, "The Distributional and Efficiency Effects of Increasing the Minimum Wage: A Simulation," *American Economic Review*, Vol. 73, No. 1, March 1983, pp. 204–211.

Katz, Lawrence F., and Alan B. Krueger, "The Effect of the Minimum Wage on the Fast-Food Industry," *Industrial and Labor Relations Review*, Vol. 46, No. 1, October 1992, pp. 6–21.

Linneman, Peter, "The Economic Impacts of Minimum Wage Laws: A New Look at an Old Question," *Journal of Political Economy*, Vol. 90, No. 3, June 1982, pp. 443–469.

Mincer, Jacob, "Unemployment Effects of Minimum Wages," *Journal of Political Economy*, Vol. 84, No. 4, Part 2, August 1976, pp. S87–S104.

Neumark, David, and William Wascher, "Employment Effects of Minimum and Subminimum Wages: Panel Data on State Minimum Wage Laws," *Industrial and Labor Relations Review*, Vol. 46, No. 1, October 1992, pp. 55–81.

Smith, Ralph E., and Bruce Vavrichek, "The Wage Mobility of Minimum Wage Workers," *Industrial and Labor Relations Review*, Vol. 46, No. 1, October 1992, pp. 82–88.

DISCUSSION QUESTIONS

1. Briefly describe the trend in the coverage rate (the percentage of unemployed workers receiving benefits) of the UI system since 1970. Discuss the factors that account for this trend.

2. Why might an increase in the UI replacement rate lead to an increased average duration of unemployment?

3. Define the social security replacement rate. Explain why the replacement rate is higher for a low-income earner than a high-income earner.

4. Discuss two reasons why the social security benefit structure might reduce the LFPR of older individuals.

5. The welfare (AFDC) system has often been criticized for discouraging work and creating "welfare dependency." Evaluate the evidence on the disincentive effects of welfare on work effort.

6. Summarize the effects of the government transfer system on the overall poverty rate. What components of the income transfer system have the largest effects in reducing poverty and which have relatively small effects?

16

THE REDISTRIBUTIONAL
EFFECTS OF PUBLIC POLICY

In the last chapter, we analyzed the array of income support systems and other programs aimed primarily at helping the poor in this country. In this chapter, we consider the overall effects of the government fiscal system on income inequality.

The first section of Chapter 16 raises the issue of why social equity may be an important social concern. It considers several philosophical positions, both for and against the proposition that the state should pursue equality as an independent social goal. Section 16.2 considers general properties of tax systems and their overall effects on income inequality.

Section 16.3 first provides a description of the system of taxation currently in place in the United States. It then considers the redistributional effects of government tax policy. Is the tax system progressive, regressive, or neutral? Does the system reduce or exacerbate overall income inequality? This section also presents statistics on the extent of taxation in the United States and some comparisons with other advanced economies.

Section 16.4 looks at the other side of the ledger, the effects of government disbursements. There are two main types of disbursements: transfer payments to individuals and actual expenditures on goods and services. This section first investigates how the government spends its revenue—that is, the relative magnitudes of the different government programs. It then takes up the questions of which groups benefit from government expenditures and what are their distributional consequences. A summary is provided in Section 16.5.

16.1 EQUALITY AS A SOCIAL GOAL

Arguments in Favor of Promoting Equality

Why should we be concerned about inequality? Why should equality be viewed as a social or political objective? Perhaps, the most compelling reason is that it is indicative of the consumption possibilities of different groups within society. Consider a simple example. Suppose there are two countries with the same average incomes. The first is an oil-rich sheikdom ruled by a royal family who owns all the oil rights. The second is a country like Sweden with very high tax rates and generous transfer programs available to the population. In the first country, it is possible that the vast majority of the population is poor, while in the second country, only a small fraction of the population may be poor. Thus, even though the average incomes are the same in the two countries, only a small fraction of the population in the first country will have very high incomes, whereas the vast majority of the population in the second country will have high incomes. This difference will be reflected only in comparative measures of income inequality between the two countries.

Another reason to be concerned about the level of income inequality of a country is that income equality is often considered an important social goal of a nation. Equality is often included as a basic public policy objective along with such other goals as allocative efficiency, economic growth, and economic and political freedom. Four distinct grounds are often cited as reasons for trying to achieve equality in a society.

The first is based on the concept of *fairness*. If a country happens to be rich in oil or other natural resources, is it fair for a small number of individuals to receive all the benefits from this "gift of nature"? If a nation's economy is very productive because of the accumulation of capital stock and technology, should not all the citizens of a nation share in the rewards of past history? Such a judgment can, of course, only be made on *normative* (that is, ethical) grounds. Indeed, the underlying notion behind the concept of fairness is that members of a society are *entitled* to certain rights and privileges, simply for being members of a society. One of these rights is an "adequate" standard of living and a "just" share of society's benefits. This is a position that cannot be proved or disproved on scientific grounds but rests on one's philosophical beliefs. However, much social and economic policy in the United States, particularly since World War II, has been made with this goal in mind.

A second ground for striving for economic equality is based on **utilitarianism.** This philosophical doctrine was set forth by the English philosopher Jeremy Bentham some 200 years ago. Its major precept is that society's goal should be to maximize the total *utility* (that is, happiness or satisfaction) of its members. This, too, is a normative judgment and depends on one's philosophical bent. Given the objective of maximizing total utility, one still needs an additional assumption to arrive at equality of income as a social

Figure 16.1 **Total and Marginal Utility with Diminishing Marginal Utility of Income**

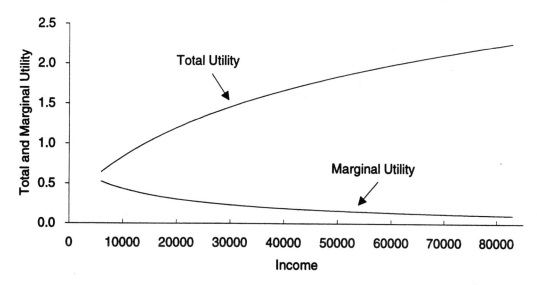

goal. One fairly plausible assumption is that income has diminishing marginal utility. Income is first used to buy necessities, but beyond some income level, additional dollars are used to buy conveniences and luxuries. Figure 16.1 provides a schematic illustration of this assumption. As income rises, total utility also increases but the added utility from an additional dollar declines.

If we make this assumption and, in addition, assume that everyone has the same utility function, it follows that distributing income equally among individuals will maximize total utility.[1] To show this, consider the case where incomes are distributed unequally. In particular, suppose that individual A receives $2,000 more income than individual B ($18,000 versus $16,000). Then, if we redistribute $1,000 from A to B (so that each now receives $17,000), then B's gain in utility will be greater than A's loss, so that total social welfare is increased. Thus, total utility will reach its highest value when everyone receives the same income.

This is also an argument for redistributing income in an equitable fashion. However, if income is perfectly equal and everyone is guaranteed the same income level, then what is the incentive to work? Too much equality may reduce work effort (and investment) and thereby the total product of society. The utilitarian argument thus implicitly assumes that labor supply and investment are unaffected by the rewards individuals receive for their

---

[1] We must also assume that individual utilities are additive and that total social welfare is the sum of individual utility levels—that is, there are no externalities present.

activity. Maximizing the total utility of society may require a distribution that is more equal than that arising from market incomes but less equal than perfect equality.

A third line of argument derives from a theory of fairness developed by John Rawls in a 1971 book entitled *A Theory of Justice.* Rawls argues that a sense of fairness or social justice can be developed only if an individual is unaware of his or her particular circumstances. This circumstance Rawls calls "the original position." In such a situation, when the person does not know his or her own income, wealth, or level of well-being, the individual is said to be behind a "veil of ignorance." Rawls argues that such an individual would favor a society that provided a minimal level of well-being (or income) to all members of society. This is also referred to as a maximin solution—that is, a system of distribution that would maximize the minimum level of income that would be available to every individual in a society.

Here it is interesting that the theory of fairness that devolves from such a philosophical system says nothing directly about the overall level of inequality that a "just society" would sustain. Rather, the theory implies that a just social order would ensure that all members of society would receive some minimal level of support. This view is more consistent with a "social safety net" conception of the role of the state in promoting equity. It would imply that the government would provide a range of transfer programs, including welfare payments, and social programs that would enable each member of a country to secure a level of income at least at the poverty line.

A fourth argument is based on self-interest. Too much inequality and, in particular, poverty may lead to an excessive amount of violence and crime in a society. Moreover, individuals may prefer not to be confronted with beggars and homeless people on a continual basis, as now happens in the major cities of the United States today. The average citizen in a country like the United States may thus feel better off with less poverty and lower inequality.

Arguments Against Promoting Greater Equality

These views do not imply that all economists (or individuals) agree that income equality is in itself a desirable social goal. There are three common arguments that have been proposed against seeking greater equality in income distribution.

The first derives from the "libertarian" viewpoint, which is also based on a notion of fairness. One must distinguish between the equality of *rights* or *opportunities,* on the one hand, and income equality or equality of *outcomes,* on the other hand. The doctrine of fairness simply guarantees that each individual has the same basic political rights and economic opportunities, particularly in access to jobs and education and training. This notion of equal opportunity is, of course, the cornerstone of much current public policy making. However, beyond this, according to this argument, society has no further obligation. Indeed, if one individual has greater drive and puts forth more work effort than a second individual, who may have greater preference for leisure, then the first individual should be entitled to greater income. Moreover, if one individual has greater ability and produces more than a second, then he should receive more compensation. If one worker is older and more experienced than a second, then it is also fair for him or her to receive a higher wage or salary than the younger worker.

Yet, it is often argued in opposition to the libertarian position that complete equality of opportunity is impossible to achieve. Consider disabled, blind, or elderly individuals, who, through no fault of their own, are unable to participate in the labor market. Should they be completely ignored by the state and made to depend on relatives or charities for their bare necessities?

Also, consider the difference in opportunities between children of rich families and those of poor ones. Rich children have greater access to education and training and potentially to jobs through family connections (see the second part of Section 7.4). Moreover, children of wealthy parents are likely to receive greater inheritances than those from poor families, and as we saw in Section 11.3, inheritances play a major role in explaining inequality in household wealth. Such differences are particularly acute between white families and minorities; as a result, the federal government has enacted special programs to remedy the lack of equal opportunity (see Section 13.5 for a description of these programs).

The counterargument to the libertarian view is that equal opportunity does not exist in society without some form of government intervention. Life is not a fair game, and to use the expression of Robert Haveman (1988), children are not "starting even." As a result, society must take specific remedial steps to counter inequality in the distribution of income.

The second argument against promoting greater income equality is related to the first. The argument is that paying higher wages and salaries to individuals who produce more serves as an *incentive* for everyone to work harder and to acquire new productive abilities and skills. As a result, the **total product** of the economy will be greater if workers are rewarded according to what they produce rather than being guaranteed an income that is not directly related to their productivity. This argument concludes that even those at the bottom of the income distribution will be better off, since the total product will be so much greater than if people received equal incomes.

This view is often referred to as the "trickle down" effect, since the higher incomes of the upper part of the income distribution will eventually cause incomes at the bottom of the distribution to rise. Briefly stated, it is that growth leads to a bigger "pie" to divide among a nation's citizens. Promoting growth will be more effective in the long run in making the poor better off than promoting current redistribution, since an expanding pie makes more income available for all, including the poor. In contrast, giving a larger slice of a fixed pie to the poor makes them better off only in the short-run.[2]

This argument hinges on the belief that a smaller piece of a larger pie will be greater in absolute terms than a larger slice of a smaller pie. This is, of course, an empirical question—that is, has history shown this belief to be true? However, even if this view is correct and the poor do experience an increase in real income even though income inequality goes up, there may still be reason to oppose the growth position. Some, for example, have argued that a person's utility may depend not only on the person's absolute income but also on his or her relative income as well (see, for example, the provocative 1985 book by Robert Frank). That is, one's satisfaction may depend, in part, on one's relative standing in the community—that is, on "keeping up with the Jones's." So even if one's income is rising in absolute terms over time, if it is declining relative to other people's income (or the median income of the country), then the person's utility level may actually decline.[3] This counterargument would thus favor greater income equality even if the trickle-down effect were occurring, since greater equality would raise the average level of utility in society.

The third argument accepts the basic utilitarian objective of maximizing the common good, but the assumption of equal needs for everyone is disputed. There are in fact two variants of this position. The Marxist principle of "to each according to his needs" assumes that people's needs differ according to their circumstances. The disabled or aged may require greater health care; a large family requires more food than a small one, and so on. Therefore, income should be redistributed in favor of those whose needs are greatest. This will then lead to the greatest overall satisfaction. Interestingly, as we saw in the last chapter, most welfare programs implicitly adopt this position, since transfer payments such as AFDC are based on number of children in the family, as well as disability and other special circumstances.

The second variant also assumes that people differ in their utility function, but here the assumption is that some people are much "harder to please" than others. The emphasis here is on how to please those hardest to please, and this may be referred to as the "elitist position." For example, some people may require a very expensive house and rare art works to have a minimal level of happiness in life. According to the utilitarian position, these people should receive greater income than those who are more easily

---

[2]There is another side to this argument, which rests on the assumption that the rich save more of their income than the poor. Thus, the argument goes, redistributing income from the rich to the poor will reduce the overall savings rate and hence the investment rate and the rate of economic growth. This will cause the overall pie to grow more slowly, and everyone, including the poor, will be made worse off in the long run.

[3]There is a very close connection between this position and arguments in favor of using a relative poverty line (see Section 4.1). In the case of the latter, the central notion is that the collection of goods that constitutes a minimally decent standard of living depends itself on the average living standard. As the standard of living grows, what the general populace considers necessities also rises. The argument here is even broader in that everyone's utility is seen to depend on the standard of living of the other individuals living in one's community.

satisfied with the simpler (and cheaper) pleasures of life. Fortunately, this view is not widely held (except, perhaps, in bankruptcy court), since it would suggest that we should transfer income from the poor to the rich.[4]

16.2 THE STRUCTURE OF TAX SYSTEMS

Whether we believe that the government should or should not be involved in the job of promoting greater equality in society, in point of fact, government fiscal policy does affect the actual distribution of income. In this section, we discuss the general distributional properties of tax systems. In the next, we particularly look at the distributional effects of the overall tax system in the United States. In Section 16.4, we discuss the distributional effects of the government's expenditure side.

Proportional, Progressive, and Regressive Tax Structures

The tax rate (or average tax rate) t is defined as the ratio of taxes paid T to income Y:

$$t = T / Y \qquad (16.1)$$

Taxes are classified into three types: (1) proportional, (2) progressive, and (3) regressive. These three types of taxes are illustrated in Figure 16.2 (where we have arbitrarily chosen the same starting point—10 percent—in each case for reasons of illustration).

A **proportional tax** is defined as one in which the average tax rate remains constant over income levels. A **progressive tax** is one in which the average tax rate increases with income level. And a **regressive tax** is one in which the average tax rate falls as income rises. It should be noted that in all three cases the total taxes paid increase with income level.[5] What distinguishes the three forms of taxes is whether the tax rate increases or declines with income.

It should be noted that in actuality, most taxes cannot be so easily categorized. In fact, as we shall see, some taxes (such as the federal income tax) may be progressive through part of the income range, turn proportional in another part of the income spectrum, and may even turn regressive at other ranges.

The marginal tax rate, MTR, is the additional amount of taxes (ΔT) paid on an additional dollar of income (ΔY):

$$MTR = \Delta T / \Delta Y \; [\text{or } dT(Y) / dY] \qquad (16.2)$$

---

[4]For more discussion of these issues, see E. H. Phelps-Brown (1988).
[5]An exception is the regressive tax, in which it is possible that after a certain income level there are no additional taxes paid.

Figure 16.2   Examples of Proportional, Progressive & Regressive Tax Structures

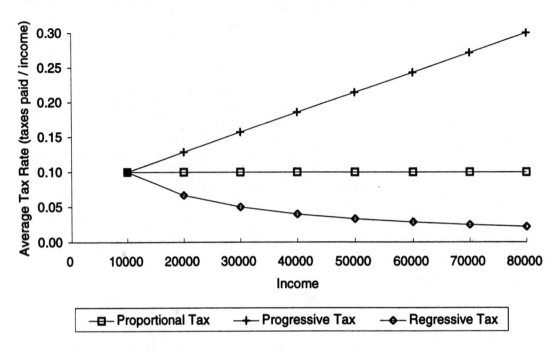

Figure 16.3 illustrates the three marginal tax rate schedules associated with each of the tax systems shown in Figure 16.2. In the case of a proportional tax,

$$t = c,$$

where c is a constant, so that $T = cY$ and

$$MTR = c.$$

In the case of a progressive tax, the marginal tax schedule will depend on the particular form of the progressive tax schedule. In the case illustrated here, where

$$t = a + bY, \; a,b > 0$$

and a and b are constant, then[6]

$$MTR = a + 2bY$$

---

[6] The derivation is as follows: Since $T/Y = a + bY$, then $T = aY + bY^2$ and $dT/dY = a + 2bY$.

Figure 16.3 Average and Marginal Tax Rates for Different Illustrative Tax Systems

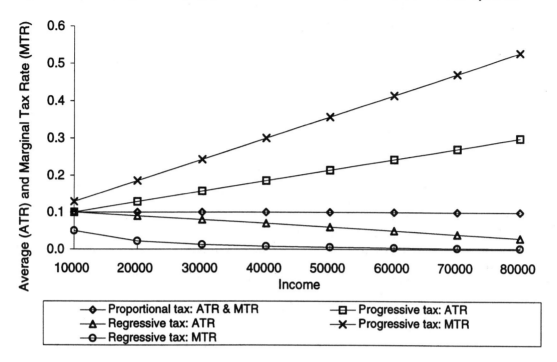

In this case, the marginal tax rate rises with income. An analogous derivation can be made for the regressive tax. In the case illustrated here,

$$t = b \,/\, (a + Y), \; a,b > 0$$

and a and b are constant, then

$$MTR = ab \,/\, (a + Y)^2$$

In the case of a regressive tax, the marginal tax rate declines with the income level.[7]

Average tax rates are more relevant when considering the effects of the tax system on income inequality. However, most of the public policy debate centers on the marginal tax rate, since it is more crucial when considering the incentive effects of the tax system. The marginal tax rate determines the net gain for an additional dollar of income and therefore directly affects labor supply and investment behavior.

---

[7]The derivation is as follows: Since $T/Y = b \,/\, (a + Y)$, then $T = bY \,/\, (a + Y)$ and $dT/dY = ab \,/\, (a + Y)^2$.

In actuality, most tax schedules are not formed as simple functions of income. Figures 16.4a and 16.4b illustrate the actual 1993 federal personal income tax scheme, both for single filers and married couples (joint tax returns). The marginal tax system is, in effect, a step function, with the marginal tax rate remaining constant along a range of income and then jumping up to a new level at the end of the range. These income ranges are referred to as "tax brackets."[8]

As shown in Table 16.1, the marginal tax rate is zero up to $6,050 for singles (assuming the standard deduction and one exemption) and up to $15,600 for married couples filing jointly (assuming the standard deduction and two children in the household). Marginal tax rates then increase to 15 percent, 28 percent, 31 percent, 36 percent, and 39.6 percent for over $250,000 in income.[9]

Table 16.1 Marginal and Average Tax Rates Based on the 1993 Federal Personal Income Tax Code

Income Bracket[a]		Marginal Tax Rate (percent)	Average Tax Rate (%)	Total Taxes Paid
Over	but less than		(at lower limit of range)	
A. Singles[b]				
0	6,050	0.0	0.0	0
6,050	28,150	15.0	0.0	0
28,150	59,550	28.0	11.8	3,315
59,550	121,050	21.0	20.3	12,107
121,050	256,050	36.0	25.8	31,172
256,050		39.6	31.2	79,772
1,000,000		39.6	37.4	374,376
B. Couples, Filing Jointly (with two children)[c]				
0	15,600	0.0	0.0	0
15,600	52,500	15.0	0.0	0
52,500	104,750	28.0	10.5	5,535
104,750	155,600	31.0	19.3	20,165
155,600	265,600	36.0	23.1	35,929
265,600		39.6	28.4	75,528
1,000,000		39.6	36.6	366,350

[a] Income levels are based on adjusted gross income (AGI).
[b] Assumes the standard deduction and one exemption.
[c] Assumes standard deduction and four exemptions (two adults and two children).

---

[8] The tax brackets are based on adjusted gross income or AGI. See the first part of Section 16.3 for details on the definition of AGI.
[9] The last two tax brackets were added in the 1993 tax law.

Figures 16.4a   Marginal and Average Tax Rates for Singles (the 1993 Federal Tax Code)

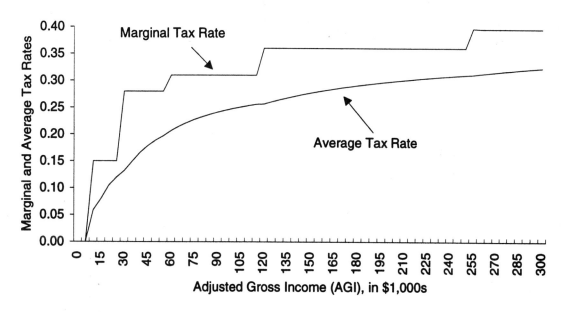

Figures 16.4b   Marginal and Average Tax Rates for a Couple with Two Children (1993 Federal Tax Code)

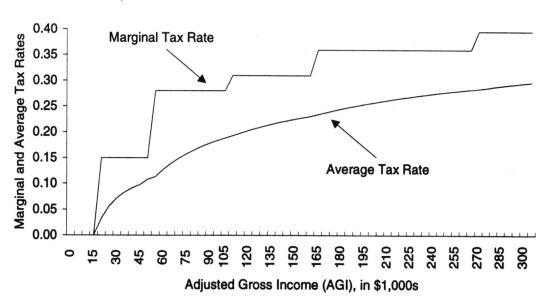

Table 16.1 also shows the average tax rates by income level. There are four important points to note. First, the average tax rate rises with income. Second, the average tax rate rises smoothly with income (there are no "discontinuities" as there are in the marginal tax schedule). Third, except for the zero tax bracket, the average tax rate is uniformly lower than the marginal tax rate. For example, at a marginal tax rate of 31 percent, the average tax rate is only 19 percent. This is a consequence of the step function structure of the marginal tax rates. Fourth, as income rises, the average tax rate approaches the top marginal tax rate (39.6 percent in 1993) in the limit.

It should be apparent that the federal personal income tax schedule is a progressive tax, since the average tax rate increases with income. This, in turn, is due to the marginal tax structure, which increases in stepwise fashion with income. However, it should be emphasized even at this point that the actual or *effective* tax rates by income level do, indeed, differ from the tax schedule as it appears on paper. This is due the availability of deductions, exclusions, tax preference items, and other so-called "tax loopholes." We will have more to say about this in the next section.

Inequality Measures and the Tax System

How does the tax system affect overall income inequality in an economy? An answer to this question requires a comparison of the distribution of before-tax income with that of after-tax income. The effect is typically summarized using one of the standard measures of inequality, such as the Gini coefficient or the coefficient of variation. We have already broached this subject in Section 3.2, where we discussed studies which compared before-tax and after-tax measures of inequality. Here, we treat the subject theoretically.

The standard measures of inequality, such as the Gini coefficient, are designed in such a way that they are scale-free. That is to say, a proportionate change in income (every family's income changes by the same percentage) will leave the inequality measure unchanged. This, we suggested, made intuitive sense, since inequality depends on *relative* income and a proportionate change in income leaves everyone's relative income unchanged.

An analysis of the effect of the tax system on inequality thus depends on the structure of average tax rates. Let us define after-tax income as Y^*,

$$Y^* = (1 - t)Y, \tag{16.3}$$

where Y is before-tax income. It should, perhaps, be apparent that a proportional tax system will leave inequality unchanged because everyone's income will decline by the same percentage. In the example above, $t = c$, a constant, and $Y^* = (1 - c)Y$. In this case, we simply have a change in scale of our income measure.

We can demonstrate this formally in the case of the Gini coefficient. In Section 3.2, we defined the Gini coefficient, G, as:

$$G = [1 - \sum_{i=1}^{k} f_i(z_{i-1} + z_i)]$$

Table 16.2 Distribution of Total Family Income By Income Class Used to Derive the Lorenz Curve and the Gini Coefficient

Income Class	Number of Families	Percent of Families	Cumulative Percent of Families	Mean Income	Total Income	Percent of Total Income	Cumulative Percent Of Total Income
1	n_1	$f_1 = n_1/N$	$P_1 = f_1$	$\bar{Y}_1$	$n_1\bar{Y}_1$	$y_1 = n_1\bar{Y}_1/N\bar{Y}$	$z_1 = y_1$
2	n_2	$f_2 = n_2/N$	$P_2 = f_1 + f_2$	$\bar{Y}_2$	$n_2\bar{Y}_2$	$y_2 = n_2\bar{Y}_2/N\bar{Y}$	$z_2 = y_1 + y_2$
. . .							
i	n_3	$f_i = n_i/N$	$P_i = \sum_1^i f_j$	$\bar{Y}_i$	$n_i\bar{Y}_i$	$y_i = n_i\bar{Y}_i/N\bar{Y}$	$z_1 = \sum_1^i y_j$
. . .							
k	n_k	$f_k = n_k/N$	$P_k = \sum_1^k f_j = 1$	$\bar{Y}_k$	$n_k\bar{Y}_k$	$y_k = n_k\bar{Y}_k/N\bar{Y}$	$z_k = \sum_1^t y_j = 1$
Sum	N	1.0		$\bar{Y}$	$N\bar{Y}$	1.0	

for k income classes, where f_i is the percent frequency of income recipients in income class i, y_i is the percent of total income received by income class i, z_i is the cumulative percentage of income up through income class i given by

$$z_i = y_1 + \cdots + y_i,$$

and z_0 is defined as equal to zero. The algebraic derivation of the Gini coefficient is illustrated in Table 16.2.

What happens when a proportional tax is imposed on income? It should first be clear that the percent frequency of families in each income class remains *unchanged*. In a sense, we are just redefining the income class boundaries. The income side is a bit less obvious. Let us consider income class i. After-tax mean income in income class i, $\bar{Y}^*$, becomes

$$\bar{Y}^*_i = (1 - c)\bar{Y}_i,$$

and the overall average after-tax income becomes

$$\bar{Y}^* = (1 - c)\bar{Y}$$

The percent of after-tax total income in income class i then becomes

$$\bar{y}^*_i = (1 - c)n_i\bar{Y}_i / (1 - c)N\bar{Y} = n_i\bar{Y}_i / N\bar{Y} = \bar{y}_i$$

As a result, y_i remains unchanged, since total income and income in income class i both change by the same percentage (they both decline by a factor of

$(1 - c)$. It also follows that z_i remains unchanged. Since both f_i and z_i are unchanged, the after-tax Gini coefficient must equal the before-tax Gini coefficient.[10]

Another point is that the Lorenz curve for after-tax income is identical to the one based on before-tax income. From Chapter 3, the Lorenz curve graphs the cumulative percentage of income, z_i, against the cumulative percentage of families, P_i. Since the imposition of a proportional tax leaves both z_i and P_i unchanged, the after-tax Lorenz curve is the same as the before-tax Lorenz curve.

What about progressive and regressive tax structures? There is no straightforward analytical demonstration of their effect on the Gini coefficient or the coefficient of variation. The forms of these taxes may vary, and in most cases, the resulting equations do not admit of tractable solutions. However, we can use the Lorenz curve technique to assess their effects. For this, we need to impose one important condition—namely, that the rank order of families remains the same on the basis of after-tax income as before-tax income. In other words, the tax must be imposed in such a way that family A with more (before-tax) income than family B must also have more after-tax income than family B. In this case, we can still classify after-tax income families in the same before-tax income classes by simply redefining the income class bracket. As a result, the tax will leave f_i and f_{i-1} unchanged.[11]

In the case of a progressive tax, income class i will, by definition, pay a higher percentage tax than lower income class $i - 1$. Consider the first (lowest) income tax. Its tax rate, t_1, must be less than the average tax rate, $\bar{t}$, for the population as a whole. Its after-tax mean income is

$$\bar{Y}^*_1 = (1 - t_1)\bar{Y}_1$$

Its share of total after-tax income is

$$y^*_1 = (1 - t_1)n_1\bar{Y}_1 \,/\, (1 - \bar{t})N\bar{Y}$$

and, as a result,

$$y^*_1 = (1 - t_1)n_1\bar{Y}_1 \,/\, (1 - \bar{t})N\bar{Y} > n_1\bar{Y}_1 \,/\, N\bar{Y} = y_1$$

---

[10] The proof is also straightforward for the coefficient of variation. Recall from Section 3.2 that the measure is defined as:

$$CV(Y) = \frac{STD(Y)}{\bar{Y}}$$

Then,

$$CV(Y^*) = \frac{STD(Y^*)}{\bar{Y}^*} = \frac{STD[(1 - c)Y]}{(1 - c)\bar{Y}} = \frac{(1 - c)STD(Y)}{(1 - c)\bar{Y}} = CV(Y)$$

[11] See the last part of this section for more discussion of this ranking criterion. It should be noted that a proportional and a regressive tax will always fulfill this rank order criterion. A progressive tax will also meet this criterion as long as the marginal tax rate is always less than 100 percent.

since $(1 - t_1) / (1 - \bar{t})$ is greater than unity. It is clear that this relation will hold for all the bottom income classes whose tax rate is below the average tax rate in the economy. As a result, for all such income classes i below the average tax rate,

$$z^*_i = y^*_1 + \cdots + y^*_i > y_1 + \cdots + y_i = z_i$$

As a result, for the bottom part of the income distribution, the after-tax Lorenz curve must lie *above* the before-tax Lorenz curve. This is illustrated in Figure 16.5.

To look at the income classes above the mean tax rate, we "flip" the Lorenz curve around. Recall from Section 3.2 that we can read the Lorenz curve from the upper right point of the square as the cumulative percentage of income received by the *top* percentiles of the income distribution. In this regard, let us consider the highest income class, k. Its after-tax mean income is

$$\bar{Y}^*_k = (1 - t_k)\bar{Y}_k$$

Figure 16.5   Lorenz Curves for Before-Tax & After-Tax (Progressive, Regressive) Inc.

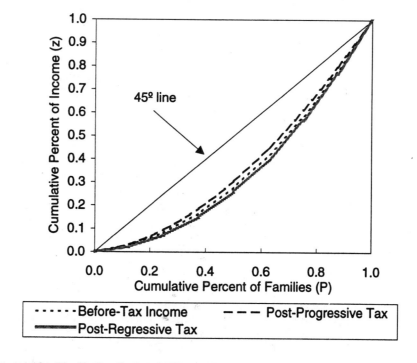

Its share of total after-tax income is

$$y^*_k = (1 - t_k)n_k\bar{Y}_k / (1 - \bar{t})N\bar{Y}$$

and, as a result,

$$y^*_k = (1 - t_k)n_k\bar{Y}_k / (1 - \bar{t})N\bar{Y} > n_k\bar{Y}_k / N\bar{Y} = y_k$$

since $(1 - t_k) / (1 - \bar{t})$ is less than unity. This relation holds for all the top income classes, above the average tax rate in the economy. As a result, for all such income classes j above the average tax rate, the share of total after-tax income received by the top income classes through j, s^*_j (the concentration of income), is given by

$$s^*_j = y^*_k + \cdots + y^*_j < y_k + \cdots + y^*_j = s_j$$

In other words, the top part of the after-tax Lorenz curve, above the mean tax rate, must also lie above the before-tax Lorenz curve. As a result, a progressive tax, subject to maintaining the rank order of income recipients, must lower income inequality.

An analogous proof demonstrates that in the case of a regressive tax, the after-tax Lorenz curve must lie completely below the before-tax Lorenz curve. As a result, a regressive tax must increase income inequality.

Vertical versus Horizontal Equity

Discussions of the distributional effects of the tax system usually deal with two different concepts of equity: horizontal and vertical. **Vertical equity** refers to a comparison of the overall after-tax income distribution with the overall before-tax distribution. In this type of analysis, we are typically concerned with whether the inequality of after-tax income is greater or less than before-tax income. The analysis of the last section is a case in point. Here, we are concerned with whether each of the three main types of tax structures—proportional, progressive, and regressive—results in an increase or diminution in income inequality. We saw that the first was neutral, the second equalizing, and the third disequalizing.

Analyses of vertical equity do not consider whether families with the same characteristics (such as income, family size, age, etc.) are treated the same or differently. This question comes under the province of **horizontal equity.** The term horizontal equity refers to a comparison of the before-tax and after-tax position of taxpayers with respect to the characteristics of the taxpayers. There are two basic principles of horizontal equity. The first is usually stated as equal treatments of equals. According to this principle, the tax system should levy identical taxes on all families who enjoy the same level of well-being (typically measured by income).

The second principle is referred to as rank preservation. The notion here is that an equitable tax system should leave the rank order of tax units unaltered. If family A was better off than family B before taxes, it should remain better off after taxes. It should be apparent that this principle incorporates the first principle but is more general. If equals are treated equally, then their relative rank will remain unchanged. However, this principle is broader, since it asserts that all relative positions must be maintained—there can be no reranking.

How do the three types of tax systems measure up with respect to this second principle of horizontal equity (assuming that the tax depends only on the income of the family)? A proportional tax, as indicated above, must be rank preserving, since all tax units experience the same percentage loss in income. Perhaps surprisingly, a regressive tax is rank preserving since a higher income family can not slip below a lower income unit. Indeed, an important feature of a regressive system is that the after-tax income of a higher income family will *increase* relative to that of a lower income unit. Thus, even though a regressive *tax violates the principle of vertical equity,* it will fulfill the second principle of horizontal equity.

Of the three, only the progressive tax is ambiguous. It is not too hard to imagine an example that will cause a higher pretax income family to slip below a lower pretax family (to take an extreme example, a 50 percent tax on middle income families and a *100 percent* tax on rich families). In actuality, most progressive tax schedules also fulfill the second principle of horizontal equity. The 1993 U.S. federal tax schedule does with respect to **taxable income.**[12] Indeed, any progressive tax schedule in which marginal tax rates increase with income level in stepwise fashion will fulfill the second principle as long as the marginal rate is less than 100 percent. The reason is that after-tax income must increase monotonically (that is, in direct relation with) before-tax income. Once the marginal tax rate hits 100 percent, this relation no longer holds. If the 100 percent limitation condition is met, the posttax income of taxpayer i will always be greater than that of taxpayer j as long as i's pretax income is greater.[13] Thus, a progressive tax fulfills the principle of vertical equity and will generally satisfy the second principle of horizontal equity, except in perverse cases.[14]

Both dimensions of equity are relevant for policy making. With regard to vertical equity, the notion that the tax system should reduce the overall inequality in the distribution of income accords with many arguments in favor of social justice. A somewhat different justification is based on the principle of the "ability to pay," which holds that taxpayers with greater resources should contribute a higher proportion of their resources to the

---

[12] However, the U.S. system may very well violate the second principle and even the first principle with respect to ordinary income or even adjusted gross income, since exemptions and deductions may not be the same for tax units with the same ordinary income or AGI.

[13] Actually, in the Swedish tax system of the 1980s, there were cases in which the marginal tax rate exceeded 100 percent. One famous case involved the Swedish film director, Ingmar Bergmann.

[14] See Berliant and Strauss (1985) and Plotnick (1985) for further discussion of these points.

maintenance of the state. This condition also derives ultimately from a sense of fair play.

With regard to horizontal equity, the unequal treatment of equals and rank reversals may generate social conflict in a society such as ours that generally views market incomes (and therefore individual ranking in the income distribution) as deserved. Tax policies that allow one family to have greater after-tax income than another with the same before-tax income goes against our usual notion of fairness. Likewise, a tax system that elevates a lower before-tax individual above a higher before-tax person may create considerable resentment. Thus, both equal treatment of equals and rank preservation appear to form part of the general notion of social justice.[15]

16.3 DISTRIBUTIONAL CONSEQUENCES OF THE AMERICAN TAX SYSTEM

Does the U.S. tax system help to reduce overall income inequality, to increase it, or to leave it basically unaltered? This is the subject of this part of the chapter. We shall begin by looking at the structure of the personal income tax and then consider other forms of taxes, including the social security tax, the corporate income tax, and sales taxes. Though the income tax is often at the center of political debates on taxation, it will become apparent that these other forms of taxation also play an important role when considering the overall distributional effects of the tax system.[16]

Tax Schedules for the Personal Income Tax

The federal individual income tax was enacted in 1913. There is an interesting history associated with this tax. The first federal tax on personal income was enacted during the Civil War and lasted from 1862 through 1871. Support for an income tax languished during the next 20 years, but because of the large fortunes made during the 1880s and 1890s, a new income tax law was passed in 1894. However, in the following year, the Supreme Court declared this law unconstitutional. The reason is that the Constitution of the United States originally forbade the federal government from levying taxes directly on individuals. Thus, an amendment to the Constitution was necessary for the enactment of a federal income tax. In 1913, the Sixteenth Amendment was ratified, which provided Congress the power "to lay and

---

[15] However, this notion of fairness rests very heavily on the belief that the pretax income distribution is deserved. A Marxist, for example, may feel that the high incomes of capitalists are the result of the exploitation of workers and therefore undeserved.

[16] Because of the technical nature of most measures of horizontal equity, our discussion here will focus mainly on issues of vertical equity. See the excellent papers contained in the volume, *Horizontal Equity, Uncertainty, and Economic Well-Being*, edited by Martin David and Timothy Smeeding (1985), for analyses of horizontal equity in the U.S. tax system.

collect taxes on income, from whatever source derived. . . ."[17] The income tax was enacted shortly thereafter in 1913.

For almost 30 years since its passage, the individual income tax applied to only a small percentage of families, since the income exemptions were very high. However, during World War II, the revenue needs of the federal government were enormously expanded, and exemptions were drastically cut. Today, over 90 percent of families are subject to the federal personal income tax, and it is the largest source of federal government revenue.

The income concept used in the federal personal income tax system is **adjusted gross income** or **AGI.** AGI differs in several ways from ordinary income. First, AGI includes realized capital gains—that is, the appreciation (or loss) of assets owned by the family that are sold during the year. This is defined as the difference between the selling price and the purchase price.[18] Second, for most retirees, social security income is excluded from AGI.[19] Third, welfare payments, food stamps, veteran's benefits, and fringe benefits received by employees from their employer (such as health insurance and pension contributions) are also excluded. Fourth, interest earned on certain state and local government bonds is, by law, exempt from federal income tax (appropriately enough, these bonds are referred to as "tax-exempt issues"). Fifth, other technical adjustments are made to the income base to obtain AGI.[20]

The actual tax schedule is applied not to AGI but to a concept called **taxable income.** This is defined as AGI less **deductions** less **exemptions.** In 1993, the principal deductions were health expenditures (over 7.5 percent of AGI), state and local income tax, local property tax, mortgage interest payments, and charitable contributions. A filer may choose between the sum of these deductions and the standard deduction provided in the tax schedule (in 1993, $3,700 for a single filer and $6,200 for a married couple filing jointly). Generally, the number of exemptions a family can claim equals the number of individuals in the family. An additional exemption is given for each person in the family over the age of 65 and for blindness. In the 1993 tax schedule, the number of exemptions is multiplied by $2,350, and this total is subtracted from AGI.[21]

The personal income tax system implicitly adopts an "ability to pay" criterion as the basis of tax payments. This is reflected in two ways. First, the

---

[17] This is not to say that there was unanimous support in Congress for an income tax. Indeed, there was staunch opposition from many conservative legislators. One apparent reason is that Karl Marx and Frederic Engels proposed a progressive income tax in the *Manifesto of the Communist Party.* As a result, many conservatives associated an income tax with communism and opposed it on this ground.

[18] In the case of tangible assets, like a home, the total value of capital improvements are also added to the purchase price in calculating capital gains.

[19] In the 1993 tax code, up to 85 percent of social security income is added back into AGI if the sum of the other components of AGI exceed a prespecified limit.

[20] For example, investments made in Individual Retirement Accounts (IRAs), Keogh plans, and 401(k) retirement plans are excluded from income.

[21] As in most of the tax code, things are not quite as simple as this. In the case of both deductions and exemptions, there are limitations imposed on the total value of each for higher income returns.

marginal tax rates are progressive with respect to taxable income. Thus, families with more income generally pay higher tax *rates* (see Figures 16.4a and 16.4b). Second, the tax schedule also adjusts for family size and composition. In Chapter 4, in our discussion of poverty, we argued that needs are based on family size (and, to a lesser extent, composition). A large family requires more income to attain the same living standard as a smaller one. This feature is captured in the use of equivalence classes to define the official poverty line by family size.

A similar notion is embodied in the tax code. This is reflected in two ways. First, the number of exemptions is equal to the size of the taxpaying unit. Larger families have more exemptions. Moreover, there are additional exemptions for the elderly and for blindness. Second, there are basically three different tax schedules provided in the tax code depending on the filing status of the taxpaying unit: (1) singles, (2) married couples,[22] and (3) single adults who are heads of households (that is, have children or other dependents living with them). Single individuals pay a higher tax on the same taxable income than married couples, even after adjusting for the greater number of exemptions that can be claimed by the latter. The rationale is that single adults should be more heavily taxed, since they do not bear the same costs and responsibilities of supporting children. Heads of households pay a tax rate that is about halfway between that of singles and married couples with the same taxable income.

The federal tax schedule has been changed frequently over time since its inception in 1913. Table 16.3 shows a history of the federal personal income tax structure from 1913 to 1993, featuring the years in which there was a change in the tax laws. The first panel shows the marginal tax rates of the lowest and top income brackets, as well as the personal exemptions for a family of four. In 1913, the marginal tax rates ranged from a low of 1.0 percent to a high of 7.0 percent, with the top bracket beginning at $50,000 (Panel A). By 1917, during World War I, the top marginal rate had been increased to 67 percent, for a bracket of $2,000,000 or more.

The top marginal rate declined during the 1920s, reaching a low of 24 percent in 1929. During the 1930s, the marginal rates increased again, and by 1944, in the midst of World War II, they reached a high of *94 percent.* The top marginal rate then declined during the late 1940s (falling to 82 percent in 1948) but was again over 90 percent during the Korean War (reaching 92 percent in 1953). During the 1960s and 1970s, the top marginal rate dropped to 70 percent (though it was raised to 77 percent in 1969, during the Vietnam War).

During the Reagan-Bush years of 1980–1992, there was a substantial reduction in the top marginal rate. The 1981 Tax Act lowered it to 50 percent,

---

[22]Actually, there are two separate categories for married couples: (1) married couples filing joint returns and (2) married couples filing separate returns. For many years, there was an advantage for a married couple to "split" their income and file two separate tax returns, since both parts would be subject to lower marginal tax rates and therefore a lower overall average tax rate. However, current provisions of the tax code have eliminated most of the advantage of income splitting.

Table 16.3   The Structure of the Federal Personal Income Tax, 1913–1993 (For Married Couples Filing Jointly with Two Children)ᵃ

A. *Personal Exemptions and Bottom and Top Bracket Rates in Current Dollars*

		Marginal Tax Rates				
		Bottom Bracket		Top Bracket		Maximum
Year	Personal Exemptions	Rate (percent)	Taxable Income Up to	Rate (percent)	Taxable Income Over	Effective Rate (percent)
1913	4,000	1.0	20,000	7.0	50,000	
1917	2,400	2.0	2,000	67.0	2,000,000	
1921	3,300	4.0	4,000	73.0	1,000,000	
1924	3,300	1.5	4,000	46.0	500,000	
1929	4,300	0.4	4,000	24.0	100,000	
1936	3,300	4.0	4,000	79.0	5,000,000	
1941	2,300	10.0	2,000	81.0	5,000,000	
1944	2,000	23.0	2,000	94.0	200,000	90.0
1946	2,000	19.0	2,000	86.5	200,000	85.5
1948	2,400	16.6	4,000	82.1	400,000	77.0
1950	2,400	17.4	4,000	91.0	400,000	87.0
1953	2,400	22.2	4,000	92.0	400,000	88.0
1960	2,400	20.0	4,000	91.0	400,000	
1966	2,400	14.0	1,000	70.0	200,000	
1969	2,400	14.0	1,000	77.0	200,000	
1975	3,000	14.0	1,000	70.0	200,000	
1980	4,000	14.0	2,100	70.0	212,000	
1983	4,000	12.0	2,100	50.0	106,000	
1986	8,000	15.0	32,400	28.0	208,560	
1991	8,600	15.0	34,000	31.0	82,150	
1993	9,400	15.0	36,900	39.6	250,000	

(continued)

and the rather famous Tax Reform Act of 1986 reduced it still further to 28 percent.[23] However, in the Tax Act of 1991, the top marginal rate was raised to 31 percent, and the first year of the Clinton administration saw the top marginal rate rising again, to 39.6 percent in 1993.[24]

---

[23]There is a slight peculiarity in the 1986 tax schedule. The top rate is actually 33 percent, for income bracket $78,400–$208,560. The marginal tax rate then falls to 28 percent, for taxable income over $208,560. The reason is that the allowable value of exemptions and deductions is gradually phased out above $208,560 of income. The lower marginal tax rate of this bracket in a sense compensates for the reduction of allowable exemptions and deductions.

[24]Panel A of Table 16.3 also shows maximum effective tax rates for the years 1944–1953. The effective tax rate, as we shall discuss in more detail, shows the ratio of actual taxes paid to AGI. During this period, the effective tax rate was capped at the indicated levels.

Table 16.3 *(concluded)*

B. *Marginal Tax Rate (in percent) by Level of Taxable Income in 1987 Dollars*

				Taxable Income				
Year	5,000	10,000	25,000	50,000	75,000	100,000	250,000	1,000,000
1944	23.0	23.0	29.0	37.0	50.0	56.0	75.0	93.0
1946	19.0	20.9	24.7	36.1	47.5	53.2	71.3	86.5
1948	16.6	16.6	19.4	26.4	33.4	37.8	57.2	78.3
1950	17.4	17.4	20.0	27.3	34.6	39.1	59.2	82.5
1953	22.2	22.2	24.6	34.0	42.0	53.0	68.0	91.0
1960	20.0	20.0	26.0	34.0	43.0	50.0	69.0	90.0
1966	15.0	17.0	22.0	28.0	36.0	45.0	60.0	70.0
1969	17.6	20.9	24.2	35.2	42.9	52.8	68.2	77.0
1975	17.0	19.0	25.0	39.0	50.0	53.0	66.0	70.0
1980	14.0	18.0	28.0	49.0	54.0	59.0	70.0	70.0
1983	13.0	15.0	26.0	40.0	44.0	50.0	50.0	50.0
1986	15.0	15.0	15.0	28.0	33.0	33.0	28.0	28.0
1991	15.0	15.0	28.0	28.0	31.0	31.0	31.0	31.0
1993	15.0	15.0	28.0	28.0	31.0	36.0	39.6	39.6

Addendum: Ratio of 1993 Rate to 1944 Rate:

	0.65	0.65	0.97	0.76	0.62	0.64	0.53	0.43

[a] Sources: 1913–1983: Pechman (1983); 1986, 1991, and 1993: Federal Income Tax Return, Form 1040, 1986, 1991, and 1993, respectively.

Students today might be astonished at how high marginal tax rates have been in the past in the United States. From 1936 to 1964, the highest marginal rate never fell below 77 percent and during periods of war hovered around 90 percent. Even during the late 1960s and the 1970s, it tended to be in the 70–75 percent range. It was not until Reagan's second term of office that the top rate returned to the 30-percent range, though in 1993 it rose back to 40 percent.

The top marginal rate is one indicator of the progressivity of the tax system, since the higher it is the greater the range in the marginal and hence average tax rates by income class. However, it is difficult to compare the relative progressivity of the tax structure across years from Panel A for three reasons. First, only the bottom and top marginal rates are shown, rather than the whole structure of marginal rates. Second, the income brackets themselves are changing over time (compare the cut-off points for the lowest and highest tax brackets), so that the range of marginal rates by themselves do not give a full indication of the degree of progressivity of the tax system.

Third, even if the tax brackets were unchanging over time in *nominal* terms (that is, current dollars), they would still be changing in *real* terms.

That is to say, with inflation occurring, a family with the same real income over time would be forced into higher and higher marginal tax brackets, even if the tax schedule remain unaltered in nominal terms. This phenomenon is referred to as "bracket creep."[25] However, tax brackets are now indexed for inflation.

To correct for inflation, Panel B of Table 16.3 shows the marginal rate schedule at constant dollar (1987 dollars) levels of taxable income for selected years between 1944 and 1993. Marginal tax rates have generally fallen at all real income levels since the end of World War II. At the bottom two income levels, $5,000 and $10,000, the marginal tax rate fell from 23 to 15 percent between 1944 and 1983. However, the decline was not continuous over time, and in some years, such as 1953, the tax rate was raised rather sharply. At the middle income level of $25,000, the marginal tax rate fluctuated between 20 and 29 percent over this period and in 1993 was almost exactly the same as it was in 1944.

At the $50,000 level, the marginal tax rate also fluctuated over time, falling from 37 percent in 1944 to a low of 26 percent in 1948, rising to 49 percent in 1980, and then falling to 28 percent in 1986, where it has since remained. Similar patterns are evident at the next three income levels.

The pattern is slightly different at $1 million of taxable income. The marginal rate declined from 93 to 78 percent between 1944 and 1948, returned to 90 percent in 1960, fell to 70 percent in 1966, 50 percent in 1983, and 28 percent in 1986.[26] Since then, it has increased to 40 percent in 1993.

Though tax rates have fallen at all real income levels between 1944 and 1993, the *relative* decline has been greater at the upper income levels. At the lowest two income levels, the marginal tax rate fell by 35 percent; while at the middle income level of $25,000, there was virtually no change. At the $50,000 level, the marginal rate was lowered by about one-fourth; at both the $75,000 and $100,000 levels, the marginal tax rate was down by about a third; while at $250,000 of taxable income, the 1993 rate was slightly more than half the 1944 rate and at $1 million, slightly more than two-fifths. Thus, the successive waves of tax reform and tax reduction acts since the end of World War II have clearly benefited the rich more than the poor, with the possible exception of the Earned Income Tax Credit, which we will discuss in the last part of Section 16.3.

Effective Tax Rates for the Personal Income Tax

The tax schedule records the relation between tax liability and taxable income. As such, it is also refereed to as the "nominal tax rate." The **effective tax rate** is defined as the ratio of actual tax payments to total taxpayer

---

[25]This is the principal reason why an increasing percentage of the poverty population were paying federal income taxes during the 1970s and 1980s (see Section 4.4).

[26]The increase between 1966 and 1969, from 70 to 77 percent, is due to a tax surcharge placed on high incomes, stemming from the Vietnam War.

income. The difference in the two concepts reflects primarily the difference between total income and taxable income.

We have already indicated two sources of difference in the two concepts of income. The first is based on the number of exemptions a taxpayer can claim, which depends primarily on the number of individuals in the family. The second is based on either the standard deduction or itemized deductions. For higher income taxpayers, the latter can be a source of considerable reduction in taxable income, particularly with regard to state and local tax payments, interest payments,[27] and charitable deductions.

A third source are exclusions to ordinary income—mainly, social security benefits, interest income on tax-exempt state and local government bonds, a portion of long-term capital gains (effective in most years, though the percentage exclusion has varied over time), certain types of pension income, and unemployment insurance receipts (in some years). Other income exclusions come from "tax preference items" such as accelerated depreciation on certain kinds of investments and depletion allowances for oil and gas drilling.

A fourth source are tax credits that can be used to offset the amount of taxes owed. These include the Earned Income Tax Credit, which applies to low-income individuals with children (see below for more details); a tax credit for child care expenses, which applies mainly to low- and middle-income families who pay for child care; and an investment tax credit (applicable in some years), which applies to self-employed workers who purchase capital goods used in their business.[28]

Table 16.4 presents estimates for 1985 showing the relation between nominal and effective tax rates by level of ordinary income. Average nominal tax rates were highly progressive, ranging from 11.6 to 48.7 percent. The next four columns show how exemptions, deductions, and tax preference items reduce the actual tax burden. Personal exemptions reduce the effective tax rate by 7.3 percentage points for the lowest income class but by only 0.1 percentage points for the top income class. This is not too surprising, since in 1985 the dollar value of exemptions depended only on family characteristics, not family income.[29]

The tax offset of deductions generally rises with the level of income. Deductions reduce the effective tax rate by 4.3 percentage points for the lowest income and 8.0 percentage points for the highest. The reason is that lower income families usually claim the standard deduction whereas richer

---

[27] Until the Tax Reform Act of 1986, all interest payments, including those for car loans, credit card debt, and other forms of consumer debt, were fully deductible. Between 1986 and 1991, deductions for nonmortgage interest payments were phased out. Today, only mortgage interest payments are deductible.

[28] A relatively recent addition to the tax code is the Alternative Minimum Tax (AMT) which provides for the payment of a minimum percentage of ordinary income for taxpayers who include tax preference items in their tax return. This provision has been somewhat effective in closing tax loopholes used by wealthy taxpayers.

[29] Since the Tax Reform Act of 1986, the dollar value of personal exemptions actually declines with income when AGI exceeds a prespecified level.

Table 16.4   Effective and Nominal Tax Rates of the Federal Personal Income Tax System, 1985[a] (percent of ordinary income)

Total Ordinary Income[b]	Average Nominal Tax Rate	Reduction due to				Effective Tax Rate	Difference Between Nominal & Effective Tax Rate
		Personal Exemptions	Deductions	Tax Preference Items[c]	Others[d]		
0–3,000	11.6	7.3	4.3	—	1.0	−1.0	12.6
3–5,000	12.6	4.7	6.7	—	1.7	−0.5	13.1
5–7,000	13.6	4.1	5.6	0.2	2.5	1.2	12.4
7–10,000	14.8	3.5	4.8	0.1	3.0	3.4	11.4
10–15,000	17.3	3.5	4.8	0.2	3.4	5.4	11.9
15–20,000	20.3	4.0	5.0	0.3	4.2	6.8	13.5
20–25,000	23.2	4.0	5.7	0.5	5.0	8.0	15.2
25–35,000	26.9	4.0	7.0	0.7	6.0	9.2	17.7
35–50,000	31.2	3.5	8.4	1.6	6.7	11.0	20.2
50–75,000	35.4	2.8	9.1	1.5	8.1	13.9	21.5
75–100,000	39.5	2.0	9.5	2.5	8.4	17.1	22.4
100–150,000	42.2	1.5	9.4	3.4	8.1	19.8	22.4
150–200,000	44.3	1.1	9.0	4.2	7.1	22.9	21.4
200–500,000	46.1	0.7	8.6	6.0	5.2	25.6	20.5
500–1,000,000	47.8	0.3	8.6	9.8	3.0	26.1	21.7
1,000,000 +	48.7	0.1	8.0	16.4	1.4	22.8	25.9
Average	30.1	3.3	7.6	1.5	6.2	11.5	18.6

[a] Source: Pechman (1983). The figures are based on averages for married couples, filing separately.
[b] Defined as the sum of adjusted gross income; excluded dividends, capital gains, and other tax preference items; tax-exempt state and local government bond interest; social security benefits, unemployment compensation, and workmen's compensation insurance; employer-provided health insurance, life insurance, and other tax exempt benefits; and other miscellaneous items.
[c] Includes capital gains exclusion, IRA and Keogh accounts, accelerated depreciation, and other tax preference items.
[d] Includes excluded social security benefits and other transfer payments; tax credits for earned income (EITC), investment outlays, and child care expenses; and the tax advantages of income splitting.

families can generally claim more itemized deductions, since they pay higher state and local taxes and mortgage interest and give larger charitable contributions.

The effect of tax preference items such as excluded capital gains, accelerated depreciation, and the various tax shelters described above on the effective tax rate is very dramatic. The tax offset is almost nonexistent for incomes below $100,000 and then increases sharply with income level, to 16.4 percentage points for incomes above one million dollars.

The other tax provisions benefit different income classes. Income splitting in 1985 helped families with incomes ranging between $35,000 and $200,000. The exclusion of social security income aided income classes $10,000 to $30,000, reducing their effective tax rate by about three percentage points. Tax credits from the EITC helped income classes below $10,000 of income (a 1.0–1.5 percentage point reduction in their effective tax rate), while the investment tax credit benefited the wealthy, above $100,000 of income (a 1.1–1.7 percentage point reduction in their effective tax rate).

On average, the result of these special provisions of the tax code reduces the average tax rate by about two-thirds, from its nominal level of 30 percent to only 12 percent. The biggest effect comes from deductions, which reduce the effective tax rate by 7.6 percentage points. In addition exemptions lessen the tax burden by 3.3 percentage points. The exclusion of transfer payments accounts for an additional 2.1 percentage points, tax preference items for 1.5 percentage points, income splitting for 3.6 percentage points, and tax credits for 0.5 percentage points.

Overall, the higher income classes benefit more from the tax reduction provisions of the tax code. The tax burden of the lowest income class is reduced by 13 percentage points, whereas that of the highest income class falls by 26 percentage points (last column of Table 16.4). The tax reduction effect rises almost monotonically with the income level of the taxpayer. The resulting effective tax rate schedule is still progressive, ranging from −1.0 to 23 percent. However, it is less progressive than the nominal tax rate schedule. We shall return to effective tax rates when we consider the effects of the total tax system.

The Payroll Tax

The second largest source of federal government revenue is the **payroll tax.** It was first introduced by the Social Security Act of 1935 and has grown enormously since the end of World War II. Unlike most other taxes, payroll taxes are "earmarked" to finance specific programs of the government, notably the social security system.

We have talked at some length about the social security system in the previous chapter from its standpoint as a transfer system. In this chapter, we consider the system from its tax side. The 1935 Social Security Act actually set up two different programs—old-age benefits and unemployment insurance. The former is technically referred to as the "old age, survivors, disability, and health insurance program, or OASDHI ("OA" for old age, "S" for survivors, "D" for disability, "H" for health, and "I" for insurance), though it is more commonly referred to as the "social security system." In 1935, the system provided only old age (retirement) benefits. This was supplemented in 1939 by survivor's benefits, in 1957 by disability benefits, and in 1966 by medical benefits for persons 65 and over (also called Medicare).

Table 16.5 highlights the tremendous increase in the social security tax since 1937. There are two dimensions to the tax. The first is the tax rate,

Table 16.5 Social Security (OASDHI) Tax Rates and Maximum Taxable Earnings, Selected Years, 1937–1993[a]

Year	Employee Tax Rate (percent)	Maximum Taxable Wage Base
1937–1949	1.0	3,000
1950	1.5	3,000
1955	2.0	4,200
1960	3.0	4,200
1965	3.625	4,200
1970	4.8	7,800
1975	5.85	14,100
1980	6.13	25,900
1985	7.05	39,600
1990	7.65	51,300
1994	7.65	60,600

[a]Source: U.S. House of Representatives, Committee on Ways and Means, *1994 Green Book*. The tax rate is shown for the employee portion only. The employer also pays the same amount, so that the total tax rate is double this amount.

which is imposed on only wages, salaries, and other forms of employee remuneration, such as tips for waiters and self-employment income. The tax is imposed equally on employee and employers, so that the total tax rate is actually double the amount shown in Table 16.5. The second is referred to as the maximum taxable wage base. The social security tax is imposed on employee compensation only up to this amount.[30]

In 1937, the social security tax was 1.0 percent on wages and salaries for both the employee and employer, and the tax was levied on earnings up to $3,000. This rate remained in effect until 1950, when it was raised to 1.5 percent. After that point, both the tax rate and the maximum taxable wage base were steadily raised. The tax rate rose to 3.0 percent in 1960, 4.8 percent in 1970, 6.13 percent in 1980, 7.0 percent in 1985, and 7.65 percent in 1990, where it is scheduled to remain for the foreseeable future. Even more dramatic is the rise in the maximum earnings level, from $3,000 in 1950 to $4,200 in 1960, $7,800 in 1970, $25,900 in 1980, and $60,600 in 1994. Since 1982, the top limit on earnings has been increased annually at the same rate as the growth in average wages, and this provision is still in effect today. Between 1937 and 1993, the tax rate has increased more than seven-fold and the maximum earnings limit by a factor of 20.

It should be clear that with respect to wages and salaries, the social security tax is proportional up to the maximum taxable earnings and then turns

---

[30]Actually, the health portion of OASDHI has no earnings limit today.

regressive. This is so because the marginal tax rate is constant up to maximum earnings and then becomes zero. As a result, the average tax rate also remains constant up to the maximum base level and then declines with earnings, asymptotically approaching zero. We shall discuss the structure of the social security tax system with respect to family income in the upcoming section, "The Overal Tax Bite?"

Unemployment insurance is a much smaller tax. Though it is a federally-mandated tax, it is administered separately by each state under federal guidelines and therefore the exact tax structure varies across states. It is generally levied only on the employer. In 1937, the federal unemployment insurance tax rate was set at one percent of payrolls on all wages. It has also been periodically raised, to 3.0 percent in 1939 (on earnings up to $3,000), 3.5 percent in 1983 (on earnings up to $7,000), 6.2 percent in 1985 (on earnings up to $7,000), and in 1993 it was 5.4 percent on earnings up to $8,000 to $10,000 in most states. Though the tax rates look high (5 to 6 percent), the earnings base is so low that the proceeds from this tax are quite small—0.9 percent of total wages in 1993.

Other Federal Taxes

Another large source of federal revenue is the **corporation income tax.** Established in 1909, this is levied directly on businesses and is based on their reported profits. The basic tax rate was raised from 38 percent in 1946 to 52 percent in 1952, where it generally remained until 1969. It has since been lowered to 48 percent in 1971, 46 percent in 1979, and 35 percent in 1993.

The federal corporate income tax schedule looks quite progressive, starting at a marginal tax rate of 15 percent up to $50,000 of earnings and reaching the top rate of 35 percent at $10,000,000. The progressivity of this schedule is generally regarded as a concession to small businesses, and since many corporation earn incomes in the millions and billions, the vast majority of corporate taxable income (over 80 percent) is subject to the top rate of 35 percent. However, as with the personal income tax, there is a gulf between the nominal corporate tax rates and the actual (effective) rates paid by corporations. Most of the difference is due to tax preference items, such as accelerated depreciation.[31] Pechman (1983, p. 144) estimates an average effective corporate tax rate of 13.1 percent in 1982, compared to a nominal maximum rate of 46 percent.

There are several other sources of federal revenue. One is the **excise tax.** This is like a sales tax, except that it is levied on a small number of items, including alcohol and tobacco products (these are sometimes re-

---

[31] As we discussed in Chapter 2, depreciation, or more technically, the "capital consumption allowance," refers to the loss of economic value of capital goods (plant, machinery, and equipment) which comes about through wear and tear and age. Corporations are allowed to "write off" the value of their capital at rates that are probably much above the actual loss in their value. This capital consumption allowance is subtracted from the gross profits of the company to obtain net profits, and the corporate income tax is levied on the net profit figure.

ferred to as "sin taxes"), gasoline and other oil products, automobiles and other vehicles, and jewelry, furs, and other luxury goods. A second is the **customs duty,** which is levied on imports. The structure of customs duties, or tariffs, is quite complex and reflects, among other considerations, the degree to which different industries can achieve protection, the tariff and other export restrictions of countries with which the United States trades, and international rules and regulations (such as the General Agreement on Trade and Tariffs—GATT) regarding tariffs.

The third is **the estate tax,** which is levied on inheritances. Federal estate taxes were first introduced in 1916, with major revisions in 1976 and 1981. The current system provides for the taxation of the value of an estate at the time of death of an individual. Moreover, the estate tax system is integrated with the gift tax, which refers to the (*inter-vivos*) voluntary transfer of assets from one individual to another. In principle, gifts are aggregated over the lifetime of an individual, and the lifetime aggregate of gifts is combined with the value of an estate at death. The estate tax applies to the full value of gifts and estates.

As of 1992, each individual is exempted from estate taxes on net worth up to $600,000. Wealth above that amount is levied at marginal tax rates, which begin at 37 percent and reach as high as 55 percent (for estates over $2,500,000). All forms of wealth are included in the tax base for calculating the gift-estate tax except pension annuities and life insurance. Though on the books the estate tax might appear to be an effective way of limiting inheritances, in fact, collections from this tax are very small, 15.2 billion dollars in 1994, or about one percent of total federal tax receipts. Unfortunately, there are so many loopholes and avoidance mechanisms associated with the estate tax that it is sometimes referred to as a "voluntary tax."

State and Local Government Taxes

State governments rely on two major sources of revenues—income taxes and general sales taxes. The vast majority of states today now have an income tax. State personal income taxes are usually modeled directly on the federal tax structure. In some states, the marginal tax rates can be quite high (in New York State, the top marginal tax rate in 1993 was 7.9 percent on $65,000 of taxable income for married couples). A few localities, such as New York City, also enact a personal income tax. In addition, almost all states follow the federal government by enacting a separate income tax on corporations. In addition, all states except Nevada have an estate tax.[32]

The main source of state revenue is the general sales tax. Almost all states today have such a tax, with rates varying from 2 to 9 percent. This tax is levied on retail sales only and is therefore paid directly by the individual consumer. Most states exempt food and medicines from the tax base.

---

[32] Many states had an estate tax in place before the federal government established a permanent one in 1916. Pennsylvania had established one in 1825, and Wisconsin had a progressive estate tax system in operation in 1903.

The principal source of revenue for local governments is the property tax. This is levied on real estate owned by individuals and businesses (that owned by not-for-profit organizations such as churches or universities is usually exempt). Some localities also enact a general sales tax. In addition, there are often "user fees" for specific services provided by local governments, such as water and sewerage and sanitation collection.

The Overall Tax Bite

What are the overall distributional consequences of the tax system in the United States? This is a consequence of two factors. The first is the progressivity or regressivity of the individual taxes that make up the tax system. The second is the relative magnitude of the various taxes. Together, they determine the overall regressivity or progressivity of the tax system.

Let us first begin with the magnitudes of the different taxes. Table 16.6 (see also Figure 16.6) shows the share of the receipts from each of the major taxes in federal government income, state and local government income, and total government income between 1955 and 1993. Payments of federal individual income taxes are the principal source of federal government revenue, ranging from 42 to 46 percent. Generally speaking, this share remained fairly constant between 1955 and 1993. Revenue from state and local individual income taxes increased rather sharply, from 4 to 15 percent of total state and local government revenue

Figure 16.6   Percent Distribution of Total Government Receipts by Source, 1955–1993

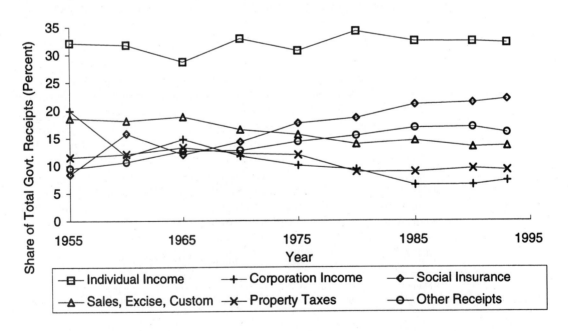

Part V   The Role of Public Policy on Inequality

Table 16.6 Distribution of Government Receipts by Source, 1955–1993 (percent)

	1955	1965	1975	1985	1993
Total federal government[a]	100	100	100	100	100
Individual income taxes	44	42	44	46	44
Corporation income taxes	27	22	15	8	10
Excise taxes	14	12	6	5	4
Customs duties and fees	1	1	1	2	2
Social insurance taxes and contributions[b]	12	19	30	36	37
Estate and gift taxes	1	2	2	1	1
Other receipts[c]	1	1	2	3	2
Total state and local government receipts[d]	100	100	100	100	100
Individual income taxes	4	7	12	14	15
Corporation income taxes	3	3	4	4	3
Sales and gross receipts taxes	27	27	27	26	25
Property taxes	38	35	28	21	22
All other[e]	27	28	29	35	35
Total government receipts[f]	100	100	100	100	100
Individual income taxes	32	29	31	32	32
Corporation income taxes	20	15	10	6	7
Sales and gross receipts taxes, excise taxes, and customs duty	19	19	16	15	14
Social insurance taxes and contributions[b]	8	12	18	21	22
Property taxes	11	13	12	9	9
Other[g]	9	13	14	17	16
Total government receipts as a percent of GDP[h]					
Total	24.3	27.8	31.8	31.8	31.6
Federal government	17.0	17.4	18.5	18.5	18.7
State & local government	7.3	10.4	13.3	13.3	12.9

[a] Sources: 1955–1980: Pechman (1983); 1981–1993: *Economic Report of the President, 1995*. The total includes both on-budget and off-budget items.
[b] Includes employee and employer contributions to OASDHI and payroll taxes for unemployment insurance.
[c] Includes earnings of Federal Reserve banks and other miscellaneous receipts.
[d] Source: *Economic Report of the President, 1995*. Total excludes revenues or expenditures of publicly owned utilities and liquor stores and insurance trust activities. Revenue from the federal government, other intergovernmental receipts, and payments between state and local governments are also excluded.
[e] Includes other taxes and charges and miscellaneous revenues.
[f] Includes miscellaneous receipts and user charges and excludes all intergovernmental transfers.
[g] Includes other taxes and charges and miscellaneous revenues as well as estate and gift taxes and earnings of Federal Reserve banks.
[h] Source: *Economic Report of the President, 1995*.

over this period. However, together, personal income taxes made up a relatively constant share of about one-third of total government revenue between 1955 and 1993.[33]

In contrast, receipts from the federal corporate income tax have fallen sharply, from 27 percent of total federal revenue in 1955 to only 9 percent in 1993. In the 1950s, this was the second principal source of federal income, but by the 1990s, it had declined to a distant third. On the state level, corporate income taxes remained rather steady at 3 to 4 percent of total state and local government revenue. Together, corporate income taxes declined from 20 percent of total government revenue in 1955 to only 7 percent in 1993.

Federal excise taxes also showed a sharp decline as a source of federal government revenue, from 14 to only 4 percent over the years from 1955 to 1993. Customs duties and fees have remained small, accounting for only 1 to 2 percent of total federal income. Among state and local governments, sales taxes accounted for 25 to 28 percent of their receipts, with the share remaining fairly constant over time. Together, sales, excise, and customs taxes diminished as a source of total government receipts, from 19 percent in 1955 to 13 percent.

With corporate income and excise taxes declining in importance on the federal level, what source of revenue made up the difference? The most dramatic growth occurred in social insurance (mainly social security) taxes, which rose from 12 percent of federal revenue in 1955 to 38 percent in 1993. It also increased from 8 percent of total government income to 21 percent. In 1955, it was fourth in importance as a source of federal receipts, but by 1970, it had climbed into second place. Today, collections from social insurance are only slightly behind those from federal personal income taxes (38 versus 44 percent). By the year 2010, social insurance payments may be the main source of federal government receipts.

On the state and local government level, the two other principal sources of revenue are property taxes and an "other" category, which principally includes user fees (for example, special taxes for garbage collection, water and sewer usage, etc., and fees for parks, mass transit, etc.). Property taxes were the most important source of state and local government revenue in 1955, accounting for 38 percent, but by 1990, their share had dropped to 22 percent. Other taxes, in contrast, have risen from 27 to 35 percent. On the federal level, estate and gift taxes and other sources have remained relatively minor as a source of revenue.

The last panel of Table 16.6 shows the share of government receipts in GDP. This is another factor in determining the distributional effect of the tax system on family income. If total taxes represent only a small percent of

---

[33]This is not an arithmetic error! The reason is that state and local government receipts have been increasing *relative* to federal receipts over this period.

personal income, then their distributional impact will be small, irrespective of how progressive or regressive the tax structure is.[34]

Government receipts as a percent of GDP increased between 1955 and 1970, from 24 to 32 percent. However, what may be surprising is that the share has remained almost unchanged since 1970, at a little less than a third. Moreover, even between 1955 and 1970, federal receipts increased rather modestly as a share of GDP, from 17.0 to 19.6 percent. The biggest growth was on the state and local government level, whose income rose from 7.3 to 12.1 percent of GDP in 1970. In 1955, the federal budget was much bigger than the total budget of state and local governments (about $2^1/_2$ times larger) but by 1990, it was only 38 percent larger. However, it should be stressed even at this point that governmental receipts include income (principally, social security taxes) that is merely transferred from one set of individuals to another. When we "net" this out of the government account and look at the real expenditure side of the government sector, the size of the government sector appears much smaller (see Section 16.4)!

Before examining the effective tax rate structure, it might be elucidating to compare tax burdens in the United States with those of other industrialized countries. There is often the sense that the United States is a very heavily taxed society. We, of course, just saw that total taxes paid in the United States as a percent of GDP have remained about constant since 1970. However, how does the U.S. tax rate compare to that of other advanced economies?

Comparisons with other OECD countries are shown for both 1981 and 1990 in Table 16.7 (see also Figure 16.7). In 1990, the United States had the second lowest overall tax rate among OECD countries (only Turkey was lower), at 30 percent of GDP. The highest was Sweden, at 57 percent. Eight countries (including Sweden) paid more than 40 percent of their national income in the form of taxes, and all except Switzerland, Japan, Australia, the United States, and Turkey paid more than a third. Interestingly, Japan, the United States' chief economic rival, had a somewhat higher overall tax rate than the United States in 1990 (though it was lower in 1981). Canada's average tax rate in 1990 was 37 percent, compared to the United States' 30 percent.

The table also shows a breakdown of the sources of taxes for 1981. The United States was slightly below average in terms of individual income taxes, corporate income taxes, and payroll taxes. However, it was substantially below average in sales taxes—5.5 percent compared to an average OECD rate of 11.0 percent.

The United States thus appears to be one of the most lightly taxed countries in OECD. However, this does not mean that other countries are worse off than the United States. Indeed, other countries receive much more in

---

[34] Ideally, we would like to show total tax collections as a share of personal income. Unfortunately, it is not possible to identify whether the sources of some taxes, such as sales and property taxes, are individuals or businesses.

Table 16.7 Tax Revenues as a Percentage of Gross Domestic Product by Source Among OECD Countries, 1981 and 1990[a]

| | 1981 | | | | | | | 1990 |
	Individual Income	Corporate Income	Payroll	Sales[b]	Inheritances Property & gift		Total	Total
Sweden	20.5	1.5	16.6	12.3	0.3	0.1	51.3	56.9
Luxembourg								50.3
Denmark	23.7	1.3	1.0	17.0	2.1	0.2	45.3	48.6
Norway	12.8	7.8	10.1	17.0	0.8	0.0	48.5	46.3
Netherlands	11.2	3.2	18.2	11.2	1.5	0.2	45.5	45.2
Belgium	15.8	2.5	14.0	12.2	0.5	0.4	45.4	44.9
France	5.7	2.2	19.3	14.2	1.3	0.3	43.0	43.7
Austria	10.1	1.4	16.1	13.8	1.1	0.1	42.6	41.6
Italy	8.9	3.0	12.1	8.3	1.3	0.1	33.7	39.1
New Zealand								38.2
Finland								38.0
Germany	10.8	1.9	13.3	10.4	0.9	0.1	37.4	37.7
Ireland								37.2
Canada	11.8	4.0	4.0	12.1	2.9	0.0	34.8	37.1
United Kingdom	11.0	3.5	7.5	10.6	4.6	0.2	37.4	36.7
Greece								36.5
Portugal								34.6
Spain								34.4
Switzerland	10.8	1.8	9.3	6.1	2.0	0.2	30.2	31.7
Japan	6.6	5.5	8.1	4.4	2.1	0.2	26.9	31.3
Australia	14.4	3.5	1.6	9.5	2.4	0.1	31.5	30.8
United States	11.8	2.7	8.3	5.5	2.7	0.3	31.3	29.9
Turkey								27.8
Average	12.4	3.1	10.6	11.0	1.8	0.2	39.0	39.1

[a] Sources. 1981: Pechman (1983). 1990: U.S. Bureau of the Census (1993). Countries are ranked according to their 1990 ratio of taxes to GDP.
[b] Includes national and local taxes.

the way of publicly provided services from the state—particularly in regard to health care, which is almost entirely paid by the government in most other OECD countries, college tuition, which is almost completely provided for by the government, and an array of income support programs.

The Overall Effective Tax Structure

We now consider the effective tax rates by type of tax. These are shown in Table 16.8 by percentile level of the population, based on the work of

Figure 16.7   Tax Revenues as Percent of GDP: Selected OECD Countries, 1981 and 1990

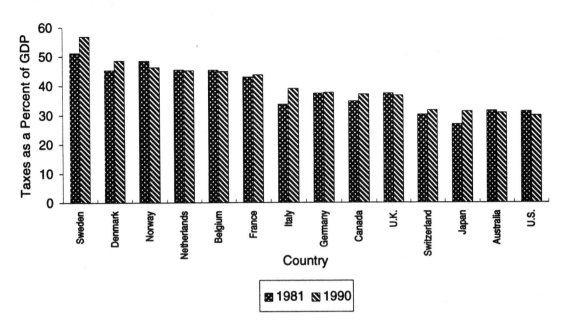

Joseph Pechman (1985). It should be noted at the outset that these calculations are based on statistical estimates. The raw data come from the Brookings MERGE file, which is a statistical match between household survey data from the Current Population Survey and actual federal tax returns provided by the Internal Revenue Service. The figures on federal individual income taxes paid are computed directly from the federal income tax returns. However, the estimates of payments of other taxes, such as payroll, property, and sales taxes, are simulated on the basis of the available data in the file (for example, sales taxes are estimated on the basis of personal consumption expenditures reported in the raw data, as well as sales tax rates by state of residence).

Moreover, assumptions have to be made regarding the *incidence* of each type of tax. For example, in the case of the corporate income tax, part of the tax is borne by stockholders in the company in the form of reduced profits (and hence reduced dividend payments and capital gains). However, part of the tax may be "shifted forward" to consumers in the form of higher prices for products of corporate enterprises, so that a portion of the tax is distributed among consumers of corporate products. Different assumptions can be made with regard to the relative proportions of the tax borne by each group. Similar problems exist with other kinds of taxes, principally sales taxes, property taxes, and payroll taxes.

Table 16.8 Effective Tax Rates by Specific Kinds of Federal, State, and Local Taxes for Each Population Decile and Top 5 and 1 Percent, 1985[a]

	Individual Income Tax	Corporate Income Tax	Payroll Taxes	Sales & Excise Taxes[b]	Property Tax	Total Taxes
A. *Most Progressive Incidence Assumptions Used in Simulation*						
Bottom decile	4.3	0.5	9.4	7.1	0.7	21.9
2nd decile	5.5	0.5	8.7	6.0	0.7	21.3
3rd decile	6.9	0.6	7.9	5.1	0.9	21.4
4th decile	8.2	0.6	7.9	4.8	0.9	22.5
5th decile	9.1	0.7	7.8	4.5	1.0	23.1
6th decile	9.8	0.8	7.5	4.3	1.2	23.5
7th decile	10.3	0.8	7.2	4.1	1.3	23.7
8th decile	11.4	0.9	7.0	3.9	1.3	24.6
9th decile	12.2	1.2	6.4	3.5	1.7	25.1
Top decile	12.7	3.6	3.6	2.0	3.3	25.3
Top 5 percent	12.7	4.5	2.6	1.6	3.8	25.2
Top 1 percent	12.8	5.7	1.4	1.2	4.4	25.5
All deciles	10.9	1.8	6.2	3.6	2.0	24.5
B. *Least Progressive Incidence Assumptions Used in Simulation*						
Bottom decile	4.1	2.8	10.8	7.3	3.3	28.2
2nd decile	5.4	2.3	9.5	5.8	2.5	25.6
3rd decile	6.8	2.0	8.6	5.0	2.1	24.6
4th decile	8.1	1.9	8.4	4.8	2.1	25.2
5th decile	8.9	1.9	8.1	4.4	2.1	25.3
6th decile	9.6	1.9	7.8	4.2	2.1	25.6
7th decile	10.0	1.9	7.4	4.0	2.1	25.4
8th decile	11.2	1.8	7.2	3.9	2.2	26.3
9th decile	12.0	1.9	6.5	3.4	2.3	26.1
Top decile	12.9	2.3	3.8	2.0	2.3	23.3
Top 5 percent	13.1	2.4	2.9	1.7	2.3	22.4
Top 1 percent	13.4	2.6	1.8	1.2	2.2	21.2
All deciles	10.9	2.1	6.5	3.6	2.3	25.3

[a] Source: Pechman (1985). The figures are based on statistical estimates from the Brookings MERGE file.
[b] Includes personal property and motor vehicle tax.

Figure 16.8a   Effective Tax Rates by Income Percentile (most progressive assumption)

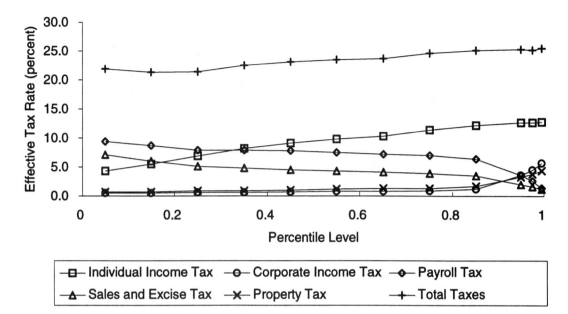

The two panels in Table 16.8 show the results of these simulations on the basis of incidence assumptions, which lead to the most progressive tax schedules and the least progressive tax schedules (also see Figures 16.8a and 16.8b). It is likely that the true effective tax structure lies in between these two extremes. However, with the exception of the corporate income tax and property tax, the results are quite similar in the two simulations.

The individual income tax is the most progressive tax, with effective tax rates varying from 4 percent for the lowest decile (10 percent of families) to 13 percent for the richest decile in 1985.[35] On average, the individual income tax amounted to 11 percent of family income in that year. The pattern of the corporate income tax is very sensitive to the incidence assumption used. If it is assumed that most of the corporate tax is borne by stockholders, then, as shown in Panel A, the effective tax rate is one percent or less for the bottom 90 percent of the income distribution and 3.6 percent for the top 10 percent (even higher for the top percentile). This result reflects the extreme concentration of stock ownership (see Section 10.3). On the other hand, if it is assumed that the tax is generally borne by consumers of products of corporations, then the tax is generally a flat (proportional) tax. In both cases, the average effective tax rate is quite small, about two percent.

---

[35] It should be noted that these results differ from those reported in Table 16.4 because of the use of the family unit here as opposed to the tax unit in Table 16.4, differences in income concepts, and other technical differences. See Pechman (1983) and Pechman (1985) for more discussion.

Figure 16.8b Effective Tax Rates by Income Percentile (least progressive assumption)

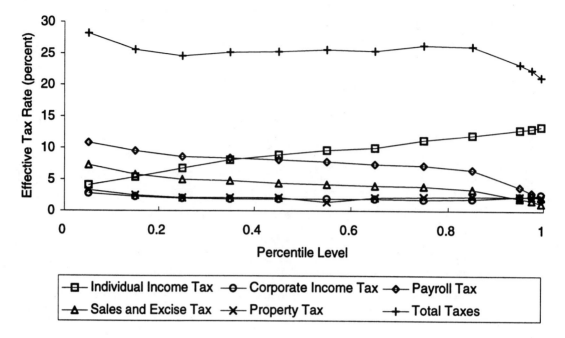

The payroll (mainly, social security) tax is mildly regressive over the bottom nine deciles and then turns extremely regressive at the top. This pattern reflects two factors. First, low-income families rely almost exclusively on wages and salaries as their source of income. As income increases, other sources of income, such as interest and dividends, become increasingly more important as a source of support. Second, in 1985, the maximum taxable wage base was $39,600. Wages and salaries above this level are not subject to the social security tax. On average, payroll taxes amounted to about 6 percent of total income.

General sales and excise taxes are steeply regressive, with effective tax rates varying from 7 percent for the poorest 10 percent of the population to 2 percent for the richest 10 percent. The reason is that the percentage of family income spent on goods and services subject to these taxes falls with family income. On average, the effective tax rate for sales and excise taxes was 3.6 percent in 1985. Property taxes are either highly progressive if it is assumed that they are fully borne by property owners (Panel A) or proportional if it is assumed that they are shifted to consumers in general (Panel B). The average effective tax rate of property taxes was about 2 percent.

Perhaps, the main point of interest is the total effect of all taxes on the distribution of income. This can be calculated by summing up the effective tax rates for the individual taxes. On average, in 1985, total taxes amounted to about 25 percent of personal income. Under the most progressive incidence assumptions, the total tax system is mildly progressive, with effective tax rates rising from 22 percent for the poorest decile to 25 percent for the richest. However, under the least progressive incidence assumptions, the total tax system is mildly regressive, with effective tax rates falling from 28 percent for the poorest decile to 21 percent for the richest. In all likelihood, the actual tax structure is generally a proportional tax on income.

How has the structure of effective tax rates changed over time? Estimates for three years—1966, 1975, and 1988—made by Joseph Pechman (1990) using the same methodology are shown in Table 16.9 (also see Figure 16.9). These are based on the most progressive incidence assumptions— namely, that all corporate taxes are borne by owners of corporate stock and all property taxes by owners of property. The average tax burden appears to have been about the same in these three years, about 25 percent of total income. However, it appears that the tax structure has become more progressive at the bottom of the income distribution but less progressive at the top.

In 1966, the effective tax rate was estimated to be 17 percent for the bottom decile, 19 percent for the second decile, between 22 and 23 percent for the third through ninth deciles, 30 percent for the top decile, and 40 percent for the richest one percent. In 1988, the effective tax rate for the

Table 16.9 Effective Tax Rates: Total of Federal, State, and Local Taxes by Population Percentiles, 1966, 1975, and 1988[a]

	Year		
Percentile	*1966*	*1975*	*1988*
Bottom decile	16.8	19.7	16.4
2nd decile	18.9	17.6	15.8
3rd decile	21.7	18.9	18.0
4th decile	22.6	21.7	21.5
5th decile	22.8	23.5	23.9
6th decile	22.7	23.9	24.3
7th decile	22.7	24.2	25.2
8th decile	23.1	24.7	25.6
9th decile	23.3	25.4	26.8
Top decile	30.1	27.8	27.7
Top 5 percent	32.7	28.4	27.4
Top 1 percent	39.6	29.0	26.8
All deciles	25.2	25.0	25.4

[a] Source: Pechman (1990). The figures are based on statistical estimates from the Brookings MERGE file. These estimates assume that all corporate income taxes and property taxes are borne by owners of these assets.

Figure 16.9 Effective Tax Rates: Total of Federal and State and Local Taxes, 1966, 1975, 1988

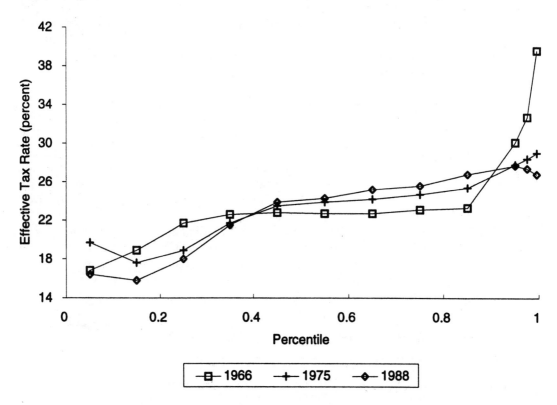

bottom decile was almost the same as in 1966, but the effective rate for the second and third deciles was lower (16 percent). Tax rates for deciles 4 to 9 were slightly higher in 1988 but lower for the top decile (28 percent). Indeed, the effective tax rate for the top one percent in 1988 was 27 percent, compared to 40 percent in 1966. This change reflects in part, the provisions of the 1986 Tax Reform Act.

Another way of posing this question is to compare Gini coefficients based on before-tax and after-tax income. If the difference between the before-tax and after-tax Gini coefficient increases over time, this implies that the tax structure has become more progressive; if the difference declines, it has become less progressive (or more regressive).

Two sets of estimates are shown in Table 16.10. The first (Panel A), from the Congressional Budget Office, is calculated from only federal taxes. In 1977, the Gini coefficient for before-tax income was 0.45 and that for after-federal tax income was 0.42, for a difference of 0.03. The difference was almost the same in 1980. However, in 1984 and 1988, the difference fell to 0.02, despite a large increase in before-tax inequality between 1980 and 1988. The federal tax structure, which was only mildly progressive in 1977

Table 16.10   Gini Coefficients of Before-Tax and After-Tax Income, 1977–1988, Selected Years

Year	Before-Tax Inequality	After-Tax Inequality	Difference
A. Before and After Federal Taxes[a]			
1977	0.450	0.419	0.032
1980	0.463	0.432	0.031
1984	0.488	0.470	0.018
1988	0.494	0.472	0.022
A. Before and After Federal Income Taxes[b]			
1972	0.468	0.445	0.023
1976	0.485	0.458	0.027
1980	0.496	0.467	0.029
1984	0.524	0.502	0.022
1988	0.567	0.544	0.023

[a] Source: U.S. Congressional Budget Office (1988).
[b] Source: Slemrod (1992).

and 1980, had become even less progressive in 1984 and 1988, a result, in part, of the declining top marginal tax rates from the 1981 and 1986 Tax Acts.

The second panel (Panel B), from Joel Slemrod (1992), is based only on federal income taxes. Slemrod also used an "expanded" concept of income, which is equal to the sum of AGI, excluded capital gains, excluded dividends, and other income adjustments. The trends are very similar to those shown in Panel A. The difference in the before-tax and after-tax Gini coefficient fell from 0.029 in 1980 to 0.022 in 1984. The difference was almost the same in 1988 as in 1984. Interestingly, Slemrod's results also show a widening gap between 1972 and 1980, from 0.023 to 0.029. According to the Slemrod figures, the redistributional effect of the federal income tax system increased during the 1970s and then declined during the 1980s, so that the difference in before-tax and after-tax inequality was almost the same in 1988 as in 1972.

The Negative Income Tax and the EITC

One proposal for helping the low-income population is the **negative income tax.** While reducing the income tax burdens on low-income families would obviously benefit them, there are two reasons why the effect would be relatively limited. First, most families with incomes below the poverty line do not pay any income taxes at all. Second, when poor individuals do pay income tax, the amounts are relatively small. Thus, even fully eliminating income taxes for this group (by, for example, raising the exemption level or standard deduction) would add little to their after-tax income.

As we discussed in the last chapter, the current method of helping poor families is through direct public transfers, such as AFDC, food stamps, Medicare, and housing subsidies. These programs target very specific subgroups of the poor (for example, AFDC is limited to families with children). Moreover, low-income families with working parents do not generally benefit from these transfer programs.

The negative income tax can be seen as an extension of the progressive structure of the income tax system to existing transfer programs. The major difference is that low-income taxpayers will now pay *negative* rates instead of low positive ones (that is, they will receive a payment from the federal government instead of making one). This is similar to the current workings of the **Earned Income Tax Credit (EITC),** in which a low-income family with labor earnings below a certain amount will receive a credit from the government. If they owe no income tax, the federal government will still refund the credit to the family (a refundable credit). See below for more discussion of the EITC.

A negative income tax could thus substitute for the various income transfer programs now in place. As a result, the system would be fairer and more comprehensive than the current transfer system. The administrative costs could also be substantially lower.

There have been different proposals for how such a tax would be structured. The simplest would work something like the following: All individuals or families would now file a federal tax return, including those whose income falls below the current minimum taxable level. As in the current system, taxpayers would compute their taxable income by subtracting the value of their exemptions and deductions from their AGI. The difference now is that if taxable income is negative, the taxpayer would be entitled to a payment from the federal government. The payment is computed by multiplying their (negative) taxable income by a new prespecified tax rate, say −50 percent.

Suppose that personal exemptions are each worth $2,000 and the standard deduction is $3,000 (see Figure 16.10). Then, a family of four with an AGI of $11,000 and taking the standard deduction would have a taxable income of exactly zero ($11,000 − 4 · $2,000 − $3,000). Such a family would pay no income taxes and receive no payment from the government. With these rates, $11,000 would be the "break-even" level. With a negative tax rate of 50 percent, a family with zero income would have a taxable income of −$11,000 and receive a payment from the government of $5,500 (half of $11,000). The $5,500 is referred to as the "basic allowance," since it is the minimum posttax income that would be allowed for a family of four.

As is apparent, the payment from the government would decline as income rises between zero and $11,000. For a family of four with $5,000,

Figure 16.10   Illustration of the Negative Income Tax

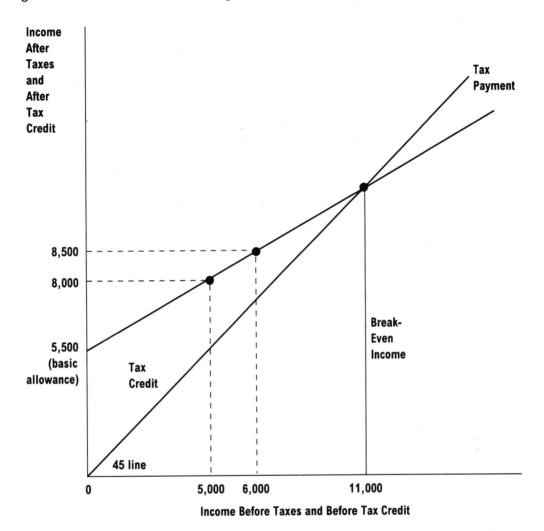

their taxable income would be −$6,000 and their payment from the government $3,000, so that their "posttax" income would be $8,000. If their income were $6,000, their posttax income would be $8,500 ($6,000 + $2,500). As a result, their posttax income would rise with pretax income, but the marginal gain would be only 50 cents for each additional dollar of income earned. For incomes above $11,000, positive tax rates would then go into effect.

As might be apparent, one criticism of the negative income tax is that it creates a disincentive for working.[36] In this example, with a "tax rate" of −50 percent, each additional dollar earned by a low-income family, below the break-even income level, will net it only 50 cents. The effective wage is thus reduced by half.

Between 1968 and 1982, the federal government sponsored four negative income tax experiments—New Jersey (1968–1972), Rural Iowa and North Carolina (1969–1973), Gary, Indiana (1971–1974), and Seattle and Denver (1971–1982). The experiments varied in their break-even level of income, but in all of them, the negative tax rate averaged about 50 percent. The results were remarkably consistent. All the experiments found a negative effect on labor supply associated with the introduction of a negative income tax, but the effects were relatively small. On average, husbands reduced their labor supply about two weeks, wives and single females by about three weeks, and youths by about four weeks (see Philip Robins, 1985, for a good summary of these results).

The EITC was introduced into the federal tax code in 1975, mainly as a way of offsetting increased social security taxes for low-income households. The credit operates as a fixed percentage (originally 10 percent in 1975) of earned income (wages, salaries, and tips) up to a prespecified ceiling ($5,000 originally), which is phased down to zero up to another fixed ceiling ($10,000 originally). The credit applies only to families who have *earned income* below a certain threshold. Moreover, the credit originally pertained only to families with children, though in 1993, it was expanded to include those without children as well.

One nice feature of this provision is that the tax credit is fully "refundable"—that is, the credit is sent to the taxpayer in the form of a check even if the credit exceeds the total tax liability of the tax filer. In this sense, the EITC operates like a negative income tax. However, its structure is different, as we will see below. Moreover, the credit depends only on earned income, not total family income.

The EITC was greatly expanded in the 1993 Omnibus Budget Reconciliation Act (OBRA93), which will be fully implemented by 1996. By 1996, the EITC is projected to cost the federal government $24.5 billion. This compares with a projected cost of AFDC of only $16 billion. The credit depends on the number of children in the family. In 1996, the maximum credit will be $3,370 for a family with two or more children, $2,040 for a family with one child, and $382.50 for those with no children.

The EITC is calculated in three income ranges: the phase-in range, the stationary range, and the phase-out range (see Figure 16.11). In 1996, families with two or more children will receive a credit equal to 40 percent of the first $8,425 of earned income and $3,370 for earned income between $8,425 and $11,000 (hence the term "stationary range"). For earned income above $11,000, the credit declines by 21.06 percent for each dollar

---

[36] A similar criticism is made about AFDC. See Section 15.5.

Figure 16.11   The Structure of the Earned Income Tax Credit for a Family of Two or More Children in 1996

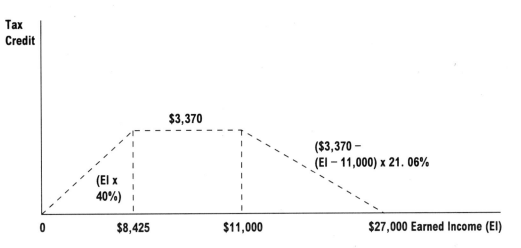

earned above $11,000. The credit becomes zero for incomes above $27,000. A family with an earned income of $6,000 (and two children), for example, will receive a credit of $2,400 (6,000 × .4); one with an earned income of $10,000 will receive a credit of $3,370; and one with earned income of $20,000 will receive $1,474.60 [3,370 − (20,000 − 11,000) × .2106].

One advantage of the EITC over a pure negative income tax is that the credit is tied to work. As a result, it has less of a disincentive effect on work. Moreover, it might actually encourage greater labor force participation on the part of low-income families, since the marginal benefit at the beginning of the schedule exceeds the marginal wage (the total gain from an additional hour of work is 1.4 times the actual wage received).

As Stacy Dickert, Scott Houser, and John Karl Scholz (1995) note, for those not in the labor force, the substitution effect associated with higher wages will provide an incentive to enter the labor market. In the phase-in range, the substitution effect provides an incentive to increase hours of work, while the income effect provides an incentive to decrease hours of work. In the stationary phase, only the income effect is operative, which leads to reduced hours of work. Finally, in the phase-out range, the net wage is now reduced by 21.06 percent for each additional dollar earned, so that both the substitution and income effect lead to reduced working hours (see Section 6.1 for more details on the income and substitution effect associated with a change in the wage rate).

According to calculations by Oren Levin-Waldman (1995), in 1994, only 28 percent of all EITC recipients had incomes in the phase-in range, 19 percent had incomes in the stationary range, and 53 percent had incomes in the phase-out range. As a result, most of the EITC recipients are in the income ranges where EITC creates a disincentive to work. However, Dickert,

Houser, and Scholz (1995) estimate that the overall effect on work hours is quite small: EITC reduces work hours by less than one percent. Moreover, when they include the positive effect of EITC on entry into the labor market, the net effect of EITC is to increase total hours worked.

16.4 THE DISTRIBUTIONAL EFFECTS OF GOVERNMENT EXPENDITURES

So far we have concerned ourselves with who pays the taxes. However, government taxes do not simply enter a "black hole" but are returned to individuals and families in two forms. The first form is government transfers, which are payments made by the government to individuals. We discussed the government transfer system in the previous chapter. In this regard, the government can be viewed as a holding company or "trust fund," which receives payments from individuals and disburses these funds to other individuals. (The social security system is, in fact, officially set up as a trust fund, which collects social security contributions from workers and employers and provides benefits to retirees.)

The second form consists of actual expenditures on goods and services made by the government, which directly or indirectly benefit individuals. Examples include education, highway construction and maintenance, hospitals, and sewerage treatment. In this sense, the government can be viewed as an enterprise which provides services to individual "clients." The major difference between the government and private enterprises (that is, corporations and small businesses) is that for most services the government does not charge fees directly to the user of the services. Rather, the costs are covered by general tax revenue, which may be collected from people who do not make use of the service. For example, public schools are usually financed through a local property tax, which is paid both by families with children and families without children. There may thus be little relation between taxes paid by individuals and the services they receive from the government.[37]

To get a complete picture of how the government affects the distribution of well-being in a country, it is necessary to look not only on the tax side but also on the transfer and expenditure side. The last chapter considered the distribution of government transfers. Here, we look at the distributional effects of government expenditures. What groups benefit from government expenditures, and how does this relate to the taxes paid by the group?

We begin by considering the functional structure of government expenditure (Table 16.11). The largest expenditure made by the federal govern-

---

[37] Many services provided by governments are paid for directly by the consumer in the form of user fees. Examples of these include toll highways, meter charges for water, local transit such as buses and subways, park admissions, and motor vehicle charges. Local governments are shifting more and more to user fees and away from general tax collection as a source of financing their activities.

Table 16.11 Percentage Distribution of Government Outlays by Function, 1981 and 1992

	1981	1992
Federal Government Outlays[a]		
National defense	23.2	21.6
International affairs	1.9	1.2
General science, space, and technology	1.0	1.2
Energy	2.2	0.3
Natural resources and environment	2.0	1.4
Agriculture	1.7	1.1
Commerce and housing credit	1.2	0.7
Transportation	3.4	2.4
Community and regional development	1.6	0.5
Education, training, employment, and social services	5.0	3.3
Health	4.0	6.5
Medicare	5.8	8.6
Income security	14.7	14.3
Social security	20.6	20.8
Veterans benefits and services	3.4	2.5
Administration of justice	0.7	1.0
General government	1.7	0.9
Net interest	10.1	14.4
Undistributed offsetting receipts	−4.1	−2.8
Total	100.0	100.0
State and Local Government Outlays[b]		
Education	35.9	36.9
Highways	8.5	9.6
Public welfare	12.9	23.3
Health and hospitals	8.9	3.5
Police and fire	5.2	9.7
Natural resources	1.5	0.9
Sewerage and other sanitation	3.7	1.6
Housing and urban renewal	1.7	0.3
General control and financial administration	4.1	6.1
Interest on debt	4.2	0.5
Other	13.2	7.6
Total	100.0	100.0

[a] Source: *Economic Report of the President, 1993.*
[b] Sources. 1981: Pechman (1983); 1992: *Survey of Current Business,* Vol. 73, No. 9, September 1993.

ment is for national defense. This constituted 23 percent of federal outlays in 1981 and 22 percent in 1992. The second biggest outlay is for social security, which amounted to 21 percent in both years. Health and Medicare together made up 15 percent of federal spending in 1992, up from 10 percent in 1981. Net interest (mainly interest payments on the national debt) amounted to 14 percent of federal spending in 1992, compared to 10 percent in 1981. Income security programs, including AFDC, unemployment insurance, workmen's compensation, and veteran's benefits, ate up 14 percent of the federal budget in 1992, about the same as in 1981. The other federal government programs are relatively small, in contrast. In 1992, for example, the following each comprised about one percent of the budget: international affairs; science, space, and technology; natural resources and the environment; agriculture; the administration of justice; and general government.

On the state and local government level, the largest budget item is education, which made up 36 percent of their combined outlays in 1981 and 37 percent in 1992. Public welfare, including welfare payments and social services, workmen's compensation, disability insurance, and medical care, comprised another 23 percent in 1992, way up from its 13 percent share in 1981 (the main reason is increased health care costs); while health and hospitals amounted to 4 percent in 1992 (down from 1981); highways 10 percent; and police and fire protection also 10 percent in 1992, almost double its share in 1981. The other government functions are relatively small.

The question of who benefits from government expenditures is not an easy one to answer. The general procedure is to take the government programs and allocate the expenditures on them to the individuals who directly benefit from them. For some government expenditures, this allocation is relatively easy. For example, educational expenses can be allotted in direct proportion to the number of school children in each family. However, the beneficiaries of others, such as national defense, international affairs, and science and technology, are more difficult to determine.

The most careful study to date on the distributional effects of government expenditure in the United States was conducted by Patricia Ruggles and Michael O'Higgins (1981), though, unfortunately, the analysis was performed on 1970 data. In many cases, the beneficiaries of government programs could be directly identified. On the federal level, social security benefits were allocated directly to their beneficiaries; veteran health benefits to disabled veterans; educational expenditures to households with students enrolled in colleges; and public assistance to welfare recipients. Agricultural expenditures were divided on the basis of farm insurance. Labor Department expenditures were distributed on the basis of wages and salaries. For highway expenditures, it was assumed that two-thirds of the benefits accrued to individual car owners and one-third to trucking. The first portion was allocated on the basis of household car ownership and the second share was distributed in proportion to household consumption, since the goods carried by truckers are eventually consumed by families. Expenditures on general federal programs, such as national defense, international affairs, justice, science, energy, environment, were divided among families in proportion to the number of individuals in the family.

On the state and local government level, school expenditures were allocated on the basis of the number of school age children in the household; higher education expenditures on the basis of the number of college students; health and hospital expenditures on the basis of the number of patients in the family; and unemployment insurance on the basis of employment status. Police and fire expenses were divided among families according to family size.

The results are shown in Table 16.12. This table shows the taxes paid by each income decile (tenths of the population ordered from lowest to highest), as well as the benefits received from the various government programs. The first line shows the average before-tax income by decile. The first line of Panel A shows that the average benefit received from the programs of the federal government amounted to $2,917 in 1970. The largest portion of this is general federal expenditures (particularly national defense), which amounted to $1,829 on average, followed by social security benefits, $718 on average, and veteran's benefits, $156. The other programs are relatively small, as noted above. The average federal tax burden in 1970 was $3,251, so that the net benefits received (the difference between the benefit level and the taxes paid) from the federal government was negative, −$333 ($2,917 − $3,251, when allowance is made for rounding error).

On the state and local government level (Panel B), the average family benefit was $2,515. The biggest source was education, where the expenditures both on primary and secondary schooling and higher education averaged $932 per family. Highway expenditures yielded an average benefit of $274, public assistance $271, health and hospitals $177, and police and fire together $151. Average taxes paid to state and local governments were $2,099, so that the net benefit received by families was $416. Combining the federal and state and local government levels, the authors calculate an average net benefit of $83, because government expenditures were slightly greater than tax receipts (Panel C).

The most interesting results are obtained by comparing the benefits and taxes of the different income deciles. On the federal level, average benefits were almost twice as great for the second decile as the first ($2,636 versus $1,451) and somewhat greater for the third than the second decile ($3,250 versus $2,636) but very similar for the third through top decile. The reason is that average social security benefits were much higher for the second and third income deciles than for the first but then tapered off with income among the upper income deciles, whereas the benefits from other government expenditures generally increased with income level. On the other hand, benefits from state and local government expenditures did tend to rise with income level, though the difference in average benefits was rather small among deciles. The main reason for this is that average benefits from public schooling expenditures were greater for richer families. On the other

Table 16.12   Average Taxes Paid to and Benefits Received From the Federal Government and State and Local Governments by Decile of Before-Tax Income, 1970[a]

	All Deciles	Lowest Decile	2nd Decile	3rd Decile	4th Decile	5th Decile	6th Decile
Mean before-tax family income	9,685	1,018	2,385	3,930	5,693	7,429	9,228
A. *Federal Government*							
1. Benefits	2,917	1,451	2,636	3,250	3,217	3,014	2,985
a. Social security	718	367	1,345	1,448	1,119	801	484
b. Agriculture	87	1	20	47	89	55	63
c. Labor	7	—	—	1	3	5	7
d. Veteran's benefits	156	41	48	85	123	141	193
e. Housing	36	52	78	76	76	43	13
f. Education	45	95	35	20	38	25	37
g. Welfare	33	18	66	102	34	23	29
h. Highways	6	1	2	3	4	5	6
i. Others	1,829	876	1,042	1,468	1,731	1,916	2,153
2. Taxes	3,251	765	951	1,321	1,864	2,455	3,150
3. Net benefits[b]	−333	685	1,685	1,928	1,352	559	−165
B. *State and Local Governments*							
1. Benefits	2,515	2,344	1,700	2,365	2,158	2,199	2,608
a. Schooling	715	192	171	417	548	694	895
b. Higher education	217	478	180	94	172	124	168
c. Highways	274	50	99	164	225	272	315
d. Public assistance	271	158	530	873	285	207	190
e. Health and hospitals	177	1,043	209	123	57	42	47
f. Fire	36	16	19	27	31	35	42
g. Police	115	50	61	89	102	113	132
h. Unemployment insurance	91	44	36	96	117	109	85
i. Housing	37	47	75	82	79	44	13
j. Others	582	266	320	400	542	559	721
2. Taxes	2,099	614	867	1,225	1,546	1,809	2,163
3. Net benefits[b]	416	1,730	833	1,140	612	390	445
C. *Total Net Benefits[b]*	83	2,415	2,518	3,068	1,964	949	280
D. *Mean Income After Taxes and Benefits*							
Dollar value	9,768	3,433	4,903	6,998	7,657	8,378	9,508
Ratio to before-tax income	1.01	3.37	2.06	1.78	1.34	1.13	1.03

(continued)

Table 16.12 *(concluded)*

	7th Decile	8th Decile	9th Decile	Highest Decile
Mean before-tax family income	11,030	13,142	16,244	27,288
A. *Federal Government*				
1. Benefits	3,010	3,135	3,093	3,402
a. Social security	466	411	379	339
b. Agriculture	70	88	70	366
c. Labor	8	10	13	18
d. Veteran's benefits	218	254	222	238
e. Housing	7	6	6	6
f. Education	37	50	54	64
g. Welfare	21	15	8	7
h. Highways	7	8	9	11
i. Others	2,176	2,293	2,332	2,353
2. Taxes	3,708	4,457	5,489	8,518
3. Net benefits[b]	−698	−1,322	−2,396	−5,115
B. *State and Local Governments*				
1. Benefits	2,563	2,859	3,089	3,161
a. Schooling	996	1,035	1,131	1,098
b. Higher education	172	232	237	306
c. Highways	331	386	404	507
d. Public assistance	137	129	119	46
e. Health and hospitals	62	59	59	59
f. Fire	42	46	51	53
g. Police	134	147	156	164
h. Unemployment insurance	104	86	119	117
i. Housing	6	6	7	6
j. Others	579	733	806	805
2. Taxes	2,402	2,772	3,230	4,446
3. Net benefits[b]	161	87	−141	−1,285
C. *Total Net Benefits*[b]	−537	−1,235	−2,537	−6,400
D. *Mean Income After Taxes and Benefits*				
Dollar value	10,493	11,907	13,707	20,888
Ratio to before-tax income	0.95	0.91	0.84	0.77

[a]Source: Ruggles and O'Higgins (1981). Figures are for families in dollars per year.
[b]Benefits received less taxes paid.

hand, the benefits from public assistance, health and hospitals, and housing expenditures were higher at the lower income levels.

As we saw in Section 16.3, taxes paid tend to rise more or less in proportion to family income. As a result, net government benefits (the difference between benefits received and taxes paid) fell off rather precipitously with income level (at least after the third decile of income), from a high of $3,068 for families in the third decile to a low of –$6,400. Net benefits were positive for the bottom six deciles but negative for the top four deciles. Moreover, in relation to before-tax income, the bottom deciles were the clear winners from government expenditures. If we add government benefits and subtract out taxes from original income, then the average income of the bottom decile more than triples, that of the second decile doubles, that of the third decile rises by about three-fourths, and that of the fourth decile by a third (Panel D). The fifth through eighth deciles see little change in their income. The ninth decile suffers a 16 percent reduction in their income level, and the highest decile a 23 percent reduction.

Thus, while the tax system by itself does not have much redistributional impact, the benefits from government expenditures do. Net government benefits clearly help the lower income classes at the expense of the upper income groups. As a result, the government fiscal system as a whole does tend to reduce inequality in living standards.

16.5 SUMMARY

Income equality is often included as a basic public policy objective. Three distinct grounds are often used to justify this position: (1) The first, based on a notion of fairness, argues that individuals in a society are *entitled* to certain rights and privileges based on their citizenship, including a share of society's output. (2) The second is derived from utilitarianism. If it is assumed that there is a diminishing marginal utility of income and everyone's utility function is identical, then equality will maximize the total utility of individuals in a society. (3) The third is a maximin position, which advocates a system of distribution that would maximize the minimum level of income that would be available to each individual in a society.

There are also two common arguments against promoting greater income equality in society. (1) The first is based on a concept of fairness, which guarantees that each individual has the same basic political rights and economic opportunities but not necessarily the same economic incomes. (2) The second is the growth position, which maintains that paying higher wages to workers who are more productive serves as an *incentive* for everyone to work harder and thus increases total output.

A governments affects income inequality both by its tax system and the distribution of its expenditures. With regard to the tax system, we generally distinguish among three types: (1) a proportional tax, in which the average tax rate remains constant over income levels; (2) a progressive tax, in which the average tax rate rises with income; and (3) a regressive tax, in which the average tax rate falls with income. We also distinguish between the average tax rate, the ratio of tax payments to income, and the marginal tax rate, the taxes paid on an additional dollar of income. A proportional tax leaves income inequality unchanged (that is, the level of after-tax inequality is the same as that of before-tax inequality), a progressive tax reduces income inequality, and a regressive tax increases income inequality.

Comparisons of the overall distribution of before-tax and after-tax income come under the province of vertical equity. A different consideration is horizontal equity, which refers to a comparison of the before-tax and after-tax position of individual taxpayers. There are two basic principles: The first is that the tax system should levy identical taxes on taxpayers with the same income. The second principle, called "rank preservation," maintains that the tax system should not change the rank order of tax payers.

The federal individual income tax has been in effect since 1913. The basic income concept is Adjusted Gross Income (AGI), which is equal to ordinary money income plus realized capital gains less interest from state and local government bonds, most of social security income, welfare payments, and other excluded items. Tax payments are based on taxable income, which equals AGI less exemptions and deductions. Different tax schedules are provided for married couples, single individuals, and heads of households.

The tax schedule is progressive, with marginal tax rates rising in stepwise fashion with AGI. The tax structure has changed frequently over time. The top marginal rate was set at 7 percent in 1913, rose to 67 percent in 1917, was reduced during the 1930s, increased to 94 percent in 1944, fell to 70 percent during the 1960s and 1970s, was lowered to 50 percent in 1981 and to 28 percent in 1986 but has since been raised to 40 percent in 1993. The reduction in marginal tax rates since the end of World War II has benefited the rich considerably more than the poor.

The tax schedule shows the nominal tax rates, the ratio between tax liability and taxable income. The effective tax rate is the ratio of actual tax payments to total taxpayer income. For the personal income tax, there are several sources of difference between the two: (1) the number of exemptions a taxpayer can claim, (2) income deductions, (3) exclusions to ordinary income, (4) income adjustments, (5) the use of tax preference items, (6) the availability of tax credits, and (7) the imposition of the Alternative Minimum Tax.

Differences between nominal and effective tax rates are quite large. The result of these special provisions of the tax code reduced the average tax rate by about two-thirds in 1985, from its nominal level of 30 percent to only 12 percent. The biggest effect comes from deductions. Overall, the rich benefit more from the availability of tax reduction provisions of the tax code. Tax liability was reduced by 13 percentage points in 1985 for the lowest income class and 26 percentage points for the highest.

The payroll tax is the second largest source of federal government revenue. When it was first introduced in 1937, the social security tax was 1.0 percent on wages and salaries for both the employee and employer, and the tax was levied on earnings up to $3,000. By 1994, the tax rate had been raised to 7.65, and the earnings limit to $60,600. Unemployment insurance is a second form of payroll tax but is considerably smaller.

Another source of federal revenue is the corporation income tax, established in 1909. The basic tax rate was raised from 38 percent in 1946 to 52 percent in 1952, where it generally remained until 1969. It has since been lowered to 48 percent in 1971, 46 percent in 1979, and 35 percent in 1993. Other federal levies include the excise tax, customs duties, and the estate and gift tax.

State governments rely on two major sources of revenues—income taxes and general sales taxes. The principal source of revenue for local governments is the property tax. In addition, there are often "user fees" for specific services provided by local governments, such as water and sewerage and sanitation collection.

Federal individual income taxes are the main source of federal government revenue, comprising anywhere from 42 to 46 percent between 1955 and 1993. Revenue from state and local individual income taxes increased rather sharply, from 4 to 15 percent of total state and local government receipts between 1955 and 1990. However, together, personal income taxes made up a relatively constant share of about one-third of total government revenue between 1955 and 1990.

In contrast, federal corporate income tax proceeds have fallen sharply, from 27 percent of total federal revenue in 1955 to only 10 percent in 1993. On the state level, corporate taxes remained rather steady at 3 to 4 percent of total state and local government revenue. Together, corporate income taxes fell from 20 percent of total government revenue in 1955 to only 7 percent in 1990.

Federal excise taxes also showed a sharp decline as a source of federal government revenue, from 14 to only 4 percent over the years from 1955 to 1993. Customs duties and fees have remained small, accounting for only 1 to 2 percent of total federal income. Among state and local governments, sales taxes comprised between 25 and 27 percent of their income, with the share staying relatively constant over time. Together, sales, excise, and customs taxes diminished as a source of total government receipts, from 19 percent in 1955 to 14 percent in 1990.

The most dramatic growth occurred in payroll (mainly social security) taxes, which rose from 12 percent of federal revenue in 1955 to 37 percent in 1993. It also increased from 8 percent of total government income to 22 percent. Property taxes were the most important source of state and local government revenue in 1955, accounting for 38 percent, but by 1990 their share had dropped to 22 percent. Other taxes and special user fees, in contrast, have risen from 27 to 35 percent.

Government receipts as a percent of GDP grew from 24 to 32 percent between 1955 and 1970. However, its share has remained almost unchanged since 1970, at a little less than a third. Moreover, even between 1955 and 1970, federal receipts increased rather modestly as a share of GDP, from

17 to 20 percent, while state and local government income surged from 7 to 12 percent of GDP.

Comparisons with other OECD countries show that the United States is one of the least taxed countries among the advanced economies. In 1990, the United States had the second lowest overall tax rate among OECD countries (only Turkey was lower), at 30 percent of GDP. The highest was Sweden, at 57 percent. Eight countries (including Sweden) paid more than 40 percent of their national income in the form of taxes, and all except five paid more than a third.

Analysis of the overall effective tax rate structure in the United States reveals that the individual income tax is the most progressive tax, with effective tax rates varying from 4 percent for the lowest decile to 13 percent for the richest decile in 1985. The payroll (mainly, social security) tax is mildly regressive over the bottom nine deciles and then turns extremely regressive at the top. Sales taxes are highly regressive, with effective tax rates varying from 7 percent for the poorest 10 percent of the population to 2 percent for the richest 10 percent. Under the most progressive incidence assumptions, the total tax system is mildly progressive, with effective tax rates increasing from 22 percent for the poorest decile to 25 percent for the richest. However, under the least progressive incidence assumptions, the total tax system is mildly regressive, with effective tax rates declining from 28 percent for the poorest decile to 21 percent for the richest. In actuality, the total tax system is likely to be a basically proportional tax on income.

Has the effective tax structure changed over time? In 1966, the effective tax rates ranged from 17 percent for the bottom decile to 30 percent for the top decile and 40 percentile for the richest one percent. In 1988, the effective tax rate for the bottom decile was almost the same as in 1966, but the effective rate for the top one percent was 27 percent. A comparison of before-tax income and after-tax income Gini coefficients also indicates that the federal tax structure, which was only mildly progressive in 1977 and 1980, had become even less progressive in 1984 and 1988.

The government provides benefits to individuals and families in two forms: transfer payments and expenditures on goods and services. To obtain a full picture of the role of the government in the distribution of well-being in a country, it is necessary to look not only on the tax collection side but also on the transfer and expenditure side. The largest expenditure made by the federal government is on national defense (22 percent in 1992), followed by social security (21 percent), health and Medicare (15 percent), net interest (14 percent), and income security programs (also 14 percent). The other federal government programs are relatively small. On the state and local government level, the largest budget item is education (37 percent in 1992), followed by public welfare (23 percent), highways (10 percent), police and fire protection (also 10 percent), and health and hospitals (4 percent).

The question of who benefits from government expenditures involves allocating the expenditures of each government program to the individuals who directly benefit from them. An analysis on 1970 data indicates that net benefits from government (the difference between benefits received and taxes paid) fall rather precipitously with income level (at least after the third decile of income), from a high of $3,068 for families in the third decile to a low of −$6,400. Moreover, relative to before-tax income, the bottom deciles are the clear winners from government expenditures. Thus, while the tax system by itself does not have much redistributional impact, net government benefits clearly help the lower income classes relative to the upper income groups.

REFERENCES

Aaron, Henry J., and Harvey Galper, *Assessing the Income Tax*, Brookings Institution, Washington, D.C., 1985.

———, and Michael J. Boskin, (eds.), *The Economics of Taxation*, Brookings Institution, Washington, D.C., 1980.

Berliant, Marcus C., and Robert P. Strauss, "The Horizontal and Vertical Equity Characteristics of the Federal Individual Income Tax, 1966–1977," in Martin David and Timothy Smeeding (eds.), 1985, *op. cit.*

———, "State and Federal Tax Equity: Estimates Before and After the Tax Reform Act of 1986," *Journal of Policy Analysis and Management*, Vol. 12, No. 1, 1993, pp. 9–43.

Bird, Richard M., "Income Redistribution Through the Fiscal System: The Limits of Knowledge," *American Economic Review*, Vol. 70, No. 2, May 1980, pp. 77–81.

Blum, W. J. and Kalven, H., *The Uneasy Case for Progressive Taxation*, Chicago, Ill., Chicago University Press, 1953.

Boskin, Michael J., "Tax Policy and Economic Growth: Lessons From the 1980s," *Journal of Economic Perspectives*, Vol. 2, No. 4, Fall 1988, pp. 71–97.

Bosworth, Barry, *Tax Incentives and Economic Growth*, Brookings Institution, Washington, D.C., 1984.

———, and Gary Burtless, "Effects of Tax Reform on Labor Supply, Investment, and Saving," *Journal of Economic Perspectives*, Vol. 6, No. 1, Winter 1992, pp. 3–25.

Bradford, David F., *Untangling the Income Tax*, Harvard University Press, Cambridge, Mass., 1986.

Browning, Edgar K., "The Trend Toward Equality in the Distribution of Net Income," *Southern Economic Journal*, Vol. 43, No. 1, July 1976, pp. 912–923.

———, and William R. Johnson, *The Distribution of the Tax Burden*, American Enterprise Institute, Washington, D.C., 1979.

David, Martin, and Timothy Smeeding (eds.), *Horizontal Equity, Uncertainty, and Economic Well-Being*, Studies in Income and Wealth, Vol. 50, National Bureau of Economic Research, Chicago University Press, Chicago, 1985.

Davies, David G., "Progressiveness of a Sales Tax in Relation to Various Income Bases," *American Economic Review*, Vol. 50, No. 5, December 1960, pp. 987–995.

Davies, James, Frances St-Hilaire, and John Whalley, "Some Calculations of Lifetime Tax Incidence," *American Economic Review*, Vol. 74, No. 4, September 1984, pp. 633–649.

Dickert, Stacy, Scott Houser, and John Karl Scholz, "The Earned Income Tax Credit and Transfer Programs: A Study of Labor Market and Program Participation," in James M. Poterba (ed.), *Tax Policy and the Economy*, Vol. 9, MIT Press for the National Bureau of Economic Research, Cambridge, Mass., 1995, pp. 1–50.

Frank, Robert H., *Choosing the Right Pond*, Oxford University Press, New York, 1985.

Fullerton, Don, and Diane Lim Rogers, *Who Bears the Lifetime Tax Burden?* Brookings Institution, Washington, D.C., 1993.

Gramlich, E., R. Kasten, and F. Sammartino, "Growing Inequality in the 1980s: The Role of Federal Taxes and Cash Transfers," in S. Danziger and P. Gottschalk (eds.), *Uneven Tides: Rising Inequality in the 1980s*, Russell Sage, New York, 1991.

Gravelle, Jane G., "Equity Effects of the Tax Reform Act of 1986," *Journal of Economic Perspectives*, Vol. 6, No. 1, Winter 1992, pp. 27–44.

Goode, Richard, *The Individual Income Tax*, revised edition, Brookings Institution, Washington, D.C., 1976.

Haveman, Robert, *Starting Even*, Simon and Schuster for the Twentieth Century Fund, New York, 1988.

Jenkins, Stephen, P., "Empirical Measurement of Horizontal Equity," *Journal of Public Economics*, Vol. 37, No. 3, 1988, pp. 305–330.

Kakwani, N., "Measurement of Tax Progressivity: An International Comparison," *The Economic Journal*, Vol. 87, 1977, pp. 71–80.

Kaplow, L., "Horizontal Equity: Measures in Search of a Principle," *National Tax Journal*, Vol. 42, No. 2, 1989, pp. 139–154.

Kern, B. B., "The Tax Reform Act of 1986 and Progressivity of the Individual Income Tax," *Public Finance Quarterly*, Vol. 18, No. 3, 1990, pp. 259–272.

Kiefer, D. W., "Distributional Tax Progressivity Indexes," *National Tax Journal*, Vol. 37, No. 4, 1984, pp. 487–514.

King, Mervyn A., "How Effective Have Fiscal Policies Been in Changing the Distribution of Income and Wealth," *American Economic Review*, Vol. 70, No. 2, May 1980, pp. 72–76.

———, "An Index of Inequality: With Applications to Horizontal Equity and Social Mobility," *Econometrica*, Vol. 51, No. 1, 1983, pp. 99–115.

Kurz, Mordecai, "Negative Income Taxation," *Federal Tax Reform: Myths and Realities*, Institute for Contemporary Studies, San Francisco, Calif., 1978.

Levin-Waldman, Oren M., "The Consolidated Assistance Program," *Jerome Levy Economics Institute Public Policy Brief*, No. 21, 1995.

Marx, Karl, and Frederic Engels, "The Manifesto of the Communist Party," 1848, in Karl Marx and Frederic Engels (eds.), *Selected Works*, International Publishers, New York, 1968.

Minarik, Joseph K., "Who Doesn't Bear the Tax Burden," in Henry J. Aaron and Michael J. Boskin (eds.), *The Economics of Taxation,* Brookings Institution, Washington, D.C., 1980, pp. 55–68.

Musgrave, R. A., and P. B. Musgrave, *Public Finance in Theory and Practice,* 5th ed., McGraw Hill, New York, 1989.

OECD (Organization of Economic Cooperation and Development), *Income Tax Schedules: Distribution of Taxpayers and Revenues,* OECD Committee on Fiscal Affairs, Paris, 1981.

———, (Organization of Economic Cooperation and Development), *Tax Expenditures: A Review of the Issues and Country Practices,* OECD Committee on Fiscal Affairs, Paris, 1984.

———, (Organization for Economic Cooperation and Development), *Taxation of Net Wealth, Capital Transfers and Capital Gains of Individuals,* OECD, Paris, 1988.

O'Higgins, Michael, and Ruggles, Patricia, "The Distribution of Public Expenditures and Taxes among Households in the United Kingdom," *Review of Income and Wealth,* Series 27, 1981, pp. 298–326.

Okner, Benjamin A., "Total U.S. Taxes and Their Effect on the Distribution of Family Income in 1966 and 1970," in Henry J. Aaron and Michael J. Boskin (eds.), *The Economics of Taxation,* Brookings Institution, Washington, D.C., 1980, pp. 69–84.

——— and Joseph A. Pechman, "Who Paid the Taxes in 1966?" *American Economic Review,* Vol. 64, No. 2, May 1974, pp. 168–174.

———, *Who Bears the Tax Burden?* Brookings Institution, Washington, D.C., 1974.

Pechman, Joseph A., *Federal Tax Policy,* Fourth ed., Brookings Institution, Washington, D.C., 1983.

———, *Who Paid the Taxes, 1966–1985?* Brookings Institution, Washington, D.C., 1985.

———, "The Future of the Income Tax," *American Economic Review,* Vol. 80, No. 1, March 1990, pp. 1–20.

Pechman, J. A., and Okner, B., *Who Bears the Tax Burden?* Brookings Institution, Washington, D.C., 1974.

Phelps-Brown, E. H., *Egalitarianism and the Generation of Inequality,* Oxford University Press, Oxford, 1988.

Plotnick, Robert, "The Concept and Measurement of Horizontal Inequity" *Journal of Public Economics,* Vol. 17, No. 2, 1982, pp. 373–392.

———, "A Comparison of Measures of Horizontal Inequity," in Martin David and Timothy Smeeding (eds.), 1985, *op. cit.*

Quigley, John M., and Eugene Smolensky, "Redistribution with Several Levels of Government: The Recent U.S. Experience," in Remy Prud'homme (ed.), *Public Finance with Several Levels of Government,* Proceedings of the 46th Congress of the International Institute of Public Finance, Brussels, 1990, pp. 125–136.

Rawls, John, *A Theory of Justice,* Harvard University Press, Cambridge, Mass., 1971.

Reynolds, M., and Smolensky, Eugene, *Public Expenditures, Taxes, and the Distribution of Income: The United States, 1950, 1961, 1970*, Academic Press, New York, 1977.

Robins, Philip K., "A Comparison of the Labor Supply Findings From the Four Negative Income Tax Experiments," *Journal of Human Resources*, Vol. 20, No. 4, Fall 1985, pp. 567–582.

Ruggles, Patricia, and Michael O'Higgins, "The Distribution of Public Expenditure Among Households in the United States," *Review of Income and Wealth*, Series 27, 1981, pp. 137–163.

Slemrod, Joel, "Taxation and Inequality: A Time-Exposure Perspective," in James M. Poterba (ed.), *Tax Policy and the Economy*, MIT Press for the National Bureau of Economic Research, Cambridge, Mass., 1992.

Suits, D., "Measurement of Tax Progressivity," *American Economic Review*, Vol. 67, 1977, pp. 747–752.

Thurow, Lester C., "The Indirect Incidence of Government Expenditures," *American Economic Review*, Vol. 70, 1980, pp. 82–87.

U.S. Bureau of the Census, *Statistical Abstract of the United States: 1993*, 113th Edition, U.S. Government Printing Office, Washington, D.C., 1993.

U.S. Congressional Budget Office, *The Changing Distribution of Federal Taxes: A Closer Look at 1980*, July 1988.

Wertz, K. L., "A Method of Measuring the Relative Taxation of Families," *Review of Economics and Statistics*, Vol. 60, 1978, pp. 145–160.

Young, H. Peyton, "Progressive Taxation and Equal Sacrifice," *American Economic Review*, Vol. 80, March 1990, pp. 253–266.

DISCUSSION QUESTIONS

1. Discuss the difference between regressive, progressive, and proportional taxes. How do average and marginal tax rates vary with income for each type of tax?

2. Define the effective tax rate. Why is the effective tax structure of the personal income tax less progressive than the actual IRS tax schedule?

3. Give two reasons why the social security tax is mildly regressive with respect to family income.

4. What is the effect of total personal taxes on the size distribution of family income in the United States?

5. What advantages does a negative income tax have over current income transfer programs? What are the disadvantages? In what sense is the EITC a negative income tax?

6. Discuss why the net benefits from government expenditure have a more progressive effect on the distribution of family well-being than taxes do.

NAME INDEX

Garbarino, Joseph W., 324
Garfinkel, Irwin, 121, 589
Germidis, Dimitrios, 37
Ghez, Gilbert, 517
Gilroy, Curtis, 598
Gini, Corrado, 63
Gintis, Herbert, 261, 262
Gittleman, Maury, 307, 330, 336
Goldberger, A. S., 253, 254
Goldin, Claudia, 533
Goldschmidt-Clemont, Luisella, 40
Goldsmith, Raymond W., 355
Goldsmith, Selma, 72
Gordon, David M., 303, 304
Gordon, Robert, 168
Gordon, Roger H., 403, 408, 411, 584
Gottschalk, Peter, 543, 544, 592
Graham, John W., 475
Gramlich, Edward M., 592, 598
Grant, Arthur, 35, 36
Green, Alan G., 319
Greenwood, Daphne, 412, 413
Griliches, Zvi, 250
Grimes, Donald R., 155
Grossman, Jean, 594
Gunderson, Morely, 538, 541, 546
Gustafson, Thomas A., 409
Gwartney, James D., 479, 483, 487, 523

Haber, William, 578
Hagenaars, Aldi J. M., 94, 95
Hager, 250
Hammermesh, Daniel S., 400, 403
Hanoch, Giora, 231, 243, 486
Hansen, W. Lee, 118, 250, 381, 382
Hanushek, Eric A., 320
Harbury, C. D., 421
Harrington, Michael, 107, 567
Harrison, A. J., 364
Hartmann, Heidi I., 533
Hartsog, Catherine E., 295
Hause, John, 250
Hauser, Richard, 108, 109
Hausman, Jerry A., 403, 408, 589
Haveman, Robert, 66, 94, 121, 584, 589, 599, 600, 615
Haworth, Charles T., 327, 487
Haworth, Joan G., 487

Hawrylyshyn, Oli, 40
Hayashi, Fumio, 420
Hayes, K. J., 74
Hearnshaw, L. S., 252
Heckman, James J., 250, 406, 470, 498, 500
Heins, A. J., 317
Hendricks, W. E., 453
Herrnstein, Richard, 252
Hersch, Joni, 526
Heston, Alan, 30, 31
Hill, Martha S., 106
Hills, Stephen, 159
Hitchens, D. M. W. N., 421
Hoffman, Saul D., 488, 528, 591, 592
Hollister, Robinson G., 594
Holzer, Harry J., 159
Hopkins, S. V., 333
Horowitz, Stanley A., 255
Hotson, John H., 37
Houser, Scott, 655
Hubbard, R. Glenn, 409, 415
Hurd, Michael D., 403, 411, 416, 417, 584
Hutchens, Robert M., 591
Hyclak, Thomas, 296
Hylton, Keith, 498

Irvine, F. Owen, 363

Jackson, John D., 251, 259
Jacobsen, Joyce P., 529
Jakubson, George, 591
Jaszi, George, 72
Jaynes, Gerald D., 464, 467, 470, 471, 475
Jencks, Christopher, 119, 247
Jennings, E. James, 317
Jensen, Arthur R., 252
Jianakoplos, Nancy Ammon, 363, 421, 475
Johnson, D. Gale, 35, 36
Johnson, George E., 321, 327
Johnson, Thomas, 584
Johnson, William R., 598
Jones, Ethel B., 251, 259
Joulfaian, David, 420
Judd, Kenneth L., 415
Juhn, Chinhui, 168, 321

Skinner, J. S., 415
Slemrod, Joel, 651
Slesnick, Daniel T., 118
Slichter, Summer, 323, 324
Slottje, D. J., 74
Smeeding, Timothy M., 78, 79, 80, 108, 109, 113, 628
Smith, Adam, 206
Smith, Donald Mitchell, 317
Smith, James D., 364, 367
Smith, James P., 480, 488, 497, 499, 519, 521, 539, 545
Smith, Sharon P., 528
Smolensky, Eugene, 66
Solmon, Lewis J., 251
Solon, Gary, 578
Sonquist, John, 399
Sorensen, Elaine, 526
Spant, Roland, 365, 384
Spence, Michael, 258
Spivak, Avia, 407
St-Hilaire, France, 412
Stafford, Frank, 295
Starr-McCluer, Martha, 474
Stephenson, Geoffrey, 78
Stevens, Ann Huff, 106
Stevenson, M. H., 453
Stevenson, Wayne, 159
Stewart, Charles, 365
Stratton, Leslie S., 470
Strauss, Robert P., 627
Stroup, Richard, 523
Summers, Lawrence H., 305, 329, 331, 332, 404, 410, 414
Summers, Robert, 30, 31

Tanzer, Michael, 446
Taubman, Paul, 250, 252, 262
Taussig, F. W., 247
Taussig, Michael K., 381, 382
Thorndike, 250
Throop, Adrian, 295
Thurow, Lester C., 441, 449, 450, 457, 486
Tobin, James, 25, 415, 484
Tomes, Nigel, 420
Topel, Robert H., 168, 579
Trinder, C. G., 421

van der Gaag, Jacques, 543
van Praag, Bernard M. S., 95
Vaughan, Denton R., 380, 381
Vroman, Wayne, 499

Wachtel, Howard M., 305
Wachtel, Paul, 251
Wachter, Michael L., 296, 305, 452
Wales, Terrence, 250
Ward, Michael P., 519, 521, 539, 545
Ward, Virginia L., 336
Warlick, Jennifer L., 416, 417
Wascher, William, 598
Weisbrod, Burton A., 118, 250, 381, 382
Weiss, Donald, 403, 408, 411
Weiss, Gertrude, 410
Weiss, Leonard W., 295, 326, 327, 486
Weiss, Randall D., 486
Welch, Finis R., 234, 264, 486, 488
White, Betsy B., 404, 410
Wicks, John, 40
Wilhelm, Mark O., 420
Wilkinson, Bruce W., 237, 239
Williams, Robert, 589
Williamson, Jeffrey G., 318, 486
Willis, Patricia, 590
Willis, Robert J., 250
Wilson, William Julius, 107, 436, 494
Wise, David A., 159, 251, 259
Wise, Donald E., 584
Wolff, Edward N., 31, 74, 118, 148, 307, 330, 352, 356, 359, 364, 370, 373, 385, 386, 387, 399, 401, 405, 409, 412, 413, 416, 417, 420, 533, 535, 537
Wolpin, Kenneth I., 259, 500

Yaari, Menaham E., 407

Yu, Ruoh Chiann, 535

Zeldes, S. P., 415
Zellner, Harriet, 530

SUBJECT INDEX